ANCIENT MAYA POLITICS

The Classic Maya have long presented scholars with vexing problems. One of the longest running and most contested of these, and the source of deeply polarized interpretations, has been their political organization. Using recently deciphered inscriptions and fresh archaeological finds, Simon Martin argues that this particular debate can be laid to rest. He offers a comprehensive re-analysis of the issue in an effort to answer a simple question: how did a multitude of small kingdoms survive for some 600 years without being subsumed within larger states or empires? Using previously unexploited comparative and theoretical approaches, Martin suggests mechanisms that maintained a "dynamic equilibrium" within a system best understood not as an array of individual polities but an interactive whole. With its rebirth as text-backed historical archaeology, Maya studies has entered a new phase, one capable of building a political anthropology as robust as any other we have for the ancient world.

SIMON MARTIN is Associate Curator and Keeper at the Penn Museum and Adjunct Associate Professor of Anthropology at the University of Pennsylvania. He was the 2019–2020 Jay I. Kislak Chair for the Study of the History and Cultures of the Early Americas at the Library of Congress. He is the co-author of *Chronicle of the Maya Kings and Queens* (2000) and *Courtly Art of the Ancient Maya* (2004).

ANCIENT MAYA POLITICS

A POLITICAL ANTHROPOLOGY OF THE CLASSIC PERIOD 150–900 CE

SIMON MARTIN

University of Pennsylvania Museum and Department of Anthropology

CAMBRIDGE
UNIVERSITY PRESS

CAMBRIDGE
UNIVERSITY PRESS

University Printing House, Cambridge CB2 8BS, United Kingdom

One Liberty Plaza, 20th Floor, New York, NY 10006, USA

477 Williamstown Road, Port Melbourne, VIC 3207, Australia

314-321, 3rd Floor, Plot 3, Splendor Forum, Jasola District Centre, New Delhi - 110025, India

103 Penang Road, #05-06/07, Visioncrest Commercial, Singapore 238467

Cambridge University Press is part of the University of Cambridge.

It furthers the University's mission by disseminating knowledge in the pursuit of
education, learning and research at the highest international levels of excellence.

www.cambridge.org
Information on this title: www.cambridge.org/9781108705233
DOI: 10.1017/9781108676694

© Cambridge University Press 2020

First published 2020
First paperback edition 2022

A catalogue record for this publication is available from the British Library

Library of Congress Cataloging in Publication data
NAMES: Martin, Simon, 1961- author.
TITLE: Ancient Maya Politics : A Political Anthropology of the Classic Period,
    150-900 CE / Simon Martin.
DESCRIPTION: New York : Cambridge University Press, 2020. | Includes bibliographical
    references and index.
IDENTIFIERS: LCCN 2019036962 (print) | LCCN 2019036963 (ebook) | ISBN 9781108483889
    (hardback) | ISBN 9781108705233 (paperback) | ISBN 9781108676694 (epub)
SUBJECTS: LCSH: Mayas–Politics and government. | Inscriptions, Mayan. |
    Mayas–Antiquities. | Archaeology and history–Mexico. | Archaeology and history–Central
    America.
CLASSIFICATION: LCC F1435.3.P7 M373 2020 (print) | LCC F1435.3.P7 (ebook) |
    DDC 972.81/016–dc23
LC record available at https://lccn.loc.gov/2019036962
LC ebook record available at https://lccn.loc.gov/2019036963

ISBN 978-1-108-48388-9 Hardback
ISBN 978-1-108-70523-3 Paperback

In memory of Diane Martin
1932–2015

CONTENTS

ILLUSTRATIONS

All images in this volume are by the author, unless otherwise stated in the in-text captions.

MAPS

TABLES

CASE STUDIES

PREFACE

In 1971 the doyen of Mayanists J. Eric S. Thompson asked why, if the key to deciphering Maya hieroglyphs had truly been found, had the trickle of initial readings not swollen into a river – instead drying up completely? That key was real enough, but the script proved decidedly jealous of its secrets. Yuri Knorozov's discovery of some core phonetic principles, first published in 1952, was not enough to fully unlock what is widely acknowledged to be the world's most complex writing system. It was not until the 1980s and 1990s that a new generation of epigraphers followed up on those initial clues and the flow of readings was resumed. Only now could the underlying structure of the script be properly discerned and the language it encoded made clear – restoring sounds to the signs, and thereby meanings to the monuments.

This book follows directly from that unravelling and the information that has flowed from it. The decipherment is still on-going and year-by-year fresh interpretations of the inscriptions allow us to read the words of an ancient people – ancestors to the millions of Maya people who inhabit the same lands today. What these texts have to say provides unique access to what was thought and done in this part of the world 2,000 or more years ago, offering the kind of data that Mayanists of yesteryear could only have dreamed of. The profound transformation that this has wrought has turned Maya studies into a historical archaeology, one as rich and robust as many more well-established ones across the globe.

It was the political organisation of the Classic Period that first drew me into Maya research and has been at the core of my interests ever since. This book represents the fullest statement of my views yet on this long-contested topic, but its aspirations go beyond that. It seeks to tackle critical questions that have long puzzled me and to explore the theoretical issues any answers to them must provoke. It is clearly not enough to produce a narrative of events, we must seek to comprehend the inner mechanisms and structures of their society. If Maya studies is to reach its full potential it will need to show how the material and textual can be harnessed and shown to work synergistically to do this. The emphasis of this book accordingly falls not on the minutiae of the decipherment but on the understandings it makes possible. Those wanting to know the full justifications behind individual readings will need to chase the relevant citations. It is addressed to the Mayanist community as a whole – scholars, students, and aficionados alike – but has the greater ambition of communicating the advances in our field to a broader audience of anthropologists, historians, political scientists, and anyone interested in comparative sociopolitics worldwide.

I have been very fortunate to be encouraged and enabled by a variety of fine scholars and good friends over the past thirty years. It was a chance encounter during a mud-splattered trip through northern Guatemala in 1990 that Anthony Aveni first urged me to pursue a professional life in Maya research. The Maya Meetings at the University of Texas at Austin would soon become an annual fixture in my calendar, where Linda Schele and David Freidel proved enormously supportive of my early efforts. Ramón Carrasco graciously accepted the petition of a little-known epigrapher to join his archaeological project at Calakmul in 1994, an engagement with this crucial site that continued for more than two decades.

My fellowship at the Dumbarton Oaks Research Library in 1996–1997 was a transformative experience that gave me the time and study materials to begin writing *Chronicle of the Maya Kings and Queens*. Jeffrey Quilter, as Director of Precolumbian Studies, was a splendid ringmaster of that rich and enjoyable year. That book took me a further two years to complete and was the product of frequent dialogues, sometimes daily correspondence, with my then-collaborator Nikolai Grube. In 2003 I took up an appointment at the University of Pennsylvania Museum, leaving my original career in design behind me. Here appreciation must go to not only the Director of the time, Jeremy Sabloff, but to the late Bob Sharer and Chris Jones – who proved to be ideal colleagues. I am grateful to have received strong support from former Director Richard Leventhal and current Director Julian Siggers, at an institution where I have been honoured to follow in a long and storied history of Maya research. In regard to this particular volume, I want to thank the Museum for its financial support and the role Steve Tinney as Deputy Director played in that.

Back in London I was very fortunate to have Elizabeth Graham and David Wengrow as the supervisors of my belated doctorate at University College London, for which Norman Hammond and Stephen Houston diligently served as external examiners. That study laid the groundwork for many of the thoughts and arguments set out in greater detail here.

Mary Miller has been a mentor and friend for over twenty-five years. The invitation to join her in developing the exhibition and writing the accompanying catalogue for *Courtly Art of the Ancient Maya* at the National Gallery of Art, Washington DC, in 2004, was only one of several key interventions she has made in my career, all of which I am profoundly grateful for.

Special thanks are also reserved for my epigraphic colleagues and friends Stephen Houston, David Stuart, and Marc Zender. Their insights into the script and various gifts in anthropology, archaeology, iconography, and linguistics have been freely shared over the years and inspired me to ever improve my own work.

In reference to this book more directly, Joel Skidmore, a learned and much-appreciated friend, read all the chapters and offered sage advice and improvements. My colleague and friend at the Museum, Naomi Miller, kindly took on similar duties, offering valuable critiques and suggestions. Others who have offered helpful information or comments, or else provided drawings or photographs are: Bárbara Arroyo, Anthony Aveni, Joanne Baron, Dmitri Beliaev, George Bey, Anna Blume, Marcello Canuto, Nicholas Carter, Albert Davletshin, Kai Delvendahl, Nick Dunning, Barbara Fash (at the Corpus of Maya Hieroglyphic Inscriptions), Antonia Foias, Charles Golden, Praveena Gullapalli, Christina Halperin, Christophe Helmke, Julie Hoggarth, Stephen Houston, Bart Jaski, Eva Jobbova, John Baines, John Justeson, Terry Kaufman, Mary Kate Kelly, Emad Khazraee, Matthew Looper (at the Maya Hieroglyphic Database Project), Karl Herbert Mayer, Patricia McAnany, Cameron McNeil, Mary Miller, Megan O'Neil, David Pendergast, Jorge Pérez de Lara (who took the stunning cover image), Dorie Reents-Budet, Franco Rossi, Alexandr Safronov, David Schele, Ivan Šprajc, David Stuart, Matthew Todd, Alexandre Tokovinine, Kenichiro Tsukamoto, Mark Van Stone, Verónica Vázquez, Andrew Weeks, Marc Zender, and Jarek Źrałka, as well as the rights departments at the Peabody Museum of Harvard University, Los Angeles County Museum of Art, and the Saint Louis Art Museum. At this point a particular mention must be made of Justin Kerr, a friend whose generous sharing of his unique roll-out vase images has hugely assisted not only my research but that of many others in our field. I am fortunate that three of his peerless photographs of Maya monuments grace this book.

David Stuart and an anonymous reviewer gave excellent feedback on the manuscript and I warmly thank them for their recommendations. Likewise, I am very appreciative to Beatrice Rehl and everyone at Cambridge University Press for their professionalism and attention to detail in bringing this book to fruition. Last, but by no means least, I thank my partner Frauke Sachse, who has helped in a great many ways and endured the entire length of this process, contributing valuable critiques and much encouragement.

This book is dedicated to my late mother, but I also want to honour the memories of four renowned and much-missed Mayanist colleagues: Robert Sharer (1940–2012), Christopher Jones (1937–2015), Erik Boot (1963–2016), and Alfonso Lacadena (1964–2018).

ONE

INTRODUCTION: THE QUESTIONS

Few issues are more central to understanding an ancient people than how they were organised politically, a topic that touches on virtually every aspect of their social, cultural, and economic life. Configurations of power are the critical frameworks within which identities, relationships, and events are formed, understood, and function both within communities and in their interactions with others. This was no less true for the ancient Maya, who occupied the Yucatan Peninsula and adjacent highlands to the south, an area now divided between the nations of Mexico, Guatemala, Belize, and the western extremities of Honduras and El Salvador (Map 1; see also Maps 2–4) – today home to millions of their descendants.

The traits traditionally used to identify the ancient Maya as a material culture had coalesced by at least 1200 BCE, and substantial monumental construction was taking shape soon after. By 500 BCE there were expansive settlements, and this florescent Preclassic Period, lasting until about 150 CE, was crowned with the growth of major cities that manifest all the core features of Maya civilisation. But it was during the ensuing Classic Period – lasting from around 150 to 900 CE, and here divided into Proto, Early, and Late sub-periods – that the region saw its highest populations, most abundant architectural and arte-factual remains, and most precocious intellectual and artistic achievements. The collapse of Classic Maya society, which began close to 800 CE and was completed by the early tenth century, left its core regions abandoned, never to be fully re-occupied. Reclaimed by a tropical forest for the last millennium,

MAP 1 Principal sites in the Maya area, which is today divided between Mexico, Guatemala, Belize, Honduras, and El Salvador. (All maps in this volume by the author, using base maps made available by NASA/JPL)

this has bequeathed us – despite various modern depredations – one of the richest and least disturbed archaeological landscapes in the world.

The nature of the Classic Maya political landscape has been a long-running question, a source of fascination and no small measure of frustration for a century or more. A sizeable number of scholars have been drawn to the problem over that time, each bringing their own datasets and approaches to bear. All have attempted to show how the enormous number of settlements, ranging in size from the mammoth to the miniscule, were composed into units and structured with others across space and time. The resulting interpretations have proved to be divergent, even deeply polarised, fuelling a vigorous debate that continues to the present day. Two disciplines, archaeology and epigraphy, lie at the heart of the endeavour, and it is clear that only their direct engagement will allow us to build a persuasive portrait of the Maya past. For a long time, our understanding of their hieroglyphic script was rudimentary, leaving physical remains as our only viable source. That began to change in the 1950s, with revelations about the historical content of the inscriptions, but it was only after the phonetic decipherment that took hold in the 1990s that the full value of the texts could begin to be realised.

The decipherment of any ancient script is a rare and transforming event, but when it illuminates the only sizeable corpus of writing from two entire continents it is a precious one indeed. The steady unravelling of the texts has opened unparalleled vistas on the beliefs, practices, history, and institutions of a New World society as it existed a thousand years or more before European contact. Maya inscriptions offer the best, indeed the only, opportunity we will ever possess to understand an ancient American people through their own words and on their own terms.

The challenge taken up in this book is to utilise these data to conduct a thorough re-analysis of Classic Maya politics. It is a surprising fact that no single, long-form work using the inscriptions for this purpose has been attempted in over four decades. This same period has seen a huge expansion of archaeological work in the region, providing an ever more complete picture of the physical remains of ancient Maya communities. Advances in survey technologies, most especially airborne laser scanning, have produced a quantum leap forward in data-gathering. This offers a wealth of new information on settlement size and distribution, revealing in unprecedented detail how the Maya adapted the landscape for agricultural and defensive purposes. The excavation of sites great and small has also led to the discovery of many new inscriptions, while our enhanced literacy means that even long-published texts provide a steady stream of fresh material. These same decades have also seen significant shifts in theoretical orientations, with the rise and fall of paradigms in the social sciences that have altered the intellectual setting within which any interpretation must take place. The time is, therefore, ripe in a number of respects to launch such a project. I will argue that the quantity and quality of evidence now in our possession, the epigraphic together with the archaeological, allows us to put long-standing differences to rest, enabling a move from basic questions of Classic Maya political organisation to the richer and deeper ones that lie beyond.

Points of scholarly disagreement have focussed on the size of political units, the degree of centralisation they achieved, and whether material or ideational factors played the greater role in their structure and behaviour. By the mid-1990s, Mayanists could choose between a vision of regional-scale entities, in which a handful of capitals with strong central governments administered tiers of provincial centres, or a diametrically opposed view of a multitude of polities with weak, faction-riven governments with domains so small that some could be traversed by foot in a single day. A third, hegemonic perspective, took its cue from the then-newly emerging epigraphic data on the differing statuses of kings and the patron–client bonds between them. This was a model that could accommodate the evidence for the highly-segmented character of the political landscape with that for significant disparities in site size, with the greater power and influence this seemed to imply.

More than two decades later, we can say with confidence that the evidence is in. It shows that there was indeed a plethora of small kingdoms, each of them notionally sovereign but, in reality, engaged in enduring struggles for autonomy and dominance over others. Especially powerful kingdoms had expansionist ambitions, at times achieving multi-generational ascendancies, but none secured a monopoly on power or consolidated their conquests into anything resembling large unitary states or institutionalised empires.

However, even though this hegemonic interpretation is one I initiated and have long argued for, it remains incomplete. To date we have learnt much about the who, where, when, and what of the system, but far less about the how and why. How could a system of multiple polities persist essentially unchanged for hundreds of years, and why were none among them willing or able to create larger and more unified formations? These closely related questions are far from the only ones to be addressed in this book, but they can be seen as the core problems that motivate it.

This study makes a fresh analysis of the data, using material newly unearthed in the field or deciphered in the greater comfort of the office or library. But equally important to the project are the methodological and theoretical positions it takes. A central premise is that Classic Maya inscriptions are not only particularistic accounts of the identities, relationships, and deeds of individuals, they are inherently mirrors to the organising principles of the societies that produced them. We can, and often do, look at recorded events as ends unto themselves, but from an appropriate standpoint they become the means through which to perceive a grammar of political life. This permits a move from political history to political anthropology, a shift that looks at particularities for what they can tell us about the rules, norms, and conventions that operationalise notions of authority, power, and legitimacy. In doing so we take on the wider imperatives of political anthropology to look beyond the parochial to see how local phenomena relate to universal ones, exploring how the communities at hand fit within the greater picture of structure and power in human society.

This volume is concerned with all facets of political organisation and behaviour, but reverses the usual focus on the structure of individual polities in favour of the relationships between them – a systemic outlook which, if not ignored, has certainly been under-emphasised in previous work. I will argue that, in classic recursive fashion, neither polity nor system can be understood independently, since each plays a pivotal role in determining the other. Political anthropology has dealt at length with the factors, both practical and conceptual, that allow communities to cohere and operate as individual units. However, it has no strong tradition of analysing multi-polity ecologies of the kind we find in the Maya region, and if we want relevant theoretical insights into this we are forced to look elsewhere, toward fields that have made such issues a central concern.

While mine is an epigraphic investigation, it is far from insensible to archaeological interests and in no manner wishes to reinforce the epistemological divide between the textual and the material. Indeed, it seeks further opportunities to bring these "two ways of knowing" together, not in the merely additive sense but, at best, as part of a dialectic in which each makes propositions that can then be compared and contrasted with the other. The sorely depleted remains of the past mean that the original place of words and objects within a unified social reality is irrevocably lost to us – we must accept that only a tiny percentage of the available fragments can be refitted today. This means that any examination of the past necessarily involves interplay between the seen and the unseen.

That issue is especially acute in the case of the Maya because of the poor preservation endemic to the tropics, which robs us of almost all perishable materials. When it comes to writing, this means that we are restricted to the subject matter found on stone, stucco, shell, bone, and ceramic, and even there little has survived unscathed from the scouring effects of heavy rain, corrosion by acidic soils, and the impacts of falling trees. With all these limitations, we must acknowledge how much falls around and between the features that can be discerned. Like the search for dark matter and dark energy, the material and force that are together thought to make up some ninety-five per cent of the mass-energy of the universe, we are often in pursuit of things that cannot be observed directly, only inferred from their effects.

The Classic Maya economy is a case in point. Because the inscriptions make virtually no reference to the topic – eschewing any direct mention of land ownership, market and exchange systems, tax and tribute lists, long-distance trade networks, and the organisation of agricultural or craft production – we must seek to understand a political system in the absence of written knowledge about how resources moved around inside and outside the polity to support the lifestyles of commoners and elites alike. Yet, while we may be blinkered, we still have the capacity to make inferences, combining our sparse epigraphic clues with archaeological, ethnographic, and comparative historical

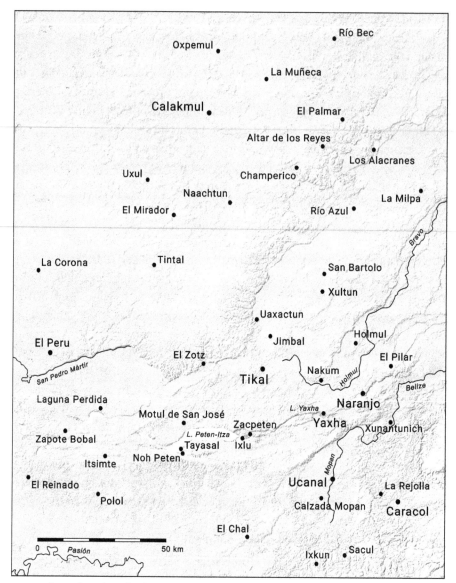

MAP 2 Central southern lowlands or Peten.

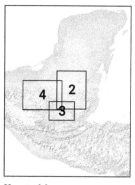

Key to Maps 2–4.

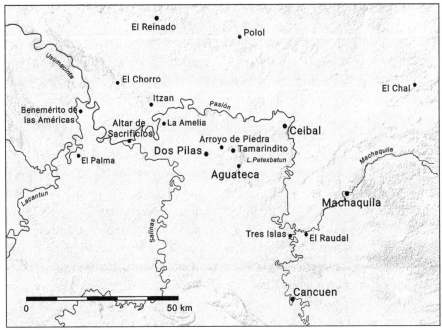

MAP 3 Southern and Petexbatun regions.

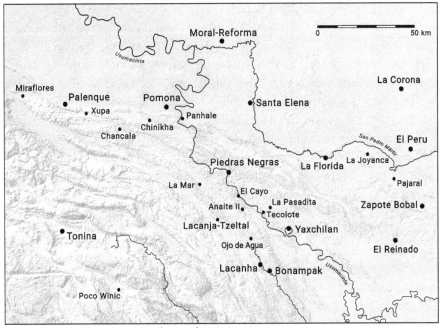

MAP 4 Western, Usumacinta, and Lacandon regions.

data to offer credible conjectures, even if certainties and finer points will always elude us.

In discussing Classic Maya politics as a generalised phenomenon, I do not mean to deny or gloss over some real variations in organisation and practice across the region and through time. However, I join others in maintaining that the consistent expression of authority in art, writing, and architecture we see across the length and breadth of the lowlands is clear evidence for a single dominant political culture. Emerging from the social and demographic collapse that brought an end to the Late Preclassic Period (400 BCE–150 CE), this new tradition developed its distinctive character during the transitional Protoclassic Period (150–300 CE), before spreading outward from the central southern lowlands – the interior of the peninsula known as the Peten (Map 2) – in a materially attested process. Its homogeneity is significant because it means that what we lack in comprehensiveness at any single centre is compensated for by the geographical expanse of its coverage and a 600-year-plus time span. The one important caveat is the marked weighting of the data toward the latter part of that range. The transition between the Early Classic (300–600) and Late Classic (600–900) eras entailed, among other changes, a substantial increase in the production of inscriptions and the kinds of topics they discuss. Here it is important to strike a balance between an idealised, but heuristically useful, synchronic approach and the reality of diachronic processes, some of which may be masked by intentional efforts to preserve tradition and present outward continuity.

This study concentrates on the nature and operation of the Classic Maya political system, placing less emphasis on its origins. We have few, if any, inscriptions from the initial founding events of the second to fourth centuries CE, and here archaeology can be our only direct source. That said, retrospective accounts of political genesis, whether historical or mythistorical in character, are of considerable interest to us, if only in casting light on the ideological self-perception of Classic Maya kingdoms. As for the famed collapse of the ninth century, that event represents an end to the regimes that produced the inscriptions, progressively robbing us of our textual "window" into the past. Although monuments were raised and inscriptions carved during this social, cultural, and political tumult, their aim was more to fortify and preserve a fading tradition than to offer a reportage of crisis. However, late texts do supply significant clues to the processes at work during the collapse, providing evidence for transformation as well as disintegration. This makes the topic worthy of a chapter-length treatment which presents evidence that runs counter to notable parts of the current consensus.

An implicit critique throughout the book regards the long tradition of exceptionalist thinking in Maya studies. By this I mean the propensity to see the Classic Maya as following their own unique star without meaningful precedents in world history and anthropology. It goes without saying that every society will have individual, culturally mediated, responses to the challenges it faces. Yet the recurring nature of those challenges, together with the base cognitive and physical capacities we all share, mean that familiar problems will often find familiar solutions, even if they are framed in distinctive ways. The dazzling virtuosity of Maya culture, its remarkable accomplishments and enduring enigmas, has a beguiling quality that we must, in some respects, resist. In the absence of an argument as convincing as the posited feature is extraordinary, exceptionalism leads us back into the kind of interpretive cul-de-sac that blocked progress in Maya research for a major portion of the twentieth century.

This relates to a wider intent to counter the exoticism attributed to the Maya in much contemporary popular culture. It is only by placing the Maya within the common thread of global history that we can appreciate their universal as well individual qualities, opening a genuine debate on what concepts of identity, ethnicity, and culture mean in ancient as well as modern times. Only by asserting a comparative equivalence can we analyse their past in the same way we would that of any other complex historical society.

My approach is to use epigraphic data as an informant, as a set of sources that must be first accessed, then interpreted and contextualised, taking an emic resource for the etic purpose of explicating an extinct sociopolitical system. We cannot collaborate with these sources in the way we would in ethnographic fieldwork, and our dialogue with them can only be of a metaphorical kind. But in our own way we can interrogate them, parsing their meaning by discerning how one text reflects upon others and the wider physical record. The textual past is never a whole or continuous narrative, but so many scattered scenes with characters, acts, ideas, settings, and relationships that we hope to restore to something like their original sequence and place within a simulacrum of their original matrix.

STRUCTURE OF THE BOOK

The arguments in this volume are developed through three parts. Part I, "Agendas in Classic Maya Politics", sets out the context, methodology, and conceptual orientation in which the remainder of the study takes place. It begins with "Modelling the Maya", a chapter that explores the interwoven history of sources and interpretation that constitute the quest to understand ancient Maya political organisation. Here each of the pivotal developments is discussed within the milieu of its times, setting out how data and theory have interacted to produce both major advances and major revisions.

The next chapter, "On Archaeopolitics", broadens the focus to discuss why certain concepts and agendas will be useful for this study, and others not. It begins with a discussion of the "state" in anthropological thought, joining the critique of formal socioevolutionary schemes that has steadily grown over the years. This is followed by a look at the recursive social models that have superseded them in several respects, discussing the amendments required to patch their omissions, especially in their understanding of hierarchy and collective agency. Lastly, it looks at how these models might be viewed within the framework of complexity theory, a field that expressly studies the relationship between wholes and parts that constitutes the central rub of this study.

Since epigraphy provides the dataset with which this book builds its understanding of Classic Maya politics, it is necessary to offer some epistemological grounding for the use of written sources. Thus, the fourth chapter, "Worlds in Words", revisits the often-uneasy relationship between the textual and the material, addressing the unique challenge faced by historical archaeologies. It takes a special interest in defining the rhetorical purposes of Maya inscriptions, and examines potential bridges between history and anthropology – viewed here as estranged cousins more illuminating in combination than they are in isolation. The end purpose here is to demonstrate how the information on events provided by texts can contribute to an understanding of both process and structure.

These presentations prime us for Part II, "Epigraphic Data on Classic Maya Politics", which begins with six chapters that each examine a major theme in the composition, operation, or interaction of Maya polities. Here the decipherment of key terms serve as points of departure for lexical and semantic analyses, elaborated through specific examples and additional iconographic, ethnographic, or archaeological materials. Where appropriate, statistical studies test for underlying patterns. Each of these chapters closes with one or more case studies that examine particular sub-themes or pertinent historical episodes in greater detail.

Part II opens with "Identity", an examination of status, office, and role in the construction of Classic Maya authority. Divided between royal and noble titles, it examines how these epithets were employed and changed through time, shedding light on the construction of political personas. Next, "Constitution" concerns the institution of kingship and the specific acts that established fields of royal action. It begins with an examination of the royal life cycle and how authority passed between generations. It then moves to accounts of political foundation, seeking to understand how individual acts grounded institutions in time and place. The seventh chapter, "Transcendence", deals with the fused nature of Classic Maya politics and religion. Among a large array of deities, some were attached to particular places and dynasties, supernatural associations that rulers used to fix themselves at the spiritual core of their communities. The eighth chapter, "Matrimony", concentrates on that singular institution to explore how unions within and between polities worked as strategies of descent or alliance. It contends, among other things, that the flexibility of strategies made possible by polygyny was a key element in the composition of inter-polity networks. "Conflict" pursues the most extreme and disruptive of political behaviours. Oriented around five key verbs, it moves from the specificity of individual events to the social purposes of warfare, contesting some common assumptions held in Mayanist circles today. The tenth chapter, "Hierarchy", sets out the direct evidence for asymmetries in status and power between Classic Maya polities, examining the terms that define the ownership and supervision of clients by patrons. This data is presented chronologically in order to track the shifting fortunes of the major powerbrokers.

The conclusion of Part II, "Coda", is a special chapter that looks at the ninth century collapse from an epigraphic perspective. While the dataset for this period is undeniably thin, it is not without value. The ambition here is less to explain the social and demographic unravelling as such, more to examine the shifts in identity that point to the political transformations of these turbulent times.

Any division by theme involves a measure of artificiality, since most of the topics described are interpenetrating. All political systems are functioning wholes whose parts can be isolated for investigative purposes but gain their real meaning only when articulated with others. Much of this connectivity is restored in Part III, "A Political Anthropology for the Classic Maya", which develops proposals for the structures and mechanisms behind the effects we see in the epigraphic and archaeological records. It opens with the twelfth chapter, "Classic Maya Networks", which begins by stepping back from historical specifics to consider the topic at a macroscale level. It asks some elemental questions about the ways that units relate to systems, seen from three diverse perspectives on networks: practical, statistical, and conceptual. It explores how cultural commonalities were produced and maintained, what diagrammatic and statistical approaches can tell us about political dynamics, and finally what the application of network theory might have to offer our topic.

The next chapter, "Defining Classic Maya Political Culture", draws together the evidence from Part II to show how a synthetic effort can produce interpretations that are both historical and structural. It discusses the ways in which kingship related to the noble cohort that supported that institution, before moving to how dynasties imprinted themselves on landscapes both physically and ideologically. Next to be explored is the character of inter-polity engagements en masse, before concluding with an analysis of the strategic goals of powerbrokers. What is apparent at the close of that section is the need for some deeper appreciation of hegemony as a political system.

"Hegemony in Practice and Theory", the fourteenth chapter, therefore focuses on the nature and principles of political division within cultural continuity. Having made only a cursory use of external parallels until now, it begins by looking outside Mesoamerica to examine four societies across the globe – drawn from the diverse histories of Fiji, Ireland, India, and Greece – that offer strong parallels for the Maya case. It seeks to demonstrate how all manner of surface differences mask underlying similarities, features that arise from the shared structural logics of multi-polity systems. We can also glean useful lessons from these often better documented societies, especially when it comes to dark matter problems such as economy. This is followed by an analysis of the mechanisms at work within multi-polity systems more broadly and what determines their historical fate. Here the argument draws on strands within political science to tackle the issue of socially-constructed rather than simply materially-driven systems.

The unity of the perspectives of Part III comes from their pursuit of the forces behind both the dynamism and equilibrium we find in the Classic Maya political ecosystem. Its primary goals are to explain how high levels of political segmentation are consistent with cultural homogeneity, how power was exercised in such a landscape, and in what ways individual units contributed to, and were shaped by, the interactive whole. Here I am not in search of a set of universal formulae to replace those that have reigned in the past, but rather a deeper appreciation of how the systemic and the contingent interact to generate political life in a complex world.

PART I

AGENDAS IN CLASSIC MAYA POLITICS

TWO

MODELLING THE MAYA

The history of Maya research is a relatively short yet eventful one, peppered with field-changing discoveries and spirited theoretical debates. To fully appreciate what is at stake in deciding on a model for Classic Maya politics, and how we reached the point we now have, it is necessary to retrace the development of interpretation through time, isolating the contested questions and explaining how scholars have marshalled evidence to support one position or another. Since data and analysis are intrinsically entwined they are here treated within a common narrative, stretching from the period of first European encounters to the state of the field today. The division into eras, latterly 20-year spans, is patently arbitrary, but it does allow section titles to capture the general character of their times.

CONQUERORS AND CLERICS, 1502–1820

The closest contact between ourselves and active Maya polities came during the Spanish invasion of the sixteenth and seventeenth centuries, the cultural as well as military conquest that laid waste to all the indigenous societies of the Americas. Elsewhere in Mesoamerica, especially in Central Mexico, extensive ethnographies were compiled as the invaders sought to understand the peoples and places now in their possession. Sadly, nothing of comparable scale and detail was collected in the Maya area, leaving a sparse record with which to work. What we have are eyewitness testimonies from some of the conquerors, and a larger and more useful body of documents compiled by the clerics and administrators who followed in their wake – those who knew and worked with Maya people who had grown up in the pre-contact era.

The first meeting between Maya and Europeans took place off the coast of Honduras in 1502, when Columbus, on his last voyage, came upon a heavily laden trading canoe (Lothrop 1927). That encounter passed off peacefully enough, but the first interactions with Maya societies on land most decidedly did not. Three Spanish expeditions explored the coastline of the Yucatan peninsula between 1517 and 1519 – the last of them commanded by the redoubtable Hernán Cortés, en route to vanquishing the Aztec Empire of Central Mexico – and landings were met with fierce resistance. Testimonies survive from each incursion (Chamberlain 1948: 11–15), but a more significant account comes from the march Cortés made across the heart of the Maya southern lowlands in 1525, staged in order to quell a Spanish rebellion in Honduras. He and his small army made its way through a forest covered by the expansive and loosely integrated polities of the Acalan and Cehach without opposition, moving on to the isolated homeland of the Itza, where he was formally received on their island capital Noh Peten on Lake Peten-Itza (Cortés 1971: 362–377; Díaz de Castillo 1967: XIV, 24–46) (Map 3).

Cordial contacts of this kind were, again, the exception. Flush with their success in conquering Central Mexico, the main body of Spanish adventurers and their native allies had, within a year, turned to the subjugation of the Maya. Pedro de Alvarado led the invasion of the highlands of present-day Guatemala, a rugged region that was, as now, more linguistically diverse than other parts of the Maya world. Although there are few descriptions of this invasion, we do have the later writings of Spanish commentators such as Bartolomé de Las Casas, governmental censuses, and indigenous works such as the *Annals of the Cakchiquels* (Carmack 1973, 1981). These describe the K'iche' Maya as having the most important polity of the time. Their military exploits over the previous century had established an extended domain, although it had lately come under pressure from their former subjects, the Kaqchikel. The K'iche' capital of Q'umarkaj (Utatlan) fell to Alvarado in 1524 and the remaining polities – including those who, like the Kaqchikel, had initially sided with the Spaniards – were crushed by 1527.

The conquest of the northern lowlands began that same year under Francisco Montejo, but was aborted twice over before success was finally achieved by a son of the same name in 1546 (Chamberlain 1948). The colonial regime established thereafter would produce a body of ecclesiastical, legal, and bureaucratic documents, including detailed surveys known as the *Relaciones de Yucatán*, while a number of indigenous works, which survive as later copies, were created in this period (see Restall 1997). Easily the richest description of life before the conquest comes from Fray Diego de Landa's *Relación de las Cosas de Yucatán* (Landa 1941 [c.1566]; Tozzer 1941). Landa, an inquisitor of considerable cruelty who rose to become bishop of the regional capital of Mérida (Clendinnen 1987), worked with several high-born Maya informants and found no difficulty in accepting that the ruined buildings scattered throughout the territory were the work of their ancestors.

When the Spanish arrived, this northern region was divided between fifteen or more *cuchcabal*, often translated as "province" but in fact identifying an individual polity. Some of these were centrally controlled by hereditary lords, but others were collectives or confederacies with differing degrees of integration (Roys 1957, 1962). The sources describe many of these units as formerly under the domination of the single centre of Mayapan. The governance of that walled settlement, whose ceremonial architecture mimics the earlier and more massive site of Chichen Itza, is said to have lain in the hands of two lineages, the Cocom and the Xiu, who required subject lords to live at their capital for part of the year.[1] An internal dispute, we are told, led the Xiu to massacre all but one of the Cocom male line around 1441, after which Mayapan was abandoned.

We learn a good deal about the aforementioned Acalan polity from a group of seventeenth-century documents, including a native language description, the Paxbolon-Maldonado Papers written in Chontal Mayan, which describe the establishment of its intrusive ruling dynasty (Scholes and Roys 1968; Smailus 1975). Acalan submitted to the Spanish Crown in 1530 and accepted Christianity in 1550, but efforts to subdue and convert the more remote polities inland, the Itza and associated groups surrounding Lake Peten-Itza, met with little success (Avendaño y Loyola 1987). It was not until 1697 that the colonial authorities tired of their resistance and sent latter-day *conquistadores* to storm Noh Peten in the final act of imperial appropriation in Mesoamerica (Jones 1998). To the east, in modern-day Quintana Roo and Belize, the Spanish had established a measure of control from 1543 to 1544 onwards, but were still pacifying areas well into the seventeenth century (Graham 2011: 156–164).

This, then, is a brief outline of what has come down to us from early years of Spanish control. Relatively reliable accounts of the pre-contact era cover no more than the last century of the Postclassic Period (900–1546 CE), a time when the great centres of the Classic Maya had already lain in desolation, their histories lost to memory, for more than six centuries. The relevance of these late data depends on what continuities can be established between the two eras, a topic of contention among scholars. Whereas some perceive notable correspondences, others see a deep disjuncture reflected in very different social, political, and economic orientations. It should also be noted that the meaning and accuracy of the documentary sources, as well as the rather uncritical interpretations of early scholars, have increasingly been brought into question, leading to the emergence of revised formulations of Postclassic and early Colonial society and its politics in more recent times (e.g. Farriss 1984; Quezada 1993, 2014; Okoshi 1994, 2009; Restall 1997; Okoshi, Williams-Beck, and Izquierdo 2006; Braswell 2003a). It is safe to say that the meagre sources we have on the last years of independent Maya political culture will continue to provide debating points for those working on the Classic Period.

PIONEERS, SAVANTS, AND SCHOLARS, 1820–1930

For the best part of three centuries, the imperial authorities of New Spain showed scant interest in the antiquity of their domains. For them, the suppression of a pagan past was both a moral and practical necessity, one that saved souls while solidifying their political and economic control. There was no legitimate place here for the curious antiquarian. The little information collected in the early years of contact gathered dust in ecclesiastical and state archives, most to be rediscovered only in the nineteenth century. The European Enlightenment did inspire a handful of explorations in the waning years of the Spanish Empire, but none were published before its collapse in the 1820s (Evans 2004: 10–36). It was only with the birth of Latin American nation states that fresh light began to fall on the region's past. Now accessible to foreigners, a small but steady stream of adventurers arrived from Europe and the United States to follow up on newly publicised reports of lost cities in the jungle.

This was a turbulent time in Western science, as debates on the origins of humankind and the literal truth of the Bible gripped public and academic circles alike. Precisely where the history of the Americas fitted into these controversies was as yet unclear, and into this vacuum of knowledge were sucked all manner of speculation and ethnocentric delusion. As news of magnificent ancient remains spread, they were explained either as the products of diffusion from the "higher" civilisations of the Old World or the work of extinct races much superior to those now living there (see Kehoe 1998; Evans 2004: 34–42, passim). Throughout the nineteenth-century it was not unusual, even for scholars who made significant contributions to Maya studies, to ascribe the great ruins to the lost tribes of Israel (Kingsborough 1831–1848), to Egyptians and Freemasons (Le Plongeon 1886, 1896), or even to refugees from Atlantis (Brasseur de Bourbourg 1868).

Yet a turning point had come in 1839, when American diplomat and writer John Lloyd Stephens and his English illustrator Frederick Catherwood disembarked in Belize City for the first of two expeditions into the interior. Their encounters with vine-choked ruins in the forest were brought to the wider world through a pair of bestselling travelogues, for which Stephens produced a compelling prose notable for its lack of exaggeration and Catherwood supplied evocative renderings of unusual accuracy for their time. Stephens had already experienced the wonders of Egypt and the Near East, and was more than willing to see the Maya as a New World counterpart of these illustrious civilisations. His speculations that the ruins were the work of ancestral Maya and that the hieroglyphs would prove to be the accounts of kings and heroes proved to be prescient – of the great ruins of Copan he wrote: "One thing I believe, [is] that its history is graven on its monuments" (Stephens 1841: 159–160).

Catherwood's drawings of architecture and monuments were aided by the Camera Lucida, but recording took a major step forward with the arrival of photography, especially with the subsequent switch from daguerreotype to glass-plate negative technology. The pioneers here were Désiré Charnay (1862), Alfred Maudslay (1889–1902), and Teobert Maler (1901–1903, 1908a, 1908b, 1910, 1911), who produced state-of-the-art images in the most rudimentary of field conditions. Maudslay and Maler were the more archaeological in their approach, producing descriptions and maps of the sites they visited – many of which were new to science – while Maudslay additionally undertook excavations and took moulds of monuments, later used to produce casts and drawings. Neither man commented to any great degree on the social significance of their finds, although Maler (1911: 55) echoed his predecessor Edward Thompson (1886: 253) in noting the many house-mounds surrounding impressive ruins such as that of Tikal. Their primary contribution was in producing accurate records of the inscriptions that would prove invaluable to the early decipherers.

The greatest of these was the German librarian Ernst Förstemann, who kept the finest of the four surviving Postclassic books, the Dresden Codex (which had probably reached Europe in a consignment Hernan Cortés sent to Charles V) in his desk drawer. He used it to make astounding progress in Maya calendrics and astronomy, publishing as many as 50 papers between 1880 and 1906. Combining its rich data with those from the new records of monuments, together with early Spanish accounts, he established the fundamental workings of the Maya calendar.[2] Even so, turning its relative dates into absolute ones by tying them to the Christian calendar remained a thorny problem. Using a few elliptical clues in the colonial documents, it was the solution advanced by Joseph Goodman (1905), modified by later scholars, and now known as the Goodman-Martínez-Thompson (GMT) correlation, that has since been broadly corroborated by radiocarbon dating and other analytical techniques.[3]

It was within these early days of Maya scholarship that a key bifurcation began to emerge. One perspective took its cue from the comparative approach of Stephens, and looked to the ways in which Maya art, architecture, and writing, however idiosyncratic, could and should be viewed within universal themes of human culture. Thus, the art historian Herbert Spinden saw no difficulty in taking depictions of captives and weaponry as evidence for warfare and as references to historical events (Spinden 1913: 23, 1916: 442–443; also

Lehmann 1907). Likewise, the indefatigable archaeologist and epigrapher Sylvanus Morley (1915: 33–36) felt sure that the inscriptions, most of which remained inscrutable, were fundamentally historical in nature.

Yet a few years later he was adopting a more cautious tone (Morley 1920: 36) and would ultimately reject this position entirely. The reason is not hard to find. As the years went by there seemed no end to revelations concerning the scope and sophistication of Maya time reckoning; each discovery bolstering the prediction that every last hieroglyph would prove to have calendrical or astronomical meaning (Brinton 1895: 32). The texts were increasingly viewed not simply as insights into an intellectual world, but as an embodiment of the Classic Maya psyche. A society that abjured any mention of worldly affairs for a fixation on the mysteries of time and the cosmos would be a strange and exotic one, and who could say where their distinctiveness ended? It was this reasoning that fuelled an enduring vein of Maya exceptionalism: the belief that their society could only be understood on its own unique terms and without reference to regional or global precedents.

Up until this time little interest had been shown in the political organisation of the numerous ruins, and the first formal proposal came from Thomas Gann, an English doctor and archaeologist. He believed the whole lowland region to have been subsumed within a single state or empire (Gann 1927: 233), locating its capital at the site of Tikal, which he judged to be a city whose population exceeded 250,000 people (Gann and Thompson 1931: 36). Yet the views of his co-author J. Eric S. Thompson could hardly have been more different, and in the very same volume Thompson argued that major Maya sites were empty of all but a priestly caste. For him, the ruins were not the cores of one-time metropolises, but ceremonial centres used to stage rituals for a peasantry whose hamlets and farmsteads were scattered throughout the forest (Gann and Thompson 1931: 199). These sharply diverging interpretations illustrate both the rudimentary state of archaeological knowledge and the breadth of the paradigmatic divide that deficit allowed.

A TROPICAL ARCADIA, 1930–1950

Over the next two decades it was the idea of a deeply esoteric and exceptional Classic Maya that gained ascendancy. There were several strands to this interpretation, none of them entirely new, which were now woven into a compelling whole (see Becker 1979, 1984; Webster 2006). Morley played a significant role in this, but it was Thompson, a scholar of intimidating erudition active in the fields of epigraphy, archaeology, and ethnography, who became its great synthesiser and populariser.

By now, the lengthy opening portions of most monumental texts were correctly understood as commemorations of a single day, as specified within a series of different calendars, counts, and cycles. The portions that followed were filled by shortened references to additional dates, each linked to one another by precise enumerations of days. Filling the space between these were sequences of glyphs, dubbed by Morley (1915: 26) a "textual residue", which defied all attempts at comprehension. A convoluted explanation of these passages as corrections bringing the Maya year into line with the true solar circuit (Teeple 1930: 70–85, following Bowditch 1910: 199) was entirely erroneous, but chimed with the growing consensus that calendrical reckoning and its associated astrological and religious ruminations were the sole topics of the inscriptions. The glyphs that resisted understanding, it was argued, did so because the script itself was an ad hoc and ideographic affair only fully comprehensible to its authors (Schellhas 1936: 133, 1945; also Thompson 1932; Morley 1937–1938: I, 106).

It seemed only logical that the specialists who once controlled this recondite knowledge would have formed the social elite, with a class of astrologer-priests holding a mass of humble farmers in their thrall. Each Classic Maya centre would be ruled by a "theocracy or a government over which the priests had complete control", in regional terms forming a "loose federation of states each ruled by a small group of sacerdotal aristocrats" (Thompson 1950: 7). All was well until their demands for temple-building labour proved intolerable and provoked a peasant revolt, a catastrophe that brought Classic civilisation to an end (Thompson 1932: 14–15). The lessons of the Italian Renaissance notwithstanding, before this disaster it was believed that its impressive artistic and intellectual achievements could not have been possible in a time of strife (Thompson 1927: 12, 1950: 6). Although it was conceded that some raiding and squabbles over borders may have taken place, relations between polities were deemed to be "quite friendly", due to the common education and shared values of their unworldly leaders (Thompson 1954: 81). When the seizure of captives occurred, it was solely for the purpose of securing victims for ritual sacrifice (Morley 1946: 70; Thompson 1950: 7). Thus, the many depictions of bound prisoners struggling under the feet of spear-brandishing grandees were not to be taken as evidence for political conflict, but rather for religious obligations mandated by the gods. It was these divinities and the priests that served them who were portrayed in such splendid fashion on the monuments, the artistry and effort consumed in carving them itself an act of devotion (Thompson 1932: 12). Thompson's commitment to a pacific model was greatly influenced by his ethnographic research (e.g. Thompson 1930) and personal friendships with Maya collaborators. To his mind their philosophy was always to "live and let live"; which he took to be an essential ethnic quality that could be safely projected into the distant past (Thompson 1954: 81).

Morley's positions differed in no substantial way, although, based on readings of contact-period data, he was prepared to accept some partnership between sacred and secular authority and as a result had more interest in practical politics. In *The Ancient Maya* he conjectured that governance lay in: "hereditary dynasties, the members of which filled not only the highest civil offices of the state but also the highest ecclesiastical positions" (Morley 1946: 50). Based on a transition in art and architectural styles, he had earlier distinguished between an "Old Empire" and "New Empire" (Morley 1911: 208) – eras that largely accord with the Classic and Postclassic Periods used today (Willey and Phillips 1958). However, "empire" was never more than a notional term invoked for its allusions to cultural greatness, and Morley's more substantive comparisons were to the Classical Greek *polis*, to the city-states of Renaissance Italy, and to those of the Hanseatic League (Morley 1946: 50, 160). At the same time, he speculated on the presence of four "principal political entities", whose capitals he judged to be Tikal, Copan, Tonina, and (as a collective or in turn) Palenque, Yaxchilan, and Piedras Negras (Morley 1946: 160–161). He also attempted a wider political ranking in a map and associated table that set out a four-class division of Maya centres "according to their supposed degrees of relative importance" (Morley 1946: 316–319, plate 19, table VII). His main criteria were the scale of architecture and number of monuments, but he also included qualitative considerations. This contributed to what now seem to be glaring anomalies. Despite its enormous size and having the largest inventory of stelae, Calakmul was consigned to the second tier due to the "little aesthetic merit" of its sculpture (Morley 1946: 319). Mayapan was relegated to the third, irrespective of the fact that, as we have already seen, it is amply attested in ethnohistorical sources as the most powerful centre of Late Postclassic Yucatan (Roys 1962). Here it was the modest scale and relatively poor construction of its ceremonial buildings that excluded it from greatness.

Any clues to political organisation were to be deduced from the archaeological and ethnohistorical record alone. As regards the texts, Morley's move to the ahistorical position is first evident in his five-volume *The Inscriptions of the Peten*, where he reviews the major developments in Maya epigraphy since 1920 – all of them calendrical in nature – and drops even the suggestion of history (Morley 1937–1938: I, 103–108). By the time of *The Ancient Maya* his conversion was complete:

> [Maya texts] are in no sense records of personal glorification and self-laudation like the inscriptions of Egypt, Assyria, and Babylonia. They tell no story of kingly conquests, recount no deeds of imperial achievement; they neither praise nor exalt, glorify nor aggrandize, indeed they are so utterly impersonal, so completely non-individualistic, that it is even probable that the name-glyphs of specific men and women were never recorded upon the Maya monuments.
>
> (Morley 1946: 262)

In 1950, Thompson published his encyclopaedic *Maya Hieroglyphic Writing: Introduction*, a masterful treatment of the calendar system and his grand judgement on the nature of the script. It featured two of his deepest convictions: that any phoneticism in the hieroglyphs was strictly limited (Thompson 1950: 46–48) and that the texts lacked historical content of any kind. The latter was dismissed in characteristic style: "To add details of war or peace, of marriage or giving in marriage, to the solemn roll call of the periods of time is as though a tourist were to carve his name on Donatello's David" (Thompson 1950: 155).

THE PRAGMATISTS, 1950–1970

The vision of priests and peasants in a forest idyll would have a powerful hold on both the public and scholarly imaginations for years to come and was further solidified by Thompson's (1954) *The Rise and Fall of Maya Civilization.* However, the 1950s more truly belong to the research that would eventually topple it. An initial spark came in 1952 with Alberto Ruz's (1954, 1973) discovery of an elaborate tomb at the end of a rubble-filled stairway deep within the largest stepped pyramid at Palenque – a resting-place fit for an Egyptian Pharaoh. As Michael Coe (1956: 393) soon noted, this grandiose memorial suggested a concentration of wealth and personal power more typical of hereditary kings than stargazing theocrats.

It was within those troublesome portions of the texts strewn with dates, day-counts, and "non-calendrical" glyphs that a German émigré to Mexico, Heinrich Berlin (1958), made the first step in uncovering Maya history. There he found that each of the major sites displayed an "emblem glyph", a three-part compound with two consistent elements, and a third variable one specific to that city.[4] These distinctive markers would lie at the heart of all future epigraphic inquiries into Classic Maya politics, but at the time he could only speculate on their meaning, considering that they might be the names of cities, ruling dynasties, or patron deities. He followed this advance a year later by recognising that some of the figures depicted inside the great Palenque tomb were captioned by personal names, so identifying the first historical individuals in Maya art and writing (Berlin 1959).

The decisive breakthrough and full negation of the ahistorical view came with Tatiana Proskouriakoff's (1960) work on the inscriptions of Piedras Negras. This remarkable study, followed by two treatments of the monuments at Yaxchilan in a similar vein (Proskouriakoff 1963, 1964), sprang from a close scrutiny of the relationships between dates and particular hieroglyphs. Like Charles Bowditch (1901: 13) before her, she noticed that the chronology covering any group of adjacent Piedras Negras monuments never exceeded a normal human lifespan, but she took the analysis much further. Within the "textual residue" she was able to isolate the names of individual rulers, recognising their dates of birth, accession, and ultimately death, as well as other prominent events such as the taking of captives. In so doing, she identified the figures portrayed on the stelae not as gods but kings, and the robed figures that attended them not as priests but queens. Her modestly titled "historical hypothesis" was so tightly argued that it found universal acceptance, with even Thompson (1960: v, 1965: 636) quickly and graciously conceding his former position. The way was now open to apply the same methods to other sites, which was progressively done at Quirigua (Kelley 1962a), Palenque (Berlin 1965, 1968a; Mathews and Schele 1974), and Tikal (Coggins 1975; Jones 1977), among others.

Banishing anonymous theocracies and replacing them with vainglorious dynasties was the crowning achievement of the "first wave" of the decipherment. Yet everything had been accomplished by little more than pattern recognition and inductive reasoning – neither Berlin nor Proskouriakoff could read a hieroglyph and, indeed, were less than sure that they represented language in any direct sense. The seeds of the "second wave" and true decipherment lay in the work of their contemporary, the Russian linguist Yuri Knorozov (1952, 1956). Reviving a phonetic approach that had faltered in the hands of others, he applied some sparse clues in Landa's manuscript to the surviving Postclassic books and uncovered several core spelling principles. Published at a highpoint of the Cold War, with one paper bearing an editor's introduction extolling the virtues of Marxist-Leninist scholarship, it is little surprise that his ideas met a frosty reception in the West. Whether attributable to Thompson's (1953, 1959: 362, 1960: vi) acerbic critiques or, more realistically, to Knorozov's own lack of follow-through, it would be some three decades before his ideas bore full fruit.

While Proskouriakoff was preparing her ground-breaking thesis, another revolution, this time an archaeological one, was taking place at Tikal. Starting in 1956, a University of Pennsylvania project, mostly under the direction of William Coe, addressed an unusually broad set of research issues for its time, excavating not only temples and palaces, but also humble households, addressing the sequential development of the site, and assessing the relationship of the core to its sustaining hinterland. The mapping of Tikal's periphery revealed dispersed but significant settlement extending in all directions (Carr and Hazard 1961) – the house-mounds spotted by the early explorers were indeed on a grand scale. This was decisive in dispelling Thompson's notion of vacant ceremonial centres (Becker 1979, 1984), and the same low-density urbanism was subsequently found, if usually on a lesser scale, in all similar surveys.

But this was not the only surprise in the environs of Tikal, where further mapping found parts of an extensive, rampart-like earthwork (Puleston and

Callender 1967). Casting doubt on the "live and let live" Maya, this inspired a revisiting of the evidence for militarism, ultimately leading to the demolition of the pacific model at the hands of combined archaeological, epigraphic, and iconographic study (e.g. Webster 1976a, 1976b, 1977, 1978; Baudez and Mathews 1979; Riese 1984a; Freidel 1986; Schele and Miller 1986: 209–240).[5] Focused as it was on a single site it is unsurprising that the Tikal project had little to say about broader issues of political organisation, although its newfound size encouraged many to see it as *the* dominant Classic Maya centre, in an understanding not so very different from that of Gann.

Archaeological work that did pursue a wider political understanding came from William R. Bullard Jr. (1960, 1964). His analysis of settlement distribution in one part of the central southern lowlands produced a size-based hierarchy of sites and projected territories under their administration. William Sanders (1962, 1963) conducted similar studies in a portion of the western lowlands (Map 4), but set the results within a more theoretical framework. This was the cultural ecology of Julian Steward (1955), a perspective that gave environmental factors a leading, even determining, role in the development of social complexity. In *Mesoamerica: The Evolution of a Civilization*, Sanders and Barbara Price (1968) blended cultural ecology with the social evolutionary "band-tribe-chiefdom-state" scheme of Elman Service (1962). They concluded that priestly governments in the Maya lowlands were for the most part chiefdoms, although Tikal had reached "state-level" by the Late Classic Period (Sanders and Price 1968: 142–145, 205).

Emblem glyphs were first used in a political model by Thomas Barthel (1968a, 1968b). He took up Berlin's observation that Copan Stela A, dated to 731 CE, featured four such compounds – those of Tikal, Copan, Palenque, and an unknown centre he called *Chan* "Snake" – where each was associated with the glyph for a cardinal direction. From this Barthel posited a "cosmological model" that envisaged a four-way division of authority between these major sites. This revival of Morley's four "principal political entities" drew on assessments of ethnographic materials from the contact and early colonial eras, which showed a recurring concern for a quadripartite organisation of space within Maya communities (Coe 1965). Among other texts Barthel brought into his analysis was Ceibal (formerly Seibal) Stela 10 from 849 (Figure 63). This also features four emblems: two of the same ones found on Copan Stela A, Tikal, and "Snake", as well as that of Ceibal itself and another unknown emblem he called *Ik'*, "Wind". He argued that this quartet was a later set of regional capitals whose central locations reflected a contraction of the Maya realm – the more peripheral sites of Copan and Palenque having by that time succumbed to the mounting collapse.

OF MAPS AND MODELS, 1970–1990

The 1960s had seen major developments in archaeological theory, and these came to the Maya area in Kent Flannery's (1972) application of systems analysis and spatial modelling. Flannery was interested in the differing information flows required by the ascending social evolutionary levels of Service (1962) and Fried (1967), with a particular focus on the pinnacle of complexity, the "state". Inspiration came from efforts in the Near East to identify administrative hierarchies through mapping the size and distribution of settlements (Johnson 1972). The key tool here was central place theory (Christaller 1933; Haggett 1965), which had been devised to chart market exchange systems, but was now re-purposed as an instrument of political analysis. Its method traces shortest-distance connections between primary and secondary sites, judging that a hexagonal lattice of nodes represents optimum efficiency in communications and, in political terms, a level of organisation consistent with states. Flannery (1972: 420–421, figure 5) applied the same procedure to the sites surrounding two major Maya centres, Calakmul and Naranjo, detecting patterns of just this kind and positing a correspondingly high degree of regional integration.

Another approach to geographic modelling came from Norman Hammond (1972, 1974), who introduced Thiessen polygons to map potential territories around Maya sites. The Thiessen method takes equidistant points between selected sites and from them draws perpendicular lines whose intersections define hypothetical boundaries and domains. Initially employed to chart the resource catchments around the site of Lubaantun (Hammond 1972: 774–775), the technique was subsequently extended to posit political domains across a swathe of the lowlands (Hammond 1974: 321–322, figure 3). Hammond joined Flannery in acknowledging the likely gap between such formulations and the real world, but their maps and diagrams were the first attempts to understand how Maya settlements might have interacted with a wider spatial dimension.

Barthel's cosmological model left several important issues unaddressed. Most of all, how were the hundreds of other Maya sites, including very large ones with their own emblem glyphs, organised within this scheme? That question was taken up by Joyce Marcus (1973), who drew together textual, quantitative, and spatial data in the first assessment of its kind, further developed in her book *Emblem and State in the Classic Maya Lowlands: An Epigraphic Approach to Territorial Organization* (Marcus 1976). She reasoned that the inscriptions of any one centre would likely mention the emblem of another to which it was beholden, but not vice versa. This methodology produced a three-tier hierarchy of sites for each projected state, with small settlements lacking inscriptions constituting a fourth. She suggested that the unknown "Wind" site was Motul de San José and, based on its size, that Calakmul would turn out to be the missing "Snake" site, and was ultimately proved correct on both counts. Regional hierarchies for the states of Tikal, Palenque, Copan, and Yaxchilan (due to the uncertainty of the Snake identification Calakmul was omitted) were defined by their constituent primary, secondary, tertiary, and quaternary sites. The spatial component to her work came in formalising the central place lattices linking Tikal and Naranjo, now reconstructed as primary and secondary centres within a single state (Marcus 1973: figure 6).

Marcus (1993, 1998) later elaborated her ideas into a more dynamic model that saw a waxing and waning of political integration. In this, a landscape of Preclassic chiefdoms coalesced during the Classic Period into five unitary states by 731 (Tikal, Calakmul, Copan, Palenque, and Yaxchilan, together with a more loosely structured confederacy in the Petexbatun sub-region), only to fracture along the "cleavage planes" of their component territories and devolve back into small chiefdoms as the ninth-century collapse approached (Marcus 1993: figure 26). Close parallels were drawn with the ethnohistorical record of contact-period Yucatan and the dissolution of political authority that followed the fall of Mayapan. Direct historical analogies such as this were strongly preferred over the kind of global comparisons gaining ground among fellow researchers in the 1990s.

Quantitative approaches to Maya political structure found their fullest expression in the work of Richard E. W. Adams and his collaborators. Estimates of the construction mass and the typological make-up of sites across the central lowlands were collected in search of hierarchical rankings between them (Adams 1981; Turner, Turner, and Adams 1981; Adams and Adams 2003). A separate strategy assessed overall site-sizes in relation to their distribution across the greater part of the region (Adams and Jones 1981). Taken together, the resulting data were believed to betray the presence of regional states headed by Tikal and Calakmul, a view subsequently expanded into eight such units across the Maya realm, each averaging some 30,000 km^2 in area (Adams 1986: 437) (Map 5a).

But this version of the Maya past was soon to be challenged by fresh decipherments, including a number from the nascent second wave of phonetic readings. Warfare emerged as a common topic of the inscriptions, expressed by a variety of glyphic terms (e.g. Riese 1980, 1984a; Sosa and Reents 1980; Schele 1982; Houston 1983a, 1983b; Stuart 1985a; Orejel 1990). Newly read texts revealed that a large number of sites engaged in military operations, their one-on-one encounters distributed across the lowlands without regard to the boundaries of projected regional states. Indeed, some of the non-local mentions of emblem glyphs that had previously been taken as evidence for political integration turned out to document quite the reverse – violent confrontations between neighbours (Stuart 1993: 326). The dates of these recorded conflicts were also significant, since they were almost completely restricted to the Late

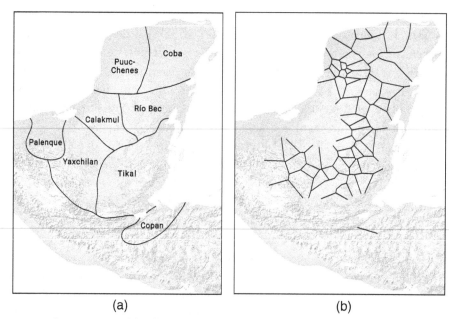

(a)   (b)

MAP 5 Contrasting models of Classic Maya political organisation: (a) The Regional State (after Adams 1986: 437); (b) The Peer Polity/Weak State (after Mathews 1991: figure 2.6).

Classic Period, precisely the point when regional states were said to have reached their maximum size and degree of consolidation.

A better understanding of the emblem glyph revealed it to be a personal title of lords governing distinct domains, each of whom claimed an exalted but equivalent status (Mathews and Justeson 1984: 216–219). While the list of unique emblems grew ever longer, the only evidence for titular hierarchies at that time was among the secondary lords that were subject to emblem-bearers (Stuart 1985b). It was the combination of these factors that led Peter Mathews (1985: 32–33, 1991: 29) to conclude that emblem glyphs were assertions of political autonomy. Charting their distribution and using Thiessen polygons to reconstruct their territories, his map showed a dense mosaic covering much of the southern lowlands, with conjectured domains pushed well into the north (Map 5b). These tesserae, roughly 1,500–2,500 km² in area (though some were much smaller), constituted the ground plans of sixty or seventy petty statelets – a radical contrast to the regional state perspective.

There had always been archaeologists who favoured a small polity view, and some of them were drawn to cross-cultural work on divided political landscapes, principally to the "peer polity interaction" model of Colin Renfrew (1982; Renfrew and Cherry 1986). The collected volume of that name included contributions from David Freidel (1986) and Jeremy Sabloff (1986), who explored how small autonomous Maya polities could have developed through processes of collective competition, emulation, and exchange. The defining feature of a peer polity is that it is "not subject to the jurisdiction of a higher power" (Renfrew 1986: 2, 4), so that the emergence of dominant polities, ultimately in the form of empires or unified states, spells the end of the system. Peer polities had something in common with the heterarchical model advanced by Carole Crumley (1979, 1987, 1995). This perspective actively contested the tenets of central place theory and its assumption that size distinctions and spatial distributions necessarily reflect hierarchical arrangements (Crumley 1976). Instead, heterarchy considers the ways in which polities within the same cultural system might be unranked or ranked in different ways. Some Mayanists would later take an explicitly heterarchical approach, particularly in regard to political economy (e.g. Potter and King 1995; Scarborough, Valdez, and Dunning 2003).

Another approach to small-scale politics came from a focus on urbanism. William Sanders and David Webster (1988) applied the typology of Richard Fox (1977) to the Maya case, concluding that sites such as Copan were examples of his "regal-ritual city". This is defined as a place of consumption rather than production, in which symbolism and ritual are important but political pragmatics remain paramount, even though central power is rather feeble. In their assessment, Copan was a chiefdom or ranked society that "crystallised" into a state only in the reign of its last true king in the later eighth century CE.

By the end of the decade the phonetic decipherment of the script had begun in earnest, with the initial trickle of readings swelling to something closer to a flood. The most important contribution of this time, David Stuart's (1987) *Ten Phonetic Syllables*, had a clear methodological impact, demonstrating how each successful reading of a sign could branch out, hydra-like, to suggest several more. With increasing access to phonology it was possible to investigate grammar, with scholars combining epigraphic data with colonial and modern Mayan linguistic sources to reveal the underlying language of the texts.[6] As one discovery followed the next, so the hieroglyphs began to provide detailed information on a number of topics, politics among them. Few advances of the late 1980s were more significant in this regard than the discovery of toponyms, research that was ultimately published as *Classic Maya Place Names* (Stuart and Houston 1994). This opened a rich seam of data meshing political events with specific places and identities, revealing that at least some emblem glyphs were based on place-names.

INTO THE BLACK BOX, 1990–PRESENT

The collected volume *Classic Maya Political History* sought to synthesise the emerging epigraphic data with archaeological research from across the region (Culbert 1991a). Several contributions addressed the issue of political organisation directly, including a review of emblem glyphs (Mathews 1991) and a summary of the site interactions known at that time (Schele and Mathews 1991). The consensus reached was that possession of an emblem was de facto evidence of independence, although T. Patrick Culbert (1991b: 140–143, 1991c: 325) expressed reservations on this point. He sided with colleagues – invariably those who worked at major sites – who favoured larger and more integrated domains (e.g. Folan 1985; Chase, Chase, and Haviland 1990). Hammond (1991) invoked a "black box" approach to the Maya polity and reviewed the full range of competing explanatory paradigms, giving early notice of the ethnographic models from Southeast Asia that would soon become major talking points.

The next generation of researchers to come to the issue, most notably Arthur Demarest (1984: 146–147, 1992: 149–156) and Stephen Houston (1992, 1993: 142–148), took the case for numerous small polities as proven, but were dissatisfied with the limitations of a peer polity model that was descriptive of a political landscape but offered little by way of analysis. The construct said nothing about the internal functioning of such polities, or explained why such a dispersed, non-hierarchical pattern of authority should persist for 600 years or more. What was it that inhibited, or even prevented, Classic-era polities from forming larger states and empires?

A key influence here was the growing evidence for great variability in individual site histories emerging from both archaeology and epigraphy. There was clearly no single trajectory of development and decline spanning the Classic era, but instead a series of fluctuating fortunes that aligned only at the ninth century collapse. Even the "Middle Classic Hiatus" – a long-perceived malaise curbing monument erection and major construction for some 80 years (Willey 1974) – was now revealed as a phenomenon overly influenced by data from Tikal, which suffered a key military defeat at its inception (Chase and Chase 1987: 60; Houston 1987: 93). The implication was that there was something innately unstable about Classic-era polities, a view that inevitably shifted attention from their external to internal dynamics. Interest alighted on ideological factors of the kind functionalists and processualists had long dismissed as mere surface phenomena.[7] Here the investments the Maya put into monumental architecture and facilities appropriate for mass public display, together with a strong imagistic and textual emphasis on ritual and perform-ance, provoked comparisons with societies in which symbolic extravagance masked political fragility.

These analogies, drawn from ethnographic and historical research in Africa and Southeast Asia, would collectively become known as "weak state" models. The first of them, the African Segmentary State, was defined by Aidan Southall (1956, 1965) as an entity in which "the spheres of ritual suzerainty and political sovereignty do not coincide" (Southall 1988: 52). Royal power is restricted to an inner core beyond which lies an unstable periphery controlled by the heads of segmentary lineages, each of whom replicates the central kingship "writ small" (Southall 1988: 64). The whole is held together not by coercive power but by charismatic authority and claims to divine sanction. The rulers' privileged access to the supernatural world is asserted through a range of devices, most of all by staging elaborate rituals at the capital. Under successful rulers the polity maintains its integrity and can even expand by conquest. However, such gains are not integrated and so are easily lost. Unsuccessful rulers not only risk usurpation, they can endanger the existence of the polity itself, as peripheral magnates desert to neighbouring kings or assert their own independence.

Closely related models from Southeast Asia were the Theatre State (Geertz 1968, 1977, 1980) and Galactic Polity (Tambiah 1976, 1977). Although Southall (1988: 53) considered these little more than variants of his own construct, it is clear that they are less reliant on kinship structures and have a more developed sense of the symbolic character of a centre-oriented polity. Indeed, for Clifford Geertz (1968: 38) symbolism was of the essence: "The ritual life of the court – the mass ceremonies, the high-wrought art, the elaborate politesse – formed not just the trappings of rule but the substance of it". Consciously modelled on a *mandala* cosmogram, such polities consist of repetitive formations that radiate outward at ever-diminishing scale and weakening attachment to the core. Stanley Tambiah (1976: 102–131, 1977), however, took issue with the idea of polities as earthbound models of the cosmos, arguing instead for a "totalisation" that privileged neither the sacred nor the secular but saw them as directly and continuously engaged. To illustrate the connection between charismatic authority and the extent of nominal suzerainty he cited a Javanese analogy, in which the brighter a candle the further its light will reach (Moertono 1968: 112; Tambiah 1977: 74). Again, expansion through conquest was possible, but was fragile and ultimately unsustainable.

These features were sufficiently close to what was known of the Maya, that one or other of the weak state concepts appealed to a broad range of scholars and was variously applied to all periods, from the Preclassic to Postclassic, and all regions, in the highlands as well as the lowlands (e.g. Demarest 1984: 146–147, 1992: 149–156; Fox 1987, 1994; Sanders and Webster 1988: 534; Ball and Taschek 1991; Houston 1992, 1993: 142–148; Houston and Escobedo 1997). Their writings brought an overtly comparative perspective to the problem, offering a credible solution to the riddle of why Maya polities remained small and why they put so much effort into ritual display.

By the early 1990s opinion about the degree of territorial consolidation attained by the Classic Maya was sharply divided. Some held firm to the idea that the landscape had condensed into a small number of large polities, while others saw a large number of small polities as an enduring feature. Only the latter seemed consistent with the epigraphic evidence now available, but this left at least one important question unresolved. Why, if every polity was more-or-less equal, were the capitals of some vastly larger, in terms of both monumental construction and surrounding settlement, than others? This was a prime rejoinder offered by regionalists, who found the idea of ascribing peer status to neighbouring sites that might differ tenfold in size more than a little perverse. However, this objection left the advocates for small polities unfazed, since their shared heterarchical orientation saw no obligatory link between size and political power. For them, distinctions of scale could equally well have other causes, such as differing religious status or length of occupation.

All small-polity positions stood on an assumption that emblem glyphs were absolute markers of autonomy, but was this really true? As further readings came to light, signs began to mount that it was not. A statement had already been identified in which one emblem-bearing king described himself as the possession of another (Houston and Mathews 1985: 27, n.2). Additionally, the accession ceremonies of some kings were followed by a passage naming a second king who bears a different emblem, connected by a term that elsewhere conveyed the sense of supervision (Schele and Freidel 1990: 155, 175).[8] Neither of these formulae seemed especially common at the time, barely a handful of cases were known, and they were taken to be ephemeral links of little political consequence.

My own interest in these seemingly aberrant statements was piqued by the disproportionate number of them that involved the "Snake" polity, the focus of my research at the time. As we have seen, Barthel had named this entity among his four regional capitals and Marcus had linked it to Calakmul; where mapping around its substantial core had by now revealed a settlement exceeding even that of Tikal in size (May Hau et al. 1990).[9] The Snake polity was emerging as the most frequently mentioned in inscriptions right across the southern lowlands, and my initial goal was to understand why this should be so. Always occupying the superordinate position in hierarchical statements, its rulers installed or sanctioned the rule of others, while other kings described themselves as possessions of the Snake king. It seemed clear that this polity was an exceptional political force, one whose greatest impact was visible not in territorial terms but in its wide-ranging network of patron–client relationships. This suggested a third way in which Classic Maya politics might be organised and understood, distinct from either the regional or weak state (Martin 1993: 12–14, 1996a: 233, 1996b, 2000a).[10] To pursue these ideas and issues further I began epigraphic fieldwork at Calakmul, under the auspices of Mexico's Instituto Nacional de Antropología e Historia and project director Ramón Carrasco, in a programme that continued for 22 years.

Additionally, I invited Nikolai Grube to join me in charting these data on a larger scale and integrating them with other forms of epigraphic information (Martin and Grube 1994a, 1994b, 1995), work that resulted in the historical compendium *Chronicle of the Maya Kings and Queens: Deciphering the Dynasties of the Ancient Maya* (Martin and Grube 2000, 2008). With the rising pace of the decipherment it was possible to seek broader patterns to political behaviour and to situate them within a detailed context. The landscape of multiple polities described by Mathews (1985, 1991) was supported at every turn, but it did not follow that these units were either equivalent in status or inherently fragile.

A review of the textual corpus and fresh finds made it possible to greatly enlarge the number of both known forms of hierarchical statement, while suggesting that a third – also used for the supervision of accession ceremonies – should join them. To the asymmetries of these relationships other kinds of evidence could be added. A strong correspondence emerged between polities appearing in superordinate positions and those successful in war. Equally, it was clear that dominant polities were usually those with larger and more impressive capitals – whether as cause or effect, size did matter. The ability of some polities to sustain political relationships over considerable distances and multiple generations argued against their having some innate structural fragility or reliance on personal charisma. At the same time, there was no evidence that emblem-bearing polities ever absorbed others to create larger integrated domains. The macro-political power on view did indeed lay less in grand territorial ambitions than it did in forging networks of elite patronage.

In this regard we drew on Edward Luttwak's (1976: 192, figure 1.2) distinction between hegemonic and territorial forms of control employed by early Imperial Rome – first applied in Mesoamerica to the Aztec Empire by Ross Hassig (1985: 92–94; Martin and Grube 1994a: 23–24).[11] Across Central Mexico, the Aztec "Triple Alliance" built a vast system of tribute-paying clients by means of short-lived conquests and long-term intimidation, blended with policies that drew newly subject nobility into beneficial networks of elite interaction (Smith 1986). No Maya entity achieved such military prowess and scale of success, but a number behaved rather like the lesser hegemons found among the small-scale polities that preceded the Aztec Empire. Here and elsewhere asymmetrical relationships were accompanied by a flow of tribute from client to patron, and the conjecture was that the same would be true for the Classic Maya.

This hegemonic perspective on the Classic Maya moved away from locational or statistical modelling, or the search for continuities with later periods and ethnographic analogy, and instead towards an understanding grounded in historical specifics. More evidence was to be found for the idea that the central lowlands saw a long-standing opposition between Tikal and Calakmul (Schele and Freidel 1990: 211). At the same time, it was clear that these influential players were by no means the only hegemons of the Classic Period and individual regions saw the rise and fall of their own powers.[12]

While the political networks each created were based on formal arrangements and specific bonds between kings, they had dynamic histories and were never codified into state-like structures (Martin and Grube 1995: 44, 2000: 18–21).

But the debate proved far from closed. Archaeologists responded with alternative models that put renewed emphasis on statistics and ethnohistorical analogy. Arlen Chase and Diane Chase (1998) revived the regional state, this time rooted not in settlement hierarchies but in an assessment of military logistics. Here three types of data were taken into account: the average distances between selected major centres, the average distances between combatants in a sample of 33 epigraphically attested conflicts, and a three-day marching distance around each major centre. The latter generates a territory some 60 km in radius, which was judged to be the maximum reach of practical military control.[13] This limiting factor results in a political landscape containing a minimum of 14 regional states, each averaging about 11,333 km^2 in area (Chase and Chase 1998: 14–17, figure 1). "Primary capitals" in this model include the sites of Tikal, Palenque, Calakmul, Caracol, and La Corona, which are distinguished from "border centres" such as Naranjo, Yaxchilan, and Tonina, secondary sites over which rival capitals vied for control.[14]

As in all regional perspectives, the link between emblem glyphs and individual political units was challenged, with a later article suggesting that widely seen emblems, such as that of the Snake, could have a religious rather than a political significance (Chase, Chase, and Smith 2009: 180).[15] Despite utilising epigraphic data in their model, the inscriptions were held to be suffused with mysticism and propaganda and thus unreliable sources for historical reconstruction. We will return to this issue in Chapter 4, but it is safe to say that scepticism about the usefulness of the texts remains strong in some quarters.

Indeed, adapting Martin Wobst's (1978) turn of phrase about the dangers of an archaeology unduly driven by ethnography, Prudence Rice (2004: 9) has warned of a potential "tyranny of the epigraphic record". In her book *Maya Political Science: Time, Astronomy, and the Cosmos* of 2004, Rice argued that priority should instead be accorded to direct historical analogy. Her proposals focussed on a Late Postclassic Period (1250–1546 CE) concept mentioned in a few colonial documents from northern Yucatan, all dating to the sixteenth century and later (Edmonson 1979, 1982; Avendaño y Loyola 1987: 39). This concerns a formulation of the Maya calendar that arranges thirteen *k'atun* – units just shy of twenty solar years – into a cycle or "wheel" encompassing 256 years. Each *k'atun* is identified by the day-name on which it ends, which in every case is *ajaw*, "lord", each distinguished by coefficients that span one to thirteen. Putatively called the *may* in these late sources, this arrangement is ascribed a political significance in which named sites are said to have served as sequential seats of authority over each *k'atun* subdivision.

Rice takes this to be a literal rather than allegorical scheme and projects it back into the Classic era, extending the model to argue that every *may* had its own governing seat, a centre that presided over a full 256-year period. For her, the "politics", including "warfare", that appear in the inscriptions belong in inverted commas because they refer less to historical dynamics than they do acts of symbolism or performance (Rice 2004: 7, 259, 271–273, 289). This includes quarrels between Tikal and Calakmul, which are viewed as ritualistic struggles staged to legitimise the hosting of a new *may* cycle. Rice concedes that among the thousand or so calendrical cycle-endings recorded in the inscriptions, not one refers to a 256-year circuit, nor is there any written reference to the seating of a new political centre at a K'atun period. However, in a response to her critics, she invokes James Scott's (1990) concept of the "hidden transcript" (Rice 2013: 686). This argues that it is precisely what is most important to a society that will be masked, omitted, or denied – meaning that it might be entirely invisible in the ancient sources.[16]

Since 1990 excavation in the Maya area has gathered pace, with many sites, large and small, the subjects of multi-year investigations. Questions of social and political organization are, of course, always close at hand, and archaeologists have continued to probe material culture in search of its wider implications (e.g. de Montmollin 1989, 1995; LeCount and Yaeger 2010; Foias 2013). New technologies are currently revolutionising our knowledge of Maya settlement and engineered landscapes; resolving some vital issues while raising others (e.g. Chase et al. 2011; Canuto et al. 2018; Garrison, Houston, and Alcover 2018). As a result of these developments, we have never had so rich and multifaceted a collection of relevant data.

To summarise, this synoptic review makes it clear that Classic Maya political organisation has been, and remains, contested ground. To make further progress, and ultimately to build a true consensus, we must succeed in the double task of building a deeper comprehension of the data and applying appropriate conceptual models to make sense of them. If successful, this would contribute to the wider understanding of the variations and similarities in pre-Modern politics worldwide.

THREE

ON ARCHAEOPOLITICS

Perhaps no other part of the ancient world has seen such a lengthy discourse about the fundamental nature of its political organisation, nor seen judgements vary so widely. Practical considerations offer some explanation for the lack of agreement, since both material and textual avenues have suffered from slow and uneven accumulations of reliable data. The difficulty of fieldwork in what are often remote and densely forested regions – where elementary archaeological procedures have long been arduous, time-consuming, and expensive – means that it has taken a good while to fully grasp the physical parameters of the problem. Equally, deciphering the script has proved to be a project of daunting complexity, in which the partial data teased out in one generation have often cast into a different light when a fuller picture emerged in the next. As a result, injections of fresh information, from either domain, have frequently not so much modified existing understandings as sent them careening in new directions.

However, it is clear that there is more to this interpretive diversity than alternative sources of data. Researchers have taken very different philosophical stands on how what survives of the past should be translated into evidence in the present, reflecting debates taking place well beyond Maya studies. Today we accept that all scholarship is historically situated and inescapably imbued with the zeitgeist of its time, something that determines not only what conceptual tools are available to us but the kinds of interpretation we can even imagine. Wherever we swim it is under the influence of deeper tides.

This study can be no exception of course and, in this chapter, I set out the particular ideas and premises that ground and guide it, whether implicitly or explicitly.[1]

ABANDONING THE STATE

As we saw in Chapter 2, a consistent point of divergence for Mayanists has been the relative strength or weakness of central authority, with its implications for the extent of its territorial control and the nature of its administrative structure. This question has persistently focused on the existence and character of the "state" as both a historical object and a transcending abstraction. No view of Classic Maya politics can avoid taking some stand on this topic.

In *The Origin of the State*, Robert Lowie (1927) argued for a "principle of continuity" that allowed virtually any scale of political association to be characterised as a state. But it was not long before Arthur Radcliffe-Brown (1940) was taking the idea of the State (his capitalisation) to task. In the preface to the founding text of political anthropology, *African Political Systems*, he called it a "fiction of the philosophers", and claimed that only governments, as organised groups of individuals, were a political reality. The editors of that volume were equally leery of the term and avoided it altogether; their only concession to classification being a division between centralised and decentralised societies (Fortes and Evans-Pritchard 1940: 5–6).

By mid-century a new movement in anthropology was taking hold, one that sought to purge the discipline of the culture–historical particularism these authors represented. The new approach was universalistic and looked for its model not in the humanities but in the sciences, adopting a logical-positivism that promised greater objectivity (White 1949). At its heart was a return to sociocultural evolution as a central explanatory paradigm, rehabilitating the ideas of Lewis Henry Morgan (1877). Morgan's escalating tiers of sociocultural sophistication, from savagery to barbarism to civilisation, were reformulated by Elman Service into his four-level progression of band, tribe, chiefdom, and state (Sahlins and Service 1960; Service 1962). In contrast to the cultural-historicists, the socioevolutionists saw the development of the state as a distinct watershed, a move from *societas* to *civitas* (Morgan 1877: 7, passim) that crossed a "great divide" (Service 1975: 3–10) between kin-based and bureaucratic forms of government.

These ideas formed the core of the processualist programme in archaeology, where the same nomothetic approach brought quantification, hypothetico-deductive testing, and "middle range" theory to the fore (Willey and Philips 1958; Binford 1962, 1965; Clarke 1968).[2] The formation of the "archaic state" was retained as a key focus, with the scale and location of ancient settlements now read as evolutionary stages etched into the ground, the veritable stigmata of sociopolitical organisation. The processualist concept of the state came to prescribe a four-tier settlement hierarchy, in which a centralised bureaucracy had superseded familial ties as an organising principle. An equation between the state as a political order and as a cultural level was often explicit in processualist writing, with "state" and "civilisation" openly employed as synonyms (e.g. Sanders and Price 1968: 44–45).

There are certainly consistencies to be found in sociocultural development, as communities acquire new means of integration and administration, simultaneously adapting to and modifying their environments, both physical and ideological. The issue is whether there is a trajectory to this growing complexity that is predictable in all places and at all times, with thresholds or "tipping points" between distinct stages. The labels band and tribe, with their origins in colonialist ethnography, were soon discarded, although in replacing them with more neutral terms the four-stage scheme was left intact (Fried 1967).[3] Real cracks in stage theory only appeared as the once-simple sequence began to atomise into sub-types, as scholars struggled to capture the variability they saw in their data (see Chapman 2003: 41–45; Yoffee 2005: 23–26). Each addition represented not greater refinement, but evidence that stage theory was falling apart. As one comparative ethnographic analysis demonstrated, given a sufficiently large sample the groupings of features thought to specify distinct levels disappeared – the variation between societies was instead "multidimensional and continuous" (Feinman and Neitzel 1984: 78). In the wake of this and similar assessments it was the turn of the chiefdom to fall from grace. A number of Americanists have kept the faith (e.g. Redmond 1998; Earle 2011), but for others the chiefdom could only be derided as an ethnocentric "delusion" (Pauketat 2007).

The neo-evolutionary position dominated the theoretical landscape from the 1960s into the 1980s, but faced increasing opposition from those who saw one-time heuristic models mistaken for "things in the world" and a once-innovative agenda turn into a sterile scientism. There were calls for a shift away from disembodied systems toward a "peopled past", one concerned as much with the ideational as the material aspects of social life (Hodder 1982, 1986; Tilley 1982; Miller and Tilley 1984; Shanks and Hodder 1995). What became known as postprocessualist archaeology, then interpretive archaeology, was influenced by both structuralism and poststructuralism, the latter overtly in the mode of critical theory (see Patterson 1989). In its search for more humanistic approaches, postprocessualism invoked the anthropologies of Geertz (1973) and Victor Turner (1974), with their views of society as an inescapable world of symbols in which meaning could only emerge from the close exercise of cultural hermeneutics.

The impact of these developments on Maya studies, such as it was, came in the enthusiasm for "weak state" models detailed in Chapter 2. What all such interpretations share, if to different degrees, is a disconnect between the rhetoric of rulership — its grandiose displays of ritual and pageantry wrapped in a quasi-divine aura — and authentic political power. This dissonance found its fullest expression in the Geertz's Theatre State (1980), which is a glorious façade behind which kings struggle to project the illusion of potency, the effort of doing so becoming the purpose of rulership itself. Yet weak state constructs have always had troubling aspects. Concerns have been raised by the disturbingly broad range of societies to which these models have been applied (Houston and Escobedo 1997: 472), which range from massive entities such as the Vijayanagara polity in fourteenth century India (Stein 1977), to tiny ones such as those of archaic Greece (Runciman 1982: 352). Something that can be scaled up and down so radically would seem to offer no real analytical utility. Weak state models, as their name indicates, did not escape the statist legacy, but merely sought to explain deficient or counterintuitive cases. What their wide adoption achieved was a period in which the idea of government was drained of pragmatism, a view dubbed by one critic as "the State *sans* politics" (Chattopadhyaya 1985: 16).

The state long escaped the censure visited upon its cousins on the neo-evolutionary scale, with even those who rejected stage theories seeing it as a real and necessary artefact in the world (e.g. Chapman 2003: 88–100; Yoffee 2005: 15–17). But contemporary challenges to the state had already emerged among political scientists, who had begun to wonder if the object that had consumed so much of their energy was really what it seemed. Their aim had always been to define its substantive qualities, but Philip Abrams (1988) argued that its usefulness came from its very lack of substance. Its purpose instead was that of a "mask" designed to obscure all manners of exploitation. Even those who believed that the state was more just than a mask saw an entity of extreme variation, a modern construct that is "largely useless for theory-building" (Ferguson and Mansbach 1996: 10). As Yale Ferguson put it: "Where we differ strongly with most archaeologists and anthropologists is with regard to their persistent use of the term 'state' to refer to a host of different polities in the ancient and medieval (pre-Westphalian) worlds ... [...] It is the political equivalent of talking about the wheeled carts on Roman roads being automobiles" (Ferguson 2002: 83–84).

Here the fault-line between political anthropology and political science neatly comes into view. Political science is openly teleological, exploring the past only to the degree that it can illuminate the present, in which the subject is always ourselves and the Western world. Political anthropology differs in its goal to understand worlds culturally and often temporally distant from us, asking what different configurations of power can teach us about human capacities, always alert to the way in which local cultural inventions complicate or disrupt the idea of universals. Yet in the recent move within anthropological and archaeological circles away from political forms and toward political relations, new areas of common ground are opening up. Here the exploration of phenomena such as ideology, authority, legitimacy, sovereignty, and conflict have largely displaced objects of analysis such as the state, city, government, economic institutions, religious organisations, and the like (e.g. Baines and Yoffee 1998), shifting attention to transhistorical and transcultural themes relevant to both disciplines.

From this perspective, Adam T. Smith (2003: 78–102) launched his comprehensive critique of the state, refuting the claims made for its universality and distinctive imprint on the landscape. For Smith, its long-dominance had distracted scholars from more important questions: "In placing the State at the heart of investigations into early complex polities, political analysis – the investigation of the formation, administration, and transformation of civil relationships – is replaced by a political cladistics in which typological classification suffices for explanation" (Smith 2003: 81).

To accept that the state is not a timeless universal, but a creature developed in and most applicable to the modern world, one deeply coloured within anthropology by its association with the neo-evolutionary ladder, is to see an impediment rather than an aid to archaeopolitical research. To be clear, this is not to reject classification of all kinds, or to deny that there are qualitative distinctions between one variety of political order and another. But it is to abandon the idea that these are systematic, predictable, and advance in lockstep, compelling us to take the messy, blurred realities in the data at face value. A political anthropology without idealised tiers is one that focuses on degrees of social complexity, examining how universal phenomena express themselves locally in culturally-fashioned and historically-contingent ways (see Tainter 1996: 13–15; Yoffee 2005: 15–16).

THE RECURSIVE TURN

In the wake of the postprocessualist critique, a renewed program for exploring the social and political in the ancient world was required. It was clear that this would need to include a shift in focus from faceless systems to one centred on individual lives and experiences, a concern with ideational as much as material forces, an orientation toward society as historical and contingent, an engagement with politics on the level of practical effects, and an approach that looked to internally rather than externally imposed change.[4] This effort would be expressed in a particular group of theoretical concerns, a revised set of thematic interests, a revisiting of material and spatial engagements, as well as in a revived interest in documents and representations.

The dominant social theories of the mid-twentieth century were at heart synchronic. Whether it was the functionalism of Talcott Parsons (1951) or the structuralism of Claude Lévi-Strauss (1963), societies were modelled as static and unchanging. Functionalism did this through a biological metaphor, in which social roles and institutions were likened to organs in the body, each designed to serve a specific task and contribute to a stable, optimised whole. Structuralism drew instead on a language model, specifically Ferdinand Saussure's distinction between *langue* (grammar) and *parole* (speech). Lévi-Strauss equated *langue* with the unconscious mind and inner mental templates that determined human behaviour, casting *parole* into a secondary role of a derivative conscious mind of mere expression.

There was never any question that this atemporality was artificial and assumed only for the purposes of analysis. As all linguists knew, language itself evolves, doing so by means of small innovations in individual speech acts that reflect back to progressively modify the grammar that otherwise governs them. However gradual change might be, structure is dynamic.

A social theory embracing this process would be one that re-imagined how individuals and societies relate to one another, contesting the idea that agency is unidirectionally determined by structure. This was realised in the work of anthropologist Pierre Bourdieu (1977, 1990) and sociologist Anthony Giddens (1979, 1984). Both argued for a duality between the two, a reciprocal interaction known as recursion. In this, agents and structures are not separate and opposed but mutually constitutive, each shaping the other through the repetition of conscious and unconscious acts. In the practice theory of Bourdieu, the emphasis fell on the ingrained and unreflective concept of *habitus*, in which small adjustments gradually alter internalised dispositions and the norms under which acts take place. Giddens similarly saw a range of embedded routines, but was also interested in conscious change performed by knowledgeable actors, together forming a process he dubbed *structuration*. Both of these perspectives were holistic in the sense that they refused to see either agents or structures as primary and antecedent. Although not a term that either employs, it is clear that dualities of this kind can only emerge from processes of interactive co-evolution.

Archaeologists pursuing that elusive peopled past sought to build these ideas into fresh agendas for interpreting the material record (e.g. Pauketat 2000, 2001, 2007; Barrett 2001; Dornan 2002; Porter 2010; also Hodder 1985). Exactly how this might be accomplished has been a matter of debate, with the labels of agency and practice applied to a worryingly broad and diffuse range of humanistic concerns (Dobres and Robb 2000). One approach reads physical remains not as products of social action but as evidence for society-in-the-making (Pauketat 2000: 123), while another sees the archaeological record filled not with the traces of past practices but only with the facilities that enabled those practices (Barrett 2001: 153).

An underlying issue here is to what extent, and in what ways, are polities mental constructs as opposed to material ones? How, indeed, do we analyse political constitution once liberated from the teleological frame of the state? Giddens's model envisaged structure as composed of two parts, rules and resources, in which the former determines the application of the latter – a partnership that constitutes "the media through which power is exercised" (Giddens 1979: 91). Importantly, resources are not only material things but also human capacities of body and mind, including knowledge. This model was subsequently refined and expanded by William Sewell (1992: 9–13), who recast rules as "schemas" in order to evade the implication of rigidity and to signal a more adaptive and inventive potential. Importantly, he insisted on a further level of recursion in which there can be no schemas without the resources that make them possible and, in turn, resources are recognised as such only because they are created or utilised by schemas. As with the capacity for agency, resources are universal – all actors possess capacities of mind and material, however vast or meagre they might be.[5]

This reformulation offers us a suitably elemental level at which we might examine and understand the composition of political societies. They would consist of the expected sets of ordering ideas, but ones that have a structural role *only* as they are practically enacted. To exercise power is to have the capacity to utilise resources via control of their corresponding schemas. In this view, structure cannot be an entirely abstract or virtual thing, since to have effects it must at some point have a material dimension, however ephemeral. The material aspect is also important because the availability of certain resources also determines what schemas, and therefore powers, are possible or conceivable. In a recursive model the two are always interdependent. In a further amendment, Sewell (1992: 16) suggests that society does not have a single structure, but multiple overlapping and interacting structures, each determining their own sets of practices "which exist at different levels, operate in different modalities, and are themselves based on widely varying types and quantities of resources". This has implications for studies of the ancient world in a number of ways and obliges us to think in a more focussed fashion both how we conceive of extinct political structures and what we can know about them today.

While enthusiastically taken up by those studying the ancient world, it often passed without comment that neither Giddens nor Bourdieu had set out to produce a universalistic model. Giddens' (1979: 2) work explicitly began as a response to socialism and capitalism and only secondarily, and somewhat vaguely, argued to have wider applications (Giddens 1984). Bourdieu (1977: 164) identified ancient practice not as habitus but as *doxa*, meaning the misrecognition of social order as a natural order, in which there can be no capacity to question social stratification – a claim that has been contested (Smith 2001).

Given all this, it is less than surprising that practice and structuration have "holes" (Ortner 2006: 129) and these are no more apparent than when it comes to politics. Structure may well be simultaneously "enabling and constraining" (Giddens 1984: 25), but that does not illuminate much about the nature of the balance between the two and the greater impact of social constraint. Although both theories profess a concern for power relations, they have very little to say about how institutions are formed, maintained, or countered (Shennan 1993). In rejecting the functionalist emphasis on role and status they introduce their own form of atemporality; since the conditions into which individuals are born, or the social mobility that might take place during their lives, are very largely set to one side. It cannot be denied that social position, whether ascribed or acquired, has a profound impact on how agents behave and what they can accomplish, and must be part of any comprehensive sociopolitical understanding (Sewell 1992: 20–21).

Nico Mouzelis (1995: 100–126) has been the most vocal critic in this regard, contending that hierarchy cannot be adequately described within a duality because, by limiting the agency of some and expanding that of others, we have a top-down effect of the kind recursive models claim to escape. However, it does not seem especially problematic to define hierarchy as institutionalised manipulation: ". . . within which certain elites worked explicitly to define the conditions under which other forms of agency could operate" (Barrett 2001: 161). The constraints hierarchies impose on individual action are achieved through enduring inequalities in power as manifested in status and role, an element of functionalism not easily relegated to a lower level of analysis.

Multigenerational institutions have their own identities and work according to their own logics and imperatives, in some sense making them "collective agents". Exactly how those collectivities are organised varies, but differential status almost always affords some actors disproportionate access to information, greater influence over decision-making, control of latent and active coercion, and through these the ability to make their goals those of others. The populace must, to some degree, be beguiled and bound to the ideals of the structure, by what we might otherwise call ideology, but also motivated to perform their appropriate parts by means of practical inducements. In terms familiar from Max Weber and Emile Durkheim, structure must be made authoritative and legitimate and, to be stable, naturalised as much as is possible. The reproduction of institutions cannot practically take place without their instantiation and re-instantiation through binding public acts, which serve to make structure not only an idea but, in symbolic terms, a visible reality (Bell 1997). It is correct to call structures self-perpetuating because those acts are the very same as those required for the ongoing life and maintenance of a political association; they, therefore, simultaneously sustain and transmit.

A COMPLEX WORLD

In the recursion of individual acts we have an engine for both the reproduction and incremental transformation of society which, if understood as taking place within a web of institutionalised inequalities, is critical to how political communities are composed and function. Yet this says little or nothing about greater social processes and how, for example, revolutionary ideas sweep through societies and reconfigure them in profound ways. It is here that we return to the role of the totalising paradigms that have been pursued and revisited over the past 150 years of the social sciences (Ortner 1984).

Within their own terms of reference and intellectual universes, each effectively claims a unique possession of insight, even truth. As a sequence of historically-situated movements, we can appreciate how and why each rose to prominence, but any assertion of priority or exclusivity rings hollow today. It is no great intellectual feat to accept that all objects of enquiry are multi-dimensional and simultaneously occupy different ontologies (Yoffee 2005: 15–16). Demurring from singular governing paradigms does not imply a rejection of their value, rather it opens the wider vistas to be found in comparative approaches and theoretical pluralism. Particular conceptual frameworks can be selected for specific purposes and explore questions of a certain kind – each having worth within its own system of logic without denying the value or legitimacy of others.

What seems relevant at this point is a conceptualisation that addresses social phenomena at the macroscale that meshes with what we see at the meso- and microscale. One paradigmatic understanding is unusually well-suited to the recursive mechanisms of agency-based approaches and the relationships they envisage between components and wholes, namely complexity theory.[6] This still-inchoate field is less a theory than a group of related perspectives that address how and why the properties of collectivities differ from those of their constituents (see Lewin 1992; Mitchell 2009). Whether complexity is, as has been claimed, a new chapter in science or whether it simply brings us face-to-face with the unfamiliar world of non-linearity and feedback effects, it speaks to a number of the issues that most concern this book; where we are also trying to comprehend what links units and systems.

Complexity builds on the familiar maxim of "wholes being greater than the sum of their parts" – a touchstone for holistic thinking since the time of Aristotle (Metaphysics, Book 8). The innovation comes in identifying processes behind this effect, which have been glimpsed for centuries but only recently defined mathematically. Science since the Enlightenment has triumphed by means of a reductionist paradigm which comprehends wholes by breaking them down to understand their component parts. While this works for a great many problems, it has made little headway in explaining some of the largest and most complicated natural systems. The manner in which billions of neurons communicate to generate consciousness and memory, how the immune system acts autonomously to fight disease, or precisely how ants are able to take different roles and work toward common goals without a command structure cannot be intuited from any single neuron, T-cell, or ant. Those systems display behaviour that is much more complex than any one part can be expected to produce individually.

It is the engagement and feedback between unit and system, the way in which they are dynamically connected, that generates these synergistic effects. To pick the simplest of examples, a flock of birds or a shoal of fish perform elaborate manoeuvres absent of central direction. Simply by monitoring and reacting to the movements of their nearest neighbours – an exchange of information – individuals collectively generate the spontaneous coherence dubbed "self-organisation" (Prigogine and Stengers 1984; Kauffman 1993). The point at which a critical mass of communicating units acquires its greater-than-the-sum properties is one complexity theorists call "emergence". This evocative but hard-to-define phase transition is where an origin- or centre-oriented system is superseded by a totality formed from the interaction of all its elements.

Human groups plainly differ from those of fish, birds, or ants, but are no less shaped by the power of their own collectives, producing forms and behaviours that are beyond the capabilities of any individual. Even though we are sentient and self-reflective, possessing a model of mind that allows us to assess what others are thinking and feed that into our own decision-making, there are multiple ways in which our activities reflect the macroscale patterning of self-organisation (Imada 2008; Castellani and Hafferty 2009). What self-organisation invites us to discard is the idea that social structures necessarily, or exclusively, arise from intentionality or design. The obvious cue here, and the source for much of this thinking, is the natural world – which, despite its lack of planning, displays remarkable coherence and order. One of the implications of complexity for the social sciences is that, whatever goals people might have, they are also subject to unseen forces that play a greater role in shaping their form and behaviour than we can readily perceive or appreciate. There are hidden sources of attraction that complex systems gravitate toward or harmonise with.

However, self-organisation is not the dominant feature of a complex world. The regions of order it creates are no more than islands in an ocean consisting of its antithesis, the non-linear dynamics known as "chaos". Chaos describes how unascertainable variations in the initial conditions of any complex system are magnified exponentially through time, with the result that there are severe limits to how far its future course can be predicted.

Meteorology is the founding and classic example. Weather can be retrospectively described, and in some senses explained, for year-upon-year if so desired, yet the ability to make accurate forecasts evaporates after little more than a week or two. This is because the forces governing the climate are of such immense scale and intricacy that, with each of its parts in a constant state of flux, it less follows a path than continually comes into being. Its current trajectory is no more than a short-term guide to its future one. Every element can theoretically contribute to this process, such that even a minute change in one might transform the course of the whole – a feature of chaos famously dubbed the "butterfly effect". This means that very large effects can have very small causes; although this necessarily involves a different understanding of "cause" than the one in common usage. Moreover, chaos is not chaotic in the usual sense of the word. Rather it is a kind of "pre-order" from which coherence can emerge under certain conditions. While general results can be predicted, the exact form that those islands of order will take cannot be anticipated, nor how they will develop precisely foretold.[7]

Chaos is clearly not confined to nature, it is just as much a feature of the social world, which takes us to contingency in history. Carl Hempel (1942) argued for a deductive-nomological philosophy of history, one that could generate laws to which all human events should conform. But no such laws have been identified and chaos explains why (Reisch 1991; Shermer 1993, 1995). Like the weather, social worlds have an incalculable number of variables, each subject to constant and unpredictable change. This means that, although we can reconstruct how the historical past unfolded, we can neither be entirely sure why it took one path instead of another nor make projections into the future that are more than probabilistic. This does not negate the search for reason, purpose, and function but, if the system in question is non-linear and subject to feedback, it does complicate the relationships we trace between causes and effects. Any of the factors we judge to be significant are dependent on a myriad of seemingly insignificant or unknown ones that form the full matrix from which events unfold (Kehoe 1998: 226). Events are not things waiting to happen so much as they are things brought into being by a particular context, at a particular moment, and in a particular place. Contingency has long been treated as a random and unquantifiable variable in history that lies outside any theoretical understanding, yet a non-linear perspective indicates otherwise.

The ideas inherent to complexity have been explored in mathematics, physics, chemistry, biology, sociology, and economics, among other fields, and also attracted the attention of anthropologists and archaeologists (e.g. Bintliff 1997, 2003; Crumley 2001; Bentley and Maschner 2003; Beekman and Baden 2005). Social scientists of many stripes see the analytical issue posed by human societies as a classic problem of complexity – in which multiple individuals act upon each other in ways that are not predictable yet not entirely random either, creating entities whose ordered forms and patterned behaviours cannot be fully deduced from their participants' intentions alone.

This compatibility between complexity and recursive social models offer alternative ways of perceiving dynamic collectives, accepting that both their ordered and disordered dimensions fit within the same conceptual realm. However, complexity is not a revelatory tool that provides easy answers for our questions. Rather it leads us toward a deeper appreciation of the properties of real world social systems and why there are harsh limits to what we can know about them, no matter how large our dataset might be. While such ideas serve only as an underlying premise for much of this book, they find more direct realisation in the final section of Chapter 12, where Classic Maya society is approached through understandings of networks and system failure.

FOUR

WORLDS IN WORDS

If the written word is to be our principal source in this study, in which historical accounts are used to shed light on the institutions that gave rise to them, then we need a fairly comprehensive sense of what that source represents. Accordingly, this chapter is concerned with the epistemological status of writing as a "window" on the past and, more specifically, the viability of using it to understand long-extinct political systems.

It begins by examining the status of historical archaeology as both a field and a method, asking what we can reasonably expect from the engagement of such rich, but deeply contrasting, resources as inscriptions and artefacts. Taking on the Maya case more directly, it then moves to consider the reliability of their texts, and how we might distinguish effects in their own time from how we use them today. These are key issues wherever epigraphic and archaeological studies jointly reference past societies, but they have an extra significance in the Maya area, where the dominant paradigm has long been a material one and where intelligible texts represent a more recent insurgency. For this reason, methodological questions that escape self-reflection in Old World contexts acquire a certain necessity here in the New. Having established these foundations, we are free to move forward to discuss a theoretical framework within which the data produced by textual analysis can move from the particular to the general, which is to say, from the realm of political history to that of political anthropology.

TWO WAYS OF KNOWING

The ease of defining historical archaeology as a field seems inversely propor-
tional to the difficulty that its two domains find in harmonising their
efforts. The meeting of material and textual studies raises profound and often
troubling questions about the historical enterprise itself: of the relative
weighting of evidence, the resolution of contradictions, and the possibility of
saying anything truly concrete about worlds that no longer exist. Today we
can point to bodies of ideas that illuminate, however dimly, the investigation
of objects or texts, but nothing that speaks to their integration. On the positive
side, historical archaeologies are fields of contrast, counterpoint, and contest-
ation, where the friction between these "two ways of knowing" offers a
dynamism not found elsewhere. More negatively, as hybrids they are often
"wracked by anxieties of alignment" (Carver 2002: 467), where the lack of
assimilation, even at times useful dialogue, has been much lamented and
appeals for "reconciliation" or "rapprochement" long been commonplace
(e.g. Dymond 1974; Arnold 1986: 36; Moreland 1992: 115, 2001: 30, 2006;
Geary 1994: 45; Ross and Steadman 2010: 4).

Past societies were like our own, in the sense that they were composed of
a myriad of collaborations and interpenetrations between words and objects.
To a degree too familiar to be readily apparent, language is instrumental to the
production of social meaning, and collective living inconceivable without the
shared systems of communication and indexical reference it provides (Searle
1995: 59–78).[1] Language mediates the social world because it is the only
vehicle through which value and meaning can be agreed, let alone conveyed.
Without a shared semiotic system, of which language is always the most
powerful, there is reality, but no social reality. This means that even the most
materially focussed explorations of the past are, whether recognised to be so or
not, a pursuit of things once part-composed in language. But with the
extirpation of a given culture, words are ripped from the domain of objects
and objects from the domain of words. What remains of both are mere traces.
We know that they were once rooted together in a common past, but there is
no necessity that the isolated fragments left to us belong together. Although
much differs from one historical archaeology to the next, this is the conundrum shared by all.

The entwined history of writing and archaeology in the Old World, with its
origins in biblical and classical studies and the long subordination of the
material to the textual, is well known (Dymond 1974; Trigger 1989; Andrén
1998; Liverani 1999; Zettler 2003; Sauer 2006). The emergence of archaeology
as something more than a "handmaiden" to documentary sources began in the
study of early and non-literate societies within the culture-history paradigm
but flowered under the processualist one that had replaced it by the 1960s.

As we saw in Chapter 3, the ambition of archaeological processualism was an expansive one, seeking to reform the field into a nomothetic science along positivist and universalistic lines. History was dethroned from its once-privileged status and chided for its theoretical shallowness (Flannery 1967; Binford 1968a, 1968b, 1977, 1983; Clarke 1968: 12).[2] The eventfulness of the past was seen as noise that should be filtered out in order to better perceive underlying, longer-term forces of change, conceived of in social evolutionary terms (Cobb 1991). The fundamental questions of social, political, and economic organisation were all believed to have material analogues that could be revealed by appropriate procedures and bodies of middle-range theory – a historicisation of the past by other means.

A key contention of the processualist approach was that the material record offers a direct point of access to the past, making it an inherently more objective and reliable avenue than the one provided by documents. But there has long been reason to question that claim. It cannot be doubted that quantitative approaches can be hugely illuminating, exposing, for example, strong correlations between systems of power and their physical manifestations. But correlations are not always so direct. We observe this in the contemporary world, where the modest scale of national capitals such as Brasilia and Canberra bear no correspondence to their political significance, but also in the ancient. The issue was already clear to Thucydides, the first writer to cast his mind forward to anticipate the work of archaeologists, writing some twenty-four hundred years ago:

> Suppose the city of Sparta to be deserted, and nothing left but the temples and the ground-plan, distant ages would be very unwilling to believe that the power of the Spartans was at all equal to their fame. And yet they own two-fifths of the Peloponnesus, and are acknowledged leaders of the whole, as well as of numerous allies in the rest of Greece. But their city is not built continuously, and has no splendid temples or other edifices; it rather resembles a group of villages like the ancient towns of Greece, and would therefore make a poor show. Whereas, if the same fate befell the Athenians, the ruins of Athens would strike the eye, and we should infer their power to have been twice as great as it really is. [*Historia* 1.10.2, translation by Dale, with some substitutions from other versions]

There is no mathematical model, quantitative analysis, or central place mapping of landscape that would reconstruct the strength and extent of Sparta's political power, a social rather than material fact. Things would be only slightly better in the case of Athens, a city many times more populous, whose power derived less from its immediate territorial possessions than it did from the extensive network of subjects it exploited.[3] What distinguishes Sparta and Athens, lost to sight in the processual approach, is their radically different cultures and sociopolitical make-ups – meaning, for us, divergent schemas that harnessed resources in contrasting ways. To be sure, this example is an extreme one, but being so it makes it crystal clear that political structures carry the force of ideas, each variable and contingent in nature with their own trajectories and histories. The degree to which we can understand them archaeologically depends on the kinds of resources that those schemas recognised and utilised and, even then, only to the degree that they are preserved or can otherwise now be detected.

Under the counter-reformation of postprocessualism, historical perspectives regained some ground as part of a new pluralism. However, this was also a time when traditional notions of an accessible past were challenged, or denied altogether, under the heightened influence of poststructuralism and critical theory (see Shanks and Tilley 1987; Patterson 1989). When archaeologists sought theories of history they usually alighted upon the French *Annales* group of social and economic historians, scholars who had turned away from narrative toward a focus on past *mentalités* (Hodder 1987; Bintliff 1991a, 1991b; Knapp 1992; see Last 1995: 141–145). Their most influential contribution was the temporal scheme of Fernand Braudel (1972–73, 1980), whose escalating durations of *histoire événementielle, moyenne durée,* and *longue durée* overtly favoured the latter; grand sweeps of geographic and climatological history that lay far beyond the life-spans of individuals. This presented clear attractions for archaeologists and their ability to track change over the long-term, although in ways that only marginally differed from the environmental interests of their processualist forebears.

One might have expected that the rise of agency and practice theory in archaeology would lead to a rehabilitation of eventfulness in the past, but such a development has been surprisingly stunted. The interest in agents and practices has been strong, where the issues at hand are generalised within a non-literate material record, but strangely absent wherever textual records with known agents and specific practices are available for study. Their histor-icity somehow absolves them of conceptual interest, textual information serving the same explanatory role that might otherwise be ascribed to theory (Andrén 1998: 3). This absence promotes the disciplinary divisions that practice theories actively sought to dissolve (Porter 2010: 169–170). A call has been made for a "historical-processual" approach in which practice is defined not in terms of near-static habitus, but as an unfolding series of events in which human creativity generates change (Pauketat 2001, 2007). This replaces the law-like processualist approach that asks why cultural processes occurred, with a more historically contingent, but limited, question of how they occurred.

WHO MADE THIS TEXT AND WHY?

To decipher a given ancient text – that is, to recover the relationships between signs and sounds, and to retrace morphology and grammar in an underlying language – can only ever be a first step. Understanding requires knowledge of the cultural codes that determined its creation, demanding a contextual as much as textual analysis. But there are further challenges to bridging the world of words to that of things, to how texts map onto a physical fabric of the past. If this was ever thought to be a straightforward procedure, then the critical debates that have coursed through literary and historical studies in the last half-century have dispelled any such fallacy (see Clark 2004: 130–155). Ancient inscriptions emerge from lost cultural matrices and are now set adrift into an unimagined future. If meaning is viewed as problematic in the modern text, then how much more must it be for the ancient one, for which our contextual knowledge is so vastly more deficient?

During the nineteenth century, it was believed that rigorous source criticism gave access to "what really happened" in the past, an ideal of objectivity underwritten by analogy to the natural sciences. But, as twentieth century physics turned away from the certainties of mechanics to the uncertainties of the quantum world, faith in that position crumbled (Bloch 1954: 17; Aron 1961 [1938]; Carr 1961; see Novick 1988). Probabilities not certainties became the currency of historical reconstruction and we were taken, at best, to Michael Oakeshott's (1983: 33, 52, 80) "what the evidence obliges us to believe" (quoted in Clark 2004: 19). Here knowledge is not absolute, but *conditional*. What we know is what our sources allow us to infer, given some ascertainable parameters and in the absence of countervailing evidence (Beards 1994). Knowledge in these terms is never fixed, but under constant review. Similarly, we recognize today that neither the identification of evidence nor its interpretation can be independent of the investigator, and that scholarship is itself historically situated. The ancients had historical sensibilities of their own, but for our purposes history can only exist in the here and now – a point applicable to all historical reconstructions, whatever their origin.

Even the most innocuous of texts have authors, agendas, and intended audiences, and one of the first steps in the historiographical method is to ask "who made this text and why?" There can be no disinterested "history for its own sake", since all accounts come from a particular perspective, are made for a certain purpose, and have some kind of reader in mind: "[H]istory is always for someone" (Jenkins 1991: 17).

Wherever writing has emerged in the world it has been developed as a tool of the powerful and used in furtherance of social, economic, cultural, and political control (Goody 1968; Lévi-Strauss 1973: 393; Moreland 2001, 2006: 140). Texts created at the behest of political authorities invariably aim to shape perceptions and advance their cause by means of persuasion, assertion, or intimidation, and seek to justify past, present, and future actions: "Political texts never record facts for the sake of recording, but for the sake of political action" (Liverani 2001: 200). They use the rhetorical strategies of oral expression (Lincoln 1994) but, objectified in material, visible form, they generate their own discursive modes and a signification that depends not only on what they say but on their physical presence in the world. In whatever way we use texts as sources about the past it is necessary to build some sense of their aims and efficacy in their own time (Moreland 2001: 26, 30–31). Having survived into that unimagined future, we must try to reconstruct the reader as much as we reconstruct the author.

These obstacles make it difficult to assess how well the content of any text conforms to an external reality, especially when we are talking about the products of extinct societies at great temporal and cultural distance from our own. In the face of such complications, we could easily content ourselves solely with the pursuit of a textual reality – a project in which we seek to paint the portrait of no more than an internally consistent ideological world (Van de Mieroop 1999: 55–56). In fact, this is where we begin rather than conclude our investigations, with the re-assembly of cultural codes noted above (Liverani 2001: 201). If, as realists, we believe that textual and material traces are productions of a single past, then we must be concerned with reconciling their contrasting representations, and work at, not wish away, the many impediments and uncertainties we encounter.

Histories can never be complete or definitive; they are always works-in-progress. They no more constitute the "real past" than a map constitutes the "real world". Each, in its own way, schematises an entity that cannot otherwise be grasped or comprehended. The truth-value of a map comes not in any contact it makes with the substance of reality, but how well its spatial proportions reflect those of its subject, and whether features of significance are placed and identified adequately via some agreed symbolic convention. We do not mistake maps for the places they represent.

When it comes to the essential feature of history, time, and the dominant mode of its expression, narrative, a more abstract metaphor is required. Here historians work as interpolators, drawing arcs between points of knowledge so as to create chains of cause and effect – a process termed colligation. But the points can be chosen and joined in different ways, with different purposes in mind. As new points emerge, or their positions are revised, they either fit an existing narrative arc or it must bend to accommodate them. If the new data are sufficiently discordant then the whole set of connections may be abandoned and better ones drawn in their place. This form of emplotment is not only a literary device, it constitutes a form of explanation (Gallie 1964; Ricoeur 1983–1984). In organising events and relations through time we necessarily build a picture of the wider world within which they occur and, however provisionally, deduce some view of why they occur. Historical analysis does not produce a series of statements about the past, but a series of arguments as to why some evidential linkages are better – more productive or more plausible – than others.

THE NATURE OF MAYA TEXTS

Maya hieroglyphic script was not the only writing system to develop in ancient Mesoamerica, but it was by far the most sophisticated, abundant, and enduring. It saw continuous use for some two millennia and is preserved today on many hundreds of monuments and thousands more portable items. The most iconic are the limestone, occasionally slate or sandstone, stelae set on public display in open plazas. But Maya writing appears on other materials and in other settings, of which some were public, but many had restricted access or were on intimate items of personal use and adornment.

The decipherment – though an incomplete project – has produced a wealth of data, significantly enriching our view of Classic Maya society, culture, and worldview (see Coe 1992; Houston 2000; Houston and Martin 2016). But we must acknowledge that "wealth" is a relative term here and, although the texts are luxuriant sources in many respects, they are impoverished in others. They are restricted in their subject matter and reflect only the interests of the ruling elite who commissioned them. Thus, they contain extensive data on chronology and ritual practices, as well as royal biographies and some limited genealogies, but the economic records that broaden our understanding of other ancient societies are entirely absent. Such lacunae can to some degree be blamed on differential preservation, with the genres we find on durable materials likely to be more restricted than those on fugitive ones such as bark-paper. This makes the loss of books especially regrettable, with only a handful of very late, mytho-calendrical examples and a number of depictions of earlier ones now extant. The lack of surviving records dealing with the lives of commoners certainly curbs any attempt we might make to build our historical understanding from the bottom-up as well as top-down – though in global terms the ancient Maya are hardly alone in that shortcoming.

There is also what I have described as the "thinness" of Maya monumental discourse (Martin 2006a: 92–95, 2019a). Despite having the full power of language at their disposal, Maya texts are notable for a lack of rhetorical embellishment and light information load. This terse and laconic style is deliberate and evidently intended to convey an unchallengeable authority that only needs to assert, not justify (see Ong 1982: 79; Wienold 1994; Van de Mieroop 1999). Where we do find longer texts they almost always betray some historical difficulty or insecurity, a need to set out a greater explanatory context and additional information. What we normally get are base armatures onto which the reader must apply pre-existing knowledge, possibly at times serving as cues for oral recitation or performance (Houston 1994: 30–31; Martin 2006a).

Inscriptions must be understood within their physical placements and viewing contexts. Some were all-textual, often those set within building interiors, but the majority were designed to work in conjunction with images, mostly royal portraits, each supplying part of the overall message (Berlo 1983; Miller and Houston 1987). The material presence of monuments in the built landscape fixed claims to rule in particular places and times. Since the great majority of them were the commemorations of calendrical junctures, they expressed the ideological fusion between time and kingship that underpinned Classic Maya royal identity and legitimacy (Stuart 1996), with their images not simple representations but active evocations of presence and personhood (Houston and Stuart 1998). Moreover, their materialisation in stone was something more than a pragmatic vehicle, given the profound symbolic and conceptual connotations that stone had for the Maya, which was perceived to be an animate force (Stuart 2010a: 286–290). While some public monuments were later broken up and buried, moved, or very occasionally remodelled (Stuart 1995: 171–176; Martin 2000b), most stood untouched in their original locations for centuries.

In sum, if we mistake such texts as historical reportage we are not only ignoring their self-aggrandising nature but their deeper mission to assert royal legitimacy through verifiable ritual performance – a momentary act frozen in image and textually set in the present tense, that was meant to be on-going, even everlasting.

The Relevance and Veracity of Maya Texts

As noted in Chapter 2, there has been a sustained debate in Mayanist circles as to whether the inscriptions constitute reliable historical evidence or not. This is clearly a crucial issue for anyone planning to use text for a political reconstruction, and whoever does so – be they epigraphers, historians, or anthropologists – should set out not only their methods but the epistemological basis of their efforts.

It was not uncommon at one time to view Maya inscriptions as "epiphenomenal". The proposition was that as the product of an elite minority the texts do not represent Classic Maya society as a whole, making them only of peripheral interest to major questions of social organisation and economic function (see discussion in Coe 1992: 272). The processualists had reacted strongly against the "tombs and temples" approach that dominated the early phases of Maya archaeology, and the concentration on monumental inscriptions was seen to perpetuate this distorting emphasis on a rarefied upper stratum.

Yet, while it is undeniable that the texts focus exclusively on the concerns of the elite, it does not follow that such concerns were divorced from those of the commoners. The texts may omit great swathes of social and economic life, but they do provide a portrait of power, defining a governmental authority whose webs of domination, obligation, inducement, and enchantment penetrated all levels of society (Moreland 2001: 94–97). The agency of kings could not exist without the agency of subjects who, whether treated as individuals or as a collective, were forced, obliged, persuaded, enticed, or otherwise motivated to enact royal projects by contributing their own mental, physical, and material resources (see also Houston and Escobedo 1997: 467; Porter 2010: 168, 177). This was not, of course, the sum total of their agency, but it was a major constituent of how complex societies adhered and acted in synchronous fashion.

Not all critics of the textual record have taken the epiphenomenal line and another influential argument has been that inscriptions of the Maya and other Mesoamericans are best understood as "propaganda" (Santley 1989: 93; Marcus 1992a). In this view, they contain bias and, worse, deceptions in which their authors ". . . manipulated dates, life spans, astronomical cycles, and real events to put myth and history into a single chronological framework" (Marcus 1992a: 15). The idea that the texts conflate real and supernatural events is important to those advancing the most recent political models: "The events they record may be little more than dynastic chest-thumping or claims to the fulfilment of quasi-historical prophetic mandates" (Rice 2004: 9), and "Once taken to be literal history by most epigraphers . . . recent readings have found texts to be infused with references to Maya cosmology, mythology, and religion . . . as well as political propaganda" (Chase, Chase, and Smith 2009: 180).

In normal usage "propaganda" is an openly pejorative term defined by its manipulative intent; its effects achieved through selectivity, exaggeration, distortion, or active falsehood. We have already touched on the overall tenor and purpose of royal texts. Since we do not expect even politicians of our own time to give impartial reports of their careers, we cannot hold it as surprising that texts produced at the behest of ancient power regimes propound the interests of those regimes. Objectivity was never their objective. It is at the darker end of the scale, basic veracity, where the legitimate concern lies.

If the inscriptions contain not simply selective but false information it would greatly complicate our efforts to trace connections between textual and actual pasts, perhaps leaving us to study only ideological rather than historical discourses. While our ability to contextualize and conduct source criticism on the inscriptions is constrained, we are not completely powerless. There are two means by which we might address the problem. An internal approach looks to relations with other texts, seeking out consistencies or inconsistencies among those amenable to such analysis. An external approach looks to verify or falsify statements based on their relationship to the physical world, as illuminated by archaeology and its armoury of analytical techniques.

To begin with the latter, an immediate obstacle is that the great majority of things recounted in the inscriptions have either left no material remnant or were largely immaterial in the first place. As noted above, much of what interests us are social rather than physical realities (Liverani 2001: 201). However, there are times when material remains can provide a powerful test for textual data. We see this at Copan, where a project under the overall direction of William Fash since 1983 has pioneered material-textual integration in Maya studies (Fash 1991a).[4] Because all major surface remains are Late Classic in date, the entire Early Classic history of the site, including the sequence of early kings named and depicted on Copan Altar Q (Figure 20a), was considered no more than "putative" (Webster and Freter 1990: 81–82). The suspicion was that simple village chieftains were being elevated to a status well beyond historical reality, or even that they had been entirely invented to justify the claims of the later kings shown on the grand stelae of the site.

This changed when tunnelling into the site's Main Acropolis revealed the layered construction of multiple previous phases, some with dedicatory inscriptions naming the very same kings listed on Altar Q (Fash 1991a; Riese 1992; Stuart 1992, 2004a). That monument portrays the founder of the dynasty, K'inich Yax K'uk' Mo', in garb indicative of Central Mexico. When excavators reached the base of the acropolis they found a building constructed and decorated in the style of Teotihuacan – the huge metropolis close to modern-day Mexico City – and, beneath its floor, a rich tomb stocked with Teotihuacan-linked grave goods (Sharer 2003, 2004). No text identifies the male skeleton within, but its bone chemistry marks him as an outsider of some kind (Stuart 2000, 2004a; Price et al. 2010) (see p.125). Moreover, all the structures consecutively built atop that tomb celebrate the memory of that same founder figure. Wherever early Maya histories have been probed in this way the results have, to date, lent credence to the inscribed record rather than discredited it.

The *cause célèbre* when it comes to the truth-value of the texts are the bones from the great tomb within the Temple of Inscriptions at Palenque, the one excavated by Ruz briefly noted in Chapter 2. Accompanying inscriptions identify them as belonging to a king we know today as K'inich Janaab Pakal I, and state that he died at the age of 80 years in 683 (Mathews and Schele 1974: 64–65; Schele 1992a: 92–96). Yet an initial osteological analysis estimated that the body was of a male aged only between 40 and 50 (Dávalos and Romano 1973: 253), with a later study reducing that to under 40 (Ruz 1977: 293). Here, it seemed, was clear scientific refutation of the epigraphic account (Ruz 1976, 1977; Pendergast 1989: 69–70; Marcus 1992a: 291, 345, 1992b: 235–237). However, subsequent analytical advances cast serious doubt on the reliability of those assessments (Urcid 1993; Hammond and Molleson 1994). A re-evaluation of the bones using modern techniques, with blind-testing, indicated that this man endured well into his second half-century (Buikstra, Milner, and Boldsen 2006; Stout and Streeter 2006). That the Classic Maya elite occasion-ally outlasted the biblical count of three-score-and-ten years would not be too surprising, since their diet and living conditions were considerably better than those of commoners (see Haviland 1967). This is more easily countenanced than the alterations necessary to doctor the biographies of kings, who are often documented at different points in their lives, and sometimes by other polities.[5]

A second aspect of this king's record has provoked suspicion: the manner in which his reign was linked to characters with unnatural life-spans in the remote past and far future. This mixing of the ostensibly historical with the patently mythical has been taken to mean that no part of the record can be seen as free from temporal manipulation (Marcus 1992a: 291, 346). Yet other ancient societies make similar links between the sacred and the profane, which are also distinguished through divergent timescales – much as the demi-god Romulus was considered the founder of Rome but lived long before the chroniclers who recounted that tradition. In fact, the readings of Classic Maya inscriptions now possible show that even though royal persons could assume ancestral and divine co-identities, these separate categories of being were carefully delineated, belying the idea that there was an intention to obfuscate the natural and supernatural.

The propaganda concept correctly identifies the self-interested objectives of royal inscriptions, but it does so in a way that projects twentieth century sensibilities into the past (Houston 2000: 169) and references a dominant ideology thesis that has been challenged on both logical and historical grounds (Abercrombie, Hill, and Turner 1980). The term does have a heritage within studies of ancient Mesopotamia (e.g. Finkelstein 1979), but there too it has been faulted, and for similar reasons (Van de Mieroop 1999: 58–59; Porter 2010: 177). To be appropriate it would be necessary to define precisely who was to be misled, how this was to be achieved, and what benefits and costs would be accrued. For the practice to be widespread it cannot have satisfied kingly vanity alone, but must have furthered political goals.

With often modest populations living in restricted territories, neither the literate elite nor the illiterate community at large could have been deceived by the suggested falsehoods, leaving only visitors from afar and future generations as viable audiences.[6] Since there was no equivalent of an Egyptian pharaoh or Aztec emperor to dictate a singular "official" account, Maya history emerges from the interweaved records of multiple kingdoms, a good number in violent competition with one another and lacking any incentive to support another's false claims.[7] In this kind of environment questions of royal credibility must arise, since empty boasts would fail to impress or intimidate one's rivals and might, in fact, be positively counterproductive.

Few events recorded in Maya inscriptions offer much political value by their manipulation (Houston 2000: 169–170), but there is one area where mendacity could be both status-enhancing and easier to effect than most. I have commented elsewhere on the significance of war records in this respect (Martin and

Grube 2000: 127; Martin 2003a). In a sample that now totals some 186 records, over 60 of them between text-producing polities, there is not one case in which both sides claim victory in the same conflict. This is surprising, since one would expect to see at least some competing claims, if for no other reason than violent engagements are often inconclusive and give grounds for both sides to claim some measure of success. That none have been recovered so far seems telling.

To date, only one conflict provokes mention by both belligerents, the defeat of Copan's Waxaklajuun Ubaah K'awiil by his own client-king from Quirigua (see p.211). Copan gives a more flowery description of his demise than the decapitation recounted at Quirigua, but concedes that he died in war nonetheless (Stuart 2005a: 385). This is not the only instance in which polities record their own defeat (see Looper and Schele 1991; Houston 1993: 108; Grube 1996: 1–6; Martin 2000c: 107–111; Martin and Grube 2000: 95; Fahsen et al. 2003). These embarrassments were recorded not for the sake of historical accuracy, but for their explanatory power: justifying the rise of new regimes following a dynastic rupture or providing the casus belli for a more decisive counterblow.

To summarise this section, the case that Classic Maya inscriptions are not impartial is unremarkable and the claim they are widely mendacious unsupported. In one area where the stakes seem especially high, warfare, we lack the contradictory claims that might be expected if kings sought every opportunity to claim personal glory, no matter how fallacious. The multivocality of the texts may have placed some check on spurious claims, but there must also be a question as to whether the harm done to kingly credibility outweighed any perceived advantage. We must not be naïve or credulous in the face of highly self-interested representations – healthy scepticism is a cornerstone of the historiographical method, and it would be foolhardy to guarantee the accuracy of every text.[8] But, in the absence of serious inconsistencies, Classic Maya inscriptions emerge as workable, if always conditional, knowledge.

Maya Texts as Patrimonial Rhetoric

If neither history nor propaganda are terms that properly capture the character of Classic Maya inscriptions and royal texts more generally, we should seek an alternative. A good option would be the "patrimonial rhetoric" coined by Richard Blanton et al. (1996: 5; see also Jansen and Pérez 2011: 505).[9] Inspired by Weber (1978: 1006–1069), this term describes the sum total of communicative strategies by which elites actualise and legitimise their power. It is a characterisation in which elite pronouncements inherently reflect their worldview and seek to advance their aims and interests, whatever their content, style, or medium. Patrimonial rhetoric can ignore the inconvenient, but it is more than empty artifice because it accurately conveys the norms and ideologies of a given system.

The term was only scantily defined at its first appearance and, with no great violence to the original intention, it can also be expanded upon in useful ways. I will include within it here not simply elite representations of past acts, but the way that the record itself becomes a constituent of them. Inscribed patrimonial rhetoric meshes events and their instantiations in a manner that makes lasting social, cultural, and political effects possible. Events that took place on a single day with a finite number of participants can now persist for centuries, well after their original points of reference are lost and all witnesses to them long dead. By assuming a visible and durable reality that the ephemera of actual events cannot, the record transcends the immediate consequences of the action to produce effects of a different order, ones that can support future generations in their on-going (re)constitution of identity and legitimacy (see also Carver 2002: 466). This is not to invoke "object agency" in the sense of an "extended mind" (Gell 1998; Latour 2005), but instead a more conventional process of semiosis: the enduring broadcasting of a signifier that has superseded its signified. This does not imply that its meaning could be fully controlled. On the contrary, at each contact with a reader it would be re-contextualised for its own time, including our own.

As we will see throughout Part II, the patrimonial rhetoric of the Classic Maya was a radically personalised one. It tells of individuals not groups, officeholders not institutions, with all political action and identity subsumed within the person of elite, usually royal, actors. In its terse and formulaic phrasing, it does not attempt to capture the uniqueness of any incident, but rather fits that incident into an existing rhetorical category defined by a limited number of verbs. In this manner, contingent and sporadic happenings are culturally configured in ways barely distinguishable from routinised rituals. Any view of wider society must be achieved through this narrow window of heroic biography and selected tropes. Even so, the inscribed rituals, battles, accessions, diplomatic visits, and the like are not the peripheral chaff of societies that were really about something else. They are schematic mirrors to a political culture whose local effects alone touched the lives of tens of thousands of people, with unspecified but very real social and economic ramifications.

THEORISING THE EVENT

The position taken in this volume is that the identities, events, and relations recorded in Classic Maya texts, far from being epiphenomenal, give central insights into the nature of Classic Maya political structure. They were not only generated and shaped by the properties of the system but, in subtle and cumulative ways, they built and perpetuated it. However incomplete and filtered through patrimonial rhetoric, the inscriptions offer the best view we will ever obtain of how individual actors and groups engaged in the establishment, maintenance, and reproduction of polities, and in this way inform us about the wider political culture of which they were part.

To make that case it will be necessary to further bridge the disciplinary boundary between history and anthropology. Despite the inescapable embeddedness of culture in time, these two fields have succeeded in carving-out discrete domains with very different theoretical perspectives and methodologies – on the one side focussed on causation and contingency within a diachronic framework, on the other on symbols and practices within a more synchronic purview. In short, the classic opposition between event and structure. The attractions of cross-fertilisation are clear (Ohnuki-Tierny 1990), since each fills a void in the other, but is more often the subject of aspiration and experimentation than regular fulfilment.

By "structure" anthropologists generally mean the rules, norms, conventions, and understandings – stated and unstated, conscious and unconscious – that collectively bind societies together and define what is proper conduct for their members and what is not. Mesopotamianist Mario Liverani (2001: 202) makes the point that political events, usually portrayed as chaotic, must also be seen as expressions of such underlying form:

> [T]his is also a plea for a different appreciation of political history. The writing of economic and social history has for long proceeded on the assumption that single events cannot be properly understood without a reconstruction of the general structures underlying them. Political history, on the other hand, has been left as a domain free for the *histoire événementielle*, as an unstructured sequence of "facts" that cannot be reduced to any system. Yet battles and treaties have their structures too, and the proper understanding of single political events can no more do without the establishment of a grid of reference and a methodology of analysis than the discrete phenomena of the economic and social worlds.

This take on the issue is important but does not address how those structures came into being, were maintained through time, or indeed what the relationship between the chaotic and the structural might be. As in all traditional structuralist approaches, structure is disembodied, *of* a given society but somehow external to it as well, and influence is unidirectional, from structure to event. Throughout the twentieth century, changing conceptions of social order defined successive analytical avenues, running through functionalism and systems theories, the language-inspired structuralism of Lévi-Strauss – where inherent mental templates determine human behaviour – and then the totalising schemes of Michel Foucault (e.g. 1977, 1980), where people are all but imprisoned by abstract outside forces.

The model of structure composed of schemas and resources, explored in Chapter 3, might also help us to address aspects of text-material interaction.[10] The aforementioned "collaborations and interpenetrations" between words and objects is a rather vague characterisation, but conceiving of schemas as necessarily language-dependent and resources as inclusive of physical things offers a theoretical description of such relations. The material record can be seen as vestigial resources stripped of their partnering schemas, and the textual record as glimpses of schemas that necessarily imply the resources that once enacted them, at least some of which would have taken physical form. While no panacea, this shifts the emphasis from divergent epistemologies to functional synergies in potentially useful ways.

To consider embodied practices in place of disembodied processes is to consider sequences of individual acts set in time and place. In short, events of the kind denigrated by theorists of almost all persuasions for a major slice of the twentieth century. This is exemplified in the view the Annalistes took of *histoire événementielle* (Bloch 1954: 13; Le Goff 1988[1978]: 12–17), with Braudel's characterization of events as "surface disturbances, crests of foam that the tides of history carry on their strong backs" (Braudel 1972–73: I.21) and "the ephemera of history; they pass across its stage like fireflies, hardly glimpsed before they settle back into darkness" (Braudel 1980: 3, 10–11, 27).[11] But if the logic of social recursiveness was to be followed to its endpoint this view could not go unchallenged. Marshall Sahlins (1981, 1985, 1991), moving beyond his structuralist pedigree, rejected the opposition between structure and event that allows the former to be privileged, arguing that, as with structure and agency, the two constantly act upon each other. In such an engagement "... what anthropologists call 'structure' – the symbolic relations of cultural order – is an historical object" (Sahlins 1985: vii).

No matter how contingent their immediate circumstances, acts are neither completely random in type nor spontaneous in timing, but arise within certain structural conditions. However, those conditions are never fixed. They develop through time, and the engine of that change is the cumulative social, economic, political, and cultural ramifications of prior acts. Some actions deliberately seek to change the system that made them possible, but all are transformative to some degree because the reproduction of the system can never be perfect. Contingency intervenes through the uniqueness of any set of historical circumstances and the ways in which actors cope with obstacles and innovate to expedite their plans – introducing the non-linear features of complexity and chaos that offer understandings of the unpredictable.

Importantly, this is a view of agency that incorporates social hierarchy, which was all but absent in the original formulations of agency and practice, and criticised as a result, as we saw in Chapter 3. It accepts that different social status reflects the different capacities of individuals to affect others and make changes to the system (Sewell 1992: 21). Moreover, those with the most power will be those that monopolise patrimonial rhetoric and therefore be the sole actors on view. Whereas we would much prefer to hear directly from a broad social range, we need to consider that this rhetoric can be an encoding of political action performed by the many, not simply the practical domination of the few.

As Sahlins (1985: xi) puts it: "[F]or societies of a certain type, the stories of kings and battles are with good reason privileged historiographically. The reason is a structure that generalizes the action of the king as the form and destiny of the society". Such characters are what he later calls "social-historical individuals" (Sahlins 1991: 63–68). By this, he does not mean Carlyle's "great men" (individuals whose exceptional qualities are believed to have an explanatory role in history) or Hegel's "world historical individuals" (conduits for the guiding "spirit" of their times). Rather, a social-historical individual is one whose structural position in a given society, at a given time, makes him or her its representative or embodiment, someone whose agency is not theirs alone but, visibly or not, entails that of a collective. Such a position depends on status, but is not exclusively one of domination, since it also invokes wider ideals of social value and group interest. Sahlins' (1985) "heroic kingship" is an example of this and Classic Maya kingship fits comfortably within that definition. In a similar vein, Mouzelis (1995: 16) stresses the importance of "mega-actors", who are "individual actors in control of considerable resources whose decisions stretch widely in time and space". This too is a description of single agents whose agency is never truly singular but extended by means of their social position into that of the group.

In defining his social-historical individual, Sahlins reaches some accommodation between agency and the structural properties of a given system. However, it is patently the case that some agents are more capable than others and that those with relevant skills will achieve more in a particular situation than another, less capable one. An ineffectual ruler will perform badly whatever the levers of power he or she holds. The spectre of the redundant "great man" view of history should not force us to deny the role of individual abilities to effect change. That personal talents are magnified in the shift from individual to collective agency is reason enough to anticipate their ramifying impact on social process.

The Sahlins programme can be useful for us, although it requires certain adjustments. Firstly, he defines an "event" by its ability to transform structures, calling actions that only reproduce structures "happenings" (Sahlins 1991: 46). His own work focuses on transformative incidents such as Captain Cook's arrival in Hawaii in 1779, which was, by any standard, exceptional. Much of what passes for political life, however, is about reproducing existing articulations of power in routine ways. Sahlins foresaw that separating incidents into two categories would be problematic (Sahlins 1991: 86, n.12), and Sewell

(2005: 210–211) resolves the problem by having events simultaneously transform and reproduce at different levels of structure(s). Thus, a major military attack could be highly disruptive on the level of an individual polity, but amount to no more than an expected fluctuation of relative power at the scale of the system. There is also a difficulty with the passivity of "happenings", since reproduction is very often a deliberate act, as in the performance of regular ceremonies and rituals. Finally, while the emphasis on events is crucial, much of the important information in Maya texts concerns identities and relations – the networks of power and allegiance generated between people, places, positions, and polities. Identities and relations are logically tied to events because they either arise from actions, or from the possibility of them.

In this study I treat identities, relations, and events alike as constitutive of structure, with events considered a single category that transform or reproduce to differing degrees. This entails a larger point, that the powerful have a vested interest in maintaining an existing order and will seek to limit or block emendations of structure that might weaken their position. This brake on social transformation was underdetermined in agency and practice before hierarchy was properly assimilated into it. We must anticipate that social changes will be under-represented within patrimonial rhetoric, even actively suppressed, for the very reason that it was designed to perpetuate an existing order.

We now have some prerequisites for the immersion into Classic Maya political records that follows in Part II. There we will draw from a large body of patrimonial rhetoric, textual instantiations that are not only reflective of a political system but contributed to bringing it into being and perpetuated its existence. The individual identities, events, and relations recorded in them are neither "foam" nor "fireflies" for our purposes, but expressions of and contributions to underlying structural properties. Those structures, which consist of mutually supportive schemas and resources, do not determine events, but they do shape what is possible and interpret the results in culturally concordant ways. The protagonists of the texts are social-historical individuals, actors whose institutional position allows them to project their agency through that of others, a collective that they diversely serve, exploit, and personify.[12]

PART II

EPIGRAPHIC DATA ON CLASSIC MAYA POLITICS

FIVE

IDENTITY

For a society to be labelled "complex" in the conventional sense it must be one touched by processes of institutionalisation, requiring that structure be embodied in designated ranks and roles. Those positions can be ascribed or achieved, distinguishing between those positions gained by birth-right and those by selection or competition.[1] A role may require certain experience, skills, or specialised knowledge that is actively learnt, but like status exists only within a matrix of human relations – no lone person can stand resplendent as king or queen. Titles, therefore, serve to specify two, sometimes overlapping, purposes, defining aristocratic privileges as well as functional specialisations. These political personas need to be maintained and communicated through the medium of symbols (e.g. Cohen 1974, 1981). Elite distinction is most often expressed by special insignia or attire, but it can include everything from subtle codes of etiquette to grandiose architectural statements. Where items can be fashioned from rare and exotic materials, or highly charged with artistry and aesthetic value, the projection of eminence will be all the more effective (Clark 1986; Robb 1999; Joyce 2000).

We must also keep in mind that identities can be dynamic through a lifetime, and gained, augmented, or lost. Although the titles under examination here define only the upper echelons of society, we are seeking to perceive the ways in which hierarchy articulated decision-making, radiating from a sovereign and a collective group of magnates, but ultimately affecting all levels of the community.

Proximity and access to the bodily person of the ruler was always an important source of power in monarchist societies, and the primary locus for these interactions was the royal court. This hosted a network of relations around the king and was the central business space of government – reflected architecturally in greater or lesser palace complexes. These spaces in Classic Maya cities, with their variety of enclosed plazas, galleried halls, storerooms, and dormitories, can be examined archaeologically, and are sketched in the numerous courtly scenes on painted vessels and a smaller corpus of carved panels. At their heart, on the privileged right side of the scenes, we usually find a lord enthroned on a bench or dais. Attending him are functionaries of lower rank, bodyguards, fan-bearers, food-servers, musicians, and dwarves, together with those of elevated status and close kin who are shown presenting ritual items, bundles of tribute, or the human booty of captives (see Inomata and Houston 2001, 2002; Miller and Martin 2004) (Figure 1). Supplied with hieroglyphic captions identifying individuals and giving their epithets, these vase paintings are an important resource for reconstructing the social and cultural functioning of these spaces.

Yet, even where titles can be read and understood in literal terms, they might not be transparent in their meaning. Clouded by layers of metaphor or shifted from one semantic domain to another over time (migrations of meaning being common in titles worldwide) we must place deeds above denotation. Moreover, it is a distinctive feature of Maya texts that officeholders are proudly on display while the institutions, organisations, solidarities, and other kinds of grouping that underlie their positions are shadowy at best. Classic Maya political rhetoric is resolutely personified and to perceive institutional structures we are obliged to work through their corporeal representatives – even at

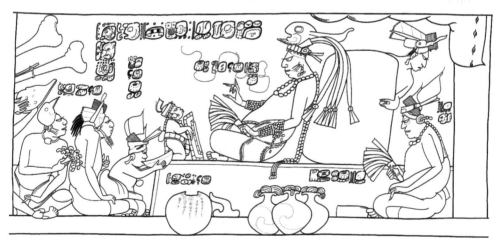

1 A palace interior with a ruler of Motul de San José and his attendants, as depicted on the cylindrical vase K1453. (Drawing by Alexandre Tokovinine after a roll-out photograph by Justin Kerr)

the level of polity identity itself. Sahlins' social-historical individuals are not free-floating agents, but grounded participants possessed of responsibilities as well as privileges. This chapter will explore the titular identities of rulers and their immediate subordinates to understand what we can of this "human architecture" of the Classic Maya polity.

ROYAL TITLES

Classic Maya royalty bore a range of epithets that proclaimed their right to rule over place and people. The commonalities to elite culture across the lowlands are more compelling than any of the variations we see, justifying the assessment of a unified tradition. The question at hand is what do titles tell us about conceptions of sovereignty and polity? How do variations in their incidence and distribution express the differing statuses of kings and their closest kin, both within the long-term dynamics of social development and the rapid shifts of contingent events? Such important and complex issues will need to be examined across more than one chapter, but we can make a start by looking at three royal titles, whose frequency and patterns of use show the leading parts they played in status definition.

Ajaw

The key term in Maya political authority was *ajaw*, best translated as "lord", but very often read by context as "ruler". It has been reconstructed for Proto-Mayan as **aajaaw*, and is attested in every Mayan language (Kaufman and Norman 1984: 115; Kaufman 2003: 84–85). Its etymology is still uncertain. It has been interpreted as an agentive *aj* joined to *aw*, "to sow", in reference to the fecund powers of lordship as the "one who sows" (Mathews and Justeson 1984: 207), but more persuasively as combining the agentive with the root *aw*, "to shout" to give the "one who shouts/proclaims" (Stuart 1995: 190–191; Houston and Stuart 2001: 59). This is under the acknowledged influence of the Nahuatl title *tlatoani*, "one who speaks" used for Aztec emperors, in which lordly utterances were the quintessence of individual power, either for acts of command or as a conduit for the will of the gods (Gruzinski 1989: 22–23). This is in line with western notions of speech acts as the key to authoritative effects (Lincoln 1994).

Alone among the epithets we will be discussing, *ajaw* survived into colonial times and even retains echoes of its meaning in traditional societies today (e.g. Ajpacaja Tum et al. 1996: 4). At the time of the Spanish conquest it clearly referred not only to the head of a given hierarchy, but also the *principales*, the indigenous nobility.[2] It is clear that the *ajaw* term fulfilled the same dual function in the Classic era and designated not only the paramount

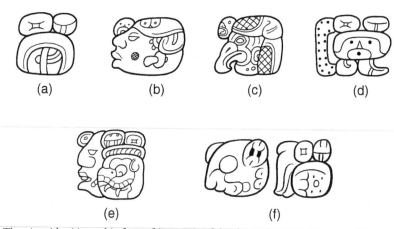

(a)   (b)   (c)   (d)

(e)   (f)

2 The *ajaw* title: (a) graphic form; (b) portrait of the deity *juun ajaw*, "One Lord"; (c) vulture form; (d) day-sign form in the spelling *k'uhul ajaw*, "Holy Lord"; (e) with the *ix* female prefix as *ix kaanul ajaw*, "Lady Snake[-Place] Lord"; (f) with the "young" prefix *ch'ok yokib ajaw*, "Young Piedras Negras Lord". (All drawings in this volume by the author, unless otherwise stated)

lords we designate as "kings", but also a broader noble class. This sense of a larger community is implicit in the epithet *baahajaw* "head lord" carried by some royal lieutenants, where *baah* signifies the leading figure among a like-named group (Schele 1990a; Houston and Stuart 1998: 79).

Floyd Lounsbury (1973) deciphered a sign present in all eras of the script as **AJAW** in one of the first practical applications of Knorozov's insights on phoneticism (Figure 2a).[3] It appears in the earliest Maya inscription yet identified, produced between 400 and 200 BCE (Saturno, Stuart, and Beltrán 2006: 1282), and in some of the very latest, such as the Madrid Codex, which is Late Postclassic (1250–1546 CE) in date. The initial identification was enlarged in subsequent work that recognised the fuller range of substitutions of which it was part (Mathews and Justeson 1984: 203–219). To Lounsbury's abstracted logogram were added humanoid and animal variants, the former the head of the deity and prototypical ruler *juun ajaw*, "One Lord" (Coe 1989; also Freidel and Schele 1988) (Figure 2b).[4]

The most important of several diagnostics of this character was a white bark-paper headband, often marked with one or more red stripes. This was elaborated at the brow by the addition of a greenstone jewel in the form of the so-called Jester God, named *huun(al)*. Usually there was only one (Figures 10a and 58), but in portrait renditions we sometimes see three in number (although usually only two are visible) (Figures 28 and 63). The Jester God was the personification of paper, a material that captured some esoteric essence of authority with deep cultural roots (Stuart 2012a). In most glyphic representations the head of this character is substituted by a sign that might be read *saak*, "seed", linked to wider concepts of fecundity and genesis.[5] The reading of the same sign switches to *ajaw* when used as a day name and, more rarely, when it is employed as the royal title itself. Other varieties of *ajaw* include a vulture (Figure 2c) and a mammal of some kind, both of which wear the identifying headband. These bands became a defining mark of *ajaw* status and their presentation *tu'baah*, "on his head/to his person/above him" was one of the main rites of lordly investiture (p.110). Indeed, the entire class of *ajawtaak* (the plural form given in the script, see Lacadena 1992: 183–184; Stuart 2004b: 1, 2005b: 55–56)[6] were identified by headbands or pars pro toto *huun* jewels used in their stead – as we see in the gathering of non-regnal lords in Room 1 of the Bonampak Murals (Miller and Brittenham 2013: 126).

While *ajaw* was a designation in its own right, it also formed the basis for a number of expanded epithets. By far the most significant of these is the famed "emblem glyph" we first encountered in Chapter 2. The Appendix offers an inventory of almost all the known examples. The importance of emblem glyphs for interpreting Classic Maya political organisation was understood from the earliest days of the decipherment (Berlin 1958), but it was the *ajaw* reading that allowed them to be recognised as personal titles (Mathews 1985: 32, 1991). With this understanding in place, attention then turned to the two other components of this three-part compound.[7]

One of these always comes first in the reading order and, because of the superimposed composition of most emblem glyphs, is normally only partly exposed on their left side (Figure 3a). Examples that are not superimposed expose the whole sign to view (Figure 3b).[8] Consisting of a snub-nosed face fronted by a stream of drops, often embedded with additional devices that signal its precious qualities, it represents the word **K'UH**, meaning "god/ divine thing" (for a more detailed description, see Chapter 7). In the context of emblems, it is used to signify the derived adjective *k'uhul*, "holy, sacred" – confirmed by some late spellings of **K'UH-lu** and **K'UH-HUL** (Jackson and Stuart 2001: 224).

Traditionally, the presence of a *k'uhul* prefix has been used to identify distinct polities, but it does not appear in all the titles serving the function of emblem glyphs, making it less than a dependable guide in this respect. In part,

(a)   (b)

3 Emblem glyphs with the *k'uhul*, "holy" prefix: (a) the standard superimposed form obscuring most of the **K'UH** logogram; (b) the separated-out form showing the whole **K'UH** logogram.

the issue is an historical one, since only a handful of polities employed the prefix before 500, and it was adopted by others in a rather ad hoc manner over the next four centuries. Some resisted its allure until the very end of the Classic Period, with no discernible implication for their political status.[9] Whatever allusion it draws to the "sacredness" of kings, it is clear that the *k'uhul* prefix worked to amplify status (Houston and Stuart 1996: 295), and that its spread was part of a wider phenomenon of title inflation. Notably, it retained an optional quality and could be omitted when writing space was limited or when referring to some lesser or opposing king. Accordingly, the Appendix makes no differentiation between "full" and "partial" emblem glyphs.[10]

The subject of the lord's authority is specified by the remaining, variable component – which I will call the emblem "referent" for the moment – appearing as x in the sequences **x-AJAW**, "x lord" or **K'UH(UL)-x-AJAW**, "holy x lord". Most of the time the referent is superimposed over the graphic form of **AJAW**, leaving only its upper two parts visible.[11] If the referent takes the form of an animal head, that of a bat or snake for example, then it can be shown wearing a headband, and this serves to spell the *ajaw* component. Technically speaking, this can be seen as a conflation with the deity or vulture head-forms.

Referents have long been assumed to be place-names, but it was Stuart and Houston (1994) who established that many were indeed the toponym of the core settlement and seat of the relevant royal court. This is the pattern we find at Tikal, Yaxha, Ucanal, Ceibal, Motul de San José, and Tamarindito among others.[12] However, it was also noted that such a linkage is not universal and in prominent cases such as those of Palenque, Calakmul, Copan, Dos Pilas, and Piedras Negras the referent and core toponym are quite different. We will examine the reasons behind this divergence in Chapter 13, having drawn on additional lines of evidence, especially the constitution of authority as a dynamic process across the landscape, to be explored in Chapter 6. However, for the present it is enough to note that a statement from the first set such as *uhtiiy yaxa'*, "it happened (at) Yaxha" (Figure 17a) is potentially ambiguous as to whether the event occurred within the site itself or in the broader territorial domain it controlled. The matter is much clarified by the second set since, with very few exceptions, such statements refer to the city serving as the main seat of power.

This means that there is scant sign of referents having an independent life as polity-names outside the confines of the emblem glyph. We, thus, encounter a key tenet of Classic Maya political identity, that the concept of a political formation was inalienably bound to that of personal sovereignty. This complicates the question of what emblem referents actually were, since an understanding of their composition does not fully illuminate the role they came to play within an active lexicon.

Although the unit *k'uhul ajaw*, "holy lord" has established itself in most writing on Maya politics and is regularly used to support the idea of "divine kingship" in the Classic Period, it should be noted that instances of this formula outside the confines of the emblem glyph are vanishingly rare and very late. It gains some popularity as a stand-alone title only in the ninth century at northern centres such as Chichen Itza (see Boot 2005: 428) (Figure 2d).

The full *k'uhul x ajaw* emblem glyph was not entirely restricted to the sovereign. There is evidence for some simultaneous use by siblings, as well as by father and son "co-rulers". At Palenque – which used the referent *baakal*, "Bone[-Place]" – the title *k'uhul baakal ajaw* was carried not only by the king K'inich Ahkal Mo' Nahb III, but by his brother Upakal K'inich, who was additionally called the *baahch'ok*, "head youth" or heir apparent (Bernal 2002a; Miller and Martin 2004: 232; Stuart 2005a: 38–40). In time, Upakal K'inich duly took the throne, in line with previous fraternal successions at this site (Stuart 2005a: 153). An earlier figure at Palenque, called Janaab Pakal, was also called a *k'uhul baakal ajaw* and, although he was never a paramount ruler, he may have been a junior one and almost certainly the conduit of royal blood to his part-namesake K'inich Janaab Pakal. A more serious complication in the case of this emblem is its contemporaneous use by the kings of other centres, firstly that of Tortuguero, 60 km to the northwest, and then at Comalcalco, which lies 152 km distant (Map 1). The degree to which these dynasties shared their origins with the one associated with Palenque remains unclear (see Case Study 1, which can be found at the end of the chapter).

For many years, emblem glyphs were perceived as static references, each predictably attached to a particular major centre. However, over time it was realised that exceptions abound and it is these instances that paint a more complex portrait of how these titles function. Emblems, it transpires, reflect an ever-changing political map and are an invaluable asset for understanding Classic Maya political dynamics through time. In addition to *baakal*, there are several other instances in which centres use the same emblem title, the best known being the sharing of the *mutul* form between ancient Tikal and parvenu Dos Pilas. We now understand that a son of the Tikal king decamped 112 km to the Lake Petexbatun region to found Dos Pilas in the first half of the seventh century, his successors later adopting an additional co-capital at Aguateca, some 12 km to the southeast (Houston 1993: 97–101; Martin and Grube 2000: 54–67) (Map 3). Whether this was a breakaway or a planned expansion, it was an intrusion into the territory of a long-established polity with its own dual centres at Tamarindito and Arroyo de Piedra, both now subordinated to the newcomer. The fraternal conflict that erupts between Dos Pilas and Tikal, which continued into the next generation, makes clear that the rightful use of the Mutul referent had become an issue of dispute.[13]

In other examples, the sharing of emblems is likely to be evidence for roving dynastic seats. Such is the case with *hixwitz ajaw*, a title that appears at the widely spaced sites of La Joyanca, Pajaral, and Zapote Bobal at different times, probably marking sequential capitals of the same kingdom (Stuart 2003).[14] Elsewhere, kings could carry two such titles, laying claim to conjoined but distinct political identities. Two emblems are used at El Zotz, although they occur much more frequently at Yaxchilan, an outgrowth or transfer that remains poorly understood (Houston 2008a, 2008b; Stuart, in Houston 2008a: 7). The *ak'e* and *xukalnaah(?)* emblems traditionally attributed to Bonampak and Lacanha, in the Lacandon region south of the Usumacinta River, are difficult to ascribe to these sites individually, and are jointly held by a few kings in the latter stages of the Classic Period (Mathews 1980: 60–61).[15] Similarly, distinct emblems associated with Cancuen and Machaquila are paired in the reign of one late monarch at Cancuen.[16] Although they are largely illegible today, La Milpa was another centre that appears to have used two emblem glyphs (Grube 1994a: 223). The highland capital of Tonina employed three, one dominant form based on the referent *popo'* (Mathews 1982: 901; Martin and Grube 2000: 179), as well as two rarely seen companions featuring the terms *sibikte'(?)* and *puhtz'am*. There were also three emblems used at Piedras Negras, where the main *yokib* or *yoykib* form was sometimes joined by *k'inil* or substituted by the very late *wayal* (Martin and Grube 2000: 141; Zender 2002: 170–176).[17] Occasionally emblems were expanded, as when El Peru adds a second term in front of its original *waka'* referent.

In a few places an emblem used for generations is suddenly replaced by another, as at Altar de Sacrificios (Houston 1986: 2) and Caracol (Martin and Grube 2000: 87). Caracol initially used *uxwitz ajaw*, "Three Mountain Lord", a form based on its local toponym, but this was later superseded by the more enigmatic *k'uhul k'antu maak*.[18] The latter highlights that not all functioning emblems feature *ajaw*, with *maak*, "man/person" substituting in this instance. At Río Azul that position is taken by what seems to be *xib*, "male" (Houston 1986: 2, 5–7), while much the same situation occurs in *k'uhul chatahn winik*, a polity of unknown location, where *winik* translates as "person".[19] Some of the more atypical titles may hark back to or continue Preclassic identities, with one candidate here being the title read *sak chuwen*, "White Artisan", which identifies Naranjo's early kings and continues to be used up to its very last legible inscription. Since these atypical forms function in very similar ways to emblem glyphs, they too are included in the Appendix.

The number of *k'uhul x ajaw* emblems has greatly increased from Berlin's initial collection of eight, today numbering at least 57 examples, or some 110 if *x ajaw* and the atypical forms are accorded equal status. Even so, the original total was higher still. There are many substantial centres for which we currently have no inscriptions and others where texts are poorly preserved, some showing the outlines of now-illegible emblems. To this day, there are poorly explored regions from which we can expect additional sites and monuments to emerge in due course, probably including some of those revealed in lidar surveys. If we were to chart the location of *k'uhul x ajaw* and *x ajaw*-bearing centres across the lowlands, it would exceed the distribution of Classic Period sites included in Maps 1–4, indicating an even denser scatter of polities than the one first laid out by Mathews in Map 5b.

Although the *ajaw* status was by default masculine, it was not exclusively gendered and adding the female classifier *ix* created titles for royal women in the form **IX-x-AJAW** (Figure 2e).[20] These generally identify the home polities of brides sent to marry elsewhere and were seldom, if ever, employed by true female sovereigns or regents. For example, ruling women such as Ix Yohl Ik'nal of Palenque or Ix Wak Jalam Chan (Lady Six Sky) of Naranjo used conventional, unmarked *k'uhul x ajaw* formulae.[21] A different prefix specifies royal heirs, where *ch'ok*, "sprout, youth" was occasionally added as a classifier or adjective to make **CH'OK-x-AJAW**, "young x lord" (Ringle 1988: 14; Houston 2009: 157, figure 5) (Figure 2f). As a plain noun, *ch'ok* had the sense of "prince" (see Houston 2009: 154–164), although, when applied to rulers acceding at a young age it could stay with them throughout their careers. For example, the Palenque ruler known to us only by the nickname Casper acceded at the age of 13 in 435, yet he carries the *ch'ok* title on his only contemporary record, a travertine bowl. There he is bearded, somewhat portly, and clearly well into his fifty-year reign (Martin and Grube 2000: 157).

Before leaving the topic of *ajaw*, we need to note its role within a dynastic consciousness. The formula in question centres on the root *tz'ak* that appears in Colonial Yukatek as *ts'akab*, "ancestry, caste, lineage, or generation" (Martínez Hernández 1929: 272; Barrera Vásquez 1980: 873) and as *–ts'ak*, "step or count of steps of parentage" (Michelon 1976: 455; see Houston 1998: 356–357). It appears in the inscriptions in the form **9-ta-TZ'AK-bu-li-AJAW** *baluun ta tz'akbuil ajaw,* where the number nine is used figuratively to mean "many" to render the overall sense of "Many in Sequence Lord" (Figure 4a). This stand-alone title may be the closest thing we have to a term for "dynasty" in the inscriptions (Stuart 2010b: 2).

Actual counts from a founding father are made where *tz'ak* is prefixed by a number denoting the bearer's place within a series, as in *uchawinik tz'akbuil*, "twenty-second in sequence" (Figure 4b). Alternatively, the position of the relevant king can be specified by attaching the appropriate number before the classifier **TAL** to produce an ordinal construction, as in *uchanlajuun tal (ajaw)* "fourteenth (lord)" (Figure 4c). Both forms are commonly called "successor titles". Though few polities record them in any systematic way, those that do provide valuable data that fix individual rulers in order and time and, where

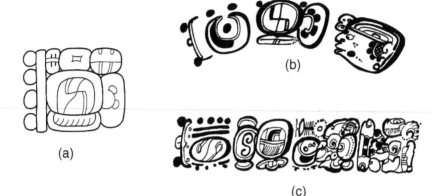

4 Dynastic consciousness expressed in counts of kings or "successor" titles: (a) Spelling of *baluun ta tz'akbu ajaw*, "Many in Sequence lord" on Palenque Palace Tablet (V1); (b) *uchawinik tz'akbuil mutul ajaw*, "22nd in Sequence of the Tikal lord" on a plate from Tikal Burial 195 (G-I) (drawing by Virginia Greene); (c) *uchanlajuun tal wak chan tajal chahk chak tok ich'aak*, "the Fourteenth (lord) was Chak Tok Ich'aak I" on K4679.

we see gaps, helpfully reveal otherwise unknown kings (Mathews 1975; Riese 1984b; Schele 1992b; Martin 2014a: table 2).

There is reason to believe that only male monarchs were registered in this way. Ix Yohl Ik'nal ruled as queen of Palenque between 583 and 604, however the numbered counts that fix her successors K'inich Kaan Bahlam II as tenth in line and K'inich Ahkal Mo' Nahb III as twelfth mesh with Palenque's dynastic history only if she is omitted. In 511, a six-year-old girl known as the Lady of Tikal was installed as queen at Tikal.[22] Although she carries the high title of *ix kaloomte'* (p.79), it is her male co-ruler and presumed consort, Kaloomte' Bahlam, who carries the designation of "19th in sequence" (Martin 1999, 2003b: 20).[23] Although there is a clear hereditary principle to Classic Maya kingship, this and another case at Tikal help to establish that successor titles are plain counts of incumbents that need not imply patrilineal descent (Martin 2003b: 29). An interesting anomaly comes with the paired emblems shared by El Zotz and Yaxchilan, since the latter ascribes different dynastic counts to each (Stuart 2007a: 31). One Yaxchilan king was the fifteenth in the line of the *pa'chan* referent but in excess of thirtieth in line of *kaaj(?)* – a clear fusion of younger and older dynasties.

Successor titles do us one further favour, providing a rough guide to the antiquity of different dynasties. If we estimate the average length of Classic Maya reigns from the two longest sequences for which we have firm starting points, those at Palenque and Copan, we come to a figure of about 22.5 years – very close to that provided by the 881-year sequence of English and British monarchs (Martin 1997a: 853–854). The caveat here is that Maya sequences are short enough to allow significant margins of error and, given the political turbulence of the Classic era, we cannot be sure that they do not span lacunae during which no king ruled. As we shall see in Case Study 6, counts could be restarted as a result of moving a royal seat, although we know of other occasions on which this did not occur. Successor titles, often surviving only as isolated examples, are known from Tikal, Copan, Palenque, Yaxchilan, Naranjo, Calakmul El Peru, Xultun, Tonina, Itsimte, Uaxactun, Altar de Sacrificios, Champerico, Oxkintok, Tamarindito Tres Islas (Cancuen), and Ojo de Agua (Bonampak/Lacanha).

Projecting backward from the respective dates of these references, we can estimate dynastic foundations that spread widely from the fifth century CE back to at least the third century BCE. However, some of these longer enumerations clearly count from divine rulers, characters who will be examined in Chapter 7. At Naranjo, for example, the accession of its founding king – which we can estimate to have taken place around 200 BCE based on two of its successor titles – is set 22,000 years in the past in one account, some 895,000 years in another (Martin 1996a: 226).[24] The same may well be true of some of the cases in which founders are identified only by emblem glyphs rather than a personal name. If these uncertain examples are put to one side for a moment, most of the earliest counts reach back to the first or second centuries CE (Martin 2003b: 5, n.6, 2016b).

The core ideology and symbolism of *ajaw* kingship were fully in place by at least the beginning of the Late Preclassic Period (400 BCE–150 CE) and may be considerably older (Freidel and Schele 1988; Stuart 2004a; Taube et al. 2010; Martin 2016b). Yet the kind of material expressions that we later associate with this status are either absent or quite limited at this time. In particular, there is a dearth of richly-stocked burials, grandiose residences, and inscribed monuments glorifying individuals – the features that originally served to define the Classic Period. The often massive Preclassic pyramids appear to have had an exclusively religious function, while many in the Classic era were mortuary shrines containing major tombs. Given how little we know about the Preclassic era, it may be premature to describe it as truly "pre-dynastic", but the evidence currently to hand suggests that the signatures of dynastic identity become widespread only in the Protoclassic Period.

Kaloomte'

The next epithet, *kaloomte'*, sits at the very summit of the Classic Maya titular hierarchy. Unlike *ajaw,* which was shared by a wider noble class, or even *k'uhul x ajaw,* which could be used by royal siblings and co-rulers, *kaloomte'* was only carried by senior or paramount kings. Moreover, of all the statuses into which Maya lords could accede, *kaloomte'* is the only one that lacks a possessed form; no such lord is said to be subject to another in this way. Epigraphers have long recognised the importance of this title without building a comprehensive understanding of it, justifying an extended treatment of it here.[25]

There are at least 275 examples of the *kaloomte'* title, representing some 119 individuals over an active history of 473 years – considerably longer if retrospective examples are included (Martin 2014a: table 3).[26] It was realised in two very different-looking but fully equivalent glyphic compounds, hereafter distinguished as its "graphic" and "portrait" forms (Figure 5a and b). Fortunately, a secure substitution with the syllabic sequence **ka-lo-ma-TE'** in a text at Copan demonstrates that *kaloomte'* was the correct reading for both (Stuart, Grube, and Schele 1989) (Figure 5c). The distinction between graphic and portrait versions lies in alternative logograms for **KAL**, signs that are usually accompanied by the phonetic complement **ma** and always by one of two variants of **TE'** – with the graphic version made especially complex by the habitual superimposition of **TE'** over one half of its **KAL** sign. Here *kal* is a verbal root appended by the agentive suffix *-oom* to form *kaloom,* meaning "the one who *kals*" or "the *kaler*". The object here is *te',* "wood, tree, stick", a term that appears in several other titles. The semantic flexibility of *te'* in Mayan languages makes a precise translation in any one context difficult.

The meaning of *kal* remains uncertain. We get a lead from the portrait form, which shows the storm deity Chahk brandishing a hafted axe, an allusion to lightning in Maya belief and artistic convention. The Postclassic Dresden Codex (pp. 59c–60c) features four axe-bearing Chahks sitting in trees aligned to the cardinal directions. As we will soon see, the *kaloomte'* title had a close relationship to the world quarters, suggesting that *te'* could refer to a cosmic arbour. Indeed, a religious significance is clear from the handful of cases in which *kaloomte'* appears as the name or title of a god. The full portrait version

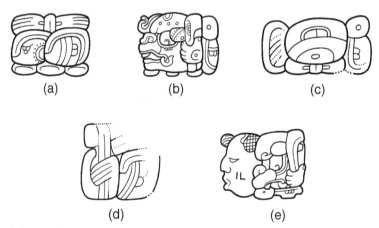

5 The *kaloomte'* title: (a) graphic form; (b) portrait form; (c) syllabic spelling; (d) axe-in-hand form; (e) female form with *ix* prefix.

emerges only in the mid-seventh century, fully 250 years after the earliest instances of the graphic form in the late fourth century. A suspicion that this innovation alludes to the basic concept in some iconic fashion is boosted by a lone early instance at Quirigua (Schele 1990b: 2; Martin and Grube 2000: 217; Looper 2003: 39–40) (Figure 5d).[27] There we find an isolated hand-and-axe in a context that makes it a clear precursor to the standard portrait form. It resembles a wider category of verbs realised as pictographic hand signs, each invoking meaning through its pose and/or the manipulation of relevant objects.[28] If the same process of sign formation is at work here we might infer that *kal* refers to "axing" in some way.[29] Relevant terms might be found in the Tzotzil cognate *chal*, "to split gradually" or Colonial Yukatek *kal* (in *kalbesah*), "to make holes", which are possibly linked to *kal*, "strength or power to do something" (Barrera Vásquez 1980: 285–287; Laughlin 1988. I.186). On this basis, a prospective reading for the original term could be "tree-splitter" or the like (Wagner 1995).

Versions prefixed with **IX** show that women also held *kaloomte'* status, of which there are 16 known holders representing some fourteen per cent of the inventory (Figure 5e). Of these, four were *ix kaloomte'* from Calakmul: two queens mentioned at the site and two princesses sent to other centres. Although the inherited status of the latter pair ensured that they outranked their husbands, neither were rulers – good evidence that *kaloomte'* was a status rather than a political office.

Nevertheless, as with *ajaw*, *kaloomte'* positions could be assumed through an enthronement ceremony, using the positional verb *chum* "to sit" in the form *chumlaj ti kaloomte'lel/il*, "is seated into *kaloomte'*-ship". Such examples are rare, however, with only one Early Classic example at Dzibanche and four Late Classic ones at Tikal (Mathews and Justeson 1984: 211, figures 2q and 2x; Stuart 1995: 206; Martin 2005a: n.16; Velásquez 2008a: 338; Martin and Beliaev 2017). On a single occasion at Palenque, *kaloomte'* appears as a derived verb. This can be understood either as the inchoative "he becomes *kaloomte'*" or the antipassive of a transitivised noun "he *kaloomte'*'s". In either case, the chronological framework dictates that this event took place on the day on which the described king underwent the normal initiation into *ajaw*-ship, which is probably how and when the great majority of *kaloomte'*-bearing kings acquired their positions. These anomalous accession statements are meaningful, since the Tikal and *kaanul* "Snake[-Place]" dynasties – the latter evidently based in early times at Dzibanche but later at Calakmul – were dominant hegemons throughout much of the Classic era, while Palenque was also a significant regional power.

A special feature of *kaloomte'* are the sub-sets aligned to each of the four cardinal directions (Figure 6). An association with *ochk'in/chik'in* "west" is by far the most common, with some 34 individuals (n = 45), while seven are

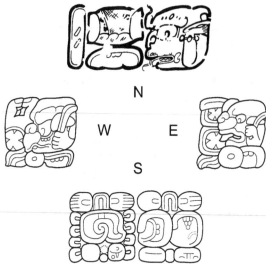

N

W   E

S

6 *Kaloomte'* in its cardinal direction forms: West (*chik'in/ ochk'in kaloomte'*); North (*xaman kaloomte'*); East (*elk'in kaloomte'*); South (*nohol kaloomte'*).

identified with *elk'in* "east" (n = 9), two with *nohol* "south" (n = 3), and two with *xaman* "north" (n = 2).[30] If these are charted across the Maya region their geographical references become clear: those specified as "south" are appropriately only seen at Copan and Quirigua (Riese 1988: figure 5; Looper 2003: 60), while "east" appears at Lamanai and probably Altun Ha (Closs 1988: 14; Helmke, Guenter, and Wanyerka 2018), and "north" at Ek Balam (Lacadena 2005: 67) (Map 1). These three directional titles could be claims to dominion over a particular world quarter, but the wide distribution of "west" in all regions casts a different light on the matter. This suggests that origin, whether real or claimed, was the more significant factor.

The most instructive case here is that of Copan in the far southeast. Here the intrusive fifth century founder of the dynasty, and several of his successors, are labelled as *ochk'in kaloomte'*. Since this early era in Copan history is closely linked to the symbolism of Teotihuacan, the inference is that this westerly version consciously invokes Central Mexican power and legitimacy (Stuart 2000: 490–494). We will examine this issue in later chapters, but for now we should simply note that the earliest contemporary references to *kaloomte'* – appearing first at Tikal and Uaxactun, and then Piedras Negras – are ascribed to outsiders who have iconographic or textual connections to Teotihuacan and outrank local kings bearing *ajaw* titles (see p.241–243).

Therefore, although the term *kaloomte'* is fully Mayan in form and is applied retrospectively to very early Maya rulers, it begins its known textual life as the exclusive preserve of foreign overlords. It is signally absent from the title strings of all the major Tikal kings of the Early Classic Period – Yax Nuun Ahiin I, Sihyaj Chan K'awiil II, K'an Kitam, and Chak Tok Ich'aak II – and it was not until 527 that a local monarch carried a *kaloomte'* epithet of their own. This sustained omission begs some explanation. It is conceivable that only lords of Teotihuacan were deemed worthy of this exaltation and, further, they may have remained Tikal's real or symbolic overlords since the time of the *entrada* event in 378 (see p.122–126). If so, it could suggest that the Teotihuacan influence that took hold over a significant portion of the Maya lowlands was no transient affair, but had effects that lingered throughout the fifth century. The *ochk'in kaloomte'* mentioned as an overlord at Piedras Negras in the early 500s also carries a *wiinte'naah ajaw* title linked to Teotihuacan. Though an isolated case, it might well imply that the great western city was still an active player in Maya politics at that time. We know that Teotihuacan did not survive as a force in Mesoamerica beyond the sixth century, with evidence that elite areas of the metropolis could have been burned and abandoned as early as 550 CE (Sugiyama 2004: 102).

Only the kings of Tikal, Dzibanche, early Calakmul, Coba, and Copan are known to employ *kaloomte'* on their own account before 600, the traditional mark separating the Early from Late Classic Periods. Over the next century they are joined by just four more (Edzna, Lamanai, Palenque, and Tonina), but after 700 the total rises by a further twelve (Bonampak/Lacanha, Chancala(?), Dos Pilas-Aguateca, Dzibilchaltun, Itsimte, Motul de San José, Oxkintok, Piedras Negras, Pusilha, Quirigua, Xultun, and Yaxchilan), and then after 800, when the collapse is fully underway, by another seven (Ceibal, Ek Balam, Ixlu, Machaquila, Nakum, Oxpemul, and Ucanal).[31] Most of this last group fall into a special category we will be examining separately in Chapter 11. Although the full sequence might need to be modified or enlarged as more data emerges, the spread of *kaloomte'* is plainly a Late Classic phenomenon in step with the growing number of sites erecting monuments.[32]

At Ek Balam in 840 a battered but visible "holy" form of *k'uhul kaloomte'* (Lacadena in Grube, Lacadena, and Martin 2003: II-36) is an innovation that differentiates the deceased dynastic founder from a reigning *kaloomte'*. In another late instance at Ucanal, ancient K'anwitznal, we see *kaloomte'* in one of only two instances of an emblem-like formula *k'uhul k'anwitznal kaloomte'*. Here it distinguishes a senior ruler from a junior one titled only as *k'uhul k'anwitznal ajaw*. These appear in the captions for two standing lords depicted on Stela 4 from 849, their contrast in scale not a marker of differing status but their relative age (Figure 7). A vessel fragment from Dzibanche refers to a unique *sukuwinik ch'ok kaloomte'* (Velásquez and Balanzario 2016), an "older brother *kaloomte'*" that could imply a co-ruling younger brother with the same title — an exception that might reflect Dzibanche's special power at the time. No actual Preclassic examples of *kaloomte'* are currently known, but it is certainly ascribed to ancient rulers. The earliest dated example appears in an ancestral, probably legendary event placed to 254 BCE, where an otherwise unidentified Snake ruler is called a *k'uhul kaanul elk'in kaloomte'* (Carter 2015: 11).[33] At the other end of the chronological scale, the very last instance of *kaloomte'* is surely the one inscribed on Ceibal Stela 13. Although undated, on stylistic grounds it was produced after 889 CE.

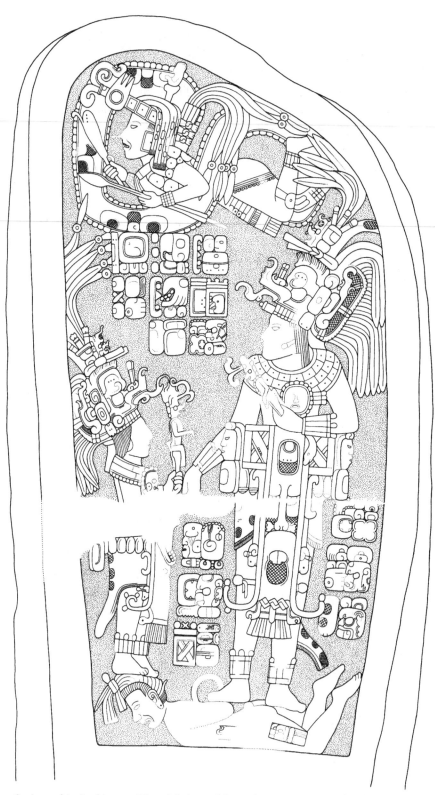

7 Senior and junior kings on Ucanal Stela 4 celebrate the 10.1.0.0.0 period ending in 849 CE. (Drawing by Ian Graham © President and Fellow of Harvard College, Peabody Museum of Archaeology and Ethnology, PM# 2004.15.6.4.9)

There are some surprising absences from the list of major kingships using *kaloomte'*, and this is probably meaningful. Although it appears in the inscriptions of Naranjo and Caracol, these examples only refer to outsiders, neither site describes its own rulers in this way. Caracol was a bellicose and powerful kingdom, but one that was at various points the client of either Tikal or the Snake dynasty of Dzibanche-Calakmul (Martin and Grube 2000: 88–92; Martin 2009a, 2017a).

At Naranjo *kaloomte'* was applied to the foreign queen regent Ix Wak Jalam Chan, as well as to her mother Ix Bulu' and her father Bajlaj Chan K'awiil, the king of Dos Pilas. It was not, however, used by her son, the Naranjo king K'ahk' Tiliw Chan Chahk, or by any of his descendants. There can be no question that this monarch was an important overlord in his own right, but one who was subject to the yet greater power of Calakmul, as we will see in Chapter 10. His grandfather Bajlaj Chan K'awiil is only ascribed *kaloomte'* status on Naranjo monuments, not on his own, where we find a reference to his subordination to a Calakmul king. A similar pattern continues with his son Itzamnaaj K'awiil, who eschews the *kaloomte'* title at his capital of Dos Pilas, but receives it at the subordinate centre of Tamarindito (see Houston 1993: figure 4.17). The next two Dos Pilas monarchs do adopt it, surely reflecting the greater degree of autonomy they enjoyed after the decline in Calakmul's power in the eighth century, when they appear to exert full control over their own clients (Martin and Grube 2000: 60–63). At Piedras Negras, Itzam K'an Ahk III (Ruler 2) was another king closely associated with Calakmul who does not use *kaloomte'*, although he ascribes it to his father, who similarly makes no mention of it on his own monuments.

In sum, when the sample of *kaloomte'* epithets is considered as a whole, patterns to their distribution and use can be discerned. While the term resembles a formal position, the evidence favours an honorific function. It is true that especially powerful kingships describe elevations into *kaloomte'*-ship, but this was employed rhetorically to emphasise an exalted status rather than to refer to an institutional office. The most significant feature of *kaloomte'* is that it was, barring one late exception, never used by rulers who were the clients of others on contemporary monuments – although it was sufficiently embedded in general notions of kingship that it could be applied to them retrospectively. It was a title that ostensibly admitted no superior and was initially restricted to only the most powerful and dominant kingdoms in their respective regions. As time wore on, however, it was adopted by a rising group of competitors, and then by lesser kingships which were by now largely unfettered from foreign overlords, reflecting the decline in larger regional power structures.

Baahkab

The spelling **ba-ka-ba** has long been understood as a royal title (Kelley 1962b: 306–307), although later it was re-analysed as the form **BAAH-ka-ba** *baahkab*, "head earth" (Houston, Stuart, and Taube 2006: 62–63) (Figure 8a). The scribes who worked on carved Chochola-style ceramics of the northwestern lowlands – especially associated with the major site of Oxkintok (Werness 2010) – sometimes wrote **ba-ka-KAB**, where the **ka** phonetic complement keys the *kab* rather than *chab* reading for the logogram for "earth, land, territory" (Figure 8b). This might well be because in most contexts the sign had already made that sound-shift and the scribes wanted to specify the older form.[34] *Baahkab* is one among a set of *baah*-prefixed titles that include *baahte'* ("head staff?"), *baahtuun* ("head stone"), *baahtz'am* ("head throne"), *baahtook'* ("head flint"), and *baahpakal* ("head shield"), which express priority within a category metaphorically associated with an object or material. As with all other royal titles, it was also used by women, usually the wives of kings in the form *ix baahkab* (Figure 8c). Additionally, there was a rare *ch'ok baahkab* version that identified child rulers (Figure 8d).

Baahkab is unknown in the Early Classic and makes a sudden appearance in the mid-seventh century, thereafter becoming extremely common.[35] As such, it illustrates the rapid spread of innovations and the tightly knit nature of Classic-era political culture. It did not attract all polities, however, and it finds no place in the title strings of kings at either Calakmul or Tikal.[36] Similarly, the kings of Piedras Negras did not carry it, although they did attribute it to one of their clients ruling at La Mar in 795. It is only in these later times that we see

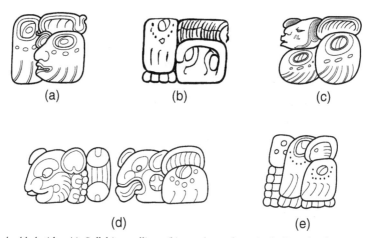

(a)   (b)   (c)

(d)   (e)

8 The *baahkab* title: (a) Syllabic spelling; (b) northern form including the logogram **KAB**; (c) female form with *ix* prefix; (d) youth form with *ch'ok* prefix and a **BAAH** logogram; (e) "holy" form with *k'uhul* prefix.

non-regnal lords adopting the form – a painted plate from the polity called either Yomootz or Yopmootz tells us that a *lakam* (see below) was also a *baahkab*. This impetus from below may be the reason *baahkab* gains a *k'uhul* prefix on a stela fragment from the highland centre of Chinkultic, dated to 771, a development that maintained the distinction between royalty and nobility (Figure 8e). The precise meaning of *baahkab* and the reason for its sudden popularity remain unknown, although its basis in "earth" means that it might allude to control over land and its resources.[37] Speculatively, its absence at certain hegemons may reflect their relative lack of interest in issues of local control in favour of the greater prize of suzerainty over other kingdoms.

NOBLE TITLES

Polity rulers took the lion's share of monumental inscriptions to exercise their own patrimonial rhetoric, but nobles, courtiers, and functionaries also found their way into the written record. They usually appear as the aides and attendants of kings, but in some areas the uppermost ranks commissioned their own monuments – if usually closely supervised by their monarch and produced by artisans under their control. From these sources and the copious body of painted ceramics we can glean a list of sub-kingly ranks and offices, which have already been the focus of much investigation (e.g. Stuart 1985b; Schele 1991a; Houston 1993: 128–136; Villela 1993; Houston and Stuart 2001; Jackson and Stuart 2001; Zender 2004; Jackson 2005, 2013; Tokovinine 2005a; Houston and Inomata 2009: 163–192; Bíró 2012b).

Cross-culturally, the non-ruling elite act as intermediaries between the paramount and his or her people, as the agents of their authority and part of the apparatus of social and economic control. Their duties typically include military service, bureaucratic administration, and sacerdotal responsibilities, work as emissaries and negotiators, tribute-collectors and suppliers of courtly needs, logistical planners for ceremonial and religious events, and managers in the construction and renewal of buildings and other public works (see Inomata 2001). Additionally, we have evidence that a range of skilled literati, including those titled *itz'aat*, *taaj*, and *aj tz'ihb*, were also closely tied to the elite group (Stuart 1989: 157; Montgomery 1995; Rossi, Saturno, and Hurst 2015; Saturno et al. 2017). Some artisans occupied high status residences close to the royal court (Inomata and Triadan 2000) and a small number carried lordly titles.

Noble epithets first appear in Early Classic texts, but are infrequent until a substantial rise in the Late Classic. Stephen Houston and David Stuart (2001: 73–74, figure 3.6) considered three potential causes for this expansion: (1) as a feature of a much larger Late Classic sample; (2) as a thematic shift that brought previously unseen actors onto the stage of history; (3) from an increase in their number, as population growth led to a greater need for administration – and favoured the second and third of these options. Marc Zender (2004: 389–390, tables 9 and 10) plotted the rise not against demography, as Houston and Stuart had done, but against the increase in monument commissions and concluded that the first option must also play a role. Obvious to all investigators is the very uneven geographic distribution of these titles. They have strong signatures along the Usumacinta River and in the western zone in general but form only pockets of prominence elsewhere, and no more than a thin scatter across very populous regions such as the central lowlands of the Peten. Such discrepancies could be a sign of differing administrative structures or of an alternative balance of power between royal and non-royal actors. We should certainly try, if we can, to explain why secondary lords in some areas exercised a patrimonial rhetoric denied to them elsewhere.

Problems of interpretation at the secondary level are more acute than they are at the primary one, since here we must try to grasp functional differentiations and how their responsibilities mesh together. Which were aristocratic rankings and which, if any, professional specialisations? Which of them denote full-time duties at the central court and which command over the provinces? Whatever these titles signify we know that individual actors could carry several of them at the same time and that several lords held the same one concurrently. As with royal titles, translation is no more than a starting point, and often a weak one at that. We will be on firmer ground if we can understand the range of actions each performed, assess how power, privilege, and responsibility were distributed, and so how each position contributed to the running of a political society. As it turns out, this is no easy task. What was once a short list of noble epithets has grown into a longer catalogue, most of them poorly understood and some quite rare. This section offers a survey and analysis of the best known.

Sajal

The first non-regnal title to be identified, initially noted by Proskouriakoff (1964: 186) in the captions of her "battle companions", was that of *sajal* (Stuart 1985b) (Figure 9a). Stuart's study described two variants distinguished by alternative versions of the syllabogram **sa** in spellings of **sa-ja-la**, together with a female version prefixed with **IX**.[38] The word *sajal* brings its own etymological uncertainty, although it could be based on the root *saj*, "to fear", with the "one who fears" reflecting the proper obeisance that a vassal should display to his king (Houston and Stuart 2001: 61). Their subordination is, as elsewhere, expressed by means of grammatical possession, with the pronoun

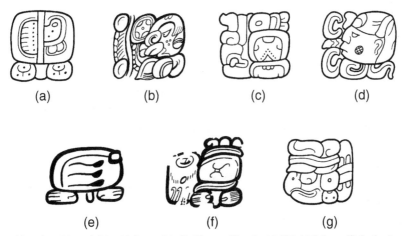

9 Noble titles: (a) *sajal*; (b) *ajk'uhuun*; (c) *ti'sakhuun*; (d) *yajawk'ahk'*; (e) *lakam*; (f) *baahtz'am*; (g) Banded Bird.

prefix *u-* added to make *usajal*, "the *sajal* of" (p.240). As with several other subordinate positions, holders acquired their titles in investiture ceremonies such as *chumlaj sajalil*, "is seated into *sajal*-ship", mirroring those performed for royalty, but usually conducted under the direct aegis of kings.

Sajal is the most numerous of secondary epithets, with over 100 examples, referring to around 78 distinct office-holders (Martin 2014a: table 4). Figural representations of *sajal* divide between those shown as the attendants of kings, participating in ceremonies or in the taking and presentation of captives, and those unfortunate enough to be prisoners themselves. Very few self-commissioned portraits of *sajal* have come down to us, and even where lengthy inscriptions detail their lives and achievements, we find them accompanied not by their own portraits but by those of their overlord and king. A case in point would be the Tablet of the Slaves from Palenque, where the text focuses on the career of the *sajal* Chak Suutz' (Schele 1991a), yet the image depicts his sovereign (Wald 1997). Another example is a small panel from the western lowlands now in the Dumbarton Oaks Collection (Coe and Benson 1966: 5–15). It offers rich information about the lives of successive *sajal* at an unidentified provincial centre subject to Piedras Negras, and features the portrait of a lord in full warrior attire. Yet it shares the same iconographic device as the Tablet of the Slaves, whereby feathers from the headdress reach up to touch the hieroglyphic name of the Piedras Negras king, a sure pointer to his identity.

Chak Suutz' was also a *baahajaw* "head lord", meaning the foremost Palen-que noble of his time, unambiguous evidence that *sajal* were members the *ajaw* class. The precise remit of *sajal*-ship is not explicit in the sources. Chak Suutz' himself was a military leader credited with victories on the Tablet of the Slaves and on the Tablet of the Scribe. The setting of the former monument in a sizeable residential compound in the heart of Palenque identifies his palatial home. However, *sajal* are also strongly represented at sub-centres well removed from the royal seat. Indeed, in governing dependencies as the heads of their own lineages this is the only secondary title to show local para-mountcy.[39] These instances are significant in that they allow us to define what sites were considered to fall within a single polity. For example, at the Piedras Negras satellite of El Cayo, ancient Yaxniil, the ruling *sajal* is described as an *aj yaxniil* "El Cayo Person", but never a *yaxniil ajaw* "El Cayo Lord", which would denote a degree of local sovereignty (Map 4).

Such nobles might have been dual-residents, alternating between service at court and presiding over their own provincial fief. Certainly, at any one time there were several active *sajal*, with the most prominent among them some-times shown with the king and picked out as the *baahsajal*. They are occasion-ally pictured in groups, as with the four *sajal* from Pomona shown in bondage on the front of Piedras Negras Stela 12 (Schele and Grube 1994; for image see Stuart 2009: 61). In total eight are known to have been seized in battle and their military responsibilities are sometimes denoted by means of titles such as "He of # Captives" and "The Master/Guardian of x" (p.205), with *sajal* the only non-regnal category to carry them.

The hereditary component to the title emerges from parentage statements. A fine panel, probably from Lacanha, demonstrates that both the father and mother of the featured *sajal* were themselves *sajal* (Case Study 2) (Figure 12). Equally, ruling *sajal* at El Cayo succeeded their fathers in office and carried the family names K'utiim or Ahk Kamiiy – some of the few examples of patron-yms in the texts. The K'utiim moniker is borne by El Cayo *sajal* through a minimum of five generations, from before 731 to at least 795 (Jackson 2005: 207–217). A dynastic identity for *sajal* also emerges on the very last example we have, an intriguing miniature stela with a portrait, dedicated in 864 in the domain of Sak Tz'i' (Miller and Martin 2004: 191, figure 51) – a kingdom whose capital has been recently identified by Charles Golden and Andrew Scherer's project as Lacanja-Tzeltal (Golden et al. 2020).[40] This memorial to a deceased noble, likely erected by his dutiful son, tells us that the deceased lord was the *waxaklajuun tz'akbuil sajal* or "18th in sequence *sajal*" (Houston, Robertson, and Stuart 2001: figure 19b). This is the only occasion on which we see a count of nobles in the same style as that used for royalty.

A cluster of *sajal* titles occurs in a small portion of the northwestern lowlands in and around the major centres of Xcalumkin and Oxkintok (Grube 1994b; Boot 2006). The looting of monuments and carved vessels, the aforemen-tioned Chochola ware, has impeded the study of their political hierarchies, which combine titles in unfamiliar ways. In this area *sajal* is an almost standard appellative in the manner of *ajaw*, with higher, kingly, ranks distinguished by the use of *baahkab* or *kaloomte'*.

Ajk'uhuun

A second epithet associated with subsidiary lords is *ajk'uhuun*, spelled **AJ-K'UH-na** with a late-appearing variant of **AJ-K'UH-HUUN** (Figure 9b). The meaning of this term has been much debated, but prominent suggestions are "one who keeps, guards", the "one who worships, venerates (the king)" (Jackson and Stuart 2001), or a priestly office of "one who worships (the gods)" (Zender 2004: 180–195).[41] There are 88 currently known *ajk'uhuun* titles, describing at least 64 individuals (Martin 2014a: table 5).

We get some of our best insights into the status and concerns of an *ajk'uhuun* from the interaction of inscriptions, iconography, and architecture at Copan (Webster 1989; Jackson and Stuart 2001: 224–225). Two major sub-groups away from the core of the site were found to include large and well-constructed buildings, 9N-82 and 9M-18, with interior sculpted benches bearing cosmic imagery and glyphic texts that tell us that each housed an *ajk'uhuun* in the service of a Copan king. The exterior of 9N-82 was in part decorated with sculpted supernatural scribes equipped with brushes and paint-pots, with an in-the-round figure of a "monkey scribe" deity deposited within an earlier phase (Fash 1989: figures 43 and 45–47, 1991b). This scribal theme is consistent with some of the attire associated with these lords: which includes brushes that serve as hairpins and bound paper, possibly whole books, tied into their headbands (Lacadena 1996: 48; Coe and Kerr 1997: 97–101). Whatever their other duties, *ajk'uhuun* were evidently the dominant lords within those compounds and closely associated with the esoteric worlds of the scribe and artist.

But *ajk'uhuun* were not simply high-minded aesthetes. An elegant portrait of one *ajk'uhuun* on a section of conch shell shows at least a mythological interest in tribute payment (Zender 2004: 330) and on three occasions they are identified as captives seized in war, where the warrior headdress of one suggests that they were active combatants. The female version, *ix ajk'uhuun*, is rarely seen, although one was a royal woman from the *kaanul* "Snake[-Place]" dynasty who married into the Yaxchilan line.

The possessed form *yajk'uhuun* "the *ajk'uhuun* of" (Houston 1993: 130) establishes such lords as subjects of the king, but on the Tablet of the Slaves at Palenque four *ajaw* of the *ajk'uhuun* rank or role are described as possessions of the *sajal* Chak Suutz' (Jackson and Stuart 2001: 219). Another instance, from the as-yet-unidentified "Site R" subject to Yaxchilan, has one individual variously described by possessed forms of *ajk'uhuun*, *sajal,* and the still-obscure *yajawte'* title (Zender 2004: 353). It is possible that all these distinctions were acquired together but, based on the data we will see in Case Study 3, they probably mark his elevation through different ranks.

There are at least two examples of accessions into the position of *ajk'uhuun*. One is described on a small stela from Tonina, where the subject was *chumjiiy ta ajk'uhuunil*, "seated into *ajk'uhuun*-ship" in 612 (Miller and Martin 2004: 188) (Figure 10a). Uniquely, this event is not immediately followed by the name of a presiding king. This lord is pictured wearing the *huun*-jewelled headband of an *ajaw* and carrying an incense bag and a curved blade fashioned from chert or obsidian.

Historically, this takes place at an interesting juncture. Just twelve days later a new ruler was invested at Palenque, Tonina's regional rival to the north. Little is known of this character, called Muwaan Mat, who presides over a period of severe disturbance at Palenque following an attack by Kaanul kingdom of Dzibanche the previous year (Looper and Schele 1991; Martin 2000c: 107–109). A few months later, in 613, the Tonina *ajk'uhuun* "witnesses" the 9.9.0.0.0 period ending, a calendrical event that was explicitly said to be *not* celebrated at Palenque (Grube 1996: 5; Stuart and Stuart 2008: 145–146). Less than two years after this in 615 we have the installation of a new Tonina king, K'inich Bahlam Chapaat, at the tender age of eight years (Martin 2001b; Martin and Grube 2008: 179). Barely five months later Palenque also sees a

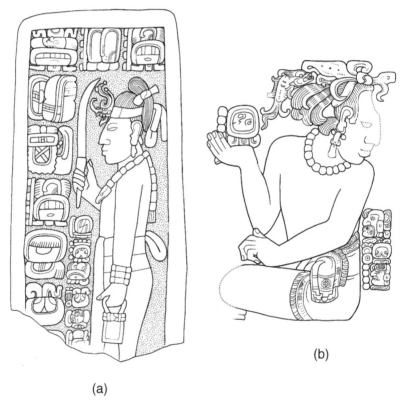

(a)   (b)

10 Nobles as ritual performers: (a) An *ajk'uhuun* shown commemorating the 9.9.0.0.0 period ending of 613 on Tonina Monument 173 (drawing by David Stuart © President and Fellows of Harvard College, Peabody Museum of Archaeology and Ethnology, PM# 2004.15.15.2.138); (b) A noble who is both a *sajal* and a *ti'sakhuun* shown in the guise of a year-bearer holding a *tzolk'in* day-sign. Pomona Panel 1.

new king, with the elevation of a twelve-year-old, the famed K'inich Janaab Pakal. It is conceivable that all these events were unconnected, but their proximity in time is striking and one must wonder if the dynastic turmoil Dzibanche visited on Palenque encompassed Tonina as well. This may be the context for the unusual prominence of the Tonina *ajk'uhuun*, who observes a ritual life with no ruling king in sight.[42]

Ti'huun / Ti'sakhuun

A further designation may be the most elevated of all non-royal titles (Case Study 3). It is spelled either **TI'-HUUN** *ti'huun* or an elaborated **TI'-SAK-HUUN** *ti'sakhuun* (Figure 9c). The pairing *sak huun*, "white paper" is readily comprehensible as the name of the royal headband, leaving only the *ti'* element at issue. *Ti'* can mean "edge", producing an enigmatic "edge (of the) white paper" which arguably could be linked to rites of investiture (Houston and Stuart 2001: 68–69). But another sense of *ti'* and its cognate *chi'* is "mouth, lips" (Kaufman 2003: 262), with verb and verbal noun derivations of "to speak" and "speech, language". Zender (2004: 210–221, tables 4 and 5) accordingly offers "speaker (of/for the) white headband", with strong sacerdotal overtones of "prophet" or "oracular priest".[43]

The known sample of *ti'huun / ti'sakhuun* is small, with 16 instances representing at least 13 individuals, but it has the longest evidence of use for any noble title, spanning 444 years. It may be the restricted sample that explains the lack of female holders. Appearances again cluster in the western part of the lowlands, although the two earliest come from the central Peten. The very first appears on the back of an unprovenanced jade plaque or "celt" dated to the end of the ninth Bak'tun (9.0.0.0.0) in 435 (Berjonneau and Sonnery 1985: pls.330, 331). The lord celebrating this event is called the *uti'huun,* meaning that he was a *ti'huun* subject to someone else identified only as the *baluun pik ajaw*, "9-Bak'tun Lord". This is a title elsewhere ascribed to the contemporary king of Tikal, Sihyaj Chan K'awiil II, since he oversaw that key juncture. We must ask if the richly attired figure carved on the other side of this jade plaque is the *ti'huun* in question, whose name appears on a matching jade celt as well, or his overlord the king. Without some explicit confirmation, such as a name spelled out in the figure's headdress, we would be on much safer ground assuming that it was a king.

It is eighty-one years before we see our next case of *ti'huun*, but it is an important one for establishing the high responsibilities and prestige of this position. Tikal Stela 8 has long presented a puzzle, with its date and the identity of the depicted protagonist both in question. Today, however, there is reason to believe that this was not a standard ruler but a *ti'huun* in the service of a twelve-year-old queen, a lord who celebrated an unconventional period ending, most likely, in 516 (Zender 2004: 333–338).[44] It is clear that nobles of the *ti'huun* status could perform major calendrical ceremonies, although this was usually noted only when the ruler was too young to do so. One suspects that this *ti'huun* – who was the namesake of a later king and carries a *unahbnal k'inich* name/title redolent of Tikal royalty – was a royal family member who played a pivotal role as an older guardian and ritual specialist during the first years of the young queen's reign. It is possible that the stone presenting/holding rites described, which were normally documented only at major calendrical junctures, were actually performed more frequently; with this perhaps the last enacted before his death and Stela 8 serving as a de facto memorial.

A similar case occurs on Tonina Monument 165, where the normal rituals to mark 9.14.5.0.0 in 716 were performed by one K'elen Hix, who was both a *ti'sakhuun* and *ajk'uhuun* (see Graham et al. 2006: 107). He carries a "holy" prefix on the former to give *k'uhul ti'sakhuun*, the only example of its kind. On this occasion, he is said to belong not to a king but to the Paddler Gods, a pair of Charon-like deities who regularly oversee calendrical rituals, here identified only by their joint title *wak chan ajaw*, "Six Sky Lord(s)" (Zender 2004: 211, 342–344). This is important not only because this "holiness" conveys the lord's high status, but also because that status seems to be derived from his intimate connection to deities. The reason for K'elen Hix's prominence again lies in the age of his monarch, who was only nine years old at the time. The incentive to memorialise the event on this particular stone came from the eventual demise of this long-serving aristocrat, who held office under three Tonina kings, which took place eight months after the 716 ceremony.

The kingdom of Pomona produces more associations between *ti'sakhuun* and calendrical rites. On the fragmentary Panel 1 at least two of them hold *tzolk'in* dates as they impersonate the solar "year-bearers" called *itzamtuun* (Stuart 2004b: 4; Martin 2015a: 191–192). This plainly demonstrates that there could also be more than a single *ti'sakhuun* at any one time, while one of them was also a *sajal* (Figure 10b). Elsewhere at Pomona, Stela 7 describes another *ti'sakhuun* engaged in a period ending dating to 751 (see García 2005: plate 6.24). The phrasing here is unusual, with the rites performed by the local king but connected to a *ti'sakhuun* by a term based on the problematic root *et/eht* – which sometimes implies a degree of agency, but other times not. This may be a character known from other monuments (Zender 2004: 328–331) and his actions at Pomona probably relate to the authority of the Palenque king K'inich Kaan Bahlam III, who also attends the ceremony recorded on Stela 7 (Martin and Grube 2008: 174). There is surely a hierarchical significance to this, but in which direction that flows remains somewhat unclear.

The very last instance is a great deal later and takes us back to the central Peten, appearing on Jimbal Stela 1 (Carter 2014a: 190). A small text, squeezed into the background of the image almost as an afterthought, identifies a *ti'huun* who *yetaj*, "accompanies" the king at the period ending ceremony for 10.2.10.0.0 in 879 (see Chapter 11) (Figure 73d). There at least, the titular structure of Classic Maya polities remained intact to the very end.

Yajawk'ahk'

Yajawk'ahk', meaning "Lord of Fire" or "Fire's Vassal", is a title found only in the far west and north of the Maya realm (Zender 2004: 195–210; Stuart 2005a: 123–125; Martin 2014a: table 7) (Figure 9d). Such lords had a strong presence at Palenque, one being the previously noted Chak Suutz' and another Yok Ch'ich' Tal, who was closely associated with Temple XIX and was perhaps a priest or administrator of some sort. The exquisitely executed stone pier within that building shows this lord kneeling before his sovereign while wearing the *huun*-jewelled band of the *ajaw*. Meanwhile, a nearby platform with two carved sides shows him attending his king's inauguration in 721 (Stuart 2005a: figure 92). Yok Ch'ich' Tal was also an *ajk'uhuun*, and this title-pair is one we encounter at Tonina and, even more frequently, at Comalcalco. There the walls of Tomb XI are adorned with nine stucco relief figures identified by partly preserved captions, with at least five, possibly all nine, holders of both titles (Zender 2004: 148–152, table 1).

Evidence for the collective nature of the *yajawk'ahk'* role is forcefully attested back at Palenque, where a censer-stand describes the accession of up to six *yajawk'ahk'* to their positions on a single day (Case Study 3). Military responsibilities for such lords are likely, but remain indistinct. Much depends on whether or not the "fiery headband" Chak Suutz' is invested with just before he begins his military campaigns is a shorthand version of the *yajaw-k'ahk'* position. We know of two such lords who were captured, both in late times. One from Santa Elena was seized by Piedras Negras in 787 and another from "Pomoy" taken by Tonina, two years later in 789.

Lakam

Another object-derived epithet comes from the word **LAKAM**, "banner" (Lacadena 2008; see Martin 2014a: table 8) (Figure 9e). It was first recognised on an unprovenanced cylindrical vessel (Kerr 1992: 640), where three such lords sit before a king of Motul de San José adjacent to the statement *tz'ahpaj upatan ux lakam yichonal*, "the tribute of the three *lakam* is set down in his sight" (Houston and Stuart 2001: 69). It is clear that they have delivered the bundled goods in the scene, but conceivably they were also involved in its collection (Lacadena 2008: 7–9).[45] The source of the term is an item of symbolic display, much like the standards that appear in Maya battle-scenes, and this could suggest some military connection (Lacadena 2008: 13). Another painted vessel points in this direction, since it shows three figures carrying fan-like feather banners and another three armed with *atlatl* spearthrowers and darts (Kerr and Kerr 2000: 937). Name captions include *lakam* titles, but these refer not to the banner-bearers but to the armed men – as if the former were heralds announcing their approach.[46] Despite their weaponry we should hesitate before identifying a *lakam* as a dedicated warrior. In a world where even long-distance traders went about their business armed in case of trouble (see Kerr and Kerr 1997: 802), this need not be their prime role.

Evidence that *lakam* were sent on long, potentially dangerous foreign missions emerges from a remarkable find at El Palmar (Tsukamoto and Esparza 2015; Tsukamoto et al. 2015). There a hieroglyphic stairway in an otherwise inconsequential residential compound on the outskirts of the site was commissioned by a lord using the *lakam* title. Its long inscription traces his line back through generations of *lakam* title-holders, each in service to the local king of the time. The motivation to produce this monumental work was an expedition the commissioner took to faraway Copan in 726, evidently a diplomatic visit of some sort sanctioned by El Palmar's overlord at Calakmul, who is also mentioned in this text (p.163 and 337).[47]

Baahtz'am

BAAH-TZ'AM-ma *baahtz'am* as well as what appears to be a variant, **BAAH-te-mu** *baahteem,* translate as "Head Throne" and suggest close contact with the business of royal audiences and receptions (Stone and Zender 2011: 97; Martin 2014a: table 9) (Figure 9f). It is not an especially common title and for the most part seems to be carried by functionaries without much institutional power – in the Bonampak murals a pair of them perform as masked mummers (Houston 2012: 165).

However, in some places it had a higher profile and one among their number even ascended, by stages, to kingship itself (Tokovinine and Zender 2012: 45–46). K'inich Lamaw Ek' was the son of a non-ruling *ajaw* and his progress is documented on a series of unprovenanced vessels originating at Motul de San José, ancient Ik'a'. All the vessels were signed by the same artist, a lord of the unidentified centre of Tuubal, and they either constitute a series of political updates or a post-facto account of events. As a *baahtz'am*, K'inich Lamaw Ek' attended the crowning of his king Yajawte' K'inich on a date now lost to erosion. Yet when we see him on another vase, in an event dated to 768, he shares visual prominence with the king and, more importantly, also boasts the emblem glyph *k'uhul ik'a' ajaw*. This marks him as a co-ruler of some kind, with only the *kaloomte'* title borne by Yajawte' K'inich setting him apart as the senior figure (Velásquez 2011; Martin 2017b). By 779 K'inich Lamaw Ek' emerges as sole ruler carrying his own *kaloomte'* epithet and the *baahtz'am* designation has finally been discarded.

"Banded Bird"

The last epithet we will be examining currently resists decipherment but consists of a logograph depicting a bird wearing a folded cloth headscarf tied with a band, at times seen with superimposed phonetic complements (Stuart 2005a: 133–137; Bernal 2009: 89–94, 103–120; Martin 2014a: table 10) (Figure 9g). Bearers of this "Banded Bird" title often appear in contexts that suggest a ritual specialisation. Dos Pilas Panel 19 is one, showing such a lord using a stingray spine to perform a penis perforation rite on a young prince (Houston 1993: 115, figure 4.19). An artefact of potential relevance in this regard is a small wooden box, carved with a text on all sides that celebrates dynasts from Tortuguero (Coe 1974; Looper 1991; Zender and Bassie 2002). Yet the main focus here falls on the accession ceremony for a Banded Bird lord called Aj K'ax Bahlam in 680, who is also pictured on the box's lid. This was clearly a personal possession and would be an ideal container to keep the tools of his profession: the small flakes of obsidian and stingray spines that served as bloodletting implements.

Our understanding of the Banded Bird title has been advanced by a broken wall panel carrying a long inscription excavated from within Palenque Group XVI (González and Bernal 2000; Bernal 2002b, 2009; Stuart 2005a: 134–135). It recounts recurring accessions into this office over a span of at least 332 years. Each bearer was installed by a Palenque ruler, beginning with the first of the line (by means of the *ukabjiiy* "he/she supervised it" expression). In addition to a personal name, each nominal phrase is completed by the sequence K'an Tok Waweel, which gives every appearance of being a family name. Joining the two patronyms previously noted at El Cayo, this encourages the idea that particular titles were the possessions of specific lineages. The multi-roomed Group XVI was evidently the business space of this position, held by specialists with a hereditary component, and perhaps a centre that serviced the ritual life of the nearby Temple of the Cross (Stuart 2005a: 136) – where one of them may also be mentioned.

The Banded Bird title was sufficiently important to be used by kings – who usually elevated its significance by adding the *k'uhul* prefix to it. Although this pattern emerges at quite an early date it becomes more popular toward the end of the Late Classic. Ajaw Bot, the king of a new Mutul dynasty at Ceibal, which was apparently an offshoot following the fall of Dos Pilas, carries such a title in four surviving examples of his name, beginning in 771 (see Graham 1996: 23). Here it is tempting to think that a secondary lord with priestly responsibilities has taken advantage of the disruption of this era to gain a kingship, but the truth of that may never be known.

CASE STUDY 1: BONES IN THE WEST

The site of Palenque, perched on a limestone shelf overlooking the plains of modern-day Tabasco, counts among the most significant of Maya cities by virtue of its well-preserved art and architecture, and, for our purposes, its extensive body of inscriptions. The target of some of the earliest explorations in the Maya area, it has contributed mightily to our understanding of the history and culture of the Classic Period (Stuart and Stuart 2008). Palenque's rich mythical foundations, treated in Chapter 7, reach back as far as 3121 BCE. These deep origins of kingship are associated with the emblem *k'uhul matwiil ajaw* and it is only in a more quasi-historical period that we see the appearance of the more familiar *k'uhul baakal ajaw* (Figure 11a). Much later accounts tell us that the first king to bear that title took office in 967 BCE, while a second was reigning in 252 BCE. The tenure of the historical founder, K'uk' Bahlam I, began in 431, the first of at least 18 Palenque kings in one of the most complete dynastic sequences we have (Berlin 1965, 1968a; Mathews and Schele 1974; Martin and Grube 2000: 154–175).[48]

The first hint of complexity to the relationship between emblem glyphs and polities came with the recognition that the *baakal* title was carried not only by the Palenque dynasty but by another at the much smaller centre of Tortuguero (Figure 11b), situated some 60 km to the northwest (Map 1). Marcus (1976: 106–109) took this to mean that Tortuguero was a second-order dependency of Palenque, but Mathews (1985: 32) argued that since both rulers shared an equivalent *ajaw* title they were either lords of like-named places or held comparable status within a single polity. Returning to the hierarchical line, Grube (1996: 6) suggested that Bahlam Ajaw, the leading figure in Tortuguero history first identified by Coe (1974: 53), was subject to the authority of his contemporary K'inich Janaab Pakal of Palenque.

Yet the lack of any explicit connection between these two characters, plus the evidence for Tortuguero attacking the home site of the Palenque king's wife, began to favour the idea of independent dynasties that laid claim to the same name (Martin and Grube 2000: 165). The divergence in their lines could have developed as early as 510, when we hear of our earliest potential Tortuguero ruler. This is soon after the Palenque kings moved their royal seat (p.130) and is contemporaneous with the reign of Ahkal Mo' Nahb I at Palenque, who begins two key dynastic histories at the site. Tortuguero

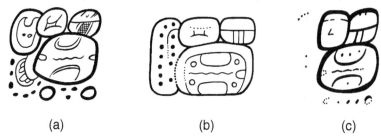

(a)   (b)   (c)

11 Three emblem glyphs using the same "bone" referent read *baakal*: (a) Palenque; (b) Tortuguero; (c) Comalcalco.

mentions *baakal* as an active historical place in one of its texts, leaving one to suspect that it lies nearby or even that it was Tortuguero itself.

The archaeological understanding of Tortuguero is poor, since its core has been almost completely destroyed by modern development (Hernández 1984). Its known epigraphic record is short-lived, with almost all of its output produced by the aforementioned Bahlam Ajaw, who reigned from 644 to 679 (Riese 1980; Gronemeyer 2006). The most notable event in his career was a "star war" attack on the westernmost Maya city, Comalcalco, in 649 (Peter Mathews, pers. comm. 1992; Zender 2001). At this time Comalcalco kings were called lords of *joykaan,* but later ones used the *baakal* emblem, a switch best explained by its conquest and political takeover (Figure 11c).[49]

That scenario has been supported by finds at Comalcalco, including that of a stone vessel naming Bahlam Ajaw dated to three years after the conflict in 652, suggestive of an enduring occupation or a transfer of his capital (Zender 2001; Zender, in Grube, Martin, and Zender 2002a: 64; Gronemeyer 2006: 61–63). Archaeological analysis shows that Comalcalco underwent a major transformation at around this time, with temple sanctuaries built in a style typical of Palenque, though with a distinctive use of clay brick in place of the locally scarce stone (Andrews 1989: 141–150). An important discovery came with a burial urn containing 36 inscribed plaques of bone and shell that celebrate the life of a leading *yajawk'ahk'* noble (Armijo, Gallegos, and Zender 2000; Zender, Armijo, and Gallegos 2001; Zender 2004: 250–263). One of many dates in these short texts falls in 776 and includes the name of a local king who uses the *baakal* epithet. Another such king is named on an inscribed brick (Hoppan 1996: 156–157), and one more on a delicately carved greenstone head that turned up in faraway Honduras (Zender, in Grube, Martin, and Zender 2002b). As far as one can tell, the kings of Palenque, Tortuguero, and Comalcalco used the same royal title from the mid-seventh century onwards, making *baakal* the single identification of royal power for a huge swathe of the western Maya realm.

CASE STUDY 2: THE RISE OF A *SAJAL* AT BONAMPAK/LACANHA

A panel believed to be from Lacanha, and certainly strongly tied to it epigraphically, offers significant data on the *sajal* status (Coe and Benson 1966: 26–35; Mathews 1980: 67–70; Miller and Martin 2004: 80) (Figure 12 and Table 1). It begins with a calendrical period ending in 746 and an appropriate ritual conducted by one Aj Sak Teles, a Lacanha *sajal* subject to a king nicknamed Knot-eye Jaguar who bears twinned emblems associated with Bonampak and Lacanha *ak'e* and *xukalnaah(?).*[50] This overlord was a native of neither locale but rather of the "Knot" site, a regional player that remains unidentified (Palka 1996). The panel goes on to name the parents of Aj Sak

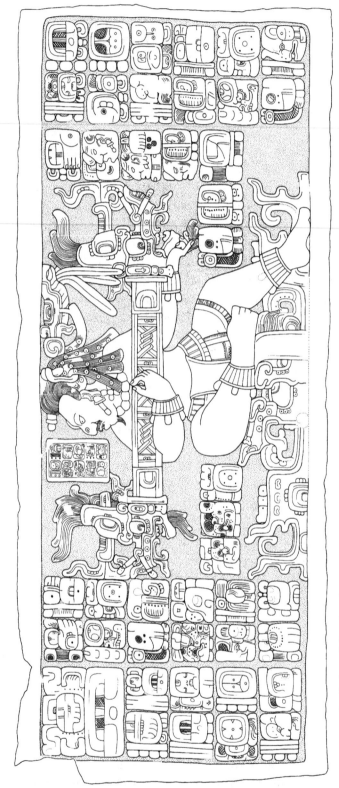

12 A relief panel that describes the seating of Aj Sak Teles into *sajal*-ship in 743. Kuna–Lacanha Panel. (Drawing by David Stuart)

TABLE I *Timeline*

Long Count	CE	Greg.	Event
9.15.11.17.3	743	Jun 4	Accession of Aj Sak Teles, He of Lacanha, as *sajal*
9.15.15.0.0	746	Jun 6	Period ending ceremony by Aj Sak Teles the *sajal* of Knot-eye Jaguar
9.15.17.2.14	748	Jul 18	Capture of the *yajawte'* of Knot-eye Jaguar
9.17.5.8.9	776	Jun 16	Accession of Yajaw Chan Muwaan as *ajaw* of Bonampak and Lacanha

Teles, who were both fellow *sajal*, suggesting the hereditary component of his position – a feature of *sajal* status that recurs elsewhere. The narrative then tracks back three years to his accession *chumlajiiy ti sajalil*, "was seated into *sajal*-ship" in 743, presumably following the death of his father. Although the depicted lord is unidentified, it seems to be Aj Sak Teles himself performing a mythic episode referred to in a small caption.

What makes this character so interesting is his subsequent career and the evidence it offers of internal political strife (Anaya, Guenter, and Zender 2003: 187–188; Miller and Martin 2004: 80). For this we rely not on the testimony of Aj Sak Teles, but on that of his son Yajaw Chan Muwaan, who succeeded to the two thrones previously held by Knot-eye Jaguar in 776 (Mathews 1980: 64).

Yajaw Chan Muwaan retrospectively ascribes these self-same titles to his father on no less than three occasions, emphasising that Aj Sak Teles preceded him as king. But how and when had Aj Sak Teles risen from the *sajal* of one centre to the sacred *ajaw* of two lines? That he performed a period ending is already a hallmark of rare distinction, but the answer is alluded to on Bonampak Lintel 3, where Aj Sak Teles is shown capturing a *yajawte'* belonging to Knot-eye Jaguar (Mathews 1980: figure 7). The date is problematic (Mathews 1980: 67–70), but a re-examination on site indicates that the Calendar Round is 3 Ix 1 Chen, a night-time event best placed to 9.15.17.2.14 in July 748. Earlier in time than the two lintel scenes it partners, this was just five years after Aj Sak Teles' elevation to *sajal*. The purpose, it seems, was to explain how his position was achieved or consolidated by means of violence, even civil war, against vassals of the previous king – social mobility at the point of a lance.

CASE STUDY 3: RANKING THE NOBILITY

Secondary lords were "owned" by their king, as expressed in formulaic statements of "a is the x of b". In Mayan syntax this requires that the relevant title "x" be prefixed by a third-person ergative pronoun: setting *u-* in front of

13 Inscribed stone censer stand from Palenque Group J bearing a portrait of Baahis Chih.

initial consonants and *y-* in front of initial vowels. The possessed version of *sajal* is thus *usajal*, while that for *ajk'uhuun* is *yajk'uhuun*. When titles already contain possession, as in *yajawk'ahk'*, "lord of fire", the pronoun is simply added to produce *uyajawk'ahk'*, "the lord of fire of". In a few cases such statements produce slim evidence for hierarchies among the nobility (Zender 2004: 163; Jackson 2005: 255–259). One of these emerges at Palenque on a small portrait censer-stand excavated in Group J (formerly Group IV), which carries a long text extending over the front, sides, and back of its flanges (Figure 13). The chronology has been surprisingly difficult to pin down, with two competing schemes set a single Calendar Round, or 52 years, apart (Table 2).[51] I am persuaded that the later one is correct, but regardless of the absolute dates this stone offers helpful data on the organisation of noble positions within the Palenque polity.

The text begins in 660 with the elevation of one Baahis Uchih to the rank of *ti'sakhuun*, an event that is *ukabjiiy* or "supervised" by his king (K'inich) Janaab Pakal. Two years later we see the inaugurations of as many as six lords – two of whom we know from later texts – into the rank of *yajawk'ahk'*, again under the direction of the king. Since all are further said to be *sajal* beholden to Baahis Uchih, we can take it that they were already holders of that title. It is unlikely to be coincidental that just three days later there is an incident involving the ruler of the rival polity of Santa Elena. If this was the military action *och uch'een* (p.213) then the group elevation seems in some way preparatory for it – in accord with occasional signs that *yajawk'ahk'* was, at least in part, a martial title (Zender 2004: 203–204, 308). The text now leaps forward some forty years to a burial whose subject is no longer legible, which was directed by the next king K'inich Kaan Bahlam II in 701. We then move on to 706 and the death of our protagonist Baahis Uchih, there called "the *sajal* of" his original master K'inich Janaab Pakal. This is a pattern that we will see again, in which the patrons that install clients are forever their overlords, even long after their deaths.

TABLE 2 *Timeline*

Long Count	CE	Greg.	Event
9.11.7.12.5	660	May 11	Accession of Baahis Uchih Aj Sik'ab as *ti'sakhuun* by (K'inich) Janaab Pakal
9.11.10.5.14	662	Dec 16	Accession of (up to) six lords as *yajawk'ahk'*, all *sajals* of Baahis Uchih
9.11.10.5.17	662	Dec 19	War?? against Santa Elena king
9.13.9.11.7	701	Sep 16	Burial of ? supervised by K'inich Kaan Bahlam, witnessed by Aj Sik'ab
9.13.14.5.1	706	Apr 17	Death? of Aj Sik'ab, *sajal* of K'inich Janaab Pakal
9.13.14.17.19	706	Dec 31	Dedication of the censer-stand?

It is by no means certain that all of these titles represent stratified ranks rather than task-specific roles, but if we track statements of ownership with the sequence of title acquisition a hypothetical order of precedence might be inferred: (1) *ti'sakhuun*, (2) *yajawk'ahk'*, (3) *sajal*, and, using a statement from another Palenque monument, the Tablet of the Slaves, (4) *ajk'uhuun*. This sketch may, or may not, reflect the true situation – *yajawk'ahk'*, in particular, may be a role – and it is possible that some other criteria are generating the appearance of ranking. However, the data we have on the order of title acquisition at Tonina does not contradict it, nor does the order in which nobles are lined up at the feet of the ruler's throne on Piedras Negras Panel 3 (Figure 24). There, in mirrored pairs radiating from a central focus we have: a *ti'sakhuun* and a *baahsajal*, followed by two *sajal*, and then a Banded Bird and an *anaab* – the last a common but poorly understood epithet.

SIX

CONSTITUTION

Chapter 5 explored the self-definition of the Classic Maya elite within a range of statuses, offices, ranks, and roles – marks of authority and entitlement that centred upon and radiated from a "holy" ruler. We now need to turn to how this collective *noblesse* went about constituting and maintaining a political community. Politics can never be reduced to a state of being since it always implies active, substantive acts that establish, maintain, and extend power relations. These acts are guided by formal and informal norms, rules, and protocols that express the structural properties of the system. To recover even an outline appreciation of these properties we must first take the textual record on offer, recognising its idealised, retrospective, and highly selective character, and then look beyond to what these tightly controlled narratives refer to only obliquely, or reveal only through statistical analysis. Very often it is the exceptions that demonstrate the rules, the anomalies and deviations that illuminate where orthodoxy gives way to exigency in a contingent world.

This chapter addresses two major topics. The first is the arc of royal life, focussing on how Classic Maya monarchy was transferred from one representative to the next. In order to see how these cycles are set in motion, the second section looks at how authority was instantiated or re-instantiated in particular places and at particular times. This tracks processes of significance for the origin and spread of Classic Maya culture. The presentation is again structured around relevant terms, here necessarily concentrating on verbs in the way the previous chapter focussed on nouns.

THE ROYAL CYCLE

The Classic Maya polity was embodied in kingship, an institution that served as the practical and symbolic fulcrum of the community and the root of its identity. Hieroglyphs for royal birth, accession, and death were all identified by Proskouriakoff (1960: 455, 460, 1963: 163) and formed the basis for her historical breakthroughs. These transformations of royal existence are still the armatures on which we build individual biographies, but the difference today is that the decipherment allows us to fill the life stories between them with many other activities and contextualise them within historical narratives.

Although all dynastic systems are predicated on consanguinity, precisely how bloodline converts into high office differs from case to case (Goody 1967, 1973). The strategic issue for each and every one is to how to achieve continuity and stability in the face of the vagaries of human reproduction and conflicting individual ambitions. Although vertical inheritance from one generation to the next tends to predominate, it is by no means universally practiced and forms of lateral inheritance are not uncommon. The vertical mode is shadowed by the certainty that it will, given occasional infertility and early deaths, break down at some point. Yet any permanent measure to widen eligibility and guarantee an available heir produces the conditions for the opposite problem, not a dearth of legitimate candidates but an excess, with all the attendant potential for rivalry and conflict.

Worldwide, the lateral mode is often used as a reserve strategy, but one that faces a structural problem in exactly how it reverts, as it must, to the vertical. However, this was not the only means to address the fragility of vertical descent. Alternatives include increasing reproductive potential in the form of additional wives – polygyny – or in the formal adoption of heirs. Strict primogeniture, which was ubiquitous among the Christian monarchies of Europe but less prevalent elsewhere, seeks to constrain the competition between siblings, but at the risk of handing power to incompetent or sickly individuals that might endanger the welfare of the whole community.

Heirs and Eligibility

The first appearance of royal individuals in the record is, as one might expect, at their birth and is signalled by the hieroglyph Proskouriakoff dubbed the "initial event". The root can be read today as *sih*, which survives as the verb "to be born" in Colonial Yukatek (Barrera Vásquez 1980: 727) – presumably related to the noun "gift" that is widespread in Mayan languages (Kaufman 2003: 786). At this introduction to the world the subject will sometimes be identified by their childhood moniker, a *ch'ok k'aba'* "youth-name", either alone or in combination with the regnal name adopted on their later assumption of power. These childhood monikers are much more prevalent when a particular ruler is the namesake of an ancestor, especially a grandfather, where they serve as a useful disambiguation. As we saw in Chapter 5, *ch'ok* was the term for princelings, the foremost identified as the *baahch'ok*, "head youth/prince". This points to a practice of designating successors during a ruler's lifetime, at least on some occasions.

There is ample evidence that the primary mode of royal descent for the Classic Maya was patrilineal. At Tikal, for example, rulership can be tracked between father and son for five generations in the Early Classic and again through four or five generations in the Late Classic (Martin and Grube 2000: 32–51; Martin 2003b). This pattern holds true in the vast majority of inscribed genealogies, the central purpose of which was to assert legitimacy based on direct descent from a previous ruler.

Where such information is not provided, we might suspect a break of some kind, especially if a particular site otherwise abounds in such accounts. Statements of parentage are very rare at some major centres, Copan and Tonina for example, though whether this indicates differing rules of succession or simply local textual traditions is unclear. Several notable kings specify that they were *not* the sons of kings, the famed K'inich Janaab Pakal of Palenque for one. He names both parents, but it is the prominence given to his mother in figural depictions, in one she hands him a crown, that strongly implies that she was the daughter of a monarch and the source of his legitimacy (Schele and Freidel 1990: 221). Both here and in another case, that of Animal Skull of Tikal (Martin 2003b: 25), the rupture follows hard on the heels of a major military defeat and seems to be a clear case of cause and effect.

The evidence for primogeniture is more limited. All we can say for sure is that where fraternal succession occurs there is no known case that violates age-order. There is an important distinction to be made between age rules and age preferences here. There need be no obligation to advance the eldest son, while at same time favouring the practice barring ineptitude or infirmity.

As we will see in Chapter 8, there is good reason to believe that Classic Maya elites were polygynous and that, while the successor was usually the offspring of a senior, paramount wife, the children of lesser wives were also eligible – which is to be expected if this was a reserve strategy to secure vertical succession. That the kings born to secondary queens paid attention to promoting their mothers' status hints at a degree of insecurity on the matter, but equally that there was nothing aberrant or discrediting about this route to power (see Martin and Grube 2000: 91, 129). Interestingly, several aged rulers were succeeded by sons born late in their lives, suggesting that older offspring had already died or had been passed over for younger, more vigorous siblings (Martin and Grube 2000: 126; Grube 2006: 162–164) (p.107). The same effect would be produced by elevating a younger secondary wife to paramountcy late in the king's tenure, conceivably demoting an existing heir.

Only a few childhood activities are documented in the texts, but one of the more important was the *yax ch'ahbaj*, "first penance" (Houston, Stuart, and Robertson 1998: 282). The term *ch'ahb* also appears in lexicons as "to fast" and "creation, genesis" and all probably stem from a common source. In Maya iconography there is clear evidence linking this term to bloodletting and the hieroglyph itself appears to be a stylised blade used for that purpose.

The earliest example appears on the unprovenanced Hauberg Stela, a monument of uncertain date from the early part of the Classic era (Stuart 2008b; also Schele 1985). It shows a masked lord manipulating a fantastic serpent, while the foregrounded passage reads *yax ch'ahb tu k'uhuul*, "first penance for his god(s)". The term appears two or even three times on Tikal Stela 10, a monument similarly dedicated to this act, which dates to the abnormal joint tenure of Kaloomte' Bahlam and the Lady of Tikal. One of these ceremonies is a back-reference to an earlier king, Chak Tok Ich'aak II, in 486 (Martin 2003b: 17). At Caracol the five-year-old heir K'an II underwent a "first penance" in 593, some 25 years before his crowning, and this was supervised by his reigning father Yajawte' K'inich II. K'an II was the son of a junior wife, a woman to whom he gave great prominence once he had taken the throne, and this was surely relevant to recording this event in stone (Martin and Grube 2000: 91).

We are fortunate that a depiction of such a ceremony survives on Dos Pilas Panel 19, dating somewhere between 727 and 741 (Houston 1993: 115, figure 4.19; Martin and Grube 2000: 60). Here a ritual specialist carrying the Banded Bird title kneels, stingray spine in hand, having perforated the penis or foreskin of a standing boy whose blood drips into a pot or basket. The current king of Dos Pilas and his queen look on, as do two lords entitled *ucha'an ch'ok*, "guardian of the youth", one of them a visitor from Calakmul. The appearance of a foreign guardian is intriguing and in this instance maps onto a patron–client relationship, since the dynasty of Dos Pilas was subject to that of Calakmul. This was part of a wider pattern of guardianship over youths (Houston 2009: 163–165), one which follows the same formula as "captor" expressions based on the term *cha'an*, "master" (Lacadena and Wichmann 2004: 140–141) or *kanan*, "care, oversight" (Houston 2009: 163) (see Chapter 9). Royal youths were evidently considered in need of protection and guidance if they were to claim their birth-right and become able rulers. The main text on Panel 19 describes the youth as a *ch'ok mutul ajaw* and he is very probably the next king of Dos Pilas, K'awiil Chan K'inich, the son of an earlier Dos Pilas monarch, bearing his youth-name.

Taken together, these "first penance" references suggest that bloodletting was a key rite of passage for royal boys, and credibly linked to their future procreative powers (Houston 2009: 165). It was exploited retrospectively to claim proper ritual preparation for office and in this carried strong political overtones. Wherever the context of these ceremonies is known there was some complexity to the succession, some reason why additional validation would be advantageous.

The mean age at accession was 28.76 years (n = 35), with the range extending from infancy to what passed for elderly by the standards of the time.[1] The very youngest was Ruler 4 of Tonina, who became king at the age of two years (Martin and Grube 2008: 183) and was suitably titled a *ch'ok baahkab*. Juvenile rulers were relatively common at Tonina, with K'inich Bahlam Chapaat elevated at eight years old and K'inich Ich'aak Chapaat at fourteen years (Martin and Grube 2008: 179, 186). Notable infants elsewhere were K'ahk' Tiliw Chan Chahk of Naranjo and Muwaan Jol of Moral-Reforma, who were both five years at their inaugurations, and the Lady of Tikal, who was six years (Closs 1985; Martin 1999, 2003c). It is plain that the qualification of bloodline overrode any practical capacity to govern, although we cannot always be sure that these children were the offspring of kings. That children were favoured over more distant adult relatives suggests that vertical inheritance at these kingdoms was enacted wherever practicable. Their reigns would clearly have empowered regents and guardians, and we have no way of knowing if some instances amounted to coup d'état by nobles setting compliant puppets on the throne.

At the other end of the scale, the oldest known acceding king was Palenque's K'inich K'an Joy Kitam II, who was fifty-seven years old when he took power in 702. His claim dates back to the inauguration of his elder brother as K'inich Kaan Bahlam II in 684, when we are told that as younger brother he *chumwaan ta baahch'oklel*, "sits in head prince-ship" (Schele 1990a: 3–4). This implies that heir apparency could be an institutionalised position. K'inich Kaan Bahlam himself was the leading purveyor of this kind of early self-validation, recorded not only in texts but on three elaborate figural panels, each of which portrays him as both an adult and as a six-year-old *baahch'ok* venerating icons associated with a local triad of deities (Bassie-Sweet 1991: 202–204).

If this emphasis on his youthful performances betrays a certain unease, what was its source? It is true that his father K'inich Janaab Pakal initiated a new patriline (Schele and Freidel 1990: 221–223), but the emphasis on Kaan Bahlam's designation as heir in 641, blended with a detailed accounting of the kingdom's mythic origins, would hardly seem to remedy that fact. Instead we might look to Kaan Bahlam's own legitimacy, asking if, born when his father was already 32 years old, he was really the first of his sons. In Case Study 4 we will look in greater depth at fraternal succession at Palenque, which occurred in three separate generations and seems to be one reason behind these kings' enthusiasm for detailing their preparations for rule (Schele 1984a, 1990a; Bassie-Sweet 1991: 200–231; Stuart 2005a: 38–44).[2]

In 662 the mighty Yuknoom Ch'een II of Calakmul – one of the characters who will appear with regularity in this study – erected Stela 9 in the main plaza of his city. Its material was unusual, a tall slab of schist or slate, which must have been hauled all the way from the Maya Mountains, the realm of Caracol some 165 km away (see Helmke and Awe 2016b: 3). The front bears a male portrait and the rear a female one, both supplied with extended captions. The main inscription opens on the monument's left edge with the birth in 649 of Yuknoom Yich'aak K'ahk' II, the eventual successor to Yuknoom Ch'een. Indeed, the richly attired lord on the face of the stela is identified as Yuknoom Yich'aak K'ahk' and specified as a *k'uhul kaanul ajaw*, "Holy Snake[-Place] Lord", the full royal title of the Snake kingdom (Martin 2009a). He would have been just fourteen years old at the time and still twenty-three years from his full elevation to rulership. Yuknoom Ch'een, just shy of his sixty-second year, had chosen his successor well in advance, probably not expecting that he would endure for as long as he did. Presumably one of the seven sons of Yuknoom Ch'een we hear about elsewhere, this adolescent boy had been made a junior king and apprentice. Interestingly, while the caption places his portrait to the year 662, it then projects forward to the next major calendrical juncture in 672 – likely to anticipate a point when Yuknoom Yich'aak K'ahk would officiate. The woman on the rear-side is most likely to be the future king's mother, but another possibility is that she is a young consort for the newly elevated lord.

A not dissimilar case is presented by two monuments at Naranjo, Stela 18 and 46, both of which were erected in 726, toward the end of K'ahk' Tiliw Chan Chahk's reign (Martin et al. 2017). Their texts focus on two *ch'oktaak*, "princes" who we can assume to be his sons. Although the rituals they perform remain obscure, there is clear intent to promote their candidacy for the succession. That their names appear in a different order on each monument suggests a desire to avoid prioritising one over the other, and we might wonder if they were biological twins. Such births would have great significance to the Maya, given that the sixteenth century epic of the Popol Vuh focuses on twin brothers who triumph over the lords of death, a myth we can track back in time for over two millennia (Coe 1989). Were the princes meant to rule together? This is unclear, but we do know that one of them, Yax Mayuy Chan Chahk, had acceded to the Naranjo throne by 744. This comes to light, unfortunately for him, only because he was defeated in battle and taken captive (Case Study 8).

Interregna

The death of a monarch has profound implications for the life of any kingdom. This must be counted not simply as the disorientating loss of a particular personage, an individual sometimes known for decades, but as the suspension of the central ordering principle of personified power. The liminal period between reigns is occupied by sharply contrasting issues of mourning and succession, on preparing the supernatural journey for the deceased while addressing where their worldly office should alight next (see Fitzsimmons 2009). This was not only an internal matter but also one of keen concern to neighbouring polities and those even further afield. Everyone would want to know the mettle of a new ruler and what he, or she, would mean for the intricate network of relations with fellow rulers.

Delays in installing successors might variously stem from long periods of official mourning and tomb construction, the time required to organise an installation ceremony, the wait for an auspicious date, struggles between rival claimants, or any combination thereof. Cross-culturally the interval between reigns is often one of intrigue and manoeuvring, as one set of personal bonds evaporates and a new series of pacts and alliances are forged. Yet politics, like nature, abhors a vacuum and we should not assume that these lacunae were as empty as they appear. Most dynastic systems distinguish de facto from cere-monially enshrined power, and coronations can be delayed for months or even years without a true absence of leadership. Even so, it is only a full consecration that transforms the candidate into the divinely charged persona, restoring a spiritual covenant as much as it does practical rule.

We have data on 24 intervals between the deaths of one Classic Maya ruler and the elevation of the next and their durations were highly variable.[3] The mean gap is 237 days, although this is skewed by the longer cases, especially one of 1,547 days, or well over four years. The shortest is fourteen days, with the typical delay being about fifty days, which must have been sufficient to complete normal mortuary procedures. A long-anticipated demise could mean that preparations were already well in hand, most of all an awaiting burial chamber, while an unexpected death might necessitate a hurried construction programme. The longer the interregnum the greater the suspicion that it silently points to dynastic machinations and disputes, even open conflict. In some cases, apparent interregna prove to be illusory and are simply the space left by a missing ruler (see Case Study 5).

The briefest possible interval is a single day, on which one king's death is immediately followed by the installation of his successor. Only one such case is known, at the site of La Corona, a subsidiary centre of the dominant Calakmul polity. K'uk' Ajaw ruled La Corona for almost three years but in 658 we are told *ikami ti ye' tuun*, literally "then dies at edge/tooth of stone" – a rare expression that evidently signifies a violent demise, perhaps a formal execution (Grube, in Grube, Martin, and Zender 2002b: 85; Baron 2013: 329; Helmke and Awe 2016a: 9–10). Significantly, the same fate had befallen the previous king, Sak Maas, perhaps casting K'uk' Ajaw into the role of usurper. That inference grows stronger when we learn that it is the son of Sak Maas, Chakaw Nahb Kaan, who becomes the same-day successor, potentially avenging his father.

The only way to avoid an interregnum of any kind is to make a *pre mortem* appointment, installing the heir while the present king yet lives. This may be favoured when an incumbent is incapacitated, or if the chosen successor is expected to face significant opposition. Classic Maya cases are rare but not unknown. In 658 K'ahk' Ujol K'inich II of Caracol acceded 29 days before the demise of the long-lived K'an II (Grube 1994c: 108). There seems to be precedent for this at Caracol. K'an II's half-brother, nicknamed Knot Ajaw but in reality closer to Saak Ti' Huun, preceded him in office, taking power in 599. His first major calendrical ceremony, in 603, is said to be *ilaj*, "seen" by their father Yajawte' K'inich II – not a term usually applied to the deceased (Martin and Grube 2000: 90). At this juncture Yajawte' K'inich is ascribed a 3-K'atun Ajaw title, stating that he had turned thirty-nine years of age, yet in later years he seems to be given a 4-K'atun mark, meaning that he had surpassed fifty-nine years (unfortunately neither a birth- nor death-date survives for this king). Perhaps most decisively, the accession of Knot Ajaw on Stela 6 is linked to that of his father by a unique phrase *yak'aw ajaw huun*, "he gives (the) lordly headband" and then *ti unen*, "to his child" (Beetz and Satterthwaite 1981: figure 7). This may well describe the father adopting his son as co-ruler (Stephen Houston, pers. comm. 1993).

Succession

The great ethnographer Arthur Maurice Hocart (1927: 70–98) pursued the cross-cultural patterns in installation ceremonies in great detail, demonstrating that both solemn ritual and theatrical performance, private mysteries and public spectacle, show startling regularities across the world and through time. Where he perceived a common origin we instead recognise the shared heritage of body and mind, a recurring cognitive pathway to how the ordinary might be transformed into the extraordinary. The near-ubiquitous interest in enthronement and crowning, in the bestowal of special insignia, objects, and apparel, takes the mundane but universal experience of tools, garments, and furniture and turns them into vehicles of symbolic distinction touched by the divine (Fortes 1967: 19). The sacralising rituals involved persuaded the populace, fellow elite, and even the initiate themselves, that they have undergone a genuine and legitimate transformation. Here it is correct to highlight the concept of succession over other aspects of the process in order to emphasise that inaugurations are, in systemic terms, acts of continuity and reproduction.

The inscriptions provide five different expressions for inauguration. The earliest seen is an enthronement based on the positional verb *chum*, "to sit", which appears on the back of a jade pectoral of the Late Preclassic or

Protoclassic Periods (Coe 1966; Schele and Miller 1986: 120). There it appears in an attenuated spelling of *chumlaj ti ajawil*, "is seated into lordship", but by Late Classic times this form was largely superseded by *chumwaan ti ajawlel* (Bricker 1986: 162; also Ringle 1985: 153–155). This same construction survived into Colonial Chontal Maya as *chumwanix ta ahaulel* (Smailus 1975: 32, 69), an endurance that approaches two millennia. It has been argued that the evolution in positional suffixes in the Classic Period is less significant than the switch from *ajawil,* an embodied abstraction of "lordliness", to *ajawlel,* another abstractive that might be somewhat closer to an office of "lordship" (Houston, Robertson, and Stuart 2001: 25–26). The suggestion is that this shift holds meaning, perhaps indicating a greater sense of institutionalisation and a growing separation of kings from a corporate community of lords (Stephen Houston, pers. comm. 2013).

A second way in which lordship could be entered was through the root *joy* (David Stuart, pers. comm. 1999), signified glyphically by the head of a bird tied-up with cloth which, due to obscuring infixes, is usually seen only as a knotted band. The most recent of several suggested translations are "to surround" or "to turn, process by circling", as in "making a procession" (Sheseña 2015: 49). This expression begins as *johyaj ti ajawil*, though it too largely switches to the use of *ajawlel* over time.

A third variety of accession employs the transitive root *k'al*, for which one translation has been "to bind, wrap", which works well within the formula *uk'alaw huun tu'baah* as "he binds the headband to his head" (Stuart 1996: 155–156). However, lexical evidence from the Ch'orti' language suggests a different root for *k'al* as "to hold", thereby offering "he holds the headband above him" as an alternative translation (Zender 2018b). The scenes associated with such events nevertheless suggest physical action, and it might be possible that in actual usage its sense was closer to "raise" or "present".[4] Some of these statements include extended names for the headband and the particular personification of paper that appears as its central crest.

There is a fourth accession verb based on the derived noun *ajaw*, "lord" as *ajawVn*, either as an inchoative "he becomes a lord" (Stuart 2005c: 72) or the antipassive of a transitivised "he rules" (Marc Zender, pers. comm. 2008). Less common than its companions, it tends to be ascribed either to mythological accessions or those of child rulers.

A last expression is based on the transitive root *k'am* or its sound-shifted equivalent *ch'am*, "to take, grasp, receive", which frequently appears as the incorporated antipassive *k'amk'awiiliw*, "*k'awiil*-takes" (Grube 1992: 211; Martin 1997a: 855–856) (Figure 20b). K'awiil was the personification of lightning, an anthropomorphic serpent whose form evolved from the axe wielded by the storm deity Chahk. He is easily identified by the polished celt or fiery torch that pierces his mirrored forehead, while one leg usually takes the form of a naturalistic snake. He could be modelled as a full-figure effigy (Figure 30) or just his head mounted on a staff, but most often appears as an axe-as-sceptre, with his extended leg forming the shaft (Figure 43). In all of these forms he symbolises the thunderous spark that constitutes nature's most dramatic sound-and-light display, a power directly associated with kingly authority. Though strongly associated with accession ceremonies, this "taking, grasping" of K'awiil was also used on other empowering occasions, including the throwing-off of client status (Stuart 2004a: 233).

These five terms evidently express different conceptualisations of kingship and describe separate acts within an extended sequence. Although only a single one is usually given, their equivalence and substitutability is made clear where they are combined or take place on precisely the same day in different texts. An example here would be the elevation of K'ahk' Tiliw Chan Yopaat of Quirigua, since on Stela E and F he "*k'awiil*-grasps", on Stela J "raises the headband above him" and on Zoomorph G "is seated into lordship", all on 30 December 724 (Looper 2003: 57, figure 2.1).

We get some idea of the actual order of events when inaugural ceremonies span more than a single day. Chak Ak' Paat Kuy of La Corona undergoes the *k'al* headband event on 8 September 689, but the *joy* binding or procession into lordship on 9 September (Stuart 2015). Indeed, that record describes a longer preparation that extended over several months. This includes a *pehk*, "to call, summon" event with his Calakmul overlord in December 688, a term elsewhere associated with journeys, conferences, and audiences (Houston 2014a).[5] We know that Chak Ak' Paat Kuy was at Calakmul in 687, since he played a ballgame with one of the king's leading *ti'huun* nobles on the occasion of the 9.12.15.0.0 period ending and the location is specifically given as *uxte'tuun chiiknahb*, the ancient name of Calakmul (Martin 2001d: 179, figure 6.5) (Case Study 6). Whether he had travelled there specially or was already a resident, the audience of 688 must have closely followed the death of his sibling and predecessor (p.188). Between the summons and the inauguration there were two kinds of dressing ceremony and also a "settling" or foundation of some location, employing a term we will come to in a moment.

The taking of a regnal name – another cross-cultural parallel of note – was a special feature of the headband event, with the new moniker described as the *uk'alhuun k'aba'*, "his headband-raising name" (Grube 2002: 325; Eberl and Graña-Behrens 2004). The new identity reflected the personal transformation of the candidate into a king, and this even extended to cases of re-installation. The king of Moral-Reforma acquired a regnal name on his accession in 661, but a new one replaces it at his re-installation in 662, while for a major calendrical ceremony in 692 he is referred to by yet another appellative, with the inference that this identity was acquired at his third installation in 690 (see p.250–253 and 265–268) (Martin 2003c).

We must also ask why these events took place on precisely the day they did. One can imagine a fair degree of planning in most cases, with an auspicious date doubtless selected by means of astrological and calendrical prognostication. At other times, circumstances may have forced impromptu affairs, as we saw earlier in the case of an apparent regicide. There are 154 dateable examples, involving all verbal expressions and statuses, which can be examined statistically (Martin 2014a: table 11, charts 1–2). A review of days and their coefficients shows that Ajaw ("Lord") was the most popular day choice (n = 17) and Kimi ("Death") the least popular (n = 1), a predictable result perhaps, while the most common coefficient was 5 (n = 21) and the least common 13 (n = 3). The most popular month was K'ayab (n = 15) and least popular Yax and Wayeb (both n = 1), the most favoured month coefficient was 3 (n = 12) and the least favoured 11 (n = 2). Despite these slight preferences, no decisive or overriding pattern can be identified.

Nevertheless, even though inaugurations took place throughout the year, when they are set against the proleptic Gregorian Calendar (GMT correlation) there is a modest but discernible dip during the rainy season, with the wet months of July, August, September, and October seeing the fewest such events (Figure 14).[6] These data suggest that whatever cultural or esoteric factors were at work, the Classic Maya could also be practically-minded and preferred, when they could, to stage events when travel was easiest and public ceremonies less likely to be spoiled by a downpour. The highest incidence in the sample comes in June, the first month with significant precipitation. This might reflect pre-emptive moves to try to miss the worst of the rains or could, given the sprouting of maize and renewed life at this time, provide a fitting agricultural metaphor for a new reign.

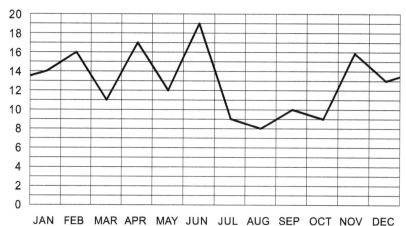

14 Accession ceremonies plotted according to the proleptic Gregorian Calendar (GMT correlation). (All charts in this volume by the author)

Given their preponderance in the texts, it is surprising that there are so few depictions of accession ceremonies. Those we have are notable for involving other participants, minimally someone who presents the king with his crowning regalia. The earliest scenes of this kind appear in the Late Preclassic murals of San Bartolo from about 100 BCE, one of which closely resembles another incised on a small bone produced as much as 800 years later – evidence for a remarkable conservatism in both the ritual and its representation (Taube et al. 2010: 60–69, figure 39b, 41b). In each case we see a caped man, who is clearly aged in the later version, presenting a headdress to a scaffold-enthroned lord. Though both scenes seem clearly to be supernatural in character, they constitute a template for lordly installations in the mortal realm. The presenter may be a priest or some similar figure of prestige and authority, but his cape is normally a diagnostic of the Underworld ruler "God L" and these events could well be part of an otherwise unknown mythological episode involving this deity. If so, it would suggest that kingship was conceptually initiated in the netherworld and part of the greater cycle of regeneration that takes place there.

Historical scenes are concentrated at only two sites, Palenque and Bonampak. An especially informative case appears on the front of a low platform found inside Palenque Temple XIX, dating to 721, where the accession of K'inich Ahkal Mo' Nahb III shows him framed by six of his nobles (Stuart 2005a: 117–123) (Figure 15a). He faces his cousin Janaab Ajaw, a holder of the priestly Banded Bird office, who holds the royal headband affixed with the image of *huun*, the sacred personification of paper. A more elaborate crown, a jade or shell mosaic "drum major" headdress, rests on a stand nearby. The accompanying captions tell us that both lords are impersonating deities, reiterated by the identifying motifs set in their headdresses. The king is acting as the Palenque patron god we know as GI (one), while Janaab Ajaw takes the role of the supreme sky deity God D. The main text on the platform recounts the mythic episode they re-enact, with *chumlaj ta ajawlel* "GI" *ukabjiiy* "God D" describing GI's seating into lordly office under the aegis of God D in 3309 BCE (Figure 15b). In one of many like-in-kind emulations in Maya art and writing, K'inich Ahkal Mo' Nahb III here compares his own inauguration to that ceremony, an event of great local importance set over 4,000 years in the past. We will hear more about accession events featuring the term *ukabjiiy*, which refers to governing supervision or aegis, in Chapter 10, where such phrases are the most common expression of asymmetrical status between kings.

This Palenque scene is very helpful when we turn to three similar ones at Bonampak, where relief panels also show lords proffering headbands to kings (Bíró 2007b). The major topic of each inscription is the inauguration of a Bonampak/Lacanha ruler, clearly identifying the richly attired and enthroned lords on the right side of all three images. The earliest, Panel 4, describes such

(b)

(a)

15 A "like-in-kind" accession from the Palenque Temple XIX Platform: (a) K'inich Ahkal Mo' Nahb III impersonates the local patron deity GI at his inauguration in 721 CE; (b) the seating of GI into lordship under the auspices of God D in 3309 BCE. (Drawings by David Stuart)

an accession in 605, while the caption to its scene introduces a character not mentioned in the main body of text, Shield Jaguar II of Yaxchilan (Figure 16a). That caption begins *ubaah ta k'alhuun*, "It is his image in headband-holding" (Zender 2018b). Necessarily not the seated monarch, the Yaxchilan king is the kneeling character bearing the headband and clearly dressed as God L, a close echo of the mythical accession scenes noted above. But the Palenque example poses a question for us: is the Yaxchilan king an underling in the manner of the actual Janaab Ajaw, or instead an overlord in the style of the God D Janaab Ajaw impersonates?

The next such event, on Panel 5, clarifies matters (Figure 16b). Here we are told that the Bonampak/Lacanha ruler's accession in 643 was "supervised" by Bird Jaguar III of Yaxchilan and, turning to the scene, this can be none other than the depicted bearer of the headband – notwithstanding his modest attire and deferential pose. Here then is Bonampak's overlord, passing the emblem of office in a performance that has, until now, obscured their hierarchical relationship. These two panels represent the only known depictions of historical supervised accessions.

The third Bonampak scene, on Panel 1, records a more straightforward accession from 683 (Mathews 1980, figure 9). Here the headband is presented by one of three lords identified with single name-glyphs, evidently true subordinates and a sign that Bonampak/Lacanha claims full autonomy at this time. Yet this scene still encodes a greater political meaning. At both Bonampak and Palenque, the bestowal of regalia by a collected nobility speaks not only of their attendance and witnessing, but of their support and approval. Even a pre-ordained heir must elicit the practical assistance that makes their reign possible, minimally requiring the acquiescence of the elite class – those who have the greatest means to make, or break, royal claims (Fortes 1967: 19).

This takes us to the ruler's control over subordinate ranks and offices, which is apparent in his supervision of their installation ceremonies. This occurred even where, as in the case of *sajal*, qualification appears to have been hereditary. It appears that any such elevation would nonetheless need the approval of the monarch, or that the ruler selected among more than one eligible candidate for a vacant position. The first of these is more analogous to the way kings were confirmed in their offices by more powerful ones, but it is also conceivable that foreign overlords similarly took some role in influencing the selection, given their vested interest in compliant incumbents.

We saw earlier how the rule of minors necessarily introduces the agency of older regents and guardians, whether they be parents, spouses, or leading nobles. While not eligible for the supreme office themselves they could act in the ruler's stead, performing activities that range from military campaigns to ritual performances. In regard to the latter, child rulers often seem to have been absent from major rites and one of the main functions of regents and guardians,

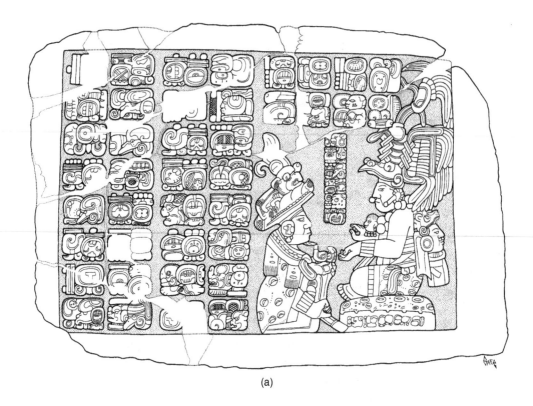

(a)

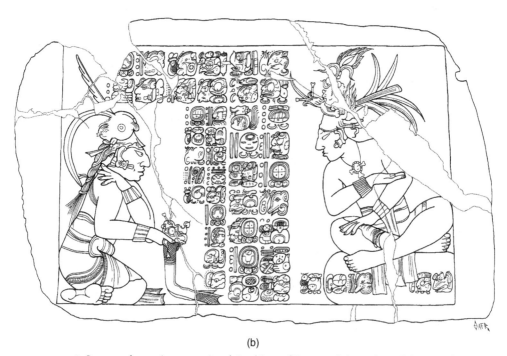

(b)

16 Sponsored accession scenes involving kings of Bonampak/Lacanha and their overlords from Yaxchilan: (a) Bonampak Panel 4; (b) Bonampak Panel 5. (Drawings by Alexandr Safronov)

in addition to their governing roles, was to maintain the on-going ritual life of the polity. This was not simply pious observance, but an integral part of its social and political maintenance.

Of the two period ending celebrations recorded after Tonina Ruler 4's accession, in 711 and 716, neither names him as their celebrant, a role he did not take until he was sixteen years old in 721. The rite of 716 had been performed by K'elen Hix, the holder of the elevated *k'uhul ti'huun* title we encountered earlier. Similarly, K'ahk' Tiliw Chan Chahk was eighteen years before he was credited with such a ceremony and on all previous occasions it was his mother, the queen regent Ix Wak Jalam Chan of Dos Pilas, who officiated and memorialised the occasions on her own stelae (Closs 1985: 73–76; Martin and Grube 2000: 74–77) (Figure 38). When the Lady of Tikal acceded at the age of six years in 511 it was another *ti'huun* who apparently held the leading position, at least until a new king and probable consort Kaloomte' Bahlam appeared on the scene in 527 (Martin 1999; Zender 2004: 333–338). Unlike her fellow child rulers, however, she is retrospectively credited with a ceremonial role and was said to preside over the 9.4.0.0.0 period ending of 514, when she was just ten years old (Martin 2014b). In later years, she conducts similar calendrical rituals but, as on Tikal Stela 12 from 527, these are recorded on a monument "owned" by Kaloomte' Bahlam.

Ruling queens are very rare in Classic Maya history, although it is certainly possible that others have simply been excluded from the record. Queen regnants use genderless royal titles in the style of kings, unlike non-ruling queen consorts and princesses who carry the *ix* prefix on such epithets. Yet, as we heard in the last chapter, even full female monarchs appear to have been omitted from the numerical dynastic lists, which continue to mark a sex distinction. The evidence to hand indicates that women gained the throne only in extremis, when the male line could only be restored through the matriline. As in the case of Ix Wak Jalam Chan, the status of queen regent and guardian to an infant son was a separate route by which women could gain power in Classic Maya society. In that particular case she uses a genderless Mutul emblem glyph of her homeland throughout her effective rule. No record of her death in 741 survives at Naranjo, but one reference to it can be found at Dos Pilas, emphasising the continued connection between these two polities (Houston 1993: 108).

The significance of royal deaths to the wider Maya world is demonstrated by Tonina Monument 160, whose long inscription is largely dedicated to the passing of foreign kings (see Mathews 2001b: table 2; Graham et al. 2006: 95–101).[7] Covering a short segment of the Early Classic Period leading up to the commissioning of the stone in 514, these include Chak Tok Ich'aak II of Tikal in 508 and what seems to be an otherwise unknown Kaanul ruler in 505.[8] Tonina, set in the western highlands, was one of the furthest centres from the heartland of the Peten, but this was no barrier to its membership of the Classic Maya elite collective and, in all probability, was referencing the elaborate familial ties that connected it to these distant realms.

FOUNDATIONS

We now turn to the acts that set cycles of royal life in motion, or restored disrupted ones, including the origins of dynasties and major settlements. The genesis of political communities in the Maya region is a difficult topic to study archaeologically due to the extensive overburden that obscures early royal centres beneath later construction. Moreover, such events usually take place before we have a viable epigraphic record and so descriptions of dynastic origins, sparse by any standards, appear only in deeply retrospective texts. Patently serving contemporary political purposes, such references often link the present with deeper ancestral, legendary, or supernatural pasts. Their goal is to attach current regimes to immutable histories and unchallengeable founts of authority that both entrench their legitimacy and offer a sense of unifying identity to their subject populations. In this section, we will be concerned with the ostensibly historical accounts, leaving overtly mythical narratives to be reviewed in Chapter 7. We will explore three verbs of importance to the concept of political foundation, indicating physical movement or the instantiation of authority at a particular locale.

In the treatment of titles in Chapter 5 we deferred discussion of places as constituents of identity, but it is precisely at this point that they become integral to our study. Just as practices are always embodied and temporal, they are always situated. This obliges us to digress for a moment to discuss the relevant terminology of place before we can engage with political action itself.

Toponyms, with their associated lexicon and iconography, were first explicated by David Stuart and Stephen Houston (1994). Their point of departure was the expression *uhtiiy*, "it happened (at)" that, outside its chronological uses, is followed by a place-name of some kind (Figure 17a). The range of base geographic terms employed within toponyms are not especially large and many names were formed as compounds with *nal*, "place/maize-field", *witz*, "hill/mountain", or *ha'/a'*, "water".[9] More significant for our purposes are the qualifying terms that offer conceptualisations of place. These are largely metaphorical and represent a stiffer challenge to comprehension. The most common, reflected in a number of graphic variants, is likely to be read *ch'een*, "(watery) cave, well" (Vogt and Stuart 2005: 157–163), although the word can also mean "hole, hollow, cistern, ditch, canyon, rock outcrop" (Tokovinine 2008: 141–142, 2013: 25).[10] It is notable that a number of major architectural complexes are built close to, or above, caves, referencing the symbolic attachment of settlements to the earth and Underworld. While the *ch'een* term occasionally refers to a literal cave in the texts, the great majority of cases do not. This is evident in contexts such as *puluuyi uch'een*, "his *ch'een* is burned" (a military attack) and *uhti tahn ch'een waka'*, "it happens in the midst of the El Peru *ch'een*" (from a monument that self-referentially describes its erection in an open plaza).[11]

This metaphorical usage is even clearer in the couplets *kabch'een* and *chanch'een*, "earth (and) cave" and "sky (and) cave", and the much rarer triplet *chankabch'een*, "sky (and) earth (and) cave".[12] These compounds appear in different but closely related contexts: *kabch'een* often grammatically possessed to mark places as owned by lords or deities, while *chanch'een* is usually appended as a qualifier to individual toponyms (Figure 17b and c).[13] The latter can be elaborated in iconic form as the pedestals or registers upon which rulers stand or prone captives lie (Figure 17d).

These combinations denote loci of cultural and political significance, although the degree to which this is a ceremonial core, a wider agricultural–urban settlement, or an encompassing territory is usually less clear. Their supernatural applications suggest that only a broad term such as "domain" can adequately fit all applications, although it could well mean something rather more specific in its relevant context (Helmke 2009: 85; Bíró 2011a: 62). For example, on a number of occasions "settlement, city" seems the better translation. There is evidence that *ch'een* served as an abbreviation for both couplets, although at other times these isolated examples may express some more nuanced meaning. Certain kinds of events (arrivals, burials, and military attacks for example) are almost exclusively associated with a lone *ch'een* term,

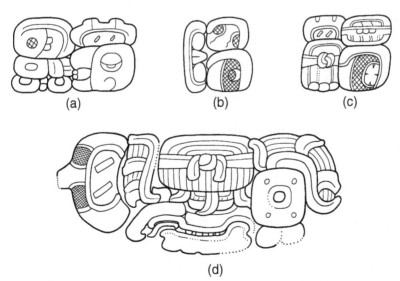

(a)   (b)   (c)

(d)

17 Place-name formulae: (a) *uhtiiy yaxa'*, "it happened at Yaxha"; (b) *ukab(u)ch'een*, "earth (and) cave of"; (c) *yax mutul chan ch'een*, "Tikal sky (and) cave"; (d) *yax mutul chan ch'een* "Tikal sky (and) cave" in the form of a toponymic pedestal.

linked via possession or the aforementioned *tahn*, "midst" construction to a named place or its kingly owner.

The resemblance of *kabch'een* and *chanch'een* to the Nahuatl couplet *altepetl*, "water (and) mountain", the core sociopolitical unit of Postclassic Central Mexico, has not passed without notice (Houston and Escobedo 1997: 471–472). The "water-mountain" concept was sufficiently embedded in Central Mexico that direct counterparts appear in adjacent cultural and linguistic zones, such as Totonac *chuchutsipi* (Ouweneel 1990: 5) and Mixtec *yucunduta* (Jansen and Pérez 2011: 14). *Altepetl* displays much the same semantic elasticity we perceive with its Maya counterparts, referring to a sovereign institution, a territorial dominion, as well as to the population that inhabited it (Lockhart 1992: 14–28; Ouweneel 1995: 761; Hirth 2003). It usually shared its name with the urbanised centre of government, although only because the two were not conceptually divided. Such central places were home to a *tecpan*, the palace or royal seat, and the origins of urban settlements lay in royal households and their supporting services, as in Weber's (1951: 66) *oikos*. At the core of an *altepetl* was a ruling lord drawn from a legitimate bloodline who presided over a hierarchy of nobles, priests, merchants, artisans, and farmers, the latter working its land in return for tribute paid in goods and services that passed up the social order. The central place also contained a temple to a polity-specific deity, and a key function of rulership was to commune with this patron and the divine world more generally.

The ability to understand where events took place has been significant in one other regard, the identification of locations active only in the Protoclassic Period. The two most prominent, neither of them securely deciphered, are known as "Moon Zero Bird" and "Maguey Metate" – the latter perhaps to be read *chicha'* (Stuart 2014a).[14] They were closely related, perhaps spatially close to one another, but it is Maguey Metate that is accorded a special significance for dynastic origins and has a good claim to be considered the Ur-Classic site (Grube 2004a: 127–131; Stuart 2004a: 216–221; Guenter 2005a; Tokovinine 2013: 79, 119–120; Martin 2016b: 531–534).

The founders of the Kaanul (Dzibanche and Calakmul), Mutul (Tikal and Dos Pilas), and Pa'chan (Yaxchilan and El Zotz) dynasties are directly associated with Maguey Metate, while a reference from the site of Namaan (La Florida) implies much the same thing. One lord associated with both locations, Foliated Jaguar, is picked out for a retrospective mention at Tikal, where he is identified as a *kaloomte'* sometime before 317 CE (Figure 18a). He is further named on two early belt assemblages, a device that serves to identify a prominent ancestor of the wearer, and appears on an early jade celt text that ended up in faraway Costa Rica (Martin 2003b: 6–7). A separate figure, Foliated Ajaw, celebrates the calendrical juncture 8.6.0.0.0 at Maguey Metate in 159 CE, as recalled at both Copan and Pusilha (Stuart 1992: 171; Braswell

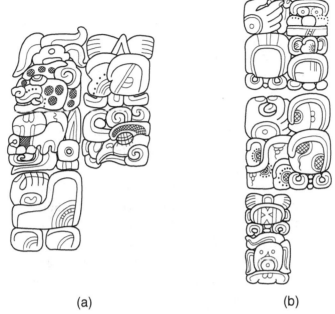

(a)   (b)

18 Two locations associated with the origins of Classic Maya political culture: (a) Fragmentary passage with a now-missing event involving the *kaloomte'* Foliated Jaguar that took place at Moon Zero Bird and Maguey Metate. Tikal Stela 31; (b) The completion of the 8.6.0.0.0 period ending of 159 CE at Maguey Metate, as supervised by Foliated Ajaw. Copan Stela I.

et al. 2004b: 229) (Figure 18b). A cluster of dates at other sites fall within a few decades of this point, including one at Naranjo in 158, and imply that something that lived long in the memories of Classic kings was happening at this time (Stuart 2004a: 219).[15]

To recap these points, narratives of the Classic era are peppered with references to places where actions occur. Collectively these invoke not a natural but a cultural geography, fashioned environments loaded with political significance. Importantly, they define ownership, in historical contexts as the personal properties of the ruling *ajaw*, which obliges us to consider their practical as well symbolic dimensions, especially economic implications over land use and tribute obligations (see Graham 2006: 114–115, 2011: 38–43; McAnany 2010: 269–304; Graham, Simmons, and White 2013) – topics we will examine properly later.

Hul, "To Arrive"

We turn now to a verb that engages us with the temporal and spatial as well as the transition from absence to presence. The intransitive root *hul*, "to arrive" – usually used in the sense of "to arrive here" – is of universal distribution in Mayan languages and therefore of great antiquity (Kaufman 2003: 1298). It was deciphered in the context of lunar notation, where it refers to the number of days that have elapsed since the appearance of the last New Moon (MacLeod 1990: 339–341).[16] That work established three separate logographic forms of **HUL**, together with syllabic renderings of **hu-li**, and suggested applications in several non-calendrical contexts. These are now known to include: the delivery of ritual objects (Chapter 7); visits to pilgrimage locations such as caves; references to exogamous marriage (Chapter 8); the submission of captives at the seat of their captor (Chapter 10); memorial visits to the tombs of ancestors; or, to be discussed in this chapter, the return from a journey, foreign stay, or exile, as well as metonymic references to dynastic foundation or re-foundation (Martin 2014a: table 12).

As these applications make plain, the term is a general one imbued with political significance only within a particular context. Significantly, a number of later texts in Yukatek and Chontal Maya languages use *hul* or its cognates in precisely this sense of political foundation, a strong sign that it was an enduring cultural trope (e.g. Roys 1933: 18; Brinton 1969: 199; Smailus 1975: 29, 100; see also Lacadena and Ciudad 2009). Indeed, the corresponding term in Nahuatl, *aci*, was used with precisely the same sense in Postclassic Central Mexico, suggesting a pan-Mesoamerican currency (see Schroeder 1991: 123).[17]

The earliest examples in the inscriptions are associated with a key historical episode from January 378. El Peru supplies the first mention of someone called Sihyaj K'ahk', a bearer of the elevated *kaloomte'* title. Eight days later he *huley*, "arrives" at *mutul chanch'een* or Tikal, 80 km to the east. Recorded in several different texts, this arrival takes place on the same day that the Tikal king Chak Tok Ich'aak I dies and, although no greater elaboration is offered, it is hard to conceive that the two events were not causally connected (Stuart 2000: 471–481, see also Martin and Grube 2000: 29–31; Martin 2001a: 107, 2003b: 11–15; Estrada-Belli et al. 2009: 238–246). A year later, in 379, Sihyaj K'ahk' installed a new ruler of Tikal, Yax Nuun Ahiin I, who was unconnected to the former patriline and instead the son of someone called "Spearthrower Owl" – who we will encounter again in Chapter 10.[18]

As Proskouriakoff (1993: 4–10) first surmised on the basis of iconographic analysis alone, these events coincided with an "arrival of strangers". This was manifested in a wave of stylistic traits and artefacts linked to Central Mexico and, more specifically, Teotihuacan. One evocative scene from an incised vessel from Tikal shows six characters in distinctive Teotihuacan dress. They are headed by four armed with spearthrowers and darts, followed by two wearing a headdress associated with high status who carry lidded vessels. They leave a place with Teotihuacan-style architecture and walk toward buildings and people with more mixed Maya features (Coggins 1975: 177–184, passim, figure 57b; Martin and Grube 2000: 29). A not dissimilar image of journeying to and from a Teotihuacan-style structure appears on one of the murals uncovered at La Sufricaya (Estrada-Belli 2011: figure 2.13).

Actual architecture of this kind appears at Tikal at this time, including a residential compound that had a central platform holding a stone representation of a Teotihuacan feathered banner, today known as the Marcador. Dedicated to "Spearthrower Owl", it bears two panels of text that give a further description of the arrival and tell us that its owner was a vassal of Sihyaj K'ahk' (Laporte and Fialko 1990: 45–62; Stuart 2000). A depiction of Sihyaj K'ahk' on a stela at El Peru shows him dressed in Teotihuacano attire (Freidel, Escobedo, and Guenter 2007: 197–203, figure 9.3), as does a portrait on a Late Classic polychrome cylinder vessel (Beliaev, Stuart, and Luin 2017) (Figure 19).[19] These representations first and foremost ascribe him a political identity rather than an ethnicity. However, his Mayan name need not be original, but could be a translation from a foreign tongue.[20]

Cumulative evidence from epigraphy, iconology, and archaeology argues for an intrusion by Teotihuacan that was dynastically disruptive and amounted to a political takeover (see p.241–243 and 353). Although centred on Tikal, its affects were felt across the central lowlands, creating what I have previously dubbed a "New Order". Signs of this first emerge at the major early centre of Uaxactun, just 19 km north of Tikal, where Stela 5 records the same arrival date in 378 and Stela 4 describes Sihyaj K'ahk's interactions with another lord, presumably a local ruler, on the 8.18.0.0.0 period ending ceremony of 396. Importantly, the one-year anniversary of the *huli mutul*, "arrives (at) Tikal" event is documented in a painted wall text at La Sufricaya, where nearby murals and graffiti show warriors in Teotihuacan-style garb

19 Portrait of Sihyaj K'ahk' in typical Teotihuacano garb on a Late Classic polychrome vessel.

clutching their characteristic spearthrower darts (Estrada-Belli et al. 2009: 237, figures 6a and b).[21]

The best information we have on Classic Maya polity formation comes from Copan Altar Q, a monument we last encountered in Chapter 4. A square block standing on four columnar legs, its sides depict the sixteen kings of the Copan dynasty in order, each sitting on an identifying hieroglyph, usually his personal name (Figure 20a). On the front face the first and sixteenth kings meet, the founder K'inich Yax K'uk' Mo' holding and perhaps presenting a sceptre or dart to his fellow monarch, symbolically legitimising his reign. The stone was commissioned in 776, but the 36-block inscription on its top looks back 350 years to early events in the founder's life (Stuart 2004a: 226–240).

It begins in September 426 with the statement *uch'am k'awiil*, "it is his K'awiil-taking", which, as we saw earlier, is usually a rite of inauguration

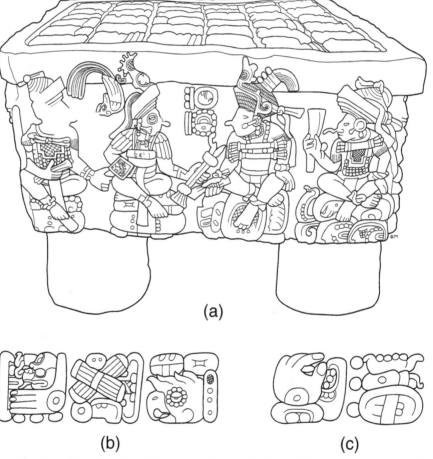

(a)

(b)   (c)

20 Altar Q and the founding of the Copan dynasty: (a) Front of the monument where the dynastic founder K'inich Yax K'uk' Mo' faces the sixteenth king Yax Pasaj Chan Yopaat; (b) Yax K'uk' Mo' takes power at Wiinte'naah in 426; (c) He "arrives at Copan" in 427.

(Figure 20b). This took place at *wiinte'naah,* a building or building-type closely associated with claims to authority from Central Mexico which has been interpreted as an "Origin House" where foundational fire rituals were conducted (Stuart 2000: 492–493, 2004a: 235–238; Fash, Tokovinine, and Fash 2009; Estrada-Belli and Tokovinine 2016: 159–161, figure 7). Three days later the newly elevated lord *tali,* "comes from" Wiinte'naah, beginning a journey that lasts 153 days. This concludes in February 427 when he *huli uxwintik,* "arrives at Copan" (Figure 20c).

There had already been some non-Maya settlement at Copan, but after these events the site was radically transformed as a new Classic Maya centre (Sharer et al. 1999; Traxler 2004). One of the earliest structures in the new site core was a Teotihuacan-style building with interior murals that invoke those at that great city. The first royal burial was cut into its floor and furnished with both local ceramics and others imported from Central Mexico and the Peten (Sharer 2003, 2004; Bell et al. 2004; Reents-Budet et al. 2004: 173). Revealingly, all subsequent structures built on this spot – each larger and grander than the last – were dedicated to Yax K'uk' Mo's memory and serve to identify him as the occupant of the tomb. Although Altar Q shows him in Teotihuacan attire, earlier, more contemporary monuments picture him as a native Maya and on a couple of occasions he bears the title *uxwitza' ajaw* that connects him to Caracol (Stuart 2007b). This resonates with the mention of a Copan king on a sixth century Caracol monument (Grube 1990), and such an origin would be in accord with the non-local body chemistry of the individual in that first royal grave, data that tentatively links him to the Peten (Price et al. 2010).[22]

Copan was not alone in its foundation event and Yax K'uk' Mo' plays the senior partner in the synchronous creation of a dynasty for Quirigua. This is described on Quirigua Zoomorph P where, on the same day that Yax K'uk' Mo' takes the emblems of office in 426, someone *itali wiinte'naah,* "then comes from the Origin House" (Stone 1983: 135; Grube, Schele, and Fahsen 1991). Three days later, on the day that Yax K'uk' Mo' departed for his journey to Copan, a monument is dedicated and the future king of Quirigua – the likely subject of the *itali* event – is invested in the name-giving headband rite by Yax K'uk' Mo'. This somewhat elliptical sequence can be read as a kingly investiture and name-giving at a distant location, probably Teotihuacan itself, which presents the creation of both the Copan and Quirigua regimes as a single planned operation (Martin and Grube 2000: 192–193, 216; Stuart 2004a: 239).

Teotihuacan connections are often related to the concept of Tollan "Place of Reeds" – a source of legitimation that turns up in sources across the Mesoamerican Postclassic and linked to the Maya term *puh,* "cattail reed" that is attested in Central Mexican-style iconography (Stuart 2000: 501–506). That symbolic connection is persuasive, but I wonder if what we see here is less a metaphor than the exercise of the real political power that inspired the Tollan idea. The whole Copan-Quirigua episode may be demonstrative of Teotihua-can's continuing role as the political master of the Maya lowlands, a half-century after the entrada.

There is a second category of arrivals that initiate or reinstate authority after a period of absence. One such case involves the twenty-first Tikal king, Wak Chan K'awiil, who "arrives" at the city in 537 (Martin 2003b: 23, n.37, 2005b: 6–8, n.13). Here the historical situation was complex. Wak Chan K'awiil was the son of the eighteenth Tikal king Chak Tok Ich'aak II, who had died in 508. Yet, as we have already seen, in 511 the Lady of Tikal succeeded as a six-year-old girl, initially with the support of a *ti'huun* noble but later with that of Kaloomte' Bahlam, identified as Tikal's nineteenth king. Why had Wak Chan K'awiil not acceded earlier, needing to arrive at Tikal in the manner of a returning exile?[23] Whatever the circumstances, and the role of an unknown twentieth Tikal ruler, he appears to present his return as a restitution of proper order by adopting the name of the Tikal dynastic founder Yax Ehb Xook at this point.

The next example is one of clear expediency. In Chapter 5 we touched upon the story of how the Dos Pilas dynasty splintered from that of Tikal to establish a new political centre in the Petexbatun region (Houston 1993: 100; Martin and Grube 2000: 57; Fahsen et al. 2003; Guenter 2003).[24] Much remains to be understood about these events, but in 650 the founding king of Dos Pilas, Bajlaj Chan K'awiil, came under attack from Yuknoom Ch'een II of Calakmul and soon after was forced to become his vassal. Dos Pilas now emerged as an "anti-kingdom" claiming the same Mutul emblem as Tikal and some of the same mythic associations. The hostility between Bajlaj Chan K'awiil and the incumbent Tikal king, his brother or half-brother Nuun Ujol Chahk, was manifested in a series of conflicts they fought over seven years (Case Study 11). After a Tikal attack on Dos Pilas in 672, Bajlaj Chan K'awiil *lok'ooyi*, "leaves/emerges", or in a second reference *bixiiy*, "went", fleeing into what would become a five-year exile.[25] Initially finding refuge at a site called Chahknaah, Nuun Ujol Chahk pursued him there the following year, driving him on to Hixwitz, modern Zapote Bobal, another client of Yuknoom Ch'een. The great king now intervenes to rescue Dos Pilas's fortunes. It was his victory over Tikal forces at Pulil in 677 that allowed Bajlaj Chan K'awiil to "arrive at Dos Pilas" on the very same day to restore his rule there.

A not dissimilar episode took place at Caracol in 680. A stucco frieze inscription found high on the massive Caana structure at that site tells of a series of battles between Caracol and Naranjo, although damage means that the narrative climax is now missing (Grube 1994c: 103–104). Recounting their own defeat, Caracol tells us that it was attacked and conquered in a "star war" action in 680 (see p.208–209). It was 168 days before the Caracol king K'ahk' Ujol K'inich II *huli uxwitza'*, "arrives (at) Caracol", returning to his abandoned and likely sacked royal seat (Nikolai Grube pers. comm. 1995; Martin and Grube 2000: 94–95).

Soon after, in 682, there was a fresh development at Naranjo with the arrival of the previously mentioned Ix Wak Jalam Chan, a daughter of Bajlaj Chan K'awiil of Dos Pilas (Houston and Mathews 1985: 14; Schele and Freidel 1990: 185–186; Martin and Grube 2000: 74). Celebrated in four separate inscriptions, in this case *hul* carries a double sense, referring both to her marriage to the current Naranjo king and – from a retrospective vantage at least – a new political era (p.176–177). But she was not alone. One account lists an entourage of supporters, presumably Dos Pilas nobles and kin, who *yit huli*, "arrive with" her.[26] Three days later she conducts a ceremony at a Naranjo temple that, when mentioned years after the event, was used to bolster her legitimacy as the de facto ruler. All this was predicated on her producing an heir, K'ahk' Tiliw Chan Chahk, in 688. Assuming power on her son's accession in 693, Ix Wak Jalam Chan is depicted alone on five stelae in various kingly poses. However, she always uses the Mutul emblem of Dos Pilas and bears no title specific to Naranjo. It is very hard to conceive that tiny, distant Dos Pilas could have masterminded these developments, and the finger necessarily points to Calakmul, the patron of her father's reign and, as we will see later, that of her son as well.

Another "arrival" event appears in the northern lowlands, where it appears within an extensive mural text uncovered at Ek Balam (Lacadena, in Grube, Lacadena, and Martin 2003; Lacadena 2005). There it describes the first stage in a process of political formation in 770, with a damaged but just legible *huli *tahn *ch'een ek' bahlam* or "arrival in the midst of Ek Balam", establishing that the ancient and modern name of the site are one-in-the-same. The initial actor here is a *baahtz'am,* a noble or functionary who belongs to a *xaman kaloomte',* a major king of the north whose emblem glyph – featuring the head of a raccoon – has yet to be attributed. Ukit Kan Le'k, who would become Ek Balam's most important ruler, enters the narrative at this point as the subject of the verb *pehk,* "to summon, invite" noted earlier. The implication is that the *xaman kaloomte'* is the overall authority under which Ukit Kan Le'k gains his new status.

The use of *hul* to connote political foundations in the inscriptions finds one last example at Ceibal in the ninth century. Here Stela 11 describes the arrival of a future ruler named (in part) Wat'ul K'atel under the *ukabjiiy* direction of an *aj k'anwitznal,* an Ucanal-based person called Chan Ek' Ho' Peet, in 829 (Schele and Matthews 1994; Schele and Mathews 1998: 183). This takes place *yetaaj* "accompanied" by an existing Ceibal king (Houston and Inomata 2009: 306) (p.288). Deep excavations at Ceibal have demonstrated that it was a centre of considerable antiquity, with major architecture dating back to the Middle Preclassic Period at around 1000 BCE (Inomata et al. 2013). In the brief history we can study through inscriptions, stretching from 721 to 889 CE, it was battered by warfare and periods of domination by other polities before standing alone as one the very last centres to preserve the Classic order (Martin and Grube 2000: 61, 63, 65, 227). Ceibal is one of the most important places to our understanding of the political changes of the ninth century and Wat'ul K'atel will return to this study in Chapters 10 and 11.

Pat, "To Form"

The verb *pat*, "to make, form" (Stuart 1998: 381–382), from Proto-Mayan **pät* (Kaufman and Norman 1984: 128), was another term denoting political constitution. An instance at Ek Balam comes 49 days after the arrival event – each of the intervening day-signs written-out in a very literal fashion – in a short statement that concludes the text. This reads *ipatlaj k'uhul talol ajaw*, "then the holy Talol lord is made". The Talol emblem glyph was used by Ukit Kan Le'k and all subsequent rulers of Ek Balam we know, and this was evidently not only his probable accession date but the formal initiation of his dynasty at the site (Lacadena 2005: 67).

In another example *pat* plays a role in the most consequential record of political instantiation yet known. In 642 K'an II of Caracol commissioned a monumental staircase that fronted one of his city's major temple platforms (Martin 2000b: 57–58, 2017a). Each component block was engraved with one, occasionally two, medallions that enclose parts of a continuous text. At some point, quite possibly when Naranjo seized Caracol for that span of 168 days in 680, it was broken up and portions removed, leaving only one small fragment to be recognised in debris at the foot of Structure B-5 (Martin 2000b: figure 12). What we know of this monument today comes from the fragments taken, in the manner of trophies, not only to Naranjo but also to Ucanal and Xunantunich; presumably distributed en route home to allied or subject polities ranged against Caracol (Map 2). Thanks to two key sections found at Xunantunich, excavated by Jamie Awe and interpreted by Christophe Helmke, we now have a good idea of its narrative purpose.

After the formalities of the opening date, we immediately come to the statement *machaj k'awiilil tahn ch'een kaanul pahtaal k'awiil(il) uxte'tuun*, "power is negated in the midst of Snake[-Place], power is formed (at) Three Stones" (Helmke and Awe 2016b: 11–19) (Figure 21). The text continues onto another block which supplies *chiiknahb,* perhaps "Coati? Lake", the second of the two-part Calakmul toponym (Martin 2017a). This passage offers a parallelism featuring the same subject, *k'awiilil,* of which the first is negative, the second positive. The -*il* suffix on *k'awiilil* is an abstractive, marking a quality or essence of the personified lightning bolt K'awiil, the character we last encountered when kings "grasped" its image at accession ceremonies. "Power" might poorly capture the nuances of the concept but conveys its general sense well enough (p.159). The real significance of this text comes in the different toponyms involved, with Kaanul, evidently the ancient name of Dzibanche (Martin and Velásquez 2016: 29–30), contrasted with Uxte'-tuun Chiiknahb, that of Calakmul (Stuart and Houston 1994: 28–29).[27] What we have here is an explicit description of the demise of Dzibanche as the Snake capital and the rise of Calakmul in its place, a transfer that had been proposed using other evidence (Martin 2005a) (Case Study 6).[28]

21 Panel describing the *machaj k'awiilil*, "negation of power" at *kaanul* (Dzibanche) and the *paahtal k'awiil(il)*, "formation of power" at *uxte'tuun* (Calakmul) on Xunantunich Panel 4.

The stairway text goes on to detail the close contacts between Caracol and the Snake kingdom leading up to this event. A second contribution of the Xunantunich material is evidence for a civil war associated with this split, one in which the Calakmul side emerged victorious (Helmke and Awe 2016a: 10–11). K'an II was, as we will see in Chapter 10, a client of the Snake kings, and the whole stairway represents his effort to establish his bona fides as a supporter of the winning side. In sum, we could hardly hope to receive a clearer signal that the affairs of the Snake kings were central to regional power dynamics, and that the shift to Calakmul was viewed as a key political event in its own time.

Kaj, "To Settle"

Our last verb is the most common referring to acts of constitution and reconstitution, one whose contexts have implied a meaning of "to set, establish" (Stuart 2004c: 2, 2005a: 184, n.62). Based on phonetic substitution evidence, the best candidate for its reading is *kaj,* which can be found in both colonial and modern lexicons as "to inhabit, live" and "to settle, remain (in a place)" (Beliaev and Davletshin 2014) – presumably derived from Proto-Mayan **kaj,* "begin, arrive" (Kaufman and Norman 1984: 122).[29]

It is used in the texts to describe foundations of a certain type. It does not necessarily refer to the original settlement of a place, or even its dedication as politically charged, but rather to personal authority instantiated or re-instantiated at that locale (Martin and Grube 2000: 157; Tokovinine 2013: 79–81). The latter is clear when we consider the antiquity of some of the places where the term appears and its recurrence at the same place under different, or even the same, kings. The Classic Maya occupied a landscape that was widely settled by their Preclassic forebears and few centres of note did not have some origins, however minor, well before 300 CE.

The earliest dated example of the term, retrospectively recorded, appears at Piedras Negras in or around 454, when a local king "settles in the midst of Paw Stone" (Stuart 2004c: 2–3) (Figure 22a). Paw Stone is the partially deciphered toponym used to designate Piedras Negras in foreign as well as local texts, but a question mark has hung over whether it constituted the whole or just part of the site. There is a clear distinction drawn between this place and *yoykib*, later *yokib*, a separate toponym that serves as the Piedras Negras emblem referent. *Yoykib* is the location for events taking place in 297 and 435, and a lord of that place is even said to have presided over mythic era-ending rites in 3114 BCE (Houston et al. 2003: 225). The lack of temporal overlap between the two toponyms most likely distinguishes separate locations: with *yoykib* as the origin and early seat of the dynasty and Paw Stone referring to the Piedras Negras we know today (Stuart 2004c: 5; Tokovinine 2008: 212–214, 2013: 74–76).[30] This would correspond well with the archaeological understanding of the site, which suggests a sudden influx of people and emergent urbanisation around a royal court midway through the Early Classic Period (Houston et al. 2003: 222–226).[31]

The same "settle, remain" verb appears at Palenque on a panel excavated from Temple XVII, where the third king of the dynasty Butz'aj Sak Chiik conducts such an event at *lakamha'* together with his presumed younger brother, Ahkal Mo' Nahb, in 490 (Martin and Grube 2000: 157; Stuart 2005a: 184, n.62; Stuart and Stuart 2008: 115–116) (Figure 22b). This is the earliest mention of the site we now call Palenque, with all previous activities performed by historical kings occurring at a place called *toktahn* (Stuart and Houston 1994: 30–31). First referenced in 435 and active in domestic affairs up to 496, Toktahn was an earlier base for the dynasty, made explicit in an important retrospective text that ascribes the emblem glyph *k'uhul toktahn ajaw* to the first and second Palenque monarchs (Bernal 2009: 123–126).[32] Archaeological knowledge of Palenque is less than comprehensive but, as at Piedras Negras, this switch to Lakamha' broadly coincides with an injection of Peten-style ceramic production to the site (Rands 1977: 174–175, 179, 2007: 34).

Three examples of our *kaj* term appear on panels uncovered at Bonampak, each in a separate episode of royal constitution (Safronov 2006; Bíró 2007b, 2011a: 58; Tokovinine 2013: 81). In the first, dated to 610, the local protagonist *lok'ooyi tu ch'een*, "leaves from his *ch'een*" and then *t'abaayi pa'chan*, "goes up

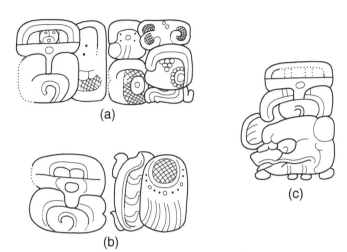

22 Selected phrases using the term *kaj*, "to settle, inhabit": (a) *kajaayi tahn ch'een ? tuun*, Piedras Negras Throne 1; (b) *kajaayi lakamha'*, Palenque Temple XVII Panel; (c) *kajaayi kaanul*, La Corona Element 33.

(to) Yaxchilan", the nearby regional power (Figure 16a). A year later a conflict of some kind, perhaps to overthrow a usurper, leads to the re-establishment of the same king's authority with *kajaayi tu ch'een*, "(re)settles at his *ch'een*".[33] Something similar recurred in 647 when a later ruler at the site *lok'ooyi usiijwitz*, "leaves Bonampak" and a few months later is restored, though no explanatory details are offered. The last case describes a third king who stages a *kajaayi tu kabch'een usiijwitz* or "settles at the *ch'een* of Bonampak" in 692, again without any further elaboration (Figure 16b). The politics of this region seem to have been especially involved, with two separate emblem glyphs used at Bonampak and several centres hosting royal seats – all interacting with a Yaxchilan dynasty that periodically held dominion over them.

An interesting act of political constitution emerges on a relief panel discovered at La Corona (Stuart 2012b), where we find *kajaayi kaanul* or "settles (at) Snake[-Place]" in 635 (Figure 22c). Unfortunately, the rest of the phrase is damaged, and the difficulty comes in deciding whether Kaanul refers to the toponym of Dzibanche in this example, or more broadly to the referent for the Snake polity derived from it. That almost all instances of *kaj* are followed by specific locations suggests the former, and here may describe complex politicking between the sites during the period of civil war (see p.328 and Case Study 6). That said, chronologically-speaking this event falls exactly where we would expect to see the reconstitution of the kingdom at the Calakmul location of Uxte'tuun-Chiiknahb, which keeps that second interpretation in play.

An instance of the *kaj* verb that appears on Cancuen Panel 1 is especially important because it is paired with *hul* and shows the intimate connection of the two terms within a narrative dedicated to political restoration. This 160 glyph-block panel was commissioned by a king called Tajal Chan Ahk and is clearly one of a pair of which only this, the second part, is currently known

(Fahsen and Jackson 2001; Guenter 2002; Kistler 2003). Its text concerns a 148-year portion of Cancuen's dynastic history, with particular reference to the influence of Calakmul. As we join the narrative mid-phrase, in 651, a missing event is overseen by the Calakmul king Yuknoom Ch'een II. Next a lord assumed to be a Cancuen native dies at Calakmul in 653, and three years afterwards a lord called K'iib Ajaw accedes into the Cancuen royal title. This event, in 656, was "supervised" by Yuknoom Ch'een and "overseen" by a group of Calakmul deities (Martin and Grube 1994a: 7) (p.163 and 250). A few months later K'iib Ajaw travels to *makanwitz*, a hill that might be a ritual location, and some months after that "arrives" and then "settles" at a range of places before concluding at the core toponym of his new home *haluum*, ancient Cancuen (Tokovinine 2013: 81). Since the archaeological time-depth at this particular location is very shallow, with the first structures of any note laid down in the seventh-century, it is quite likely that these events amount to the physical foundation of Haluum (Barrientos et al. 2002; Barrientos 2014, 2015).[34] Thereafter, Cancuen developed a very atypical layout for a Maya city, with no large stand-alone temple pyramids and little in the way of monumental public spaces. Construction effort was instead concentrated on an enclosed, fortress-like, royal court whose final form in the later eighth century ranks among the largest in the entire Maya area.

CASE STUDY 4: FRATERNAL SUCCESSION AT PALENQUE

Sibling succession occurred at several Classic Maya kingdoms but only one, Palenque, puts rhetorical emphasis on the practice, giving rare insights into the branching of a dynastic line. The Early Classic kings Butz'aj Sak Chiik and Ahkal Mo' Nahb I were born in 459 and 465, respectively, suggesting that they were brothers or half-brothers. The importance given to the latter in later texts is a strong sign that descent to the next generation flowed through his bloodline. In the Late Classic, K'inich Janaab Pakal I died after a 68-year reign in 683 and was succeeded 132 days later by his son K'inich Kaan Bahlam II. On the same day, the new king's younger brother was installed as *baahch'ok*, or heir apparent, eventually to succeed him as K'inich K'an Joy Kitam II in 702.

The next Palenque king, K'inich Ahkal Mo' Nahb III, was sired by neither brother but was instead the issue of a non-ruling lord called Tiwol Chan Mat. Such was Tiwol Chan Mat's importance to K'inich Ahkal Mo' Nahb that one representation of the king's accession in 721, the Tablet of the Slaves, shows the father presenting the royal headdress to his son (Wald 1997). This was, however, a contrived scene, since we are elsewhere told that Tiwol Chan Mat met his end in 680. His burial rites were overseen by K'inich Janaab Pakal, and a convincing case has been made that Tiwol Chan Mat was a third son of that

long-lived king, a figure who died prematurely, making K'inich Ahkal Mo'
Nahb the grandson of K'inich Janaab Pakal (Ringle 1996: 55).[35]

K'inich Ahkal Mo' Nahb's royal blood clearly did not allay the concern that
descent had deviated through a non-ruler. This can be discerned from a stucco
tableau once fixed to the back wall of Temple XVIII, which goes to special
lengths to justify his position. It consisted of a multi-figure scene accompanied
by a large number of appliqué hieroglyphs and, although found in a sorry state
of collapse, careful reconstruction has yielded some significant information
(Ringle 1996). The scene is dated to 679 and once showed an enthroned ruler,
certainly K'inich Janaab Pakal, faced by a line of figures composed of K'inich
Kaan Bahlam, K'inich K'an Joy Kitam, and Tiwol Chan Mat. The first two are
captioned with their pre-accession names, and all three are described as *ch'ok*,
"youth, prince". Stuart (2005a: 152–153) reads the second-person text spoken
by another figure as *tihmaj awohl atz'akbuji*, "you are pleased (that) you order
them". The claim, it seems, is that K'inich Janaab Pakal had ordained that the
succession should pass through all three of his sons, with the full plan thwarted
only by the early demise of Tiwol Chan Mat a year later. In this way K'inich
Ahkal Mo' Nahb III's legitimacy is wedded to the will of the great king. Even
though his father had not survived to become a ruler, he was intended to be
one and was therefore a suitable conduit for royal blood.

Fraternal inheritance evidently recurred in K'inich Ahkal Mo' Nahb III's
own generation. Much is revealed by the magnificent carved platform inside
Temple XXI (González and Bernal 2012), which offers a scene dominated by
the revered K'inich Janaab Pakal once again (Figure 23). Seated to either side

23 The future kings K'inich Ahkal Mo' Nahb III and K'inich Janaab Pakal II flank their
grandfather K'inich Janaab Pakal I. Detail of Palenque Temple XXI Platform. (Drawing by
David Stuart)

of him are two lords of equal physical stature: one identified as K'inich Ahkal Mo' Nahb III and the other as Upakal K'inich, the latter carrying the *baahch'ok* title as well as Palenque's full *k'uhul baakal ajaw* emblem. Pointedly, both are given their childhood names via the *ch'ok k'aba'* formula, indicating that this was an idealised, but likely genuine, historical event conducted when the presumed brothers were children at the court of their grandfather (Miller and Martin 2004: 232). We know that by at least 742 Upakal K'inich had succeeded as king, re-using the name K'inich Janaab Pakal to memorialise the great patriarch (Bernal 2002a, 2002b).

CASE STUDY 5: ERASING THE PAST IN THE YAXCHILAN "INTERREGNUM"

In her treatment of Yaxchilan's history, Proskouriakoff (1963: 163, 1964: 180) noted a gap in its dynastic sequence between 742 and 752, a span separating the long rule of Shield Jaguar III from that of his energetic son Bird Jaguar IV. Though not the interregnum once supposed, this is an era of special interest for us. We now know that there was an intervening king, Yopaat Bahlam II, who visited Piedras Negras with a group of nobles in 749 (Martin and Grube 2000: 127, 149).[36] This visit is recounted on Piedras Negras Panel 3, arguably the most innovative and thematically complex monument to survive from the Classic Period (Figure 24). Commissioned by K'inich Yat Ahk III in 795 or soon thereafter, it ostensibly focuses on the 1-K'atun (20 Maya year) jubilee of a predecessor at Piedras Negras, Itzam K'an Ahk IV, some forty-six years earlier.

There is, however, a barely concealed underlying topic: Piedras Negras's relationship with Yaxchilan through the greater part of the Late Classic. In a first-person speech Itzam K'an Ahk IV appears to remind the visiting Yopaat Bahlam and his party that Bird Jaguar III of Yaxchilan (identified as Yopaat Bahlam's grandfather) was installed or re-installed by Itzam K'an Ahk III in 654 (p.254). Yopaat Bahlam's presence at the jubilee is itself a deferential gesture in line with Piedras Negras' view of a rightful asymmetry between the two kingdoms. Unspoken here is the long history of antagonism between them. Other texts tell us that within the Late Classic alone, Shield Jaguar III captured a Piedras Negras *sajal* in 726, while in 759 Bird Jaguar IV seized the Piedras Negras heir T'ul Chiik who, not coincidentally, is pictured as a boy on the right side of Panel 3 (Alexandr Safronov, pers. comm. 2006). The intended audience for Panel 3 would be well aware of these events and the reality that Yaxchilan was often anything but a loyal client. Indeed, this topic of Piedras Negras–Yaxchilan relations may be motivated by renewed hostilities, since within a few years K'inich Yat Ahk III would himself fall victim to Yaxchilan, seized by its very last king sometime before 808 (Stuart, in Houston et al. 1999: 14).

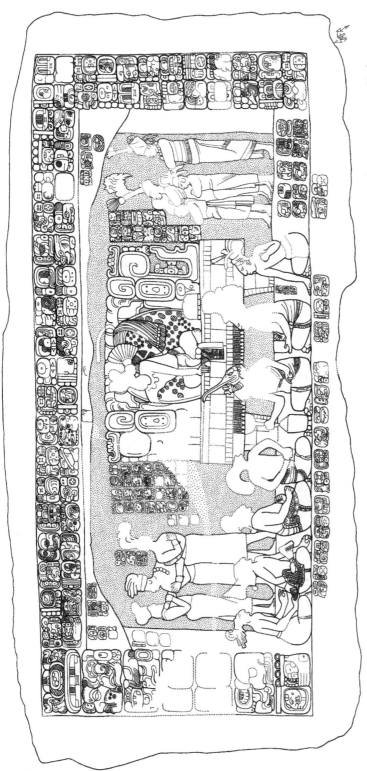

24 Itzam K'an Ahk IV of Piedras Negras addresses Yopaat Bahlam II of Yaxchilan and attending nobles on their visit to Piedras Negras in 749. Piedras Negras Panel 3. (Drawing by Alexandr Safronov)

This is a critical background to understanding the Yaxchilan "interregnum" and the disappearance of Yopaat Bahlam II from Yaxchilan's monumental record. There is good reason to suppose that he was a son of Shield Jaguar III, probably the issue of Shield Jaguar's paramount wife, Ix K'abal Xook, whereas we know that Bird Jaguar IV was the son of a lesser queen born when Shield Jaguar III was in his sixties (Case Study 10). After Bird Jaguar IV acceded in 752 he embarked on a vigorous monumental programme that retrospectively placed himself at the centre of events during the previous ten years, including battle honours, as well as still earlier rituals conducted with his father (Mathews 1988: 205–217; Schele and Freidel 1990: 262–287; Noble Bardsley 1994; Martin and Grube 2000: 128–130). To re-tell Yaxchilan's history, Bird Jaguar IV reset old monuments, had missing or destroyed ones for his grandfather Bird Jaguar III re-carved, and created a grand dynastic narrative in the form of a 480-sign hieroglyphic stairway (Stuart 1995: 171–176; Nahm 1997; Martin 2000b). From all these records Yopaat Bahlam is signally absent. In fact, the hieroglyphic stairway text was carved over another, now-obliterated text contained in roundels, and this earlier version is a excellent candidate for a work of this presumed half-brother.

The nature of the inferred conflict between them is beyond reconstruction, but their very different relationships with Piedras Negras can have been no small matter. Indeed, one of the motives behind Panel 3 may have been a desire to set the record straight by deliberately highlighting the expunged Yopaat Bahlam. Those looking for propaganda in Maya texts need look no further than Bird Jaguar IV's efforts at self-promotion, transparent to us over a millennium after the fact. That said, it must be noted that his sins are more those of omission rather than commission (Houston 2000: 170), since he does not backdate his inauguration so as to eliminate the vacant years. That gap is left plain for all to see.

CASE STUDY 6: ON THE TRAIL OF THE SERPENT KINGS

Although not the first kingdom to come to scholarly attention, that of *kaanul*, "Snake[-Place]" has risen to dominate discussion of Classic Maya political history. Berlin (1958: 118) noted the snakehead form in his foundational text on emblem glyphs, but he passed over it with the single comment "a site unknown to me". That obscurity was not lifted even as it began to emerge as the most prevalent royal title in the written corpus, appearing at sites right across the lowlands. Where, researchers asked, did this once-famous kingdom call home?

Calakmul first emerged as a candidate because it was the largest city to lack a known emblem glyph (Marcus 1973: 913), but the extreme erosion of most of its numerous monuments – the local limestone being especially porous and brittle – meant that the attribution could not be speedily confirmed. With the aid of an unprovenanced text the birth-date of the Snake king Yuknoom Yich'aak K'ahk' II was recognised on Calakmul Stela 9 (Mathews 1979). However, the accession of the same king was already known from another looted monument and after that stone was traced to El Peru this site became the favoured candidate (Miller 1974; Graham 1988: 125–126). The question was further muddied by the steady appearance of a large number of looted monuments featuring Snake emblem glyphs. With several contenders still in play, the mystery capital gained the suitably mysterious nickname of "Site Q" (see Schuster 1997).

It was only with the discovery of glyphic toponyms and the recognition on two Calakmul monuments of the twin place-names intimately tied to the Snake dynasty, Uxte'tuun and Chiiknahb, that attention rightfully returned to the central Peten (Stuart and Houston 1994: 28–29). Efforts to identify the Snake emblem on standing Calakmul monuments produced several contenders (Marcus 1987: 173–176), but it was not until the onset of deep excavations across the site, directed by Ramón Carrasco, that unambiguous examples came to light and the issue could finally be brought to a close (Martin 1996d, 2008a) (Figure 25a).[37]

Or could it? In 1993 excavations at the site of Dzibanche, situated 126 km to the northeast of Calakmul, uncovered blocks of a stairway carved with captives and accompanying inscriptions (Figure 26). Those texts showed as many as six serpent emblem glyphs – by now read as k'uhul kaanul ajaw, "Holy Snake[-Place] Lord" – each of them attached to a ruler called Yuknoom Ch'een (Nalda 2004; Velásquez 2004a, 2005, 2008a) (Figure 25b). The Calendar Round dates on these blocks floated without an anchor in the Long Count, but the style of the carving suggests an early timeframe, perhaps as far back as the fourth century CE.[38] Dzibanche can be counted among a cluster of northeastern Peten sites with early references to the Snake dynasty, with examples also seen at El Resbalon, Yo'okop, and Pol Box (Carrasco and Boucher 1987: 5; Martin 1997a: 861; Esparza and Pérez 2009: 9) (Figure 25c). Even though Dzibanche has no surviving stelae and thus far provided only a small number of inscribed finds, Erik Velásquez has identified four additional

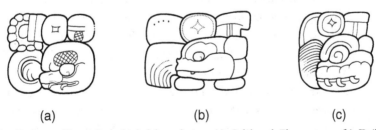

(a)   (b)   (c)

25 The Snake emblem glyph k'uhul kaanul ajaw. (a) Calakmul Element 39; (b) Dzibanche Monument 13; (c) El Resbalon Block BX25.

26 A captive taken by Yuknoom Ch'een I. Monument 5 from the Dzibanche Captive Stairway.

Snake emblem glyphs there.[39] One of them can be dated, with the mention of a Kaanul king who reigned in or close to 573 CE (Velásquez 2004a: 99–100).[40]

Just as Dzibanche's Early Classic candidacy was strong, so Calakmul's was weak. The Snake kingdom had patently been a major player in Early Classic power politics, with notable rulers such as Tuun K'ab Hix and Scroll Serpent exercising dominion over other kings (p.245–246). Yet despite almost three decades of excavations at Calakmul not a single early Kaanul name or title had been uncovered in a contemporary context. Just a handful of Early Classic texts were known at the site and close examination of one uncovered by the team of William Folan, Stela 114 from 435 (Pincemin et al. 1998), complicated matters by revealing an entirely different emblem glyph featuring the head of a bat (Martin 2005a: 9–10).[41] The ruler with that title is depicted on the front of the monument, but a second reference in the main text to a *kaloomte'* and *chiiknahb ajaw* refer to what could well be a separate character.

This Bat emblem glyph is not an isolated example, since another such title is seen at Uxul, 32 km to Calakmul's southwest – there paired with a *kaloomte'* epithet in 632 – and at least two more are found on monuments at Naachtun, situated some 35 km to the southeast (Grube 2005: 95–98; 2008: 220). Wherever the Bat dynasty was based then or later, and Naachtun must be a contender, it clearly once had wide influence in this region. Even so, when its Snake counterpart comes onto the scene it promptly disappears from sight.[42]

That switch coincides with the reign of the long-lived and politically dominant Yuknoom Ch'een II, a namesake to that early king at Dzibanche. Despite following in a long line of Snake kings he becomes the starting point for a new dynastic count, with his successors Yuknoom Yich'aak K'ahk' II calling themselves the "second in sequence" and Yuknoom Took' K'awiil "third in sequence". Some important reconstitution of the kingdom had clearly taken place at Calakmul during the reign of Yuknoom Ch'een or that of his immediate predecessor (Martin 2005a: 11). A further hint to that effect appears at Naranjo, where someone we know as Yuknoom Head is oddly described as *kaanul ajaw ta uxte'tuun*, "Snake[-Place] Lord at Calakmul". The passage is explicable only if the Kaanul seat in question requires disambiguation from a more familiar one, which is to say Calakmul instead of Dzibanche (Tokovinine 2007: 19–21). Since Yuknoom Head is also an *aj chiiknahb*, "Chiiknahb Person" he may have already been based there.

The 2016 finds at Xunantunich, detailed earlier in this chapter, have offered unexpected confirmation of this transfer between the two cities. Specifically, one text describes the nullifying of power at Kaanul and its formation at Uxte'tuun Chiiknahb (Helmke and Awe 2016b) (p.128–129). A fragmentary Dzibanche inscription mentions Kaanul as a toponym and this adds further weight to the idea that this was the original "Snake[-Place]" where the dynasty was first formed and from which it took its name (Martin and Velásquez 2016: 27–30). It should be noted at this point that the vowel in the -*Vl* "place" suffix is not specified in the script and, while Kaanul has now become customary in the literature, Kaanal or even Kaaniil are other viable readings.

What provoked the move? Again, discoveries at Xunantunich provide an answer, although only by reading one of its texts in conjunction with portions of the same one found at Naranjo (Helmke and Awe 2016a). One passage describes a battle in 636 in which Yuknoom Head triumphs over the Kaanul king Waxaklajuun Ubaah Kaan – whose superior status is signalled by the *k'uhul* prefix to his emblem that Yuknoom Head always lacks.[43] That clash took place just 58 days before the inauguration of Yuknoom Ch'een. This proximity enhances the prospect that Yuknoom Head is simply the pre-accession name of Yuknoom Ch'een, who would have been a thirty-six-year-old at the time of the battle (Martin 2005a: 11, n.9). Whatever the truth of that, the civil war was finally concluded with the death of Waxaklajuun Ubaah Kaan in 640, and thereafter Yuknoom Ch'een stood alone as the undisputed Kaanul sovereign.

The reign of Yuknoom Ch'een and his two successors represent the golden age of the Late Classic Snake dynasty and between them they commissioned as many as 42 stelae at Calakmul. Although always more abstemious in its monument-making, troubled Tikal erected just two known examples over the same period. The political dominance of the Calakmul kings ranged far and wide as they built an elaborate network of subject polities, a key topic of this volume. Calakmul itself was an ancient city that had flourished in its Preclassic iteration as far back as 400 BCE (Folan et al. 1995; Carrasco 2005; Carrasco and Colón 2005). Its Early Classic phase is not well understood, but it was a vibrant place and its rulers were important enough to possess their own *kaloomte'* title. But it was during the seventh and eighth centuries that the core of the city was extensively refashioned by the Snake kings into a capital befitting their imperialistic ambitions (p.348–350).

Despite starting a new dynastic count, the kings of Calakmul did not forget their forebears in the north. One of the ways in which the earlier Snake kings

27 Codex-style vase listing nineteen successive kings of the Kaanul dynasty, K6751. (Photograph © Museum Associates/ LACMA Conservation Center, by Yosi Pozeilov)

appear to have been memorialised was on a set of "codex-style" vases that provide a list of up to nineteen of their number (Martin 1997a) (Figure 27). Twelve whole pots of this kind are known from the illicit art market, while a few sherds from one more turned up among over 700 fragments of codex-style ware excavated at Calakmul (Martin 2008a, 2012a; Delvendahl 2010; García Barrios 2011). Their standardised texts give names, titles, and accession dates, though these come with plenty of interpretive problems. Some of the names one might expect to see are missing, perhaps obscured behind alternative monikers, while their untethered Calendar Round positions float in time and are usually unreliable.

The latter problem is in part the result of multiple copying errors, with differences even between two vessels executed in the same hand.[44] Significantly, the list features a Yuknoom Ch'een as the tenth king, a not unreasonable position for him to be the protagonist and commissioner of the Dzibanche Captive Stairway. Later in the sequence we find kings named K'ahk' Ti' Ch'ich', Sky Witness, and Scroll Serpent as the sixteenth, seventeenth, and nineteenth in line, the same order as kings of those names seen on monuments.

The accession date ascribed to K'ahk' Ti' Ch'ich' in the longest sequence, on K6751, matches another that can be reconstructed from an inscribed wooden lintel at Dzibanche, the only legible survivor of a set that originally spanned the doorways of one of the city's highest temples. The ruler's name falls on a missing section, but what we have describes his elevation to the status of *kaloomte'* in 550, just six years before the historically known K'ahk' Ti' Ch'ich' first appears in the inscriptions (Martin 2017b; Martin and Beliaev 2017).[45]

Our painted king list concludes with Scroll Serpent, and this may have a particular significance. A king of that name is retrospectively cited on two Calakmul monuments as he celebrates the period ending of 593, one of which might connect him to the birth of Yuknoom Ch'een and imply that they were father and son.

For the better part of a century Calakmul was undeniably the most important place on the Maya political map, but its success was not to last. There are
signs of major disruption as early as 751, with the king depicted on Stela 62
using the Bat emblem in place of the Snake (Martin 2005a: 9). Moreover,
while the front face of this monument is complete, its sides were outlined for a
text that was never carved. The much larger and finished Stela 88 celebrates
the same date, but depicts a queen wearing the full royal panoply – the two
monuments together suggesting a complex state of affairs.[46] At about this time
at least one series of inscribed blocks featuring a Snake dynast of this era was
broken up and buried in construction fill (Martin 2008a). It was also at this
point that we see a revival of the local toponymic title *chiiknahb ajaw*, last seen
in the Early Classic, and this is the only title we have for the king who was
installed not too long after 751 and erected two especially tall stelae in 771
(Martin and Grube 2000: 114–115).

As the Snake kingdom's power began to wane some nearby centres set up
monuments on a consistent basis for the first time. Oxpemul, a sizeable hilltop
site 27 km to the north, restarts its tradition following a long hiatus in 731. Its
new stelae have rulers who carry a local toponymic *ajaw* title, but this was soon
joined by the Bat emblem glyph as well as the *uxte'tuun kaloomte'* epithet
(Grube 2008: 197–215). First seen at Calakmul in the Early Classic Period, the
latter had been the exclusive preserve of Snake kings for almost a century.
Another one-time satellite 23.5 km to the northeast of Calakmul, La Muñeca,
commences its own stela programme in 780 and continues to erect stones until
at least 889, although little more than their dates are now legible. This upsurge
of monument-making across the Calakmul region comes to northerly
Chactun in 731 (Šprajc 2015) and something similar occurs at Nadzca'an at
much the same time and certainly by 830 (Carrasco and Wolf 1996: 72). Signs
of Calakmul's weakening grip on the region might first be seen at El Palmar,
where a fairly steady monumental record begins only in 711.

While all these sites can be broadly characterised as Peten-style, important
changes were underway. The centre of Río Bec, 56 km to the northeast of
Calakmul, gives its name to an architectural style of elaborate cut-stone
facades, plainly connected to those at Chenes region sites such as Santa Rosa
Xtampak and Dzibilnocac further north. Río Bec style spread across a wide
region and flourished in the later eighth and first half of the ninth centuries. Its
distinctively decentralised form of elite settlement marks a major departure
from the standing norm, and is a clear sign of the cultural as well as political
decline of the old order in the Peten. Calakmul was not immune to these
developments, as it introduces some aspects of Río Bec architecture and shows
increased imports of northern ceramics (Carrasco 1998).

Dated stela commissions at Calakmul continue until 810, but not one of
these later carvings has a preserved name or title. It is not inconceivable that the

Kaanul lineage re-established itself at the site. Certainly, we know that the dynasty was active in some form up until 849, when the last known holder of its title appears at Ceibal (p.260). Whoever ruled Calakmul at this time did so under much reduced circumstances and a falling population, with those that remained retreating to the core as the hinterland was steadily deserted (Braswell et al. 2004a) – a pattern we see elsewhere. Even so, some monuments were produced during this final swansong. The small Stela 65 has no surviving text, but has stylistic traits that put it well into the ninth century. Another diminutive stone, Stela 61, has a text but its date remains uncertain and there is no sign of an emblem glyph. Two even smaller monuments, Stela 84 and 91, are surely later still and show a distinct change in lordly attire and a marked deterioration in quality. The texts they carry either imitate writing or are simply too crudely executed to be read. They include squared signs with numbers set beneath them, features indicative of the second half of the ninth century (p.290–293). The ill-proportioned image carved on one last stone, Stela 50, was made by someone with no formal training, or indeed talent. At some unknown point in the tenth century Calakmul was finally abandoned to the forest.

The evolving story of research into the serpent kingdom is a good illustration of how epigraphic and archaeological information can be tallied, sometimes in surprising ways, as initial estimations meet a messy and always dimly lit reality. New information is constantly emerging from field finds and the on-going decipherment, allowing us to continue testing interpretations. One of many unanswered questions concerns the scope of the Snake dynasty's influence to the north and its relationship with the Classic Period centres who vied for dominance there. Another is the nature of the early relationship between Dzibanche and Ichkabal, a huge Preclassic centre situated just 11 km to the east. Although current evidence points to Dzibanche as the origin of the Classic-era Snake dynasty, we can still hope for a better epigraphic understanding of that site and an assurance that some still more complex historical scenario is not at work.[47] There have already been several twists and turns on the trail of the serpent kings and, even now, we might not be at the end of them.

SEVEN

TRANSCENDENCE

Like all institutions, polities are physical things only in certain restricted senses. They can be materialised in practical facilities and visible symbolic expressions, both manifestations of the bundled schemas and resources that compose their structure. Yet in their conditioning of individual and group behaviour within idealised communities, polities emerge from, and essentially remain, "states of mind" (Yoffee 2005: 38–41). If we are to appreciate the sources of legitimacy and empowerment integral to governing authorities, we must turn our attention to how those minds saw politics as inherently entwined with the transcendent. The Classic Maya were far from alone in believing that political communities encompassed supernatural beings and the ancestral dead, not simply as distant abstractions but role-playing constituents.

Excavation can tell us something of how these beliefs were expressed materially, as in the elaborate construction of tombs and shrines for the veneration of dead kings, decorated temple platforms, or caches of ritualised objects. But it is art and writing where we find specific data on how royal identity was suffused with religiosity, with most Classic Maya images and texts alluding to spiritual life to some degree. These productions seldom recount mythic episodes directly, and theological discourses not at all, but rather convey the ways that the world of the sacred sanctioned kingly action. We can see these as self-serving programmes that naturalised stratification and inequality using the authority of the divine, but can be equally persuaded that elite and commoner alike viewed them as authentic expressions of the entwined character of the secular and sacred (Durkheim 1915).

My purpose here is not to explore Classic Maya religion as a totality, but to concentrate on how particular beliefs and practices underpinned the identity and authority of kings, kingdoms, and the wider political system. I am, therefore, interested less in meaning than in practical effects. This is akin to Milner's (1994) concern with sacredness as a status resource and Cohen's (1981) analysis of dramaturgy as an instrument of elite distinction. Both are concerned with differential social power and are ultimately dependent on the familiar notion of a social contract, an obligation – even burden – in which the ruler's performance of services on behalf of the community was the rationale for their privileged existence. The following treatment falls into two sections: the first focussed on how kingship was defined in relation to the divine world, and the second on how those ideas were manifested in links to particular supernatural personas.

DIVINITY AND KINGSHIP

Monarchy among the Classic Maya is usually characterised as a "divine king-ship". This label evokes more than privileged access to the supernatural realm and the ability to mediate with, or channel, divine essences and powers, it implies some perceived union with ethereal powers. However, since the abandonment of Frazer's original criteria for the concept, most of all ritual regicide, it lacks any great precision in the literature and permits a range of different interpretations (Frazer 1890; Feeley-Harnik 1985: Graeber and Sahlins 2017). One point of contention in Mesoamericanist circles is whether this communication with, and experience of, the transcendent is best categorised as shamanistic or sacerdotal (Freidel and Schele 1988; Schele and Freidel 1990; Freidel 1992, 2008; Kehoe 2000; Klein et al. 2002; Stuart 2002; Zender 2004: 56–79). The issue is an important one because it is so closely attended by questions of sociocultural development – with the shaman-king traditionally viewed as a primitive stage en route to more sophisticated forms of institution-alised priesthood.

But shorn of that evolutionary baggage, these universalistic labels seem overly dichotomous, with neither an ideal fit for the kind of immersive exchanges we see in the Mesoamerican record. Recent comparative work on the sacred in royal authority (e.g. Brisch 2008) only highlights the extent to which different study areas are wrestling with similar issues of definition and meaning, engaged in similar debates as to the relative weight of word and image and how well these reflect ancient thought.

A foundational study by Stephen Houston and David Stuart (1996) set out the epigraphic evidence for the interaction between Maya kings and divinities through a core set of terms and visual devices. This and subsequent work allows us to address what was a "god" and what was only "god-like", to illuminate the practices with which the elite engaged with the divine, to understand something of the position kingship took in the order of the cosmos, and to appreciate the liminal space ancestors occupied between humans and truly supernatural beings.

Divine Things

A fault-line that still lingers in the field concerns the appropriateness of the term "god" to describe suprahuman entities in Mesoamerica. Older ideas of a Maya "pantheon" (Schellhas 1904; Thompson 1970) have been critiqued by those who see the unwarranted imposition of an Old World concept on the New, preferring to see not deities on a Greco-Roman model but embodied forces of nature and deified ancestors (Proskouriakoff 1978: 116–117; Marcus 1992a: 270; Baudez 2002). That position is not without merit, and there is reason to question universalistic models of religious belief and experience (Houston and Inomata 2009: 193–195). However, research has shown how mythological narratives once thought to be late introductions are actually of considerable antiquity (e.g. Bardawil 1976, Coe 1989), and it is plain that it is the character and behaviour of otherworldly agents, not simply their bodily form, that have been modelled on humans and human society. To reject the term "god" in these cases is to sacrifice much in the way of cross-cultural comparison. What the abundant epigraphic and iconographic materials now reveal is a complex theology inhabited by different categories of being operating within a multi-dimensional cosmology that we comprehend only in part.

The most important epigraphic contribution in this regard has been the decipherment of the hieroglyph associated with truly divine figures. In its most complete form it takes a quasi-anthropomorphic form, with a blunt-nosed face joined by lines of dots or beads (see Figure 3b), which are elaborated in many cases by a shell or the sign reading *k'an*, "precious" (Taube 1992a: 27–31). This compound sign was first read as **K'U** by William Ringle (1988) and later refined to **K'UH** by Stuart (in Stuart, Houston, and Robertson 1999: II-41); an interpretation first mooted by Barthel (1952: 94). *K'u/K'uh* is a word consistently translated in colonial dictionaries as "*dios* (god)", and today there is copious evidence that it anciently had the sense of "god/divine thing" (Houston and Stuart 1996; Prager 2013). Its origins are to be found in Proto-Mayan as **k'uuh*, which means "sun" and "radiance" in a range of Mayan languages in use today (Kaufman 2003: 458–459; Marc Zender, pers. comm. 2011). The later cognate *ch'u* is the basis of the extended form *ch'ulel*, a spiritual essence or energy that is translated as "soul" or "spirit" in post-contact ethnographic sources (e.g. Guiteras-Holmes 1961: 72; Vogt 1969:

369–371). Where the beaded motif appears as a flowing stream in Classic Maya art – often shown spilling from the hands of kings – it has been interpreted as the ancient analogue of this vital force, one which could be manifested as water, incense, or even human blood (Stuart 1988).

The scribes were careful to distinguish the *k'uh* status from other forms of otherworldly entity, including a range of embodied phenomena and the demon-like characters called *wahy* (Houston and Stuart 1989; Grube and Nahm 1994; Calvin 1997; Stuart 2005d: 160–165). Crucially, no historical rulers, even the long-deceased founders of major dynasties, are characterised as *k'uh*. The boundary between the natural and supernatural was, therefore, not as permeable as some extravagant artistic representations invite us to believe. Kings did, however, possess a kind of mystical essence, expressed as *ch'ahb ak'ab*, "genesis (and) darkness". The same obscure metaphor turns up in statements of parentage and David Stuart (2005e: 278) has suggested that it alludes to the procreative powers of monarchs, something rendered null and void by their capture in war, as we will see in Chapter 9.

The decipherment of the adjectival form *k'uhul*, "holy, sacred" led to understanding emblem glyphs as titles specifying a particular quality of Classic Maya kings – clear support for the general affinity between divinity and kingship. However, we have previously seen that this *k'uhul* prefix underwent a historical development with strong elements of status inflation to its use and spread. It is difficult to detect a distinction between kings that were marked by this term and those that were not, since they are all ascribed the same symbols of rank, perform the same rituals, and had the same interactions with the divine realm. In short, the introduction of the prefix is more a rhetorical embellishment, at times a statement of relative rank, than a meaningful transformation of the kingly ideal.

Engaging the Gods

Maya kings interacted with the transcendent in various ways, most directly when gods were brought into being by the act of *tzak*, "conjuring" (Houston and Stuart 1996: 300–301; Prager 2013: 359–369). Illustrations of these rituals typically show the manipulation of fantastic serpents or centipedes, from whose gaping mouths gods or ancestors emerge (Figure 33). There is evidence that perforations of the skin and the spilling of blood, an offering that was subsequently burnt, was closely associated with these "visionary" scenes (Schele and Miller 1986: 175–196). One of the more common entities conjured in this way was K'awiil, the embodied lightning bolt that encapsulates an essence of power we heard about in Chapter 6 (Taube 1992a: 69–79; Martin 2006b: 172–173; Prager 2013: 370–371; Valencia 2015). It is little surprise that his was an energy lords sought to harness and project. Indeed, some major lords were posthumously referred to as K'awiil, presumably as an honorific implying that they have absorbed or incorporated its force.[1]

On other occasions deities are invoked by means of masks, costumes, and insignia; performances that are described with the still poorly understood expression *ubaahil aan/ahn* (Houston and Stuart 1996: 297–300; Houston 2006; Prager 2013: 190–203). Such impersonations among the Aztec were not simply dramaturgical, they induced the god's presence in the body of the subject in the same way as it did within a physical effigy – with a single term *teixiptla* used for both the living performer and static model (Townsend 1979: 28). Dressed in their godly guise, Maya rulers conducted performances, at times probably for a select few, at others in full sight of the greater populace. Other lordly rituals took place *yichonal*, "before" or "in the sight of" named deities, and at other times they were *ilaaj*, "seen" by them, terms treated more fully in Chapter 10 (Houston and Stuart 1996: 301; Prager 2013: 381–395). Among the most frequent of such divine observers were the Paddler Gods (p.165 and 296), characters associated with transporting the Maize God to the Underworld, and in late times the pair are shown floating in the sky within billowing clouds.

The responsibility and political significance of such ritual duties should not be underestimated. In societies that believed intimate, transactional relations with deities were required to sustain the whole community – most especially in the case of local patron gods – failure would reflect badly on the kings who served as their primary interlocutors. When kings were seen to deliver on the social contract they enjoyed a splendid existence, but equally any perceived breakdown in divine providence might lead them be held accountable and delegitimised as a result (see Iannone 2016).

Lords of Time

The degree to which the institution of kingship was considered a part of cosmic order is of central interest to us. The twentieth and last day of the *tzolk'in* calendar was named *ajaw*, "lord" and reflects an understanding of kings as instantiations of time (Stuart 1996, 2011a; Houston et al. 2006: 85–89; Martin 2019a). All major round dates in the Long Count calendar, known as "period endings", fall on the day *ajaw* and a portrait of the presiding ruler can replace the ordinary day sign in elaborated renditions of such dates, emphasising that synergy (Figure 28).

The rhythmic procession of the Long Count, with days, months, and years meshed to produce a linear count stretching many trillions of years into the past and future, was the dominant component of a monumental inscription, sometimes consuming almost all its textual space. The verb that follows describes one of several rites appropriate to these occasions and a key role of kingship, and the elite more generally, was to conduct them on a regular basis.[2] The acts of erecting standing stones or of scattering incense were re-enactments of those performed by the gods in the deep past, and were constitutive of the present universe. They must be seen as foundational to the ways that kings sustained the current order and formed part of the fabric of time itself.

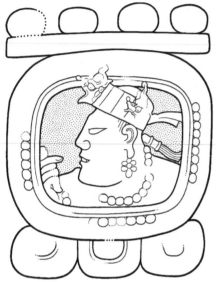

28 The day 9 Ajaw in the *tzolk'in* calendar, showing the sign for *ajaw*, "lord" replaced by a portrait of the monument's commissioning king. Unprovenanced altar from the Itsimte area in the Museo Nacional de Antropología, Guatemala City.

One key representation of these ideas comes on an altar discovered by Ivan Šprajc at the now-eponymous site of Altar de los Reyes (Grube 2003a, 2008: 180–183; Houston et al. 2006: 95; Tokovinine 2013: 106–108) (Figure 29). This stone was originally ringed by 13 emblem glyphs, with those of Tikal, Calakmul, Palenque, Edzna, Motul de San José, Chatahn, and seemingly Altun Ha still legible.[3] The sequence is introduced by a partially readable possessed form of *saak (?) tz'am*, "seed throne", while an eroded text on the top of the altar evidently refers to these kingships as *k'uhul kab uxlajuun (x)* or "holy lands, thirteen-?".

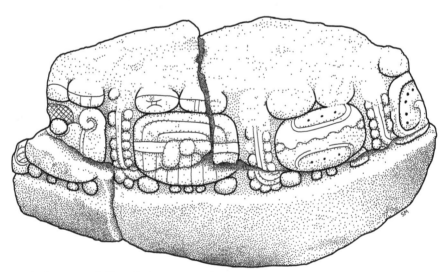

29 A fragment of Altar de los Reyes Altar 3, showing four of the 13 emblem glyphs that originally ringed this monument. From the left: Calakmul, Tikal, Palenque, and probably Altun Ha. (After a photograph by Ivan Šprajc)

This stone is analogous to the "K'atun Wheel", the calendrical display of thirteen *ajaw* dates that together encompass 256 years, found in some Maya documents of the Colonial era (see p.34). There are other pre-contact antecedents for this idea, best seen in a Postclassic sculpture of a turtle (the central metaphor for the surface of the earth) whose carapace is surrounded by 13 *ajaw* day-signs (Taube 1988).

What we have at Altar de los Reyes is a symbolic arrangement of kingships substituting for these temporal-cosmic divisions, not a literal scheme of passing political authority but an idealisation employing the most powerful real-world kingdoms. In a similar vein, the array of four kingdoms aligned to cardinal directions on Copan Stela A did not, as Barthel (1968a, 1968b) supposed, define geographic segments that accorded with expansive political domains, but an ideological statement that reflects politics only to the degree that Tikal, Calakmul, Palenque, and Copan itself bestrode the four quarters as the foremost powers of their time.[4]

Ancestors Above and Below

What we know of the afterlife of the Classic Maya elite must be assembled from scattered clues, since we lack any comprehensive explication of the topic. In outline, it follows an agricultural metaphor and the cycle of maize cultivation, a story that finds close parallels in the sixteenth century Popol Vuh epic of the K'iche' Maya (Taube 1985, 2003, 2004a; Martin 2006b, 2012b). Interment represents a descent into the netherworld analogous to the sowing of the dry kernel, which is sometimes pictured as a skull. In a cave beneath a mountain, symbolised by the tomb and its encompassing pyramid, the soul is separated from the body and rises, much as a germinating seed sprouts and emerges into the light. The Maize God himself, Juun Ixiim, finds symbolic expression in the swaying stalk of the mature plant, his head the cob and hair the flowing corn-silk. It is the harvest of the cob that brings decapitation, but the detached soul allows a rebirth in a bejewelled and flowery paradise in the heavens, where men are fused with the sun and women the moon and look down from the sky. The bones of the ancestors remain underground to enrich the soil and ensure its fertility.

The hieroglyphic term for both "ancestor" and "grandfather" was *mam* (Stuart 2007c[2000]) and parents as well as founding kings are shown fixed within solar or lunar frames according to gender. These same downward-looking, observant characters also appear on shell pectorals, their names introduced with *yuuh mam*, "the jewel of (the) ancestor" (Houston et al. 2006: 50–51). The humanoid masks shown in cutaway or "x-ray" fashion in depictions of performance are likely those of forebears, while the maskettes suspended on belts are sometimes identified by a hieroglyphic headdress as an earlier predecessor or the name of the wearer's own father. While the iconography of ancestor veneration can be flamboyant and supernatural in tenor, they rarely seem to inhabit the same domains as deities.

Part of Patricia McAnany's thesis in her book *Living with the Ancestors* (McAnany 1995: 143–154, 163–165) is that land and its resources were under the control of lineages, adding a strong economic dimension to any consideration of ancestry and descent. The burial of the dead within houses or separate shrines served to assert proprietorship over places and their produce. Royal dynasties do what they can to usurp this system by placing their lineage over all others and make the fruits of inheritance not property per se, but political power. In the process, royal ancestors become the fictive kin of the community and demand group veneration.

PATRON GODS AND PATRON ANCESTORS

Gods particular to individual kingdoms were first recognised at Palenque, where the divine beings dubbed GI, GII, and GIII were each the focus of one of the three temples known as the Group of the Cross (Berlin 1963). Thanks to much subsequent research we know more about these patron deities than we do any others (Kelley 1965; Lounsbury 1976, 1980, 1985; Stuart 2005a: 158–176, 2006a) and they will be a recurring topic in the discussion that follows. Patron deities were long an underexplored topic, but a growing body of knowledge derived from a combination of epigraphic, archaeological, ethnographic, and ethnohistorical data has brought their role into greater relief (Baron 2013, 2016). Wherever we find tutelary gods in the world they express a series of recurring themes that directly engage religious sponsorship with society and politics (Weber 1978: 413–415).

Classic Maya patron deities were "owned" by kings, as expressed by means of the same grammatical form we saw earlier. In this, *k'uh* is marked by the third-person pronoun together with the suffix used for intimate possession to render *uk'uhuul*, "the god of", or equally reversed in sequence as "his/her god". In almost all cases the possessors are rulers, but at least one *yajawk'ahk'* noble is said to own the gods he propitiates, while a *ti'huun*, the K'elen Hix we met in Chapter 5, belongs to a pair of gods, perhaps a status appropriate to his role as caretaker or regent (Zender 2004: table 6, 344). These expressions of belonging never appear with universal gods, such as those of the sky, the sun, storms, and the various deities of the netherworld, only with their lesser aspects and the distinct minor gods tied to localities and individual dynasties.

Royal Prototypes

Each of the Palenque Triad were variants or localised aspects of universal divinities, with GI a version of the piscine storm deity that is associated with the rising sun, while GII is the infant form of personified lightning called *unen k'awiil*, "Baby K'awiil", and GIII is associated with the solar deity K'inich Ajaw. In several deep-time narratives we are told that they were not eternally present, but rather born at a place called *matwiil* within a few days of each other in 2360 BCE. All were the "creation" of another character linked to Juun Ixiim, called in part Muwaan Mat, who was born in 3121 and acceded to lordship – described as the *unaahtal*, "first" such event – in the manner of a human king in 2324 aged 797 years (Stuart 2005a: 180–183).[5] This supernatural being carries the emblem glyph *k'uhul matwiil ajaw*, which is also used by the historical kings of Palenque to express their antique affiliations. Although Muwaan Mat exists in the distant past and has an unnatural lifespan, he performs familiar royal acts, including the conjuring of gods, and falls into a special category of ancestral royal deities.[6]

A deep-time ruler of much the same type appears at Naranjo (Mathews 1977; Martin 1996a: 226; Baron 2013: 169–171, 2016: 59–60). Carrying the *sa'al* emblem glyph of Naranjo, one text places the accession of this character – whose unread name I will gloss here as "Square-nosed Serpent" – some 22,000 years in the past, while another sets it back over 896,000 years. A third, more historical timeframe is suggested by his role in the local count of kings, with one monarch stating that he was his thirty-fifth successor, another his thirty-eighth (Schele 1992b: 140). On Stela 45 at the site the Square-nosed Serpent is shown floating in disembodied form at the top of the scene, the name-glyph on his crown identifying the Naranjo king Naatz Chan Ahk and indicating that their identities have been fused (Tokovinine and Fialko 2007: 10). We know this device from an analogous case on Tikal Stela 31, where the Sun God is merged with the king Yax Nuun Ahiin I, the deceased father of the kingly protagonist standing below (Taube 1992a: 54–55). The name of the Square-nosed Serpent appears among those of at least one later ruler and, interestingly, the same seems to be true for a lord of Holmul, a lesser kingdom with strong Naranjo ties (Tokovinine 2005b: 354–355).

The Tikal dynasty had its own remote deity-ancestor in the form of Sak Hix Muut (Martin and Grube 2000: 50; Stuart 2007d; Baron 2013: 173–174, 2016: 60–61). This character makes its earliest appearance in iconic form on the front of Tikal Stela 29 in 292 CE and his latest in a text carved in 859 on Ixlu Altar 1 (Jones and Satterthwaite 1982: 114–116, figure 81c) – a site whose rulers take up the Mutul emblem glyph of Tikal after the decline of that great capital (p.162). The association therefore endures for almost six centuries, although in mythic terms the relationship was considerably longer. An oversized inscription that adorns the rear and side entablatures of Temple 6 (where individual hieroglyphs reach almost a metre in width), placed at the south-eastern limits of Tikal's ceremonial core, begins with Sak Hix Muut presiding over the completion of the fifth Bak'tun (5.0.0.0.0) in 1143 BCE (Berlin 1951; Jones

1977: 53). In this and later events it carries its own Mutul emblem glyph, as well as other names and titles distinctive to the Tikal dynasty. Another text describes an event at Tikal as taking place "in the *ch'een* of Sak Hix Muut", a further demonstration of this figure's intimate connection with the site and its lineage (Stuart 2007d). While an emblem glyph places it as an archaic founder, the type of actions it performs and its presence within a god list at Ixlu would likely point to *k'uh* status. At this early 1143 BCE date Tikal did not yet exist. If the area was populated at all it was with the early farmers and villagers who had moved away from the main rivers to colonise the interior of the Peten.

All three of these kingly gods served as spiritual cores for their respective kingdoms and their hazy position between supernatural agents and the ancestral dead is somewhat analogous to situations described in Postclassic Central Mexico: "Frequently the patron deity was merged with the deified 'first founder', usually portrayed as a notable participant in the early history of the group. These ostensibly deified ancestral founder-leaders were usually referred to by the generic name *altepeyollotl*, 'heart of the community', or *altepeteotl*, 'community god'" (Nicholson 1971: 409).[7] In sum, for the Classic Maya there was a category of ruler distinct from a patron god who predated historical sequences and initiated specific kingships in a legendary or mythical past.

These references to "deep time" raise the issue of what was notable or distinctive about the religious ideas of the Classic as opposed to those of the Preclassic Period. The highly significant discovery of mythological murals at San Bartolo make it clear that much of the core of Maya cosmology and belief was in place by 100 BCE, with good reason to believe that it is far older (Saturno, Taube, and Stuart 2005; Taube et al. 2010). The Classic Period did not therefore introduce major change to the belief system, but rather assimilated existing ideas about the lordly relationship to the divine into a reconfigured, overtly dynastic, system (see p.323).

Effigies and Embodiments

A near-ubiquitous feature of Mesoamerican divinities is the instantiation of their essence, spirit, or being within effigy figures, sacred bundles, or other material housings (Hvidtfeldt 1958; Townsend 1979: 23–36). Various physical representations of gods are depicted in Classic Maya art, with K'awiil perhaps the most popular of subjects (Figure 30). Some are shown unwrapped from cloth or loosened from tied bundles or back-slings – the latter seemingly the most common way to transport effigies. A good example of the latter appears at Xupa, a satellite of Palenque, where a panel fragment shows a woman bearing a god-image in a back-sling, while she carries a small stacked object that elsewhere serves as a stand or dais, its miniature size indicating that it is intended for the effigy in this case (Miller and Martin 2004: 105, plate 48).

The inscriptions are seldom explicit when it comes to the use of material representations, their concern is much more with the immanent agency of the deities themselves. We have the spelling *winbaah* as a disarticulated stucco glyph at Palenque, a word that survives in Yukatek Maya as "image, figure, portrait" (Houston and Stuart 1996: 302–306; see Barrera Vásquez 1980: 923). A text on Dos Pilas Stela 15 describes the gifting of an effigy from Dos Pilas to Ceibal in 721. It concerns the *nahwaj*, "display, presentation" of some kind of *baah*, "image" of GI-K'awiil, a deity that combines the piscine storm god and the embodiment of lightning, which was an enduring divine patron at Ceibal (Houston et al. 2006: 67) (p.162).[8] Preceding the *baah* sign is another of unknown reading that

30 The presentation of an effigy of K'awiil, the embodiment of lightning and a key expression of royal power. Palenque Temple XIV Panel.

resembles a composite stand similar to the one shown at Xupa. This kind of stacked bundle also has potential analogues in the murals of San Bartolo, thus reaching back to Preclassic times (Saturno et al. 2005: figure 9, 30a, b).

The gifting of a god image from one kingdom to another also seems to be described on Caracol Stela 3. The god in question already appears in local lists, one just three years earlier, so the gift is presumably a new representation of it (Baron 2013: 199, 2016: 62). The relevant verb is *hul*, "to arrive" and the source of the donation was the Kaanul or Snake kingdom. Among the Aztec "alliances between states were confirmed by the exchange of cult effigies" (Townsend 1979: 34), and here the gift was from patron to client.

We see the practice of transporting deities in a sling once again on a carved column from the Campeche region of the northern lowlands, this time in a mythic context where the aged ruler of the Underworld, God L – whose associations include trade and travel – carries K'awiil on his back (Taube 1992a: figure 41a). The analogy to the carrying and swaddling of infants here is in no way coincidental, since a familiar way to define relations between deities and rulers was with *ubaah ujuuntahn*, "the cared/precious one of", the same term used to describe the relationship between children and their mothers (Houston and Stuart 1996: 294). Mesoamerica abounds in the juxtaposed ideas of gods as powerful and dangerous, but at the same time vulnerable and needful of care (Hughes 2016, also Martin 2002).

Such care included the giving of clothes, jewels, and headdresses, which is attested for the Palenque Triad on an all-textual panel in the Temple of Inscriptions at the site (Macri 1997: 91–92; Stuart 2005a: 166–167). Though not specified as such, here we are clearly dealing with the dressing of effigies, objects that may typically have been made of wood or some other perishable material, given their absence in the archaeological record here and elsewhere. A rare survival comes in the four staff-mounted models of K'awiil found in Burial 195 at Tikal (Moholy-Nagy 2008: 55–56, figure 232). The wood from which they had been carved had rotted away completely, but their form was preserved by their blue/green-painted stucco coatings, recovered intact from a layer of hardened mud. Case Study 8 describes over-sized effigies that were carried on litters, and these must also have been made of lightweight and highly perishable materials.

The portability of embodiments would have been especially relevant when migrations established new settlements and political domains, as amply described for Postclassic Central Mexico (e.g. Nicholson 1971: 409–410; Schroeder 1991: 122–123, 145–147). When the Mexica are shown journeying from their homeland they carry sacred bundles tied across their backs in much the same manner as the Maya (see Boone 1991: figure 8.3). These wrappings contained relics and magical paraphernalia, as well as an image of their ethnic god Huitzilopochtli.

For the highland Maya of Guatemala, a similar diaspora is described in the Popol Vuh, reflecting a pan-Mesoamerican trope. Here the four lineage founders of the K'iche' each receive their tutelary god at Tulan – the legendary source of political legitimacy for much of Postclassic Mesoamerica – and carry away their effigies on their backs (Christenson 2003: 211–212). Significantly, the failure of one of these men to sire male heirs meant the extinction of his lineage as well as his god, which disappears from the story at this point (Christenson 2003: 212, n.554). This connection serves to emphasise the link between such gods and lordly bloodlines over and above those of localities or communities. That these late accounts are archetypes rather than historical accounts only emphasises that they express central concepts of political legitimacy, the means by which authority could be uprooted, transported, and sown again in fresh lands (Smith 1984; Boone 1991; Sachse and Christenson 2005; Sachse 2008).

Gods' Houses

A key activity and component of settled space was the construction of shrines to house deities and venerate ancestors; buildings not infrequently set on the eastern side of plaza groups or the eastern portions of site cores (Becker 1971, 1999; Haviland 1981). Texts inside some of those shrines describe their dedication and ownership, at times specifying them as the *otoot*, "dwelling" or *wayib*, "sleeping place" of particular gods (see Stuart 1998: 376–379, 399–402). Similarly, ancestral shrines among the Postclassic K'iche' of the highlands were called *warabal ja*, "sleeping houses" (Carmack 1981: 161; Freidel, Schele, and Parker 1993: 188–189). This suggests dormitories in which deities or ancestors were thought to rest between their periodic emergence and display in ceremonies and parades. The concept is illustrated by small shrine models uncovered at Copan (Grube and Schele 1990; Andrews and Fash 1992: figures 16 and 17; Houston and Inomata 2009: 200–201; Prager 2013: 446–453). These show the generic *k'uh* anthropomorph standing in the doorway of a thatched building, while texts on the roofs and sides describe each structure as the *wayib* of a patron god of the Copan dynasty.

For a full-size version of a god house we can turn to the aforementioned Tikal Temple 6, where a monumental text on the back of the structure's tall crest or roofcomb describes it as the *wayib* of Sak Hix Muut (Houston and Stuart 1989: 11–13; Stuart 2007d; Baron 2013: 174). That passage dates the dedication of the building to 766, making it the work of the little-known twenty-eighth Tikal ruler, although elsewhere the text makes clear that he was reworking a structure originally built by his father Yihk'in Chan K'awiil in 735 (Martin 2015b). This was less than a year after the king's accession and his building was actually modifying a still earlier temple that lies just one metre below its surface. As we will later see, Yihk'in Chan K'awiil was a conqueror whose political successes were manifested in a major redevelopment of Tikal (Martin 1996a: 233, 2001c: 186, 2003b: 31).

We can identify a similar process at Palenque. There the three lavishly decorated temples of the Cross Group, whose inner enclosures house carved relief panels and long inscriptions combining dynastic and mythic information are said to be the *pibnaah*, "sweatbath/oven" of the Triad gods (Houston 1996; Stuart 2006a: 109). Dedicated together in 692, they were built by K'inich Kaan Bahlam II and constituted his major architectural contribution to the city. They came just five years after his most important military triumph, which was commemorated inside one of them, the war-themed Temple of the Sun dedicated to GIII (Case Study 12) (Figure 31). At both Tikal and Palenque, we might therefore detect not simply grateful propitiations to influential deities, but expressions of the recently acquired economic wherewithal to carry them out.[9]

A political dimension to the construction of *wayib* temples also emerges in recent work at La Corona, home to a dependent dynasty of Calakmul from which most of the "Site Q" monuments originated (Stuart, in Schuster 1997). In 2005 a perfectly preserved, two-part panel was found inside the ruined structure labelled 13R-5, and its extensive text offers valuable connections

31 Palenque's Temple of the Sun, one of three temples that make up the Group of the Cross, which was dedicated to the local patron deity GIII in 692. (Photograph by Linda Schele, courtesy of David Schele)

between historical and archaeological evidence (Canuto et al. 2006; Baron 2013; also Guenter 2005b; David Stuart, pers. comm. 2005). The panel concerns the dedication of a patron god's *wayib* by the local ruler K'inich Yook in 677. But the panel also mentions the dedication of three earlier *wayib* by his father Chakaw Nahb Kaan in 658, each ascribed to one of La Corona's patron deities. The best candidates for these buildings are the line of three structures adjacent to 13R-5, and archaeological and epigraphic data combine to tell us something about their development and historical significance.

As Joanne Baron (2013: 352–361) notes, their joint dedication came just thirty-five days after Chakaw Nahb Kaan's accession to the throne of La Corona and the same-day killing of the previous ruler K'uk' Ajaw, as detailed in Chapter 6. Excavation confirmed that these three buildings amounted to a single contemporary phase and that they were remodellings of existing structures. Adding a veneer only 50 cm deep in places and surmounted by wattle-and-daub superstructures, this suggests that they were hastily made. Clearly, Chakaw Nahb Kaan wanted to imprint himself on the site by putting up a major work as soon as he practically could – much as Yihk'in Chan K'awiil was to do at Tikal. However, the earlier phases of the three La Corona buildings, which are Early Classic in date, contain wealthy burials, a sign that they were previously used as ancestral shrines. The speedy emphasis on gods over ancestors may have served a political purpose for the new king, redirecting or blocking the veneration of those dead lords, perhaps linked to the dynastic struggle made clear by Chakaw Nahb Kaan's violent path to power.

Patrons of War

Unsurprisingly, Classic Maya kingdoms were much concerned with their fortunes in war, the ultimate guarantor of their liberty and means of material gain, and this was a thematic focus of several patron deities and their sub-variants.[10] A leading concept here is that expressed by the metaphorical couplet of a flint-blade and shield; an icon that could be possessed by deities as well as conjured in the same manner that deities themselves were conjured. Thanks to occasional substitutions of syllabic spellings its component logographs have been deciphered: with **pa-ka-la** providing the key to reading **PAKAL**, "shield" (Kelley 1968: 257–258) and **to-k'a** likewise revealing **TOOK'**, "flint" (Houston 1983a).

The martial connotations of this combination were first noted by Jean Genet (1934: 24–27).[11] He compared its appearances in the Postclassic Maya codices with metaphorical terms in Colonial Maya documents and literary sources from Central Mexico, arguing that it represented the general idea of "war". This is an issue which we will return to in Chapter 9, but for the moment we will simply consider *took'pakal* as an emblematic representation of martial power. It appears in a number of illuminating iconographic contexts, notably where a representation of it is unwrapped from a bundle as a virtual deity (Schele and Miller 1986: 115–116) (Figure 32).

32 The presentation of a *took'pakal*, "flint (and) shield" war icon. Palenque Palace Tablet. (Drawing by Linda Schele, courtesy of David Schele)

Yaxchilan Lintel 25 supplies a vivid representation of a conjuring involving the *took'pakal* and a text that directly links political rejuvenation to a local deity (Figure 33). The scene is dominated by a sinuous beast, part-snake part-centipede,

33 Yaxchilan's Shield Jaguar III, armed with spear and shield and wearing the mask of the Teotihuacan storm god, is "conjured" in the form of the city's principal patron deity by his wife Ix K'abal Xook. Yaxchilan Lintel 25. (Photograph by Justin Kerr)

from whose maw emerges a portrait of the king Shield Jaguar III armed with a lance and shield. Meanwhile his wife, whose bloodletting rite has invoked the apparition, looks on (Freidel, Schele, and Parker 1993: 308–309; Martin and Grube 2000: 125; Miller and Martin 2004: 100, 108; Stuart 2005e: 279–281). The king wears a mask and headdress drawn directly from the iconography of Teotihuacan and, indeed, the whole image is drenched in the style of that once-great, but by that time fallen, metropolis of Central Mexico. The event takes place on the day the king acceded to office in 681 and the text describes the scene with *utzakaw uk'awiilil utook'(u)pakal aj k'ahk' o' chahk*, "She conjures the power of, the flint and shield of, Aj K'ahk' O' Chahk" – this being the leading patron deity of Yaxchilan. The appearance of *k'awiil* in the abstractive form *k'awiilil,* signifying some essence or quality of the lightning bolt, is the same embodiment of power and authority we saw on Xunantunich Panel 4. In this case it tells us that the king stands as the human instantiation of Aj K'ahk' O' Chahk's martial power.

Taken as a whole, Lintel 25 is an overt claim to Yaxchilan's rebirth as a sovereign entity, a kingdom which was, at the point this scene was carved in 723, emerging from many years of silence and probable subordination to a foreign power (Miller 1991; Martin and Grube 2000: 121–126). That this particular image, among all of the many royal tableaux at Yaxchilan, is rendered *à la mode mexique* is especially telling. The Classic Maya, as a whole, clearly perceived Teotihuacan as both an indomitable military icon and source of political legitimation, not simply by dint of its reputation but because of their own contacts and asymmetrical relationship with that great city in the Early Classic Period (p.122–126 and 241–243).

This takes us to a much wider body of images in which Classic Maya kings don the garb of Teotihuacan warriors (Stone 1989). These costumes frequently depict the Teotihuacan war serpent deity, called Waxaklajuun Ubaah Kaan by the Maya, often in the form of an enveloping plated headdress in which the face of the wearer appears in its open maw (Taube 1992b, 2000) (Figure 34a). There were also occasions in which direct impersonation of this god took place (Houston and Stuart 1996: 299) or it was "conjured" into being (Freidel, Schele, and Parker 1993: 309–310) (Figure 34b). This last ritual, in particular, demonstrates that the Maya were not simply evoking the general idea of Teotihuacan militarism, they were actively enlisting its most potent war god into their own service. Although only partially preserved today, Tikal Temple 1 Lintel 2 was once a splendid example of Central Mexican iconography in wood, featuring a towering effigy of Waxaklajuun Ubaah Kaan (a fragment of the name survives in the text) above a portrait of a local king suitably bedecked in Teotihuacan war-gear (Schele and Freidel 1990: 209; Taube 1992b: 68–69; Stuart 2000: 490). The giant figure is more clearly seen in a contemporary graffito on the wall of a palace building at Tikal (Trik and Kampen 1983: figure 52b).

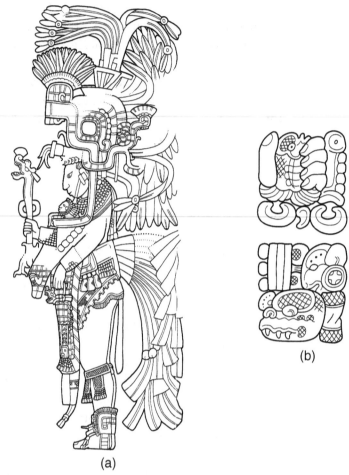

(a)

(b)

34 The Teotihuacan war serpent Waxaklajuun Ubaah Kaan as invoked by the Classic Maya: (a) Worn as a costume on Bonampak Stela 3; (b) A "conjuring" of this deity described on Copan Stela I.

Other lintels at Tikal are in better condition and these offer profound insights into the significance of patron gods to warfare (Martin 1996a, 2000c: 113–122). As we will see in Case Study 8, the depicted structures are palanquins that carried the king under the symbolic protection of a god, and a major topic of the accompanying texts is the capture and subsequent display of effigies and their litters. This forms part of a Mesoamerican, indeed worldwide, pattern in which human struggles are played out in a supernatural plane, where the political identity invested in models of tutelary gods made them targets for seizure.

In the Bonampak battle mural of Structure 1, Room 2 we see a box carried aloft in the midst of the fighting (Miller and Brittenham 2013: 100) (Figure 44, at far right). It seems to be saluted or blessed by someone bearing a feathered whisk in one hand and a severed head in the other. Clearly something of value, the box might have an analogous role to that of the patrons at Tikal and contain a god image or sacred bundle, making it another kind of "participant" in the battle.

The Yaxchilan patron Aj K'ahk' O' Chahk appears in another context, this time one that reveals something of the religious rationalisation of warfare (Houston et al. 2006: 123). On Lintel 35 at that city a subordinate of the Dzibanche king seized in 537 is said to be *uwe'iy*, "the eating of" both this god and a fellow Yaxchilan patron. The implication is that the deities were sustained by defeated foes, probably at the moment of their ritualised death.

A further aspect of patron deity identification arises in a comparison of texts from Naranjo and Yaxha. Yaxha Stela 31 records the capture of a ruler of Ucanal by the local king K'inich Lakamtuun in 796 that was, unusually, "supervised" by one or two versions of the "Jaguar God of the Underworld" (JGU).[12] The same local patron or patrons appear in very different circumstances just three years later on Naranjo Stela 35, here at the climax to a series of battles fought between the two kingdoms in 799.[13] The inscription begins with a primordial *puluuyi*, "burning" event that tells of a mythic immolation of the JGU by four young gods (Schele and Mathews 1998: 148). Scenes on painted vases supply depictions of the same event with a matching deep-time date. The front of Stela 35 shows a re-enactment of the myth, with the kneeling Yaxha king in the role of the JGU and the Naranjo king, suitably equipped with a giant torch, as the agent of his demise (Martin 1997b; Martin and Grube 2000: 82). One passage specifies that someone, presumably the defeated Yaxha king himself, is decapitated inside a deity temple.[14] Both here and in another version of the same event on Stela 12, the agent is the victorious king of Naranjo.

These texts demonstrate that mythological tropes had a part to play in the conceptualisation of Maya warfare. However, this specific myth seems to have been prompted opportunistically by Yaxha's close association with the JGU – an association Naranjo itself shared through another aspect of this deity – and in that sense, was contingent rather than part of some formulaic charter for war. Indeed, it is notable how *rarely* war is presented within a supernatural paradigm in Classic Maya patrimonial rhetoric, this case is all but unique.

Shifting and Adding Patrons

By tracking the references to patron gods through time it becomes clear that their associations to kings or kingdoms were not fixed. Changes in a given line-up of deities are significant where they coincide with transfers of regime or other developments in which political reality impinged on a theological construction.

Though the evidence is limited, we see such a case in the migration that brings a Mutul line originating at Tikal first to Dos Pilas and then Aguateca.

A glimpse of the newcomer's divine identity comes on Dos Pilas Stela 9, where a portrait of Bajlaj Chan K'awiil shows him wearing a feathered backrack containing the image of a supernatural feline called *wak hixnal winik*. Such assemblages are worn by the Maize God in his localised or kingdom-specific variants, and this spotted cat is identified as the one attached to Tikal in its accompanying caption – as we will shortly see in a fuller examination of this complex in Case Study 7 (Figure 35). Another monument, one of the much-destroyed panels from the main three-sanctuary temple at Dos Pilas, refers to a star deity that is very prominent at Tikal, though also like one that serves as a founding king at Dos Pilas's older neighbour Tamarindito (Houston 1993: 100–101).[15]

Similarly, when Bajlaj Chan K'awiil's son Itzamnaaj K'awiil succeeds him in 698 he is said to do so in the company of a set of gods only otherwise seen at Ixlu some 161 years later (Mathews 2001a[1979]: 399). We have already noted that the Ixlu dynasty was itself a splinter or descendent of that at Tikal, one that continued the veneration of ancestral gods such as Sak Hix Muut. At Dos Pilas, Itzamnaaj K'awiil would later begin to pivot toward a deity distinctive to his local Petexbatun and Pasión regions, GI-K'awiil, whose veneration seems to have been specially focussed on the ancient centre of Ceibal. On the same day in 721 that the king gifted or unveiled an effigy of this god at Ceibal he dedicated a stela to it at Aguateca (Stuart and Houston 1994: 90–92; Houston and Stuart 1996: 301–302; Baron 2013: 450–455, 2016: 90–91). By the time the Mutul kings of the Petexbatun were ruling from Aguateca in 741, GI-K'awiil was preeminent within their pantheon and oversaw their period ending rituals. The same god is said to oversee the accession of Aguateca's vassal at the small centre of La Amelia, home to another Mutul lord. In securing the services of this deity, the new regime seems to have balanced contrasting notions of local and lineage-based divinity, its efforts to embed its authority in a new land casting some faint light on the transposability of regional and dynastic gods.

The wide distribution of the *baakal* emblem in the western Maya region offers a further opportunity to observe the relationship between political authority and patron deity concepts. By the middle of the seventh century Palenque, Tortuguero, and Comalcalco claimed a common title and show other forms of connection, including their architectural styles (Case Study 1). The little we know of Tortuguero gods (Gronemeyer and MacLeod 2010: 59; Baron 2013: 532–535) shows no overlap with those of Palenque, a clear hint to their political separation. A much fuller inventory of tutelary gods comes to us from Comalcalco, where the pendants from Urn 26 describe ten or more deemed worthy of veneration. Interestingly, among them is Unen K'awiil, the god we know as GII at Palenque (Marc Zender, pers. comm. 2000; Zender 2004: table 6, figures 69 and 70). Unen K'awiil was an intimate of Palenque kings and the stucco piers of the Temple of Inscriptions show a series of historical monarchs, each cradling the infant lightning god. With Comalcalco 152 km distant from Palenque it is difficult to see how localism can have been a factor in the appearance of Unen K'awiil there and much easier to accept that the attachment stemmed from their shared dynastic title.

In a ceremony performed in 656 a lord is elevated to the rulership of the Cancuen polity, a centre almost 234 km to the south of Calakmul – as detailed in Chapter 6. This is not only supervised by the Calakmul king Yuknoom Ch'een II, it is "overseen" by a list of Calakmul deities. To be sanctioned by foreign gods in this way, in the complete absence of Cancuen's own dynastic deities, admitted as much in its own account, identifies Calakmul at the site of the ceremony (Guenter 2002: 6). Moreover, this suggests a strong political dimension in which subordination could be embedded not only in secular but divine power (Baron 2016: 168–169).

We will conclude this review at Copan, the centre with the richest collection of divine protectors. Two of the most prominent, Baluun K'awiil and Chan Te' Ch'oktaak, appear by the middle of the sixth century and are steadily joined by others over the next 200 years (Baron 2013: 219, 416–448; Prager 2013: 372–375). Indeed, each ruler makes a point of augmenting the list with his own additions – though whether these are promotions from the lower echelons of Copan's supernatural inventory or true innovations is unknown. The reign of the thirteenth king Waxaklajuun Ubaah K'awiil is typical in adding two gods, Mo' Witz Ajaw and K'uy Saak Ajaw, to which he devoted special iconographic programmes on particular stelae.

A fascinating development came in 2011 with the discovery of a hieroglyphic stairway at El Palmar detailing a local dignitary's visit to Copan in 726, noted in Chapter 5. Although the context is not entirely clear, the three most prominent Copan deities are listed in that text and the visitor's interaction with them was clearly a matter of importance. A further outside mention of Copan deities comes at Quirigua in 738, though in much less agreeable circumstances since it relates to the capture and execution of Waxaklajuun Ubaah K'awiil by his one-time vassal (Houston and Stuart 1996: 302; Looper 1999: 268–269, 2003: 78–79). Stela I at Quirigua records a date six days before his beheading that involves two of the Copan gods named at El Palmar. Although the verbal phrase here is poorly understood, the implication is that Waxaklajuun Ubaah K'awiil's divine support was in some way undermined, perhaps in a manner like those on the Tikal lintels in Case Study 8, where the seizure of gods parallels that of their owners.

Copan recovers from its setback and its interest in patron gods reaches a new pitch in the reign of its sixteenth and last true king, Yax Pasaj Chan Yopaat. He makes his own additions and in two texts refers to the collective as *koknoom uxwintik*, "guardians (of) Copan" (Stuart, in Stuart, Houston, and Robertson 1999: II–59; Houston and Inomata 2009: 204; Baron 2013: 219; Prager 2013:

372–375). This phrase is unique to Copan and it is hard to know if the concept is so familiar as to escape mention elsewhere, or whether the king is consciously extending the ambit of dynastic gods to a locality.

Yax Pasaj Chan Yopaat is also responsible for the greatest spectacle of otherworldly oversight at Copan, which comes on a carved step inside Temple 11 (Schele and Miller 1986: 121–126, plate 36). Here the king's accession in 763 is attended by massed ranks of gods and ancestors, each shown as lords sitting on their own name-glyphs. Although there are distinctions to the figures' costumes and accoutrements, these are not systematic and the overall sense is that they form a common body summoned from whatever unworldly quarter they reside in. It is surely relevant that Temple 11 stands on an earlier phase with its own dedicatory step identifying it as a *k'uhul naah*, "holy house" of the Copan dynasty, of which the first six kings are named as its "owners" (Prager and Wagner 2008). The earliest ancestral king on both monuments is the historical founder of the dynasty K'inich Yax K'uk' Mo'. Though he is never deified as such, the sacral character of the dead king is manifested through multiple versions of the Structure 16 mortuary shrine that covered his (probable) tomb (Taube 2004b). Like other male ancestors, he is here equated with the sun god K'inich Ajaw and the iconographic programmes make clear that his identity had been fused with that of the avian solar realm.

CASE STUDY 7: PATRON MAIZE DANCERS

In addition to the gods who reside in particular locations, those intimately connected to dynasties as prototypical kings, and those adopted as patrons of war, there is at least one further category of divinity linked to individual Classic Maya kingdoms. The handsome young Maize God was a universal deity of fertility and fecundity, his natural cycle of harvesting, sowing, and sprouting serving as the central metaphor of life and death for Maya kings (Taube 1985). However, like many other supernatural beings, the Maize God had different aspects or permutations and these included localised varieties responsible for the sustaining bounty of a certain place, or more precisely the domain of a particular kingship.

The life-size, swaying stalks in the cornfield readily evoke the idea of dance, and the god of maize was perceived to be a dancer who wore elaborate costumes whose tall "backrack" symbolised a layered cosmos. Rulers donned that same attire to emulate his performance, no doubt one of many efforts to propitiate an abundant harvest. Although royal impersonators are occasionally depicted on monuments (p.162), most of the images we have are of the god, or rather gods, on painted cylinder vases (Reents-Budet 1991; Grube 1992; Houston, Stuart, and Taube 1992; Looper, Reents-Budet, and Bishop 2009: 117–131; Tokovinine 2013: 115–122) (Figure 35). Numbering between one and

35 The Tikal-specific version of the Maize God featuring its jaguar patron in the backrack and a caption that describes his "ascending" at Mutul. K503.

four on each vessel, each of them dances with an accompanying dwarf or hunchback, regular companions of the corn god.

What distinguishes the dancing maize deities as separate versions are the small creatures that nestle in the midst of their backrack cosmograms. These are identified in their appended glyphic captions and specify the place or kingdom to which each refers. The example illustrated here is the same spotted cat noted on Dos Pilas Stela 9, whose caption reads *ubaah juun ixiim *wak hixnal (winik)* or "The image of One Maize, Six Cat-Place (Person)", completed here by the pairing *t'abaayi mutul*, "ascends (at) Tikal". There are several variants of this final section, another gives the passage *tahn ch'een k'uhul mutul ajaw*, "(in the) midst of the domain of the Holy Tikal Lord". Evidently local maize gods emerged in the heart of the kingdom or, in still another version, acceded to the ultimate lordly rank of *kaloomte'* there. We find the same *wak hixnal winik* version of the deity delicately incised on animal bones from Tikal Burial 116. These scenes depict the universal myth in which the corn deity is ferried across a primordial body of water by the two Paddler Gods, en route to the Underworld. This shows us how a local divine consciousness was embedded within a wider mythscape, such that the two could effortlessly coexist.

The contrasting version for Calakmul was called *juun ixiim wak chanal winik*, "One Maize, Six Sky-Place Person", which usually appears in the backrack in the form of an anthropomorphised serpent. Interestingly, the same hybrid appears in the costume worn by the client king of La Corona (Stuart 2015).[16] This is a small but valuable insight into the way that subject dynasties, doubtless linked to their overlords by blood ties, were integrated not only politically but in terms of religious beliefs. In this way La Corona, whose lords otherwise venerated its own local deities, was still part of an overarching divine scheme.

The great majority of the maize dancer vessels are painted in the distinctive red-on-white style produced in or close to Naranjo. Yet the corn deity specific to that kingdom is either absent or is one of the creatures not identified by a legible caption – we see various unattributed monkeys, dogs, gophers, vultures, squirrels, peccaries, among other beasts in these contexts. The key point to note is that two kingdom-specific dancers predominate, those distinguished by the spotted cat of Tikal and the serpent of Calakmul. Indeed, in most cases these are the only featured dancers. An illustrative example here is the finely executed vase excavated at Buenavista del Cayo (Houston, Stuart, and Taube 1992). Its rim text names its owner as the Naranjo king K'ahk' Tiliw Chan Chahk and it may well have been a gift to the ruler of this secondary centre and small polity. Even so, its twin corn gods are those of the two great hegemons.[17] In another case, the grandson of that same Naranjo king was the owner of a plate excavated at Holmul, which shows the Tikal maize deity dancing alone. Why was such interest lavished on these two polities in particular?

The Naranjo line could certainly claim links to both, being related to the Mutul dynasty of Dos Pilas through blood and to the Kaanul dynasty of Calakmul by its political allegiance. However, on some higher, transcendent level it plausibly represents an effort to conceptualise the pre-eminence of these players. The kingdoms buffeted by Tikal and Calakmul through time, as Naranjo certainly was, seem to have rationalised their ascendency in symbolic terms, as a core dyad sanctioned on a divine plane. That this is an idealised concept is all the more clear when one considers that the great majority of these vessels date to the late eighth century. By that time only Mutul held real political power and a grand duopoly could be no more than a wistful remembrance.

CASE STUDY 8: GIANT EFFIGIES AT TIKAL

The largest wooden artworks to survive from the ancient Maya world, without much argument the finest as well, are a series of lintels that once spanned doorways within the sanctuaries of three of Tikal's tallest stepped pyramids (Jones and Satterthwaite 1982: 97–103). They consist of abutted beams of sapodilla wood, deeply carved and burnished to a glossy finish on their undersides. The scenes and texts on the lintels from Temples 1 and 4 convey key information about patron deities and the use of effigies (Martin 1996a, 2000c). All show enthroned kings enclosed by a towering figure atop a tiered and decorated platform. One of these objects shows lashed poles at its base, identifying the structures as litters or palanquins carried by teams of bearers, as confirmed by graffiti from the walls of other Tikal buildings (Jones 1987: 108). The over-sized figures are not, therefore, imagined apparitions but physical models, doubtless made from lightweight wood, paper, and textile, like those we might find on a carnival float or the giant litters used to parade the images of Catholic patron saints in Latin America today.

Texts accompany the scenes and in each of the three well-preserved examples the central topic is warfare, recounting Tikal victories over Calakmul (on Temple 1 Lintel 3), El Peru (on Temple 4 Lintel 3), and Naranjo (on Temple 4 Lintel 2). These carry detailed accounts, by Classic Maya standards at least, which contribute information of historical importance (see Chapter 9). Here, however, I will focus attention on the light they cast on the role and meaning of patron deity systems.

Temple 1 Lintel 3 celebrates the achievements of Jasaw Chan K'awiil I, who defeated the Calakmul king Yuknoom Yich'aak K'ahk' in 695 in a *jubuuyi utook' pakal*, "his weapons are knocked down" event (Schele and Freidel 1990: 205–207). This success marked a historical turning point and the start of an extended process of decline for Calakmul, counterpoised by a rise in the fortunes of Tikal (Martin 1996a: 233; Martin and Grube 2000: 44–45). On the same day as this victory we learn that *baaknaj yajaw maan*, "Yajaw Maan is captured". Inscriptions at Calakmul and elsewhere tell us that Yajaw Maan was an important patron deity of the dynasty and we can conclude that some representation of it was taken into battle and seized by the enemy.

The text goes on to describe a ceremony performed forty days after the battle that involved the lifting or carrying of the litter, called here the *nuun? bahlamnal*.[18] Since *bahlam* is "jaguar" it presumably describes the giant jaguar effigy in the scene and identifies that palanquin. The same carrying verb and named subject are recorded on Calakmul Stela 89 from 731, confirming its connection to the site and indicating that such models were made and remade for generations.

Supernatural beliefs have had an influence on the conduct of warfare and its interpretation throughout history, with battle outcomes attributed to divine will or even to the result of contests between rival tutelary deities (Weber 1978: 413). It is not unusual for such gods to be represented in effigy form on the battlefield and later lost to enemy action (for one of a number of Mesopotamian cases see Liverani 2001: 104).

This practice was also a recurring one in Mesoamerica, not least among the Aztec (Hassig 1988: 8–10). Not only did they carry their own divine effigies into battle (Sahagún 1979: II.8.17), but their wars involved the seizure of the enemy's gods, which were returned to the Aztec capital of Tenochtitlan and installed in a building called the *coateocalli* that was dedicated to such divine captives (Durán 1967: 2, 439; Townsend 1979: 36; Hassig 1988: 105). This was a strategy by which they "absorbed and usurped the cults of the vanquished, undermining their claims to an independent spiritual identity" (Houston and Stuart 1996: 302).

Effigies were no less important to the Postclassic Maya. The early chronicler Villagutierre Soto Mayor (1985: 540) tells us that the Itza Maya of the central lowlands "had two other idols worshiped as gods of battle; one called Pakoc and the other Hexchunchan. These were carried when they went to fight the *cinamitas*, their neighbours and mortal enemies . . .". Other parallels are found in the highlands, where the K'iche' took an image of their supreme god Tohil to the battlefield, but were defeated and forced to surrender it (Carmack 1981: 138; Otzoy 1999: 178). It is also from K'iche' sources that we learn that kings could be taken into battle riding a litter – indeed, one ruler is said to have been knocked down from one and killed (Fuentes y Guzmán 1932–1933: 7, 39–40; Carmack 1981: 140).

Jasaw Chan K'awiil was succeeded by his son Yihk'in Chan K'awiil in 734 and the new king continued the struggle against Calakmul, capturing one of its kings or high nobles before 736 (Martin 2005a: 11–12, figure 9). Within a decade, Yihk'in Chan K'awiil had exploited his growing superiority to attack two of the Snake kingdom's most important clients, El Peru and Naranjo. The first of these is recorded on Temple 4 Lintel 3, which describes a "star war" victory at the site of Yaxa' in 743 (Table 3). This was not the well-known site of that name on Lake Yaxha but a namesake said to be *elk'in waka'*, "East (of) Waka'" or "Eastern Waka" – Waka' being the toponym that can be attributed to El Peru, 80 km due west of Tikal (Martin 2000c: 119–122). One candidate here might be Laguna Perdida, a large lake with a site on its shores 61 km from Tikal, whose limited inscriptional record shows some ties to El Peru. The triumphal party subsequently returned to their city, with the statement *ihuli mutul*, "then arrives at Tikal", although this is not entirely fixed in time (if this was on the day after the action then Yaxa' must be somewhere closer to Tikal).

This conflict resulted in the *baakwaj*, "capture" of the El Peru king's personal deity, a version of the death god Akan. Tikal chose to celebrate the success in 746, exactly three *haab* years later, an occasion on which Yihk'in Chan K'awiil was carried on the splendid serpent throne shown in the lintel scene.[19] The latter is here called "the god of" the Tikal king, suggesting its appropriation, his performance constituting the symbolic transfer of its powers from El Peru to Tikal (see Baron 2013: 210).

These themes are repeated on Temple 4 Lintel 2, which recounts the campaign Yihk'in Chan K'awiil launched just 191 days after his success over El Peru (Martin 1996a) (Figure 36). The target on this occasion was Naranjo, 40 km to the east of Tikal. Although there had been close links between the two kingdoms in earlier times, since at least 546 Naranjo had been under the domination of the Snake dynasty and had been an opponent of Tikal in the seventh century. In February 744, the Tikal king conducts a preparatory rite of

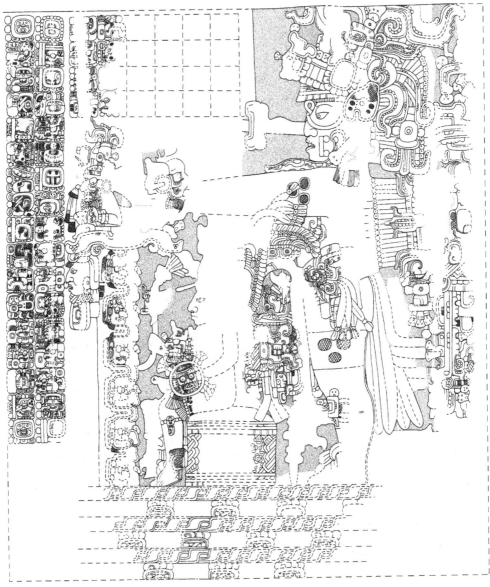

36 Yihk'in Chan K'awiil of Tikal seated within a captured palanquin featuring a giant effigy of the Naranjo war patron. Tikal Temple 4 Lintel 2. (Drawing by William R. Coe, University of Pennsylvania Museum)

some kind and then arrives at Tuubal (Zender 2005a: 14). Since the assault on Naranjo came only a day later this information should help to locate this unidentified centre, for which the city now known as Nakum is the best, if not the only, candidate.[20]

The subsequent attack on Naranjo is described, in rather elliptical language, as a "star war" against the *ch'een* of Naranjo's divine ancestral king the Square-nosed Serpent (p.151). This is followed by another capture event and the names of several deities belonging to Yax Mayuy Chan Chahk, the Naranjo monarch who was almost certainly a son and successor of the great K'ahk' Tiliw Chan Chahk, gaining power sometime after 727 (Martin et al. 2017). Damage to the text on Lintel 2 cuts short our view of the celebratory rites that took place in 747, but enough remains to know that Yihk'in Chan K'awiil was borne on a *tz'unun pi'it*, "hummingbird litter" – an object that takes first position in the list of supernatural captives (Figure 37a).[21]

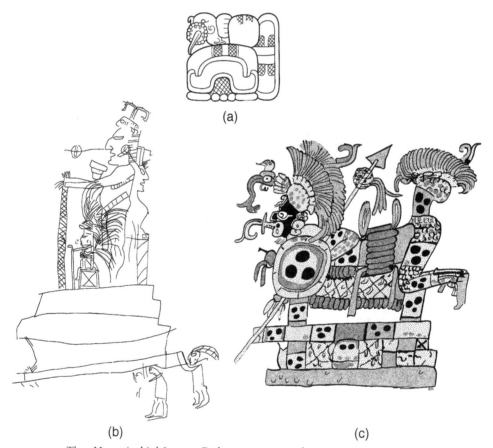

(a)

(b)   (c)

37 The Hummingbird-Jaguar God war patron of Naranjo: (a) Hieroglyph for the hummingbird palanquin from Tikal Temple 4 Lintel 2; (b) Graffito in Tikal Structure 5D-65 Room 9. (Drawing by Michael E. Kampen, University of Pennsylvania Museum); (c) The Naranjo war palanquin pictured on the vessel K7716

The giant figure on the lintel lacks any immediate resemblance to a hummingbird, and what we see instead is an anthropomorphic jaguar deity equipped with a prominent feline ear, a cord looped around the eyes indicative of the Jaguar God of the Underworld, and a body marked by groups of three dark spots. Crucially, the platform base is decorated by recurring *sa'al* signs, the heart of the emblem glyph and political identity of Naranjo. Wherever it might be carried, the god stood on the ground of the kingdom it protected.

As in the case of Temple 1 Lintel 2, we have a graffito that shows the same object, this time clearly carried aloft by bearers (Figure 37b). Both versions show a projection from the figure's head with a disk partway along it, an object that is damaged on the lintel and only cursively etched in the graffito. Its significance is revealed by a painted vessel, K7716, providing a third version of this effigy. This image is significantly earlier, produced for the long-lived Naranjo king Aj Numsaaj Chan K'inich, who was in power from 546 to at least 612. The scene shows him sitting on a canopied throne. Behind we see a black-faced jaguar deity, armed with a spear and shield and marked with the same sets of three spots, lying in a prone position atop a palanquin roof (this is either visually compressed to fit the limited height of the vessel, or more likely accurately portrays a partially assembled structure that would have included the king's throne) (Figure 37c). As Karl Taube (pers. comm. 2001) points out, the projection is clearly an elongated bird's beak, while the disk, here shown edge-on, is recognisable as the pierced flower that is diagnostic of hummingbirds. Each of these pictured effigies, therefore, represents a hummingbird-jaguar deity that served as the war patron of Naranjo.[22] The vase representation further establishes its extended history at this polity, where it was clearly invoked by generations of its kings.

What the Tikal lintels collectively convey is the importance put on seizing rival deities in war and the performances that celebrated and retold these events. Such triumphs – in the original Roman sense of the word – were not only self-glorifications, they sought to nullify or abrogate the spiritual power of their vanquished enemies. The painted Naranjo vessel confirms that such litters were local productions which, however cumbersome, must have been exposed to capture in war (though the El Peru version may be a separate case). In whatever way they were employed, as transport to the battlefield, as command posts, or battle standards, they express a belief in divine protectors with supernatural powers, a force they hoped to enlist to their aid.

Yihk'in Chan K'awiil's lintels focus on the fate of gods, but his Stela 5 and its partnering Altar 2 demonstrate that these serve as mirrors to the fortunes of

TABLE 3 *Timeline*

Long Count	CE	Greg.	Event
9.15.10.0.0	741	Jul 1	Period ending (anchor date)
9.15.12.2.2	743	Aug 2	Star war against Yaxa' (Elk'in Waka')
9.15.12.2.3	743	Aug 3	Unknown event followed by a return to Tikal
9.15.12.11.12	744	Feb 8	Ceremony performed and then a "descent" to Tuubal
9.15.12.11.13	744	Feb 9	Star war against Naranjo
9.15.15.2.3	746	Jul 18	God impersonation and palanquin ceremony for El Peru victory
9.15.15.14.0	747	Mar 12	Palanquin ceremony for Naranjo victory

their respective kings. The altar is now shattered but features the same rope border that elsewhere holds captives at Tikal (Jones and Satterthwaite 1982: 17), while the stela shows a prone and bound Yax Mayuy Chan Chahk, his name emblazoned in a caption above this head (Martin 1996a: 231, figure 11). Behind the pieties and supernatural sub-texts there lay the brutal business of taking, and sometimes dispatching, rival kings.

EIGHT

MATRIMONY

If we are to understand the inner articulations of power in the Classic Maya polity, and how they extended outward to interact with others, we must address the familial bonds through which these were realised and reproduced. We need, in short, to examine how ties both within and between Classic Maya polities were established through marriage and their resulting progeny. Superficially narrow in focus, this topic actually engages broad issues of kinship, legitimacy, succession, and power relations – forming a bridge between the preceding chapters that focus on the individual polity and those to come that concentrate on how they engaged with others. Every dynastic group seeks to maintain itself and, wherever possible, enhance its fortunes by manipulating its reproduction. This involves overt planning and negotiation in the expectation of, among other things, forging alliances, generating heirs, and securing resources.

Social anthropology drew much of its initial grammar and substance from kinship structures and their traceries of consanguinity and affinity (e.g. Radcliffe-Brown 1941; Fox 1967; Lévi-Strauss 1969), and the extent to which these are enmeshed in power relations makes them a concern of political anthropology as well (e.g. Fried 1967). Ethnographic research worldwide has revealed the astonishing variety of kin concepts and practices of which human groups are capable. Yet at the same time there are recurring, virtually ubiquitous, patterns to how the aristocracies of complex societies emerge and perpetuate themselves. There is an on-going contrast between structures of descent that focus on ancestry and structures of alliance that stress the strategic relations between groups. This is formalised in the opposition between lineage and house models of society (for the debate in the Maya case see Gillespie 2000a, 2000b; Houston and McAnany 2003: 36–37; Watanabe 2004), although the distinction can only be one of degree. Indeed, as we seek to define ruling kin groups we are often drawn to the ways that descent and alliance coexist in a productive tension.

The precision of the inscriptions offers a powerful tool to examine these questions. Even so, the aforementioned problem of the "unseen" remains acute, since the links exposed in the texts are patently mere fragments of a far greater whole. Occasionally they allow us to assemble a partial family tree or trace descent through the male line for a few generations. But the wider familial organisation of the polity, the matrix of collateral lines and other noble blood, is almost entirely hidden. We are also utterly dependent on retrospective sources that give us the outcomes of particular unions, but little or nothing of the machinations that led up to them – least of all, of course, of the many plans that came to nought. If records of warfare give us winners' history, then those of genealogy present the history of successful strivers and survivors; those who, through legitimate right, good fortune, personal aptitude, or ruthless manoeuvring, achieved ascendency and became history-makers.

The issue of royal marriage has naturally drawn the attention of Mayanists, and a number of studies have sought insights from available archaeological or epigraphic materials (see Marcus 1973: 914, 1976: 157–179, 1987: 135–147, 1992a: 249–259; Molloy and Rathje 1974; Haviland 1977; Schele and Mathews 1991: 243–245; Bricker 2002; Josserand 2002, 2007; Martin 2008b). In reassessing the topic here, we have the advantage of both an enhanced dataset and a richer historical context within which to interpret it. I will begin with the kinds of evidence that allow us to identify marriages, before moving to a discussion of royal polygyny. This is a practice that has received very little attention in Maya studies until now, but whose ramifications are, I believe, of considerable relevance to understanding the Classic system. From there we move to how marriage reflects distinct power relations within and between polities. As usual, points are illustrated by examples and supplemented by case studies that explore the issues in greater contextual depth.

IDENTIFYING MARRIAGE

Sources on marriage fall into five types, of which four emerge directly from the texts and the fifth as an inference from iconography. These are: (1) statements identifying parents or other close relatives; (2) references to "his/her spouse"; (3) unions implied by a bride's "arrival" at the home of her future husband; (4) references to betrothing or wedding ceremonies; and (5) figural scenes in which males are shown in the company of one or more females. Each will be discussed in turn and examined both in rhetorical and historical terms for what they tell us about the reproduction of dynastic groups.

Genealogies

By far the most numerous testaments to marriage are those in which a ruler, or more rarely a noble, names his or her parents – a feature first identified by Christopher Jones (1977: 41–42). The terms in his initial examples are today read *yal*, "child of (mother)" and *umijiinil*, "child of (father)", although these are just two within a set of comparable kinship terms that appear in substitution with one another (Schele, Mathews, and Lounsbury 1977; Stuart 1985c, 1997; Bricker 1986: 106–107; Mathews 1988: 208; Hopkins 1991; Stewart 2009). There are at least 166 surviving parentage statements from at least sixty-two different sites, spanning almost five centuries between 376 and 864.[1] The unmistakable purpose of these statements is to legitimise their subject, usually by demonstrating that he, or very rarely she, is the progeny of a previous king. The names and title phrases of the progenitors may be lengthy, but with few exceptions they are restricted to a single generation. Immediate descent was therefore key and, at least in the monumental record, longer genealogical recitations are avoided even when kings possessed extensive royal pedigrees.

Although some polities routinely provide statements of parentage, others do so rarely or not at all. For instance, despite the large corpus of well-preserved monuments at Copan, Quirigua, and Tonina, these sites provide meagre genealogical data. Whether this reflects some idiosyncratic reticence or, more meaningfully, unorthodox patterns of descent, endemic succession struggles, or the rule of intruders lacking a claim to local legitimacy, may never be known. A suspicion of abnormality grows when genealogical data is absent for a particular king, while being standard practice for others of the same polity. Where only the mother's name is given we have particular grounds to suspect that a break in the ruling patriline had taken place – especially if such cases align chronologically with a decisive military defeat (Jones 1991: 116–117; Martin 2003b: 25).

Other relationships are less commonly specified, but where they are they can be very useful in reconstructing family trees. Here *mam*, "grand-father/grandson" (Stuart 2007c[2000]) is a case in point. At Tikal, the king Chak Tok Ich'aak II is three times identified as the *mam*, "grandson" of a king of Naranjo (Martin 2005b: 8, n.15; Tokovinine and Fialko 2007: 10–13). Since we already have an extended Tikal patriline for Chak Tok Ich'aak, it follows that his mother must have been a Naranjo native – representing only one among several connections between these major kingdoms (Martin 2005b: 7–8).

A further term, as yet undeciphered, links mothers to their offspring in the formula "mother (of child)" (Mathews 1980: 61, Stewart 2009: 44–46). It mostly appears in passages where dowager queens are supporting the rule of their sons, stressing the importance of on-going maternal bonds – although it is a form that became popular only after about 720, with twenty-seven examples in all. Less common are *yichaan*, "mother's brother" and the sibling terms *sukunwinik*, "older brother" and *itz'inwinik*, "younger brother" (Stuart 1997: 5–8, 2005a: 32–33). These last two are used to mark distinctions between fraternal candidates for the throne, demonstrating that birth-order was of some significance.

"His/Her Spouse"

The term for "spouse" in the inscriptions, *atan*, is almost invariably seen in its possessed form of *yatan*, "the spouse of". Although Berlin (1968b: 15) recognised its sense it was first read phonetically by Lounsbury (1984: 178–179). In the Postclassic Period codices it is sometimes spelled with the syllable sequence **ya-ta-na**, but Classic-era sources always render it with a logographic root in the form **ya-AT-na** (see Figure 40).[2] Today, *atan* only appears as "wife" in the Yukatekan branch of Mayan languages (see Kaufman 2003: 8). It is notable that the ten instances of *yatan* or *yatanil* in the Dresden Codex all involve the same female, usually called Sak Ixik "White Woman" in her captions and presumed to be the young Moon Goddess. In each case, it links her to a different male deity pictured in the accompanying scene, a licentiousness that could point to "sexual partner" as the closest sense of the term.[3] Classic Period examples are not especially plentiful but, as we shall shortly see, they do provide key data on the multiple wives taken by the upper echelons of Maya society.

Here Comes the Bride

The interdynastic marriages we have convey a strong patrilocal system of residence with women moving to their husband's polity. The inscriptions emphasise this point when brides-to-be are the subjects of the metonymic verb *hul*, "to arrive" (MacLeod 1990: 339–341), a term we explored for its political connotations in Chapter 6 (Figure 20c). Examples from La Corona – to be discussed in detail in Case Study 9 – make this doubly clear since the same women that arrive also appear in *yatan* relationships (Martin 2008b).

We have already noted the "arrival" of Ix Wak Jalam Chan of Dos Pilas at Naranjo in the summer of 682, referring both to her marriage and, if only retrospectively, an important political move (Schele and Freidel 1990: 184–186) (p.127). She would be the mother of the next Naranjo king but, despite the survival of fifteen monuments from this era, her ruling husband receives only a single mention (Martin et al. 2017). In all other cases the suppression of his memory is achieved by simply avoiding normal practice and naming neither parent.[4]

In 693 her five-year-old son, K'ahk' Tiliw Chan Chahk, was elevated to kingship, leaving no doubt that his father was dead by that time. It is clear that Ix Wak Jalam Chan now assumes the position of queen regent and rules on behalf of the boy (Closs 1985: 74–76). Indeed, immediately after his inauguration she begins military campaigning in his name, attacking a number of lesser sites and battling larger ones (Schele and Freidel 1990: 189; Martin and Grube 2000: 76). Two of her stelae show her trampling enemies underfoot in the style of a warrior king, a motif only otherwise seen with queens at Calakmul (Figure 38). The impression we get is that she was compelled to protect her position and that of her son by conquering sites that might normally be clients of Naranjo, as well as defending their regime against major competitors such as Tikal, Yaxha, and Ucanal.

This sequence of events cannot be properly understood without knowledge of Naranjo's regional rivalries and ties to greater powers. As we have also heard, just two years before Ix Wak Jalam Chan's arrival Naranjo seized the capital of long-time foe Caracol. The report of this defeat in 680 comes from Caracol itself, in a now-incomplete text that would have likely gone on, in standard fashion, to describe some successful retaliation (Martin and Grube 2008: 73) (p.128). But Calakmul is the crucial player in what happened next, since it is the stated overlord of K'ahk' Tiliw Chan Chahk as well as that of Ix Wak Jalam Chan's father at Dos Pilas (see p.250, 255). While the precise chain of events is lost, the upheavals of this period were clearly settled to the advantage of Calakmul, which ultimately was in control of affairs and the guarantor of the queen's position.

38 The Naranjo queen regent Ix Wak Jalam Chan tramples an enemy underfoot in 702. Naranjo Stela 24. (Drawing by Ian Graham © President and Fellows of Harvard College, Peabody Museum of Archaeology and Ethnology, PM# 2004.15.6.2.45)

Nuptial Ceremonies

One might expect nuptial or prenuptial rites to be topics of interest to Maya chroniclers but, on the contrary, they are barely mentioned at all. The best-known examples come from Piedras Negras and concern the union of Chooj, the child-name of the future king K'inich Yo'nal Ahk II, and Ix Winikhaab Ajaw of Namaan – the kingdom of La Florida that lies almost 50 km to the east.[5] On Piedras Negras Stelae 1, 3, and 8, as well as on a series of shells found in the king's tomb, the textual focus falls on two events separated by a few days in 686 (Stuart 1985c). The first is given as *mahkaj* in one instance and Stuart has linked this to *mak*, "to sign up, contract" found in Modern Tzotzil, while also considering a ritualistic use of a sense already attested in the glyphs of "to cover/enclose" (Laughlin 1975: 225; Stuart 1985c: 178–179; Kaufman 2003: 866–867; Zender 2005b: 4–6). Interpreted as "betrothal", the event is overseen by a woman whose relevance to the story is not immediately clear. It is followed a few days later by the verb *nahwaj,* which probably means "is presented" and could well refer to the new bride's public display. A further *nahwaj* event on the shell, apparently describing a much later marriage for K'inich Yo'nal Ahk in 729, was this time overseen by Ix Winikhaab Ajaw. If the pattern holds true for the earlier example then it implies that that overseer was another consort of the king.

Statements of this kind are so rarely recorded that we must suspect that they are only provoked by unusual circumstances. Such can be detected in the only other example of our "betrothing" term, this one on a stela from Tres Cabezas, Guatemala (Martin and Fialko n.d.). Here a three-year-old girl, the Lady of Tikal, is involved in the same *mak* event in 507, a rite that presaged her elevation to queen-ship in 511 at the tender age of six years (Martin 1999, 2003b: 18–21). We know that her probable father died at a relatively young age and, even though she had a younger brother, she received the crown. We also know that she was associated with at least two men, one a noble of the *ti'huun* rank who was perhaps her initial guardian or regent, and another, Kaloomte' Bahlam, who became her co-ruler and Tikal's nineteenth king (Martin 1999, 2003b: 20–21; Zender 2004: 333–339). One means of securing power in her name would clearly be marriage, and the Tres Cabezas stela – commissioned when she was still only ten years old – almost certainly marks her betrothal to that older male, whose name is now missing on this damaged stone.

A candidate for "wedding" might appear in a lone example on Bonampak Stela 2, whose scene shows the king Yajaw Chan Muwaan flanked by two richly dressed women (Mathews 1980: figure 2). Since the leftmost figure has a caption that identifies her as a Yaxchilan princess, the uncaptioned woman to the right must be the one that the adjacent main text describes as a "namesake" of the woman otherwise identified as the mother of Yajaw Chan Muwaan. The initial verb in this passage, dated to 789, is the passive form **nu?-pa-ja** *nuhpaj,* presumably based on the root **nup* "to join" (Kaufman 2003: 64). It has been proposed that marriage is its intended sense here, although the identification of the opening **nu** syllablogram is not entirely secure (Houston 1997a: 292; Bíró 2011b). While the overall syntax remains somewhat murky – there is an intervening verb – the passage might well describe a new bride for the king who happens to share his mother's name.[6] Significantly, this woman occupies the privileged right side of the scene, facing her husband, a position that invariably identifies the main focus of a given monument (see Houston 1998: 341–344).[7]

Marital Iconography

This brings us to the final category of evidence, scenes in which males are depicted in the company of richly attired females who observe or participate in their performances. The greatest number of such scenes come from Yaxchilan and its satellites where, for example, its king Bird Jaguar IV is shown with four separate women, each captioned with names and titles, three of them identified as foreign princesses (Mathews 1988: 220–221, passim; Martin and Grube 2000: 131) (Figure 39). The dates on which these women appear with the king

39 Bird Jaguar IV and his spouse Ix Mut Bahlam of Zapote Bobal both engage in ritual bloodletting, she from her tongue and he from his penis. Yaxchilan Lintel 17. (Photograph by Justin Kerr)

overlap, demonstrating that they are coeval rather than sequential relationships. This is further demonstrated by a small group of scenes, none well-preserved, that show two or more of these partnering women together (e.g. Houston et al. 2006: 6, figure 2). The clear supposition is that these are all official wives.[8] We will return to the case of Yaxchilan and its marriage patterns in Case Study 10.

Other male–female pairings are those seen on separate but adjacent monuments, such as the stelae pairs that are a recurring pattern at Calakmul (Marcus 1987: 135–147; Stewart 2009: 85–88). Given the political pre-eminence of this dynasty, these unusual declarations of royal partnership are not easily regarded as an idiosyncratic localism. Instead, they seem designed to give an elevated expression of bilateral unity, perhaps indicative of the delicate balance of collateral lines within a dominant polity whose primary marriages were, as far as we know them, endogamous. Although erosion robs us of much data on Calakmul spouses it is significant that they carry high titles, not only *ix baahkab* but the localised *uxte'tuun ix kaloomte'* – expressions of status that are unique in a home account.[9]

Finally, there is also a tradition of single stelae that bear male and female portraits on their sides so as to flank a central portrait. Tikal was the main exponent of this form and in all cases these appear to be the parents of the featured ruler (Coggins 1975).[10] A fine example here is Tikal Stela 40, where K'an Kitam is framed by his father Sihyaj Chan K'awiil II and mother Ix Ahiin K'uk' (Valdés, Fahsen, and Cosme 1997).

POLYGYNY AND ITS EFFECTS

The multiple women shown with some kings have led a good number of Mayanists to infer that the Classic Maya elite was polygynous.[11] However, we do not have to rely on inference, since direct evidence for such a practice emerges on a group of texts from the Puuc region of the northwestern lowlands. Xcalumkin Jambs 8 and 9 were found at the base of a large elite residential complex from which they had fallen (Graham and von Euw 1992: 170–171). Although both inscriptions are incomplete, their sense is clear. The first includes a statement of possession *yotoot ix baakel*, "(The) house of Lady Bone ...", and evidently refers to one of the structures from this palace. A closely related second text probably comes from another doorway of the same building. Here we find *ix baakel uchan yatanil itz'aat*, "Lady Bone, fourth wife of (the) *itz'aat*". The last element here is a title that denotes a person of learning or artisanship commonly carried by rulers, the nobility, and what we might loosely call the intelligentsia (Stuart 1989: 157).[12]

It is at least conceivable that an unfortunate husband could see the death of three wives before taking a fourth (even without the uxoricidal tendencies of a

Henry VIII). But confirmation that polygyny is at work comes in another text from the Puuc region, this one carved on a column now in the museum of Hecelchakan (Mayer 1991: pl.101) (Figure 40). Superficially it looks much like the jamb text, but contains a key switch from an ordinal to a cardinal construction, running *yotoot ux yatan sajal*, "house of the three wives of (the) *sajal*" (see Grube 1994b: 339). This makes the building concerned, presumably a complex with a number of separate chambers, the abode of three contemporaneous spouses. If at least some of the rooms in palace groups can be shown to be dedicated to housing elite wives, it raises the interesting question of whether a major purpose of these discrete cell-like dormitories, so typical of royal courts, was to provide individual accommodation for the king's spouses and concubines in a veritable harem.[13]

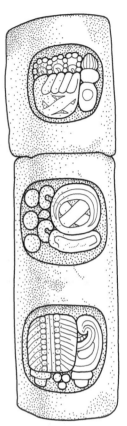

40 A direct reference to polygyny: *yotoot ux yatan sajal*, "House of the three wives of (the) *sajal*". Unprovenanced column in the Hecelchakan Museum.

Polygyny was the norm among the Postclassic Mixtec, Zapotec, and Mexica elite of Central Mexico (Spores 1974: 303, 1984: 69; Whitecotton 1977: 145; Carrasco 1984: 44; Lind 2000: 576; Hassig 2016), where it played a major role in maintaining and expanding hierarchical relations among rival dynasties.[14] Similarly, it was a Postclassic Maya practice attested among the Itza of the lowlands (Jones 1998: 81, 405) and the K'iche' of the highlands – whose ruler had a senior wife of high-status but also several secondary ones, predominantly drawn from other groups and territories, including conquered ones (Las Casas 1909: 624–625; Carmack 1981: 63–65, 150).[15] Wherever we find polygyny it is typical for status distinctions between consorts to produce a ranking, with one holding principal position – although this is often dependent upon producing a viable heir (Westermarck 1921: 3, 29, 46).

There is a wealth of ethnographic sources on polygyny worldwide, which have been mined in search of its purpose and social significance, finding explanations in cultural factors as well as in economics and demography (e.g. Clignet 1970; White 1988; White and Burton 1988; Bretschneider 1995). However, only a few of these studies have addressed the type of power relations inherent in royal polygyny (Musisi 1991; Betzig 1993; see also Hassig 2016), issues that are greatly amplified in multi-polity landscapes. Polygyny is significant because it radically expands the parameters of marriage as a political tool, allowing diversified strategies denied to monogamous systems (Carrasco 1984: 74–75).

Hardly less significant is the greater number of legitimate offspring that can be expected from multiple wives, providing children who will become actors/pawns in the next generation of politicking. Although all will be descended from the same ruling father, they will be distinguished by the rank of their mothers and carry separate affiliations to internal or external kin groups. The heavy Classic Maya emphasis on naming mothers as well as fathers, noted above, would have real purpose in a polygynous system, where identifying a particular woman would communicate her unique set of associations (Palka 1999: 42).

In dynastic marriage, daughters became the currency in a certain kind of political transaction, with each providing an opportunity for the patriline to link itself to others to varying degrees of advantage. The economic dimensions of these transfers remain deeply obscure: we cannot know if there were offsetting costs to such exchanges – the payment of a dowry or bride price, or whether royal women brought independent wealth or landholdings with them. Documented Mesoamerican parallels should alert us to these "unseen" components of what were doubtless complex and situational negotiations.

We might glimpse the expanded production of sons in La Corona Panel 1's mention of the *wuk tikil ch'oktaak yunen kaan ajaw*, "Seven youths, sons of (the) Snake lord" (David Stuart, pers. comm. 2005). The father here is the long-lived Yuknoom Ch'een of Calakmul, and the same text goes on to discuss two princes who presumably count among them – one of whom, Yuknoom Yich'aak K'ahk', would eventually succeed him. Although our sources on Calakmul genealogy are generally poor, Yuknoom Ch'een appears to have had at least two, perhaps three, identifiable wives.

But the La Corona count begs a rather larger question: what became of those "spare" sons and so many like them? Males who did not rise to kingship are barely mentioned in the texts, but we must try to deduce their place in the system nonetheless. Even if a restrictive rule of succession was enforced – primogeniture from the paramount wife for example – a significant number of royal sons offer the potential for disruptive, even fratricidal, rivalries. In fact, the evidence for primogeniture is limited and it is well to remember that in many societies competence, especially in military affairs, was valued more highly than birth-order. Accordingly, there may be advantage to having a pool of regnal candidates from which to select the most able or, in Darwinian fashion, to have one fight their way to the top. Those excluded from the throne would need alternative occupations, whether it be within the courtly life of polity administration, risking life and limb in the military, or withdrawing to the relative calm of an artistic, intellectual, or religious life (Houston and Stuart 2001: 74, 76). Ethnohistorical cases for these avenues abound both in Mesoamerica and elsewhere, as they do for sons without an inheritance moving to take power at other centres. Whatever the options open to Classic Maya *ch'ok,* they are only dimly reported.[16]

One unusual but revealing case appears at Uaxactun, where the shattered Stela 14 lists the parents of what can only be the local ruler. Here the mother's name has no distinguishing place of origin, but the father's name includes *aj mutul*, "Tikal Person". The political fortunes of Uaxactun and Tikal were closely tied for much of the Classic Period, experiencing monument hiatuses of almost equal length from the mid-sixth to the end of the seventh centuries. The erection of Stela 14 in 702 comes at a decisive moment because it both terminates the local hiatus and comes soon after Tikal has re-asserted itself militarily by defeating Calakmul in 695. There is persuasive evidence here that Tikal "seeded" a new Uaxactun dynasty.

STRATEGIC DIMENSIONS OF MARRIAGE

The major distinction in marital strategy is that between *endogamous* and *exogamous* unions – in this context whether they are intra-dynastic or inter-dynastic (Marcus 1992a). Both have roles to play in the promotion of dynastic interests, and while monogamous systems normally require a choice between the two, polygynous ones permit a diversified strategy.

Exogamous Marriages

Exogamy allows dynastic groups to enhance their position by means of favourable matches with other polities. The primary distinction here comes in the relative status of the participants: whether it is an *isogamous* relationship that links peers, a *hypergamous* one in which the man or woman marries into a more powerful polity, or the reverse, a *hypogamous* one in which he or she moves to marry from a greater to a lesser polity.[17] It needs to be kept in mind that the balance of power and prestige could shift over time and, moreover, that individual marriages may be only one link within a chain of inter-polity connections. Although women were a form of currency they were not necessarily passive players. We can easily imagine incoming wives as de facto diplomats and proxies for their kin, perfectly placed to relay intimate knowledge of affairs at their new home, be it a client, ally, or overlord.

With so much political advantage at stake and so many dynasties available with which to create symmetrical and asymmetrical alliances, we would expect the Classic Maya to be tenacious matchmakers and exogamous marriage a key tool of statecraft. However, its scarcity in the record was first highlighted by Schele and Mathews (1991: 245), who noted just nine sure or probable cases. The corpus now available pushes that figure to some thirty-five today (Martin 2014a: table 14), but given the larger sample size this is still a rather low proportion of around fifteen per cent compared to recorded marriages as a whole.[18] Either some factor inhibits interdynastic unions, or they are significantly under-reported. Mentions of the maternal grandfathers of two Tikal kings during the Early Classic Period point to the latter. One was a king of Naranjo, the other of Xultun, but in neither instance do their daughters, the respective partners of K'an Kitam and Chak Tok Ich'aak II, carry the identifying titles that would reveal them to be exogamous brides. The implication is that a much higher incidence of interdynastic marriage occurred but is now hidden to us. We will return to this important issue in Case Study 10.

Isogamous relations are by far the most challenging to identify since we must know the relative fortunes, prestige, and wider inter-relationships of both parties with precision and at a specific point in time. The attribution might seem safest when the partners are major polities at great distance, and one thinks here of the putative Palenque-Copan union that traverses some 425 km, but even here we cannot assume parity.[19]

In political hypogamy powerful dynasties marry their offspring into weaker ones to create new, or deepen existing, relationships with the goal of producing a fused bloodline that will rule in subsequent generations. When the weaker party seeks, or is obliged to accept, a hypogamous partnership they gain the benefits of a cooperative elite group, but also introduce foreign interests and loyalties that can further erode their autonomy and entrench their inferior status.

A good example of such relations comes at El Peru, where the king K'inich Bahlam took a Calakmul princess as his spouse. Her status as principal consort is reflected in possessing her own monument, Stela 34, which was originally paired with her husband's Stela 33 in the same manner as that used to portray royal couples at Calakmul itself (Miller 1974; Marcus 1987: 135–147, 1992a: 251–253; Wanyerka 1996). Her personal name was one used by Snake dynasty women on at least two other occasions and she carries the appropriate title of *ix kaan(ul) ajaw*, as well as the *ix kaloomte'* that marks her exalted rank. The main text on the sides of Stela 34 has been badly damaged by looters but can be reconstructed in part. It begins with her *huli*, "arrival" on a missing date that might not have been too long before 677. It may then name her parents, although only that of her father Yuknoom Ch'een is now legible. On the front of the monument the succession of her presumed brother or half-brother, Yuknoom Yich'aak K'ahk', to the Calakmul throne in 686 is described, as well as her own ritual performances at the 9.13.0.0.0 period ending of 692. The political context of this marriage, and the key to the relative standing of the two kingdoms, is supplied by Stela 34's partner monument Stela 33, which tells us that K'inich Bahlam acceded under the *yichonal*, "oversight" of Yuknoom Ch'een, on a date now lost (see p.254).

In the contrasting scheme of hypergamy, kings acquire brides from kingdoms of lower standing and strength. Lesser dynasties may volunteer to enter such relations in exchange for a favourable alliance, but others are likely forced into doing so, notably after their defeat in war. Here we see the asymmetry of hypergamy at its starkest, as the newly dominant seek to solidify their gains in ways barely distinguishable from hostage-taking or bride-capture (see p.207).

Relations of this sort can be detected at Naranjo, where two kings married women from recently defeated polities. K'ahk' Tiliw Chan Chahk is credited with burning the site of Tuubal in 693, even though he was only a five-year-old at the time and, as we have heard, the action must have been at the behest of his mother Ix Wak Jalam Chan. He would later marry and sire a child with a Tuubal princess, Ix Unen Bahlam, and we can take it that this arrangement arose as a consequence of the conflict. Such relations could also span generations, as we see in the marriage of this couple's son, K'ahk' Kal Chan Chahk, to a woman from neighbouring Yaxha. This city had been seized and burned by his father in 710 and its ruler driven away (see p.212–213). The fact that war between Naranjo and Yaxha re-ignites in the next generation, as the son of this Yaxha queen, Itzamnaaj K'awiil, invades Yaxha in 799 and beheads its king, presumably an affine of some kind, speaks to the feeble nature of interdynastic marriage and its failure to unite the interests of habitual adversaries (Martin and Grube 2000: 74–82).

Endogamous Marriages

The great majority of Classic Maya rulers for which we have records were born to women with no discernible foreign affiliation, and are therefore assumed to be scions of the home dynasty or its associated nobility. In avoiding the unequal exchanges and outside influence innate to most forms of exogamy, endogamy offers a number of tangible advantages. Marrying-in is a powerful means of shoring up an internal powerbase and uniting rival factions. If pursued through closed-system, agnatic marriage, the natural growth of the royal lineage would be curtailed and eligibility for the throne kept to a narrow range of candidates.

This practice was exemplified in the Mexica royalty's system of cross-cousin marriage, whose purpose in resisting outside claims to power was clear to the early Spanish chroniclers: "[R]elatives married each other so that the rulership would not go elsewhere" (Relación de la Genealogía 1941: 254, quoted in Carrasco 1984: 57). It is very unusual to learn about the familial connections of Classic Maya endogamous brides, with the best data by far emerging from Yaxchilan, shortly to be described in Case Study 10.

CASE STUDY 9: SNAKE LADIES AT LA CORONA

A single monument, La Corona Panel 6, offers a comprehensive sampler of hypogamous ties between a major power and one of its satellites. A finely

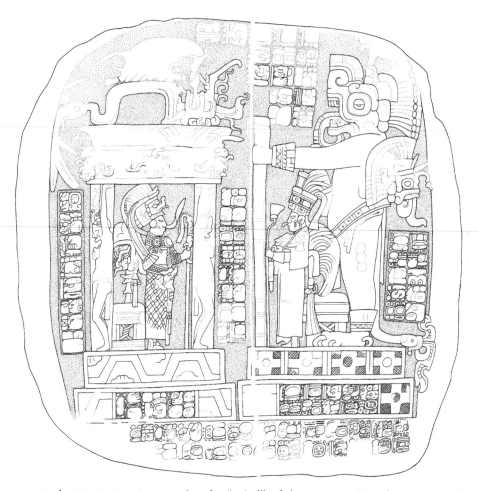

41 A monument commemorating the "arrival" of three separate Kaanul princesses at La Corona. The figure portrayed to the right is the first bride in 520, borne on a palanquin depicting the Teotihuacan war serpent-jaguar. To the left a local queen stands within a temple or pavilion as she celebrates the period ending ceremony of 731. La Corona Panel 6. (Drawing by David Stuart)

detailed relief, now in the Dallas Museum of Art, shows two women inside structures equipped with thrones, each atop a tiered platform (Figure 41). The woman on the left is dressed in the netted jade skirt and blouse of the lunar-associated Maize Goddess, and stands within a temple-like pavilion richly bedecked in supernatural imagery (most noticeably the aged world bearers who support its roof). Her counterpart on the right is dressed in Teotihuacan-style garb and is enclosed by a giant anthropomorphic serpent-jaguar, a version of the Teotihuacan war deity the Maya called Waxaklajuun Ubaah Kaan. Oversized beasts of this kind are often fabricated effigies borne on litters or palanquins, suggesting that this too may be a portable assembly (for more on this topic see Case Study 8).

The text flows around the scene to fill most of the intervening space and is, with a few exceptions, well-preserved. Panel 6 had been ascribed to La Corona due to the recurring references to its toponym Sak Nikte' ("White Flower") and mentions of known members of its dynasty. However, in 2012 excavations at the site directed by Marcello Canuto and Tomás Barrientos uncovered even more decisive evidence, the discarded carcass from which the carved face had been sawn during the rampant looting of the 1960s.

The inscription begins with the most recent event, before switching back to two earlier eras, together forming three parallel passages (Martin 2008b: table 1). Each proceeds with: (1) the verb *hul*, "to arrive (here)", (2) the name of a female protagonist, (3) the location arrived at, (4) the possessed term *yatan*, "the spouse of", (5) the name of a male, (6) a term probably to be read *yatik* that functions as "the daughter of (father)", (7) a second male, (8) the possessed term *yal*, "the child of (mother)", and (9) the name of a second female. All the relationships serve to link the initial female protagonist of each passage to additional characters.

Chronologically, the narrative begins in 520 with the arrival of a woman who is designated the *unaahtal ix kaan(ul) ajaw*, "First Snake Lady" (here, as elsewhere, *ix ajaw*, "Lady" is used as the female version of *ajaw*, "Lord") which, on current evidence, we presume was a native of the Dzibanche kingdom (Martin 2008b: figure 2) (Table 4). Sak Nikte' is identified as the place of her arrival and then her family relationships are set out, beginning with the name of her new husband. This same lord appears in a retrospective section of La Corona Stela 1 that details an event in the year 544, where he bears a version of the title *k'uhul sak wahyis*. We lack a good translation for this epithet, which is carried not only by La Corona lords but by others in this region who were subject to the Kaanul kings.

Returning to Panel 6, since the next relationship term, *yatik* (Christian Prager, pers. comm. 2008), introduces the father of the female protagonist in the second of our parallel passages, we can be confident that it does so in all cases (Martin 2008: 6). The word *atik* survives in the Mayan language outlier of Wasteko (Huastec) – spoken on the Gulf Coast of Mexico – as "daughter" in

TABLE 4 *Timeline*

Long Count	CE	Greg.	Event
9.4.5.6.16	520	Feb 6	Arrival of the "first" Kaanul princess
9.12.6.16.17	679	May 4	Arrival of the "second" Kaanul princess
9.14.9.9.14	721	May 1	Arrival of the "third" Kaanul princess
9.15.0.0.0	731	Aug 23	Period ending celebrated by Yajawte' K'inich of La Corona
9.18.0.16.16	791	Sep 13	Arrival of a Tikal princess

the specific context of "child of man" (Marc Zender, pers. comm. 2016). The father here is Tuun K'ab Hix, a ruler of the Kaanul kingdom who is mentioned at Yaxchilan in 537 and Naranjo in 546. The illegible name of the bride's mother completes the sequence.

The next arrival takes place over 150 years later in 679, where the woman is identified (in a different numbered construction using *tz'ak*, "to set in order") as *ucha tz'akbuil ix kaan(ul) ajaw* or "Second Snake Lady". The formula from the earlier arrival is repeated, with Sak Nikte'/La Corona given as her destination, followed by the name of her husband by means of the *yatan* term. This character, named in part K'inich Yook, was the ruler of La Corona from at least 675 until 683. The next *yatik* term introduces the famed Calakmul king Yuknoom Ch'een, the dominant figure in the lowlands at this time. Clear evidence for a daughter–father relationship comes on a looted La Corona panel recently returned to Guatemala, where the son of K'inich Yook is identified as the *mam*, "grandson" of Yuknoom Ch'een and the *al*, "child" of a generically named Calakmul princess (Martin 2008b: 5, figure 5). La Corona Panel 1 tells us that the Calakmul king *yichonal*, "oversaw" the accession of K'inich Yook – emphasising his control over this minor dynasty (David Stuart, pers. comm. 2005) (see p.239–240). Panel 6 continues with the name of the second arrival's mother (which is barely legible, but does not resemble that of the only sure consort of Yuknoom Ch'een we know) and apparently goes on to detail additional kin, including a male, Janaab, who later ruled the site under the name Yajawte' K'inich and was the commissioner of this monument.

The third arrival takes place in 721 and gives a more elaborate reference to La Corona, appropriate to its position opening the inscription: *huli tahn ch'een sak nikte'*, "arrives (in the) midst of the domain/settlement of White Flower". This woman's husband is that same Yajawte' K'inich, while her father has a damaged name-glyph that closely resembles one ascribed to the contemporary ruler of Calakmul, Yuknoom Took' K'awiil, although only in foreign contexts. Again, the name of the mother is no longer fully legible. The text later describes the bride's participation in the 9.15.0.0.0 period ending of 731 celebrated by her husband. In the process, she is described as the *u(y)ux tz'akbuil ix kaan(ul) ajaw* or "Third Snake Lady" and an *ix kaloomte'*, the female version of this honorific title carried by major kings that is passed on to their progeny.

The two women pictured in the scene would appear to be the most recent (at left) and the earliest (at right) Snake princesses, in a rare but by no means unique conflation of narrative time. In regard to the palanquin structure itself, it is conceivable that major marriage events were marked by grand processions into the bride's new home. Its Teotihuacan design would not be out of place at Dzibanche, where stucco reliefs in Central Mexican style have been uncovered, in one case decorating a whole pyramid, that date to much the same period. As an aside, this is an important hint that Dzibanche did not fall outside the post-378 New Order in the Peten. The woman on the left is referenced in an adjacent caption, which dates her actions to the 9.15.0.0.0 period ending of 731. We would expect her to be the most recent arrival, but nothing in her name phrase suggests that she is and this could well be a different local queen instead.

Panel 6 is remarkable enough, but a further find adds an important post-script. La Corona Altar 4 was found in a battered and broken condition, although David Stuart's initial field investigation in 1997 was able to demonstrate that it focuses on the arrival of yet another elite woman. This event took place in 791, but much else in this text is badly weathered, including the woman's name and titles. However, in 2010 members of the Proyecto Arqueológico La Corona uncovered a missing fragment that could be fitted back into the stone (Barrientos et al. 2011: 170–172, figure 8). This contained the titles of *ix mutul ajaw* and *ix kaloomte'*, demonstrating that this woman was from the royal line of Tikal and, given her elevated rank, necessarily the daughter of a Tikal king. That the switch in martial affiliation between Panel 6 and Altar 4 mirrors the changing fortunes of the two great powers of the central lowlands, reflecting the decline of Calakmul and renewal of Tikal, seems a necessary deduction.

To summarise, the La Corona data is unique in its detail and chronological depth, offering a close-up view of hypogamous marriage patterns at a secondary centre. The high status of the Calakmul-Dzibanche brides sent to La Corona speaks of its strategic importance for the Snake polity, at least for certain points of its history.[20] That significance coincides with the unusually large inventory of monuments from the site, which is hugely disproportionate to its size both in terms of its urban core as well as the extent of its settlement (Barrientos et al. 2011). Home to a dynasty displaying all the pomp and circumstance of regular Maya kings, it pointedly lacks an emblem glyph – not even the minimal version of *sak nikte' ajaw*. If we were to stick rigidly to the criteria sketched out in Chapter 5, La Corona would hardly meet the requirements for polity status. In the finely calibrated grades of Classic Maya lordship, which we struggle to translate into the tidy categories of our own political vocabulary, La Corona more resembles an exclave or special function dependency during the period we know about.

A hypothesis that might explain its anomalous features emerges from a look at the locations of sites subordinate to Calakmul in the central Peten, which include an arc running from the fringes of the Calakmul polity at Uxul, down through La Corona to El Peru, Dos Pilas, and Cancuen. These could well represent way stations or at least secure passage on an overland route linking Calakmul to the southern highlands (Freidel et al. 2007; Canuto et al. 2011; Canuto and Barrientos 2013). David Freidel has dubbed this hypothesised highway the "royal road", in reference to the Spanish *Camino Real* that once cut through the Peten in much the same way. The southernmost section, from Dos Pilas to Cancuen, would be an easier river highway up the Pasión River. Today we can fill in some gaps in this ancient chain with the addition of two polities lying between El Peru and Dos Pilas: Zapote Bobal (Martin and Reents-Budet 2010; Vepretskii and Galeev 2016) and El Reinado (Stuart 2012c) – both of which refer to Calakmul in the late seventh century and were plainly immersed in its hegemonic network.

CASE STUDY 10: MARRIAGE STRATEGIES AT YAXCHILAN

If we want to observe the interplay of endogamous and exogamous relationships then Late Classic Yaxchilan offers a prime opportunity. Figure 42 sets out the known pattern of marriage and descent for a 179-year period through five generations of kings. The sequence begins in Yaxchilan's "dark age" spanning 613–723, an era that lacks surviving inscriptions, even though contemporary records at other centres attest to the presence of an active dynasty for much of this time (Martin and Grube 2008: 121–123).

In retrospective accounts the throne was taken by Bird Jaguar III in 629, and it was a son produced very late in the reproductive life of his principal queen, Ix Pakal, that eventually succeeded him as Shield Jaguar III (the Great) in 681. It was still four decades before the long-lived Shield Jaguar emerges as a newly empowered and prolific king and this period is especially vacant in historical terms. His first major project was Structure 23, a large building looking out on

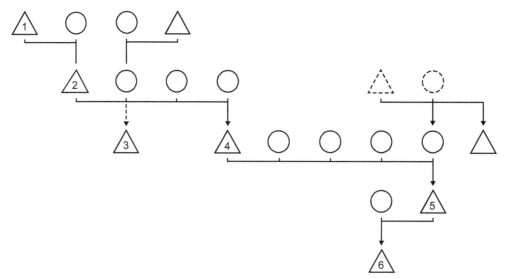

42 A partial family tree for the Yaxchilan dynasty traced through the reigns of six Late Classic kings: (1) Bird Jaguar III (629–669+); (2) Shield Jaguar III (681–742); (3) Yopaat Bahlam II (749); (4) Bird Jaguar IV (752–768); (5) Shield Jaguar IV (769–800+); (6) K'inich Tatbu Joloom IV (808).

the main plaza equipped with carved lintels above each of its three front-facing doorways (Tate 1992: 203–208; García Moll 2004; Miller and Martin 2004: 99–101, 106–108). Although the king appears on all of them, so does his consort Ix K'abal Xook, who occupies the focal right side of their scenes and is the main protagonist in acts of ritualised self-harm, the presentation of war-gear, and the conjuring of a fused king-and-patron deity (Figure 33). Indeed, accompanying texts describe her as the owner of the building and link her to the king via a possessed form of the "inverted-vase" title, an unde-ciphered term carried by most wives and mothers.

The lintel above a side-door is entirely textual and offers unique documen-tation on her family. Its syntax is a little obtuse, but it names her parents, two female associates who accompany her in dedicating the doorway (one of which seems to be a sister), and probably a son as well (McAnany and Plank 2001: 111–113; Josserand 2002: 123, 2007). Her father is of non-royal *sajal* status, placing him at the head of a local noble line. He carries the same K'abal Xook name, which evidently functions as a patronym here – an insight into sub-royal onomastics and valuable because monarchs eschew any mention of family names. Taken as a whole, Structure 23 represents the single most elaborate celebration of a woman in Maya history and speaks to some tangible role for her in the rejuvenation of the polity, and perhaps some indebtedness to her family.[21]

In 738 a woman by the name of Ix Sak Biyaan was honoured with another monumental building, Structure 11, whose only carved lintel identifies her as an *ixik ch'ok*, "young woman" (Martin and Grube 2000: 126; McAnany and Plank 2001: 113–114). She is linked to the by-now aged Shield Jaguar by means of the same possessed "inverted-vase" as Ix K'abal Xook, but we know nothing more about her. Just four years later the king was dead and a ten-year "interregnum" had begun.

As we saw in Case Study 5, today there is evidence that most or all of this obscure interval was ruled by a king called Yopaat Bahlam II, very likely the crowned son of Ix K'abal Xook. Mentioned at Piedras Negras in 749 on the occasion of a state visit there, he lacks any monuments at Yaxchilan itself and there is a prima facie case that he was actively expunged from its record. The next king was a son of Shield Jaguar who took the name Bird Jaguar (IV) in 752. He embarks on a vigorous programme of self-legitimation that included the creation of retrospective records, among them new stelae for his long-dead grandfather Bird Jaguar III, and several re-workings of earlier monuments (Martin 2000b: 56–57; Martin and Grube 2000: 128–132).

One of his first projects was an annex to Structure 23, designated as Structure 24 (Tate 1992: 197–199). Its all-textual lintels supply a collective royal memorial, with death-dates for his grandmother in 705, his father in 742, and his mother, a hitherto unmentioned wife of Shield Jaguar we know as Ix

Uh Chan, in 751. Structure 24 also commemorates the death of Ix K'abal Xook in 749 and the text concludes with a ceremony at her tomb in 755, a sure sign of her revered status. But this was to be the very last reference to her as Bird Jaguar begins to promote his own mother, a woman who would eventually receive nine mentions on seven monuments, including two portraits on her own stela and three more on lintels that depict her with her husband.[22] The date of their marriage is unknown, but their earliest joint appearance is in 697 – well before Bird Jaguar's birth in 709 – as if to emphasise their long-standing relationship (Mathews 1988: 213). She twice carries an *ix elk'in kaloomte'* epithet, but on one occasion, on Stela 10, she is additionally described as an *ix kaan(ul) ajaw* or a princess of the Snake kingdom (Schele and Freidel 1990: 270) (Figure 2e).[23]

One might expect that a direct tie to this titan of the Classic Maya world would be trumpeted rather than simply noted, and this singular reference contrasts with the much less consequential *ix ajk'uhuun* title that is ever-present in her name. But by the 750s and 760s the Snake kingdom was greatly diminished and we can surmise that the connection now offered little political capital. The more interesting question concerns the relationship between the two polities at the time the marriage was contracted, and whether it came before or after Calakmul's watershed defeat in 695.[24]

A further Bird Jaguar project, Structure 21, bears lintels that emulate those of Structure 23 in the rituals they illustrate, but populates them not with a local consort but two foreign brides. There were three such women in total, two from the kingdom of Motul de San José and another from Zapote Bobal, all of whom were given extraordinary prominence. To judge from the latter king-dom's defeats at the hands of both Bird Jaguar's grandfather and father – most recently in 732, when one of its lords was captured and its king submissively visited Yaxchilan (Martin and Reents-Budet 2010: 5, n.8) – this link was a hypergamous one. The relationship with the former is less clear. There are signs that Motul de San José, strategically located in command of Lake Peten-Itza, had significant ties to Tikal, its king naming himself as a Tikal client in 701 (see p.255).[25]

Bird Jaguar also gave marked precedence at his capital to another constituency, several nobles of the *sajal* rank, who are depicted together with the king, often in the role of military captains. This might also be linked to Bird Jaguar's abnormal succession, as if rewarding lords whose support made his bid for power possible (Proskouriakoff 1964: 189; Mathews 1988: 217). His military claims were modest, most of his captives come from unknown sites, but were emphatic in their presentation, with constant repetition of the title *aj winik baak*, "He of 20 Captives".

Bird Jaguar's questionable ascent presumably explains his unusual interest in having his chosen son succeed him – as we saw earlier, it is rare for heirs to be

43 Bearing a K'awiil sceptre, Bird Jaguar IV appears with his wife Ix Chak Joloom. She holds a bundle which in this context probably contains sacred paraphernalia. Yaxchilan Lintel 1. (Drawing by Ian Graham © President and Fellows of Harvard College, Peabody Museum of Archaeology and Ethnology, PM# 2004.15.6.5.1)

identified or promoted during a king's lifetime. The very last monument Bird Jaguar commissioned at Yaxchilan, Lintel 9 from 768, shows him in the company of Chak Joloom, a *sajal* dubbed the *yichaan ajaw*, or "uncle of the lord". We can be confident that the lord in question is the king's son and heir, Chelew Chan K'inich, because of the inscribed scenes inside Structure 33, the most magnificent surviving building at Yaxchilan.[26] There Lintel 1 celebrates the king's accession in 752, showing him together with the sister of Chak Joloom, the hitherto unseen queen Ix Chak Joloom (Figure 43). A caption at lower right identifies her as the "mother of Shield Jaguar" – the future regnal name of Chelew Chan K'inich. On Lintel 2, above the central doorway, we see the king with his son as a five-year-old boy, who is nonetheless credited with a full sequence of royal titles. This provokes a question: is this Bird Jaguar lavishing attention on his heir, or are we instead looking at an elaborate self-legitimation by Chelew Chan K'inich/Shield Jaguar himself? The important tomb beneath the front steps of Structure 33 is very likely to be that of Bird Jaguar and, if so, the whole programme of the building must be understood as a memorial shrine. Probably completed only after his death, there was every opportunity for his son to use it to embed his own power.

He duly succeeded as Shield Jaguar (IV) in 768 or 769, and continued Yaxchilan's idiosyncratic approach to monument making. He portrays himself with his mother on several occasions, while also producing long-after-the-fact depictions of his father and grandfather with their dynastically consequent spouses. Unlike these forebears, however, he produces no identifiable images of his own queen or queens. We know of one only from the parentage of his son, K'inich Tatbu Joloom IV, whose sole record is the poorly executed Lintel 10, the last monument created at Yaxchilan in 808.

We can see that Yaxchilan's rich representations of royal partnerships present innovative strategies that respond to changing political imperatives. They begin with Shield Jaguar III, who announces the end of his kingdom's long silence by showering attention on his paramount consort, Ix K'abal Xook. These fix her ritual performances to a message of royal regeneration, while also honouring her local lineage. Tradition and convention were cast aside in pursuit of an objective we cannot fully comprehend so long as the cause of Yaxchilan's "dark age" remains uncertain.

Under Bird Jaguar IV inventive approaches accelerate, with his father's programme replicated in part, but put to quite different purposes. This time the orientation was not endogamous but exogamous, with a similar set of rituals staged with foreign brides. No discernible hierarchy emerges between these women, and their multiplicity argues against any role in generating an heir. They more resemble a harem of marital rather than martial conquests, opportunities to boast of favourable connections to polities that were likely of significance for his place in the Maya world. That Bird Jaguar's fourth wife is thrust into the limelight for the sole purpose of supporting their son's right to rule shows the rhetorical calculation at work. There also seems to be method in the lavish treatment of his mother, Ix Uh Chan, which came not from her ability to legitimise him, but rather the need to upstage or eclipse her co-wife Ix K'abal Xook. The significance of that great queen could not be disputed, but she must have been an uncomfortable reminder of Bird Jaguar's questionable claim and the "lost line" of her issue. That Shield Jaguar IV in large measure continued this program of dynastic remembrance could suggest that anxiety over the rightful descent between grandfather and father persisted, with implications for his own position.

Exogamous brides abound here as nowhere else, but so do hints as to why their numbers may be deceptively low in the wider record. In the period we have data for at Yaxchilan there is a distinct suggestion that endogamy was preferred for the principal wife and mother to the heir. When this pattern was disrupted and the child of a lesser queen acceded there followed a sustained flurry of self-justification (although we cannot judge if the taint of usurpation was a still greater spur here). The foreign origin of this mother was only casually acknowledged and were it not for a single surviving reference we would happily have assigned her a local origin. If reflected elsewhere, under-reporting would be an important factor behind the startlingly scarce incidence of female exogamy, if a necessarily unquantifiable one.

Yaxchilan's distinction is the way it used the monumental record to address female-centred issues of descent and alliance. The statistics here are emphatic, since the figural representation of women at Yaxchilan dwarfs that of any other polity, constituting around one third (n = 39) of all such images in the corpus of Classic Maya monumental art.

We see a select few royals in the textual record, but polygyny virtually guarantees that Classic Maya courts heaved with potential candidates for the throne. Figure 42 presents the bare bones of a royal genealogy for Yaxchilan, but the exponential effect of a comparable group of wives and their children through all of its history would produce a far larger and more complex family tree. This suggests one final, intriguing possibility. Since the number of wives taken, and corresponding offspring produced, is proportionate to the husbands' rank in almost every polygynous system, it means that as each generation passed the descendants of kings should constitute an ever-greater percentage of the total population. Even if some exogamy is taken into account, this would be a decisive in making some populations, especially those of smaller polities, not fictive but actual relatives of the ruling group and therefore provoke a particularly intense kin-based loyalty to them.[27]

NINE

CONFLICT

Divided political landscapes such as that of the Classic Maya are, with a relentless regularity, filled with competing ambitions and deeply felt animosities. The periodic rupture of hidden fault-lines exposes where the pressure points and conflicting interests lay at any one time. War is one of the most complex of all social phenomena. While violent conduct may seem chaotic and emotionally driven it is, in the end, grounded in a calculation between the risks and rewards sufficient to motivate a life-threatening activity. Nonetheless, wherever we find it, warfare is shaped by powerful cultural understandings that dictate its form and meaning and these comprise an equal part with any pragmatic understanding.

To re-assess Classic Maya warfare is to take on questions that have long proved controversial. Answers to them would be profoundly revealing of a political system. Was combat exclusively the affair of a professional elite, or did it engage sizeable portions of the population? To what degree was it motivated by conceptual as opposed to practical factors? Was war constrained by ideas of cultural affinity that limited physical damage and loss of life? What, at root, were the goals behind fighting, and did they change through time? Regarding this last issue, was there a rise in the frequency and intensity of conflict as the Classic Period progressed and, if so, did it provoke the collapse that overtook society in the ninth century? Newly available epigraphic data turns a beam of light on at least some of these issues.

To examine this topic the current chapter is divided into five sections. The first two offer an overview of how Mayanists have dealt with physical and imagistic data pertaining to warfare, and the journey from idealistic interpretations to pragmatic ones. The third looks to the glyphic and lexical evidence for conflict, supported by examples that illuminate their significance and meaning. The fourth examines a dated sample of war records from a statistical point of view, addressing long-standing debates about conceptual and practical influences on the timing of conflict. The last section draws on epigraphic, iconographic, and archaeological evidence to make some assessment of the role of warfare within Classic Maya society. The concluding case study presents the data we have for a single prolonged war involving three main protagonists.

WARFARE IN CLASSIC MAYA STUDIES

Given all the imagistic evidence for Maya militarism it is confounding that a generation and more of scholars were persuaded, or simply acquiesced to the idea, that this was a pacific society. Some of the first monuments to emerge from the forest showed near-naked captives, trussed in heavy ropes, lying contorted and trampled beneath the feet of their oppressors (see Figure 49a). These unfortunates gape and grimace, some with nails torn from their fingers or garrottes at their necks readied for throttling. Their pain and humiliation is contrasted with their preening victors, dandies in their fabulous feather crests and monster-mask headdresses, suitably armed with heavy lances and shields.

Pointing to these features, Robert Rands (1952) questioned the prevailing wisdom, but his voice went if not unheard then certainly unheeded. When the great battle mural of Bonampak – which, extending over three walls, is one of the largest and most naturalistic panoramas of combat in the ancient Americas – was written-up by Thompson he opined: "I think the terms 'battle' and perhaps even 'fight' are too grandiose to describe this action" (Ruppert, Thompson, and Proskouriakoff 1955: 51) (Figure 44). Seen through the tint of his particular spectacles it was a mere raid, the pious in search of a few sacrificial victims to satisfy their stern and demanding gods.

A paradigm shift would come, but only slowly. Proskouriakoff distanced herself from Thompson in believing that individual captures and engagements like those recorded at Bonampak did have "political importance" (Proskouriakoff 1963: 155). The identification of defensive works around certain sites would provide an important archaeological counterpoint (Puleston and Callender 1967; Webster 1976a, 1976b), while iconography played its part in focussing attention on the aforementioned brutalisation of prisoners (Baudez and Mathews 1979; Schele 1984b; Miller 1986: 112–130). The interpretive door thus cracked was flung wide by a wealth of newly deciphered inscriptions in the 1980s (Riese 1980, 1984a; Schele 1982; Houston 1983a, 1983b; Stuart

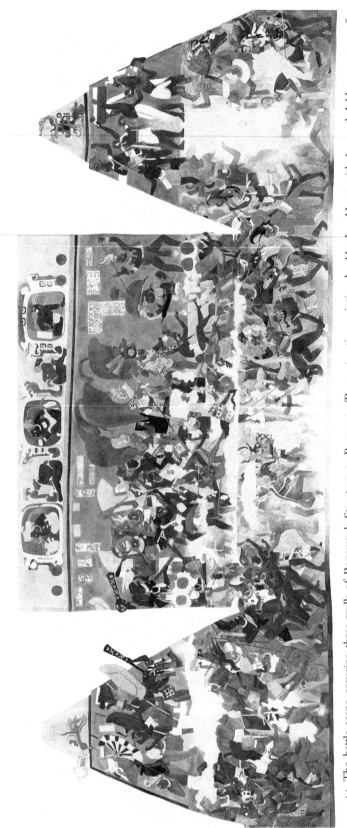

44 The battle scene covering three walls of Bonampak Structure 1, Room 2. (Reconstruction painting by Heather Hurst with Leonard Ashby, courtesy of Mary Miller)

1985a; Schele and Miller 1986: 209–240; for a review see Webster 2000). Even so, the laconic nature of the texts, their sparse provision of detail and explanation, together with some early problems of interpretation, suggested the prevalence of warfare without illuminating its political, social, and economic import.

Although by now accepted as widespread and meaningful, differing views on Maya warfare quickly emerged. Cultural ecology, which looked to the explanatory power of the environment, made the first contribution. David Webster (1975, 1977) took up and modified Robert Carneiro's (1970) argument that population growth and the scarcity of productive land fuelled violent competition. This, in turn, led to greater social complexity as war leaders capitalised on their new-found position to entrench their power in times of peace – an idea whose antecedents reach back to Hume if not well before (see Haas 1982: 25–28; also Sanders and Price 1968: 95–97). Webster (1993, 1998, 1999, 2000) posited that low resource diversity of the lowland environment offered little economic incentive for political consolidation, with the result that emerging polities were small and unstable. Since conquest could not be sustained, conflict took the form of endemic raiding instigated by intra-polity factions as a form of status rivalry. Here battle prowess bestowed higher rank and, as a result, greater access to local resources.

Looking at the same evidence, George Cowgill (1979) took a contrary position, perceiving much stronger polities that strove to achieve unification through conquest. However, in his view their failure to produce a single dominant power led to an enduring "warring states" era in which conflict became ever more nihilistic, eventually driving the whole society into ruin. Based on the late defensive features found across the Petexbatun region, Arthur Demarest (2004) has also pointed to an escalation in warfare as the root cause of the collapse, which for him began with inter-polity clashes but descended into a more chaotic and destructive social and class struggle.

Images of heroically posed and flamboyantly costumed combatants, as epitomised by the Bonampak murals, suggested to many that war was restricted to elite participation and of limited ambition (see Adams 1977: 153; Demarest 1978: 106; Schele 1984b: 44–45; Freidel 1986: 106–108; Schele and Mathews 1991: 245–246; Hassig 1992: 73–77; Stuart 1993: 333). By way of explanation, Demarest (1978) advanced the concept of "situational ethics". This was a set of principles that constrained conflict within a closely knit cultural zone but expanded it in more deadly and destructive forms against culturally distinct peoples. Specifically, this was placed at the meeting point of the southern and northern lowlands, inspired by the major fortifications at the site of Becan.

This argument was influential on the emerging model of peer polities, in which warfare was viewed as a regulating mechanism that preserved small-scale autonomy (Freidel 1986). Here campaigning was a central pursuit of kingship, indeed an essential feature of royal ideology. Frequent yet limited in its goals, it focussed on status-enhancing seizures of captives, subsequently sacrificed to the gods, and emphasised boundary maintenance over territorial aggrandisement. Fighting was conducted by highborn specialists under the hand of ideological charters with strong celestial influence (Freidel 1986: 107; Schele and Miller 1986: 220; Schele and Freidel 1990: 441). Interest in the theatricality of war was just as keen in the weak state scenarios that followed the peer polity interaction model, although this time the impediment to expansion was not just a constraining ideology but anaemic levels of political cohesion (e.g. Demarest 1992: 144). The arguments for ritualised and religiously motivated combat did not pass without criticism from the more materially-minded, who perceived a continuation, in new clothes, of much the same exceptionalism championed by Thompson and Morley (Webster 1993: 432–440).

The question for us now is which, if any, of these viewpoints does the current evidence best support? How might we penetrate the traces of war we see in text, image, and the material record to comprehend its forms and purposes?

MAYA WARFARE IN THE MATERIAL RECORD

There are limits to how much archaeology can tell us about Classic Maya warfare. Battles, even major assaults on population centres, can leave no physical traces to speak of, as damage to buildings was repaired, discharged weapons recovered, and the bodies of the fallen carried away.[1] Cemeteries of war dead are unknown and other signs of mass killing, caches of severed heads for example, are rare and ambiguous in their meaning. Very few of the skeletons excavated from tombs and other burial contexts, not all of them high-status, show obvious battle injuries. Finds of burned or demolished structures can be suggestive of conflict, but stubbornly resist certainty given that "termination rituals" can produce identical effects (see Brown and Stanton 2003; Iannone, Houk, and Schwake 2016).

To date, the exception proving the rule comes at Aguateca, which offers a time-capsule of the very moment of violent site destruction. Takeshi Inomata's excavations of burned buildings across its central district found many of their contents, valuables as well as everyday items, still in situ (Inomata 1997, 2008; Inomata and Stiver 1998; Inomata et al. 2002). Despite having a naturally defensive chasm on one side and a steep escarpment on the other, with the wider settlement protected with lines of palisades atop low walls erected late in its history, Aguateca fell to attack shortly before 810 – just as the collapse process was beginning to bite. This fascinating record survives only because it constitutes an absolute abandonment; no one returned to clear debris, repair damage, and start life anew. The bodies of some of those who died were given cursory burials, but others were left in the sun to rot.

Worldwide, fortifications are the most obvious and physically enduring signs of political insecurity. In the northern lowlands, freestanding walls surround the Late Postclassic settlements of Tulum and Mayapan (Lothrop 1924; Shook 1952; Russell 2013), but similar structures also appear at a number of earlier sites (Webster 1978; Dahlin 2000). Sometimes these take the form of two concentric rings that enclose a "killing zone" between them. A double wall of this type is depicted under assault in a mural scene at Chichen Itza dating to the late ninth century (Bolles 1977: 199, 202–203) (Figure 45a). A not dissimilar one protected the core of Ek Balam, a major centre 51 km to the northeast that preceded Chichen Itza as a regional power (Ringle et al. 2004: 507–511) (Figure 45b).[2]

Defences in the south more often consisted of ditches and banks, where spoil excavated from bedrock was heaped toward the side to be protected, forming a rampart. These would have been made still more formidable if surmounted by wooden palisades. Such simple but labour-intensive constructions are notoriously difficult to date, yet it is interesting how many of them, including the impressive moat at Becan, appear to be Preclassic in origin (e.g. Webster 1976a, 1976b; Matheny 1987; Johnston 2006: 190–191; Ford 2016). During the Late Preclassic the greatest city of its day, El Mirador, built a substantial wall around much of its ceremonial core (Matheny 1987: 19; Medina 2012). Our knowledge of Preclassic political history is effectively zero, but works of this scale imply a not insignificant degree of conflict (Inomata and Triadan 2009; Inomata 2014).

The cores of some Classic Period cities were situated on raised ground, but many were set on more-or-less level terrain and their settlement dispersed widely in all directions – neither feature showing a great eye toward defence. The vast majority had no formal fortifications and walled cities in the true sense were absent altogether.

The most notable barrier almost certainly commissioned in this era is the one found at Tikal (Puleston and Callender 1967). Set as much as five kilometres from the site core, a long bank and ditch earthwork, crossed by occasional causeways, demarked a large rural zone rather than an urban core. A re-examination of this feature extended its length to some 26 km, tracking a western line to match the one originally identified to the north (Webster et al. 2004, 2007). While demonstrating the massive ambition of the project, this later study noted that the northern course does not always follow an ideal topographical line and that some stretches on the western side were left unfinished.

The two lines converge on steeply rising ground, the beginning of a chain of hills that define the northern boundary of a wide valley extending west

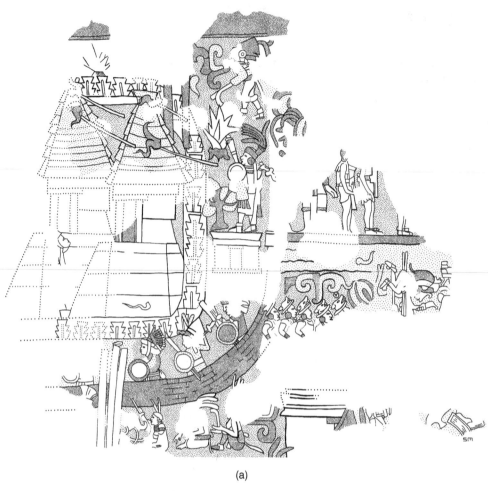

(a)

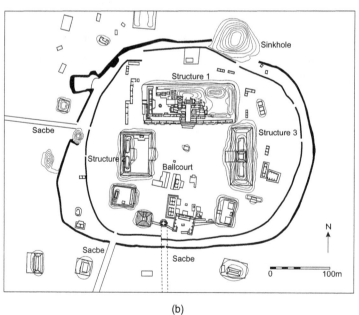

Sinkhole

Structure 1

Sacbe

Structure 3

Structure

Ballcourt

N

Sacbe

Sacbe

0   100m

(b)

45 Double-wall systems in the northern lowlands: (a) Mural showing an assault with flaming darts against the core of a site featuring two temples. Las Monjas, Room 22, Chichen Itza (after Adela Breton); (b) Map of the core area of Ek Balam (based on maps in Vargas and Castillo 2014: figures 21.1 and 21.40 and Ringle and Bey 1988: 20–21)

towards El Zotz. Lidar survey now reveals that some of the ridgetops over-looking this valley were home to major fortifications, of which La Cuernavilla is the most significant (Garrison, Houston, and Alcover 2017, 2018). Encircled by deep trenches and enclosing little internal architecture – features increasingly seen in lidar scans elsewhere – these are not protected settlements so much as strategic fortresses from which a force could dominate a surrounding area, or else refuges used only in times of special threat. The same survey also revealed a dense network of watchtowers and/or signalling posts set on levelled hilltops, evidence for a sophisticated surveillance system. The dating of these efforts is as yet unknown, but since they commanded the western approaches to Tikal they could well have been dedicated to its greater security.

Planned defensive landscapes, if on a much smaller scale, have also been identified in the border zone between Yaxchilan and Piedras Negras (Golden et al. 2008: 265–266; Scherer and Golden 2009, 2014). Here we find valley passes that have been obstructed with the low walls that once secured palisades, while hilltops were the location for lookout stations. Nearby settlements such as Tecolote and La Pasadita, the latter known to be home to Yaxchilan *sajal*, were perched on high ground with clear defensive intent. Dating to the latter parts of the eighth century, these features hold particular promise for text–material interactions, given the rich record of conflict between these two polities. Revealed only by detailed ground survey, frontier defences in this kind of terrain might not be exceptional.

As we enter the ninth century more drastic and hurried measures appear in the record, often, as at Aguateca, shortly before final abandonment. Court structures and temples at Dos Pilas, for example, were torn down to form the rubble footings for more palisades, in this case a double line (Demarest et al. 1997: 233–236). Such barricades, often running right through elite compounds, have been reported at a good number of sites now and seem to have been a common response to the terminal crisis (e.g. Medina 2012). A few populations survived by withdrawing to lake peninsulas which, cleaved from the shore by ditches or water-filled moats, became artificial islands.[3] Examples of these are to be found at Punta de Chimino on Lake Petexbatun and Zacpeten on Lake Salpeten (Demarest et al. 1997: 238–242; Rice, Rice, and Pugh 1998: 225–227). The former succeeded Aguateca as the last active Classic settlement in the Petexbatun region.

To summarise, fortifications provide the best physical evidence of Maya warfare, works that appear across the lowlands and the full span of time periods. They show great variability in form and were patently designed on an individual basis to serve specific local needs. Lidar mapping has proven adept at identifying elevated fortresses set away from population centres and, to judge from what we have seen thus far, future work will only increase their number. Construction dates indicate an ebb and flow of perceived threat, with highpoints in the Late Preclassic and at the end of the Late Classic – both periods that ended in political, social and demographic collapse.

WORDS OF WAR

For all the challenges of interpretation and the obvious gulf between actual events and the written testimonies to them, epigraphic records of warfare offer a source of unmatched specificity. They identify protagonists, both victors and victims, as well as different types of engagement and their timing accurate to the day. Any epigraphic study of conflict must work outward from a comprehension of the relevant terminology within its semantic and narrative context. Accordingly, this section is organised around the most common war verbs, which serve as a framework for the discussion of a wider group of conflict-related terms as they arise.

Chuk, "To Seize, Tie-up"

One of Knorozov's successes came in linking the images of bound prisoners in the Postclassic codices with captions containing the syllabically spelled compound we can read as **chu-ka-ja** (Knorozov 1958: 471–472) (Figure 46a).[4] *Chuk* is a widely-distributed root in Mayan languages with meanings of "to tie-up", "to catch", and "to take" (Kaufman 2003: 904), and it is this sense of seizing and binding captives that we find in the inscriptions. Without endorsing Knorozov's language paradigm as such, Proskouriakoff (1960: 470, figure 8a, 1963: 150, figure 1) took up this identification – bravely so given

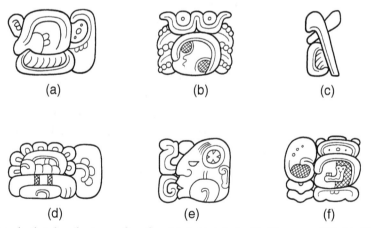

46 Six verbs that describe types of warfare: (a) *chuhkaj,* "seized"; (b) star war "?"; (c) *ch'ak,* "to damage, attack"; (d) *jubuuyi,* "downed"; (e) *puluuyi,* "burned"; (f) *och uch'een,* "enters the domain/settlement of".

Thompson's blanket rejection – and used it in her historical reconstructions. She recognised that the glyphs emblazoned on the thighs of prisoners on Yaxchilan Lintel 8 were personal names, and that one of those names recurs in the accompanying text directly after the *chuk* term.

Although a transitive root, the appropriate active form *uchukuw*, "he seizes him/her" is very rarely seen and it is the passive *chuhkaj*, "he/she is seized" that predominates. Since the name of the captor is omitted, any credit for the action must come via a connecting term such as *ukabjiiy*, "he/she supervised it" or "the doing of" (explained more fully in Chapter 10). On other occasions the link is provided by a possessed noun, which Proskouriakoff (1963: 152) understood in principle and was later read as **u-ba-ki** *ubaak*, "the captive of" (Fox and Justeson 1984: 42).[5] Other spellings use logographic **BAAK** in one of two versions, a stylised long bone or a skull, both signalling homophonic *baak*, "bone" (Stuart 1985a: 98). Even though the noun's martial sense has disappeared from modern languages, it was preserved in the causative verb *baksah*, "to capture in war" in Colonial Yukatek (Barrera Vásquez 1980: 29). In the Classic Period we also see "count of captives" titles such as *aj wuk baak*, "He of Seven Prisoners" (Stuart 1985a) and *aj baak,* literally "He of Prisoner(s)" (Grube 1996: 8).

Another important title introduces a captive's name with **u-CHA'AN-nu** or **u-cha-nu**, read *ucha'an*, "master/guardian of" (Proskouriakoff 1963: 152; Alfonso Lacadena, pers. comm. 1997; Lacadena and Wichmann 2004: 140–141). Frequently these "captor titles" refer back to pre-accession qualifications for rulership and are the only evidence we have for those particular conflicts.

One monument combines several of these forms in a carefully staged interplay between text and image (Figure 47). The carved underside of a lintel, with some of its original blue and red colour still adhering, it comes from an as yet unknown site in the sphere of Yaxchilan (Stuart 1995: 296–297). It shows the king Shield Jaguar IV within a palace building, signalled by its lashed curtains or awning. There he is enthroned on a bench that bears his name and titles, written in reverse, beginning with his youth-name of Chelew Chan K'inich and followed by his captor's title *ucha'an tajal mo'*, "Guardian of Torch Macaw". The scene shows him receiving his vassal Aj Chak Maax, who offers up a shell, a token of preciousness that often accompanies gifts and tribute. Since Aj Chak Maax appears on the prestigious right-hand position we can be sure that this stone was his commission and decorated one of his buildings, although he denotes his inferior status by setting the king at a higher level. At the foot of the scene sit three prisoners, their names given in nearby inset captions. After the date, the main text gives *chuhkaj baah wayib ukabjiiy aj chak maax*, describing Aj Chak Maax's taking of the leading captive, Baah Wayib, in 783.[6] Three days later we are told *nahwaj ubaak ti yajaw*, "his captives are

47 A noble called Aj Chak Maax presents three captives to his overlord, Shield Jaguar IV of Yaxchilan in 783. Unprovenanced panel now in the Kimbell Museum of Art, Fort Worth. (Photograph by Justin Kerr)

displayed/presented to his lord". Perhaps a regular practice by which warriors gained merit and personal honour, this suggests that the unfortunates could be gifts and hint at the economic value of high-status prisoners – of which we will hear more (p.232).

Chuk is the most commonly recorded military action, with fifty-eight dated and another fifteen undateable cases appearing between 564 and 808 (Martin 2014a: table 15). Its history is even deeper given that the earliest examples, from

Dzibanche, might be dated in terms of style to as early as the fourth century CE (Case Study 6). While the term itself focuses attention on a personalised seizure, it was always part of a larger action. It might be noted in this respect that the great battle mural of Bonampak is captioned by a single *chuk* event. Sometimes *chuk* verbs accompany other war expressions as addenda that specify the leading prisoner taken in the action concerned, while a war verb of any variety might be illustrated by images of trussed prisoners. A good many pictured captives have captions that provide their names and titles, often identifying conflicts unattested in narrative inscriptions. While these contribute to our overall knowledge of Classic Maya warfare, many of them reflected in Figure 75, in lacking dates they fall outside the chronological analyses that we will be conducting here.

A very small percentage of depicted captives are female (n = 3). Their treatment is no better than that of their male counterparts. One is tied with rope and her dress cut with flapped holes, a second is trampled beneath the feet of her female abuser, while a third is shown bound and half-naked – breaking the taboo against female nudity outside mythic contexts (Martin 2009a; Reese-Taylor et al. 2009: 52–53, 58–59) (Figure 48).[7] We must wonder about the ultimate fates of these women. The seizure of highborn females for enforced marriage is a recurring practice worldwide. However, the abject humiliation they suffer in these scenes seems more akin to the symbolic crushing of the maternal bloodlines they embody.[8]

In the case of male captives, it was long assumed that all met a grisly end in ritual killing, but we now know that some not only survived imprisonment, they were restored to their thrones. The best example of this is Yich'aak Bahlam of Ceibal, who was seized when his capital fell to Dos Pilas in December 735. He is shown bound and trampled on monuments at both Dos Pilas and Aguateca, but within a few years he re-appears at his home city conducting ceremonies as

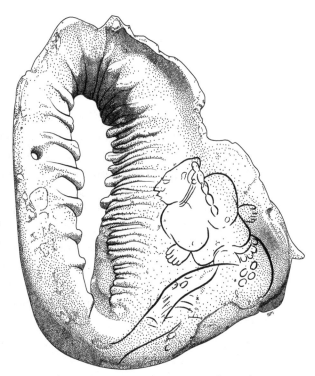

48 Female captive on an unprovenanced conch shell. K4499. (After a photograph by Justin Kerr)

king – albeit under the oversight of his conquerors (Martin and Grube 1994a: n.20; 2000: 61, 63; Stuart 1995: 324–326).

Star war "?"

A compound featuring the sign for "star" framed by beads or dots and set over the sign for "earth" has long aroused interest for its astronomical potential, its associated dates scrutinised for how they relate to the movements of planets, most especially Venus (Thompson 1950: 228; Kelley and Kerr 1973: 197–199; Kelley 1977: 38–42; Closs 1979, 1981) (Figure 46b).

Yet in many contexts it appears with war-related glyphs and symbolism, suggesting that a core reference is to conflict (Mathews in Sosa and Reents 1980; Riese 1980: 38–39, 1984a: 274–280). As the evidence for this connection mounted a group of scholars sought to reconcile the two lines of enquiry, developing a model in which warfare was timed to coincide with planetary motions (Lounsbury 1982; Schele 1982: 99; Schele and Miller 1986: 214, 217; Justeson 1989: 105–109; Aveni and Hotaling 1994; Nahm 1994). This was crystallised in the nickname "star war" and linked to militaristic motifs from Central Mexico, especially those associated with the storm god the later Mexica knew as Tlaloc (Schele and Freidel 1990: 146–147, 444–446; Schele 1991b; Carlson 1993). This "Tlaloc-Venus complex" posited an ideology of celestially timed war-making that employed distinctive weaponry, most of all the *atlatl* spearthrower, as part of a package of features imported from Central Mexico in the late fourth century CE.[9]

With no phonetically transparent substitutions identified thus far, the star war root remains unknown.[10] The symbolism of the glyph offers a clue to the concept at its core, since the beads framing the star represent streams of water falling onto the earth. This starry rain has been linked to meteors, which were identified with war, malevolence, and misfortune throughout Mesoamerica (Stuart 1995: 310). Some contexts clearly indicate that we are dealing with an idea derived from myth. In these, the verb captions a scene in which the Maize God rides in a canoe propelled by the Paddler Gods, a journey that ends in its sinking (see Freidel, Schele, and Parker 1993: figure 2:26). One version, on a painted polychrome vessel, elaborates the narrative by showing the canoe paddled through a star-sent storm (Marc Zender, pers. comm. 2016). Supernatural episodes such as these have often been confused with war events in past studies, and re-analysis requires that they are separated, and non-martial instances excluded (Martin 2014a: table 16). Such a view steps away from any specific cosmic events and towards the broader realm of metaphor.

It has long been clear that star wars often denote the most momentous of encounters, including those resulting in the capture of kings and the fall of dynasties. Grammatically, the victim can be either a place or a person, with a variety of different phrasings and formulae employed.[11] Toponyms are the most common subject, and in several cases these are the referents featured within the emblem glyphs of opposing polities. Some show a glyphic super-imposition in which the vanquished referent is set directly beneath the starry rain of the verb (Mathews 1991: 24–25). When Ceibal falls prey to Dos Pilas, its toponym is additionally introduced by the preposition *ti*, specifying a "star war *at* Ceibal". Elsewhere, as in the attack on Naranjo by a member of the Snake dynasty, the verb with a superimposed Naranjo referent is followed by a possessed *uch'een* and the name of the defeated king, thereby directly equating an emblem referent with the elusive *ch'een* term. Elsewhere, *uch'een* can itself be superimposed into the verb. Further light on its meaning is shed by an instance at Tonina, where the star war victory over Sak Tz'i' – the "White Dog" dynasty based at Lacanja-Tzeltal – takes place against the expanded *ukab(u)ch'een* of its king (Martin 2004b: 108).

On other occasions star wars take a different possessed subject: the conjoined signs for a flint-blade and a shield, the metaphorical *took'pakal* we last encoun-tered in Chapter 7 (Figure 32). The pairing appears in its full martial form as a shield backed by crossed flint-tipped spears within the Temple of the Sun at Palenque (Figure 31), where it serves as an object of veneration in a war-themed patron deity shrine. It plainly has a symbolic or conceptual value, but there is cause to question that Jean Genet's early interpretation of "war" is the most appropriate one.

The existence of the titles *baahpakal*, "head shield" and *baahtook'*, "head flint" in military contexts could well imply that there were groups of warriors called "shields" and "flints" – in the same manner as *baahch'ok*, "head youth" and *baahajaw*, "head lord" implies other youths and lords (Miller and Martin 2004: 27, figure 12h).[12] More than one such *baahpakal* stands before the king in a scene of captive presentation in the murals of Bonampak (Houston 2012: 165). The Classic Maya *took'pakal* metaphor might have a dualistic sense, signifying an abstract expression of the king's martial power as well the physical realisation of that power as a body of armed men.[13] In either case, when a possessed *took'pakal* is the subject of the star war verb there are grounds to suspect that the defeat of an army, the king's "weapons", is the intended sense (Martin 2001c: 179).

Ch'ak, "To Damage, Attack"

The pictograph of a hafted axe invites a relatively narrow range of interpret-ations (Thomas 1882: 126; Brinton 1895: 103–104), with warfare one of the more compelling (Kelley 1976: 135; Riese 1984a: 272–274) (Figure 46c). Thomas's suggested reading of *baat*, "axe" held sway for over a century until the recognition of its verbal role and phonetic complementation led Jorge

Orejel (1990) to propose *ch'ak*, "to chop". In Yukatekan languages this word appears as "to chop with an axe", while Ch'orti' has *ch'akem*, "hacked, wounded", evidently descended from Proto-Ch'olan **ch'aak*, "injure" (Wisdom 1950: 43; Barrera Vásquez 1980: 122; Kaufman and Norman 1984: 119; Kaufman 2003: 872). A fully syllabic rendering of the passive form **ch'a-ka-ja** *ch'ahkaj*, "is chopped" was identified soon afterwards and offered persuasive support for Orejel's idea (Looper and Schele 1991).

With few exceptions in the Classic era, logographic **CH'AK** appears with its appropriate phonetic complement **ka**, in either its fish-fin or whole fish form. Here its presence is motivated less by the needs of lexical distinction or as an aid to its reading than by the desire to fill-out the awkwardly shaped axe image into a more convenient lozenge shape for the script.

All *ch'ak* war verbs are applied to toponyms, describing such-and-such a place as "injured/damaged" or perhaps simply "attacked" (Martin 2014a: table 17). Two examples involve assaults by the Snake dynasty on the Palenque capital Lakamha', one in 599 and the other in 611 (Martin 2000c: 107–111).[14] These are the longest-range campaigns yet identified, reaching over 247 km from Calakmul, but if launched from the Snake capital of this period, Dzibanche, an even more impressive 369 km (Map 1, see Case Study 6).[15]

The 611 attack represents the pivotal episode within the 617-glyph long inscription of the three interior panels that give their name to the Temple of the Inscriptions. Completed by K'inich Kaan Bahlam II in 692, they represent a textual memorial to his father K'inich Janaab Pakal I – whose body was found buried deep within the pyramid in the tomb discovered by Ruz – and describe the ritual servicing of the city's three patron gods and a political history that explains his father's route to power. Here the 611 defeat is followed by the death of Ajen Yohl Mat, the then-ruler of Palenque, in 612 and the elevation of someone who named himself after the deep-time founder of the kingdom, Muwaan Mat. The reign of this mysterious character is accompanied by explicit statements of calendrical rituals and rites for local gods that were *not* performed and a general lamentation *sataayi k'uhul ixik sataayi ajaw*, "loss of the holy ladies, loss of the lords" (Grube 1996: 5–6; Martin and Grube 2000: 161). Muwaan Mat could well have been a puppet ruler installed by the victors, and it is telling that he does not seem to have a place in Palenque's count of kings. These troubles come to an end with the accession of the twelve-year-old K'inich Janaab Pakal in 615, and it was his indirect claim to rule, lacking descent from a previous king, that seems to motivate this lengthy discourse.

The *ch'ak* statement could be personalised by exchanging the relevant place-name for the possessed location *uch'een* followed by the name of its defeated owner. The earliest example, in fact the earliest firmly dated military action thus far, appears on Tikal Stela 10 and is placed to 486 (Martin 1999: 5, 2003b: 16).[16] The full phrase here runs *ch'ahkaj uch'een maasal ajaw*, "the domain/

settlement of the Maasal lord is attacked". The only truly personal applications of *ch'ak* are references to decapitation in the form *ch'ahkaj ubaah*, "his head is chopped" (Houston and Stuart 1998: 78). The inclusion of these in several previous lists of war actions has been misleading, since they are executions performed on prisoners and do not necessarily occur on the date of their capture. The illustrative case here is the beheading of the Copan king Waxaklajuun Ubaah K'awiil at the hands of his one-time vassal K'ahk' Tiliw Chan Yopaat of Quirigua, which took place six days after what appears to be the actual date of his defeat (Marcus 1976: 134–140, Looper 1999: 268–269, 2003: 234).

Jub, "To Take/Knock Down"

Linda Schele (1982: 106–107) first noted the close relationship of a particular glyphic compound to captive-taking, but it was only after the decipherment of the complete syllable string **ju-bu-yi** that the verb root *jub* could be read (Grube, in Schele 1992c: 223; Martin 2014a: table 18) (Figure 46d). It appears in Modern Ch'ol as *jubel*, "to take down" (Aulie and Aulie 1978: 68), while in Yukatekan languages the cognate *hub* has a range of negative connotations, most notably Mopan's "to knock down" (Hofling 2011: 223). Like the star war verb, *jub* can be applied to a possessed *utook' upakal* – the defeat of an army in a metaphorical or literal sense. Since it never takes *uch'een* or a specific location as its subject, *jub* is the best candidate we have for a field battle fought away from major settlements.

A critical instance of the *jubuuyi utook'pakal* event is the one describing the clash between Calakmul and Tikal in August 695, which can be considered among the most consequential of the Classic Period. Noted in Case Study 8, it is one of only two known defeats of the Snake polity. Even though its king Yuknoom Yich'aak K'ahk' survived the battle, it marks the beginning of a steady decline in its political fortunes, as its ability to install foreign kings ebbs away and its dominance is at least partially replaced by that of Tikal. The 695 action is associated with the capture of an image of the Calakmul deity called Yajaw Maan in an earlier example of the same god-capture formula seen at Tikal a generation later. It is interesting and significant that thirteen days after the battle a captive is displayed at Tikal (Schele and Freidel 1990: 205–208), where he is apparently captioned as an *aj sa'al*, making him a native of Naranjo rather than Calakmul (Martin 1996d, 2003b: 30). If so, this offers a rare glimpse of collaborative campaigning between a patron and one of its clients.

Pul, "To Burn"

Another term specifying conflict consists of a human head with a "sun" motif set into its temple and flames issuing in front or above (Schele 1982: 103–104)

(Figure 46e). None of its martial examples offer a clue to its reading, but its substitution with **pu-lu** in a ritual usage establishes **PUL** as the logogram in question (Stuart 1995: 320–322). As the transitive verb *pul*, "to burn" it survives in a variety of Ch'olan Maya languages today (Aulie and Aulie 1978: 96; Kaufman and Norman 1984: 129). Outside war contexts it can describe mythic burning events, the foremost being the immolation of a jaguar deity. On at least one occasion in a re-enactment in which a defeated king takes the place of the feline god (Martin and Grube 2000: 82) (p.161). Like *ch'ak*, *pul* is exclusively applied to locations in war contexts, either directly or via the *uch'een* formula that introduces the name of the defeated opponent.

To what does the "burning" refer? A temple in flames served as a pictographic emblem of conquest for the Mexica and appears in their manuscripts in conjunction with a toponym that denoted the defeated town or city (see Stuart 1995: 330). Stone structures of the kind found in Maya site cores might not seem very combustible, but they would have contained wooden and textile furnishings that would have burned well. But more to the point, the great mass of any Maya settlement consisted of pole-and-thatch buildings that were highly flammable. Indeed, the mural painting from Chichen Itza noted above shows thatched temples under a rain of flaming darts (Figure 45a). If we examine how the instances of *pul* fall across the tropical year we see that no currently known example occurs in the months of July, August, October, or November (Figure 52e). These are some of the wettest parts of the year and would be consistent with the idea that thatched roofs, soaked for much of this time, were the main reference in these actions, with *pul* having a literal not symbolic meaning (Martin 2009b).[17]

There is a poignant case on Naranjo Stela 23, towards the end of the period in which Naranjo conducts a fiery rampage through the eastern Peten (Martin and Grube 2000: 76). In 710 K'ahk' Tiliw Chan Chahk burned the nearby capital of Yaxha, described using the *puluuyi uch'een* formula. The name of the Yaxha king is preceded by *ma' ch'ahb ma' ak'abil*, "without genesis, without darkness", the negated form of a metaphorical couplet linked to a king's procreative powers (p.146). This tells us that whatever this mystical possession represents, defeat and capture nullifies it, rendering a king spiritually impotent (Stuart 2005e: 278). The Yaxha king's nominal follows and is perhaps to be read Joyaj Chahk (Tokovinine 2013: 34, figure 21a). The text goes on to give the self-contained statement *waxaklajuun k'in ajawin*, "18-day reigns". This seems to refer to the short tenure of the victim, implying an accession date for him on 9.13.18.4.0 (Nikolai Grube, pers. comm. 1995).

The next section describes the denouement of the action and is marked with the previously noted verb *lok'*, "to emerge", which includes the senses of "eject" or "abandon". In this case we find it in the phrase *ilok'ooyi yitaaj yatan ix mutul ajaw*, "is ejected with his spouse (the) Tikal Lady".[18] This unusual supplement serves to highlight Yaxha's links to a kingdom Naranjo had twice battled in 695, the great rival and antagonist of Naranjo's overlord Calakmul.

The implication is that Naranjo and Yaxha were not only local rivals but were divided by their wider loyalties to regional hegemons. In this vein, it has long been noted that the twin pyramid complex at Yaxha is modelled after those at Tikal. After this banishment, the Stela 23 text duly records K'ahk' Tiliw Chan Chahk as the agent of all these events and concludes by describing rituals involving the exhumation of an earlier Yaxha king and the scattering of his bones on an island (Grube and Schele 1994: 4–5). This information evidently provides some relevant subtext to the war, which seems to have been designed to remove a newly installed neighbour.

The most interesting instance of the *lok'* verb may well be the one that has K'awiil Chan K'inich of Dos Pilas as its subject (Houston and Mathews 1985: 18; Houston 1993: 117, figure 4–21). Recorded on Tamarindito Hieroglyphic Stairway 2, this "ejection" in 761 seems sure to reflect a significant military reverse, although the opponent responsible is not clearly stated. This episode could well mark the early abandonment of Dos Pilas and a retrenchment to Aguateca, given that this king's Dos Pilas Hieroglyphic Stairway 1 was left unfinished, with a number of its glyph-blocks outlined but never carved. Other important instances of *pul* and *lok'* – as well as *t'ab,* which describes acts of "ascent" to particular locations – appear on two earlier hieroglyphic stairways at Dos Pilas, where a great war narrative tracks the kingdom's fortunes through a portion of the seventh century, examined in Case Study 11.[19]

Other War Verbs

There are some other verbs for hostile action that, though uncommon, should be mentioned here. The intransitive verb *och,* "to enter" (Stuart 1998: 387–389) appears in a variety of contexts, taking a martial character where it has *uch'een* as its subject (Martin and Grube 2000: 76, 181; Martin 2004b: 105–109) (Figure 46f).[20] Proceeding from our earlier discussion of *ch'een* we can gloss *och uch'een* as "enters the domain/settlement of".[21] Two contexts go a long way to revealing its meaning. The first comes on the series of stairway blocks excavated at the site of Dzibanche, where texts show *och uch'een* followed by the names of the bound captives pictured in their scenes (Nalda 2004: 32–55; Velásquez 2004a: 87–96) (Figure 26). In most cases the verb is *och uch'een,* but in a few *chuhkaj,* "is seized" replaces it with no alteration to the scene. In the second example, on the front of Stela 21 at Naranjo, we see the local king trampling his enemy underfoot in a standard motif of victory, with the caption reading *ubaah ti ochch'een yopmootz(?)"* or "he is in (the act of) *ch'een*-entering Yopmootz" (Figure 49a and b).[22] The body of the trampled king, his eyes closed to indicate death, is tagged with a name-glyph also visible

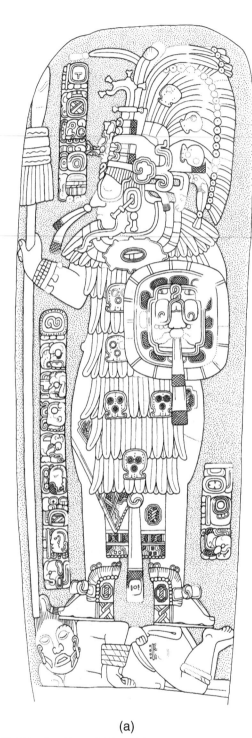

(b)

(a)

49 K'ahk' Tiliw Chan Chahk and the *ochch'een* "domain/settlement-entering" of "Yopmootz" on Naranjo Stela 21: (a) Front face (drawing by Ian Graham © President and Fellows of Harvard College, Peabody Museum of Archaeology and Ethnology, PM# 2004.15.6.2.37); (b) Detail of the caption reading *ubaah ti ochch'een yopmootz(?)*, "His image in (the act of) *ch'een*-entering Yopmootz".

in a badly damaged *puluuyi uch'een* phrase on the rear face of this monument. The *och uch'een* expression evidently refers to an invasion, on this occasion leading to the capture and killing of the opposing king.

Analogous to the *baksah* verb mentioned earlier, the noun *baak*, "captive" was the basis of a derived intransitive verb in the inscriptions. This is formed as *baakwaj* or its variant *baaknaj* (Schele 1991c: 2; Martin 1996a: 227, 2000c: 112; Lacadena 2004: 185, 193). Both appeared in our discussion of captured god images in Case Study 8, but on one other occasion, the Tikal Rock Sculpture, *baakwaj* refers to the seizure of a Holmul lord in precisely the context we might expect to find *chuk* (Martin 2000c: 111–113, 2003b: 31–32, figure 1.18).[23]

The final verb to be treated here appears in the active transitive form *unakaw*, "he battles, conquers it" in a single example at Dos Pilas (Grube and Schele 1993). The root *nak* is only attested as "to battle, conquer" in contemporary Tzotzil Maya (Laughlin 1988: 267–268), but in Colonial Yukatek we find the agentive title *nakom*, "conqueror" as a key military position in the preceding Postclassic Period (Landa 1941: 122; Relaciones de Yucatán 2 1898–1900: 185–186, 208–209). These terms presumably have a common origin and indicate that the *nak* root had a wider distribution at one time.

STATISTICAL ANALYSIS OF MAYA WARFARE

As we have seen, epigraphy presents us with several different types of military action, the names of participants, and sometimes the location where the engagement took place. That many are accompanied by dates fixed to the day offers an excellent opportunity to conduct a statistical analysis of their chronology. The five main verb categories above describe 165 separate episodes of conflict, of which 141 can be dated and are suitable for such a study.[24] This is a larger dataset than any assembled thus far and it allows us to revisit some of the competing models of Classic Maya warfare to see how well they stand up to renewed examination. The analyses on which those models relied variously suffered from small samples, limited verbal categories, and errors in dating and identification. Since it is difficult to evaluate and compare studies that differ so much, some of them reaching opposite conclusions, I will note their sample size and the percentage to which they match the current dataset wherever it can be calculated.

Previous Statistical Work

The first lists of battle events were assembled by Schele (1982) in her doctoral research, a substantial compendium of hieroglyphic verbs. However, it was Berthold Riese (1984a: figure 16) who first collected war-related terms in a dedicated study. His 46 actions contained some duplicates and misidentifications, bringing that figure down to just 24, making for only a fifty-two per cent correspondence with the current sample. Soon after, John Justeson (1989: 105–109, table 8.8) focussed on the astronomical significance of dates associated with the star war verb, identifying twenty-three such events as military actions, although of these only ten, or forty-three per cent, stand up today. His distributional analysis suggested a "war season" running from mid-November to mid-February. Schele and Mathews (1991: table 10.4) looked at warfare in terms of regional interaction, collecting 16 conflicts in which both victor and vanquished were identifiable polities, with a seventy-five per cent match to the dataset used here.

Ross Hassig (1992: 97) re-examined the issue of seasonality and posited a distinction between "conquests" that were clustered between December and early June, and "captures" that were grouped in two periods, spanning late November to March, and then August to September. The first set numbered twenty-five cases and consisted mostly of star wars, although of these only fifty-two per cent were correctly identified and dated, while the second set, numbering forty-three cases, were mostly *chuk* captures that achieved an accuracy of seventy-four per cent (Hassig 1992: 219–221, n.35, 36).[25] The same year Joyce Marcus (1992a: 430–433, table 11.1) used historical accounts from the Colonial Period to argue for a preference for dry season warfare, illustrating her point with a collection of twenty-three events from the texts that fell between November and May – although only fifty-two per cent of them would be recognised as conflicts today.

A larger-scale study came from Werner Nahm (1994), who concentrated on the question of Venusian influence. He looked solely at star war and *chuk* events, with samples of twenty-five and forty-two and an accuracy that can now be judged to eighty per cent and seventy-eight per cent, respectively (Nahm 1994: tables 1 and 2). His charts suggested clusters around particular "months" of the 584-day Venus year he was proposing, but little or no correspondence to points in the visible motion of the planet from earth such as superior or inferior conjunction (the points at which Venus disappears while travelling behind or in front of the sun, respectively, both of variable duration) (Nahm 1994: figures 3 and 4). In a comparable assessment of the solar year he detected reduced war activity during the maize planting in May and a complete cessation during the harvest between mid-September and the end of October (Nahm 1994: figure 5). He noted the surprisingly high frequency of conflicts during the middle of the rainy season, interpreting them as short-lived affairs that could be distinguished from longer campaigns falling in drier parts of the year.

A direct challenge to Nahm's data and analysis quickly emerged. Lorren Hotaling (1995) excluded events whose Long Count positions had been reconstructed from Calendar Round dates alone, together with all actions in campaigns apart from the initial engagement, arguing that follow-on actions would distort any specific instigation by Venus. In their place, he added some star war events that Nahm had set aside as non-martial, producing a sample of fifty at a barely improved eighty-two per cent accuracy. Hotaling's study disputed any correspondence to posited divisions of the Venus year (Hotaling 1995: figure 6), while supporting the same wet-dry pattern for the solar year – even after exchanging Nahm's Julian calendar for the seasonally attuned proleptic Gregorian version (Hotaling 1995: figures 4 and 5).

In a paper presented in 1995, Peter Mathews (2000: 151, table 3) also plotted warfare against the solar year, although only for a sub-region stretching from Yaxchilan to points further west. Using a sample of fifty-four unspecified conflicts, he found no noticeable seasonal pattern to the data, but in a second chart that spanned the length of the Classic Period he did detect a major uptick in incidents towards the end of the era (Mathews 2000: 128–129, table 1). In an unpublished paper, Mark Child (1999, cited in Webster 2000: 96) claimed a sample of 107 episodes of warfare and argued for the same acceleration in conflict leading to a peak at around 800, thus implicating endemic warfare in the ninth century collapse.

It was clear from the beginning that very few star war events fell directly on Venus nodes, and the scholars who argued for the influence of this planet allowed wide margins to accommodate the vagaries of observation. This lack of strict correspondence would eventually inspire a review of the whole concept of celestial influence. Gerardo Aldana (2005) conducted a re-analysis of the star war data, demonstrating the absence of any discernible connection to Venus phenomena. He employed a sample of twenty-seven events, although his accuracy of seventy per cent was actually less than the lists of Nahm and Hotaling he critiqued (Aldana 2005: table 3). A subsequent study using an updated listing of twenty-seven star war events, with a much-improved accuracy of eighty-eight per cent, supported Aldana's conclusions (Villaseñor 2012: 37, graph 5, table 2).

Variation over the Classic Period

The simplest way in which we might examine the new dataset is to place it in chronological order to track records of warfare over the course of the Classic Period. It has been appreciated for some time that such accounts are rare in the Early Classic – even when assessed within a reduced sample – but rise abruptly after 550 to become a notable feature of Late Classic inscriptions (Houston 1993: 138; Miller 1993: 408; Stuart 1993: 333; Mathews 2000: chart 1).

This is duly reflected in my sample (Figure 50a). In fact, given the retrospective nature of the many early episodes, even this understates the issue. Perhaps only *five* records in the sample were actually recorded during the Early

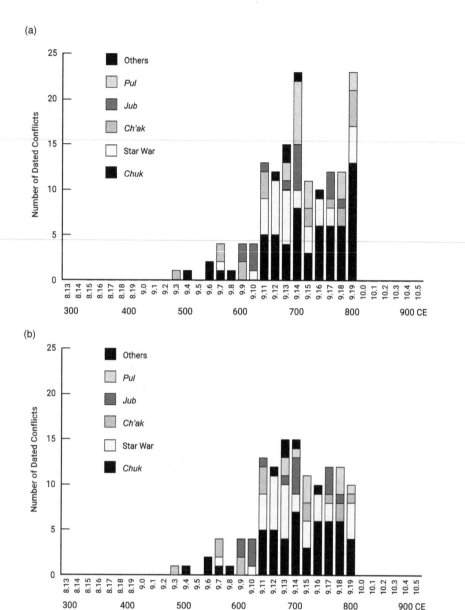

50 Records of warfare arranged according to K'atun eras and divided into five thematic types: (a) The full sample; (b) The sample minus three monuments (Naranjo Stela 22, Yaxchilan Hieroglyphic Stairway 5, and Naranjo Stela 12).

Classic Period itself.[26] Nevertheless, given the quantity of early war iconography and archaeological indicators, principally depictions of bound captives known to reach back into Protoclassic times if not before, as well as the early defensive systems noted earlier, it is widely accepted that warfare had long been a feature of Maya society. The point at issue is whether the Late Classic upsurge was a rhetorical development spurred by changing ideas about royal prowess and validation, or whether it reflects a genuine increase in the tempo and significance of war in society (see Houston 1993: 138; Stuart 1993: 333–336).

A number of scholars suggest that warfare did indeed increase, with its greatest effects felt at the close of the Late Classic as a symptom of mounting social and political breakdown (e.g. Adams 1977: 223; Demarest 1978: 108, 1993: 111, 2004, 2013a; Cowgill 1979; Schele 1991d: 87). Statistical data for an acceleration, with a highpoint in 800 that coincides with the first signs of political collapse, have clearly lent weight to that proposition. A peak of this kind certainly appears in the sample collected in Figure 50a, but there is reason to question its significance and the inferences drawn from it (Martin 2009b).

Here it is instructive to look at an earlier peak in the chart, the one representing 22 conflicts recorded between 692 and 711. This is the period the Maya defined as the fourteenth K'atun of the tenth Bak'tun that spanned 9.13.0.0.1 to 9.14.0.0.0, marked on the chart as "9.14". Our first response might be to ask what social or political factors provoked this well-above-average incidence. However, the explanation is a single monument, Naranjo Stela 22 from 702, which lists nine military actions, constituting fully forty-one per cent of the total for that period. While this record has much to tell us about Naranjo's activities at that time, it does not point to a systemic increase in violence.

The same is true of the final peak as well. There just two texts, Naranjo Stela 12 and Yaxchilan Hieroglyphic Stairway 5, both from 800, account for fourteen actions and represent seventy-four per cent of the war records between 790 and 810, the K'atun ending on 9.19.0.0.0. The stela details four separate engagements in a single war between Naranjo and Yaxha in 799, while the stairway lists at least ten of the sixteen separate captures claimed by the commissioning Yaxchilan king. These conflicts have local implications, but cannot be used to generalise about Maya society as a whole. If, purely for analytical purposes, we were to omit these three monuments we would see no marked increase in conflict throughout the period for which we have such records – indeed even a fall for the final K'atun (Figure 50b).

It should also be noted that the last dateable account of military action took place in 808, over a hundred years before the last inscription of the Classic era. The sporadic records created during this troubled terminal century of lowland society were the products of an ever-decreasing number of active polities, are almost universally brief, and focus to a large degree on ritual action, as we will see in Chapter 11. An explosive level of conflict may well have accompanied the collapse process, indeed we have archaeological evidence suggesting as much in several locations. However, since such events left no mark in the written corpus we cannot use epigraphy to make that case.

Conceptual Factors

Historical and ethnographic studies worldwide demonstrate that violent conduct can be influenced, or even seemingly induced, by supernatural beliefs. These can be framed in terms of auguries, omens, and prophecies that suggest advantageous or "proper" times to launch an attack, or else in claims of a mystical offence, such as sorcery, that serves as a casus belli for war. There are a huge variety of possible conceptual factors, but several of the most common suggested for the Classic Maya are amenable to testing using the current sample.

As we have already seen, it has long been believed that the positions of celestial bodies could be portents of war for the Maya, at times reaching the stronger claim of cosmological determinism. Venus was a particular focus here and it was thought that star war events clustered in significant phases of its 584-day synodical cycle. Floyd Lounsbury's (1982) dating of the battle depicted at Bonampak and his interpretation of its wider iconographic programme had a decisive influence here. Yet, as the decipherment advanced most or all of this argument unravelled. Lounsbury's date was never tied to an actual star war verb and, in any case, was erroneously reconstructed (Stuart 1995: 308).

Aldana's (2005) statistical reassessment highlighted the difficulties in sustaining the idea of Venus-driven conflict and I have repeated his analysis with the improved dataset now at our disposal. This involves producing radial plots representing a 583.923-day synodic year of Venus, one with star wars alone and another, for comparative purposes, where all five main war verbs have been collected together (Figure 51a and b).

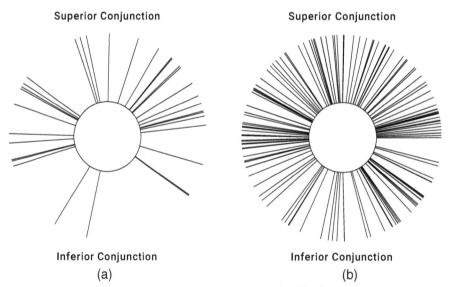

Superior Conjunction

Superior Conjunction

Inferior Conjunction

(a)

Inferior Conjunction

(b)

51 Warfare charted in a circular plot representing the Venusian 584-day year according to the GMT correlation: (a) star war events; (b) five main war events.

The former, in line with that prior work, shows no consistent alignments to any critical points in the Venus cycle, while the latter shows a comprehensive 360-degree distribution. That said, it is too early to say that there is no patterning whatsoever. In Figure 51a we can discern a bias toward the upper half of the chart and preliminary testing casts some doubt on this being a random distribution.[27] It is difficult to know quite what to make of this result since, as aligned to the GMT correlation, much of the relevant segment corresponds to the time when Venus is at greatest distance from us and dimmest in the sky. Indeed, at least one plot falls within superior conjunction, when Venus is invisible to us. Other plots, by contrast, fall when the planet is especially bright, defeating any idea that could have been a relative absence of Venus that interested the Maya. Even Figure 51b contains groupings that are hard to rationalise as statistically arbitrary, and the distributions of the different verbs – not accessible in this view – have their own anomalies. The best we can say at present is that the issue deserves further investigation and more sophisticated kinds of analysis, hopefully with a still larger dataset.

Whatever auspicious date selections may have been divined from celestial phenomena, presumably involving other planets and stars as well, it is clear we are talking about the kind of circumstantial specificity common to such prognostications, not prescribed cultural imperatives. It therefore remains highly probable that practical rather than esoteric considerations always took precedence (Martin 2001c: 18).

We know that the contact-era Maya used their calendar not only to schedule rituals and ceremonial events but as a mechanism for divining the future and selecting propitious days. With this in mind the sample was tested for any significant concentrations of numbers, days, or months. This first involved an examination of year-bearers – the sets of four possible *tzolk'in* days on which a new *haab* year could begin – that Landa (1941: 147) described as influential on warfare (Martin 2014a: chart 8).[28] Next, the incidence of different *tzolk'in* days or *haab* months was scrutinised to see if there were any particular preferences among them, and their coefficients similarly collected to see if these formed any meaningful distributions (Martin 2014a: charts 9 and 10).

The results of all of these tests were negative or very weak. Wars were less common in years that began on the day Ik' compared to its fellow year-bearers of Manik', Eb, or Kaban (coming in at thirteen per cent, where twenty-five per cent would be the mean expectation).[29] Additionally, there seems to be a slight preference for actions to take place on the day Ix (at twelve per cent, when the mean would be five per cent). In this context Ix is a term for "jaguar" and the symbolism of an aggressive predator might well be seen as auspicious. When the sample is arranged by individual verbs the only noteworthy feature is the quantity of star wars that took place in the month of

Muwaan (twenty-one per cent, when the mean is just six per cent). However, this is a phenomenon almost exclusively centred on the site of Dos Pilas (six out of seven cases), which recounts three of its own actions and three of others (John Justeson, pers. comm. 2010). It is this unusually elevated incidence of Muwaan that produces the spike in star war events during December, which we will soon encounter in Figure 52b.

To bring this topic to a close, if the timing of warfare was influenced by particular alignments of Venus or calendrical positions then the effect is not strongly reflected, indeed not evident, in the sample. There are near-limitless opportunities to read significance into different phenomena, whether natural or cultural, and interactions between different contributory factors would be impossible to reconstruct. The Maya certainly believed in supernatural influence over military affairs and surely consulted diviners, soothsayers, and astrologers in search of maximum advantage – from their perspective both prudent and logical moves. Yet the degree to which this slides towards determinism in some scholarship seems to say more about our exoticisation of ancient people than real world practice.

Practical Factors

The practical issue that could most easily influence the timing of warfare is the distribution of wet and dry seasons through the year. The rainy season in the lowlands generally stretches from late-May or June to November, with peak precipitation between June and September. This is typically interrupted by a lull caused by changes in average sea temperature, known in Spanish-speaking parts of the region today as the *canícula*. Of variable duration and timing this comes in some portion of late-July and/or August (Page 1938: figure 161b, c; Magaña, Amador, and Medina 1999). Rain returns and continues through the autumn and winter with declining frequency, turning into a pronounced and reliable dry season by the turn of the year. Within these broad patterns there are regional and topographical differences, with the southern lowlands (the only zone for which we have epigraphic data on conflict) experiencing the highest rainfall.

It is widely assumed that any conflict involving long-distance travel will be inhibited during the rainy season. Today a single heavy downpour converts forest tracks into cloying mud, while a longer spell turns riverbeds into torrents. When the rain is sustained, low-lying land can be inundated for weeks or months at a time. It is notable that of the eleven battles that lock together the histories of Dos Pilas, Tikal, and Calakmul between 648 and 679 in Case Study 11, only one took place during the rainy season according to the GMT correlation.

Seasonal rainfall has another important effect because it determines the greater part of the agricultural cycle. In the most important cultivation phase spent fields are cut and burned to release their nutrients in the spring and sown with maize, beans, and squash shortly before the rains begin in late-May or June (Dumond 1961). There is some maintenance to keep the crops free of weeds, pests, and animal predation, but the real labour only returns with the first harvests in September and October. Any general mobilisation of men for military operations, above and beyond that of a core of elite warriors, would face challenges during planting and harvest time. Famously, it has been claimed that the Maya rebels who had seized much of the Yucatan Peninsula by June 1848 were forced to abandon their march on the regional capital of Mérida and return home largely in order to sow their fields (Reed 2001: 110–111).

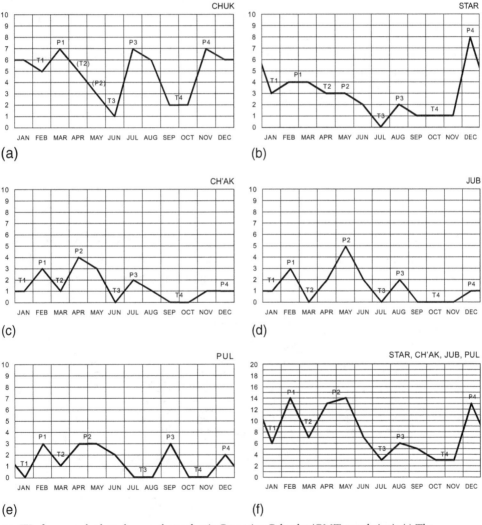

52 Warfare records plotted across the proleptic Gregorian Calendar (GMT correlation): (a) The *chuk* verb; (b) The star war verb; (c) The *ch'ak* verb; (d) The *jub* verb; (e) The *pul* verb; (f) A plot that combines star war, *ch'ak*, *jub*, and *pul*.

By organising the data across the solar year we can test whether seasonality had any detectable effect on recorded warfare. Here I have created a chart for each of the main five verbs distributed across the proleptic Gregorian year, according to the modified GMT correlation (Figure 52a–e). We must be mindful that the sample sizes are rather small and not statistically robust. Even so, they do not produce randomised profiles but instead show ones with common features. For example, it will be noted that all five charts show a double trough, wherein war events reach their lowest levels in June–July (T3) and again in October–November (T4). We can also see that *ch'ak*, *jub*, and *pul* all reach their peak incidence in April–May (P2), also sharing closely matching fluctuations in the period from December to March (T1, P1, T2). Although less pronounced, star war events have a similar trajectory (with the exception of the previously noted December outlier). If these were random oscillations we would expect them to even-out when combined, but instead the conjoined star war, *ch'ak*, *jub*, and *pul* plots in Figure 52f form a synchronous signature, with the same set of troughs in January (T1) and March (T2) and peaks in February (P1) and April–May (P2). The corollary of the summer's double trough (T3, T4) is an intervening rise in conflicts in August (P3). This effect is far stronger in the case of *chuk*, which has a marked double trough but deviates from the other verbs in reaching its initial peak in March and then undergoing a steady decline until the summer (Figure 52a).

Two straightforward observations follow from this analysis: that Classic Maya warfare took place throughout the year, but that its intensity varied substantially depending on the season. If we combine the data from all five verbs in Figure 53 we see a persistence of the general profile from Figure 52f, with the now-familiar set of peaks and troughs. If we then add a plot to represent rainfall we see an inverse correspondence between precipitation and

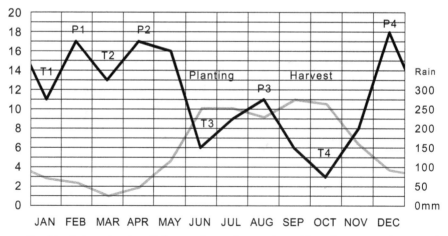

53 Combined chart showing all five warfare verbs together with a plot representing annual rainfall in the southern Maya lowlands.

conflict at crucial points in the year. Generally speaking, the wettest periods are those with the least violence and the driest the most.[30] We even see a correspondence for the mid-rainy season P3 feature, which coincides with the dry-spell of the *canícula*.

These results are consistent with a difficulty-of-travel hypothesis noted earlier, yet they would also be in accord with an agricultural one, since the depths of T3 and T4 correspond fairly closely to the main times for planting and the onset of the harvest, respectively. It may well be important that an interpretation restricted to the difficulties of transport cannot explain the variations between December and March, when rainfall is light. If these fluctuations are not influenced by precipitation per se, could the P4–T1 and P1–T2 features be evidence for greater complexity within the subsistence cycle?

The swidden or "slash-and-burn" method of maize cultivation practiced in the Maya area today requires shifts in field location and long fallow periods to allow the shallow soils of the region to recover and to reduce the effort required in weeding (Dumond 1961). Even though population levels for the Classic Maya cannot be precisely enumerated, it has long been accepted that swidden agriculture would be wholly insufficient to feed the number of people living in Late Classic times and that farming strategies must once have been more varied and intensive. Intensive techniques require investments in water management and soil enrichment, as well as the exploitation of foodstuffs other than maize, squash, and beans. These would include year-round root crops such as manioc (*Manihot esculenta* Crantz) and sweet potatoes (*Ipomoea batatas* (L.) Lam.), as well as fruits and nuts from orchards and managed forest, and the varied produce of near-house plots and kitchen gardens (see Bronson 1966; Turner 1974; Netting 1977; Dunning and Beach 1994; Fedick 1996; Farrell 1997), production that made the dispersed Maya city an "agro-urban" landscape (Isendahl 2012).

Significantly, early Spanish travellers in the southern lowlands describe not one but two, three, or even four maize crops per annum (Villagutierre Soto Mayor 1933[1701]: 8.12; Avendaño y Loyola 1987[1696]: 13, 41; see Hellmuth 1977: 427, 435, 436). One sixteenth-century source tells us that maize was ready to harvest in mid-April (Archivo General de Centro America 1937: 141, in Hellmuth 1977: 424), a time when the swidden cornfield of today is filled only with parched stalks ready for burning.

Maize crops produced without the benefit of the June to October rains give smaller yields and usually require both particular hardy varieties and added moisture, with mulching a method attested in recent times (Drucker and Fox 1982: 185). Such crops could have been grown in near-house plots, but the investments in water management we see – of which terracing, check dams, canals, and raised fields are among the more easily discerned – may have played a role in making dry season maize crops viable.[31] Recent lidar surveys have hugely expanded the evidence for engineered agricultural landscapes, revealing many upland slopes modified into terraces and low-lying areas reticulated with spidery canals (e.g. Chase et al. 2011; Canuto et al. 2018; Garrison, Houston, and Alcover 2018). The latter indicates that the swampy *bajo* areas of today once saw an almost industrial scale of food production spreading over hundreds of square kilometres. Any food production outside the main wet–dry cycle would have been a major contribution to the subsistence base of the Classic Maya. Indeed, it was probably instrumental to the population increase that took place, and thus the essential enabler of Late Classic society.

If four of our verbs show a degree of consistency across the year, shown in Figure 52f, what lies behind the divergences of the *chuk* pattern in Figure 52a? Despite its concordance with the major T3 and T4 troughs, as we have seen it differs significantly in April and May, when its recorded incidence falls sharply at just the time most others reach their P2 highpoint. This is compounded by an even greater difference at the P3 peak in August, where the signature for *chuk* is so much stronger than those of all other verbs. Both features are explicable if we concur with earlier authors that when capture events appear by themselves they typically refer to actions of limited scale. In April–May, when other types of conflict were taking place, the lesser act of seizing prisoners could be rhetorically overwhelmed and fall out of the record despite captive-taking being no less prevalent. We saw grounds for this earlier, in noting the number of other war events illustrated by captives without their seizure being specified in the texts. A similar rationale explains the vigorous spike around August, since the brief dry-spell of the *canícula* presents an opportunity for limited warfare, but its unpredictability and the still-wet conditions underfoot would remain an obstacle to major campaigns.

Interestingly, in those cases where a *chuk* event serves as a same-day addendum to another action (n = 9), only one occurs in the P3 window between July and September, very atypical for its overall incidence. Moreover, if we define campaigns as two or more actions fought by the same party within 30 days (n = 9), none fall in the P3 period. Neither of these observations has a high statistical value, but they are at least consistent with the hypothesis that isolated *chuk* events more-often-than-not signal lesser actions.[32]

In summation, it is possible to detect significant inhibitions on warfare during two periods, in the summer and again in the autumn – a finding that supports previous assessments of a dry–wet seasonal pattern to Classic Maya conflict. The impediment posed by rainfall was surely very important, but cannot account for December–March variation, where the demands of intensive cultivation emerge as one potential explanation. Given the evidence for two or more maize crops across the southern lowland region in the contact period, this group of peaks and troughs could be the ghostly traces of extra growing cycles (Martin 2009b).[33]

There is more than one way in which agriculture might produce this effect on war-making. In summarising evidence on the timing of warfare in colonial sources from the northern lowlands, Ralph Roys (1943: 67) wrote: "Wars were short, and the usual time was between October and the end of January. This was the cool season, when there was little or no agricultural activity and when food would be found in the enemy's granaries" (see also Landa 1941: 217). The drier climate of the north may always have restricted farming in that part of the year – the aforementioned Colonial-era references to multiple maize crops relate only to the south – so this period could well have been free of agricultural labour. But it is the reference to food stocks that raises the point of interest here. Having secured one's own supplies it was possible to use men newly freed from the fields to threaten the stores of others. Falling upon enemy granaries would not only sustain or enrich the invaders, it would deprive the assailed community of the food and seed-corn upon which it depended.

Crop ravaging has been a feature of pre-Modern war worldwide and, when appropriately timed, could prove a crippling blow (for comparative material from Classical Greece, Fiji, and Ancient China see Hanson 1998, Kuhlken 1999: 275–276, and Walker 1953: 44, respectively). The practical difficulties of destroying or plundering growing crops are not inconsiderable: maize is usually harvested when the plant is still green and resistant to burning, while theft from the fields would constitute a harvest of its own. Even so, the Spanish practiced both in their conquest of the southern lowlands, at times chopping down corn and pulling up root crops, at others carrying these prizes away (e.g. Archivo General de Centro America 1937: 141, 144; in Hellmuth 1977: 424).[34] The destruction of verdant crops is explicitly mentioned in the *Annals of the Cakchiquels* of the Postclassic Highlands, where "young corn was burned" by one invading force (Maxwell and Hill 2006: 216).

Nevertheless, the most efficient time for attack would always come after the harvest was in and the corncribs filled. The P1, P2, and P4 peaks could be connected to these junctures – moments when there was not only available manpower but also a key resource to extort, loot, or destroy. The huge Tikal earthworks were clearly intended to enclose a settled agricultural landscape rather than the royal court and urban core alone. Barriers must be manned to be effective, and if this was truly a defensive structure then posting sufficient numbers over such a lengthy pair of lines would have been quite a challenge. They might only have been intended to be manned and operate when crops were at their most vulnerable (Martin 2001c: 184–185).

The synchronous quality of seasonal factors, with dry periods being the easiest for travel, the least demanding of labour in the fields, as well as when food stocks were most vulnerable, would produce a compounded effect. Agricultural warfare can only have been one among several strategic components – and here we must include not only subsistence targets but also craft and cash crops such as cotton or cacao – but it should at least be considered among the mix of proximate or ancillary goals of conflict influenced by seasonality.

INTERPRETING CLASSIC MAYA WARFARE

Examining the epigraphic record from lexical and statistical points of view offers some clues to the character and aims behind organised violence among the Classic Maya, but we will need to draw on other sources before a fuller picture becomes possible. It is safe to assume that, however refracted through social and cultural norms, it is the linked goals of survival and procreation that constitute the ultimate causes of social conflict and the engine powering much political action (Thayer 2000, 2004; Gat 2006). Proximate causation, that is, the aim to gain or defend territory, status, honour, wealth, and the like, together with the powerful emotions they invoke, are to be understood as secondary phenomena in this light.

But this sociobiological perspective is not one that addresses or explains situated historical processes. Pragmatic understandings of warfare are important, and long too little emphasised in Mayanist studies, but such critical activities take place at the meeting point of subjective and objective consciousness, a realm where culture makes the decisive contribution (see Nielsen and Walker 2009). If one needs any evidence of this one only has to recall the enormous god effigies depicted at Tikal (Figure 36). These reflect beliefs about conflict that had effects as real and influential as any practical objective. In looking for the "true" goals of warfare we must not neglect how closely the warrior ideal was woven into the fabric of Classic Maya kingship and the ways in which that role symbolised the success and security of the entire community. Simultaneously part of the bargain in which the populace surrender power and wealth to the elite, and the means by which that elite cement and enforce their control, violence is the ultimate arbiter of who holds power and who does not.

Scale and Frequency

What can be said about the scale of Classic Maya warfare? Here the inscriptions offer no direct information, at no point describing the number of combatants or resulting casualties. Seen more than once, the phrase *nahbaj ch'ich' witzaj jol*, "blood is pooled, skulls are piled up" is certainly evocative and suggestive of mass casualties, but is best regarded as a formulaic exercise in rhetoric, if not poetics.

However, the texts do reveal that certain actions were assaults on polity capitals that resulted in the seizure of kings and the overthrow of dynasties. It is difficult to conceive that such attacks, violating the inner cores of polities, were not resisted by as many defenders as could be brought to bear, since to argue otherwise would be to dispute the very notion of community and collective identity. In order to succeed against such targets, it follows that an attacking host would usually need to be similarly numerous.

This would be consistent with the data we have for the Postclassic Period, where some wars involved significant numbers of combatants, with a core of elite specialists supplemented as needed by a larger body of men drawn from the general populace. This is described for the pre-contact northern lowlands (Roys 1943, 1957: 6) and is entirely in line with the conquistadors reports of massed Maya opponents (Cortés 1986: 21–22; Diaz del Castillo 1967: 23–24). For the highlands, the *Annals of the Cakchiquels* describe invading Maya armies as "innumerable" and as "not just 8,000 nor 16,000" (Carmack 1981: 138; Maxwell and Hill 2006: 197, 199, 204, 221). Both are formulaic expressions not to be taken literally, but they nonetheless signal more than elite participation. This would certainly conform to comparative historical data worldwide, where engagements range from minor skirmishes to major campaigns, and objectives can vary from merely making a show of force and testing the strength of a rival, to efforts at their complete conquest or annihilation. There is no reason not to assume similar variation among the Maya.

Evidence for major wars might not be entirely restricted to the epigraphic record. The difficulty of identifying specific actions from physical remains has already been noted, but if their effects were sufficiently severe some might be captured in larger archaeological patterns. We know that a number of sites went through cycles of florescence, depopulation, and rejuvenation (e.g. Hammond 1991: figure 11.3) and such fluctuations could well represent the shifting fortunes of war. Here we need to consider rare but severe episodes of societal devastation, of a kind familiar from world history but seldom advanced for the Maya (Martin 2001c: 176). The abandonment of Dos Pilas during the eighth century might be best explained as this form of episodic event rather than as the beginning of an incipient regional collapse.

We cannot know how many conflicts went uncelebrated in the inscriptions or have since been lost through erosion or intentional destruction. Maya centres also differ radically in their interest in martial symbolism and that could suggest, thematic preferences notwithstanding, variations in bellicosity. When we chart the records through time we get the sense that warfare was recurring but by no means continuous, with sizeable spans of ostensibly peaceful coexistence – or at least cold rather than hot wars (see also Webster 1998: 329).

The lowly origins and status of many highlighted captives, who often hail from otherwise unheard-of centres, is revealing since kings would surely boast of their most prestigious successes. Such contests must reflect peripheral skirmishes far removed in scale or consequence from the strategic conflicts of the major political players. A case in point would be Yaxchilan, a city whose many textual and imagistic claims to military achievement have persuaded some that it was a "conquest state". However, while the litany of successes accorded to Bird Jaguar IV (who bears the title "He of Twenty Captives") and his son Shield Jaguar IV ("He of Sixteen Captives") successfully burnish the image of great warrior-kings, the texts reveal that very few of their victories were of more than local significance. Most of their victims are best regarded as the lords of minor communities that lay in the interstitial zones between more powerful ones. Never fully incorporated into one or other of their neighbours, their allegiance switched back-and-forth between them. Appropriately, the area to the south of the Usumacinta, the home of Yaxchilan, seems especially well-stocked with petty kingdoms.

Did Classic Maya warfare change through time? As we saw earlier, contemporary textual records of conflict arise rather suddenly at the beginning of the seventh century and maintain a relatively steady incidence (once distorting anomalies are removed) until disappearing at the beginning of the ninth. To judge from the aforementioned defensive works and early depictions of captives, war had been a feature of Maya culture since Preclassic times, so this rapid emergence could be seen as an entirely rhetorical one. The drive for kings to advertise and immortalise their martial achievements in historical rather than purely symbolic terms – the explicative inscription joining or supplanting the simple image of the bound captive – marks a new specificity that takes events outside an idealised heroic narrative and puts them instead within a discourse situated in contemporary time and space. Also noted earlier, while populations remain unknown in absolute numbers, they underwent an exponential rise during the Late Classic Period, reaching a peak sometime close to 800 (see Santley 1990: figure 16.2). The number of identifiable polities likewise rose, and in close alignment with that growth.

Some have argued that this "filling-in" of the landscape in political and demographic terms suggests that much of the best agricultural land was occupied and that the conditions for resource scarcity, and therefore competition and insecurity, were increasing. While lidar evidence confirms the high population projections, running into many millions of people, it also indicates that some regions were only lightly settled and not terraformed for intensive agriculture (Canuto et al. 2018)—there was always available land.

Whatever the resource situation, the cheek-by-jowl placement of polities would make all kinds of interaction more important, with rhetorical jockeying and the projection of intimidating reputations, for both external and internal consumption, evidently now a pressing concern. This would mean that certain political stimuli gave rise to martial accounts within the broader increase in textual production.

If the art and writing of war are examined within their wider historical context, certain interesting correspondences emerge. The first iconographic allusions to warfare show kneeling captives bound at the wrists, or similar figures lying prone behind the feet of unarmed lords engaged in ritual performance. Images where victorious lords bear weapons and military garb emerge only in the fourth century, when they are restricted to those dressed in Teotihuacan-style attire brandishing clubs, spearthrowers, and darts. Depictions that reference the power of Central Mexico would recur for the remainder of the Classic era, but it is the entrada that introduces this particular subject matter.[35] Images in which Maya kings bear lance and shield and wear the native panoply of war-making join them only from the sixth century onwards, a development that broadly coincides with the first textual references to warfare. We will return to potential explanations for these developments in Chapter 13.

If warfare was as central to Late Classic life as text and imagery seem to imply, then the dispersed layouts of their cities and rarity of urban fortifications in this period is marked. However, not all societies that experience prolific warfare invest in formal defences (Webster 1993: 423). We see this in the Postclassic Valley of Mexico where, aside from some large specialised fortresses (Armillas 1951), there is very little sign of permanent physical barriers, despite the documentary evidence for frequent conflict. But the character of warfare does appear to change in the Maya realm at the end of the eighth and during the ninth centuries, with the proliferation of hurriedly-built walls and palisades. A good number of the last populations in the lowlands evidently felt a need for the kind of physical protection that previous generations had not.

Aims and Outcomes

The epigraphic evidence is clear that territorial expansion, in the sense of victorious polities absorbing defeated ones to enlarge their zone of direct administrative control, was extremely rare and cannot be seen as a prime objective. In consequence, if warfare had acquisitive benefits they must have been garnered by other means.

One interaction between epigraphy and archaeology supplies an important clue. In several instances we see explosive site growth, attested in terms of monumental construction as well as an increase of the expanse and density of settlement, which comes directly after victories described in the texts. An especially convincing cause-and-effect relationship comes in the case previously noted at Quirigua, when its king seized and executed his former overlord from Copan in 738. The victor thereafter transformed the entire Quirigua site core, creating a huge new plaza that would host the tallest collection of Maya monuments ever erected (Sharer 1978: 67; Martin and Grube 2000: 218–221;

Looper 2003: 81–83, passim). Similar correlations between urban expansion and accounts of war have been suggested for Caracol (Chase and Chase 1989: 13–16), as well as for both Tikal (Martin 1996a: 233, 2001c: 186, 2003b: 31) and Calakmul (Martin 2001d: 186). Particular construction projects, such as Palenque's Group of the Cross, also came hard on the heels of an important military success and suggest the same correlation (see p.155). The question is: by what process was war success translated into material wealth, monumental construction, or population increase?

Scenes painted on vases show warriors presenting bound captives to kings, frequently accompanied by bundles, cloth-stacks, plumes, and shells that elsewhere appear in tribute scenes – suggesting that this is booty or the initiation of tribute payments (Stuart 1995: 296; Miller and Martin 2004: 187). While the seizure of high-ranking individuals was emblematic of the defeat of their forces or communities, it has also been argued that such captives themselves had economic significance (Miller 1993: 408–409; Miller and Martin 2004: 166). This was realised by the transfer of existing tributary relations from the vanquished to the victor (see also Graham 2006: 118–119, 2011: 40–43) or by their direct ransom (see also McAnany 2010: 278–283).[36] This would be especially true of decisive triumphs that led to political subordination.

Importantly, among the Postclassic Maya of the northern lowlands we know that disputes over tribute payments were one of the main cited causes of war (Relaciones de Yucatán 2 1898–1900: 209).[37] Yet, even if we accept that tribute was the principal mode of wealth transfer, it would not exclude other forms of enrichment from war, be it plunder or agricultural looting, enforced labour obligations or full enslavement – which was a common consequence of war in the Postclassic era (Landa 1941: 123, passim; Roys 1957: 6). There is one slim glyphic pointer that may refer to booty seized in warfare. On a Naranjo monument, a defeated king of Yaxha is the subject of the phrase baakwaj yikaatzil, "his cargo is captured" (Stuart 1995: 361; Beliaev, in Stuart 2019) – although it is possible that this refers instead to a "ritual bundle" that had religious significance for the Yaxha kingdom.

Another interesting and significant reference to the aftermath of war in Classic inscriptions involves the pehk, "to summon" term. One day after seizing a Bonampak/Lacanha king in battle in 693, the victorious ruler of Sak Tz'i' called together a range of lesser figures identified only by their toponyms, including a former ally of the vanquished lord. As Dmitri Beliaev and Alexandr Safronov (2004, 2009) note, the implication is that they have been compelled to switch their allegiance to a new overlord. From this rather minor episode we can extrapolate to imagine the consequences of much grander conflicts. Success at that level would likely have brought with it a slew of political subjects and allies beholden to the defeated party, and with them an influx of wealth much beyond that offered by the victim alone.

As important as war records are for identifying particular adversaries, the absence of such accounts constitute their own source of data. There are, for example, no extant records of military action between a group of kingdoms that run in a broadly north–south line (Uxul, La Corona, El Peru, Zapote Bobal, El Reinado, Dos Pilas, and Cancuen) during much of the seventh and eighth centuries (Case Study 9). As we will see in Chapter 10, each of them was subordinated to the more powerful kingdom of Calakmul at this time, and this could well indicate that this domination had a suppressive effect on conflict between them.

Without some stability and structure to the distribution of power between polities, such as a hegemon might provide, warfare has the potential to be highly disruptive and difficult to keep in check. In acquiring resources or settling disputes by violence all those touched by such strategies are in danger of being drawn, by degrees, into a self-perpetuating cycle of hostility and fighting. Since each polity can never know enough about the intentions of its neighbours to feel entirely secure, war-readiness is a sensible precaution. But because military preparations are always ambiguous, with even the most defensive of measures offering an offensive advantage, this can provoke like-in-kind escalations from others who feel similarly threatened. Efforts at greater security can therefore become destabilising and counterproductive, especially so in multi-polity environments where many close-at-hand communities would mean many potential threats. Suspicion and fear can build to a point where pre-emptive attack seems a rational and necessary initiative – thus completing a paradox in which a desire to avoid war leads to that very result. This phenomenon has been called the "security dilemma", and it is a recurring threat in cases where polities have no other means of survival than self-reliance (see p.368).

We still have much to learn about Classic Maya warfare. Yet we are now refining our questions, searching for answers that are compatible with both the textual and physical evidence, and opening ourselves to the comparative historical and ethnographic data that reveals patterns and suggests specific interpretations. We must appreciate not only the immediate or short-term goals of conflict, but its longer-term political objectives. There is good reason to believe that the greatest benefits of war accrued from dominance over subject kingdoms, and that the establishment of power hierarchies was the principal route to material enrichment.

CASE STUDY 11: WAR AND EXILE ON THE STAIRWAYS OF DOS PILAS

The most comprehensive war narrative we have for the Classic Maya was inscribed across two hieroglyphic stairways at Dos Pilas (Figure 54). These extended texts recount campaigns covering a twenty-one-year period, telling

54 Dos Pilas Hieroglyphic Stairway 2 West. (Photograph by Merle Greene Robertson, courtesy of Mesoweb)

of both triumph and disaster in the emergence of a new polity in the Petexbatun region (Houston et al. 1992; Houston 1993: 108; Fahsen et al. 2003; Guenter 2003) (Map 3). Hieroglyphic Stairway 2 (HS.2) was found at the base of the largest temple platform at the site, facing the public space of the Main Plaza. It is composed of three sections, a central portion that begins the story and takes it up to 643, with flanking eastern and western portions – which are carved in a different style and were doubtless later additions – that continue events up to 682. Hieroglyphic Stairway 4 (HS.4) occupied a more intimate space within the palace at Dos Pilas. Its four lower steps were completed in 682, while the upper fifth step was added in 684 to celebrate the 3-K'atun birthday of the Dos Pilas king Bajlaj Chan K'awiil, the commissioner and lead protagonist of the whole programme. Augmented by other inscriptions at the site, and a wider understanding of the historical characters and places involved, we can build an unusually detailed picture of the way warfare could disrupt the lives of Classic Maya kingdoms.

The central steps of HS.2 concern the early life of Bajlaj Chan K'awiil, although key parts are now too eroded to read. The action gets going in 648 with a date recorded on both HS.2 and HS.4, though each contributes different parts of the story (Table 5). There is a battle success for Bajlaj Chan K'awiil against an unknown rival, a separate capture, and the death of a third

TABLE 5 *Timeline*

Long Count	CE	Greg.	Event
9.10.15.4.9	648	Feb 8	A victory for Bajlaj Chan K'awiil, the *ajaw* of Yuknoom Ch'een of Calakmul. Death of Tikal lord
9.10.18.2.19	650	Dec 24	Star war on Dos Pilas by Yuknoom Ch'een of Calakmul
9.11.4.5.14	657	Jan 16	Star war on Tikal by Yuknoom Ch'een of Calakmul, Nuun Ujol Chahk flees to Sak Pa'
?	657>	?	Unknown event involving Yich'aak K'ahk' attended by Bajlaj Chan K'awiil and Nuun Ujol Chahk
9.11.9.5.19	662	Dec 26	Defeat of Tab Joloom of Koban
9.11.11.9.17	664	Mar 3	Capture of Tajal Mo' by Bajlaj Chan K'awiil
9.12.0.8.3	672	Dec 12	Star war on Dos Pilas by Nuun Ujol Chahk, Bajlaj Chan K'awiil flees to Chahknaah
9.12.0.16.14	673	Jun 1	Burning of Dos Pilas and another site
9.12.1.0.3	673	Jun 30	Star war against Chahknaah, Bajlaj Chan K'awiil flees to Hix Witz
9.12.5.9.14	677	Dec 17	Star war on Pulil, Nuun Ujol Chahk flees to Paptuun
9.12.5.10.1	677	Dec 24	Star war on Pulil by Yuknoom Ch'een, Bajlaj Chan K'awiil arrives at Dos Pilas same day
9.12.6.16.17	679	May 4	The army of Nuun Ujol Chahk is brought down by Bajlaj Chan K'awiil
9.12.10.0.0	682	May 11	Dance by Yuknoom Ch'een with Bajlaj Chan K'awiil

individual specified as a Mutul lord. It is a pity that this episode is so obscure, since it presumably plays a crucial part in the internecine conflict that soon erupts within the Tikal royal household and therefore explains later events.

The next record, two years later in 650, is a decisive reverse for the Dos Pilas ruler, as his site is attacked and overrun by Yuknoom Ch'een of Calakmul. Since this Kaanul king would soon emerge as the most powerful in the whole Maya lowlands it is no surprise that Bajlaj Chan K'awiil was forced to flee. We are told that he goes to *k'inich pa'witz*, the name of nearby Aguateca, a cliff-top site with impressive natural defences that would later serve as a second capital for the polity. A subordination statement in which he admits to "belonging" to his Calakmul counterpart is attached to the earlier conflict episode of 648, though it presumably reflects a submission made in 650 or soon thereafter (see p.250).

In a reign of unparalleled success, Yuknoom Ch'een attacks Tikal in 657 and achieves the same result, seizing the city and ejecting its king Nuun Ujol Chahk, the sibling or half-sibling to Bajlaj Chan K'awiil. Both appear to be sons of an obscure Tikal king, K'inich Muwaan Jol II, who reigned during Tikal's bleak silence in the early seventh century. Next, on a date too damaged to read but falling between 657 and 662, there is some form of ceremony performed for the Calakmul heir Yuknoom Yich'aak K'ahk', then a boy aged only eight-to-thirteen years. Located at Yaxa' – perhaps the great city of that name in the eastern Peten – its most significant feature is the attendance of both Mutul kings, presumably at the command of Yuknoom Ch'een (Guenter 2003: 18–20). On the face of it, Calakmul now dominates both claimants to the Mutul kingship and has imposed a degree of reconciliation between them, however limited.

The narrative then turns to Bajlaj Chan K'awiil's own military exploits, with victories in 662 and 664. The first of these against a lord of Koban, a place-name we find today in the foothills of the highlands well to the south, while the second was against someone ascribed a title resembling the referent of Machaquila, but is probably something else.

The peace enforced by Calakmul was not to last, and by 672 Nuun Ujol Chahk had restored his independence and strength to such an extent that he could attack and seize Dos Pilas in a star war that forced Bajlaj Chan K'awiil into another exile, this time at an unidentified site called Chahknaah. The war resumed the following year, 673, when Nuun Ujol Chahk "burns" Dos Pilas as well as a second now-illegible place, and 29 days later takes Chahknaah in another star war. The Dos Pilas king this time takes refuge at Hixwitz, the kingdom centred on modern Zapote Bobal. Since this was another Calakmul client it would have offered a safe haven while keeping him close to his occupied realm. His exile continued until 677, when Yuknoom Ch'een re-enters the fray and takes a centre called Pulil from Nuun Ujol Chahk, who is in turn forced to flee. A second attack on Pulil the following month was required, but thereafter Bajlaj Chan K'awiil could finally make good his return to Dos Pilas after a five-year absence.

The denouement and climax of the text takes place two years later in 679 and describes Bajlaj Chan K'awiil's "knocking down of the flint(s) and shield(s)" of Nuun Ujol Chahk. The Tikal ruler evidently survived the encounter, but one of his lesser lords or allies, Nuun Bahlam, was taken captive and is depicted at the foot of Dos Pilas Stela 9.[38]

For Dos Pilas this was a saga of survival and fortitude against a formidable enemy and a shifting relationship with the leading hegemon of its day, whose support came at the price of political subordination. Bajlaj Chan K'awiil was prepared to supply all manner of uncomfortable, even humiliating facts, including his defeats and exiles in addition to his dependence on the greater might of Calakmul. Since this is patrimonial rhetoric the climax is, naturally enough, his ultimate victory over his Tikal relative – a success that would, for him, justify the catalogue of misery and misfortune that led up to it.

TEN

HIERARCHY

Thus far, we have examined the titular composition, sustaining practices, and cohering concepts of the Classic Maya polity, before moving to its external relations in the form of interdynastic alliances and warfare. But we have not yet exhausted the range of inter-polity contacts in the inscriptions, and a final category takes us to the heart of how individual kingdoms were drawn into larger political configurations. Here I explore the asymmetrical relations of power that suffused the divided landscape of the Classic Maya.

That evidence takes four forms. The first two are statements in which the actions of one monarch are "supervised" by another or in a similar formula "overseen", most tellingly in the case of accession ceremonies. A third is comprised of those statements where the "witnessing" of one king's actions by another carries a hierarchical implication, and a fourth is where kings explicitly describe themselves as "owned" by others. The first section of this chapter examines these terms and their usage, while the second describes individual episodes collectively in chronological order. The aim there is to produce an outline narrative that allows us to track the political dynamics of the Classic era, appreciating the rise and fall of individual fortunes. As usual, concluding case studies will examine some of these arising issues in greater detail and within a fuller context. This is especially desirable in this chapter, since hierarchy is at its most comprehensible when intersecting with other relationships and events as part of an overtly historical process.

RELATIONSHIPS OF RANK

Supervision

The first of the relevant formulae is based on the root *kab* or its cognate *chab*, which likely survives in Modern Tzotzil as the intransitive verb *chab*, "to cultivate, plough" but more directly as the transitive "to govern, guard, watch over" – the latter forming the basis for many occupational titles that involve agency and responsibility (Laughlin 1988: 184–185; Stephen Houston, pers. comm. 1996).[1] In the script this is represented by the logograph **KAB/CHAB**, "earth" (the precise dating of the *k* > *ch* shift in Ch'olan languages is unclear (see Law et al. 2014), but the former will be preferred here) suggesting to some that the root had its semantic origins in working the soil and tending crops and only later extended to broader forms of supervision (Stuart 2010b: 3). The alternative is that this sign was borrowed as a handy homophone.

The scribes show a preference for passive phrasings that describe an action and its patient but omit the agent. The identity of this agent is very often supplied in a following statement headed by the *kab* term, establishing a somewhat detached, guiding role rather than one of direct engagement. In the inscriptions, it is often spelled with the string **u-KAB-ji-ya** for *ukabjiiy* and is traditionally considered to be a transitive verb, as in "he/she supervised it", although a relational noun that amounts to a simple "by" has also been considered (Law 2006: 72–73) (Figure 55a). It appears in a wide variety of contexts, including calendrical ceremonies, monument and tomb dedications, as well as the full range of warfare events, and in all cases supplies the ultimate authority under which an action takes place. An instance that makes this sense

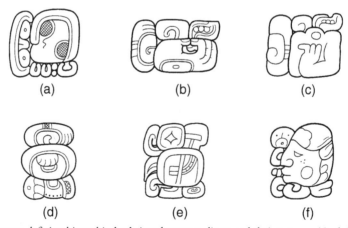

(a)   (b)   (c)

(d)   (e)   (f)

55 Key terms defining hierarchical relations between clients and their patrons: (a) *ukabjiiy*, "he/she supervised it"; (b) *yichonal*, "before, in the sight of"; (c) *yichonal*, using the prospective logogram for **ICHON**; (d) *yila'*, "he/she witnesses"; (e) *yajaw*, "the lord of"; (f) *yajaw*, "the lord of".

of detached supervision plain comes on Caracol Altar 23, where the seizure of captives by a lesser royal, perhaps a sub-kingly brother or son, is said to be *ukabjiiy* the reigning king (Chase, Grube, and Chase 1991: figure 23). Although the term can describe the agency of supernatural actors or ancestors, such instances are extremely rare.

A number of different royal actions could be supervised by a foreign king, including calendrical rituals, the presentation of costuming, and particular expeditions, but by far the largest category (some sixty-eight per cent) consists of inauguration ceremonies (Martin 2014a: table 20). While all instances of outside supervision are indicative of differential status, these investitures point most directly to hierarchical ties and will be our focus here.

Oversight

The second term, spelled **yi-chi-NAL**, is an inalienably possessed noun that introduces a higher status actor, be it another lord or a deity (Stuart 1997: 10; Houston and Taube 2000: 287–289) (Figure 55b). A cognate form, *yiknal*, survives in Modern Yukatek (Barrera Vásquez 1980: 265–266, 977) and offers helpful insights into its meaning. William Hanks (1990: 91–93) describes its role in defining a field of perception based on bodily presence and activity, concerning not only things directly in one's line of sight but as they engage an assembly of people and objects. The Classic-era form can be translated as "in front of" or simply "before", with the sense of "overseeing". It shares a close resemblance to a compound that appears in almost identical contexts, the difference being that the **chi** syllabogram (for which there was a choice of two equivalent signs) is replaced by a glyph showing an arm bent across a chest (Figure 55c).[2] Marc Zender (in Stone and Zender 2011: 59) interprets the gesture sign as logographic **ICHON** with the sense of "front" and views **yi-chi-NAL** forms as under-spellings of *yichonal* with the same set of meanings. Although the issue of the unstated medial vowel remains hard to resolve, *yichonal* will be preferred for both spellings here.[3]

In no instance does *yichonal* directly substitute for *ukabjiiy* and this seems to be clear evidence for their semantic distinction. To what degree the political relationships involved differed is harder to say. It could be that *yichonal* conveyed a sense of direct engagement or personal presence, while *ukabjiiy* established a broader aegis that could describe direct contact but was not required to do so. There is no obvious pattern regarding the incidence of the two terms in their political contexts, and neither the physical distance between the two protagonists' home sites nor the relative size and importance of their polities seems to be a factor. The most significant point is the relatively late introduction of *yichonal*, which is largely a Late Classic innovation in the script and infrequent until the end of the seventh century, although it is applied retrospectively to earlier events. Indeed, after 741 *yichonal* is the only term used to distinguish foreign authority in accession events (Martin and Grube 1994a: 15; Martin 2014a: table 21). Outside of its political contexts *yichonal* becomes the pre-eminent term describing the oversight of kingly ritual by deities.

Witnessing

Another term will be relevant to our discussion. Based on the verbal root *il*, "to see" (Kaufman and Norman 1984: 121) its logographic form **IL** depicts an eye and it also appears in a variety of syllabic spellings (Stuart 1987: 25–27; Houston and Taube 2000: 286–287) (Figure 55d). It is used to indicate the presence, but only passive participation, of someone in a foregoing event. The term is not used in supernatural contexts and, as far as one can tell, refers to literal observation in the same moment and place. A common example would be that of a dowager queen mother witnessing rituals performed by her ruling son. The motivation in such cases can hardly be a sentimental one, and we can surmise that such women were powerbrokers who had engineered the rise of their offspring and remained significant political players during their reigns.

Within hierarchies *il* is used where patrons observe the actions of their clients, with an implication of supervision. Yet it also works in the reverse case, where clients witness acts performed by their patron, with no such implication. Since it makes no distinction in rank by itself, one can only appreciate its political significance by assessing its circumstances, considering both the nature of the event, its participants, and its location (Martin 2014a: table 22).[4]

Possession

In Mayan languages possession is marked by prefixing the third-person pronoun *u-* before consonant-initial words (achieved in the script by adding any one of the fourteen or more signs that have the value **u**) and *y-* before vowel-initial words (by means of the signs **ya**, **ye**, **yi**, **yo**, or **yu**, depending on the vowel). For example, in expressing a hierarchical relationship between a *sajal* noble and his king we see the possessed form **u-sa-ja-la** *usajal*, "the *sajal* of" (Houston and Mathews 1985: figure 12b; Stuart 1985b) while, in the case of an *ajk'uhuun*, possession produces **ya-AJ-K'UH-HUUN-na** *yajk'uhuun*, "the *ajk'uhuun* of" (Houston 1993: 132–133; Jackson and Stuart 2001: 219).

As noted in Chapter 5, these constructions serve to define relations of rank within polities, but our focus in this chapter falls on possessed forms of *ajaw* as it is used as a royal title. This was identified grammatically by Stephen Houston (in Houston and Mathews 1985: figure 12a and c, n.2), with a phonological understanding of the prefix **ya** that supplies the pronoun in **ya-AJAW** *yajaw* added by Victoria Bricker (1986: 70). Spellings of this term can take several forms, employing different combinations of logographic and syllabic signs (Figure 55e and f).[5] There are currently at least 22 examples of possessed *ajaw* relationships ranging over some 334 years, from firm dates of at least 392 to 726 CE in the record we have (Martin 2014a: table 23).

HIERARCHY AND HISTORICAL PROCESS

Hierarchy in the Early Classic Period, 300–600 CE

The earliest hierarchical statements appear in the central lowlands in the late fourth century CE and take us back to the entrada event described in Chapter 6. There the first instance of *ukabjiiy* comes when Yax Nuun Ahiin I accedes at Tikal in 379, an event said to be the doing of the *kaloomte'*, Sihyaj K'ahk' (Stuart 2000: 479). We last encountered Sihyaj K'ahk' on his "arrival" at Tikal in 378, an event that coincided with the death of the incumbent king Chak Tok Ich'aak I (see p.122). Two other inscriptions from the reign of Yax Nuun Ahiin state that he "belonged" to Sihyaj K'ahk' by means of the possessed *yajaw* construction. That Yax Nuun Ahiin was both installed and owned by Sihyaj K'ahk' establishes a direct connection between these two kinds of subordination, the latter evidently a consequence of the former.

For the reasons set out in Chapter 6, these statements suggest the seizure of Tikal by Teotihuacan by one means or another. It is surely significant that both known portraits of Sihyaj K'ahk' show him dressed as a Teotihuacano (see Figure 19), while all four images of Yax Nuun Ahiin depict him in like-manner (see p.123). Sihyaj K'ahk' was the prime agent of this political takeover and his standing is reflected elsewhere in the region. For example at Naachtun, where the king is named as one of his vassals (Nondédéo et al. 2016), and at Bejucal, where he said to be the overlord to a local ruler in 382. He is cited in a similar but damaged context at Río Azul in 392.[6] This meshes with other indications of the establishment of a New Order in the central lowlands, with Teotihuacan or its agents subordinating or reconfiguring certain Maya regimes to its liking (Martin and Grube 2000: 30; Martin 2001a: 111; 2003b: 12–13).

Directly after the accession statement on Tikal Stela 31, and still under the authority of Sihyaj K'ahk', a second passage deals with the empowerment of "28 *pet*", with *pet* a word that can mean "province" (Stuart 2010b: 6). This could well relate to the "28 *ajawtaak*" who sometimes bear witness to calendrical rituals, perhaps an idealised number of peers that represent the greater elite community. This is either a claim that Yax Nuun Ahiin is now master of those other realms or, more likely, that Sihyaj K'ahk' himself installed their rulers. Both events are said to have taken place at the Wiinte'naah, a structure that Yax Nuun Ahiin *t'abaayi*, "goes up (to)" directly before these ceremonies.

In all likelihood, this is a building located at Tikal, perhaps a replica or substitute for one at Teotihuacan that provides a legitimating locus of power for the Maya lowlands.

There was a second key figure behind the New Order, another *kaloomte'* called "Spearthrower Owl"—a name now known to read *jatz'oom ku(y)??*, "Striker Owl??". Raptors armed with shields and darts are seen in the art of Teotihuacan and this name combination featuring an *atlatl* spearthrower appears in several contexts in the Maya lowlands after 378. For example, it forms the focal motif on the Marcador, commissioned in 416, the previously mentioned Teotihuacan-style banner model found in a Teotihuacan-style residential complex at Tikal (Figure 56a). Two other Maya rulers specify that they were subject to the person using the Spearthrower Owl name via the *yajaw* expression, one from the unidentified Maasal kingdom and another who may have ruled at Río Azul (Figure 56b and c).[7] These and other references contribute to the sense that this figure stands as the overall authority under which the entrada took place. Crucially, he is said to be the father of Yax

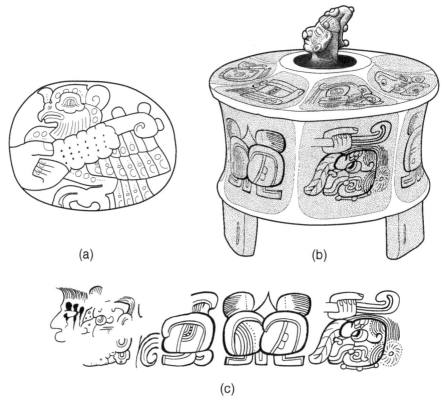

(a)   (b)

(c)

56 "Spearthrower Owl", a name associated with Teotihuacan: (a) Central motif on the Tikal Marcador; (b) Stucco-covered tripod vessel in Teotihuacan-style naming Spearthrower Owl as a *kaloomte'*. K7528; (c) Section of the text on K7528 in which a Maya ruler states that he is the *yajaw*, "vassal" of Spearthrower Owl.

Nuun Ahiin, making his patriline the seed from which a new Tikal dynasty would sprout.[8] The text on the Marcador tells us that he came to power in 374, while a reference on Stela 31 tells us that he died in 439, clearly at an advanced age. The inference that has been drawn is that he was the ruler, or minimally a leading lord, at distant Teotihuacan (Stuart 2000: 482–487; Martin 2001a: 108, 2003b: 13–15).[9]

The next example of hierarchy in the inscriptions also relates to dynastic foundation and Teotihuacan, but this time in the far southeast. The inauguration of Quirigua's first king took place in 426 under the *ukabjiiy* supervision of K'inich Yax K'uk' Mo', the founder of the Copan dynasty (Stone 1983; Grube, Schele, and Fahsen 1991: 110; Stuart 2000: 492).[10] The appropriate phrase begins with a monument dedication followed by an *uk'alhuun* headband ritual, all of which occurs at Wiinte'naah – in this case most likely a place or structure at Teotihuacan itself. There follows a journey of 152 days that took both lords to the modern borderlands of Guatemala and Honduras, where Maya dynastic rule was intrusive and part of a deliberate project of polity formation (see p.124–126).

One further link to Central Mexico comes from Piedras Negras in 514, where Panel 12 describes the local king as celebrating the period ending 9.4.0.0.0 with a *chok ch'aaj*, "incense scattering". Dressed as a Teotihuacano, the Piedras Negras monarch is shown holding one tethered captive while receiving three more, including the kings of Yaxchilan and Santa Elena (Martin and Grube 2008: 141). In this way, he announces military success in both the east and west (Map 4). In place of a personal name the triumphant figure is at this point simply called the *yajaw ochk'in kaloomte'*, "lord of the West *kaloomte'*", stating that he is subject to an overlord (Martin 1996c, 1997a: 860, 2014a: figure 197b). A rather later monument from the site, Panel 2 from 667, revisits this era and identifies the *ochk'in kaloomte'* in question as one Tajom Uk'ab Tuun. In the accompanying text we learn that this figure oversees, by means of the *yichonal*, "before, in sight of" term, the Piedras Negras king Yat Ahk II as he receives Teotihuacan-style *ko'haw* war helmets in 510 (Figure 57). The retrospective scene shows Yat Ahk and his young heir, both in Teotihuacan-style attire, presiding over kneeling youths from Bonampak, Lacanha, and Yaxchilan – evidently clients upon which he has bestowed gifts of helmets and other war gear.[11]

Piedras Negras Panels 2 and 12 can be seen as partner monuments, both claiming regional dominance under the real or symbolic patronage of Teotihuacan in the early sixth century (see O'Neil 2012: 166–168). Helpfully, the 510 event is also mentioned on a fragmentary wooden box, discovered in a dry cave near the village of Alvaro Obregón in Tabasco, a short distance from Piedras Negras (Anaya, Mathews, and Guenter 2003; Zender 2007). This describes Tajom Uk'ab Tuun as a *wiinte'naah ajaw*, the marker of Teotihuacan

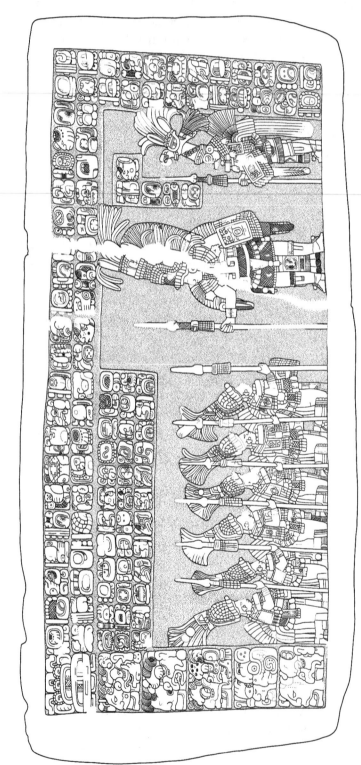

57 The king of Piedras Negras and his heir preside over young lords from Yaxchilan, Bonampak, and Lacanha in 510 CE. Piedras Negras Panel 2. (Drawing by David Stuart)

affiliation. Interestingly, a further reference to Wiinte'naah on the box is set
155 days before the *ko'haw* ceremony, which closely approximates the time it
took for Yax K'uk' Mo' to journey from that same place to Copan almost a
century earlier. Piedras Negras has long been known for the heavy stylistic
influence of Teotihuacan on the portraits of its rulers (Stone 1989), but in this
instance we appear to see claims of actual contact with that city in the early
500s. Rhetorically, Tajom Uk'ab Tuun here fills much the same supervisory
role as Sihyaj K'ahk' did at Tikal, implying that the Central Mexicans
remained an active source of power and prestige for at least some Classic Maya
into the sixth century, 132 years after the entrada.

A surge of Teotihuacan-inspired styles took place immediately after the
events of 378, influencing the iconography not just of Tikal but of centres right
across the Maya realm. Resonating for the next four centuries, the Maya use
and adaptation of Central Mexican symbolism would endure long after the fall
of the great metropolis itself.[12] With few exceptions, its styles and motifs
were kept distinct from Maya forms, thereby putting acute emphasis on its
"foreignness" (Stone 1989). Scholars have long debated whether this speaks of
military adventurism or a purely ideological influence.[13] I have described the
case for the former in several places in this volume. That the Maya employed a
Teotihuacan war deity in support of their own martial causes, as we saw in
Chapter 7, is a testament to its perceived potency.

Under the New Order, Tikal became a yet larger and more opulent centre
and we can suspect, though not demonstrate epigraphically, that it exercised a
wide regional hegemony throughout the fifth century. The Tikal king Sihyaj
Chan K'awiil II is linked to a counterpart at Ucanal at some point between
411 and 456, but their connecting term is undeciphered (Martin 2003b: 16,
figure 1.10). Another trace of Tikal's influence might appear at Tamarindito in
534, where the local king celebrates the 9.5.0.0.0 period ending seemingly
under the supervision of someone else, whose name closely resembles one used
by the Lady of Tikal.[14] She, and her consort, were the first native Tikal *ajaw*
known to carry the *kaloomte'* title.

It may be no coincidence that it was at about the time central Teotihuacan
was burned, c.550–600, that new players came onto the Maya stage to
challenge that status quo (see also Willey 1974: 423). The most important of
these was the Kaanul dynasty, which was evidently based at Dzibanche during
the Early Classic Period. Explicit evidence for its growing political influence
comes in 546, when we learn that the Naranjo king Aj Numsaaj Chan K'inich
(Aj Wosal) took office under the auspices of the Kaanul king Tuun K'ab Hix
(Schele and Freidel 1990: 175; Martin and Grube 1994a: 7).[15] That record
appears on Naranjo Stela 25, a retrospective text that celebrates the long-lived
Naranjo monarch's 3½-K'atun or 69-year jubilee. Back-calculating from
various dating clues, he could have been no more than 12 years old at the

time of his elevation, probably younger. His father is mentioned on several occasions and he is the first figure we see using a version of the Naranjo emblem glyph. Previous Naranjo kings were associated with a title thought to read *sak chuwen*, which is first seen in the Early Classic and continued in use until the fall of the dynasty some three centuries later.

Confirmation of the enduring subordination of Aj Numsaaj Chan K'inich to the Kaanul dynasty comes from the remarkable Naranjo Stela 47, a find made by archaeologist Vilma Fialko and her team in 2014 (Figure 58). This supplies the same accession date, but in place of a conventional inaugural rite describes a "dressing for the ballgame", referring to the protective equipment worn by players which the Naranjo king is shown wearing in the guise of the Hero Twin Juun Ajaw. The supervising agent of the event is again Tuun K'ab Hix, but this time he is listed together with three other kings, collectively specified as the *chan tz'akbu k'uhul kaan(ul) ajaw*, or the "four in sequence holy Snake[-Place] kings" (Martin et al. 2016). The given order continues through Aj Saakil, Sky Witness, and Scroll Serpent – each of whom we know as overlords to other kingdoms.[16] Their naming here must either represent a ceremony they collectively attended as children or, more likely, conflates time to list the four successive patrons of the Naranjo king, emphasising that he was a steadfast client for more than sixty years.

58 The Naranjo ruler Aj Numsaaj Chan K'inich impersonates Juun Ajaw, one of the mythical Hero Twins, in his role as ballplayer. The accompanying text names the king's four successive overlords from the Kaanul kingdom. Naranjo Stela 47. (Drawing by Alexandre Tokovinine)

How pervasive was the practice of supervised installations? That they are under-represented in the corpus is indicated by the accounts of a Caracol king's inauguration in 553. Yajawte' K'inich II came to power under the *ukabjiiy* direction of a Tikal ruler (Grube 1994c: 106), who can be identified as Wak Chan K'awiil (Martin 2005b: 3). We learn of this from texts on Caracol Stela 6 and Altar 21, which were commissioned in 603 and 633, respectively, by the two sons who in turn succeeded Yajawte' K'inich. Yet his own record of the ceremony on Stela 14, erected just a year after it took place, includes no mention of his subordination, or indeed makes any reference to Tikal. He clearly felt no obligation to present this information to a contemporary audience, even though it must have been common knowledge. Our understanding of Caracol's tie to Tikal is entirely fortuitous, arising as Yajawte' K'inich's sons sought to explain the shift in Caracol's loyalties from the Mutul dynasty of Tikal to that of its arch-rival, the Kaanul dynasty of Dzibanche.

It is worth stressing that references to hierarchical status, like any incident or relationship in the inscriptions, always suit a purpose pertinent at the time of their commissioning. In Yajawte' K'inich's blithe omission we lose any expectation that the extent of Classic-era power networks will be fully revealed in the inscriptions that have come down to us, and they could well be far more prevalent than we currently know. This would be especially true for the many minor polities, most of which produced only a few monuments. Much here falls into the category of the "unseen".

Within three short years relations between Tikal and Caracol collapsed and Altar 21 tells us the latter suffered a *ch'ak* assault at the hands of its erstwhile overlord in 556 (Houston 1991: 40). We know very little about nature of the bonds that tied client to patron here and elsewhere, but this suggests that a repudiation of them ran the risk of a retaliatory response. Whether as cause or effect, Caracol was thereafter aligned with the Kaanul kingdom. In this same year of 556, El Peru Stela 44 tells us of the accession of a local king who was "owned" by one K'ahk' Ti' Ch'ich' (Stanley Guenter, pers. comm. 2013). Although the titles of this character are too damaged to read, we now know that this was part of the longer name of the Kaanul king Aj Saakil (Martin and Beliaev 2017).

Importantly, the subordination of the El Peru kingdom to Dzibanche comes a scant six years before the decisive Tikal star war defeat of 562 recorded on Altar 21. There is good reason to believe that these developments are connected. The previous ruler of El Peru, father to the commissioner of Stela 44, was called Chak Tok Ich'aak, a name that is only otherwise used by kings of Tikal. We know that client kingdoms had a propensity for mirroring the names of their patron power, if usually at a generation's remove. This could well place El Peru as a one-time vassal to Tikal, and its switch in allegiance a sign that Tikal was losing its grip over nearby clients in the build-up to its defeat (David Freidel, pers. comm. 2016).

Who was responsible for reducing Tikal to silence for generations? The name of the protagonist is damaged, but it can be said with certainty that the surviving outlines are not those required for Yajawte' K'inich and, moreover, the accompanying royal title cannot be that of Caracol. Instead, our suspicions must fall elsewhere, to those who benefited most in geopolitical terms, namely the Kaanul dynasty of Dzibanche.[17] Those surviving details are consistent with the names and emblem of either K'ahk' Ti' Ch'ich' Aj Saakil or his successor Sky Witness. We first hear of Sky Witness when he installs a ruler at Los Alacranes in 561 (Grube 2008: 195), making him a prime suspect (Martin 2005b: 3–5). However, he might not have been the true or only Kaanul king at this time. K'ahk' Ti' Ch'ich' is named in a later section of the Altar 21 text (Sergei Vepretskii, pers. comm. 2017) and his responsibility for the war would make sense of a further record, seen on a vessel painted in the style of Naranjo dating to the later sixth century. This names K'ahk' Ti' Ch'ich' as the overlord of a *k'uhul mutul ajaw* – which is to say, a full Tikal king – by means of another *yajaw* formula (Martin and Beliaev 2017). This monarch is otherwise unknown to us and if he ever ruled at the city, perhaps as a puppet following the conquest, he was later struck from Tikal's numbered dynastic count.

The next *yajaw* statement in the corpus also involves the dynasty of the serpent. It appears within a lengthy stucco frieze text at the site of Holmul, the greater site to which La Sufricaya is attached, which mentions several successive rulers of that centre (Estrada-Belli and Tokovinine 2016). The then-current Holmul sovereign is said both to be the vassal of an unspecified *kaanul ajaw* and a grandson of Aj Numsaaj Chan K'inich of nearby Naranjo, suggesting that he fell within the orbit of both kingdoms. There are no preserved dates here, but the general timeframe should fall somewhere around 580. More recently, a jade jewel depicting the Maize God was found in a tomb at Holmul, its incised inscription showing that it was once owned by a Kaanul king (Francisco Estrada-Belli, pers. comm. 2016). This was probably a diplomatic gift and part of the reciprocal, but asymmetrical, exchanges between patron and clients.

Hierarchy in the Late Classic Period, 600–900 CE

We previously heard about the only scenes to show supervised accession events, those on Bonampak Panels 4 and 5 (Figure 16a and b). The earlier of the two describes the inauguration of a local king in 605, although the presiding patron of the event does not appear in the text but within the scene instead. Dressed as the Underworld ruler God L, identified by his cape and owl-crowned hat, Shield Jaguar II of Yaxchilan here presents the candidate with a *huun* headband. Other features of this text are intriguing. It begins by telling us that the coronation took place at *usiijwitz*, "Vulture Hill" or Bonampak itself (Stuart 2006b). But the main topic is how the Bonampak ruler was forced into exile at Yaxchilan in 610, returning just over a year later to defeat a likely usurper and reclaim his throne (Bíró 2007b: 35) (p.130–131). This would have delivered the kingdom back into the fold of its overlord as well.

The damaged Santa Elena Monument 1 describes an event conducted by the local king that, although it certainly could be clearer, resembles a kingly *uk'alhuun* accession statement. Whatever its nature it takes place under the direction of Palenque's Ajen Yohl Mat, placing its date to no earlier than 605 and no later than 611 (Grube, in Grube, Martin, and Zender 2002b: 16).[18] This is the earliest non-retrospective date associated with a Palenque king and shows that its influence reached well into the Tabascan plain at that time, with Santa Elena some 93 km distant from Palenque.

Caracol makes additional mentions to Kaanul rulers and their affairs at this time. Yajawte' K'inich's younger son K'an II came to power in 618, an event that is said, rather unusually, to be supervised by a set of deities. These belong to a now illegible actor, perhaps an earlier Caracol dynast. Just under a year later we know that the new king was engaged in some action under the aegis of the Kaanul ruler Yuknoom Ti' Chan, but its nature was long obscure (Figure 59). Close examination of the monument in question shows the outlines of a *k'alhuun* headband-raising statement which, as we have heard, was normally an accession event in its own right. The presence of a "second" accession was puzzling until a sequence of events recorded at Moral-Reforma, which revealed that such ceremonies could re-occur at the behest of powerful overkings (p.250–253). This offers a resolution to the conundrum and tells us that Caracol had become officially subject to the Snake kingdom by at least 619 (Martin 2008c). In rhetorical and symbolic terms, K'an II appears to balance his admission of subordination by taking the unusual step of stressing his prior installation under the direction of Caracol's own gods.

In 626 and again in 627 K'an II battled with Naranjo, single episodes in an extended war (Grube 1994c: 103–104). Later in 627 he attacked an unidentified location *yitaaj* or "with" the Kaanul lord we know as Yuknoom Head, a phrasing that signals allied action.[19] The Kaanul king at this time was Tajoom Uk'ab K'ahk', and on the same day as that conflict he performs a ballgame ritual, likely of the kind associated with martial celebrations and the dispatching of prisoners (Miller and Houston 1987: 52–63). Tajoom Uk'ab K'ahk' died three years later in 630, and within a year Yuknoom Head was in action again, this time enacting a star war conquest of Naranjo in 631 (Martin and Grube 1994a: 11, 21, 2000: 72–73, 92). Initially, it appeared that Naranjo had simply rebelled from its subordinate status.

59 The *k'alhuun* headband ceremony of K'an II of Caracol in 619, as supervised by Yuknoom Ti' Chan of the Kaanul kingdom. Caracol Stela 3.

However, we now appreciate that the situation was rather more complex. The key factor is that when Yuknoom Head next takes to the field in 636 it is to battle and defeat Waxaklajuun Ubaah Kaan, the immediate successor to Tajoom Uk'ab K'ahk' and the legitimate king of Dzibanche (Helmke and Awe 2016a: 10–11). A clash between two members of the Snake dynasty indicates a civil war and, although Waxaklajuun Ubaah Kaan survived this encounter, he was seized at some point and put to death in 640.

If the Kaanul dynasty's record in installing subject rulers was already notable, it blossomed anew once its capital was relocated to Calakmul (Case Study 6). Yuknoom Ch'een II was the central figure in the reconstitution of the Snake kingdom at the ancient centre of Uxte'tuun Chiiknahb, and his lengthy reign was indisputably the highpoint of the late Kaanul dynasty. The new powerbase led to greater engagement with the western and southern lowlands, which we see first in a series of military campaigns fought in the Petexbatun region. The initial focus there was the site of Dos Pilas, whose ruler Bajlaj Chan K'awiil was a scion of the Tikal dynasty who had, for reasons that remain unclear, moved to the Petexbatun by about 643 (Houston 1993: 102–110; Martin and Grube 2000: 56–57; Fahsen et al. 2003; Guenter 2003; Martin 2003b: 25–29). In 650 Yuknoom Ch'een attacked Dos Pilas and, although Bajlaj Chan K'awiil evaded capture, he soon capitulated to become a vassal of the Calakmul king (Houston 1993: 108). These events established Bajlaj Chan K'awiil as a Tikal "anti-king" at the head of his own polity.[20] Calakmul and Dos Pilas would thereafter pursue cooperative wars against Tikal, which included the Yuknoom Ch'een victory that allowed an exiled Bajlaj Chan K'awiil to return to his capital in 677 (Case Study 11).

The authority of Yuknoom Ch'een had by then extended to Cancuen, a site on the Pasión River in the southernmost portion of the lowlands and a strategic gateway to the resource-rich highlands (Maps 1 and 3). As we saw in Chapter 6, the narrative of Cancuen Panel 1 begins with events taking place at Calakmul, including the inauguration of a new Cancuen king called K'iib Ajaw in 656. This is phrased, uniquely, as *yichonal* a set of Calakmul deities as well as *ukabjiiy* Yuknoom Ch'een. A few months later K'iib Ajaw leaves for an extended journey that ends at places close to Haluum, ancient Cancuen, to formally establish or re-establish royal authority in the area. The installation of the next Cancuen king in 677, also conducted under the auspices of Yuknoom Ch'een, lacks this elaborate narration and we can take it that the kingdom was now properly constituted. Dedicated in 799, Panel 1 has a distinctly nostalgic air to it, harkening back to political associations long past and a world of once-powerful hegemonies that had, by that time, faded from sight.

The most illuminating additions to understanding the role of the *yichonal* "before, in sight of" term have come from a single monument, Moral-Reforma Stela 4 (Martin 2003c) (Figure 60). Its rear text opens in January

60 Muwaan Jol with two captives on the front of Moral-Reforma Stela 4.

656 with the birth of a princeling whose father carries the emblem glyph of Moral-Reforma and was presumably the reigning king at that time. A count of just five-and-a-half years takes us forward to 661 and the boy's succession as ruler, indicated by the verb *ajawaan*, "becomes a lord" that describes some other childhood accession rites.[21] A second statement supplies *uk'alhuun k'aba'*, "his raised headband-name", a reference to a newly acquired regnal name. This is standard fare, but the next phrase offers something unexpected.

Less than a year later, on 5 April 662, there is another *k'alhuun* headband presentation event, this time prefixed by the number "2" that signifies "the second" in verbal contexts (Figure 61a). The name of the subject here is different, in part reading Muwaan Jol, but a connecting day-count between the birth and this accession makes doubly clear that this is the same person now bearing his new name. This second inauguration is appended by *yichonal* and the name and Kaanul title of Yuknoom Ch'een. The text goes on to give the location of the ceremony, although this is now too damaged to read. The narrative moves next to Muwaan Jol's adult life and a military encounter in or around 687 that produced the two captives who are depicted with him on the front of the monument. Three years after this, on 11 July 690, Muwaan Jol undergoes a "third" headband event (Figure 61b). Once again, the investiture has a supervising patron introduced by *yichonal*, but this time it is K'inich Kaan Bahlam II of Palenque. The location of the ceremony is given as *baakal*, the referent in the Palenque emblem glyph (see Case Study 1). This statement indicates that the ceremony occurred somewhere within the Palenque polity,

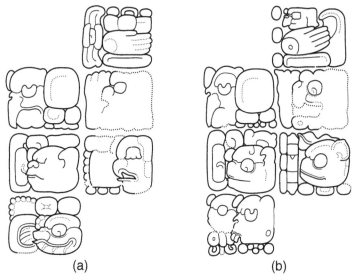

(a)   (b)

61 Two supervised accessions of Muwaan Jol recorded on the back of Moral-Reforma Stela 4: (a) "Second" headband ceremony overseen by Yuknoom Ch'een II in 662; (b) "Third" headband ceremony overseen by K'inich Kaan Bahlam II in 690.

in all probability at its capital Lakamha'. This in turn implies that the previous installation also took place at a foreign locale, either distant Calakmul or a nearer centre subject to it.

The text ends with a commemoration of the 9.13.0.0.0 period ending, just two years later, yet its celebrant has a name different to all of those inscribed thus far. To introduce a new character at this point would run counter to any known narrative structure, and the count of days leading to that date in 692 explicitly ties it to the first accession event. The only plausible explanation is that this is the same person, now using a third nominal. Conceivably, each *k'alhuun* event involved the bestowal of a new name, the shift instigated by the presence of a new overlord.

This sequence of events offers an exceptional window into the history not only of Moral-Reforma, but Classic Maya political practice in general. Here is direct evidence that individual kings could, and did, move between the spheres of opposing powers and that these transfers in allegiance were instituted via formal rites of re-investiture. The only way to understand the reasons behind these specific events is to take a wider regional perspective, the purpose behind Case Study 12.

Secondary installation ceremonies, such as those at Caracol and Moral-Reforma, could solve a historical riddle posed by Piedras Negras Panel 3 (Figure 24). This intricately carved monument, which in many ways echoes a scene of courtly life we might find wrapped around a painted vessel, shows the local king Itzam K'an Ahk IV (Ruler 4) presiding from a wide throne over several groups of lesser lords (Houston and Stuart 2001: 69–73). The main focus among these falls on the three dignitaries at left, visitors from the regional rival of Yaxchilan. The problem comes in a small, incised text, a second-person speech of the seated king – one of very few such examples on a stone monument – who refers to something done by *amam yaxuun bahlam*, "your grandfather Bird Jaguar" (Stuart, Houston, and Robertson 1999: I:19). The text goes on to state that this same Bird Jaguar was installed in office by one of the Piedras Negras kings called Itzam K'an Ahk (Mathews 1988: 230; Martin and Grube 1994a: 8). This event is plainly set in the past, but no attempt to correlate these names and the possible dates of the accession at their respective polities offers a match.

However, if we assume that Yopaat Bahlam II – the Yaxchilan monarch present and mentioned in the main text of Panel 3 – is the person addressed (the short caption identifying the leading visitor is now effaced), then his grandfather was very likely to have been Bird Jaguar III. According to Yaxchilan's accounts, most of them produced by Bird Jaguar IV, Bird Jaguar III reigned from 629 until at least 669. One reference that may legitimately date to his lifetime comes on a panel found at Bonampak that describes his installation of a ruler using a Bonampak/Lacanha emblem in 643

(Figure 16b).[22] Conceivably, Piedras Negras Panel 3 asserts that Bird Jaguar III was re-installed or sanctioned by a newly dominant Itzam K'an Ahk III in a ceremony we can calculate to the year 653. Whatever the truth of this, the major message of Panel 3 is a history lesson delivered to the visiting delegation, perhaps one in deliberate contradiction of the record by-then-extant at Yaxchilan (Martin and Grube 2000: 127, 149, see Case Study 5).

Uxul commemorated the 9.11.10.0.0 period ending of 662 on two stelae, both of which describe Yuknoom Ch'een's *yichonal* oversight of the local ruler's scattering of incense (Grube 2008: 224–226). The location is unspecified, but it is exceedingly hard to believe that this modest Calakmul satellite hosted such a momentous event, or that the central ritual actor was not the great overking himself. We are left to conclude that it took place at Calakmul, presumably as part of a larger gathering of client kings who repeated the same rites in his presence. A precedent for this comes from the visit Bajlaj Chan K'awiil of Dos Pilas paid to Calakmul in 682 on the occasion of the 9.12.10.0.0 period ending, where he accompanied the by-then aged Yuknoom Ch'een in a dance performance (Houston 1993: 108).

Yuknoom Ch'een oversaw the accession of the El Peru ruler K'inich Bahlam II on a date now lost to us (Martin and Grube 1994a: 15, 2000: 109), and also gave him a daughter in marriage (see p.184). El Peru monuments pay special attention to dynastic affairs at Calakmul, recording the birth of Yuknoom Ch'een and the accessions of Yuknoom Yich'aak K'ahk' and Yuknoom Took' K'awiil.[23]

Yuknoom Ch'een was also overlord to El Peru's neighbour to the south, Hixwitz, a polity whose royal seat lay at Zapote Bobal at the time (Stuart 2003). There Stela 1 describes the accession of its king Janaab Ti' O' at the age of 14 in 663. No higher authority is mentioned at this point, but five years later, in 669, Janaab Ti' O' is installed for a second time, now under the oversight of Yuknoom Ch'een (Vepretskii and Galeev 2016) – a sequence very much like the one we saw at Moral-Reforma. An isolated block of hieroglyphic stairway, presumably robbed from Zapote Bobal, names the same client and patron again connected by *yichonal*, and this almost certainly refers to the same event (Martin and Reents-Budet 2010). David Stuart (pers. comm. 2010) points out that a partly eroded inscription at El Reinado could name Janaab Ti' O' as the possessed *ajaw* of Yuknoom Ch'een.[24] Zapote Bobal Stela 1 next counts forward to 695 for a now illegible event that took place at Uxte'tuun during the reign of Yuknoom Yich'aak K'ahk' (Vepretskii and Galeev 2016). This gives us good reason to think that Janaab Ti' O' continued as a Calakmul vassal, and it is notable that an unprovenanced vessel naming Janaab Ti' O' is in the distinctive "codex-style" produced at one of Calakmul's other subject polities in this same era (Guenter 2003: n.9; Martin and Reents-Budet 2010: 4).

The guiding hand of Calakmul suzerainty can be detected once again when a daughter of Bajlaj Chan K'awiil travels to Naranjo to marry its king in 682 (see p.177). This is made explicit when her son, the five-year-old K'ahk' Tiliw Chan Chahk, takes the Naranjo throne in 693, at which point he is described as belonging to Yuknoom Yich'aak K'ahk' (Martin and Grube 1994a: 9, 2000: 75). Just two years later, in the summer of 695, Calakmul suffered a significant blow as Yich'aak K'ahk's forces were defeated by those of Jasaw Chan K'awiil I of Tikal (Schele and Freidel 1990: 205) (p.167). It is doubtless no coincidence that this success is soon followed by evidence of Tikal's restored political muscle, with the new ruler of its southern neighbour Motul de San José describing himself as an *ajaw* possessed by Jasaw Chan K'awiil in 701 (Martin and Grube 2000: 45–46; Tokovinine and Zender 2012: 50, figure 2.2).

A year later, in 702, the king of Bonampak/Lacanha expresses his subordination to the Tonina ruler K'inich Baaknal Chahk (Houston and Mathews 1985: figure 12, n.2), which seems to stem directly from the latter's campaigning in the Lacandon area (Houston and Mathews 1985: figure 12, n.2; Miller and Martin 2004: 141) (Figure 62a and b). These events will be explored in

(a)   (b)

62 The king of Bonampak/Lacanha describes himself as a *yajaw* or "the lord of" the Tonina king K'inich Baaknal Chahk on an unprovenanced column: (a) Photograph (*Column with Hieroglyphs,* 715; Maya, Mexico; limestone with pigment; 22 7/16 x 9 1/16 inches; Saint Louis Art Museum, Gift of Morton D. May 384:1978); (b) A "roll-out" drawing of the text.

Case Study 13, where a series of *yajaw* relationships show us how Tonina tried to wrest regional control from Palenque. While this chapter concentrates on the power relationships between major kingdoms, here we can see the bonds that connected leading and lesser lordships, which were doubtless common to the point of ubiquity. Centres with their own ruling *ajaw* that were situated close to some more significant centre might normally form part its effective "home" domain. Yet we see that such associations were not so fixed that the loyalty of peripheral sub-kingdoms could not be willingly, or forcibly, transferred to a different patron.

Dos Pilas maintained its links to Calakmul into the eighth century but was already operating a smaller-scale hegemony of its own. Evidence for this comes in 711–731 with Itzamnaaj K'awiil's *yajaw* ownership of the king of Arroyo de Piedra, part of an original Petexbatun polity paired with Tamarindito, centres whose regional power had been usurped by the intrusive Mutul breakaway (Houston and Mathews 1985: figure 12, n.2; Houston 1993) (p.73). The site chosen for Dos Pilas was not especially advantageous from an agricultural point of view and its inhabitants put little effort into modifying the landscape to improve its yields (Dunning, Beach, and Rue 1997: 263). Tamarindito, only 7.5 km away, had better soils and moreover had, over the years, enhanced its productive capacities by building terraces and check dams. There is potential here for exploitation, as the interlopers drew on the resources of a nearby "breadbasket".[25] Throughout its short history Dos Pilas more resembles a special-purpose political centre than it does one with an organic place in the landscape.

In every instance of polity-level hierarchy described thus far it has been the client who provides an account of their own subordination. The only exceptions I have been able to find appear on Naranjo Stela 2, where K'ahk' Tiliw Chan Chahk – as we have just seen, himself the vassal of Calakmul – makes gives an account his regional dominance. In this he first oversees the probable accession of a king from Ucanal in 712, then tells us that he owns the king of the still-unidentified Yopmootz polity at his installation ceremony in 713. Case Study 14 examines this interesting anomaly in more detail.

El Peru Stela 27 describes the accession of a local king under the supervision of the next Calakmul king Yuknoom Took' K'awiil (Martin and Grube 1994a: 8). While the date is now lost, it must have occurred after 698 and before 736, the point by which a different ruler had assumed the Snake throne (Martin 2005a: 11–12). This is the last occasion on which we see Calakmul exert this kind of political sway, and this once-expansive power would soon disappear from view. Its increasing impotence was such that just two years after Stela 27 was commissioned in 741 the king of El Peru was captured by Tikal – one of the decisive moves it made to fill the dominant position vacated by Calakmul.

Two of our few glimpses into the political organisation of what is today southern Belize come at the site of Nim Li Punit. On a date that can be reconstructed to 724, Stela 2 describes the *uch'amaw k'awiil*, "he grasps K'awiil" accession of a new king.[26] This is performed *yichonal* a king of the "water scroll" polity, the somewhat elusive entity for which Altun Ha remains the best candidate (Wanyerka 2009: 468; Helmke, Guenter, and Wanyerka 2018). Though of modest size and without surviving monuments, the wealth and importance of Altun Ha is implied by the great quantities of jade found in its burials (Pendergast 1990), one of them bearing a text featuring the "water scroll" emblem. Appearing among the thirteen major kingdoms listed at Altar de Los Reyes (p.148), at least one of its rulers carried the *elk'in kaloomte'* title, signalling that it was a leading power of the eastern Maya realm.

The same king of Nim Li Punit goes on to conduct the period ending ceremonies of 731 *yitaj*, "with" a ruler who bears the Copan emblem glyph prefixed with the sign *ihk'*, "black". Although this suggests a connection to that city, this darkened form served as an alternate emblem glyph for Copan's long-term client kingdom of Quirigua – here followed by either a name or relationship to what may be a second character.[27]

The Quirigua king at this date was the well-known K'ahk' Tiliw Chan Yopaat. It was he who radically transformed the monumental signature of Quirigua, which had been a fairly minor centre up to that point. The pivotal event of K'ahk' Tiliw Chan Yopaat's tenure came, as we heard earlier, in 738 with his seizure and beheading of the Copan king Waxaklajuun Ubaah K'awiil (p.163, 231). Yet in one of the retrospective accounts of his accession in 724, the Quirigua king took care to mention that he was installed by Waxaklajuun Ubaah K'awiil, making this a story of betrayal in which a vassal rebelled and fashioned his minor provincial seat into a rival for mighty Copan (Stuart 1992: 175).

Did Quirigua act entirely alone? Perhaps not. Quirigua Stela I was commissioned by K'ahk' Jol Chan Yopaat in 800, but its text revisits the rebellion to describe the defeat or capture of the patron gods of Waxaklajuun Ubaah K'awiil. This is tied directly to the period ending ceremony K'ahk' Tiliw Chan Yopaat conducted two years earlier in 736, which we are told involved someone named Wamaaw K'awiil. He is identified as the ruler of Chiiknahb, which is to say Calakmul (Looper 1999: 270–272, 2003: 79).[28] Sadly, the connecting term between the two kings is unique and as yet undeciphered. Wamaaw K'awiil had succeeded Yuknoom Took' K'awiil sometime after 731, and we see the new king with the expected Kaanul emblem glyph and *kaloomte'* title pictured on a panel from Hixwitz (Tunesi 2007: 15–16, 19).[29] This kind of ballgame, involving two kings, has hierarchical significance (see p.338) and suggests that Calakmul's shrinking realm did not evaporate overnight – meaning that it might still have been influential in Quirigua's bid for independence.

A passage on Naranjo Stela 46 attests to the *yilaaj* witnessing of a local ritual in 726 by the kings of Calakmul and Dos Pilas (identified only by their emblems), a clear sign that these polities remained closely involved in the affairs of Naranjo throughout the reign of K'ahk' Tiliw Chan Chahk (Martin et al. 2017). The same "seeing" term could be used to describe interactions between kings and nobles, as on a stairway block once set at La Corona where an *ajk'uhuun* dedicates a building observed by Yuknoom Took' K'awiil.[30] The reversible nature of this expression is made plain on another block featuring the same two actors, where this time the noble witnesses a now-missing action performed by the king (compare Mayer 1978: pl.29 to 1980: pl.27). Similarly, when Yuknoom Yich'aak K'ahk' rose to the Calakmul throne in 686, his Dos Pilas client Bajlaj Chan K'awiil was on hand to observe the proceedings (Houston 1993: 139; Martin 1997a: 852; Martin and Grube 2000: 57). Such important ceremonies presumably occasioned a gathering of many subject lords.

Dos Pilas initially profited from Calakmul's decline, expanding its power to encompass Ceibal and Cancuen (Johnston 1985; Houston 1993: 114–117; Martin and Grube 2000: 61–63). At this same point, Dos Pilas starts to employ a version of the Mutul glyph rarely used at Tikal, a small but deliberate effort to carve out a distinctive identity for the rebel kingdom. Still more significantly, its kings now carry the *kaloomte'* epithet in contemporary contexts for the first time. In 735 its then-king Ucha'an K'in Bahlam seized Ceibal together with its monarch Yich'aak Bahlam (Houston and Mathews 1985: 17) (see p.207). That this event brought enduring control is made plain on the Ceibal Hieroglyphic Stairway, set in the heart of the defeated city, whose central actor is the next Dos Pilas ruler, K'awiil Chan K'inich. The stairway text records the calendrical rites he conducted at Tamarindito and Ceibal in 746, as well as his witnessing of a Ceibal princeling's elevation to *ajaw* status in 747.

By now, or shortly thereafter, Dos Pilas took over the patronage of the Cancuen kingdom, overseeing Tajal Chan Ahk's accession in 757 (Fahsen, Demarest, and Luin 2003: 712). As we learn from Cancuen's Hieroglyphic Stairway, this took place at Dos Pilas and it was four days before the newly anointed ruler returned to his home city (Tokovinine 2008: 94, 2013: 16). This repeats the pattern we saw at Moral-Reforma, where the installation ceremonies of vassal kings could take place at the home seat of an overlord. We cannot know how common this particular practice was and it may, like supervised accessions in general, be significantly under-reported.

Tajal Chan Ahk commissioned the previously mentioned Cancuen Panel 1, which centres on the sponsorship of his predecessors by Calakmul kings, but he makes no mention of his own subordination to Dos Pilas. This is unsurprising, given that the political situation had radically altered by the time this monument was dedicated in 799. By then, Dos Pilas had been abandoned and its alternate capital at Aguateca was about to suffer the same fate. By contrast,

Tajal Chan Ahk's fortunes were on the rise and having gained some degree of control over Machaquila – seemingly in a conflict conducted by his leading noble – he incorporates its emblem glyph into his title phrase (Demarest, Barrientos, and Fahsen 2006: 832; also Guenter 2002). Some have argued that Cancuen Panel 3 shows Tajal Chan Ahk enthroned at Machaquila in 795, although that might be contested. In any case, this incorporation did not outlive him and we find no trace of it at Machaquila, which saw one of its own kings succeed in 799.

Although the number of recorded hierarchical relationships had held up relatively well during the first half of the eighth century, from here on they become much less common. We briefly see the minor kingdom of Sacul enter the macro-political stage when its king performs a key ceremony, the "taking" of a palanquin, "before" and therefore in subordination to the king of Ucanal in 760. The same Ucanal ruler likely also exercised control or oversight at El Chal. Having long suffered defeat or subjugation at the hands of its larger neighbours Naranjo and Caracol, we here see Ucanal finally asserting itself in the region.

The next inaugural sponsorship, also using the *yichonal* term, comes in the murals of Bonampak, where the penultimate ruler of Yaxchilan, Shield Jaguar IV, oversees the elevation of a new king in 790 (Houston, in Miller 1995: 62). For the very first time the initiate shares a contemporary *kaloomte'* title with his overlord, suggesting a less imbalanced relationship between them. The two polities were already military allies. Three years earlier, in 787, the preceding Bonampak ruler had joined Shield Jaguar IV in battling the dynasty of Sak Tz'i' from Lacanja-Tzeltal, and had also married into the Yaxchilan royal line (Mathews 1980: 64–67; Bíró 2005: 26).

Back in 717, Sak Tz'i' had served as overlord to Bonampak/Lacanha, and by at least mid-century was itself subordinated to Piedras Negras. We discover this indirectly from El Cayo Panel 1, where a Sak Tz'i' lord called Aj Sak Maax installs an El Cayo *sajal* in 763 (Martin and Grube 2000: 151; Bíró 2005: 20–24). El Cayo lies only about 14 km upstream from Piedras Negras and was otherwise a direct dependency of that capital (see p.88). Even on Panel 1, Piedras Negras remains the overall authority to which an El Cayo *sajal*-in-waiting travels at the age of eleven years a couple of months earlier, perhaps to reside at its royal court. The implication is that Sak Tz'i' has been assigned territories to administer on behalf of Piedras Negras, a rare glimpse of a three-tiered regional hierarchy.

The last record of direct supervision might come at Caracol. Here, in an eroded but broadly legible text on Altar 13, the king we know as K'inich Toobil Yopaat is the subject of a *ch'am* "taking/receiving" event in 817, under the evident oversight of someone called Papamalil or Papmalil.[31] This character ruled at Ucanal and the event took place at that centre, emphasising the asymmetry between the two lords. Interestingly, Papmalil is never ascribed the Ucanal emblem glyph but does carry an *ochk'in/chik'in kaloomte'* title, making him a high king from the real or symbolic "west" (pp.79–80). Some measure of his importance can be deduced from the simple fact that his name and title are inscribed three times on Altar 13, whereas those of the Caracol king appear only twice. If we were to judge by the carved scene alone, and another on Altar 12, we would mistake Papmalil as a supplicant to the Caracol king. However, as we saw in the supervised accessions depicted at Bonampak, representations designed for home consumption are inflected with patrimonial rhetoric and not reliable guides to relative status (p.115). Papmalil appears in three other contexts at Caracol, one referencing his *ebeet*, "messenger" and two others suggesting that the polities collaborated in war (Grube 1994c: 95–96).[32]

To this we must add a reference on Naranjo Stela 32, dated to 820, where Papmalil is again given the *ochk'in/chik'in kaloomte'* epithet and owns a palanquin that the commissioner of that text, the Naranjo king Waxaklajuun Ubaah K'awiil, is carried upon (Carter 2014a: 213–214). This is surely related to the palanquin pictured in the scene, whose front steps carry a text referring to two presentations of tribute in 815 (p.340). Waxaklajuun Ubaah K'awiil had acceded in 814, but the day before he performed a pre-accession dressing rite under the oversight of a *k'uhul peet ajaw* "holy palanquin lord". Given the context, this could be a supervising deity or, if not, an oblique reference to Papmalil. Whoever this person was it clearly implies that Naranjo, like Caracol, was under the hand of some outside authority. Although Papmalil outwardly seems to be a standard ruler, his unusual name – unlike any borne by a previous Classic Maya king – and lack of a local title makes one wonder if there is something alien about his regime nevertheless (p.295–296).

Some of the final attested cases of *il*, "to see" are the most interesting and significant. As we saw in Chapter 6, a lord called Wat'ul K'atel arrived at Ceibal in 829 at the direction of an Ucanal lord. We know that by that point the polity had already revived its original emblem glyph, which had fallen into disuse while the city served as the capital for one of the petty Mutul kingdoms that arose in the wake of Dos Pilas's fall (Martin and Grube 2000: 64–65; Carter 2014a: 196–197). In 849 Wat'ul K'atel commissioned a group of five stelae to celebrate the period ending 10.1.0.0.0, placed in and around a cruciform temple richly decorated with stucco sculpture known today as Structure A-3 (Smith 1982: 12–59; Schele and Mathews 1998: 175–196). The most famous of these monuments is Stela 10 (Figure 63), whose text features the names of three foreign kings, those of Tikal, Calakmul, and Motul de San José. Other A-3 monuments add a fifth ruler representing an unknown polity called Puh and a sixth that refers to the Lakamtuun polity based at El Palma by that time – although in that case using the *yeta(j)*, "with" connecting term (Stuart and Houston 1994: 37).[33]

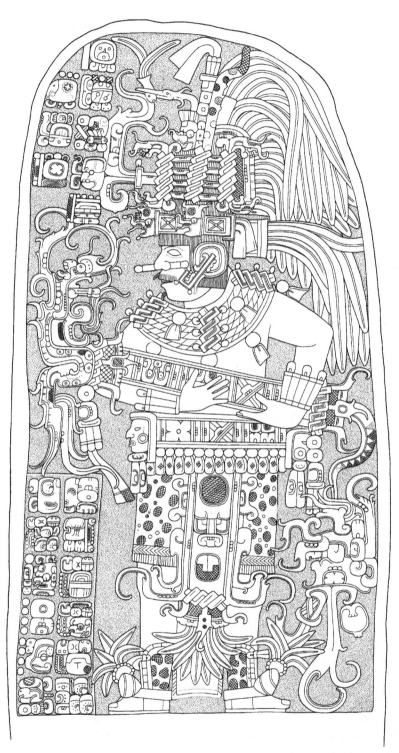

63 Wat'ul K'atel celebrates the period ending 10.1.0.0.0 in 849. Ceibal Stela 10. (Drawing by
Ian Graham © President and Fellows of Harvard College, Peabody Museum of Archaeology and
Ethnology, PM# 2004.15.6.17.10)

As we saw in Chapter 2, Barthel compared the set of emblems on Stela 10 with another carved over a century earlier on Copan Stela A, which together formed the cornerstones for his concept of a quadripartite division of the Classic Maya world. However, when the text of Stela 10 was finally read it became clear that it only referred to these other kings as "witnessing" the calendrical ceremonies conducted by their Ceibal counterpart (Stuart 1993: 327).

Still, in making that necessary correction we cannot pass over the profound political message that remains in this record. That these foreign kings were physically present at Ceibal is emphasised by the end of the Stela 10 text, which states *uhtiiy tahn* "Ceibal" or "it happened in the midst of Ceibal". As the magnet to which other rulers are obliged to travel, Wat'ul K'atel here sets out his claim to be a great king (see also Guenter 1999: 136). That so modest a centre as Ceibal could command so lofty a guest-list speaks to a radical transformation of the political landscape in the ninth century, and we shall return to the wider significance of this and other late records in the next chapter. It can be no surprise that Wat'ul K'atel is the first king of Ceibal known to bear the *kaloomte'* title. Although the institution of kingship would linger in the lowlands for at least two generations more, the ceremony of 849 was the last great political moment claimed by the Classic Maya.

But Structure A-3 and its stelae constitute one further symbolic statement. The central monument set inside the building, Stela 21, refers to the foundation of the current Long Count era in 3114 BCE, and the whole programme can be seen as model of the four-sided Maya cosmos, each stela aligned to a cardinal direction (Stuart 2016). It is doubtless no coincidence that the place-name of Ceibal is directly related to that of the key supernatural location for this ancestral event, making its commemoration here all the more poignant and appropriate. In sum, although the programme of Ceibal Structure A-3 comes in the dying days of the Classic Maya political society, it is a fascinating and intricately composed last testament.

CASE STUDY 12: THE CONTEST FOR EASTERN TABASCO, 659–692 CE

The instances of multiple accession ceremonies at Moral-Reforma, one of them under the direction of Calakmul and another under that of Palenque, are revealing and significant in their own right. However, if we are to understand their full relevance, explaining why they occurred at this particular place and at these particular times, we must move to a broader historical process rooted in regional competition.

The Usumacinta River flows westward through the Lacandon region past Yaxchilan and Piedras Negras, through some turbulent rapids and a steep-sided canyon, before emerging from a V-shaped split in a high ridge – today called Boca del Cerro "Mouth of the Mountain". From there it spills onto the alluvial plain of eastern Tabasco, where it meanders before joining the San Pedro Mártir River, a placid waterway that provides the easiest and most direct route between the central Peten and all points to the west.

This area boasts no grand capitals but instead a number of mid-sized centres situated close to these two rivers: principally those of Pomona, Santa Elena, and Moral-Reforma (Map 4). The earliest notice of the region comes from Piedras Negras, where Panel 12 shows a bound Santa Elena lord in 518 or earlier (Martin and Grube 2000: 141). A little under a century later, at some point between 605 and 611, one of Santa Elena's monuments describes its king performing some ceremony, possibly his own accession, under the auspices of Palenque's Ajen Yohl Mat (Table 6). We have no other evidence for Palenque's political activities at this time, but this mention alone suggests that it had significant political clout in the area. Palenque and Piedras Negras were regional rivals, probably clashing militarily in 603 (Stephen Houston, pers. comm. 1998) but more clearly in 628, when Piedras Negras displays a Palenque captive carrying the *ajk'uhuun* title (Miller 1991; Grube 1996: 4–5; Martin and Grube 2000: 142–143). Since he is displayed together with a lord of Sak Tz'i' this centre may have been an ally or client of Palenque at this time.

We now move to the year 659 and a conflict that constituted the foremost claim to military competence and personal glory for the Palenque king K'inich Janaab Pakal I. It was inscribed in the heart of the Palenque royal court on the steps of House C, the focal point of its main reception space, the East Court (Figure 64a). Six captives seized on 11 August 659 were depicted on the east face of House C's supporting platform, identified by adjacent captions as well as by name elements inserted into their headdresses (Schele 1994: 4–5, figure 4). Each holds his arm across his chest in a gesture of submission and has strips of cloth or paper drawn through his earlobes, a mark of defeat (Baudez and Mathews 1979: 36) (Figure 64b). Although all the captions reference toponyms, these are unknown except for Pipa', a location intimately associated with Pomona some 51 km to the east of Palenque (Schele 1994: 8–9; Stuart and Houston 1994: 46, figure 56).

Yet the stairway text makes clear that these are secondary victims taken *yitaaj* or "with" the main subject of the *chuhkaj* capture verb, a ruler of Santa Elena called Nuun Ujol Chahk (a namesake to the contemporary king of Tikal). His portrait is hidden in plain sight on the adjacent northern balustrade of the stairway, identified as such by the *chahk* storm deity headdress he wears (Martin 2014a: figure 182a and b). Nuun Ujol Chahk is mentioned in two other texts at Palenque where, six days after the fighting, he *huli lakamha'*, "arrives (at) Palenque" under the *yichonal* oversight of Janaab Pakal (Schele 1994: 3; Martin 2004c). There are other cases in which arrivals follow close on the heels of captures, where we can understand them as acts of formal

(a)

(b)

64 East side of House C, Palenque Palace: (a) View across the East Court, with the hieroglyphic stairway flanked by portrait balustrades; (b) Prisoner sculptures identified by their headdresses and intervening captions carved into the platform façade.

arraignment or submission (Martin 2010b: n.13). Given the prominence accorded to this event – it was also retold on a censer stand (Martin 2004c) and in a now-fragmentary stucco text (Houston and Stuart 2008) – the major outcome of the conflict from Palenque's perspective was the subjugation of Santa Elena.[34]

The text on the House C steps links the fighting of 659 to a much earlier assault on Palenque by the Kaanul kingdom in 599, when *ch'ahkaj lakamha'*, "Palenque is chopped" (Martin 2000c: 110–111, 2010b: 77, n.10). This is followed by a reference to the three patron deities of Palenque, who were *yalej*, "thrown down" (Grube 1996: 3). Why would Janaab Pakal want to remind his audience of a major reverse that took place four years before he was born? As we have already seen, the devastating defeat delivered at the hands of the Kaanul dynasty in 611 was used to justify Janaab Pakal's rise to power in 615 (see p.210), and we can expect any similar reference to have a political purpose of its own. The answer may lie in an obscure section of the text following the attack, which features an earlier lord of Santa Elena called Nuun Hix Lakam Chahk.[35] One wonders if he was implicated in the assault in some way, perhaps as an ally of the Kaanul invaders, making the battle of 659 something of a retribution in Janaab Pakal's eyes (see also Stuart and Stuart 2008: 159).

There is a hint, rendered speculative through poor preservation, that the Kaanul dynasty responded to Santa Elena's new submission to Palenque. The rear face of Calakmul Stela 9 shows a local queen trampling another woman, identified as such by her long tresses and the female prefix to her name in the accompanying caption (Martin 2009a). The verb in that text is the standard *chuhkaj*, "seized" while the date correlates to 8 September 659.[36] What survives of her nominal phrase concludes with a compound featuring two signs (**wa** and the remains of a bird's head) familiar from the toponym of Santa Elena. This capture falls just 32 days after Janaab Pakal's victory on the House C steps and 26 days after Nuun Ujol Chahk's arrival at Palenque – a proximity that lends weight to, but cannot confirm, a connection.

No events are recorded in the region for the year 660, but on 11 May 661 Moral-Reforma saw the accession of Muwaan Jol as a five-year-old boy (Martin 2003c: 46) (see p.252). Later that year, on 26 December, a text inscribed in the eaves of Palenque House C records the dedication of that building, suggesting that its triumphant programme of texts and sculptures was in place by that time (Schele 1994: 7–8).

The next year, 662, would prove especially eventful. On 11 February a Calakmul lord took part in a fire ceremony recorded on Piedras Negras Stela 35, but damage prevents us from knowing who this was (Grube 1996: 8, figure 8b). Its significance is signalled by the highly unusual feature of having its own Long Count date, which is unprecedented for a non-local agent.[37] Just six days later on 17 February, the same monument tells us that the Piedras Negras king Itzam K'an Ahk III staged a star war assault against Santa Elena. Palenque would be engaged in fighting soon after, seizing one captive on 29 March and another a day later. These were celebrated with two large prisoner portraits among a group flanking the stairway of House A, directly opposite House C across the East Court. Although the texts carved on their loincloths do not identify them, the close timing of these actions to the Piedras Negras campaign must raise the strong suspicion that they were connected to it in some way. Just ten days later on 5 April the second inauguration of Muwaan Jol took place at Moral-Reforma, with Yuknoom Ch'een of Calakmul named as its supervising patron (Martin 2003c: 46). There is no reference to a military campaign here, but Calakmul's intervention clearly changed the status quo – conceivably overturning a prior overlordship of Palenque.

The most parsimonious interpretation is that all these incidents were connected and that Piedras Negras and Calakmul were engaged in a coordinated effort to assert or restore their dominance over parts of eastern Tabasco. Subsequent events would appear to confirm that any control Palenque achieved over Santa Elena had indeed been brief.

On 19 December 662, Palenque makes reference to yet another lord of Santa Elena on a small censer stand and, while the appropriate verb is cursively inscribed and none too clear, it could well refer to an *och uch'een* military action (Zender 2004: 308) (see Case Study 3). This would certainly strike a chord with additions Janaab Pakal made to the west-facing rear of House C, which were inspired by some additional success of this kind.

Today all that can be seen are seven widely separated texts carved directly into the slabs of its basal platform (Figure 65a and b). The first six feature names and titles of Santa Elena natives, one of them an *ajaw*, "lord" and the other five *ch'ok*, "youths, princes". Strangely isolated, these references have always been difficult to explain. The solution can be surmised from the gaps between the blocks of this platform façade, which are approximately the same shape and size as those on the east side of the building occupied by sculpted portraits. Those on the west were presumably designed to hold sculptures in the same way, with intervening captions identifying the depicted prisoners just like those on the east side (Martin 2004c, 2010b: 79–80). The western sculptures were either removed at some later point, were modelled in perishable stucco (as were figures on the south side of the West Court), or were simply never installed in the first place.[38]

The seventh and final text on this façade names a lord of Pipa' who is said to have died on 17 July 663 (Schele 1994: 8–9). That date offers a valuable pointer to the timeframe of this campaign, which apparently involved Pomona as well as Santa Elena, falling about seven months after the event recorded on the censer stand. In celebrating this new success on House C Janaab Pakal presents

(a)

(b)

65 West side of House C, Palenque Palace: (a) View across the West Court; (b) Close-up of the gaps in the platform façade with inscribed captions naming lords of Santa Elena.

it as a continuation of his regional triumphs and a further testimony to his
military prowess.[39] It is not clear if this sequence of events left Santa Elena in
Palenque's hands once more.

There is silence on these issues for some twenty-seven years, but the "third"
installation of Moral-Reforma's Muwaan Jol in 690 demonstrates a key shift in
the political firmament (Martin 2003c: 47). Once again, this ceremony takes
place *yichonal*, "before" a foreign king, but this time it is the Palenque ruler
K'inich Kaan Bahlam II, the son and successor of K'inich Janaab Pakal. The
ousting of Calakmul's influence – assuming that it had continued up until this
point – corresponds to a wider decline in its fortunes, and it would soon suffer
its major defeat at the hands of Tikal in 695. Palenque, by contrast, was on the
rise after Kaan Bahlam achieved a signal victory over Tonina in 687 (Martin
and Grube 2000: 180–181). In describing that engagement as *och uch'een* we are
told that it involved a penetration of Tonina territory, perhaps even the capital
itself. The simultaneous disappearance of its king means that it could well have
resulted in his death.

A material correlate to this revived power was manifested in the major
programme of construction at Palenque. Three temples, forming the Group of
the Cross, were each dedicated to one of its patron deities and commissioned
together on 11 January 692. The war against Tonina was specifically celebrated
in one of them, the military-themed Temple of the Sun (see Figure 31), but
given even greater prominence within Temple XVII, a nearby battle memorial
where the victory was recounted on a relief panel as well as in a stucco
appliqué text (Martin and Grube 2000: 181). As we will see in Case Study
13, by 692 Kaan Bahlam had built a hegemony that reached not only into
eastern Tabasco but far along the southern bank of the Usumacinta River,
gained largely at the expense of Piedras Negras.

So what does this fragmentary story, assembled from texts created with
no intent to produce an overall narrative, tell us? Although various inter-
polations are necessary and certain aspects remain unclear, these closely spaced
events offer an unusually "thick description" setting the sanctioned accession
statements on Moral-Reforma Stela 4 within a historical matrix. It points to
a struggle for control of eastern Tabasco during the mid- to late-seventh
century, with the polities of Pomona, Santa Elena, and Moral-Reforma
battling on their own behalf, but at points succumbing to the intrusive
ambitions of Palenque, Piedras Negras, and Calakmul. This dynamic may well
have a longer history, since the willingness of the Kaanul dynasty of Dzibanche
to launch long-distance expeditions against Palenque in 599 and 611 may also
be attempts to neutralise its regional influence. Indeed, Ajen Yohl Mat's
involvement at Santa Elena after 605 suggests that the assault of 599 was less
than a fatal blow to Palenque's aspirations, perhaps provoking the more
decisive attack of 611.

TABLE 6 *Timeline*

Long Count	CE	Greg.	Event
?	c.608	?	Investiture(?) of Santa Elena king by Ajen Yohl Mat of Palenque
9.11.6.2.1	658	22 Oct	Itzam K'an Ahk III of Piedras Negras receives 5 war helmets
9.11.6.16.11	659	11 Aug	Capture of Nuun Ujol Chahk of Santa Elena and 6 others by Palenque's K'inich Janaab Pakal I
9.11.6.16.17	"	17 Aug	Arrival of Nuun Ujol Chahk at Palenque
9.11.7.0.3	"	12 Sep	Capture of a Santa Elena(?) woman by Calakmul
9.11.8.12.10	661	11 May	First investiture of Moral-Reforma king (aged 5)
9.11.9.8.6	662	11 Feb	Calakmul lord performs a fire ceremony, presumably at Piedras Negras
9.11.9.8.12	"	17 Feb	Star war defeat of Santa Elena by Piedras Negras
9.11.9.10.12	"	29 Mar	Display of a captive at Palenque
9.11.9.10.13	"	30 Mar	Display of a captive at Palenque
9.11.9.11.3	"	9 Apr	Second investiture of a Moral-Reforma king (aged 6) under Calakmul's Yuknoom Ch'een II
9.11.10.5.17	"	19 Dec	War(?) against Santa Elena by Palenque
9.11.10.16.7	663	17 Jul	Death of Pipa' lord (given with the names of Santa Elena prisoners)
9.12.13.4.3	685	17 Jul	Itzam K'an Ahk III presented with a war helmet by a Calakmul captain
9.12.18.5.0	690	8 Jul	Third investiture of Moral-Reforma king (aged 34) under Palenque's K'inich Kaan Bahlam II

CASE STUDY 13: TONINA'S CAMPAIGNS IN THE LACANDON, 692–702 CE

Our next case study takes up where the previous one left off, and charts events after K'inich Kaan Bahlam's victory over Tonina and his re-installation of the king of Moral-Reforma. The main purpose here is to show how statements of possession, in this case *yajaw*, "the lord of", define political allegiances and chart the ebb and flow of regional hegemonies.

A new Tonina king, K'inich Baaknal Chahk, took power in 688 and pursued the Palenque war, gaining the upper hand within four years (Table 7). Most of what we know of this comes from Tonina Monument 172, which shows a bound prisoner identified by a headdress featuring the head of a *mo'*, "macaw" marked by the projecting torch of the lightning deity *k'awiil* (Miller and Martin 2004: 185) (Figure 66a). This same K'awiil Mo' name appears as a stucco glyph that must once have been part of a further celebratory inscription and is seen again in the caption to a contorted prisoner on a stairway riser block (Figure 66b and c).

The ropes that extend to either side of K'awiil Mo' on Monument 172 might originally have linked prisoners depicted on adjoining panels. It carries a 16-glyph text that begins with a star war on 4 October 692 that bested the "flint(s) and shield(s)" – the armed forces – of a Palenque lord named only

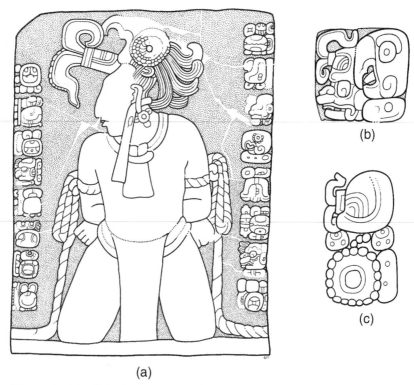

66 The captive K'awiil Mo' who was seized at Tonina's battle with Palenque in 692: (a) As depicted on Tonina Monument 172; (b) His name as a disarticulated stucco hieroglyph; (c) An alternative spelling of his name on Tonina Monument 27.

as Aj Pitzil "Ballplayer". This was part of the pre-accession name of Kaan Bahlam. Since victors had every incentive to clearly identify the rival king they had defeated this understatement is surprising and might be interpreted as a gesture of disrespect, or even a denial of his legitimacy. The Palenque emblem glyph follows but, as is often the case with royal foes, the *k'uhul*, "holy" prefix is omitted. The inscription goes on to tell us that K'awiil Mo' was seized on the same day and that this was the work of Baaknal Chahk. Neither the status nor origin of K'awiil Mo' is specified, but we can take it that he was a high-ranking Palenque noble or military leader, or if not some close confederate. Another text refers to a second prisoner taken that day, named Buk' Saak. He is the subject of an over life-size sculpture-in-the-round found close to the Tonina ballcourt (Stuart 2011b).[40]

Just as Kaan Bahlam's earlier triumph had elevated Palenque's political prospects, so Baaknal Chahk's riposte expanded the horizons of Tonina, a story we can piece together from the sizeable body of records he produced. One monument, now very fragmentary, was a frieze depicting a line of crouching prisoners, who are identified both in an inscription running along its base and, in several cases, by nametags carved into their thighs. The former features dates for their seizures, though most are specified only by a *tzolk'in* position rather than a full Calendar Round. This type of abbreviation was usually employed when dates were closely spaced in time, as in a single campaign.[41]

One of these victims was Chan Maas from a site likely to be read *pepe'tuun*, the name of modern-day La Mar (Montgomery 1994: 326; Zender 2002: 176–182).[42] Situated to the south of the Usumacinta (Map 4), it was closely linked to Piedras Negras, which records the accession of a La Mar ruler in 763. The connection between the two centres is even more apparent in 794, when a *pepe'tuun ajaw* of the *baahkab* rank joins the Piedras Negras king in a joint campaign against Pomona (Schele and Grube 1994). Returning to Tonina, the unfortunate Chan Maas is depicted in another three-dimensional sculpture (Stuart 2011c), while a relief portrait very likely supplies his capture date, falling in March of 693, less than six months after the success over Palenque (Mathews 2001b: 2).

A second victim on the frieze was called Sak Bahlam, whose origin is now too eroded to fully discern, and a third was Yax Ahk (Ayala 1995: 207, 225). A better-preserved depiction of the latter shows him bound and dressed in the guise of the Jaguar God of the Underworld (Miller and Martin 2004: 171, 182). There his nametag identifies him as an *ajaw* of *anayite'*. Today Anaite is a name attached to a set of rapids on the Usumacinta as well as a stream that flows into it and a large lake set back from the river. It was adopted by Teobert Maler to label two ruins, Anaite I and Anaite II – the latter a substantial site at the western end of the lake about 25 km or so from Yaxchilan (Maler 1901–1903: 98–99). As noted by Peter Mathews (in Ayala 1995: 207), it is reasonable to suppose that modern Anaite and ancient *anayite'* are one-in-the-same and, like Yaxha/*yaxa'* in the eastern Peten (Stuart 1985e), this is a name that has endured for over a millennium.

Baaknal Chahk's main commemoration of these campaigns was in and around Tonina's ballcourt, which he renovated in 696 and again in 699 (Ayala 1995: 187; Stuart 2011b). The flanking walls of the playing alley were now equipped with six sculptures of captives that projected over representations of rectangular feather-trimmed shields, each bearing its own inscription (Becquelin and Baudez 1979: figures 82 and 91; Freidel, Schele, and Parker 1993: 372–374; Ayala 1995: 224–225). Surviving examples identify the same cast of prisoners, with Buk' Saak, Sak Bahlam, Chan Maas, and Yax Ahk all represented. Significantly, their expanded captions include possessed titles revealing that most, likely all of them were the vassals of a Palenque king. We learn that Buk' Saak was an *ajk'uhuun* of the deceased K'inich Janaab Pakal, while Yax Ahk and Sak Bahlam were both *ajaw* belonging to K'inich Kaan Bahlam – here again identified by his pre-accession name (Martin and Grube 2000: 170, 181–182; Martin 2001b).[43] The text for Chan Maas is incomplete and only a small portion of the *yajaw* glyph survives, but it must surely have followed the same pattern and also set La Mar within Palenque's orbit at this time.[44]

What these references expose is a deep penetration of Palenque authority into the Lacandon, a region where overlordship was more commonly assumed by either Piedras Negras or Yaxchilan. That Tonina's campaigns displaced them and instituted its own dominion in this area is confirmed by a small unprovenanced column, now in the Saint Louis Art Museum, which comes from Bonampak, Lacanha, or some nearby centre (Figure 62a and b). Dated to 715, it celebrates the thirteen-year anniversary of rule for a local king with the *ak'e* emblem glyph and describes him as the *ajaw* of Baaknal Chahk. Since the Tonina ruler was dead by 708, this inscription ties him to the initial inauguration in 702 and further demonstrates – in a pattern we also saw in the case of Buk' Saak – that clients were considered to have a bond to those who installed them that extended beyond that patron's death. It remains to be seen if a Tonina affiliation continued into the reign of Baaknal Chahk's successor Ruler 4, as the dedication in 715 might suggest.

That a kingdom as far to the east as Bonampak/Lacanha could become a direct Tonina client is a testament to the success of Baaknal Chahk's expansionist programme and is, at the same time, evidence for the weakness of Yaxchilan. As Bonampak and Lacanha's neighbour, Yaxchilan was variously its antagonist and overlord but at this point was still within a long monument hiatus, for which defeat and foreign subjection remain by far the likeliest explanations (Miller 1991; Martin and Grube 2000: 121–123).

TABLE 7 *Timeline*

Long Count	CE	Greg.	Event
9.12.15.7.11	687	13 Sep	Defeat of Tonina Ruler 2 by K'inich Kaan Bahlam of Palenque
9.12.16.3.12	688	20 Jun	Accession of K'inich Baaknal Chahk of Tonina
9.12.19.16.5	692	13 Feb	Capture by K'inich Baaknal Chahk (Tonina Monument 157)
9.13.0.10.3	692	8 Oct	Defeat of Kaan Bahlam, captures of K'awiil Mo' and Buk' Saak
9.13.1.0.4	693	18 Mar	Capture of Chan Maas of La Mar
?	?	?	Capture of Sak Bahlam
?	?	?	Capture of Yax Ahk of Anayite'
9.13.4.6.7	696	3 Jul	Earlier dedication of the ballcourt
9.13.4.13.10	696	23 Nov	Capture of Huus
9.13.7.14.7	699	25 Nov	Later dedication of the ballcourt by K'inich Baaknal Chahk
9.13.10.8.4	702	10 Jul	Accession of Etz'nab Jawbone the *ajaw* of K'inich Baaknal Chahk
9.13.14.12.14	706	17 Sep	Birth of Tonina Ruler 4
9.13.16.16.18	708	29 Nov	Accession of Tonina Ruler 4

CASE STUDY 14: NARANJO'S PATRONAGE OVER DEFEATED POLITIES, 698–713 CE

Naranjo Stela 2 was commissioned by K'ahk' Tiliw Chan Chahk to celebrate the first K'atun anniversary of his reign in 714 (Figure 67a). It shows him in full Central Mexican-style garb, equipped with a shell-plated helmet, square shield, and pair of spearthrower darts. The lightly incised side texts of the monument are today rather pitted and worn, but nevertheless include one certain and one probable inauguration statement using possession and supervision formulae, respectively.

The first of these, dating to 712, shows a verb whose scant surviving outlines resemble *k'ahlaj huun*, "the headband is held/raised" (Figure 67b; Table 8).[45] The name of the subject is similarly damaged, although we see the ear of an animal, perhaps that of *bahlam*, "jaguar". Better preserved is his title of *k'anwitznal ajaw*, "Yellow Hill Place Lord" that identifies him as the ruler of Ucanal, the polity whose hilltop capital lies some 34 km to the south of Naranjo (Map 2). This statement is linked by means of the *yichonal*, "before" expression to K'ahk' Tiliw Chan Chahk, establishing his oversight and sanction.

Significantly, an Ucanal monarch with "jaguar" in his name, Itzamnaaj Bahlam, is twice mentioned on Naranjo Stela 22 where, some fourteen years earlier in 698, he suffers a *puluuyi uch'een*, "his settlement/domain is burned" defeat. This success is attributed to the ten-year-old Naranjo king, although undoubtedly performed under the regency of his mother Ix Wak Jalam Chan, a woman who appears with full royal regalia on several other monuments from this period (Closs 1985: 71, passim; Schele and Freidel 1990: 183–193; Martin and Grube 2000: 74–77) (Figure 38). The front of Stela 22 shows Itzamnaaj Bahlam kneeling and bound in a scene dated to 702 that, if taken literally, would mean that he was a prisoner kept for four or more years. There his caption specifies that he is *ma'ch'ahb ma'ak'abil* "without genesis, without darkness" – the negated form of a kingly essence, something that has been lost in his defeat and subjugation (see pp.146, 212).

We cannot know if the character who appears to accede on Stela 2 is the same as that shown in bondage on Stela 22 ten years earlier, although the repeated *k'alhuun* installations at Moral-Reforma, as well as the restoration of the Ceibal king following his capture, offer at least the possibility that it was. It may be significant that an unprovenanced polychrome cylinder vase in Naranjo-style names an Itzamnaaj Bahlam of Ucanal as its owner (Reents-Budet 1994: 300–302). Even though the vessel cannot be dated with accuracy, its style is consistent with this period and appears to be a royal gift bespeaking a positive relationship between the two polities at the time. Whether the same king or a successor, Stela 2 indicates that Ucanal was still under the yoke of Naranjo some fourteen years after its original conquest.

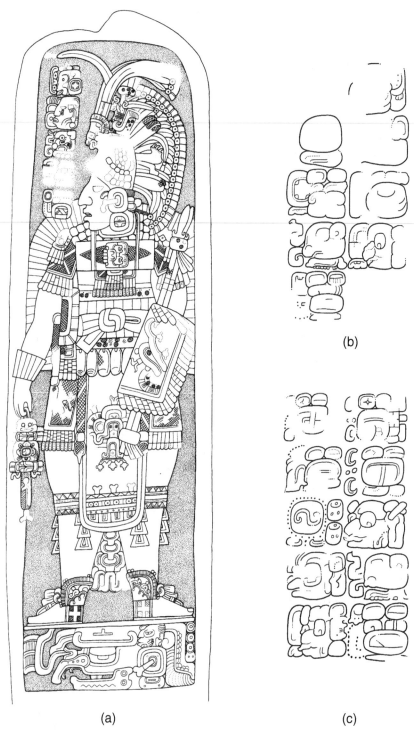

(a)   (b)   (c)

67 K'ahk' Tiliw Chan Chahk records his patronage over the Ucanal and Yopmootz polities on
Naranjo Stela 2: (a) Front face (drawing by Ian Graham © President and Fellows of Harvard
College, Peabody Museum of Archaeology and Ethnology, PM# 2004.15.6.2.4); (b) Probable
accession of an Ucanal king under the supervision of the Naranjo king in 712; (c) Accession of
the Yopmootz king as a vassal in 713.

In 713, a little over six months after this event, Stela 2 next recounts a clear royal inauguration involving a king called Yajawte' K'inich, a bearer of the emblem glyph of Yopmootz (Figure 67c). This statement employs the verb *ajawaan*, "to become a lord" applied to some child kings and goes on to state that the Yopmootz ruler is the *yajaw*, "the lord of" K'ahk' Tiliw Chan Chahk. Yopmootz has yet to be identified, but (as we heard in Chapter 9) six years earlier, in 706, the Naranjo king had "entered" it. Its then-ruler is the unfortunate shown on the front of Stela 21 as a trampled captive with the closed eyes indicative of death (Figure 49a). Stela 2 leads us to wonder if a king-less seven years there ended with the installation of a compliant replacement.

In summary, Naranjo Stela 2 records two occasions on which K'ahk' Tiliw Chan Chahk proclaims authority over the kings of recently defeated polities, at least one and probably both of which are installation ceremonies. Since accounts of patrons declaring dominion over their clients are otherwise conspicuous by their absence, it is unclear why he departed from convention to do this. Given his record of attacking and seizing his neighbours (see Schele and Freidel 1990: 186–195; Martin and Grube 2000: 76) his power over these two kingdoms is unlikely to be exceptional. As we saw earlier, K'ahk' Tiliw was installed as king at the age of five as the client of Yuknoom Yich'aak K'ahk' of Calakmul (Martin and Grube 1994a: 9, 2000: 75–76), a king who had inherited wide political dominion of Yuknoom Ch'een in 686. It is quite possible the rhetorical priority behind K'ahk' Tiliw's statement of supremacy on Stela 2 was to assert his like-in-kind status to his more famous overlord, his Teotihuaca-noid costume intended to cast him as the regional "imperator".

We have good reason to think that Calakmul's patronage of Naranjo continued beyond Yuknoom Yich'aak K'ahk's death in 697. K'ahk' Tiliw's subordination to him was not recorded until 711, suggesting that it was a still source of pride or validation at that time. More importantly, Yuknoom Took'

TABLE 8 *Timeline*

Long Count	CE	Greg.	Event
9.12.15.13.7	688	7 Jan	Birth of K'ahk' Tiliw Chan Chahk *yajaw* Yuknoom Yich'aak K'ahk'
9.13.1.3.19	693	1 Jun	Accession of K'ahk' Tiliw Chan Chahk
9.13.6.10.4	698	8 Sep	Burning of Ucanal, capture of its king Itzamnaaj Bahlam
9.13.14.4.2	706	29 Mar	Entering and burning of Yopmootz, capture and death of its king Nine-X
9.14.0.10.0	712	23 Jun	Accession? of an Ucanal king *yichonal* K'ahk' Tiliw Chan Chahk
9.14.1.2.9	713	18 Jan	Accession of Yajawte' K'inich of Yopmootz *yajaw* K'ahk' Tiliw Chan Chahk
9.14.3.1.19	714	29 Dec	K'ahk' Tiliw Chan Chahk's 1-K'atun jubilee

K'awiil, the next ruler of Calakmul, appears on Naranjo Stela 46 in 726 – even if only identified by his royal title. There he joins the king of Dos Pilas in witnessing ceremonies that endorse the candidacy of two princes at Naranjo, probable sons of K'ahk' Tiliw, indicating that the Snake dynasty continued to be the power behind the Sa'al throne (Martin et al. 2017) (see p.258).

ELEVEN

CODA

To bring our examination of primary sources in Part II to a close we come to a special chapter – more of an extended case study – that deals with the demise of Classic Maya society. It is difficult to address such a profoundly complex and still far from comprehended topic in brief, but it is important to appreciate the ways in which the epigraphic record can contribute to our understanding. Indeed, it will be argued here that the texts are a valuable and underestimated resource in this regard.

There are two significant impediments to appreciating that worth. The first is the greatly reduced output of inscriptions, a feature of an ever-decreasing number of active polities. As a result, the corpus available for study in the ninth century is a mere fraction of what we have for the eighth.[1] Next, the texts that we do possess are almost always shorter and less informative than those produced in earlier times. Historical content of all kinds sharply declines and some themes, such as warfare, disappear altogether. What remains is an emphasis on calendrical ceremonies and ritual performance, the perpetuation of traditions reaching back a thousand years or more. In this striving for continuity the monuments stood in silent defiance of the calamitous changes taking place all around them.

The archaeological data on this is clear. Excavations across the Classic Maya lowlands supply bountiful evidence for a surging population that rose to a peak by about 800 before undergoing a vertiginous decline. The process was by no means a uniform one, but it eventually reached all corners of the Maya lowlands, leading to the effective abandonment of entire regions by the early tenth century.[2] Even those few Classic Period sites that persisted into the Postclassic usually saw their occupations fall by ninety per cent or more.[3]

Numerous explanations for the collapse have been proposed over the years without any achieving a consensus (see Culbert 1973; Webster 2002). Even though a great quantity of data is available, drawing it together into a single coherent picture across all regions has proved an elusive goal (Demarest, Rice, and Rice 2004a, 2004b; Arnauld and Breton 2013; Iannone, Houk, and Schwake 2016). That the phenomenon was multi-causal and an internal one now finds little if any dissent. Some researchers have emphasised "top-heavy" social decay amid the stresses of over-population, giving primacy to inter-necine warfare that escalated into ever more destructive forms (p.199). More widely accepted has been the idea that it was first and foremost the relationship between the Maya and their environment that disastrously unravelled. The depletion of natural resources due to over-exploitation was the initial scenario, but today it is the evidence for recurring droughts, with implications for food supply and public health, which is receiving the most attention as a destabilising factor.

CLIMATE AND THE COLLAPSE

Pioneering studies into the paleoclimatology of the Yucatan Peninsula (Gunn, Folan, and Robichaux 1995; Hodell, Curtis, and Brenner 1995; see also Gill 1994, 2000) identified episodes of marked aridity between the eighth and eleventh centuries, and subsequent work has only put that finding on an ever-firmer empirical footing (e.g. Medina-Elizalde et al. 2011; Kennett et al. 2012; Evans et al. 2018). Yet, while the portrait these studies paint is broadly consistent, the precise timing, duration, severity, and sub-regional distribution of these droughts, as well as the degree to which they actually resulted in famine, have still to be fully determined (Yaeger and Hodell 2008; though see Hoggarth et al. 2017).

Not all scholars accept that drought played such a decisive role. An early objection that many of the strongest ninth century societies were to be found in the driest zone, the northern lowlands, has been partially assuaged by data suggesting that droughts in the south might not have had commensurate effects in the north (Douglas et al. 2015). Given that the populations there were somewhat lower and more familiar with a dry environment, they might have rebounded more quickly when conditions improved (Dahlin 2002). Even so, the limited signs we have for the late clustering of settlement around dependable water sources in the south is cited as one reason to reserve judgement, while the evidence for late period malnutrition is as yet patchy and indistinct.

What needs to be kept in mind is that the drought scenario rests not simply on the intensity of these multi-year episodes, but on an assessment that the high population levels of the Late Classic had made the Maya acutely vulnerable to any significant disturbance to their finely honed, but rain-dependent, agricultural system. This means that even a modest drop in precipitation over several years might have been sufficient to spark serious food shortages and societal distress (Medina-Elizalde and Rohling 2012) – a timeframe that might be too short to leave much of a material signature. Similarly, untoward climate effects in one part of the Maya world could have sparked a breakdown that spread unchecked to less affected ones.

Fortunately, we can expect ever-more accurate and areally comprehensive climatological data to emerge in the years ahead, with season-by-season, perhaps even month-by-month, estimations of rainfall throughout the region and across the temporal range a not unrealistic prospect. But we will still need to avoid seeing a strictly mechanistic connection between climate and society (e.g. Yaeger and Hodell 2008: 227–230; Houston and Inomata 2009: 292–295, 318). There can be no monocausation in a complex world, nothing exists outside a myriad of interrelationships. Environmental change is only one, if important, variable, whose impact comes from the way that it engages with other conditions and parameters. Whatever understanding of the collapse is now possible, it will be one in which social, cultural, and economic factors entwine with environmental ones, as a historical process and a holistic phenomenon. The goal of this chapter is less to seek causes for the collapse than, as far as we are now able, to better comprehend the political dynamics of this baleful time.

A CHRONOLOGY OF CRISIS

For a control on the sequence and timing of the breakdown we can turn to the monumental record. Figure 68 shows the arc of dated commissions from the end of the third to the beginning of the tenth century across the Maya region, with the southern and northern regions distinguished.[4] The Late Classic Period saw a considerable increase in output, but it should be noted that a good number of Early Classic monuments were deliberately broken and buried, meaning that totals in that portion of the chart are somewhat reduced. Our interest here, of course, is the steep decline at the other end of the arc.

Regimes begin to fall silent at the very end of the eighth century, with some of the more notable terminal dates coming at Pomona in 790, Palenque in 799, Cancuen in 800, El Peru in 801, La Corona in 805, Yaxchilan in 808, Piedras Negras, Quirigua, and Edzna in 810, Comalcalco in 814, Naranjo and El Palmar in 820, and Copan in 822.[5] There is no overriding direction or geographic focus to these failures, although it has long been noted that many

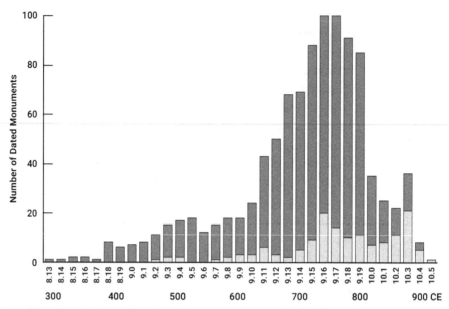

68   Chart showing the total number of monument commissions by K'atun (twenty Maya-year) periods, divided into the southern lowlands (dark grey, n = 856) and northern lowlands (light grey, n = 151).

of the earliest take place on the western waterways. Some polities in the eastern half of the Peten, the northern lowlands, and a pocket in the western highlands survived until the end of the ninth century, a scant few into the tenth. Final dates appear, for example, at Machaquila in 840, Xunantunich in 849, Oxkintok in 860, Tikal in 869, Caracol in 884, La Muñeca, Xultun, Uaxactun, and Ceibal in 889, Uxmal in 907, and Tonina in 909.[6]

Even if final dates do not precisely correlate to political failure in all instances, this fine-grained sequence gives a clear impression of what took place. It demonstrates that the collapse was not a single catastrophic event, but a process that unfolded over a hundred years and one that saw much regional variation (e.g. Ebert et al. 2014). Figure 69 plots the terminal dates from the last seventy centres to appear in the record (shown in black), commencing in 800, with the names of some of the better-known ones picked out. Here the decline in the number of active polities appears to be a steady one, showing neither an early spurt nor a later escalation. It is as if the eclipse of each eroded the position of the remainder, like a spreading contagion from which the next weakest, in its time, sickened and succumbed.

Yet a concentration on terminal dates is misleading. First, of the sites in this sample almost one third (n = 23) erect their first or only known inscriptions in this period. We cannot read a seamless cultural continuity into such ex novo political developments. Second, the picture is skewed by a late resurgence in the north (n = 20), which obscures the scale of the southern decline. Lastly and

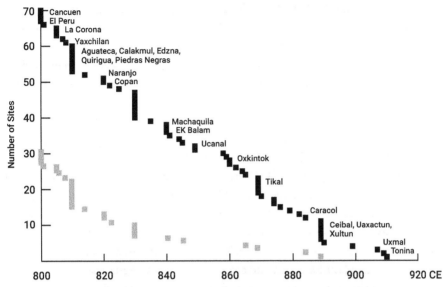

69   Chart showing the final monument dedications after 800 CE at seventy Classic Maya sites in all regions (in black). A second set (in grey) consists of the terminal dates found at thirty-one long-established cities in the southern lowlands exclusively.

most decisively, the chart underplays the importance of the period between 800 and 830 and, specifically, the years leading up to and a little beyond 810, the year of the Long Count position 9.19.0.0.0.

This is the point by which the majority of polities had ceased a continuous monument tradition and, even if they subsequently restarted one, did so only after a good number of years. Tikal, for example, erects stelae fairly consistently in the Late Classic Period until 810, after which it puts up just one more stone in 869. Tonina offers another case, since its last carved monument in 909 must be seen in the light of the abrupt halt to its continuous record in 806 – the following century seeing only two isolated commissions in 837 and 906. Ceibal's spotty monumental record saw a half-century gap between 800 and 849 and, similarly, at highland Chinkultic a monument erected in 810 was not followed by another until 844. Another lacuna came at Calakmul, where stylistically late monuments suggest a two-decade halt to its regular tradition after 810. If we reduce the sample in Figure 69 to those southern sites that were already well-established and did not experience long silences, while adding the last pre-hiatus dates for those that did, we get an idea of how the original Classic Maya centres fared in what was by far the most important and densely settled region (in grey).

To convey the scale and significance of the 810 watershed one need only list sites active in the later eighth century that ceased all monument production on, or not too long before, that date: Aguateca, Altar de Sacrificios, Bonampak, Cancuen, Coba, Dos Pilas, El Cayo, El Palma, El Peru, Itsimte, Ixkun,

Ixtutz, La Corona, La Florida, La Mar, La Milpa, Moral-Reforma, Motul de San José, Naachtun, Nim Li Punit, Palenque, Piedras Negras, Poco Uinic, Polol, Pomona, Pusilha, Quirigua, Sacul, Tamarindito, Xcalumkin, Yaxchilan, Yaxha, Zapote Bobal, and one could certainly add others. Classic Maya society continued in some form, but there can be no doubt that the heart and soul of it had been torn out.

One of the best illustrations of the early ninth century phenomenon comes at Yaxchilan. In 800 Yaxchilan commissioned the large and impressive Structure 20, which was equipped with three carved lintels, six original and re-carved stelae, and the 182-glyph-block Hieroglyphic Stairway 5. Yet by 808 it could only produce the paltry, single-doored Structure 3 and its stylistically degraded Lintel 10, the site's last inscription. Between the reign of two kings, father and son, a major diminution of Yaxchilan's cultural and material wellbeing had taken place, providing us with a rather precise index to the onset of distress.

Something even more dramatic can be discerned at Aguateca (Inomata et al. 2004). There two stelae mark the period ending of 790, and the next major calendrical juncture, in 810, was meant to be commemorated by Altar M and its partnering Stela 12. Altar M consists of the single *tzolk'in* day-sign 9 Ajaw appropriate for this 9.19.0.0.0 date, but its crude state demonstrates that it was never completed. The 4.4 m high Stela 12 was smoothed in readiness for carving but not even begun. In this they are consistent with their find-spot at the base of the largest temple pyramid at the city, which had clearly been abandoned in the midst of construction – found with only two of its tiers completed and a temporary access ramp leading to its partial third.

This is only one of a number of reports of structures left half-built across the lowlands, sometimes with stones stacked neatly nearby ready to be laid. At La Milpa, for example, an extensive programme of works – which included elite residences, temples, and a new ballcourt – underway in both core and peripheral areas, were stopped and never restarted (Hammond and Tourtellot 2004: 300).[7] The hugely accomplished mural programme of Bonampak Structure 1, whose last date falls in 791, is another unfinished work, with many of its glyphic captions outlined but never filled in (Miller and Brittenham 2013: 74, figure 123). Two things are clear: there was no lack of prosperity in these places and their failure came with little prior warning.

This critical period evidently left its mark in the north as well, with the most important centres of the seventh and eighth centuries also going dark (Guenter 2014: 265–267). The last legible date at massive Coba in the eastern half of the peninsula comes in 780. The last dated stelae at western Edzna comes in 810, with its later monuments carved in distinctively different "non-Classic" styles. Oxkintok had an extended period of success, but by the end of the eighth century construction and monument-making had switched from the core of the site to its margins, suggesting a newly empowered and wealthy nobility (García 1991: 70–75). It will be remembered that this northwestern region had long had a strong emphasis on the *sajal* title, and that might be relevant here. Activity across the site came to halt in about 820 and when it restarted in 849 new monument formats were introduced, some bearing images of warriors in new styles of dress.

In at least some places the end was violent. In Chapter 9 we heard about the hasty building of fortifications, testaments to a steeply rising level of threat, as well as the final assault on Aguateca. But there is also evidence for violence specifically directed at the elite at the turn of the ninth century. At Cancuen, whose last date comes in 800, bodies accompanied by greenstone jewellery as well as other signs of wealth and status were buried in three improvised locations, a gulley and two artificial pools (Barrientos 2014: 604–619). The larger of the pools became the grave for at least 31 individuals, including two children, many of whom had died from trauma to the head or body.

Researchers have been right to explore the innumerable complexities, neglected continuities, and regionalised trajectories of the collapse process, looking beyond a simplistic catastrophism. However, although the whole phenomenon did indeed take a century or more, there is reason to believe that it began rather abruptly. This makes the ninth century less an extended decline than a lengthy coda, the postscript to some grave and unforeseen turn of events. We might justifiably call this the "early ninth century crisis" and, although it has been noted elsewhere (e.g. Martin and Grube 2000: 226–227; Martin 2003b: 35; Houston and Inomata 2009: 300; Guenter 2014: 294), it has yet to replace the idea of a simple steady decay.[8]

A NORTHERN RENAISSANCE

It was the people of the northern lowlands, so long in the shadow of their southern brethren, who produced the last great flowering of Classic Maya civilisation (Map 1). It is this half-century-long revival that we see in the final uptick in monument dedications in Figure 68.

The dynasty established at Ek Balam became the eastern region's leading light by the end of the eighth century (Ringle et al. 2004), supplanting Coba in that role.[9] The lavish stucco sculptures that adorned the Ek Balam acropolis combine the flamboyance of the Chenes regional style – typified by monstrous serpent mouth doorways – with the stucco figural modelling perfected in the Peten (Vargas de la Peña and Castillo 2006). Dated inscriptions at Ek Balam continue until 841, although as late as 870 there is a reference to one of its rulers at a site peripheral to Chichen Itza (Voss and Eberl 1999: 126–127). Chichen Itza first rose to prominence as an eastern outpost of a mixed Chenes-Puuc style (see below), though its imprint was then rather modest compared to what the site became in the tenth century (an era that will not be discussed here).[10] Inscriptions at Chichen Itza begin in the middle of the ninth century and this, together with a new programme of construction, suggests that it had replaced Ek Balam as regional hegemon, though not necessarily by absorbing it.

But the true heart of the northern resurgence lay to the west among the low hills of the Puuc region (e.g. Carmean, Dunning, and Kowalski 2004). Among the most prominent cities here were Sayil, Kabah, Kiuic, and, the jewel in the crown, Uxmal. Though building on earlier histories, these and other Puuc centres reached their artistic highpoint and peak population from the middle of the ninth century to the first decades of the tenth. Inscriptions in the Puuc, like all those in the north, are few in number, often badly preserved, and seldom concerned with political history (Grube 1994b, 2003b; Graña-Behrens 2002, 2006, 2018). In consequence, we know almost nothing about how these closely-spaced centres were organised. However, due to its greater size and finer construction, Uxmal has long been assumed to have been preeminent among them.

The celebrated architectural style of the Puuc is characterised by elaborate upper façades composed of finely-cut stone blocks set as a mosaic veneer, a method with clear ties to the Chenes and the Río Bec traditions. It is also noteworthy that the stelae commissioned by Puuc kings adhere to all the major conventions of Classic Maya ritual performance and representation. One late Uxmal king's name even includes the spelling of Ch'olan *chan*, "sky" rather than the Yukatekan *ka'n* we would expect to see in this northern zone (Wichmann and Davletshin 2006: 105; Law et al. 2014: 363–364) – evidence that the *ajawtaak* of the north fully identified with the prestige culture of the south. Although one can certainly discern influences from Central Mexico and the Gulf Coast by at least the mid-ninth century (e.g. Kowalski 2007), the Puuc florescence was grounded in a shared Classic Maya heritage.

TURBULENCE AND TRANSFORMATION IN THE HEARTLANDS

The story of the final century in the south is one of starkly contrasting fortunes. On the one hand we see the continued withering of once-vibrant cities, presumably provoking dislocations and migrations of their one-time inhabitants. On the other, we see centres that either weathered the initial crisis or rebounded quickly from it go on to prosper—growing in population and returning to programmes of construction and monument-making.

The instability of these times is suggested by the transfer of some surviving regimes to more defensible locations. The last known inscription at Pomona comes in 790, but by 830 a king using its *pakbuul* emblem glyph had erected a single stela at the elevated redoubt of Panhale some 8 km away. He uses a traditional Pomona royal name and mentions an event that took place some

60 years earlier – linking him to the site's former heyday. To judge from one damaged *sa'al* emblem glyph on a stela at the hilltop centre of Xunantunich, part of the Naranjo line may have shifted 13 km to the southeast by 820. By 849 the *ik'a'* polity of Motul de San José had moved 11 km across Lake Peten-Itza to occupy the peninsula site of Tayasal as well as its adjacent island (later the Itza capital Noh Peten and today the town of Flores). The late occupation of smaller fortified peninsulas was noted in Chapter 9.

But this story is not only about discord and disintegration, there are also notable innovations in the material culture of the elite. A number of sites show architectural developments that broke from existing norms with, for example, the appearance of tiered circular temple platforms and the expansion of "C-shaped" open-fronted buildings. More widely distributed were changes in pottery, with a significant eastward and northward spread of fine paste ceramics, wares whose temperless technique originated on the Gulf Coast (Rands 1973: 59; Forsyth 2005: 14, figure 4). One of these types, Pabellon, predominantly found in the Peten, was mould-made and bears "non-Maya" figural scenes, somewhat in the vein of another mould-made tradition using fine pastes, Río Blanco ware from the Gulf Coast (Wyllie 2002: 98–104, 121–122, 209–213). This reflects one of several moves away from Classic Maya iconographic orthodoxy, especially in the latter ninth century. Although some of these shifts have correspondences with those taking place in the northern lowlands (e.g. Kowalski 1989), nearly all find their ultimate inspiration in Central Mexico and along the Gulf Coast.

To give an overview of the varied impact of these changes we can look at a selection of sites for which we have not only inscriptions but also some relevant archaeological knowledge. In Case Study 6 we heard about the inversion of the Calakmul region, with growing impoverishment at this once-great capital contrasted with the blossoming of former satellites such as Oxpemul and La Muñeca (Map 2). Tikal's one late monument from 869 was not accompanied by any significant construction and, in terms of population and maintenance, the city was by then a shadow of its former self (Valdés and Fahsen 2004). Between 859 and 889 the small peripheral centres of Ixlu and Jimbal erected their first monuments, claiming a connection to the Tikal line by using its Mutul emblem glyph. Uaxactun was faring little better than Tikal. An active dynasty is indicated by its small all-textual stelae of 830 and 889, but its population had slumped and only one major structure can be assigned to this period, and that was left unfinished (Smith 1950: 47–48).

Conditions were much healthier at Caracol, which shows no sign of the early crisis and is unique in commissioning three monuments to mark the period ending of 820. Building work continued at the tallest platform at the site, Caana, whose upper floor was raised some 4 m and surrounding buildings re-modelled (Chase and Chase 2004: 345). To judge by their traditional names, Caracol had maintained its dynasty, who put up monuments (of indifferent quality) in 830, 849, 859, and 884 (Houston 1987; Grube 1994c; Chase and Chase 2015). The material culture of the ruling elite suggests that they kept themselves aloof from the general populace, but they remained in contact with the high-born elsewhere and were subject to outside influences. The best illustration of the shifting cultural sands at Caracol is the huge stucco masks applied to the front of Structure B5-sub, directly facing Caana (Ishihara, Taube, and Awe 2006: 216, figures 2 and 3). There representations of the Water Lily Serpent, a native deity of water and fertility, were covered over in the ninth century by goggled-eyed visages of Tlaloc, the storm and water deity of Central Mexico. Population levels and prosperity held up relatively well until a violent destruction of the site core was followed by abandonment around 900.

Xultun, an especially large and little-explored centre to the northeast of Tikal, was another to continue a monumental tradition after 810, erecting stones to celebrate period endings in 830, 859, and 889 (Map 2). These show none of the foreign-tinged stylistic developments we find elsewhere and follow a template that had been in place at the city since at least 731. Finds of fine paste and mould-made ceramics have been minimal to date, with only a few sherds of the latter (Franco Rossi, pers. comm. 2019).

A robust revitalisation took place at Ucanal (Laporte and Mejía 2002: 43–45, passim; Halperin et al. 2019). The city saw a rising population and fresh construction activity, among which was a circular platform set atop an older square-plan pyramid. Fine paste wares commonly turn up in excavations, including mould-made types, as well as a number of imported vessels from the northern lowlands. The presence of some distinctive green obsidian from Central Mexico also speaks to far-flung contacts. Of the monuments from this period only Stela 4 from 849 now survives in legible condition (Figure 7), but its imagery is notable for the Mexican-style warrior who occupies a cloud above the two lords' heads – a motif we will turn to presently. Ucanal was only one of a number of buoyant centres in the greater Mopan River Valley (Laporte 2004). One of these, Calzada Mopan, may be larger than Ucanal and, while it has produced no inscriptions to date, was presumably a significant player. Similar growth also took place further up the valley at Ixtonton, which has a stela that may date to 825. Both these sites had an "abundance" of fine paste ceramics in their central areas, used veneer mosaic masonry of the kind distinctive of the north, and built circular structures (Morales 1993; Laporte 2004).

The strongest florescence in the Peten was likely the one that took place at Nakum, set on the Holmul River midway between Tikal and Naranjo (Źrałka 2008: 27–146; Źrałka and Hermes 2012). All the structures in its impressive South Acropolis were rebuilt at this time (Figure 70), and a circular platform added just in front of this complex. Around eighty per cent of the settlement

70 The South Acropolis at Nakum is the largest known redevelopment project conducted in the ninth century southern lowlands. To the right, just outside this view, stands the circular platform Structure 12. (Rendering by Breitner González)

surrounding the city was occupied in the ninth century, with many plaza groups newly built to accommodate an expanding population. Peripheral sites were also well-occupied and, given the progressive depopulation of the region it is not unreasonable to suppose, as archaeologists here and elsewhere have done, that the expanding centres were drawing migrants from nearby failing ones. Certainly, the lifestyles and material culture of the commoners show little change, with the innovative additions largely restricted to the high-status inhabitants of central areas. There the Nakum elite used fine paste and mould-made ceramics, including the Pabellon variety, with some pots made from the same moulds as vessels found at Uaxactun. In a potential link to developments in the Pasión region, one of Nakum's monuments, Stela 5, has a distinct resemblance to Ceibal Stela 17 – both showing a lord in full Classic attire on the right facing a differently dressed character on the left holding a staff.[11] Despite the fine finish of its architecture, a feature shared with other late sites, Nakum's final inscriptions show a marked decline in execution and legibility. This is a sure sign that the literate and learned cadre so central to the Classic phenomenon was by then in sharp decline or already expired.

Machaquila also defied the wider trend (Map 3). A continuing tradition of stela dedications is matched by new architectural commissions, which included the same northern-style façades of veneer masonry we see elsewhere (Ciudad et al. 2013). Ceramic finds, however, suggest a strong continuity with the local production of the seventh and eighth centuries; with those imports we do see coming from the east. Freed of Cancuen's assertion of political union, a new Machaquila king had taken the *ochk'in kaloomte'* title as his personal name in

799. While not unknown in earlier times, this is an interesting choice given the western influences now emerging. The next king briefly uses *kaloomte'* as a title in 815, but his successor by 825 makes no such claim. Up until now the Machaquila regime seems to have been quite traditional, but the later stelae of this ruler, in 835 and 840, acquire more "foreign" characteristics and a weakening of Classic Maya conventions (Chase 1985: 106–109; Just 2006; Lacadena 2011; Carter 2014a). Activity in the site core comes to an end just before the resumption of monuments at Ceibal.

Ceibal has a complex history and evidently played a key role in ninth century developments. Not long after 800 it experienced the same crisis as its neighbours and was partially burned, leaving damaged and unfinished monuments in a manner not entirely unlike those at Aguateca (Bazy and Inomata 2017: 92–93; Inomata et al. 2017). However, Ceibal did not lose all its ties to Classic kingship, with mention of a local ruler on Stela 11 in 829 (p.127).[12] This is the person who accompanies Wat'ul K'atel when he arrives at the site, and his presence may be the reason the newcomer does not commission any carvings of his own until 849. Like Altar de Sacrificios, 55 km down the Pasión River – another centre re-energised after an initial failure – this era was characterised by a concentration of Pabellon and other fine paste ceramics (Adams 1971; Sabloff 1975; Tourtellot and González 2004; Bazy and Inomata 2017). Ceibal's population was never large by the standards of the great Classic cities, but now reached its peak. Renewed effort was put into monumental architecture, which included the addition of a large tiered circular platform set at the end of its own causeway (Smith 1982; Willey 1990: 265–269). The importance of the site is suggested most clearly by the 17 stelae it produced from 849 onwards, by far the most impressive inventory of the late period.

These carvings are famed for the number of "foreign" iconographic traits they carry. Such features first appear on the stelae that make up the assemblage of Structure A-3 from 849 (pp.260–262). Each shows Wat'ul K'atel in standard Classic Maya regalia, but his facial features fall into two distinct types. Some are conventional, with prominent nose and sloping forehead, the latter a result of the cranial modification conducted in infancy. Others have a distinctly different physiognomy, showing blunt noses and flat foreheads, as well as the otherwise absent feature of facial hair (Graham 1973: 211) (Figure 63). With all scenes fixed to a single day, Wat'ul K'atel essentially pivots his identity and ethnic associations, "code-switching" from one stone to the next.[13] In the years thereafter the art of Ceibal would depart ever further from the Classic canon (Figure 71). Indeed, its last stelae, likely erected at the cusp of the tenth century, abandon the Maya calendar and offer a "Mexicanised" aesthetic closely aligned to what we see on Pabellon vessels (Figure 71). These final carvings would hardly seem out of place if found hundreds of kilometres to the west.

Based on their work at Ceibal and Altar de Sacrificios, respectively, Sabloff and Willey (1967) and Adams (1971: 162–165, 1973) took these features as evidence for an invasion of the southern lowlands, a notion that can be traced at least as far back as Thomas Joyce (1914). They suggested an advance up the Usumacinta River, sourced from either the Maya northern lowlands, Central Mexico, or the Gulf Coast. Thompson used some of the same data to build his "Putun" hypothesis (Thompson 1970: 3–47; also Graham 1973: 213–215). This posited the involvement of a Chontal Maya-speaking group from the Gulf Coast that were heavily influenced by Central Mexico. It was argued that these were the entrepreneurial traders who reconfigured coastal commerce in the ninth century, who also made aggressive moves to secure strategic locations and resources inland – accounting for the presence of Chontal speakers in the Usumacinta and Pasión River regions when the Spanish arrived there in the sixteenth century.[14]

71 The final decades of monument production at Ceibal show a Gulf Coast and Central Mexican aesthetic much removed from the Classic Maya canon. Ceibal Stela 18 from 889. (Drawing by Nicholas Carter after James Porter)

However, even if the fine paste tradition originated on the Gulf Coast, later chemical analyses demonstrated that Pabellon pots were not imports but produced along the upper Usumacinta or lower Pasión rivers (Rands, Bishop, and Sabloff 1982; Bishop 1994; Foias and Bishop 2005) – in other words, close to or at Ceibal and Altar de Sacrificios, consistent with the mould fragments uncovered at the latter (Adams 1971: 51). The "foreignness" of their surface designs and their counterparts on monuments also underwent a reassessment (e.g. Stuart 1993: 336–344; Schele and Mathews 1998: 175–196, 351–352, n.6; Demarest 2004: 114–117; Tourtellot and González 2004: 77–81, passim; Just 2006; Carter 2014a). One response was to question whether the changes in art, architecture, and ceramics were not some natural evolution in Maya style or, if accepted as foreign, seen as Maya kings appropriating outside identities as they sought new sources of unity and prestige – clutching at ideological straws in desperate times.

READING THE NINTH CENTURY

The difficulties in pursuing an epigraphic approach in this last century of the Classic era were explained at the beginning of this chapter, but it proves to be a far from fruitless exercise. No one text proves to be all–illuminating but, when read in conjunction with art and architecture, these spare inscriptions have a cumulative effect, offering some important leads to the political forces at work.

The aforementioned changes to elite culture coincided with the appearance of rulers whose names were unlike any of those employed for the previous six centuries of the Classic Period. Formed from strings of syllabograms, they produce words without ready parallels in the Ch'olti'an language of the script. In the case of Wat'ul K'atel, it has been suggested that this unfamiliar name was actually an attempt to render a non-Maya language (Mathews and Willey 1991: 58). Although Wat'ul K'atel bore a local emblem glyph several other lords with such names did not, instead sporting the elevated *kaloomte'* title alone, usually in its "west" version, spelled either as *ochk'in* or *chik'in*.[15]

The previously noted Papmalil of Ucanal was one such figure, and another was called Olom (Guenter 1999: 104–109). The latter "witnesses" the end of the 10.0.0.0.0 *bak'tun* on Uaxactun Stela 13 in 830 – an unusual phrasing since kings are normally either the agents of appropriate rites or they observe subordinants performing them.[16] Indeed, the next phrase in that text supplies the appropriate ceremony, where its celebrant seems to be just such a local ruler. When a later king bearing the Uaxactun emblem glyph, Jasaw Chan K'awiil (a traditional moniker he shared with a close-contemporary at Tikal), performs the calendrical ceremonies on the site's last monument, Stela 12, in 889 he does so *yetaj* or "accompanied" by a second character.[17] This person is an *ochk'in/chik'in kaloomte'* whose name is again an unfamiliar collocation of signs. To these instances we should add the ruler presiding at Nakum in 849, whose partially effaced name includes a further syllabogram sequence without an emblem – although this time he is a *kaloomte'* of the *elk'in*, "east" (Martin, in Źrałka et al. 2018: 22). Almost forty years after the last mention of Papmalil we hear of a namesake on Ixlu Altar 1 in 859 (long misdated to 879), where he is identified as a *kaloomte'* of the *xaman*, "north" (Awe and Helmke 2017).[18]

As early as mid-century some royal identities had begun to change in still more radical ways. Now we see rulers whose nominal phrases incorporate numbered signs from the 260-day ritual calendar, a naming practice popular among the Mayas' neighbours to the west. Yet the truly extraordinary thing is that this is not the native *tzolk'in* system but one of those western cousins, its signs instantly recognisable from their squared outlines (Proskouriakoff 1950: 153). Sometimes their coefficients appear beneath them, a uniquely western feature. Similar signs appear on the gold disks dredged from the cenote at Chichen Itza, but their origin clearly lies along the Gulf Coast. There, for example, they identify characters portrayed on Río Blanco vessels and similar wares found as far north as the great city of El Tajin (Wyllie 2002: 201–232, passim, tables 9.1 and 9.25; Pascual and Velásquez 2012: figures 5–9).[19] A few stylistic traits originating in this part of the world turn up in Maya art of the Late Classic Period, and there seems to have been interregional contact in both directions.

The first dated examples of square day-names in the Maya area are found on Ucanal Stela 4 from 849, where they appear within two otherwise conventional Maya royal nominal sequences (Thompson 1970: 42) (Figure 7). The same kind of mixed name is carried by the lord of the aforementioned minor Tikal satellite of Jimbal, the last to lay claim to the Mutul title, who erected stelae in 879 and 889 (Figure 72). He is identified as a son of Olom on both Stela 1 (Guenter 1999: 155) and Stela 2, in both cases equipped with his *ochk'in/chik'in kaloomte'* title. Square day-names appear at Ceibal too, in the conjoined name of yet

72 Jimbal Stela 1 shows the last Mutul-titled ruler at the 10.2.10.0.0 period ending ceremony of 879. Note the square day-names halfway down the adjacent text. (Photograph by Christopher Jones, University of Pennsylvania Museum)

another *ochk'in/chik'in kaloomte'* on Stela 13, and they also serve to identify non-Maya storm gods or their impersonators on Stela 3.[20] One of the last two Maya day signs at the site, on Stela 18 from 889, is rendered within a squared cartouche in a conscious, almost playful, mixing of the two systems (Figure 71).

One more dualistic name is seen on the unprovenanced cylinder vessel K6437, which depicts a courtly scene in a pared-down late style (see Kerr and Kerr 2000: 967). Its rim text describes a traditional Maya god impersonation rite in which the subject is named first with two square day-names, then the Maya sign sequence **pe?-to-lo,** followed by *chik'in kaloomte'* (Figure 73a).[21] Intriguingly, this same "Petol" name is incised in a caption identifying the captive portrayed on Tikal Stela 11 from 869

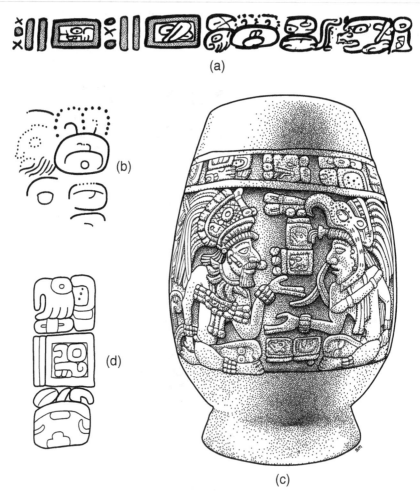

73 Anomalous names of the ninth century: (a) Combination of square day-names with the syllabographic string **pe?-to-lo** and *chik'in kaloomte'* in the rim text of K6437; (b) Caption to the captive on Tikal Stela 11 with the **pe?-to-lo** name; (c) a Pabellon vessel with lords identified by square day-names from Uaxactun Burial A41; (d) Text on Jimbal Stela 1 that identifies a *ti'huun* noble with a square day-name.

(Figure 73b). Given the close timing and uniqueness of this name, we have good reason to suspect that this is the same person.

Painted polychrome vases such as K6437 were fast disappearing by this point and this example must be counted among the last in their 300-year line. In their place come the mould-made vessels, many finished by hand, which depict a limited number of lordly and mythological scenes. While this shift is represented by Pabellon in the western and central regions, it overlaps with other types made using the same technique but from non-fine paste clays, including one now dubbed Ahk'utu' (Helmke and Reents-Budet 2008). Especially common in the east, modern-day Belize, the scenes these vessels carry are much more closely related to Classic Maya traditions than those on Pabellon pots, and may well predate them. More than one replicated Ahk'utu' vase identifies Olom as its owner and commissioner, thus aligning the new style to the emergence of kings with anomalous names and dating it to about mid-century.[22]

Aside from their square day-signs, Pabellon ceramics generally carry pseudo-glyphic designs that imitate, often only very vaguely, the look and arrange-ment of Maya hieroglyphs (Wyllie 2002: 286–302; Werness 2003).[23] However, an atypical but important Pabellon vessel excavated at Uaxactun includes a literate Maya inscription around its rim while labelling the four lordly figures in its scene exclusively with square day-names (Figure 73c). The use of a square day-name as a sole identifier turns up again in the tiny "addendum" on Jimbal Stela 1, where it names a *ti'huun* noble who accompanies the king in his period ending ritual (Carter 2014a: 190) (p.92–93) (Figure 73d). A link between the syllabically spelled names and square day-signs comes when we return to the parentage of that Jimbal monarch, since the name of his mother on both stelae clearly includes a squared sign (Carter 2014b: 173). While Olom does not carry such a boxed glyph there, a damaged example does appear in his extended name phrase on an unprovenanced Ahk'utu' vessel.[24] This suggests that the two kinds of anomalous identifiers could be part of a single phenomenon and have a common source.

The critical points to note here are that the lords with anomalous names exercise a near-monopoly on the high *kaloomte'* epithet, as well as appearing in contexts that either suggest or state their superiority over those bearing more conventional names.[25] We have previously heard how Wat'ul K'atel staged a royal congress at Ceibal in 849 attended by the kings of Tikal, Calakmul, and Motul de San José, attesting to a dramatic upending of the old political order (p.260–262). We have also heard how his regime was set up via the agency of Ucanal in 829, the centre from which Papmalil hosted and presided over acts performed by the kings of Caracol and Naranjo from 817 to 820 (pp.259–260). Olom and a second later *ochk'in/chik'in kaloomte'* mentioned at Uaxactun similarly outranked local rulers in 830 and 889, while at Ixlu the second

Papmalil is mentioned as he oversees the period ending ceremonies conducted by another Mutul-titled king in 859.[26] Additionally, the scene on Ixlu Stela 1, also from 859, rewards a closer look. It shows the expected portrait of the king, but also a character behind him who is bearded, wears a contrasting headdress, and sits before an apparent throne (Chase 1985: 111; see Jones and Satterthwaite 1982: figure 80). Could this be a depiction of the presiding *xaman kaloomte'* mentioned on Altar 1?

An early suggestion that new political forces were in play comes in the far west at Tonina (Guenter 2014: 216). There Ruler 8, who was ruling by the 780s, does not employ the *kaloomte'* title boasted by his predecessors. Instead, on Monument 95 from 806, his final commission, he ascribes it to someone with an otherwise unknown emblem glyph based on the term *waakchin*. The term connecting the two lords is the familiar *yichonal*, "before, oversee", which denotes a hierarchical relationship in all comparable contexts. Thus, in this last record before the local hiatus lasting until 837, Tonina expresses its subordination to an unknown power.

THE CHALLENGE OF INTERPRETATION

The ninth century evidence is undeniably challenging, verging at times on the confounding. With both traditional and innovative elements prominently on display, mixed in a temporal and geographic patchwork lacking any easily discerned pattern, it is little wonder that scholars have come to very different conclusions about its meaning. Still, we know that hidden somewhere within this disparate scatter of data there must lie a narrative that connects them – the task, as ever, is to find it.

The preceding two sections have shown how the changes in elite culture were not distributed evenly among the enduring centres of the southern lowlands. There is a correspondence between the most successful sites and those equipped with circular structures, which are also places where we find some of the densest concentrations of fine paste and mould-made ceramics. Moreover, in all cases where we have the appropriate textual record, these same places were home to rulers who bear anomalous names and *kaloomte'* titles. At precisely the same time, we see kings with traditional names who were rarely distinguished by *kaloomte'* epithets. These characters ruled centres without circular structures that show only scatterings of fine paste wares.

For the purposes of this discussion I will distinguish these two groups as the "new elite" and "old elite", respectively. Separated in this way, the ninth century landscape loses some of its more perplexing aspects. In the wake of the early ninth century crisis a once-uniform political culture had become a variegated one in which different regimes expressed different kinds of identity. If the Classic Maya were self-selecting these contrasting new and old ideological strategies, then those opting for radical change flourished, while many of those who did not followed a downward path to impoverishment, depopulation, and an early extinction.

There are a number of issues to address at this point, the most obvious being the aberrant names and art-styles, and with them the ever-elusive question of identity. Any judgement here presupposes that it is possible to ascribe cultural, ethnic, or geographic associations to people living over a millennium in the past – in the knowledge that identities are not necessarily fixed, are often multiple rather than singular, and can be ascribed by others as well as being self-determined. It will be noted that our problem in the ninth century is not entirely unlike that in the fourth to eighth centuries, where we have a similar mix of identity-based issues regarding the "strangers" linked to Teotihuacan. There we seek to distinguish actual outsiders from those who simply assume outside identities, and grapple with the historical processes that gave rise to both kinds of representation.

Approaches to the ninth century problem divide along the lines of our sources, with distinct, if connected, iconographic, epigraphic, and archaeological avenues. The first of these involves aesthetic and stylistic assessments, but strictly in the sense that these can be objective properties fixing particular forms and motifs within coherent symbol systems grounded in place and time. The archetypes and cultural matrix for many of the late non-standard features we see undoubtedly lie in the west, in Central Mexico but especially along the Gulf Coast.

On the face of it, there is an inconsistency in the monumental programmes of the new elite, where a striving to observe and preserve conservative ritual practice is complicated, if not undermined, by their jarringly atypical personal identities and stylistic shifts. We can only conclude that such dissonance is vital to their message, or instead that it could simply not be avoided. In keeping with the current consensus, we might ask if the drastically deteriorating conditions of the ninth century encouraged some Maya rulers to acquire additional, non-Maya, identities to signal their links to foreign groups who supported their positions, whether in practical or symbolic terms. But it is one thing for Maya lords to acquire extra identities, quite another for them to fully exchange their own markers of selfhood for alien ones – which would have to be the case on the Uaxactun vessel and the noble on the Jimbal stela. Free of preconceptions, we would hardly hesitate to conclude that these were outsiders.

But more tangible evidence for outsider status comes from the nomenclature itself. Although the Papmalil name is strange to the script, it finds analogues in western Mayan languages, especially Chontal, which employs the prefixes *pa-*, *pap-*, and *papa-* as male classifiers in surnames (Feldman 1983: 46, 48; John Justeson and Terrance Kaufman, pers. comm. 2019; also Thompson 1970: 47).

The Chontal Paxbolon-Maldonado Papers contain examples of such forms, including leading lords named Paptucun and Papcan (Scholes and Roys 1968: 386, 395).[27] A similar review of Chontal surnames in the early Colonial Period shows that an -ol suffix appears among them (Feldman 1983: tables 2 and 3), which could well be relevant to the similarly unfamiliar Petol moniker. Following this vein further, it is especially interesting that among those Chontal speakers living along the Usumacinta and Pasión rivers in the 1500s and 1600s, some thirty-five to forty-five per cent of the calendrical names they employed were derived from Nahua, the language that stretched from Northern and Central Mexico to several other parts of Mesoamerica (Feldman 1983: 46; Justeson et al. 1985: 54). The antiquity of this practice is unknown – we have no data whatsoever between the tenth and fifteenth centuries – but it is not implausible that the acquisition is an old one that took place on the Gulf Coast where the two language groups meet. The seductive prospect is that Chontal nominal practices could explain the appearance of both the syllabographic and square day-names.

This linguistic evidence, if as strong as it appears, would be decisive in linking characters already suspected of outside ties to a specific cultural group and region. While still open to critique and revision, it is no longer so easy to dismiss Thompson's proposal of a Chontal-Putun intrusion into the southern lowlands out of hand. Precisely how the new elite achieved their dominant status, taking direct control at some centres and exercising influence over others, is not apparent in the data. However, it is clearly significant that their first appearances follow so closely on the heels of the early ninth century crisis, suggesting either that they quickly exploited the opportunity it presented, or were themselves its instigators.

If these were newcomers they were by no means antagonistic toward the heritage of Classic Maya kingship, indeed quite the reverse, they actively embraced and expounded it. This would be so much less of a challenge if, as Thompson (1970: 43) believed, they were Maya who already had some direct knowledge of the Classic ideal. Mythical scenes on mould-made ceramics include a much-curtailed Maya pantheon that largely focusses on God L and K'awiil – a pairing associated with the regeneration of crops as well as travel and trade (Martin 2006b: 169–176); characters who were doubtless already well-known on the Gulf Coast. The stelae of the new elite put particular emphasis on the traditional Paddler Gods, figures shown within swirling clouds in the sky – a motif that first appears at Tikal in 771 (Figure 72). However, they are now either joined or replaced by other characters in the same cloud settings, warriors in foreign attire who brandish spearthrowers and darts (Figure 7).

The most important single celebration of native religion was that performed by Wat'ul K'atel at Ceibal in 849. With the central monument of his programme focussing on the founding of the current era in 3114 BCE, a core

Classic Maya concept, we see a grand cosmological statement as well as a
political one (Stuart 2016). That Wat'ul K'atel went to such lengths at a time of
upheaval and disintegration is significant, and we might even ask if it represents
an active effort at Classic revitalisation – a renewal and re-centring of the Maya
world at his city and in his person.

On three of his five monuments around Structure A-3 Wat'ul K'atel
portrays himself as an unalloyed Maya king, and this has long ranked high in
the list of reasons to doubt a foreign origin for him. Stanley Guenter's
unpublished study of 1999 (104–109, 134–135) notes the anomalous name of
Wat'ul K'atel, as well as the unusual status of Papmalil and Olom, expanding
upon these features to argue in favour of the Putun invasion scenario.
Regarding the conventional Maya portraits of this time, he draws a comparison to the Greek conquerors of Egypt, who sought acceptance from their new
subjects by depicting themselves as native Pharaohs performing age-old religious rites (Guenter 1999: 153). One might add here that these new overlords –
Romans, Persians, and Assyrians too – carried full Pharaonic titles, and it was
primarily the phonetic spellings of their personal names that betrayed them as
foreigners. The remaining two portraits of Wat'ul K'atel are, as we have heard,
utterly different and, despite their traditional costuming, make no effort to
conform to the Classic ideal. It is as if the "mask" has been slipped aside in an
open acknowledgment that this was all a performance, an admission that he
was indeed a stranger in the land.

One of the most distinctive archaeological features of the new elite is their
association with circular structures. Such buildings are found throughout
Mesoamerica, where their meaning varies depending on their epoch and
region (Pollock 1936; Szymański 2010). Their sudden appearance in the Maya
lowlands, having been absent for centuries, signals the introduction of some
new spiritual practice or specific deity. Indeed, scholars have previously linked
round platforms at Ceibal and elsewhere to a "cult" of the feathered serpent
Quetzalcoatl/Kukulkan and a religious movement that swept across Mesoamerica at this time (Ringle, Gallareta, and Bey 1998: 219; see also Pascual and
Velásquez 2012). The specific connection drawn here is to the circular temples
dedicated to the wind deity Ehecatl-Quetzalcoatl distributed throughout
much of Postclassic Central Mexico (Pollock 1936: 162; Taube 2001:
112–114; Szymański 2010: 56–61). Ringle, Gallareta, and Bey (1998: 213–214)
attribute the spread of this cult to a variety of mechanisms, including militarism, migration, proselytisation, and contact through long-distance commerce.

This is also linked to the diffusion of so-called "international style" (in its
Late Postclassic form known as Mixteca-Puebla), which increasingly hom-
ogenised regional traditions within an overriding Central Mexican aesthetic.
Indeed, we might ask if the rise of new religious ideas and the international
style more reflect the political and cultural dominance of western societies than

it does a transformation sought out by the Maya. Here we are reminded of the Gulf Coast imagery on Pabellon pots, whose manufacture in the heart of the Maya lowlands would seem not to weaken, but rather strengthen, the case that they were the product of culturally distinct people, reproducing motifs familiar from their distant homelands.

Despite the sweeping effects of the early ninth century crisis along the Usumacinta and Pasión rivers, the first significant cultural developments to reach the interior of the peninsula evidently came not from the west but from the east. It has been noted that a sizeable number of circular structures from this period crop up along the Hondo, Belize, and Sibun Rivers – waterways that offer access to the Peten from the Caribbean – part of a suite of northern features that suggest major shifts in commerce, inward migration, or military opportunism and with these same Chontal associations (Harrison-Buck and McAnany 2013; Harrison-Buck 2016; also Chase and Chase 1982; Chase 1985: 105, passim; Awe and Helmke 2017). The upper tributaries of the Hondo and Belize courses ultimately take you to Nakum, Ucanal, Calzada Mopan, and Ixtonton, clearly implying that these locations were also oriented toward the commercial, cultural, and political routes leading to the east and north.

In Postclassic times the Chontal Maya were circumpeninsula travellers who established trading communities on the island of Cozumel and as far down the eastern coast as the mouth of the Motagua River and the Gulf of Honduras (Thompson 1970: 7–8). This makes the early appearance of new elites with Chontal-style names at eastern Peten sites less strange than it might otherwise appear. The epigraphic link between Ceibal and Ucanal in 829 would have strategic significance, since it traverses the land bridge between waterways flowing toward the Gulf Coast on the one hand and the Caribbean on the other. The leading role played by Ucanal again suggests that the eastern approach was of greater importance, at least initially.

Even if marked by power differentials, the new and old-style regimes in the Peten coexisted for much of the final century. Some "legacy" Classic Maya kingdoms were subjects or collaborators in the new hybrid landscape, while others might have survived as a recalcitrant rump ever-seeking to restore the old order.

We might step back at this point to the caption on Tikal Stela 11 (Figure 73b). Tikal's continuous monumental tradition had concluded in 810 with Stela 24 and Altar 7, stones that were found smashed and missing most of their images and once-long inscriptions (Jones and Satterthwaite 1982: 52, figures 38–41).[28] When we next hear of a king bearing the Mutul title he is the compliant guest at the great Ceibal gathering of 849. Stela 11 marks the end of the six-decade monument hiatus at Tikal and was commissioned to celebrate the rule of Jasaw Chan K'awiil II in 869 (Jones and Satterthwaite 1982: 29–31, figure 16). It bears cloud-borne Paddler Gods, but not the weapon-bearing versions and, while it has a late border design, it shows not a glimmer of foreign influence. The dedicatory cache set beneath it shows a direct continuity in Tikal traditions. Did the isolated production of this stela pivot on the capture of Petol and reflect a successful act of resistance in which one of the old elite briefly triumphed over one of the new?

In light of the evidence examined in this and the previous section, we might wonder anew if these changes are the manifestations of powerful bodies of intruders. Thompson (1970: 5, 47) envisaged a "Macedonian aggrandisement", in which a militaristic group swept aside a culture by then past its prime. Other advocates of foreign intrusion have speculated that outsiders first arrived as mercenaries to fight in an increasingly nihilistic struggle between the Classic kingdoms. To entertain the possibility of meaningful foreign presence, rather than simply foreign influence, in the ninth century southern Maya lowlands is a controversial position today. But new data, unavailable to its original advocates, argues that the case should be re-opened. Ideally, isotopic and genetic analyses will allow us to test for foreign presence – although it is well to keep to mind that we may be in search of proportionately small numbers of people, who could have assimilated with the local population rather quickly, and might not have shared the same inhumation practices.

To conclude and summarise, I hope to have shown that ninth century inscriptions can make a meaningful contribution to the study of the collapse. The data they provide combines with others to show that a thriving socio-political order experienced a rapid-onset emergency close to the turn of the century, reflected in a wave of early abandonments and the start of a demographic freefall. Within a short space of time what remained of the Classic Maya political landscape was reconfigured and new centres came to the fore. In the south these regimes expressed previously unseen features which, while they incorporated many local ideas and practices, drew on others with origins on the Gulf Coast. Whether these specific developments are linked to climatological events or are independent of them has still to be determined. We may well be looking at complex interactions in which climate trends precipitated social problems or exacerbated existing ones, creating opportunities for some and narrowing options for others on a region-by-region basis. Whatever forces were acting on the system, and the sequence in which they occurred, they were ones no strategy or ideology could ultimately resist and one-by-one the ninth century survivors also disappeared.

By the first part of the tenth century all the defining characteristics of Classic Maya civilisation, in both the southern and northern lowlands, had finally perished. Few settlements of any size had more than a vestigial population, and those that did reflect new modes of authority, changes in material culture, religious expression, and trade patterns, marking a full transition to the Post-classic Period.

PART III

A POLITICAL ANTHROPOLOGY FOR THE
CLASSIC MAYA

TWELVE

CLASSIC MAYA NETWORKS

Having assembled a sizeable dataset in Part II, we now move forward in Part III to its analysis, synthesis, and conceptualisation. Multi-faceted problems invite cross-disciplinary approaches, and Part III engages in methodological and theoretical pluralism as it seeks ways to bring anthropology and history into a closer communion. At various junctures in this volume I have emphasised the importance of looking at the Classic Maya less as a series of separate polities than as a unified political culture. We have reached the point where that assertion needs to be more fully explored and its implications fleshed out.

Accordingly, this chapter looks at what a macroscale, holistic approach can add to our investigation, as seen through three very different applications of the term "network". We begin by considering the practical means of communication necessarily implied by strong cultural commonalities. Next, we turn to what can be learned from a statistical and distributional analysis of political connections in the epigraphic record. A third section looks at network issues from the viewpoint of complexity theory, an approach expressly focussed on the relationship between unit and system. Networks share certain common properties and exploring the ways in which these are manifested in the Maya case shows us how historical specifics reflect phenomena operating at much greater scales.

WAYS AND MEANS

The remarkable uniformity of Classic Maya society across more than 250,000 km² of the lowlands is one of its most distinctive features. Today we recognise an impressive list of shared traits, at the level of the general populace as well as that of the elite, demonstrating a clear consistency of material and intellectual culture. The continuity of artistic style alone tells of a unifying aesthetic, with minimal variation from one end of the Maya world to the other. So much was noted over a century ago by Morley (1915: 15): "The architecture, sculpture, and hieroglyphic writing of all the southern centers is practically identical, even to the borrowing of unessential details, a condition which indicates a homogeneity only to be accounted for by long-continued and frequent intercourse". Now that we have appropriately dated material for northern Classic centres such as Coba, Oxkintok, Xcalumkin, Edzna, Ek Balam, and others, we can extend that observation to the whole Maya lowlands. To be sure, there are local variations, stylistic quirks, and selective thematic interests, but the unity of principles and repetition of "unessential details" – which could almost have sprung from the hand of a single master artist – endorse Morley's view, which he discerned from just a fraction of the material available to us today.

The question is what enabled and mediated this phenomenon? What were the modes and pathways of transmission? No assessment of an interactive whole can be complete without an understanding of the links that forged it, the means by which its defining knowledge and practices were circulated and propagated. Absent a central political authority, the mechanisms for disseminating ideas must occur outside a directed system and arise instead from enduring patterns of collaborative and emulative behaviour.

Without beasts of burden or wheeled vehicles the logistics of transport and communications in Mesoamerica differed substantially from those in the Old World. With relatively few navigable waterways and limited circumpeninsula sea travel – at least during the Classic era – the movement of people largely relied on walking and the movement of goods on what could be carried. The tumpline was the ubiquitous technology of the latter, allowing burdens to be taken on the forehead and neck as well as on the shoulders and back (Figure 74). While astonishing weights can be borne by those with a lifetime's training in such labour, there can be no comparison to the load-bearing capacities of horses or oxen. There are considerable social and economic ramifications here. The production of all kinds of high quantity but low value goods, utilitarian pottery for example, are much more likely to be locally produced than widely exchanged. Moreover, if geography is understood not in terms of absolute distance but in the time taken to travel from one point to another, then the ambition of journeys, the expense of moving goods,

and the size of political units must
all be scaled-up before meaningful
like-for-like comparisons with Old
World societies can be made.

It is hard to look beyond the
tangled scrub and forest of today to
a time when roads would have criss-
crossed the entire region. Save for
the linear causeways that radiate out
from major settlements to cross *bajos*
or seasonal swamps, most of them
Preclassic in date, together with the
thoroughly exceptional 98 km-long
elevated road between Coba and
Yaxuna, few signs of such a network
now survives.[1] Many routes would
have been simple tracks, but more
substantial surfaces of cleared bedrock or tamped *sascab* (crushed limestone) – the kinds of pathways that
guide tourists through many a Maya
ruin today – would be relatively easy
both to construct and maintain, and
would be effective in all but the
heaviest of rains. It was these low-
tech highways, not the extravagant
causeways, which are captured in the
multiple varieties of *bih/be*, "road"
described in the early lexicons (e.g. Bolles and Folan 2001; also Keller 2009).[2]

74 Bearer using a tumpline depicted in the Chiik Nahb
murals of Calakmul. (SM/Proyecto Arqueológico
Calakmul)

Their routes would have remained well trodden for centuries, but once
abandoned would have decayed rapidly, reclaimed by a voracious forest within
a few short years. In this regard, it should be noted that in the late seventeenth
century the Spanish drove a road through the heart of the Peten, linking
Campeche with Guatemala (Jones 1998: 111, passim). The ruins of a few way
stations can be used to roughly trace its route, but nothing of the road itself
now remains. Following in the footsteps of pioneering work elsewhere in the
New World tropics (Sheets and Sever 1991), the kind of advanced topographic
analyses and remote sensing now coming to the fore in Maya archaeology will
doubtless allow us to chart the ancient routes and junctions at some point,
laying bare the arterial system of a civilisation.[3]

But roads themselves are never more than conduits, it is the human traffic
they carry where the connective essence must reside. Road systems of a

practical kind connect one settlement to another like links in a chain. Since long-distance journeys would take days, weeks, or even months to complete, travellers would necessarily have passed through many settlements, bringing them into contact with the locals as they traded for provisions and camped-out overnight. The larger sites may even have had formal facilities, the equivalent of inns and hostelries; though if so they were probably situated in the peripheries of sites to keep strangers at arm's length. Important intersections would experience heavier-than-usual traffic, with a flow of arrivals and departures that pulsed to the rhythm of ceremonies, festivals, and market days fixed by the calendar. Social and political implications abound here, since long-distance travel would necessarily have crossed numerous frontiers and domains. Though never entirely free of danger, a reasonably free flow would require some guarantee of safety through major parts of the network, in which the more powerful political entities surely played some role.

We have a good idea of the cast of characters that stretched along the Classic Maya roadways. There would be tribute-bearers loaded with cloth, cacao, and still more precious items, passing jobbing porters burdened with sundry commodities, including pine torchwood and salt brought from afar. They would be joined by merchants specialising in high-value exotica and crafted wares, couriers carrying news, messages, and diplomatic gifts, parties on their way to nuptial ceremonies, pilgrims en route to sacred sites, and little doubt itinerant healers, bards, and troupes of actors and musicians into the bargain. From time to time roads would clear of ordinary travellers to let pass bands of adrenaline-fuelled warriors trying to outpace news of their advance. At less frenzied moments, the same thoroughfares saw the stately progress of noble emissaries, princes, and kings, borne on elaborate litters with a suitable entourage of bodyguards, retainers, and accompanying baggage-trains.

All this traffic would produce a mixing of people and ideas, but the key travellers for our concerns would be the bearers of learning: the *itz'aat, ajtz'ihb, taaj,* and *ajk'in,* the scholars, scribes, artists, astrologers, and priestly keepers of the calendar. It was primarily through them, and the books they carried, that cultural knowledge and intellectual developments would have been disseminated, crossing not only political but linguistic boundaries, to reach the furthest corners of the Maya realm.

What we still need to understand are the mechanisms of this knowledge transfer. We know that some sculptors in the service of kings were "lent" to provincial centres to produce monuments for dependent elites (e.g. Houston 1993: 135, 2016: 403), and conversely that subject domains could contribute artisans to the core (Martin, Houston, and Zender 2015; Houston 2017). We can imagine a similar system of royal patronage in which the learned literati were attached to royal courts and communicated with others in a manner akin to that of diplomatic exchange. But such a tightly controlled set of contacts, necessarily subordinated to political considerations, seems inadequate for the region-wide networking that produced such affinity, which demands inter-actions of an altogether more expansive and fluid kind.

In Medieval Europe, the Roman Church supplied a highly organised cultural as well as religious exchange system that bonded the disparate and often warring kingdoms of the age into a single international order. But flows of knowledge need not be so institutionalised. In Classical Greece and Renais-sance Italy the requisite sharing arose from the mobility of a class of intelli-gentsia and haute artisans, a loosely defined group whose personal identities transcended their origins and any fixed political affiliation (e.g. Raaflaub 2004: 206; Malkin 2011: 28–30; Pongratz-Leisten 2011: 3–11). Here the elite acted not so much as owners but as consumers of advanced knowledge, and wealthy patrons competed to host the most skilled practitioners.

We see something of this kind when Quirigua broke the bonds of its subjection to Copan, immediately thereafter commencing a programme of monumental art-making, within a few years producing the tallest group of stelae in the Maya world. These were carved in a distinctive style that made copious use of anthropomorphised "full-figure" hieroglyphs – the most complex form of the script – produced with a skill and inventiveness that surpassed even that of their original mentors at Copan. Was this unnamed virtuoso of Maya art and writing already residing in this provincial backwater awaiting such an opportunity, or is it not more likely that he was drawn there by the newly independent and wealthy Quirigua king intent on proclaiming his power in the most impressive manner possible?

MAPPING THE SYSTEM

If we know some of the means by which a cultural totality could be forged and sustained, what can we say about the overall form of that entity? Can we quantify connectivity, information flows, and power dynamics at a system-wide scale? Some of the comings and goings described above found their way into the epigraphic record – high-status visits and rampaging armies in particular – but the remainder, trade ties, pilgrimages, intellectual and artistic exchanges, and the like, leave no more than shadows in the inscriptions and are part of our dark matter problem. What we have is a significant body of patrimonial rhetoric, which at least allows us to paint a portrait of power. Moreover, some of these connections might serve as proxies for absent data, for example where hierarchical ties imply tribute-flows and asymmetrical gift exchanges.

To gain some sense of the greater system we can take the contacts between the most active and connected centres and represent them in diagrammatic form (Figure 75). The advantage of graphic displays such as this is the ease with

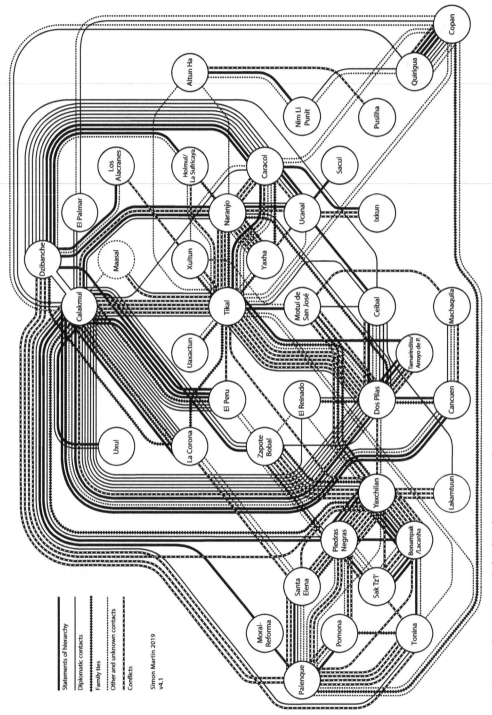

75 Diagram showing recorded political interactions during the Classic Period.

which one can appreciate distributions, gaining an immediate impression of
the range, intensity, and diversity of contacts. I have visualised inter-polity
relations in this way before, each time with the aim of sidestepping geographic
and territorial concerns in order to focus on network structure. The present
version has antecedents in the two editions of *Chronicle of the Maya Kings and
Queens* (Martin and Grube 2000: 21, 2008: 21), but has been updated to reflect
new finds and to expand the number of featured participants. It now comprises
40 polities connected by 282 links. The latter are divided into five categories:
hierarchical relationships, diplomatic and other cordial contacts, familial ties,
conflicts, and finally those that are poorly understood, only partly legible, or
for some other reason difficult to assign elsewhere.[4]

It is necessary to be clear about what kind of a "map" this is, and what it is
not. The diagram shares the limitations of its predecessors. It is a sample of
recorded interactions and, therefore, influenced by agendas of patrimonial
rhetoric and the physical survival of inscriptions. By only including the most
textually loquacious players, its geographic range is necessarily confined to a
band that runs through the western, central, and eastern parts of the southern
lowlands and its adjacent highlands. Its temporal conflation means that it
cannot convey historical dynamics and, for the sake of simplicity, it does not
indicate the directionality of its ties. Finally, it gives no hint to its heavy
weighting toward the Late Classic, the era when texts were most numerous
and political themes most commonly discussed. For these and other reasons,
the diagram cannot stand alone as a realisation of the data, but must be
complemented by other forms of analysis and display.

Even with these caveats and disclaimers, the sample is of sufficient size and
time-depth to expose significant patterns. What most strikes the eye are the
highly-connected nodes of the Kaanul dynasty, based first at Dzibanche and
then at Calakmul. Their joint count of links is substantial, but certainly
understates the original total due to the small number of texts thus far
uncovered at Dzibanche and the extreme erosion of surface monuments at
Calakmul. To illustrate this point, Figure 76 shows the total number of links by
polity, but distinguishes home references to other polities (in grey) from the
mentions of that polity made elsewhere (in black). This reveals that over
ninety-six per cent of the connections featuring the Snake kingdom appear
in the inscriptions of other centres. Foreign references might be seen as a less
self-interested index of the impact that one polity had on the affairs of others,
offering a better guide to the "fame" of a given kingdom.[5] By this measure, the
position of the Dzibanche-Calakmul axis is especially elevated, its outside
mentions constitute over 240 per cent of that its nearest rival, Tikal.

If we investigate the thematic categories in total a similar story emerges.
Amply reflecting their political pre-eminence, Dzibanche-Calakmul features in
thirty-five per cent of all recorded hierarchical ties, while in diplomatic

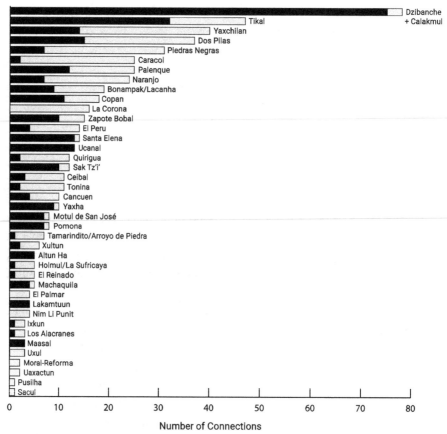

76 Political interactions arranged by polity. The foreign references to each polity are shown in black, while home references to other polities are shown in grey.

contacts – many of which are linked to hierarchy – the proportion is a still more impressive fifty-seven per cent. Familial ties come in at twenty per cent of the total, while conflict turns out to be a more modest thirteen per cent (other and unknown connections also amount to thirteen per cent). These proportions are influenced by the home–foreign imbalance, since hierarchical and diplomatic contacts typically come from outside sources, while warfare is a topic concentrated in home accounts (to illustrate the point, only one locally-referenced inter-polity conflict of the Snake kingdom makes it into the sample).

Despite these biases, we have some quantification of the Snake dynasty's political influence and it indicates how completely it exceeded that of its rivals. By contrast, one would hardly imagine that Tikal was a great power at all from its share of direct hierarchical ties, which come in at a paltry seven per cent, while its recorded cordial encounters amount to just ten per cent. Family connections reflect greater influence at twenty-four per cent, while episodes of conflict come in at twenty-one per cent (others and unknowns amount to a sizeable twenty-six per cent). Whatever the actual strength of Tikal, it is plain that its rhetorical stamp on the region was much weaker than that of its main competitor, even when mitigating factors such as its limited production of monuments are taken into account.

Figure 77 shows the distribution of contacts through time as a histogram, arranged by K'atun, the unit of twenty Maya years. The Late Classic bias of the sample is very obvious here, with no more than nineteen per cent of the links dating to before 600. Broadly speaking, we can discern a 100-year highpoint in the recording of interactions lasting from the mid-seventh to the mid-eighth century. While the five different types of contact – not displayed here – vary throughout the full sample, the major contribution to this increase is the rise in diplomatic links – which are, as previously noted, a corollary of hierarchical relations in most cases.

It is when we separate out the interactions of Dzibanche-Calakmul (highlighted here in black) that we can appreciate not only the scale of their politicking but also its temporal profile. The Kaanul kingdom first emerges as a force towards the end of the Early Classic Period, with its share of recorded interactions reaching a dominant sixty-six per cent between 554 and 593. After a brief dip to thirty-three per cent in 593–613, it maintains a fifty-five per cent or sixty per cent share in all K'atun periods up to 692 – with neither its civil war nor shift in capital dulling its political fortunes. However, after its defeat in 695 its influence begins to ebb, such that its share in 692–711 falls

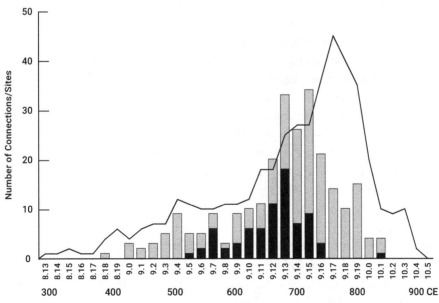

77 Histogram showing the distribution of recorded political interactions through time, with those of the Kaanul kingdom highlighted in black. This is overlaid by a plot representing the number of southern lowland sites dedicating monuments.

to twenty-seven per cent, slipping a little more to twenty-six per cent in 711–731. After the reverse of c.734 we see a sharper drop to just fourteen per cent by 731–751. In the next K'atun, lasting from 751 to 771, its presence on the "international" scene disappears entirely, coinciding with a dynastic crisis at Calakmul that saw the Snake kings lose power, at least for a time (Case Study 6). Although a crude measure, these results are nevertheless testimony to the rise, flowering, and fall of the Snake hegemony, all completed well before the end of the Late Classic Period.

Its decline briefly affects the overall levels of connectivity, but interactions between other polities are still rising, reaching a new peak between 711 and 731, the K'atun ending of 9.15.0.0.0. If we compare the histogram of connections in Figure 77 to that of the output of monuments in Figure 68 we can see how far the two are out of step. This demonstrates that the rise in connectivity is not merely the artefact of an increased sample size. But it is when we add an additional plot to Figure 77, this time representing the number of different sites erecting monuments in this same southern zone, that we see how starkly the profiles are out of sync. The two datasets track one another relatively well until the peak of 9.15.0.0.0, after which they significantly diverge: the number of connections dropping at the same time as the number of sites are entering the record are climbing. The latter reaches its zenith between 751 and 771, up to four decades after connections had begun to fall.

A review of the forty-five southern centres active during this peak time show that the majority were well-established places. However, these have been joined by others emerging from a long silence, as well as those who appear to erect monuments for the first time, a few of which may have been recent site foundations. In most instances, though, we can explain the absence of earlier monuments at newly active centres only if they had been buried or destroyed, or if these sites had hitherto been unable to commission any. The proportion of smaller centres producing inscriptions continues to rise into the ninth century, even as the overall total number falls away. Some of this can be attributed to the movement or break-up of dynasties, as where the Mutul emblem glyph of Dos Pilas is adopted by rulers at Ceibal in 770 and La Amelia in 802, and the identical title used by Tikal appears at Ixlu in 859 and Jimbal in 889, as we saw in Chapter 11.

As we enter the ninth century it is only natural to scan the data horizon in search of gathering storm-clouds. The difficulty is that signs of incipient collapse are seldom unambiguous and their identification is tainted by our foreknowledge of what was to come. However, in this instance the offset between histogram and plot in Figure 77 is a clear and significant data-point, demonstrating that Classic Maya society was changing in some important regard well before the onset of the early ninth century crisis. There are, as some scholars have suspected, some deeper roots or a prelude to the collapse – even if these shifts were not appreciated by actors at the time.

The upsurge in the recording of political interaction, c.650–750, coincides with the era in which hegemonic activity was at its most visible and consequential. Indeed, I believe we can take it that the two are inherently linked and that this type of record was driven by these kinds of activities. It follows that this century constitutes the era of maximum political integration in the Late Classic Period. The deterioration of Calakmul's hegemony in the first part of the eighth century, replaced only in weaker fashion by Tikal, can be interpreted as the first sign of a wider dissolution of Classic Maya political culture. The most plausible explanation for significantly more polities coming into view after 730 is this weakening of macro-political structure. Lords once constrained by powerful neighbours and enveloping hierarchies could assert their new-found liberty through a new or renewed monumental tradition, elevating themselves to the level we take to be independent kings.

NETWORKS IN A COMPLEX WORLD

What I have engaged in above is a form of social network analysis, a relatively common approach within archaeology and anthropology, but only one of several methodologies that fall under the general rubric of graph theory. It had long been assumed that the varied datasets and research questions of the many fields interested in networks would leave them wholly unrelated. However, in the late 1990s research made possible by greatly increased computing power demonstrated that networks themselves have properties, even laws, that are independent of the topic under investigation. Thus, the molecular-scale formation of ice, the spread of epidemics, reversals in magnetic polarity, economic bubbles, and many similarly diverse phenomena prove to have common principles, their universality stemming from a previously unexplored region of graph mathematics (Barabási 2002; Strogatz 2003; Watts 2003). This approach to networks is a branch of complexity science and, as such, relates to the phenomena of self-organisation, chaos, and emergence last encountered in Chapter 3.

If these network principles are indeed universal, then they should apply to social webs as much as they do any other. The prospect at hand is that we can know something about the structure and behaviour of a system distinct from our understanding of the historical specifics from which it is composed. Such ideas have been seeping into the humanities, even into studies of the ancient world (Brughmans 2013: 645–648; Knappett 2013: 7). An illustrative example is Irad Malkin's *A Small Greek World: Networks in the Ancient Mediterranean* (2011), which points to the close analogies between the growth and interaction of Classical Greek colonies and the principles of network theory, with its lexicon of hubs, spokes, and clusters. Malkin rightly cautions that the meagre quantity of data from antiquity means that we can never have a deep statistical basis to our research, and that a network approach must go beyond the bromide that "everything is connected" (Malkin 2011: 25). Even so, this thinking offers a fresh perspective on some familiar problems.

Hubs and Small Worlds

The polities in our diagram have been selected for their high levels of connectivity, thereby excluding many links to lesser polities or secondary sites. If we were to add the entirety of known connections it would bolster the link totals of some already well-placed polities but, more significantly, add a sizeable number of new ones possessing a low number of links. The most common number of connections would be one, followed by two, three, and so on. If we drew a plot for those data, essentially an expanded version of Figure 76, we would have something closely resembling a "power law" distribution, a distinctive curve in which there are far more low values than there are high ones.

Power laws are of particular interest to network theorists since they cannot arise from a randomised sample and are typical of many human-made systems. Instances of the latter include the relative size of cities, the distribution of personal wealth, the popularity of websites, and the layout of airline routes (Barabási 2002). As the last example exemplifies, where those data can be drawn as a network they show a few dominant hubs connected to many peripheral nodes. Important Maya hubs such as Dzibanche-Calakmul and Tikal certainly rose to their positions by virtue of their own efforts within a particular historical frame. However, given that power law distributions occur so frequently in social networks, the presence of many connected polities might alone predict, a priori, that the system would have a small number of high-degree hubs and many low-degree ones. Which polities fill those positions on the scale, and how they came to do it, is of sublime indifference to the phenomenon.

What lies behind the power law distributions that correlate to hub structures remains unclear. One candidate is "preferential attachment", which stipulates that nodes gather new connections in direct proportion to how many they already possess (Barabási 2002: 84–90). At the formation of a system, contingency will give some nodes a small advantage and this is magnified as the system grows, such that just a few nodes acquire most of the new links ("the rich get richer"). As a result, early members of a network have a distinct edge over those joining later. Certainly, centres such as Tikal and Dzibanche had precocious early dynasties, and that could have given them an advantage over the newer ones with which they competed. But since latecomers can and do rise to dominant positions in all such systems, antiquity is not a sufficient explanation. Latecomers typically blossom because of some advantage of their own and, in Darwinian fashion, prove to be *fitter* than their more established rivals ("the fit get rich") (Barabási 2002: 93–107). Maya polities were competitive, and the most powerful actively sought to prevent others from achieving that same status – a good illustration of the agency that no purely mathematical node can possess.

In the natural world power laws are common only in phase transitions, those points at which apparent disarray turns into coherence or vice versa. This ties power laws to emergence and self-organisation (Barabási 2002: 77–78), situating their subjects within the dynamic region between order and disorder dubbed the "edge of chaos".[6] In social terms, this marks some point of balance between the entirely centralised and the entirely decentralised, in which the benefits and costs of each are in some manner offset. This leads us to conclude that a middling hub structure has some distinct advantage or practicality compared to the alternatives at either end of the spectrum. The larger point is that if power laws are a product of complexity, they reflect a principle of self-organisation in which competing units fall, without deliberate planning, into a hub-based pattern generated solely by their interactions.

If Maya polities interacted only with directly adjacent ones we would have a serial near-neighbour network, where the spread of ideas and information would be slow and unlikely to reach all parts equally. But the diagram makes clear that the "wiring" of this landscape is quite different and features a high proportion of long-distance ties. This takes us into the realm of "small world" networks, a phenomenon in which even a limited number of extended links exponentially increases overall connectivity (Watts and Strogatz 1998; Watts 1999, 2003; see Braswell 2005).[7] The result is a huge reduction in the distance between nodes in the system, counted not in kilometres but in the number of intervening steps, making an emergent totality a viable proposition.

Yet, in a feature that mathematical nets need not consider, virtually all long-distance connections in the Maya area must, as noted above, traverse the domains of other polities. This implicates them as enablers, or at least low-friction corridors, for the flows of people on their way to business elsewhere. Communication between geographically distant nodes in such a case cannot be the same kind of "shortcut" it is in a mathematical small world network, since it necessarily engages wider parts of the system.

The ties found in social networks are not all of equal strength or of similar kind, again in contrast to those in mathematics, and this is reflected in the division into the five types in Figure 75. It is to be expected that "closer" nodes – a description that need not refer to physical distance – will generally have stronger ties than others. The point of interest here is that it is the *weaker* ties that have much the greater role in creating system-wide connectivity

(Granovetter 1973). This is because the capacity to maintain strong ties is limited in the real world, they are "costly" in several senses, and their number is finite as a result. Weak ties, by contrast, are much easier to form and less effort to maintain, and as a result can be much more numerous. The diagram we have is sure to be dominated by strong ties sufficiently important to be reflected in patrimonial rhetoric, and so in order to envisage the whole network one must infer a far greater number of weak ones. The knowledge flows carried by emissaries, intellectuals, priests, artisans, and other kinds of cultural specialist would represent exactly this type of weak connection. The journey of the El Palmar *lakam* to faraway Copan might be one of the few to be captured in the texts.

In the Classic Maya case, we have evidence that a limited group of innovators broke with Preclassic norms to create a new political order during the turbulent Protoclassic Period. Structurally autonomous and self-replicating polities grew in number and, once they reached a certain critical mass, effectively lost their attachment to a centre and became an interactive whole. A sign that we have an emergent system freed from the direction of its originators can be glimpsed where innovations take place at the periphery rather than the core. The unique portraiture in modelled stucco and relief carving that develops at Palenque in the seventh century, or the distinctively baroque three-dimensional sculpture at Copan in the eighth, were sui generis phenomena at the edges of the Maya world with no antecedents elsewhere. As we have seen, Classic Maya political culture was a strong force for conformity, but no social reproduction can be perfect, and the essence of recursion is that there is always an element of transformation. Whether by unconscious error or deliberate amendment, changes modify that culture, just as speech acts do a governing grammar. An innovation will have a particular locus, even an individual creator, but at a deeper level it is no more than the contingent manifestation of a potential already inherent to the system.

Chaos and self-organisation can be thought of as the yin and yang of complexity. One tells us why the progress of systems is subject to compounded contingency and cannot be predicted in any detail through time, the other the ways in which systems can, if the conditions are right, fall into coherent synchronies absent of any guiding hand. The hierarchies that develop between political communities can be considered a manifestation of self-organisation, in the sense that they arise not from a grand plan or outside direction but from their interactions alone. Those hierarchies proceed to regulate the number, distribution, and behaviour of polities in ways that maintain their individual existence and, therefore, the system itself. Change in the system is usually slow and incremental, but holds within it the possibility of radical transformation, seismic shifts that correspond in the Maya case to what we identify as distinctive Preclassic, Classic, and Postclassic Periods.

Recognising these "unseen hands" in no way negates the sentient dimension to social and political organisation. Societies and individuals constantly adapt their behaviours within the feedback process, trying first one strategy and then another, pursuing those that produce a desired or otherwise beneficial result. Sociopolitical organisation might be seen as an interplay of subjective and objective understandings, of intentionality as well as sheer accident and necessity, in which the direction of the group rather than that of the individual predominates.

Cascades and Traumas

In whatever other manner we might choose to characterise the ninth century collapse, it represents a complete and irrevocable network breakdown. Network theory has particular understandings of how complex systems fail and these offer ways to think about such processes outside of their historical specifics. One of these focuses on how the interdependencies that make networks robust in almost all circumstances can, under unforeseen ones, turn into a source of weakness (Barabási 2002: 110–121, 209–211; Watts 2003: 109, 189–194; Mitchell 2009: 255–257). It is precisely because complex systems are highly connected that one failure can induce others and lead to a "cascade". Although its progress may be imperceptible at first, if left unchecked its exponential accumulation will ultimately overwhelm the entire system. Failures of this kind are not so much things "waiting to happen" as they are things brought into being by the contextual forces acting on the system. As an example, some seemingly insignificant fault on a powerline can be magnified by other mishaps to the point that it spreads to cut supply across regions or whole nations. Cascade failures have starting points, and in that sense origins, but these need not have much importance in their own right – it is how they contingently interact with the wider system that makes them count.

But clearly not all network failures can be attributed to an insidious growth of problems, others are undone by something closer to blunt trauma. When a violent storm brings down powerlines it is a specific outside force which the system was insufficiently resilient to bear. Even here, however, cascades might be at work, as the sturdiness of a network is undermined by cumulative deficiencies that are only manifested as such when put to the test, otherwise having no apparent consequences.

Networks with an even distribution of links are more vulnerable to failure than those with strong hub structures, where the loss of a few links is proportionately low and more easily sustained (Barabási 2002: 121, passim). However, if a major hub does fail it has a much greater impact than the demise of an ordinary node, immediately breaking the system into smaller and less cohesive islands. The power law distribution is flattened as the peak values disappear, with the result that a network once posed between the centralised and the decentralised veers sharply toward the latter.

We have long focussed attention on how Maya society moved from abundant success to abject failure, but just as crucial a question is why no meaningful recovery took place. The Maya had survived major traumas in the past, most especially the Preclassic–Classic transition that saw sites abandoned across the lowlands amid the birth of a new political order. But now there was no reconstitution. Instead, a once-teeming landscape emptied of people, leaving settlements great and small to be reclaimed by a rejuvenated natural world. The subsequent Postclassic society, conspicuously lacking in dynastic kingship, took root elsewhere, in the northern lowlands and the highlands to the south – regions that played only a minor role in the Classic florescence. Only later did the Maya build on small enduring populations in the Peten to stage a reoccupation, although even then settlement was concentrated around the central lakes.

That the failure advanced without meeting the resistance of a strong hub structure could point a finger back to the demise of the Dzibanche-Calakmul hegemony, the largest and most cohesive political organisation of the Classic Period, a hegemonic empire that was the closest thing to a "Maya Imperium". The pull between centralised and decentralised configurations of power – to be further discussed in Chapters 13 and 14 – resulted in a triumph for less integration. This weakening in the eighth century would have left a dispersed and fractious political landscape more susceptible to failures, whether slow cascades or sudden traumas, in the ninth.

What lay behind this dissolution? One candidate is the soaring population. The hegemonic strategies that worked well at one scale might well have lost their effectiveness at another – as ever more assertive lesser kingdoms now commanded the weight in numbers that favoured resistance over compliance. It is possible that what we see is the low point of a cycle which would, had the collapse not intervened, ultimately have swung back to more integrative schemas and brought powerbrokers back to the fore. But the especially fragmented landscape at the time of the early ninth century crisis can hardly have favoured any coherent or united response to the threats they faced. This low point in political integration should not be discounted as a significant contributor to the fate of the Classic Maya.

We might attribute the conspicuous success of the Classic Maya to their position in the dynamic zone where structural order and disorder meet, the edge of chaos. As both the figurative and literal sense of that term suggests, success here teeters on the brink of failure, where a seemingly minor misfortune or misstep might tip a previously flourishing system into the abyss.

The inference we might draw here is that the centuries of Classic-era florescence, with all its economic surpluses and soaring populations, was not only the consequence of a certain culture and sociopolitical system, it was continually dependent upon them. The organisation of society, its intellectual health, and its ability to support a burgeoning populace were all entwined. Once rent asunder it could not be reconstituted.

THIRTEEN

DEFINING CLASSIC MAYA POLITICAL CULTURE

Although the inscriptions contain bountiful self-representations of royal performances, personas, and encounters, they by no means present an exegesis on the political system as such. To build a view of five centuries and more of societal success we must look beyond these individual expressions to the way that they synergise with other sources, revealing patterns that can only be appreciated in the assemblage. This chapter therefore moves to draw together the different themes examined in Part II so as to offer a synthetic interpretation of Classic Maya political culture, both as it was constituted in the specific unit and the interactive whole.

KING AND COHORT

Monarchy was the central and defining feature of political authority for the Classic Maya and can be traced through its principal manifestations as the individual title-holder (king), the institution (kingship), and the community (kingdom) that he or she commanded, served, and embodied. Indivisible, all pivoted on the physical and metaphysical body of the ruling *ajaw*, "lord". It was bloodline that legitimated candidates, but it was only through ritual action that he, or rarely she, was imbued with the quality of *ajawil* or *ajawlel*, "lordliness" and the sacralised office of "lordship" that followed from it.

Beneath the plumed headdresses and jade ornaments we find a concept of kingship that would be very familiar to Frazer, Hocart, and other noted comparativists. The occupant assumed a fixed social and cultural status, a predetermined role that demanded a lifetime's performance of its script and use of appropriate props – the theatricality of kingship that led Geertz (1980: 120) to call it a "thespian art". The clothes truly make the man or woman as the panoply of crowns, jewels, capes, thrones, sceptres, and other regal accoutrement serve as the visible anchors around which the abstraction of authoritative rule coheres. Such visual distinctions facilitate the reciprocal compact between lord and people: symbols identifying the king's responsibility for communal material and spiritual wellbeing and the reciprocal fealty and flow of resources that supports the governmental hierarchy – so familiar to us from Hobbes and Rousseau. That quid pro quo underpins the system and gives it its ultimate legitimacy, one that generates the willingness to undertake the group action that constitutes the king's extended agency.

Kingship was further materialised in the built environment, the practical and symbolic functions of which were fused and reflexive. Temples, palaces, plazas, and monuments announced a royal space whose accretional development turned power and prestige, history and memory, into tangible artefacts – durable sources of legitimation to those who saw and passed through them. Additionally, the creation and maintenance of those places by the greater populace was an expression of the engagement between ruler and people, highlighting their active collaboration in instantiating his or her power.

In Weber's (1951: 66) conception of the *oikos*, the city is the extended household of the monarch, its population greater or lesser service-providers to a palace economy. The royal seat was the hub of social and courtly business as well as the arena for rites and performances that promoted group identity and cohesion. It was always a religious as well as a physical abode: home to the tombs and shrines of ancestors and "sleeping places" of dynastic and local deities.

These notions of kingly place were bound within the spatial metaphors of *kabch'een*, "earth (and) cave" and *chanch'een*, "sky (and) cave" described in Chapter 6, which were seen as individual possessions of the ruler. The absence of any word in the written corpus for "polity/kingdom" only highlights the fact that the Classic Maya political community was never conceptually uncoupled from a personal dominion (*l'état c'est moi* indeed).

Those relationships between people and places were expressed in ritual practice not least because it is through tangible public acts that proper procedure could be collectively witnessed. It was the king's performances with spiritually charged objects that activated the higher compact between royalty and the divine – not simply as communication with the transcendent, but in actively bringing divine things into being.

The possession and care of specific dynastic and local deities endowed kings with powers quite apart from their place in a greater cosmos inhabited by a remote pantheon. A private religion can serve no political ends, and to successfully legitimise and empower monarchs it must also be the religion of the community, one whose ritual maintenance is therefore a public service for the common good (Baron 2016). Stephen Houston et al. (2003) draw these concepts within Durkheim's (1961: 8, 29, 90) "moral community" as a counterweight to more recent academic concentrations on factionalism, exploitation, and resistance. This does not imply that people were autonoma yoked unthinkingly to the same all-pervasive ideology, but it does posit that the greater part of society subscribed to common aims and values, in which the justifications for inequality were "naturalised" and inscribed in a cultural logic.

As explained in Chapter 5, the sacralised properties expressed by the addition of the *k'uhul*, "holy" prefix to emblem glyphs are not as straightforward as they once appeared. Notably, not one text tells of an inauguration into the status of *k'uhul ajawlel*, "sacred kingship", and the independent *k'uhul ajaw* title was almost exclusively very late in date. When the prefix to emblems appears in the fourth and fifth centuries it tends to differentiate the largest and most dominant kingdoms, with an expansion to those of lesser standing mostly occurring between the sixth and seventh centuries. It continued to be optional to some degree and its presence or absence signals no great qualitative distinction. Indeed, we might see its spread as the same process of title inflation that we see in the late appearances of *k'uhul kaloomte'*, *k'uhul baahkab*, and *k'uhul ti'huun*. Thus, despite the past emphasis on the concept of divine kingship among the Classic Maya, the evidence does not point to this type of quasi-deified status. To understand the sacralised nature of Maya kingship we would do better to look at the intimate relationship between rulers and the gods – examining their roles as the divinely sanctioned propitiators, interlocutors, and "carers" of deities.

The rhetorical focus on a paramount ruler may at times mask a more complex picture of senior and junior kingships, at least at the more powerful polities that could claim the *kaloomte'* status for their kings. Holders of the position *baahch'ok*, the heir apparency, could also be of *k'uhul x ajaw* status and, thus, ostensibly equivalent in rank to the senior king – save for that *kaloomte'* title he alone bore. The kin relations here could be father and son or brother and brother, the latter usually distinguished as older and younger. Something not too dissimilar is attested centuries later for the Postclassic Maya highlands (Las Casas 1909: 615–617).[1] There the ruling structure of the K'iche' polity, based at Utatlan, consisted of a supreme king together with a king-elect, each from a separate lineage, with their sons holding the ranks of major and minor "captain", presumably a military command. Each lord would advance in turn from one position to the next up the hierarchical chain, ensuring that only experienced and proven candidates reached the top – although if they were judged insufficiently capable they could be passed over.

The evidence at hand is consistent with an essentially two-class sociological model (e.g. Thompson 1954: 81; Sanders and Price 1968: 160; Farriss 1984: 167; Marcus 1992a: 221), with the lords a (theoretically) endogamous caste separate from the commoners. Although the great majority of named *ajaw* in the inscriptions were rulers at one level or another, the term actually denoted an elite class of which all nobles were members and permitted to wear its emblematic markers.[2] This collective *ajawtaak*, with the king in some sense the first among equals, points to, but does not yet fully illuminate, historical processes of great relevance to the formation of the Classic system (Freidel and Schele 1988; Martin 2016b).

Epigraphically and iconographically, we know that the *ajaw* status originated in the Preclassic, but in archaeological terms this period shows much less evidence for status differentiation – as exemplified by palatial residences, tombs stocked with riches, and self-glorifying monuments tying kings to the calendar and cosmos – than we find in the subsequent Classic (see p.77). While it is too early to call the Preclassic exclusively "pre-dynastic" – here one thinks, in particular, about the deep history of some successor titles – at most early sites ruling authority was materialised in much less conspicuous ways. The Protoclassic, that tumultuous period covering the collapse of Preclassic society and the birth of the Classic, was one in which the relations between *ajaw* lineages appear to have shifted and a single bloodline gained precedence over others. Emblem glyphs and successor titles are two reflections of that concentration of power, although the force of circumstances meant that the paramountcy often passed through the hands of different families or dynasties (to use the strict sense of that term).

The studies of nobles by Zender and Sarah Jackson offer contrasting but ultimately complementary perspectives, casting light on their religious roles and communal power-broking, respectively. The necessary conclusion is that the aristocracy formed a corporate group in which temporal power and sacred responsibility were indivisible. To be a lord carried the obligation to actively maintain the physical and spiritual wellbeing of the community through ritual practice, as partners with – sometimes as substitutes for – the monarch.

Images of piety and courtly refinement should not, however, distract us from their connection to violence; many lords were warriors as well as priests. Command of armed men, which is to say control over the "means of violence" (Sanderson 1995: 96), is the ultimate guarantee of political power and the *ajawtaak* formed a key section of the king's war-host. While we hear of military specialists bearing the titles of *baahpakal* and *baahtook'*, whose elite status is not explicitly stated and therefore uncertain martial epithets are only carried by *sajal*. The provincial bases of many *sajal*, effectively placing them at the polity borders, may have kept their military duties to the fore as the first line of defence.

The texts are mindful to advertise the king's sanction of advancement to all the major elite offices, even where the qualification appears to have a hereditary basis. In such societies, it would be vital to manage the aspirations and capacities of the cohort, to both reward and placate, balancing the entire group that none grow too powerful or resentful, bringing the most able to the fore while accommodating ancestral rights and privileges. The ability to award or deny status constitutes one of the key prerogatives of sovereigns, the bestowal of multiple titles one option at his disposal. The king would have relied on his title-holders to enact his will and was, in many varied ways, dependent on their loyalty and cooperation. It goes without saying that the relationship between them was marked by rank distinction, but there were also strong elements of co-dependency.

This does not mean that relations were uncontested, especially if a weak or ineffectual king was unable to meet the expectations of his nobles. As much of the recent comparative discussions of palace communities have reminded us (e.g. Houston and Stuart 2001), courts were centres of intrigue where loyalties were suspect and the wary ruler kept almost as close an eye on his inner circle as he did on surrounding kings. To judge from the visual evidence, Classic Maya kings had something to fear. A good number of palace scenes on painted cylinder vessels depict watchful bodyguards crouched behind the ruler's throne, literally minding his back (Miller and Martin 2004: 43, 187) (see Figure 1). Was this a precaution against foreign assassins, or those far better placed to strike, the embittered relative or thwarted noble? These few sketched-in figures are enough to persuade us that there was nothing in the sacral character of kings that rendered them safe from regicide.

The idea of a ruling cohort that fused kings and nobles has much in common with the one described by the political theorists North, Wallis, and Weingast (2009). In their "natural state" – essentially all pre-Modern polities – the primary objective is the control of violence, which is monopolised neither by kings nor by states (as in Weber's famed definition) but by an "elite coalition". This narrow segment of society works together to maintain its power, with the king as much, or more, their representative as their leader: "Even when one actor within the dominant coalition is designated king or is in fact more powerful than the others, that actor is never more powerful as an individual than the coalition of his peers. The king or ruler only becomes powerful if he or she heads a powerful coalition" (North et al. 2009: 31).

This is an important perspective on the issue, but we should not take the idea of solidarity too far. We need to bear in mind that the balance of relations within every coalition would differ, and we have enough comparative material worldwide to convince us that the king–noble relationship could be one of outright competition, as noted above. Who holds the upper hand at any one time depends on a great many variables, not least the personal talents and charisma of the ruler.

Much interest has been directed at what happens when elite solidarity breaks down and its inherent tensions rise to the surface, especially for the part this could have played in the ninth century collapse. The visual prominence given to secondary lords on the monuments of Yaxchilan, where kings are shown in the company of their *sajal* not only at provincial sites but within the capital itself, has been interpreted as a sign of diminished royal authority (Schele 1991d: 86–87). This is seemingly mirrored in larger and more elaborate construction at the ceremonial and palatial cores of those peripheral centres (Golden and Scherer 2013: 414). Similarly, the ornamented palaces of two *ajk'uhuun* from the late history of Copan (Webster 1989) and monuments erected at the peripheral centres such as Los Higos were taken as signs of mounting decentralisation, with a growing population providing too many qualified candidates for too few positions in the hierarchy (Fash 1991a: 175–176; Fash and Stuart 1991: 172–175, 178). Elsewhere, as at Caracol, Ceibal, and Nakum, some of the very last monuments show kings sharing the political stage with other lords.[3]

The late rise in the scale and decorative embellishment of lordly residences finds its highest expression in the composition of sites in the Río Bec region. These centres, not least Río Bec itself, flourished in the late eighth and ninth centuries, when the power of nearby Calakmul was in precipitous decline (see p.141). They show a large number of high-status residences dispersed across the landscape with no discernible hierarchical arrangement between them. The suggestion is that this reflects a new kind of community that had turned away from singular rule toward that of a lordly collective (Michelet, Nondédéo, and Arnauld 2005; Nondédéo, Arnauld, and Michelet 2013). These sites have monuments, and seemingly at least some vestigial form of kingship, but this architectural layout could nonetheless represent some intermediate step in the dissolution of the Classic system, as kings were consigned to near-irrelevance and the *ajawtaak* reclaimed their long-notional equality. The new wealth of these secondary lords, expressed in that increased residential grandeur, is key since this was presumably only possible by garnering income that had previously flowed into royal coffers.

It must also be noted that the sharp distinction in status between lord and commoner we see in the texts is not wholly reflected in material terms, especially in these later times (Jackson 2005: 36, 460–462). Although we can clearly identify high-status residences, the archaeological record shows much finer gradations in the sizes of other homes and signs of wealth than a strict division would imply (Chase 1992; Sharer 1993: 94; Palka 1995: 42; Chase and Chase 1996).

The answer would appear to lie in economic disparities, a situation in which leading commoners – court officials, leading artisans, architects, military specialists, successful merchants, and the like – approached or even exceeded the living standards enjoyed by the lower levels of nobility. The Classic Maya would not be the first society to see aristocratic privilege challenged by an industrious bourgeoisie. Elites of modest means implies downward social mobility, such that a burgeoning middle class could be constituted as much by nobles on the way down as commoners on the way up (Hassig 2016: 144). Such appears to be the case in the Central Mexican *altepetl* where: "The top nobility lived in large sumptuous palaces with numerous servants and clients, whereas the lowest nobles probably lived a life little different from many commoners" (Smith 2000: 587).[4] The possession of titles without the resources that must once have supported them marks a breakdown in the social and economic obligations that originally tied producer to lord and vice versa.

DYNASTY AND LANDSCAPE

The paramount lord and his immediate family, the dynastic lineage, were set apart from the nobility not by their *ajaw* status but by their exclusive right to use emblem glyphs in the forms *x ajaw*, "lord of x" or *k'uhul x ajaw*, "holy lord of x". Where historical processes led to the transfer or division of these ruling lines, producing geographically distant claims to what had originally been localised titles, it becomes clear that emblems came to refer to dynastic identities rather than designations of territory or community. We can use the texts to explore the varied ways in which *histoire événementielle* intervened to configure and reconfigure such identities within spatial as well as temporal dimensions. Processes of polity formation, division, transfer, conjoining, and dissolution can all be discerned and tracked via the dynamics of emblem glyph usage.

To the material markers that show Classic Maya political culture developing from its Preclassic antecedents – the aforementioned emphasis on elite burials and inscribed monuments together with innovations in art, architecture, and ceramic styles – we can now add a small but tantalising set of textual references (p.120). Two key, if still shadowy, locales that were only active between 81–320 CE were of great importance to this development, at least in the patrimonial rhetoric of later times. Wherever these places were situated, the founders of prominent dynasties such as those of Kaanul and Mutul were linked to them, while similar references by other lines seem to have much the same implication. The focus on one particular calendrical juncture, in 159, suggests that it represented some milestone moment or convenient benchmark for the developments that followed. One area, perhaps one lineage, seems to be credited as the source of much Classic-style dynastic rule and thereby the genesis of new polities.

Polities are not formed from slow processes of accretion, but from decisive acts of creation or coalescence (Houston et al. 2003: 214). The difficulties of studying foundational episodes have already been described, but we can look at two cases from a later period where the archaeological and epigraphic records combine in helpful ways. Surveys in the Lacandon region, the area bisected by the Usumacinta River, have revealed significant Preclassic occupation dispersed among many small sites, most of which had been abandoned by 350 CE (Golden et al. 2008; Kingsley et al. 2012: 112–113) (Map 4).

This was closely followed by an aggregation of settlement around newly formed nucleated centres at Piedras Negras and Yaxchilan, whose architecture and ceramic styles were drawn directly from those of the central Peten.[5] This is consistent with the intrusive nature of the Classic phenomenon here and the profound difference in social and political structure between this and what came before. These new magnets for settlement were the result of what has been dubbed a "royal strategy". This was a set of policies that initiated and embedded both the fact and the ideal of dynastic rule through materialisation and a command of landscape: "On arrival in its new seat, a dynasty constructed monumental architecture not only as a symbolic projection of authority, but as a key means of organising society around a royal court and of entrenching such beliefs and practices in fixed spaces" (Houston et al. 2003: 215). The events in this area are reflected, if faintly, by textual references to the ceremonies of an early Piedras Negras king in 297 and the later "settling" at the site we know as Piedras Negras in 454.

A similar royal strategy can be discerned at the south-eastern periphery of the Maya world, where the centres of Copan and Quirigua were established as part of a single project. Texts describe ceremonies of investiture for both kings at a distant locale – apparently Teotihuacan – in 426, followed by a journey that took them to their respective centres in 427. We can find traces of these processes archaeologically, where deep tunnelling at Copan (Sharer et al. 1999) and trenching at Quirigua (Jones and Sharer, forthcoming) have exposed the configurations of these original royal settlements. Indeed, both have produced candidates for their founders' tombs, each buried in the floor of a temple shrine at the eastern edge of their cores. The evidence currently suggests that this act of colonisation into a non-Maya area came from the Peten, with the royal line of Copan having originated at Caracol (Stuart 2007b). Yet the way that both text and image tie the project to the authority and prestige of Teotihuacan is startling. That this was the chosen mode of legitimation, in preference to all the deep historical and mythistorical sources available to the Maya, speaks not simply to the cultural deference paid to these foreign conquerors but, I suspect, to a political grasp that was still felt in the fifth century.

In these ways, Classic-style dynasties expanded out from the central area, although, given the emergence of new royal lines and the infilling of territory throughout the era, the process did not really cease until this proliferation of polities more resembles disintegration. The period at which we see the largest number of active, monument-making sites is that between 751 and 771

(Figure 77), although there is no serious decline until 810, the benchmark for the onset of collapse. On-going processes of political transformation were outlined in Chapters 5 and 6, where it is often the anomalous rather than the standard applications of emblem glyphs and other royal titles that reveal the most.

In Case Study 1 we saw how Palenque, Tortuguero, and Comalcalco used the *baakal* emblem glyph simultaneously during the seventh century and into the eighth. The appearance of this title at Comalcalco evidently came as a result of its conquest by Tortuguero, an event that displaced its original referent of *joykaan*. The situation at Dos Pilas and Tikal in Case Study 11 was more complex, as their rulers' claims to the Mutul title split along fraternal lines, with the breakaway Dos Pilas subject to overlords at Calakmul who supported them in a multi-year conflict. The Mutul schism proved to be a permanent one, lasting right up to the general dissolution of the ninth century, by which point the title passed to smaller upstart neighbours in both cases. Tikal and Dos Pilas kings may have contested exclusive rights to the Mutul epithet, but cannot in any practical sense have claimed to exercise sovereignty over the same realm. The use of the Mutul title by the Dos Pilas princess Ix Wak Jalam Chan at Naranjo is concrete evidence that dynastic affiliation was the sole operating principle.

No dynastic split and transfer was more consequential than the one that saw Kaanul relocate its seat of power some 126 km from Dzibanche to Calakmul (Case Study 6). This may have arisen from another fraternal dispute but, whatever the motivation, civil war led to the establishment of Calakmul as a new home for a venerable dynasty. A local Dzibanche line may well have continued to use the Snake title and be ruled by a surviving branch of the lineage, possibly as part of an extended or discontiguous kingdom. Yet architectural activity at that site was sharply curtailed after the split, and the monumental core at Dzibanche is essentially an Early Classic production (Enrique Nalda, pers. comm. 2004; Nalda and Balanzario 2014). Recognising the ability of one polity to transform itself in this way compels us to abandon whatever remains of the static and territorial understanding of emblem glyphs, necessitating a move toward Classic Maya political units as "royal houses" (Martin 2005a: 12).[6]

The movement of governing seats is a recurring strategy worldwide, accomplished either by building an entirely new site or transforming an existing one. One type, the "disembedded capital", describes a deliberate uprooting of the centre of government from its traditional networks of support, often stripping away ancillary functions such as commerce, industry, and large residential populations in the process (Joffe 1998). The purpose was to solidify the regime's control by physically distancing, and thereby disenfranchising, obstructionist factions and vested interests. The classic example here is Akhenaten's creation of Akhetaten (El-Amarna) in around 1343 BCE. By moving the capital to a virgin site Akhenaten sought to neuter the influence of traditional priestly authority at the former capital of Thebes, and to establish a new powerbase for his religious revolution.

While disembedded capitals look to solve internal problems, a second type of relocation has more outward-looking and strategic objectives (Fox 1977: 70).[7] The kingdoms of Early Medieval India supply some relevant instances. There major conquests enlarging the core territorial domain of the victor, though rare, could be consolidated by transferring the capital to a newly redefined central position (Kulke 1995a: 253–254).[8] This is seen when the Rastrakutas founded the city of Manyakheta in 818 CE, deliberately situating it halfway between their own homeland and that of the Calukyas they had previously defeated and absorbed. Sometimes associated with efforts to reconfigure the administration of the polity and exploit newly acquired resources, such moves were restricted to only the most powerful "imperial" Indian kingdoms.

We gain another perspective on the meaning of cities, transfers, and royal ideology from ancient China where, according to traditional accounts and dating, the Shang dynasty shifted its capital six times between 1766 and 1384 BCE (Chang 1974). Moves were facilitated by the conceptual basis of royal capitals: "The city was the institution, not the site, and its movements from site to site were obviously at the king's option. The layout and structuring of the new capital were designed to serve him as the centre of attention" (Chang 1974: 5). Ancestral shrines and their treasures held pride of place in the new foundations, while identical names were used for the settlement, its ruling lineage, the members of that lineage, and occupants of the settlement. "Thus, the immortality of the king may be said to lie in the immortality of the group, his lineage and his clan, which moved about in space, rather than the immortality of the architecture, which merely served a transient purpose" (Chang 1974: 8).

Classic Maya lords moved across the landscape and established new ruling seats, not only within an era of polity foundation but as part of on-going processes – acts referenced in the inscriptions with the "arrival", "formation", and "settling" terms examined in Chapter 6. Of these, the most telling comes with the negating, forming, or conjuring of k'awiilil, the personification of royal power into its purest form, lightning. The supplanting of Dzibanche by Calakmul is made explicit in these terms. No doubt the creation or recreation of each Classic Maya capital had its own contingent causation, whether it be internal strife and fissions, pressure from local rivals, the expansionist ambitions of non-ruling sons, the pursuit of enhanced resources, or some other perceived advantage or necessity. Even so, we need to square the disjunction between the embeddedness of kingship in concepts of locality with the ability to expediently reconfigure the bonds between lords, lands, and populace. How were such uprootings enacted and justified?

These movements necessarily imply an entourage of supporters, a body of *ajawtaak* together with a larger attachment of retainers and armed men. But another key accompaniment was sacred paraphernalia, the ritual bundles and effigies of dynastic deities that were central to the ideological contrivances of a royal strategy (Houston et al. 2003: 238). It was the personal nature of bonds between lords and gods that strikes to the heart of the conceptual possibility of royal migration – patron gods were transportable not because they could be invested in baggage-sized objects, but because they could now be possessed by people rather than places.

Evidence supporting this view was assembled in Chapter 7 with the ubiquitous "belonging" of gods to lords and the overall intimacy between divinity and the generation of royal identity and authority. These data were augmented by comparative material from Postclassic Highland Guatemala and Central Mexico, where a defining component of migratory narratives was the need to carry and install sources of divine power at each new settlement. In describing the migration of K'inich Yax K'uk' Mo' to Copan the retrospective Altar Q describes a "resting" of *k'awiil ochk'in kaloomte'* at the new site. This could simply be a titular reference to the king, one consistent with his Teotihuacan associations, but the concept of *k'awiil* as embodied power raises the possibility that it is instead a deity image on this occasion (Stuart 2004a: 238).[9] An important clue of a different type comes from Comalcalco, where the patron divinities venerated in its post-conquest *baakal* era include Unen K'awiil, the infant lightning god. This character only otherwise appears at Palenque, where it served the same tutelary role for their *baakal* kings – an indication of the enduring attachment of particular gods to particular dynastic identities.

Were transfers of the elite matched by those of commoners, or were the nobility free agents who moved to assume control over existing, sedentary populations? Migration is a poorly understood topic in the Maya area, given that the markers for population shifts are faint, with close similarities in utilitarian ceramics making for great difficulty in discerning autochthonous change from material imports or incoming producers. The isotopic analysis of human remains offers better prospects, and the growing sophistication of such technologies might yet advance beyond the broad regional signatures we have at present. We do know that the site of Aguateca experienced an influx of people when it was established as a royal centre in the early eighth century and an exodus when it was attacked at the beginning of the ninth (Inomata 2004). However, the material culture of those particular populations says little about their origins, and nothing at all about whether they moved there willingly or were compelled to do so.

The relationship between emblem referents and their locational settings has been most thoroughly explored by Alexandre Tokovinine (2008: 162–227, 2011, 2013: 61–86), who traces their intersections with the concepts of *kabch'een* and *chanch'een* – work paralleled in a number of respects by that of Peter Bíró (2007a, 2011a, 2012a).[10] There is agreement with the general point that referents identify royal houses rather than territorial units, but both emphasise that all such terms began as toponyms, places from which dynastic lines traced their origins, irrespective of where they might subsequently have journeyed. One apt comparison captures the fluidity with which identities of place can be transferred to those of families, dynasties, and regimes, and can thereafter roam across the landscape:

> Here I evoke a well-known example from the history of Europe, namely the case of the Habsburgs. While they originated from today's Switzerland, and [were] named after a castle there, later they ruled in Austria, Spain and Hungary. These new territories were never renamed as Habsburg, though the dynasty rarely called itself otherwise. Eventually, the Habsburgs lost their possessions in Switzerland, but not their name. Also, the house split into more than one branch which kept using the Habsburg name in different territories (Bíró 2012a: 60, n.11).

The distinction between emblem referents that match core toponyms and those that do not – the two sets outlined in Chapter 5 – is therefore explained as royal houses that have a local foundation as opposed to those that have migrated from near or far (Bíró 2007a: 97, 99, 2012a: 59; Tokovinine 2008: 225–227, 2013: 85–86). Thus, dynasties like those of Tikal, Yaxha, and Ceibal claimed in situ descent from ancestral founders, while those who ruled at Calakmul, Dos Pilas, and Cancuen acknowledged that they are transplanted lines whose roots lay elsewhere.[11] Whether those places of origin were real or grounded in myth has been a matter of some debate (Stuart and Houston 1994: 75; Tokovinine 2013: 72–74; Helmke and Kupprat 2016). Even though a few sites took the names of mythic locations, almost all referents appear to be earthly localities to which supernatural meaning and deep histories were subsequently attached (Martin and Velásquez 2016: 27–28).

If we plot the geographical distribution of the two sets we see an admixture, but also a faint but discernible concentration of the first group in the heart of the southern lowlands (Martin 2014a: map 9). The implication is that this is a ghost-like trace of the diaspora of elites from the core to the periphery. Archaeological evidence that the central zone served as the crucible of Classic-style developments comes with the outward movement of Peten-style ceramics which coincided with the formation of new Early Classic polities (see Forsyth 2005: 11, figure 2).[12] In many cases the production of ex novo polities outside the original heartland must have come from the fissioning of bloodlines. Here royals who could not succeed in their homeland, or were sent out in a deliberate policy of expansion and colonisation, founded new dynasties that took the names of the places they settled or seized. An illustrative case is that of K'inich Yax K'uk' Mo'. Even though one of his titles identifies him as a native lord of Caracol, when he takes up his new seat in the far southeast he adopts a quite different political identity.

To track the process more fully we would need both a larger sample and a deeper understanding of naming practices, because not only dynastic names but, from time to time, place-names seem to be transferable, producing a complex situation for disentangling origins and derivations. There is some evidence too that dynastic names made one further semantic shift to become idiomatic references to polities, though seen only in relatively late times and far from systematically employed. One thinks here of the *aj kaanul* who attends the bloodletting event on Dos Pilas Panel 19 (p.105) or the *baakal* location given for the third accession of the Moral-Reforma king (p.252–253). These could be references to the origin places of the Calakmul and Palenque dynasties, respectively, but in these particular contexts are more easily explained as derived toponymics.[13]

But such exceptions provoke a necessary question: what should we infer from the absence of polity-names in the proper sense? At this point definitional issues come into play, with a questioning of whether the Classic Maya had polities as we would normally understand them (Bíró 2007a: 95; Baron 2016: 170–171), or whether emblem referents are connected to the notion of polity in any meaningful sense (Tokovinine 2013: 67). There is a clear risk here of confusing our own, etic categories with the indigenous conceptions of political community to which we decide to attach those terms. Classic Maya political communities were objects whose nature must be discerned, over a millennium after the fact, from the way that identity maps onto materiality and practice in ways that they themselves set out for us.

To take a case raised by Tokovinine (2013: 66–67), we know that the dynasty based at Tamarindito and Arroyo de Piedra lived in propinquity, that is, cheek-by-jowl with the line from Tikal installed at Dos Pilas and Aguateca. Within a very short space of time, probably immediately, the territory of the original pair was entirely enveloped within the effective domain of the intruders (Map 3). While this informs us that one community and its *k'uhul x ajaw* could exist inside that of another, it should not trigger the conclusion that the kings of Tamarindito-Arroyo de Piedra did not rule a polity.[14]

Political enclaves and exclaves were by no means unusual in Mesoamerica, where they reflect a spatial consciousness deeply at odds with the bounded territoriality integral to modern nation states. Communities subject to different Postclassic Central Mexican *altepetl* could be interspersed with no regard to contiguous territory (Gibson 1964: 44–47, figure 2), their political alignments depending instead on personal ties between noble lines. A similar principle was reproduced in the patchwork of *altepetl* composed into regional hegemonies and, most of all, in the grander quilt of the Aztec Empire (Smith 2000: 587). The same non-contiguous allegiances are amply attested among the Postclassic

Maya of Yucatan (Quezada 1993, 2014; Okoshi and Quezada 2008; Graham 2011: 29–46), a pattern very similar to the overlapping lineage connections that defined political loyalties in Bronze Age China (Chang 1983: 374).[15]

A telling, if extreme, illustration of enclaves in Mesoamerica is the case of Tlatelolco, a Mexica commercial centre that occupied the same small island on Lake Texcoco as Tenochtitlan, seat to the Aztec emperor (Barlow 1987). Breaking from its sister city in 1337, Tlatelolco established itself as an *altepetl*, even as it grew into a single conurbation with Tenochtitlan and was increasingly surrounded by the vastness of the Aztec Empire. Yet its independence was such that when Tenochtitlan decided to re-absorb Tlatelolco in 1493 it was obliged to do so by conquest. We might note in passing that enclave polities are no strangers to the modern world, the rare sovereign isolates of San Marino and Lesotho to name two.

The greater point in regard to the Tamarindito-Arroyo de Piedra example is not the political status of enclaves per se, but whether the term polity should be restricted to wholly autonomous entities. We have, it may be recalled, a statement that a king of Arroyo de Piedra was the vassal of another at Dos Pilas – one small part of the data in Chapter 10 dispelling the idea that even major Classic Maya kingdoms enjoyed complete independence. If a criterion of total autonomy were to be comprehensively applied, we would quickly find ourselves very short on polities. What is really at stake here are degrees of sovereignty, a key issue to which we will be turning in Chapter 14.

As interesting as enclaves are exclaves, sites with a direct attachment to a distant power. La Corona was a close semblant of one that lay beyond Calakmul's immediate zone of administrative control. La Corona is a fascinating and enigmatic site, small in terms of both monumental architecture and surrounding settlement, but extravagantly endowed with inscribed monuments (Canuto and Barrientos 2013; Stuart, Canuto, and Barrientos 2015). Almost all of the latter were anciently uprooted and reset in new locations, probably in the ninth century. Together with previously known looted monuments, they tell us that La Corona had its own dynastic *ajaw* bloodline, that its kings performed all the standard royal rituals, and that they venerated their own patron deities.

However, at no point do they use an emblem glyph of *sak nikte' ajaw*, instead employing the *k'uhul sak wahyis* title carried by some other Calakmul clients.[16] This poorly understood epithet was regionally restricted and predates the move of the Kaanul kingdom to Calakmul. On balance, we should regard La Corona as a polity, even if it barely seems to meet the minimum requirements discussed in Chapter 5. It might be necessary to also consign it to a separate category of subordinate exclaves, one whose shared dynastic symbols signal an especially close colonial bond (see p.166).

The La Corona texts give an extraordinary prominence to Calakmul, detailing the many ways in which the two centres were connected. These include intermarriage, joint ritual activities, royal visits in both directions, and the installation of at least one La Corona ruler under the Calakmul king in 675 – doubtless a regular occurrence. This outsized significance for such a small centre suggests strategic importance, perhaps because it fell on a communication route Calakmul had established with sites far to the south, skirting an area of Tikal control, as discussed in Case Study 9. The late shift to a Tikal affiliation for La Corona, noted there, is especially significant in this light, suggesting its continued relevance to cross-regional traffic and perhaps some symbolic importance as well.[17]

ENGAGEMENTS

Throughout this book, I have stressed the importance of perceiving the Classic Maya polity not in isolation but as part of a collective body. That perspective is built from what we know of inter-polity contacts, the cooperative as well as the conflictive, the fleeting as well as the enduring. We must assimilate the evidence for marriage, diplomacy, warfare, economics, and shared cultural traits, and consider them as flows of people, materials, and information across the landscape, blurring their separation as topics by viewing them together under a higher-order umbrella of "engagements". This way of thinking encourages us to see each of these activities as a means rather than an end, with the pursuit of objectives potentially to be achieved through alternative methods or by synergised strategies.

In a system of multiple polities, each negotiating its position vis-à-vis its neighbours and more distant powers, as well as managing the internal dynamics of ranking lineages, the choice of any royal marriage partner would be a highly calculated one. In Chapter 8 we discussed how dynastic marriage operates within two dimensions, horizontally to generate alliance and vertically to secure descent. The scale and relative importance of these axes vary depending on the goals in mind and the circumstances at hand. For all the incompleteness of the epigraphic record, its rhetorical choices – what it chooses to say and not to say – give access to some of the main conventions and aims underlying marriage.

In the alliance mode the effects are immediate, whereas an orientation towards descent could take many years to bear fruit, if at all. For all the energies and care put into matchmaking, the hopes behind any particular union could be thwarted by all manner of exigencies, with plans abandoned and remade before ever reaching the written record. The rarity of recorded rites of betrothing and union clearly indicate that political alliance was not a rhetorical priority, and only the ultimate elevation of offspring to rulership gave them significance. The elite would also have been aware that efforts to create political alliances or reduce hostility through intermarriage were often short-lived or wholly unsuccessful. As seen in the case of Naranjo and Yaxha, common blood could be a feeble inhibition to its shedding in battle.

Polygyny is a schema that maximises the resources offered by marriage in two respects. First, it opens the door to a mixed strategy in which the political advantages of one kind of partnership can be blended and counterpoised with those of another. Here endogamy meets the needs of internal cohesion – solidifying a powerbase by keeping the bloodline within a local cabal so that "the rulership would not go elsewhere" – while exogamy engages with the opportunities of regional networks. The second effect of polygyny is simply to increase the supply of legitimate offspring, which feed into the next generation of marital manoeuvring and present opportunities for more strategic matches within a widening web of kin ties. The inherent weakness of polygyny is that in extending legitimacy to several women and their children it fosters destabil-ising competition for the succession. But this problem can be mitigated by the historically well-attested solution of establishing one wife as paramount. If her offspring were routinely favoured, half-sibling rivalries could be kept in check – in theory if not always in practice.

These strategies are only visible in the case of daughters, leaving the situation with most sons much less clear. Some resided at court as princely *baahch'ok* in the service of their ruling brothers and as kings-in-waiting, occasionally as junior kings. But other "spare" males were presumably absorbed into lesser positions within the polity, engaged in exogamous matrilocal marriages, or went out to create new dynasties in a dispersal of princes who could not inherit at home. All three processes were probably at work, but none of them is strongly reflected in the record. With polygyny increasing the supply, the percentage of princelings would have steadily grown and required some management of their number. At some point a rule of disenfranchisement would need to kick in, a degree of separation from the patriline at which royal status was lost, lest the polity be overrun with entitled descendants.

We might expect exogamous marriage to be a prime integrative mechanism across the Maya landscape, in particular that powerful polities such as Calakmul and Tikal would extend hypogamous ties to help solidify their position. The relative rarity of such links raises important questions about how the goals of descent and alliance were balanced by the Classic Maya. On the one hand, we have to consider under-reporting by offspring who did not find their mother's foreign origins politically beneficial and worth publicising, on the other that endogamy was truly the preferred pattern for principal, heir-bearing wives. If the latter scenario predominates then the sample would faithfully reflect that fewer rulers were born to foreign women. Where a king does take a hypogamous partner as his principal queen it could be a sign of especially close affiliation or deep subordination. Exogamy would normally be concen-trated at the secondary level, where incoming brides played a part in interdynastic manoeuvrings in the alliance dimension but were not expected to contribute to the dimension of descent. Several of the exogamous unions we do see may never have been intended to produce an heir and did so, and entered the record, only after some unexpected misfortune.

Yet there is good reason to believe that the first scenario plays a significant role and that exogamous brides are indeed under-represented in the corpus. Not only is the origin of Ix Uh Chan of Yaxchilan left unstated on eight of the nine occasions on which she is mentioned, but the references to foreign maternal grandfathers for two Tikal kings reveal that two royal mothers were outsiders even though they carried no titles that identify them as such. This means that the default assumption that spouses with no given affiliation were local is unwarranted, and we are left unable to gauge the true percentage of interdynastic unions.

Marital unions are one of the more visible products of diplomacy, but all parties in a multi-polity system must put effort into personal contacts with their neighbours and more distant powers (Schele and Mathews 1991). These exchanges offer the chance to influence opinion and share information, settle disputes and negotiate agreements. Such contacts were rarely the stuff of patrimonial rhetoric, though the group of Yaxchilan lords attending the court of Piedras Negras is one exception (Figure 24). Most examples are seen on painted vessels, where we find visitors with titles of *ebeet*, "messenger" or *muut*, literally "bird" but meaning "messenger" or "emissary" (Houston et al. 2006: 241–251) (Figure 78).

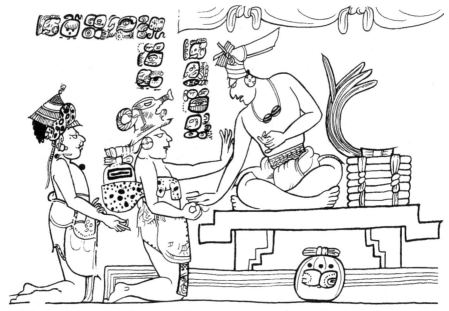

78 An *ebeet* messenger in the service of Yuknoom Yich'aak K'ahk' of Calakmul delivers a gift or bundle of tribute to a Tikal lord on the vessel K5453. (Drawing by Mark Van Stone after a roll-out photograph by Justin Kerr)

In this vein, the murals of Room 1 at Bonampak show a line of visiting *ebeet*, seemingly tributaries from lesser kingdoms (Houston 2012: 164; Miller and Brittenham 2013: 77–78). Most fit within the pattern of hierarchical interaction noted in Chapter 10, in which kings or their representatives visit foreign sites to witness the rituals of their patrons.

Perhaps the most interesting and unexpected contact comes on the hiero-glyphic stairway at El Palmar, with the journey of a lordly *lakam* to faraway Copan in 726 (p.94). The visitor would certainly have seen the first version of the Copan Hieroglyphic Stairway, commissioned by Waxaklajuun Ubaah K'awiil in 710.[18] That inscription, already hundreds of glyph-blocks in length, was a dynastic history of such scale and ambition it must have been the talk of the Maya world. Indeed, upon his return the *lakam* built his own, considerably more modest, set of inscribed steps detailed his own lordly lineage in a simple, but still rather telling, example of how the periphery could inspire developments at the core.

But what was the purpose of his visit? The text does not say directly, yet toward its conclusion there is a curious reference to the "guardianship" of Waxaklajuun Ubaah K'awiil (Tsukamoto and Esparza 2015: 45). Guardianship could arise as a consequence of defeat and capture in war (p.205), or to the poorly understood realm of protective lordly supervision (p.105).[19] Damaged and missing portions of the inscription leave the identity of the guardian open to debate and gives no real lead as to which kind of relationship this was. It is certainly tempting to see the *lakam* noble as the possessor in question, but the relevant section is closely followed by the name of Yuknoom Took' K'awiil of Calakmul – without doubt the overlord of El Palmar – and he presents a more compelling candidate.

Whatever this enigmatic tie represents, it connects the political affairs of the far southeast to those of the central Peten. This is not unique. Copan is among four kingdoms mentioned on two small bones recovered from the tomb of the Tikal king Jasaw Chan K'awiil, the others being Palenque, Edzna, and Altun Ha (Barthel 1968a: 187–189; Tokovinine 2008: 243–244, 2013: 87–89; Pallán 2012: 98–99; Helmke, Guenter, and Wanyerka 2018: 122–124). Although the meaning of these texts remains opaque, the geographical distribution of these kingdoms to the south, west, north, and east – reminiscent of the four cardinally specified polities on Copan Stela A, created at much the same time (p.25) – serve to place Tikal at a symbolic centre.[20] Perhaps in the wake of its triumph over Calakmul in 695 we are seeing a Tikal-centric view of the eighth century Maya world. The symbolism may also coincide with a historical reality, perhaps even identifying allies that contributed to Tikal's victory. Tikal's ties to Copan might even be relevant to the suspiciously timed mention of Calakmul's Wamaaw K'awiil at Quirigua just two years before the rebellion of 738, an event that took place little more than a decade after the El Palmar mission to Copan (see p.257).

Inter-polity contacts could also be manifested in ritualised sport. Here several varieties of ballgame were covered by the single verb *pitz*, "to play" (Miller and Houston 1987; Stuart 1987: 25). One form involved the torture and execution of war captives, another a mythic re-enactment in which lordly players took on the guise of the Hero Twins or their Underworld foes. Our interest focuses on a third type, royal visits and the games that were played, whether symbolically or in reality, between different kings. In a number of cases these carry hierarchical overtones. For example, we have ballgame scenes from La Corona, Zapote Bobal, Uxul, and El Peru that show Calakmul kings interacting with their vassals (Martin 2001d: 179; Miller and Martin 2004: 91; Tunesi 2007; Grube and Delvendahl 2011; Lee and Piehl 2014: 95–98). An example in which a Calakmul monarch plays against his counterpart at distant Tonina may, or may not, be less asymmetrical (Stuart 2013; Helmke et al. 2015).

A major goal for diplomacy would be to defuse the potential for conflict among so many closely spaced polities. Warfare is an engagement of immense complexity, whose proximate causes can be diverse and highly contingent. The emergence of a substantial body of epigraphic data, combined with iconographic and archaeological information, illuminates some portions of the issue while still leaving much in shadow. We know that warfare was a recurring feature of Classic Maya life, but the lack of detail in the texts makes it hard to appreciate why it was initiated, how it was conducted, or precisely what it sought to achieve.

The analysis in Chapter 9 found strong support for earlier proposals of a seasonal distribution to conflict, as well as an absence of any discernible cosmological determination. Variation across the year is certainly related to the ease or difficulty of travel in its contrasting parched and sodden periods, but we should not discount the contribution of the synchronous agricultural cycle to motivate the theft and destruction of crops, or for its impact on the availability of men for larger scale campaigns. The analysis also serves to question the frequently made assertion that textual records of warfare reached a peak at the very end of the Late Classic Period – a conclusion that relies on just two atypical inscriptions. If both these and one mid-era outlier are disregarded the sample instead points to a fairly consistent incidence of recorded warfare from the beginning of the seventh until the beginning of the ninth century. The re-examination of the data confirms the long-noted rarity of Early Classic war accounts that, as a major thematic innovation of the Late Classic, demands explanation.

Since warfare itself clearly has a deep history in Maya culture, attested not least by major Preclassic fortifications, our interest must focus on why it increasingly became a topic of the inscriptions. The move from the heroic generalities in iconography to the specified successes in text was a deliberate transformation in patrimonial rhetoric for which fashion seems an insufficient motivation. The phenomenon does not occur in isolation, since it is matched by changes in the representation of martial themes, which were almost exclusively associated with Teotihuacan-dressed warriors throughout the fifth century but – later "quotations" aside – generally shifted to Maya-style representations from the sixth century onwards.

The answer, I suspect, lies in historical processes. Society and politics were beginning to change at this time, with strong demographic growth and an expanding number of political players. The rise of Dzibanche, the first Kaanul capital, is evident by the mid-sixth century and must be seen in the context of changes at Tikal and the withdrawal of its foreign sponsors. It is probably no coincidence that by far the earliest known narrative of campaigning – which is to say one that specifies dates and verbs, together with the names of both an agent and his victims – is the Captive Stairway at Dzibanche. As we saw in Case Study 6, its dating is uncertain, but its style suggests that it could be as old as the fourth century. Might this reflect the first stirrings of a military machine, a kingdom with a special proficiency in war that would ultimately carry it to regional dominance?

The developing competition between Tikal and Dzibanche would have had rippling effects for a larger number of polities, which were forced to negotiate or align their positions accordingly; not least because these powerful actors pursued advantage in distant realms. What was missing from earlier views of Classic Maya warfare was a sense that conflict could have these broader strategic aims and lead to longer-term shifts in regional power relations. The hegemonic model conceives of polities both willing and able to engage in this kind of competition, and capable of realising the sustained benefits that can accrue from violence or the threat of violence.

Even so, this does not mean that warfare in the Classic era was necessarily rife. If we look to the polities subject to Calakmul in the seventh century there is a marked lack of recorded conflicts between them, suggesting that one consequence of hegemonic success could well be a curtailment rather than an exacerbation of violence. By reducing competition between their subjects, dominant powers would create zones of common interest that encouraged communication and cooperative behaviours. This reduction in the security threat would maximise economic gains, providing subject elites with some measure of compensation for the exactions of their overlord, who naturally benefitted most of all.

If we are looking for a motor for political violence we have to look at these economic ramifications (p.231–232). Worldwide, expansionist political systems that lack the coercive and bureaucratic structures to achieve integration, or simply eschew their logistical costs, pursue tribute as their primary means of economic exploitation (Amin 1976: 13; Wolf 1982: 76–88; Haldon 1993). Indeed, the comparative evidence is so consistent that we might easily conclude that an express purpose of hierarchic orders was the upward transfer of wealth and resources from clients to patrons.

The first signs of a Classic Maya tribute system emerged on painted vessels, where scenes of courtly life frequently include visitors to an enthroned ruler who present tied bundles or stacks of cloth (Schele and Miller 1986: 144, 153, 218; Reents-Budet 1994: 262). These items are often topped by symbols of wealth and preciousness: *Spondylus* shells or sprays of rare quetzal feathers. Additionally, sacks are occasionally marked by bar-and-dot numerals in units of *pik* or 8,000, a feature typically reserved for loads of cacao beans, which were widely used as a currency in historical times (Houston 1997b) (Figure 78). One scene even includes a scribe or official who appears to be checking the tally of received goods in a book (Schele and Miller 1986: 144). Explicit textual evidence later emerged, including references to the words *pat/patan*, "tribute" and *tojol*, "payment" (Stuart 1995: 352–374, 1998: 384, 410–416), as well as *yubte'*, "tribute cloth" (Houston, in Stuart 1995: 359). In one vase scene three officials of the *lakam* rank deliver – literally *tz'ahpaj*, "plant, set down" – a load of *patan* at the foot of a king's dais (Stuart 1995: 356).[21] We earlier heard about tribute deliveries to a dais or litter (p.260), in which large numbers of *ikaatz*, "cargo, bundles" containing precious feathers and pelts were *ak'*, "given" (Le Fort and Wald 1995).[22]

Tribute systems are documented throughout Mesoamerica, where they were the basis of political economies at the local, regional, and pan-regional scale. Exaction was the presiding objective behind the expansion of the Aztec Triple Alliance, a rapacious conqueror intent on enriching its imperial core at the expense of other polities, some at great distance (e.g. Berdan 1975; Calnek 1982; Hassig 1985, 1988; Voorhies 1989; Berdan et al. 1996). Individualised demands were made of subject tributaries that took account of local resources and travel distance, ensuring that bulk subsistence goods, raw materials, craft-worked valuables, and labour were delivered to the capital Tenochtitlan according to a strict schedule. This was no innovation in the region, but an existing practice taken to new heights. The way in which tributary polities were required to deliver non-local resources presents a particular kind of economic control, one which stimulated regional commerce (Berdan et al. 1996).

Aztec rulers also made significant investments in agricultural infrastructure and water management, including dykes and aqueducts, converting tribute income and labour into lasting economic enrichment and thereby political leverage. It has been argued that control over water supplies, including the building of reservoirs, was also a means of tribute conversion for the Maya, an instrument of kingly power embedded in royal ideology through water-focussed supernatural associations and their appropriate rituals (Lucero 1999, 2003; Lucero and Fash 2006).

Whatever scale a Classic Maya tribute economy attained it must be considered within a more diverse mix of economic activities and obligations. Although archaeology and ethnohistory teach us a good deal about the fundamentals of Maya subsistence and practical living, precisely how the agrarian base was organised in terms of land-tenure and ownership, how produce was distributed and exchanged, the role and scale of long-distance trade in bulk goods and preciosities, local resource exploitation and manufacturing specialisations, the emphasis on cash crops such as cacao and raw materials such as cotton – all of which offered a prospective tax base to support the royal court – remain among the darkest of our dark matters (see McAnany 1993, 2010; Jones 1999; Graham 2002, 2006, 2011; Masson and Freidel 2002; Houston and Inomata 2009: 218–249, 250–256; Garraty and Stark 2010; Hirth and Pillsbury 2013; Smith 2014; Baron 2018a, 2018b).

A topic of much contention has been market exchange in the Maya area, where archaeological (Masson and Freidel 2012; Hirth and Pillsbury 2013; King 2015) and epigraphic (Martin 2007b, 2012c: 80; Tokovinine and Beliaev 2013) data are finally beginning to lift a veil. Phosphate residues suggest that markets were held in an open plaza space at Chunchucmil (Dahlin et al. 2007; Dahlin 2009) and in similar locations at other sites (Terry, Blair, and Coronel 2015). Such locations were probably a common venue for such activity, where temporary stalls composed of pole-supported awnings and unfurled mats would be all that was necessary in terms of facilities. However, an extensive masonry complex with covered colonnades in the East Plaza of Tikal has been identified as a permanent marketplace (Jones 1996, 2015). Its first phase was constructed sometime before 700, but it underwent considerable redevelopment during the eighth century, expanding from a concentric central complex to surround the larger plaza on several sides (Jones 1991: 119).

Much smaller, stall-like spaces have been found within the central plaza of the minor site of El Pueblito (Juan Pedro Laporte, pers. comm. 2008), as if those temporary awnings and mats had now been petrified in stone. It has been argued that substantial facilities like those of Tikal may have impeded the recognition of comparable, but less impressive, installations elsewhere (Becker 2015).[23] Indeed, lidar surveys are beginning to suggest that dedicated marketplaces might be more common than previously thought, at least in the northern zone (Ruhl, Dunning, and Carr 2018).

At Calakmul, Ramón Carrasco has excavated a large restricted-access quadrangle covering some 2.5 hectares dubbed the Chiik Nahb complex (see Figure 81). It features long rows of north–south aligned buildings, with at least one placed east–west that is colonnaded in the style of Tikal. Situated on the centreline is a three-tiered platform, Structure 1, that had been overbuilt and renewed on seven occasions. Its third version was covered in an unprecedented series of paintings showing scenes of men and women engaged in the acts of

79 View of the murals painted on the southeast corner of Structure Sub 1–4, the focal building of the Chiik Nahb market complex at Calakmul. (SM/Proyecto Arqueológico Calakmul)

serving, consuming, transporting, and displaying foods and other materials, including textiles and ceramics (Carrasco, Vázquez, and Martin 2009; Carrasco and Cordiero 2012) (Figure 79). The proportion of women, which constitute about a third of the participants, is the highest seen in any programme of Maya art.

The captions applied to the "presenters" of goods are mostly labels that identify specialisations, including *aj ixiim*, "maize person", *aj jaay*, "clay vessel person", *aj waaj*, "tamale person", and *aj mahy*, "tobacco person" (Martin 2012c). One of these scenes shows a male with a basket and spoon labelled *aj atz'aam*, "salt person" – portioning out a commodity presumably transported from the coast, given that rock salt from the highlands was considerably more distant (Figure 80).[24] These ascribed terms are similar to those used for Maya market vendors today and the nature of the pictured scenes strongly suggests that the Chiik Nahb complex was a dedicated marketplace (Martin 2007b, 2012c: 80, Martin, in Boucher and Quiñones 2007: 48).[25] In all probability, Structure 1 was a market temple or administrative building and the paintings a lively evocation of the activities that took place all around it. The style of the paintings and the depiction of particular pottery forms are broadly in line with the ceramics excavated from that building phase and can be placed to 620–700 (Boucher and Quiñones 2007: 49).

Thus, although many Mayanists have resisted the idea of large-scale commercial engagements and the significant movement of goods across the region,

80 Scene from the northeast corner of Chiik Nahb Structure Sub 1–4 at Calakmul, featuring an *aj atz'aam* or "salt person". (SM/Proyecto Arqueológico Calakmul)

fresh evidence compels a reassessment of that position. It is interesting and surely significant that it should be Calakmul and Tikal that exhibit major market infrastructure of this type. We can venture that hegemonic powers built these complexes as strategic efforts to centralise regional exchange networks under their control and were further manifestations of their political ambitions.

Finally, if the Classic Maya polity was indeed embedded in networks and interdependencies in the way I have described them – in which analysis needs to be focussed on the cohesive whole as much as it is on the constituent parts – then we will need to consider the ideational bonds that generated and maintained that collective sense of identity. To do so it will be useful to adopt and adapt Durkheim's "moral community" concept, raising it to this culture-wide level as an encompassing "moral order" to the Classic Maya system.

By this I mean shared rules, norms, protocols, standards, and conventions of engagement in the widest sense; the ethical values by which kingdoms co-identified and co-existed in their world, as they were embedded in shared understandings of the cosmos, time, and the place of kingship within both. Indeed, the conceptual order set out in the arrangement of thirteen kingships on the circular stone at Altar de los Reyes, a representation of space-time as royal-ritual circuit, unified yet separate, might be seen to encapsulate that very notion. Whatever led the Protoclassic-era *ajawtaak* to generate new political practices and spread from the central southern lowlands, they did so carrying a set of ideas about what lordship entailed and laid claim to, providing a template from which the king and cohort-based Classic polity was propagated.

The overt expressions of that political culture are to be found in the works of that lordly cohort. But another, much less visible, group was pivotal for the development, preservation, and expansion of its ideals and the creation of those expressions: the literati. Seldom nobles themselves, these professionals serviced courtly business, keeping the records required for diplomacy, financial accounts, and the chronicling of historical events. More than this, they conducted the active scholarship necessary for astrological and calendrical calculation and its interpretation, supplying the various needs of divination and ritual. In this way they served as a collective cultural memory and consciousness, both a repository for core concepts and where intellectual and artistic innovations took place. It was the engagement and discourse of these scholars, savants, theologians, aesthetes, and learned practitioners across the Maya world, discussed in Chapter 12, which produced the cultural unity of a people, society, and civilisation.

ASYMMETRIES OF POWER

The evidence presented thus far establishes that the Classic Maya were, from beginning to end, divided into many small polities and that there were significant disparities in power between them, with some exercising a far-reaching ability to subordinate others. Communities which behaved as sovereign entities in every other sense of that term were prepared to acknowledge that their rulers were owned by others, or that their coronations were sanctioned or directed by such outsiders.[26] Having combined the hierarchical statements with military records in Case Studies 11–14 we can appreciate their close connection, serving to establish that asymmetrical relations were predominantly pragmatic and political rather than idealised and symbolic.[27] But what allowed those asymmetries of power to develop and to what degree did coercive and voluntaristic factors draw subjects into the thrall of a suzerain? What were the contributing social, political, and economic factors behind those textual and material expressions?

The first point to make is that the Classic Maya system described here is hardly out of character for the Mesoamerican region. One can take notice of the situation prevailing in the fifteenth-century Valley of Mexico, where 80–100 distinct *altepetl* were linked into a dense network in which patron–client relationships were commonplace, indeed, verged on the universal: "Every people seems to be the vassal of another and stronger one" (Davies, in Bray 1972: 164). The sources are littered with accounts in which high lords installed lesser lords and vassals (e.g. Ixtlilxochitl 1952: I:119–289, II:104; Chimalpahin 1965: 113, 218–219, 222–223, 233; Schroeder 1991: 83). To quote only one, the sixteenth century indigenous writer Chimalpahin tells us: "The kings of Anáhuac said, 'The Chalca are our forebears; long ago, all the *tlatoque* [plural of *tlatoani*] came here to be installed, and 25 *altepetl* were subjects of the Chalca'" (Schroeder 1991: 152). Indeed, there is even an account of such a system among the Postclassic Maya. Bartolomé de Las Casas (1909: 616), writing soon after the conquest of the highlands of modern-day Guatemala, describes one K'iche' ruler of the fifteenth-century as having "placed, confirmed, approved, and authorised all the lords, rulers and jurisdictions of the provinces and neighbouring kingdoms, such as Tecuciztlán (Rabinal), Guatemala (Kaqchikel) and Atitlán (Tz'utujil)".[28] When it comes to Mesoamerican power politics, Classic Maya practice seems not so much the exception as the rule.

The point of formalising political relations in this way is to convert naked power into authority, insofar as coercion can be made legitimate – creating duties and obligations where previously there had been none. We might still read the underlying situation as exploitative, but it has been moved from intimidation to some higher level, and as such invokes very different processes. With Case Study 14 providing the only exceptions, vainglorious references to a ruler's own political dominions are entirely lacking in the texts, with all statements of inter-polity hierarchy recorded by clients. Running counter to the expectations of propaganda, it is necessary to ask what motivated vassals to record their own subordination? Some may have wanted to curry favour with their overlords with a show of obeisance, while others may serve as a warning to rivals, both within the kingdom and without, that the king had a powerful protector. Where we can discern the purpose with confidence it is explanatory, offering background information to help explicate or justify a contemporary context, especially when that focuses on a shift of allegiance.

These shifts and the interweaving of power politics and warfare are vital to understanding the forces at work in building and breaking hegemony – processes we see at work in the heart of the central lowlands. We are told that the king of Caracol was installed in office by his counterpart at Tikal in 553, an event that goes unrecorded on contemporary Caracol monuments and only fortuitously documented in two later accounts. As soon as 556 Tikal launches an attack against a now only partially legible victim that seems to be a lord of Caracol. This appears to supply the narrative casus belli for a more decisive action, the star war assault on Tikal that took place in 562. That defeat evidently had dire consequences for Tikal, initiating its 130-year monument hiatus and an interruption to its dynastic line – perhaps even the installing of a compliant ruler subject to its conqueror (Jones 1991: 117–118; Martin 2008c, 2017b; Martin and Beliaev 2017). Although the name of that victor is almost illegible, the finger must point to the major beneficiary of Tikal's downfall, the Kaanul dynasty, which thereafter rose to pre-eminence in the lowlands. In 619 a recently elevated Caracol king, a son of the one installed by Tikal in 553, had his rule sanctioned by the king of Dzibanche, confirming the switch from one hegemonic sphere to that of another.

In the second half of the fifth century Tikal and Naranjo were linked by marriage, with one Tikal king making several references to his descent from a Naranjo monarch through the maternal line (Martin 2005b: 8, n.15; Tokovinine and Fialko 2007: 10–13). This implies a political connection, yet when we next hear of Naranjo's interests they lie elsewhere, with Dzibanche installing a boy-king at the city in 546. The loyalty of this character was maintained through the reigns of four successive Kaanul overlords, lasting until at least 612. However, the outbreak of the Kaanul civil war soon after 630 made Naranjo a target and it was seized by one of the rival claimants in 631. Our knowledge of this action comes via two accounts produced by Caracol, which cites it in association with its own war successes over Naranjo in 626 and 627. This clearly suggests that Caracol supported the Calakmul-based Kaanul faction, the winners of the internecine struggle.

What these fragmentary episodes reveal is something more than the simple turbulence of antagonistic kingdoms. We have installation ceremonies defining hierarchical relationships that were subsequently negated and met with a violent response. That clients chose to secede and resist is a strong argument for the compulsory nature of patron–client relations, since purely consensual ties could have no penalty for departure. It also suggests that the terms of these relations were sufficiently onerous that escaping them was worth the risk of retaliation. At least in the case of Caracol, the breakdown of its relationship with one hegemon was directly followed by a new one with its bitter rival.

This mirrors what we see out in the west at Moral-Reforma and a sequence of events that constitute a veritable smoking gun for the hegemonic interpretation of Classic Maya politics – given that it includes features anticipated by the model that were unseen until its contents came to light (Martin 2003c). Whereas the switching of allegiance from one patron to another can only be detected between two reigns at Caracol, Moral-Reforma describes such a move within a single tenure. It offers the further revelation that transferring kings underwent formal ceremonies of "reinstallation"; repeated crownings that involved the bestowal of alternative names. A new fealty could evidently require a transformation of royal identity, the persona beholden to one overking cast aside for another.

This single account allows us to make certain deductions about the shift in relative power between Calakmul and Palenque, but the ability to draw on texts from other sites in Case Study 12 provides a multivocal perspective and permits us to do much more. Collectively they portray a wider struggle between the polities of present-day Tabasco and a trio of outside powers, Palenque, Calakmul, and Piedras Negras. Military action against Santa Elena, Moral-Reforma's near-neighbour, is followed by the latter's subordination to Calakmul by a matter of weeks in 662, while Moral-Reforma's realignment to Palenque in 687 follows hard on the heels of the military renewal of that kingdom and within a year or two of the death of its original Calakmul patron.

But what was Calakmul's interest in the Tabascan plain, an area distant from any direct security concern – one that had also featured in the Dzibanche attacks on Palenque in 599 and 611? Deep alluvial soils make Tabasco prime agricultural land, and it was renowned in historical times for its abundant cacao crop. But its unique geographical feature is the confluence of Usumacinta and San Pedro Mártir Rivers. Whereas much of the Usumacinta is fast-flowing and impeded by rock-strewn rapids, the San Pedro Mártir is a placid watercourse that provides the easiest passage between the central lowlands and the western Maya world. This, in turn, offers access to the Gulf Coast and Central Mexico and the cultural and commercial contacts they represent.

A similar interest can be discerned a few years earlier when Calakmul orchestrated the renewal of kingship at Cancuen. Positioned on the upper reaches of the Pasión River, at a southern gateway to the resource-rich highlands of modern-day Guatemala, Cancuen would be an ideal location to secure trade routes. Indeed, excavations demonstrate that this site was deeply involved in the importation, processing, and transhipment of at least two distinctive highland products, obsidian and jade (Demarest 2013b; Demarest et al. 2014). The unusual design of Cancuen, with its isolated and outsized palace, is plausibly linked to its specialised function as an economic outpost; perhaps by housing elites who actively managed distant trade relations and/or local production. The site came into its own and expanded its palace only after Calakmul's eighth century decline, presumably because it now had independent control of its commercial life. In former times Cancuen would be the last stop on the proposed north–south "royal road" linking Calakmul to the highlands via a series of client kingdoms (p.189–190). Such distant projections of power make most sense as strategic interventions that put flows of resources and communication routes under Kaanul control.

It is important to note that Calakmul's intervention in Tabasco was conducted in concert with Piedras Negras, one of the occasions in which we see an ally or affiliate actively supporting a major power. This might reflect the logistical difficulties of operating at a distance of some 160 km from home, and it will be recalled that the still more distant Dzibanche might have been allied with Santa Elena in one of its two expeditions against Palenque. Santa Elena itself could marshal a confederated force, as we saw from the varied origins of the captives that were seized together with its king in 659. Earlier, Caracol went into battle "with" a Kaanul lord in 627, while the pivotal clash between Tikal and Calakmul in 695 produced a Naranjo prisoner – a further indicator of joint campaigning by major kingdoms.

Yet only a few other cooperative alliances can be identified in the inscriptions, far fewer than we might expect to see in a multi-polity system, where a major hegemon such as Calakmul should have been able to muster a composite army drawn from its many clients. One explanation for this absence is suggested by the records at Dos Pilas, discussed in Case Study 11. Its long war against Tikal was largely synchronous with the one its Calakmul patron fought against the same enemy, which the texts treat as entirely separate campaigns. Here the focus of patrimonial rhetoric on the heroic efforts of a single commissioning king could serve to separate and under-represent joint actions and the contributions of subordinate allies. Moreover, if client kings regularly contributed warriors to a patron's army rather than taking to the field themselves, the anomaly of the missing alliances would be even easier to explain. A third possibility to consider is that the ideology of warrior kingship placed an emphasis on almost gladiatorial individual over allied action, thus maintaining a certain purity of king-upon-king and deity-upon-deity encounters in at least some instances.

Suzerains bore the title *kaloomte'*, the only status ranked above that of *k'uhul x ajaw* kingship. Its antiquity is unknown, although it certainly could have had an early origin, perhaps identifying rulers at Preclassic mega-centres such as El Mirador. Alternatively, it was taken up only in the Protoclassic Period, when the growing asymmetries between dynastic kings produced the need for some further status differentiation. Although drawn from a supernatural concept, a gloss of "high king" or "overking" reflects the pragmatics of its usage. It is significant that the kings of hegemonic Tikal, Dzibanche, and Palenque are the only ones said to have acceded into this status. When the grander hegemonies began to break down in the eighth century what was already an honorific title emerged at lesser centres. We might take this to be a proliferation and debasement of a once-great epithet. However, the phenomenon matches the decline of macro-political organisation more generally and therefore simply indicates the higher status to which lesser polities could now aspire, the intimidating presence of the pan-regional powers having faded away. Moreover, its last appearances are key to understanding the rise of new power-brokers during the stricken ninth century.

A look at the architectonics of the leading Classic Maya centres suggests ways in which hegemonic power may have been materialised. Calakmul was a Preclassic city with major monumental construction reaching back to at least 400 BCE, evidently becoming the seat of the Kaanul dynasty only a millennium later around 636 CE (Case Study 6). During this Late Classic stage of its history investments were made in ceremonial and mortuary buildings, including new phases of its two massive Preclassic pyramids. Marketplace infrastructure has already been noted in the form of the Chiik Nahb complex, but the great majority of the new construction effort went into the gargantuan court spaces that dominate the final plan of the city – quite unlike anything else in the Maya world (Figure 81).

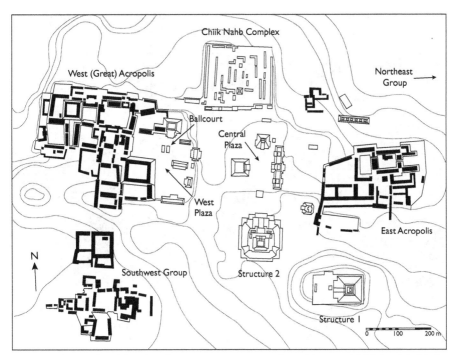

81 Map of central Calakmul with its expansive court-style architecture highlighted in black. The surrounding settlement is dispersed over some 30 km².

The West or Great Acropolis alone covers some 115,584 m², six times the area of the Central Acropolis at Tikal and fourteen times that of the Palace at Palenque (Delvendahl 2010: 614). Adding Calakmul's East Acropolis, Southwest Group, and another complex in the Northeast more than doubles that space. The West Acropolis is the only part to have been investigated archaeologically to date (Campaña 1998; Delvendahl 2010: 613–671). Comprised of seventeen courtyards and as many as eighty individual structures, some on two or even three levels, this concentrated complex could have accommodated many hundreds of people (Figure 82). Ceramic evidence suggests that the main body of it was built in more or less one phase during the seventh century, with some later alterations in the eighth – placing the project in close accord with the political transformation of the site revealed in the inscriptions.[29]

I have previously highlighted the disproportionate scale of these Calakmul courts, which dwarf the combined spaces at other major centres such as Naranjo and Caracol, and are matched only by the total at Tikal, although there in a more dispersed arrangement (Martin 2001d). The argument was that these disparities are too great to be explained within normal variation and that they must in some way manifest the paramountcy of Calakmul and Tikal. There are several options for how the expanded elite population implied by such large facilities might reflect political power. One could be the

82 Structure XXI, a multi-level building in the West Acropolis of Calakmul, under excavation (note the worker at top left for scale). (SM/Proyecto Arqueológico Calakmul)

administration of tribute, a factor that created large resident bureaucracies at the major capitals of Postclassic Central Mexico (Calnek 1982: 58–59). Yet their size is surely too substantial to have served that purpose alone, and a different function is hinted at in data from the Calakmul subsidiary of La Corona. The heir to its throne *bixiiy*, "went" to Calakmul in 664 and stayed for some three-and-a-half years, returning only upon the death of his father, who he apparently succeeded twenty-five days later.[30] If Calakmul routinely hosted the offspring of its many clients it would certainly have needed considerable residential space of a quality befitting their status.[31]

This invites parallels from elsewhere in Mesoamerica, where required residency at the seat of an overlord regularly served as a strategy of political control. Young heirs were typically hosted and educated to inculcate loyalty, while at the same time their presence sought to ensure the good behaviour of their kin. The system established by the Aztec Triple Alliance (Tenochtitlan, Texcoco, and Tlacopan) illustrates the point: "[M]andatory attendance of the lesser lords or their children at the three great courts served to prevent 'thoughts of insurrection and rebellion'" (Offner 1983: 98, quoting Ixtlilxochitl 1952: II, 165). This also invokes comparison with the Postclassic Maya capital of Mayapan, whose dominant Cocom lineage is said to have required subject lords to reside in the city, bringing "all their affairs and business", to be supported by tribute supplied by their home territories (Landa [1582], in Tozzer 1941: 24). We see relocations of this kind and for this purpose across

the world – Edo-period Japan for one – and they are a feature of "administrative cities" in the typology defined by Richard Fox (1977: 68–69). It is
therefore perfectly plausible that Calakmul and Tikal, if only during the peak
of their powers, sought to secure their dominions by keeping a sizeable
community of de facto hostages at their capitals (Martin 2001d: 186).

While smaller than that at Calakmul, the court-style architecture in the
heart of Dzibanche is quite extensive for the Early Classic dating of its
major architecture and it has much the same concentrated design (Nalda and
Balanzario 2014: figure 2).[32] This suggests that Dzibanche had a similarly
outsized requirement for high-status space. Linear buildings to the southwest
of the site core may even be evidence for a market district that predates the one
Calakmul established with the Chihk Nahb complex. If that proves to be the
case, it would only enhance the idea that hegemonic status correlated with
being a regional exchange centre, and that this was the model from which
Calakmul took its cue.

Even though we now believe that it was internal conflict that led to
Calakmul replacing Dzibanche as the main Kaanul capital, why Calakmul in
particular emerged as its successor is unclear. There were probably a great
many contingent factors at work, most beyond recovery.[33] However, some
part of the motivation might be gleaned from an examination of the political
interaction diagram that distinguishes the eras that the dynasty ruled from these
two respective centres (see Figure 75). The sample is limited and, as noted
earlier, greatly weighted to the Late Classic, but it nonetheless suggests that
Dzibanche's strongest diplomatic and hierarchical contacts were to the east,
while its contacts to the west were mostly hostile. Calakmul had eastern
connections of its own, but was much more active in building diplomatic
links in the west and south. The more central location of Calakmul in the
southern lowlands, only 100 km from Tikal, might have facilitated access to
areas previously beyond the Kaanul dynasty's effective range of operation.

It is certainly significant that the lofty hegemonic status the Snake dynasty
enjoyed at its original capital was transferred intact to that of its successor,
which thereafter matched or even exceeded its influence. This demonstrates
that whatever advantage had propelled the polity to dominant status in the first
place, its original location and resource base was not, or was no longer, a
determining factor. What was this advantage? It could have developed a long-
term potency in the arts of war, investing in military expertise in much the
same way as did ancient Sparta. Still, the populations under its direct control
would never have been especially large and it could therefore command no
overwhelming weight in numbers. This indicates that any such prowess would
still have relied on its ability to bind and orchestrate associates, allies, and
subjects into a force that could maintain and expand its power over the better
part of two centuries.

This would mean that the Snake dynasty succeeded in large measure because of the social strategies that made it the head of another kind of elite coalition – not one that linked the elite of a single polity, but that of many. The *ajawtaak* of the polity shared a specific dynastic affiliation, yet they were at the same time members of a wider corporate group spanning the entire Classic Maya world; the kind of class-based confraternity David Freidel (2018: 370) characterises as a "sodality".

It is no coincidence that the supervised accession and possession statements pertaining to *sajal*, *ajk'uhuun*, and the rest, were repeated at the higher level between ruling *ajaw*. In essence, hegemons were seeking to replicate the internal coherence of the polity in an external context. Yet there was a radical contrast in the kind of bonds that were possible within polities and those without. Nobles and kings were tied together by a strong force of long-term mutual interest predicated on the unquestioned legitimacy of blood descent. Kings were bound to other kings within the sodality by a much weaker force in which loyalties and commitments were more dependent on transient interests and the exercise of a coercion that always chaffed against the idealised autonomy of all polities. The difference in the strength of these two forces is essentially what defines the boundaries of a polity as a polity – the strong hierarchy of the kingdom distinct from the weak hierarchy of the hegemony.

Historically, by the middle of the seventh century Calakmul exercised firm control over its immediate environs, grading into differing degrees of suzerainty over a larger region, before breaking into more weakly attached, affiliated, or discontiguous subjects at greater distances. The rulers of its most proximate centres were unable to use the prefix *k'uhul*, "holy" in their *ajaw* titles, or were obliged to use other non-*ajaw* forms to distinguish themselves. Yet, since these rulers retained the symbolic capital of Maya dynastic rule – at times exercising limited degrees of diplomatic action of their own – they are far from components in an integrated state, which demands centralised administrative control.

Here it is better to imagine the gravitational pull of an immense stellar object. Its closest satellites would be locked in fixed orbits from which they could not deviate, whereas those further out followed more elliptical trajectories in which their attachment ebbed and flowed. Errant satellites, usually but not always the most distant, could be captured for a time, but were apt to break free as soon as the power of the core weakened. Any of these orbiters might be drawn away, willingly or unwillingly, to circle a rival star. Many satellites possessed systems of their own, in the way that the Calakmul clients Dos Pilas exercised patronage over Tamarindito-Arroyo de Piedra and Naranjo oversaw Ucanal and Yopmootz.[34] These, in their turn, would have controlled their own circles of still lesser satellites. The whole system was held in place by the commitments of self-professed clients pursuing their perceived best interests, although it ultimately relied on the intimidating strength and diplomatic craft of the core. Because subjects retained their own royal lines, armed forces, and aspirations for independence, their attachment to their overlord was inherently feeble and might be broken when a suitable opportunity arose. I perceive the political history of the Late Classic, in particular, as one shaped by the stresses and strains of these opposing forces and attractions.

Calakmul's great rival Tikal enjoyed its initial heyday in the fourth, fifth, and first half of the sixth century, when the system of Classic-era polities was still developing and it was in contact with the faraway power of Teotihuacan in Central Mexico. Although we await a clearer picture of the precise meaning and consequences of the entrada of 378, the finds of recent years have only enhanced the impression of an intrusive power that disrupted existing Maya political structures (Stuart 2000). The huge influence that Teotihuacan there-after exerts on Maya representations of authority and militarism, the memory of it reverberating as a part of the Maya symbolic repertoire long after the great city's fall, all speak of something more profound than simple emulation or quotation. A more compelling model sees Teotihuacan at the head of a hegemonic empire that subjected the Maya to its will, reconfiguring govern-ance in the region and instituting a system of distant overlordship (Martin 2001a). We do not know how many Teotihuacanos might have made the long trek to the central Maya lowlands, but they need not have been very numerous if they were working with subjects or allied groups rather closer to Tikal, perhaps including cooperative Maya polities.

Exactly how long Teotihuacan's influence was felt, rather than simply recalled, in the Maya area remains unclear. Sparse clues from Piedras Negras, which evidently received high-status gifts and rhetorically expressed some subordination to it, suggest that Teotihuacan had political currency until at least 514. It seems meaningful that none of the famed Tikal kings of the Early Classic Period are ascribed a *kaloomte'* title. It was not until 527 that *kaloomte'* re-appears at Tikal and thereafter is employed fairly consistently for the remainder of the Classic Period.

Another phenomenon that might be linked to the disappearance of foreign overlordship is the emergence of rich textual records of warfare at precisely this point – to continue the arguments initiated in the previous section. We have depictions of trampled prisoners in the Early Classic and can be confident that there was inter-communal violence. Yet, it might not go too far to suggest that the New Order had a suppressive effect on major conflict, conceivably constituting a Pax Teotihuacana, at least for a time. From the middle of the sixth century onwards, however, things changed decisively. Tikal now had a serious adversary and the explicit statements of hierarchy we first saw in relation to Teotihuacan emerge in wholly Maya contexts for the first time – at least in the record that survives to us.

Tikal's fortunes, as we have seen, soon took a turn for the worse, as it was increasingly hemmed-in and defeated by the Kaanul kings and their clients. The Tikal hiatus was not "a rehearsal for the collapse", but a stark reflection of its embattled position and straitened circumstances. The break with the Dos Pilas faction was a particular thorn in its side, given their allegiance to the kings of Calakmul. Yet despite suffering conquest in 657, and probably a short-lived subjection thereafter, the record shows that for much of the seventh century Tikal was far from cowed and resisted its many enemies, sufficiently confident to campaign at distance. When it experienced a stronger revival at the very end of the seventh century, one that would eventually transform the city architecturally, it was built on the back of military success – besting Calakmul twice-over and then defeating two of its major clients, Naranjo and El Peru. In 771 and again in 790 Tikal built especially large "twin pyramid complexes" to commemorate the K'atuns completed in those years, perhaps a scale designed to accommodate sizeable gatherings of dependent kings and their retinues. Yet this restored Tikal sphere, which may have endured until the collapse set in at the start of the ninth century, shows no sign of rivalling the scale of that achieved by the serpent kingdom.

Assembling all the evidence at our disposal, there is good reason to believe that Classic Maya inter-polity hierarchies were, at root, coercive organisations that employed intimidation as much, or more, than actual violence, but from which secession could be met with a retaliatory response. The precise nature of the relations between patron and client were doubtless highly variable, but the traditional identities and dynastic governments of subordinated kingdoms were consistently preserved or soon revived. Some defeated kings were killed, but others, even those shown as humiliated captives, could be made into compliant vassals and restored to their thrones. Powerful hegemonies typically attract voluntary affiliates, especially if such a connection offers security or economic benefits to the elites of weaker polities. The distant regions in which a hegemon such as Dzibanche or Calakmul intervened suggest that great powers were interested in more than purely local networks and sought to influence wider resource and communication routes.

Although it cannot be assumed a priori, there is often a correlation between the power exercised by a given political capital and its physical size (see p.50). There could be several social and economic factors at work here. They include the fruits of military success in the form of booty, slave-taking, or forced inward migration – that is, an increase in human capital, including skilled artisans – but a greater factor is likely to have been the supply of tribute and corvée labour provided by client polities. Both the scale and architectural typologies of sites such as Calakmul and Tikal appear to reflect their hegemonic activities and their positions at the head of hierarchies. Where significant political power is not represented materially, as at modestly sized

Dos Pilas, it probably reflects not only its relatively short occupation but its subordination to a still greater master and the upward movement of resources that implies. Although no Classic Maya polity approached the scale or strength of the Aztec imperium, there are enough commonalities to posit that similar principles of political economy applied in the Maya area.

Even if I have successfully identified and justified hegemony as the presiding character of Classic Maya macro-political organisation, we are left in want of a robust understanding of the principles that underlie it. To advance toward that goal we need a broader basis to our knowledge of this kind of system, casting a wider net to learn what we can from comparable systems worldwide and then to the theoretical work that might help us to understand them. These will be the topics of Chapter 14.

FOURTEEN

HEGEMONY IN PRACTICE AND THEORY

If hegemony was indeed the overriding mode of power shaping macro-political structure for the Classic Maya, we need to know more about its working principles. A political landscape that was essentially heterarchical but pervaded by great asymmetries in power is by no means unusual in world terms. Indeed, if we maintain our focus on political relations over those of political forms, we can identify a variety of historically known societies that were organised and functioned in very similar ways.

In the first section of this chapter, I select four such examples for comparative purposes. Their usefulness comes in the way in which we see certain patterns and behaviours recur, suggesting that intricate historical phenomena are the contingent manifestations of underlying structural logics and cognitive pathways. The second section is a broadly-based analysis of hegemony as a mode of political power, with a particular focus on the theoretical perspectives that might aid our enquiry. A concluding third section applies these principles to the Classic Maya case and examines how they were, or were not, manifested and culturally interpreted.

HEGEMONY FROM A GLOBAL PERSPECTIVE

Fiji, 1750–1874 CE

To emphasise that hegemonic power relations are not restricted to a particular era, geographic scale, level of complexity, or topographic environment, we

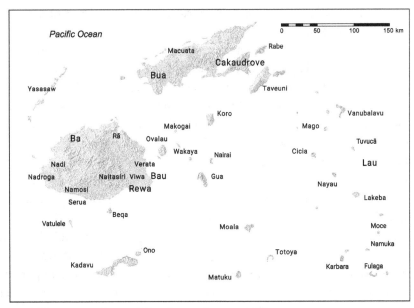

MAP 6 Major *vanua* and *matanitū* in nineteenth century Fiji.

can turn to a very different case, the Pacific islands of Fiji (Williams 1859; Sayes 1984; Routledge 1985; Thomas 1986; Sahlins 1991) (Map 6). An archipelago with a combined land area of 18,274 km², Fiji was first sighted by Europeans in 1643, although for the next two centuries contacts were intermittent and focused on trade and religious conversion rather than colonial appropriation. Over that time, the islands were settled by foreign merchants and missionaries whose journals and letters provide first-hand accounts of indigenous politics in action, as well as recording oral histories reaching back into the pre-contact era.

Traditional Fijian society was composed of lineages or clans housed within fortified villages of varying size, each ruled by its own hereditary lord or *turaga*. Several such settlements were grouped into units called *vanua*, with several of these further gathered into *matanitū* – units that the early European writers called kingdoms or states – under a single lord or king. In fact, the six-to-twelve *matanitū* extant at any one time were rather fragile and dynamic entities, largely held together by force. Beyond the home *vanua* of their paramount rulers subject *vanua* held different statuses. The highest, *bati*, described those who had joined more or less voluntarily, whereas *qali* were often those defeated in war, and the lowest, *kaisi,* occupied a status verging on slavery. Wealth accrued to the centre by means of tributary obligations, with the greater burden falling on *qali* and *kaisi* members. *Bati* were usually situated in border regions and took more responsibility for military defence, with the result that they enjoyed greater freedom, sometimes possessing their own circle of tribute-paying clients (Thomas 1986: 19–27). Central control of vassals varied in intensity, but the ruler of even a modestly important *matanitū* is reported to have installed the rulers of his lesser *vanua* (Hocart, in Kaplan 1995: 26–27).

Hocart, who worked on Fiji in the early twentieth century, considered the *matanitū* a "ritual polity", since the focus of the people's veneration was the king himself – who was called a *kalou tamata*, "human god" (Hocart 1933: 244–245). However, it was not that the king himself was divine so much that his body served as the vessel for the principal deity of the polity. This entity sacralised the king's every action, first in bringing the community into being and then maintaining its on-going existence. As such: ". . . his whole life is one course of ritual" (Hocart 1933: 245). Patron gods were considered to be the founders of lordly lineages and could be accessed through rituals conducted at temples by priestly specialists (Kaplan 1995: 48–50).

The sea was no barrier to social or political integration and there was frequent exchange between islands, even far-flung atolls: "Groups moved about, mixing with one another in a way which emphasised the importance of kinship ties and the acknowledgment of a common ancestor and tutelary deity" (Routledge 1985: 30). When the seat of a *matanitū* shifted location, as it did in the case of Cakaudrove, it could even transfer from one island to another (Routledge 1985: 16). There were no easily defined borders to a powerful *matanitū* like that of Bau, whose large fleet of war canoes established a writ stretching across many islands and counted other *matanitū* among its clients. Based on a small islet off the coast of the largest island Vitilevu, Bau imposed levies of tribute on subjects near and far – enforced, when necessary, by punitive raids. It required even friendly lords and tributaries to live at its capital, and heirs to subject seats were brought up there to "imbibe a suitably Bauan orientation of mind" (Routledge 1985: 43).

Bau played an instrumental role in the best-documented event in pre-colonial Fijian power politics, its war with the neighbouring *matanitū* of Rewa, which flared up at various points between 1843 and 1855 (Routledge 1985: 68–88; Sahlins 1991: 48–60, 2004: 13–124). Here pitched battles, sieges, massacres, and acts of treachery, all conducted within a complex interplay of kin networks, led to eventual victory for Bau. The Bau king, who had benefitted from the additional alliances brought by his conversion to Christianity, ceded the islands to the greater power of the British Crown in 1874.

Ireland, 400–1169 CE

Across the world and much earlier in time, another point of comparison is offered by Early Medieval Ireland (Byrne 1973; Charles-Edwards 2000: 522–585; Jaski 2000). Written sources reaching back to the fifth century CE describe this island of 84,421 km^2 as home to small polities called *túatha*. Perhaps 150 in number, each containing a few thousand people and spanning

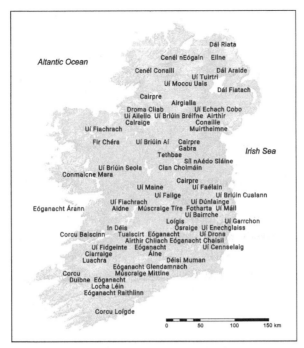

MAP 7 Major clan names and *túatha* in Early Medieval Ireland.

25 km or so, they were usually identified by lineage or clan names, many of which had turned into place-names (Map 7). Their rulers carried the title of *rí*, the Old Irish form of the Indo-European root for "king", equivalent to the Gaulish *rix* and Latin *rex*. The office was hereditary and originally possessed its own tutelary deity, typically a goddess who represented the land of the *túath*, to whom the *rí* was symbolically wedded at his installation (Jaski 2000: 57–58) – a tradition that lingered long after Ireland's conversion to Christianity at the end of the fifth century. Still, very few *ríg* (plural of *rí*) were their own masters and almost all were subject in the first instance to a *rí túath*, the "overking" of a number of separate *túatha*. These lords were in turn ranked beneath a *rí ruirech,* a "king of overkings", a category powerful enough to engage in island-wide struggles for hegemony.

> It is only at this level of organization that military power, diplomatic ability and thus overall political success led to larger political units, that were, for the greater part, much less stable than the localized *túatha* but could become as large as to consist of half or more of the island of Ireland, and were under the control of a single king like Brian Bóruma or at least a single royal dynasty like the Uí Néill or the Eóganacht.
>
> (Karl 2006: 194)

Despite the lack of formal integration, the web of hierarchical bonds ensured a densely-connected landscape, with personal ties between patron and client initiated in official ceremonies of submission and installation (Ó Corráin 1972: 35–37; Byrne 1973: 39, 43; Jaski 2000: 207). A client's obligations included paying tribute, attending gatherings at the seat of his patron, and contributing men to his war-host. To ensure loyalty hostages were held against the good behaviour of their kin, and it was a point of pride that any important king should hold many notables "in fetters" (Jaski 2000: 102–104). The influence of overkings on their subject *túatha* varied, but some were able to exploit succession struggles to intervene and choose their own preferred candidates (Ó Corráin 1972: 30–32).

Unlike the levels of kingship noted above, the position of *ardrí*, "high king" had no legal basis and amounted to no more than an acknowledgement of relative superiority that ultimately stood on a force of arms; it was "never an institution, but merely a prize to be won" (Byrne 1973: 261). Even those celebrated as a *rex Hiberniae*, "King of Ireland" achieved no more than partial suzerainty. The successor to a *rí ruirech* did not automatically inherit his dominions and it was usually necessary to threaten or conduct military raids to achieve their continued submission (Jaski 2000: 102–103). As a result, great political networks sometimes collapsed soon after the death of their creators. Major dynasties might build durable confederacies, but at some point all suffered military reverses that sapped their prestige and led to the defection of clients. None of the six-to-eight *ríg ruirech* ascendant at any one time went on to forge integrated regional polities, even though their hegemonies increasingly corresponded to the separate *cóiced* – a term often translated as a "fifth" but better understood as "portion" – of Ulster, Connacht, Leinster, and Munster, and probably the central Mide. Thus, we find that "... the king of Cashel is acknowledged as the sole overking of Munster, and is even given the right to install all the kings in 'his' province" (Jaski 2000: 207).

The complexities of royal inheritance and succession led to the frequent fissioning of dynasties, causing relocations as the landless sons of powerful families who could not inherit at home displaced weaker kings, who in turn settled in the territories of others. This led to the transfer of political identities from one region to another: "... the kings of Cenél nEogain were still called kings of Ailech, although through the process of segmentation the ruling dynasty no longer resided there" (Jaski 2000: 198). While the fortunes of dynastic powers ebbed and flowed, and the practice of overkingship became more formalised, there was no essential change to this system until Irish independence was brought to an end by the Anglo-Norman invasion of 1169. Even thereafter, the *túath* and its ranks of stratified lords continued in some form, only gradually evolving into a version of the medieval feudalism that prevailed in England and much of Western Europe.

India, 750–1250 CE

The Indian sub-continent, extending over some 4,400,000 km², offers a long and rich political history, with periods of greater or lesser integration sparked by both autochthonous developments and intrusions of people and ideas from outside. From the fourth century CE the Gupta dynasty made itself the apex of a wide-ranging imperial system, but the decline of its power from the end of the sixth gradually gave rise to a large number of kingdoms and dependent sub-kingdoms. In the period that stretches from 750 until 1250 this landscape consisted of a mosaic of territories and their ruling lineages, with complex and rather fluid relations between them (Chattopadhyaya 1985; Kulke 1995a; Heitzman 1997; Thapar 2002: 363–370, 405–424, passim; Ali 2004: 32–37) (Map 8).[1]

> This dynastic configuration, entailing multiple power centres in sub-continental regions, marked the consolidation of a pattern which had begun during Gupta times, and which would remain stable for the next half a millennium under dynasties like the Gurjara-Pratiharas, Palas and Rastrakutas, Calukyas, Colas and Paramaras. The battles fought between these imperial houses rarely resulted in or even had as their goal the direct annexation of substantial territory any great distance from the core regions of these kingdoms. They resulted rather in the giving of gifts, the offering of tributes and the profession of loyalty within an explicitly acknowledged scale or hierarchy of kingships. (Ali 2004: 32)

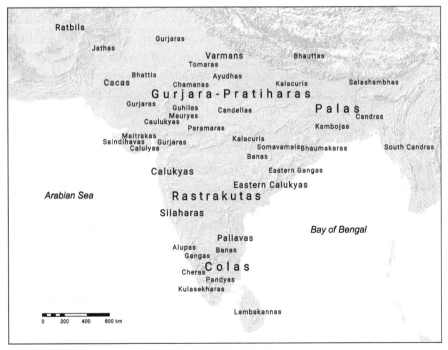

MAP 8 Major dynastic groupings in Early Medieval India.

From early times, Indian rulers carried the title *rāja*, one of the same set of Indo-European cognates as *rex*, *rix*, and *rí*. But hierarchies of kingship generated the higher epithets of *rājarāja* or *mahārāja*, "king over kings" and *mahārājadhirāja*, "great king over kings", or the even more elevated *cakravārtin*, "overlord of the entire earth" (Inden 1981: 102; Ali 2004: 33–34). The latter was another chimerical title that, at best, described the most powerful king at any one time rather than a true universal ruler (Chattopadhyaya 1985: 10–11). Manuals on Hindu rulership such as the *Arthaśāstra* give exacting accounts of the etiquette of royal hierarchy, describing grand audiences at the seat of an overlord in which each sub-king was allotted his seat according to a rigid plan reminiscent of a *mandala* cosmogram. Yet these are to be understood as idealised visions that only partly reflected the messy political realities of the times. Hierarchical relations were established through intimidation or force, the compulsion that lay behind the refined bathing rituals in which overkings would install a client king (Inden 1990: 241, 260). Such a client, having submitted, was "allowed to retain his domains more or less intact" (Inden 1981: 114; see also Kulke 1995a: 248; Thapar 2002: 423; Ali 2004: 35–36). Subject kings were often required to send their sons to be educated at the palaces of their overlords, with the aim of instilling loyalty while keeping a hostage close at hand.

Kingdoms were known by the names of their ruling lineages and were not confined to a fixed territory, made clear when dynasties transferred to new locations or sent offshoots to establish centres of non-contiguous control (Chattopadhyaya 1985: 10–15; Kulke 1995a: 253–254). Major political centres began as royal courts whose expansion sparked a process of urbanisation, first in attracting artisans and traders and then a priestly class and devotees drawn in by newly constructed public temples (Kulke 1995a: 244). The legitimacy of all kings relied on genealogical claims to ancestral founders, but they also attached themselves to local deities that they elevated to the status of dynastic patrons and absorbed into the identities of major Hindu divinities. Over time kings acquired a more sacral character as they took the role of earthly representatives of these gods and built patron temple complexes that served, in part, as royal cult centres (Kulke 1993, 1995a: 244, 258–260).

Early Medieval Indian dynasties sparred with one another and occasionally vanquished a rival, enlarging their core domain as a result, without ever approaching the universal *cakravārtin* kingship to which all, in principle, aspired. As the period wore on northern India fell under the control of Muslim sultanates, with Hindu kingdoms increasingly restricted to the south. Resistance to further Muslim encroachments ultimately led to the rise of the Vijayanagara Empire, which unified southern India to a significant extent in the 1300s.

Greece, 750–338 BCE

Ancient Greece was an early source of parallels for the Classic Maya system and it is fitting that we now turn our attention there, if with rather different analogies in mind.[2] The examples described thus far have all been monarchies, but the type of government has only a marginal bearing on the structure and operation of hegemonic systems. In Classical Greece, the quintessential political community was the *polis*, a unit composed of a central urbanised place and its rural hinterland that typically coalesced from a collection of villages (Ehrenburg 1960; Thomas 1981; Ferguson 1991; Hansen 1998, 2006, 2007; Vlassopoulos 2007). Emerging in recognisable form by 750 BCE, there were ultimately as many as 1,500 *poleis* distributed on the Greek mainland and Aegean archipelago, as well as along the coast of Anatolia and scattered across the Mediterranean and Black Seas (Map 9). The territory directly controlled by each could be as little as 10 km², although some were much larger.[3] A number were governed by monarchies or tyrannies, though by Classical times most *poleis* were either oligarchies or democracies, with many riven by competing factions and cycling between two or more styles of government.

Warfare was not infrequent and ranged in scale from neighbourly skirmishes to long-distance collaborative campaigns. A *polis* capital could be invaded, sacked, or razed to the ground, but its resilience as a localised concept was such

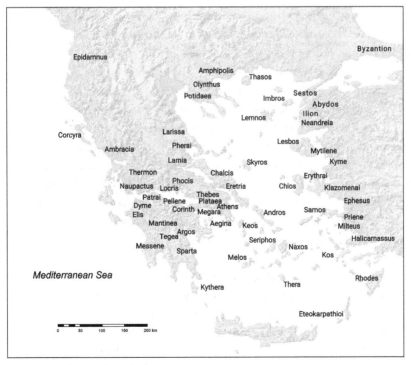

MAP 9 Major *poleis* in Classical Greece.

that it was often reconstituted at the first realistic opportunity, even if that was after a span of centuries. The basis of the Classical Greek *ethnos*, their sense of collective identity, was a shared language and culture, including a common set of religious beliefs with a rich tradition of mythic narratives. Additionally, each *polis* had one or more supernatural patrons, usually variants of those in the wider pantheon specified with compounded names and localised origin myths (Brackertz 1976; Sourvinou-Inwood 1990; Cole 1995). The rituals and festivals associated with these divine protectors were major foci of *polis* life, with most performed at a dedicated temple in the centre of the city, with the fortunes of the polity interpreted, in some measure, as the favour or disfavour of these deities.

Cultural cohesion arose from close communication between *poleis* – many of which were set at easily accessible coastal locations – that took place on both formal and informal levels (Giovannini 1994; Rutherford 2007; Malkin 2011; Mack 2015). A class of *theôrai* or "sacred ambassadors" represented their *poleis* at religious festivals, forming networks with some diplomatic and information-sharing functions. There were no permanent embassies, but there was a network of *proxenoi*, literally "proxies", consisting of local notables granted official status as representatives for foreign *poleis*. As with the *theôrai*, they facilitated political contacts and together expressed the cultural unity of the *polis* system. Still, the great majority of extramural contacts were unofficial and involved the circulation of traders and migrants among the many open cities such as Athens, which hosted large numbers of foreign residents (Ober 2015).

There was a persistent contrast between the ideal of *polis* autonomy and the reality of wide power differentials between them: "The world of the ancient Greek city-states was never a system of equal independent *poleis*, but a complicated hierarchy of *poleis*, some independent, some not, but all with a good deal of self-government, in internal affairs at least" (Hansen 2006: 130). Accordingly, there was a distinction between independent *autonomoi poleis* and dependent *hypekooi poleis*, with the latter obliged to pay tribute to a *hegemon* either on an annual basis or as a special exaction in time of war. Larger political groupings ranged from imperial formations, to leagues orchestrated by a dominant *polis*, or to cooperative alliances and confederacies. All *poleis* were subject to dynamic historical processes and shifts between different statuses and regional configurations, often several times in a generation.

The development of political hierarchies was accelerated by successive Persian invasions in 492, 490, and 480/479 BCE. These sparked a collective response from the Greeks, who gave overall command of their forces to first Sparta and then Athens, the leading powers on land and the sea, respectively. Already emerging as a major commercial centre, Athens went on to establish a league of mutual defence across the Aegean Sea. But in short order this alliance was transformed into an empire dedicated to the extraction of tribute.

The garnered wealth, from up to 330 *poleis* at one point, was used to fund a large navy that further entrenched Athens's power, as well as a splendid refurbishment of its ceremonial core that both reflected and promoted its imperial persona.

Sparta, on the Peloponnesian peninsula to the south, was a centre of diametric opposites. Personal wealth was frowned upon, coinage outlawed, and very little effort put into monumental construction. Its success was built on an austere and rigid sociopolitical order that, by enslaving its neighbours and using them as agricultural workers on its land, allowed it to dedicate its own manpower to the sole purpose of maintaining a professional army. Sparta exercised an intimidating but far less extractive hegemony over other polities on the peninsula and some well beyond.

Athens and Sparta clashed in the famed Peloponnesian War of 431–404, which eventually resulted in the defeat of Athens and ascendency for Sparta (a triumph in no small measure funded by the Persian Empire).[4] But a dyad of competing hegemonies was soon restored by the rise of Thebes, which reconstituted its former pre-eminence within the Boeotian region in central Greece and began to challenge Spartan interests. A Theban army succeeded in defeating Sparta in 371, liberating its slave workers and restoring them to their own *polis*, thereby destroying the parasitical Spartan order. Yet, apart from this, the wider system of *poleis* was maintained. Decisive change came only after the Greek defeat and general capitulation to Philip of Macedon in 338. *Poleis* continued into Hellenistic times, and even beyond the Roman conquest of 146, but the pattern of relations between them was by then decisively altered and competitive hegemonies had come to an end.

THE LOGICS OF POLITICAL DIVISION

These brief excursions to Oceania, Europe, and Asia offer a group of well-documented political systems with strong resonances for the present study. Though diverse in many respects, each zone exhibits a significant degree of shared identity, metered in closely aligned material and intellectual cultures, linguistic ties, and religious beliefs. At the same time, they are typified by enduring political divisions that saw the coexistence of tens, scores, or even hundreds of discrete units. Most of these units replicated the administrative and economic structures of their neighbours, the security and power interests of each made possible by their own armed forces. Nevertheless, imbalances in power meant that their independence was always to be understood in relative terms. The recurring factor in such asymmetries was greater military strength, which allowed suitably endowed polities to dominate and exploit their lesser rivals, achieving a measure of control over their behaviour and resources without absorbing them territorially. There was usually a good degree of regional coherence around major powers, with the greatest influence exerted over near-neighbours – a feature the Greeks called *synteleia*. But beyond this nuclear domain networks could extend outward in a non-contiguous fashion, with distant clients, affiliates, allies, and exclaves set at varied degrees of attachment to the core.

Political environments of this type have a dual character: on the one hand marked by the instability of particular configurations of power – the fluctuating fortunes of their component polities – while on the other the system itself could endure for centuries. A "dynamic equilibrium" suitably describes the situation. Importantly, this kind of system is not simply a stage en route to greater levels of integration. In the examples outlined above any such move was faltering and usually reversed, with the reproduction of the system often only brought to an end or set into irreversible decline by outside forces possessed of greater resources and/or divergent ideologies. This can, for us, be characterised as schemas that recognise and activate resources in innovative or alternative ways.

This discussion raises a number of questions, but perhaps the most pressing is what generates and preserves this equilibrium? Why, despite ample signs of power differentials between these polities, did none out-compete their rivals, absorbing their neighbours to forge larger and more integrated domains? The following sections explore hegemonic relations within multi-polity landscapes with these recurring issues in mind, moving from descriptive to analytical and theoretical perspectives. It argues that parallels between our featured cases and the Classic Maya are neither superficial nor coincidental but arise from common structural logics and the responses these provoke. Although we are now orienting ourselves towards systemic concerns, we are not in the process abandoning historicity. Indeed, returning to Sahlins, the structures we seek are "historical objects" fashioned by the long accumulation of actions and their consequences that cannot be reduced to sets of rules and formulae. We can attempt to discern underlying principles, but must acknowledge that the precise composition and play of schemas and resources will always be contingent and unique.

The Nature of Multi-Polity Systems

To accept that the Classic Maya were divided into numerous polities embedded within wide-ranging hierarchical configurations means that we must give up the socioevolutionary and symbolic armatures that respectively supported the strong and weak state, thus leaving a theoretical void. To truly occupy that space, we need to go beyond listing the characteristics of a political ecology to try to explain why it survived, indeed thrived, for so long. Political division has been common in many cultural zones throughout history and, of course, remains with us in the present day. However, the fixation on the character and composition of the "state" in so much anthropological and archaeological thought of the twentieth century meant that the investigation of interconnections and the higher-scale ordering of polities have been sorely neglected by comparison.

We should begin by noting the prior work on multi-polity systems by historians, whose interest has been spurred by familiar cases such as those of Classical Greece and Renaissance Italy. Although most of those studies retain a narrow and particularistic focus, a few comparative investigations of city-states have explored what their commonalities might signify and offered some useful insights (e.g. Griffeth and Thomas 1981). Of late, perspectives have widened to include a sizeable number of "city-state cultures" in two volumes produced by the Copenhagen Polis Centre (Hansen 2000b, 2002). In those the city-state model is applied to virtually all multi-polity contexts, even where the label seems only mildly applicable. Despite statements to the contrary, this shows how much Greece remains the archetype behind the cross-culturalism (c.f. Hansen 2000a: 598–611). In political theory more generally we find relevant labels of "multi-state systems" (Walker 1953), "systems of states" (Wight 1977), or "state systems" (Wesson 1978). In most of these the emphasis falls on identifying antecedents for the world of modern nation-states, for which the past offers precedents and suggests operating principles.

We can appreciate that the nation-states of today make for a multi-polity system par excellence – filling not islands, or even continents, but the entire globe. Though some profound differences between each of them remain, the recurring dynamics that arise between numerous interacting polities leads to notable consistencies as well. Chapter 1 remarked on the feeble record of political anthropology when it comes to such environments, while the historical studies mentioned earlier have seldom if ever offered generalisable models. For real theoretical help we must look elsewhere. The obvious place to start is in the contemporary domains of political science and its derivative international relations – the latter specialising, naturally enough, in associations and interactions between polities.

As was outlined in Chapter 3, political anthropology and political science have traditionally occupied different cultural and temporal territories, with surprisingly little commonality and cross-fertilisation. Yet, however narrowly focussed on power relations in the twentieth and twenty-first centuries, the field of international relations has dwelt at length with the very questions we are concerned with here, and in the process generated a number of interesting ideas. It is the higher-level theorising, work that explores universal themes, underlying principles, and historical groundings where the most useful work for our purposes is to be found. The key to gainful comparative study will be to avoid uncritical projections of contemporary phenomena into the past, mistaking the familiar for the universal. If we keep our attention on the core phenomena of power, authority, and legitimacy – features independent of historically circumscribed forms and a substrate to the political that is neither teleological nor deterministic – we can hope to avoid the potential pitfalls.

All multi-polity landscapes, including that of modern nation-states, are "anarchic" in the social scientific rather than common sense of the word, meaning simply that they lack an overarching authority or external order to regulate conduct. It is in its analysis of anarchy, and its counterpart hierarchy, that international relations offers some useful conceptual tools. The study of how polities interact with one another has, of course, been of scholarly interest since antiquity, but it only emerged as a distinct academic discipline in the twentieth century. Like any maturing field, it has evolved into several schools of thought and it is necessary to explore what these differing approaches have contributed to its development.

In realist and neo-realist traditions, materialism is seen as the prime mover in political systems, with the overriding objective for all polities being survival. The variant of defensive neo-realism sees polities in constant pursuit of security, best achieved by means of a "balance of power" mechanism (Waltz 1979), while that of offensive neo-realism puts its emphasis on the sole goal of maximising individual state power (Mearsheimer 2001). Realism is much concerned with uncertainty: in particular, the difficulty of determining the true intentions of rivals and potential aggressors, and therefore the necessity of preparing for worst-case scenarios. One outcome of this is the mutual insecurity we touched upon in Chapter 9, the phenomenon of escalating suspicion, fear, and pre-emptive action known as the "security dilemma" (e.g. Jervis 1978; Waltz 1979; Ember and Ember 1992; Gat 2006: 97–100).

The constructivist school in international relations is a more recent development that has sought to challenge many core realist assumptions. Constructivism points to the ways that real-world politics are pervaded by many kinds of social knowledge and inter subjective understandings. To this way of thinking political behaviour is not determined by material conditions alone, but also by the recognition of perceived interests as well as reflective responses to the behaviour of others.

Alexander Wendt (1992) has argued that there is no inherent logic to anarchic landscapes leading to insecurity and conflict, but rather "anarchy is what states make of it". In *Social Theory of International Politics*, Wendt (1999: 246–312) modifies and refines that broad claim by advancing three "cultures of anarchy", ideal types that represent alternative environments for multi-polity systems, namely Hobbesian (conflictive), Lockean (competitive), and Kantian (cooperative) (after Wight 1991). Which culture predominates depends on how deeply it has been internalised by means of outside coercion, rational self-interest, or a belief in a system's essential legitimacy. Following the leads of sociology and anthropology, constructivism in political science embraces recursiveness, whereby the actions of participants and the structures that surround them are co-determinative, each reciprocally shaping the other – as described in Chapter 3. Constructivism is replete with its own body of critics, but it is clear that this approach is a complex and culturally sensitive one with which political anthropologists should find much common ground.

The ideas of a group of liberal realists known as the English School, whose work presaged constructivism in a number of respects, also need to be highlighted. Their interest lies in the interplay between realist and idealist perspectives, and is particularly oriented towards historical precedents and processes, making its contributors arch comparativists (Bull 1977; Wight 1977; Watson 1992, 2007; Buzan 2004). Although the concept of an "international community" can be found in the seventeenth century, it became a particular focus of the English School. In *The Anarchical Society*, Hedley Bull (1977: 9–19) developed an analytical distinction between "systems of states" and "societies of states".[5] Both are complexes of multiple interacting polities, but only the latter operate within communal principles and agreed codes of conduct. As Bull and Adam Watson (1984: 1) describe it:

> [A] group of states (or, more generally, a group of independent political communities) which not merely form a system, in the sense that the behaviour of each is a necessary factor in the calculations of the others, but also have established by dialogue and consent common rules and institutions for the conduct of their relations, and recognise their common interest in maintaining these arrangements.

We can, for example, interpret the diverse yet thoroughly interconnected polities surrounding the ancient Mediterranean as a system of states. But such a system lacks the common institutions and cohesion typified by one among their number, Classical Greece, which serves as something of an exemplar of the society of states type. Here a shared cultural identity and self-constructed ethnicity worked to generate a political solidarity linked by a set of core values. Such close congruities may not be required, but they certainly facilitate the intimate ethos of English School societies of states. A central tenet is that member polities recognise the legitimacy of all other members, which has profound consequences for their strategic behaviour.

Bull (1977: 16–17, passim) was principally concerned with identifying the basis of "international order". He suggested that three inter-related factors are salient: (a) rules, in the sense of agreed principles such as the mutual recognition of sovereignty; (b) institutions, meaning not formal organisations but "patterned activities" that formalise and promote those rules; and (c) an ongoing common interest in maintaining the system. He also speculated on the motivations behind the emergence and maintenance of order, in particular pointing to violence and the fear of violence, which persuades polities and their leaders to accept constraints on their liberty in exchange for reduced threats to their wellbeing – the latter a usefully vague term that I use here to encompass security, living standards, and collective morale. It is where Bull notes the potential of common values as well as common interests that his analysis hints at a cultural dimension.

On the system/society distinction turn a series of important issues, not the least of them the aims and intensity of competition. Violence and the threat of violence may be no less prevalent in a society of culturally bonded polities than in a system of culturally estranged ones. However, more is at stake in the latter because the ultimate survival of the polity rests on pragmatic concerns unmitigated by ethical considerations. In a society of states conflicts can be devastating, but there are at least some norms that constrain aggressive conduct and limit its consequences – even if these "rules" are not followed at all times.

A society of states is more than a set of proscriptive conventions, it has wider implications for co-existence. Such societies go beyond the immediate self-interest of rational actors, recognising, for example, the subtler political craft of obligation and the deferment of reciprocation and reward. What is the source of such cooperative behaviour? The ties that bind the members of a society of states are left largely unexplained in English School thinking (e.g. Watson 2007: 110), exposing a critical gap in its capacity to enlighten us. Among Wendt's triad of socially-adhering factors – coercion, calculation, and belief – the latter is identified as the most stable, but goes without much elaboration or explication beyond "common sense" (Wendt 1999: 296). In any case, belief is much too broad a term to be useful to us in this instance, and here I instead employ the "moral order" introduced in Chapter 13. This is a specific set of ideas, an intersubjective social script with a strong ethical dimension, an ideology that codifies and justifies particular constellations of power.

While the source of morality is certainly a question for philosophers and psychologists, that should not preclude its investigation by social scientists. It can certainly be argued that morality was part of the emerging evolutionary tool-kit that enabled us to cooperate within the relatively simple hunter-gatherer societies of the deep past. Here kinship was of critical importance, but the number of participants was sufficiently high to overstretch the genetic imperatives of true consanguinity. Group identity and morality substitute for close kinship, making larger societies cohesive "super-families". Proclivities long-engrained within us in this archetypal "state of nature" are not easily discarded. We have brought them into complex societies where, vastly transformed by cultural evolution, those posing the most disruptive potential – such as aggression – have been put under greater control and, wherever possible, redirected toward the communal good. Thus, we need not see ethics and a sense of natural justice in altruistic terms, but rather ask what advantages such beliefs might offer and infer from them the way that cooperation and reciprocation are deeply embedded in our psyche, intrinsic to our success as a social species.

Sovereignty, Autonomy, and Hegemony

The legitimacy of modern nation-states is predicated on a concept of sovereignty established by the Peace of Westphalia, a series of treaties that brought Europe's Thirty Years War to a close in 1648. Traditionally defined as supreme authority over a given territory and community, sovereignty has long been a concern among a variety of disciplines, including philosophy, history, and political science (Hinsley 1966). It has more recently come to the attention of a political anthropology seeking to shed its colonialist heritage and define a poststructuralist concept of politics (e.g. Hansen and Stepputat 2006; Smith 2011).

Even the most cursory of examinations shows that this seemingly straightforward concept is riddled with inconsistencies and gulfs between principle and practice. Even in consensual agreements polities bargain sovereign rights away to outsiders, surrendering control over parts of their operations while maintaining that over others. As a result, contemporary scholars are inclined to see sovereignty as "divisible" (Agnew 2005: 441), a "composite concept" (Hui 2004: 83), or even an "organized hypocrisy" (Krasner 1999, 2001: 19). One cause of this conceptual ambiguity is that political leaders are compelled to satisfy different constituencies – both internally and externally – even though the interests of those groups may sharply diverge. Sovereignty survives as a single idea only so long as it can mean different things to different audiences and, whatever its absolutist claims, is in most cases variable, context-specific, and gradated.

Although we have concentrated on the modern world here, these issues are no less relevant as we reach back into the ancient. It is the malleable and ambiguous nature of sovereignty that casts anarchy into a more complex light. While anarchy accurately describes the demarcation of distinct polities absent of overarching control, it says little or nothing about the distribution of power between them and, therefore, the degrees of sovereignty they exercise. We need to understand how sovereign status is curtailed or enhanced by asymmetries in power, as reflected in the terms autonomy and its counterpart hegemony (Lentner 2005).

In ancient Greek *hegemonia* referred to a form of "leadership" which was distinct from *arkhe,* whose sense was closer to "control" or "dominion" (Perlman 1991; Wickersham 1994; Lebow and Kelly 2001: 594–603). Initially, *hegemonia* had a consensual basis, in which those assuming the position of hegemon did so on perceived merit as the best able to serve the interests of the collective. Yet hegemons soon came to exercise *arkhe* – as we saw in Athens converting its league into an empire – and this had become common enough by the Roman Period for *hegemonia* to be freely translated as *imperium* (Lebow and Kelly 2001: 595).

Another Greek term, *autonomia*, defined as the state of "living within one's own laws", started as a reference to the full self-determination of a polity under its own government. However, this too underwent a migration of meaning as it acquired the more restricted sense of jurisdiction over internal affairs alone (Hansen 1995; Low 2007: 188–199; c.f. Ostwald 1982). The shift is evident in the otherwise oxymoronic "autonomy-under-hegemony" that prevailed throughout Classical Greece, in which powerful polities made certain demands of weaker ones, but seldom interfered with their internal structure or operation.[6] Autonomy lays claim to a specific meaning but, like sovereignty, in practice its accuracy and appropriateness varies depending on what domain of the political is in question.

In short order, therefore, the use of both terms shifted from the idealistic to the pragmatic and from an absolute meaning to a relative one. In the modern world, where relations between nation-states are rife with disparities of wealth and power, hegemony retains this plasticity, describing a range of relations from the nominal and consensual to the coercive and exploitative. Even where we can observe these relations directly they remain hard to quantify, not only because they affect different constituencies in different ways, but because many of the most important effects are not material but psychological.

The neo-realist Kenneth Waltz (1979: 114–116) envisaged just two structural modes, anarchy and hierarchy, which all political systems mix to differing degrees. The English School's Adam Watson (1992: 120–125) preferred to see a spectrum, ranging from complete independence at one end to total incorporation within a pure imperial order at the other. Between these two extremes he distinguished forms of dominion, suzerainty, and hegemony based on how deeply superordinants interfered in the affairs of their subordinants (Buzan and Little 2000: figure 8.2) (Figure 83). Aware of historical precedents, Watson looked to the ways that dominant polities combine different strategic relationships, for example exerting firm control close to home but a weaker grasp at distance (Buzan and Little 2000: 125–128).

Whereas Waltz (1979: 91–92, 126) argued that the paramount objective of all polities is survival, since nothing is possible without it, Watson (1992: 14) added a desire for order and the pursuit of peace and prosperity.[7] In this, he sought to identify a motor behind the pendulum swings between anarchic and hierarchic poles. Anarchy offers maximum self-determination, but at the price of an insecure existence in which self-reliance is the only survival strategy. The kind of strict hierarchies we find in territorial empires offer greater stability and security, but at the cost of vexing constraints on liberty and economic

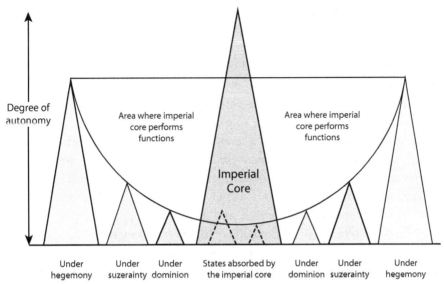

Degree of autonomy

Area where imperial core performs functions

Area where imperial core performs functions

Imperial Core

| Under hegemony | Under suzerainty | Under dominion | States absorbed by the imperial core | Under dominion | Under suzerainty | Under hegemony |

83 Adam Watson's model of political hegemony. (After a visualisation in Buzan and Little 2000: figure 8.2)

exploitation. It is the push and pull between these extremes that makes a middling "propensity to hegemony" a common compromise in Watson's model (Watson 1992: 123–125). It might be noticed that this zone of balanced priorities is much like the position between order and disorder discussed in Chapter 12, where maximum social benefits can be found sitting astride the tenuous "edge of chaos".

Similar reasoning to Watson's informs the approach of David Lake (2007, 2009), who rejects the assumption that the international order is essentially anarchic, arguing that multi-polity systems are always structured by hierarchies, whether they are acknowledged or not.[8] In his view, the legalistic framework within which modern state sovereignty was formulated unrealistically excludes hierarchy, which as an artefact of contingent power variables will inevitably emerge. Although Lake's focus falls on consensual ties, it usefully points to the way that hierarchy in the absence of laws amounts to a "contractual" arrangement between superordinants and subordinants, one that formalises and legitimises an asymmetrical status quo. Other political theorists have explored the means by which dominant polities maintain their position by means of unequal reciprocation or inducement, as well as processes of socialisation. In the latter, polities seek to shape the perceptions of their clients, persuading them to accept the righteousness of their subordination as well as that of the hegemonic system as a whole (Ikenberry and Kupchan 1990). This approach concentrates on subject elites rather than populations en toto and, it is argued, can succeed only when incentives mask or distract from the coercion at work.

In hegemonic power we are, therefore, looking at a complex and amorphous phenomenon that has different goals, employs varied strategies, and draws on resources specific to the case in hand. Each example needs to be understood within its own cultural, social, and economic context because these domains affect what kinds of power over others are possible. Although hegemonic power is one ultimately rooted in violence, its ramifying effects also generate voluntaristic arrangements – so long as these are to the advantage of the hegemon. Whereas formalised empires can be materialised in various ways, some of which might be recovered archaeologically, the structure of hegemony is such that the resources marshalled by its schemas will leave little, if any, direct trace and it more closely resembles a psychological artefact composed of perceptions, promises, and threats.

Areas that international relations theory has difficulty in addressing, even within constructivist work, are the conceptual factors that enable, support, or promote hierarchy, including the ways in which they act to normalise and naturalise relations of power. Particular shortcomings are the discipline's tepid treatments of ideology, culture, and an understanding of historical process, not simply historical precedent. This is where political anthropology, with its micro as well macro outlook, can make a distinctive contribution; one that looks to bridge materialism and idealism, structure and practice, society and the individual.

A Balance of Power

We have so far defined some structural characteristics of hegemonic power within a multi-polity system without addressing the mechanisms that limited its scope, leaving the persistence of small polities still to be explained. Where their endurance has been recognised as a specific problem, historians (Griffeth and Thomas 1981: 197), anthropologists (Sahlins 1991: 78–79), and political theorists (Walker 1953: 59–68; Kaplan 1957; Waltz 1979) have essentially reached the same solution, namely a balance of power mechanism. As Wesson (1978: 31–32) explains it:

> [W]hen multiple sovereignties oppose one another within the framework of shared culture, their power relations acquire a limited stability commonly summarized under the concept of the balance of power. [. . .] Generally speaking, the larger the number of fairly equal independent units and the more widely power within the system is divided, the less improvement one actor can expect by getting the better of another and the more potential resistance will be evoked by efforts toward hegemony. The basis of the balance of power is the fear of loss of independence, hence most members are hostile toward any that threaten to gain the ascendency.

In this classic understanding of the mechanism, the rising power of a dominant polity raises the spectre of a momentum that might ultimately absorb all members of the system. This drives weaker polities to increase their own capabilities ("internal balancing") and/or to form alliances in order to collectively thwart the ambitions of their common foe ("external balancing"). The result is that an emerging threat breeds its own countermeasures, and balance is maintained or restored. It is thought by some that the expectation of such a response would alone place some check on the ambition of an aspiring power. It is further argued that balance will emerge even without a conscious effort or strategy to do so, arising as the structural effect of each polity striving to maintain its own independence (Waltz 1979: 121).

Although this version of a balance of power dominated realist thinking for over three decades it later came under sustained criticism. Opponents highlighted the lack of fit between the theory and the historical cases on which it professed to be based (Vasquez 2003), and emphasised those parts of the world where balancing did not take place and hegemonic powers went on to achieve complete mastery (Kaufman, Little, and Wohlforth 2007; Wohlforth et al. 2007). What was under assault here was not balancing processes per se, only the claim of their ubiquitous success in the past, present, and future – which now seems an untenable position.

To understand why equilibrium might be maintained it is necessary to study cases where it was not, meaning that we must understand how dominant powers come to triumph over their former peers. Here it is illuminating to look at ancient China and compare the Spring and Autumn Period (771–481 BCE) with the subsequent Warring States Period (481–221 BCE). The former resembles the global case studies we examined earlier. Although notionally gathered under the authority of the Zhou king, in reality power was devolved among 200 or more separate units called *guo*, of which 15 or so of the larger and more powerful held others in subjection and jostled for pre-eminence (Walker 1953; Hsu 1990; Lewis 2000). For some three centuries, these polities engaged in a familiar catalogue of treaties, tributary networks, interdynastic marriages (where polygyny gave rise to succession disputes), the taking of hostages, and the harbouring of elite exiles. Developing from fortified settlements, throughout their history they continued to be defined more by their capitals than by their rather elastic territories.

All *guo* co-identified as a fraternity, following codes of conduct and maintaining collective institutional structures, which together amounted to a "surrogate for international law" (Pines 2012: 14). This system included diplomatic conferences that arbitrated disputes and coordinated military campaigns against outsiders. At a deeper level, these structures reflected the concept of *li*. Originating in ritual practice, *li* was centred on the belief that things on earth should reflect an ideal cosmic order, in which each person pursues balance and occupies his or her place within formal conventions of status and permitted behaviour. This even applied to political action.

> Harmonious co-operation and co-existence could only be achieved by
> close observation of propriety. *Li* therefore governed not only the
> conduct of individuals, but also that of states. Serious violation or even
> incompetent observation of *li* in interstate relations could have put the
> moral authority and legitimacy of a ruler into question, and may even
> have brought collective condemnation of, or war against, the perpetrator
> state (Zhang 2001: 50).

Although warfare was endemic, the major powers clashed only occasionally
and the fighting principally concerned their efforts to impose control over
lesser *guo* (Lewis 2000: 365–367). If one of the leading players approached
ascendency it was checked by alliances between its rivals in a conscious effort
to prevent the consolidation of its power (Walker 1953: 52). The number, size,
and behaviour of polities was, therefore, regulated as much or more by the
success of a balance of power mechanism as it was the proscriptions of a *li*
moral order or any vestigial authority held by the Zhou king.

At an assembly in 667 the then-dominant ruler of Qi was elected to a
position of leadership, a status the Zhou king conceded by conferring upon
him the title of *ba* "senior one". Initially the *ba* status stood as a defender of the
ancient régime, but in creating new loyalties and inter-polity agreements it
soon superseded royal authority and was assumed by a succession of hegemons
drawn from the *guo* of Jin, Wu, and Yue: ". . . the entire history of the *ba*
system was a process of realigning states . . . for the sake of establishing a new
multistate order. The purpose of this system was originally supposed to be to
restore royal authority; however, rather than restoring it, the *ba* system
replaced it" (Hsu 1990: 551–562). By the fifth century political culture was
changing in decisive ways. The collection and redistribution of resources
through gift-giving, tribute, and corvée labour formalised under the Zhou
was steadily transformed into a market economy. The *ba* system disappeared as
guo rulers now refused to concede leadership, however symbolic, to one of
their competitors within a pseudo-fraternal scheme. The political landscape
transitioned into one of bitterly opposed alliances and hegemonies.

As the Spring and Autumn Period gradated into that of the Warring States
the power of monarchs increased at the expense of the nobility. Yet rulership
was itself in the process of changing, with an underlying dynamic that
decoupled sovereignty from the body of the ruler and shifted it to the body
politic instead (Hui 2005: 175). Warfare became more brutal and destructive, as
the goal of reducing rivals to client status was abandoned in favour of large-
scale conquest and annexation. Although several polities came close to complete ascendency, it was Qin that eventually overcame all its remaining
competitors to create a universal empire, in reality a single polity, in 221 BCE.

Victoria Tin-bor Hui (2005) examines the reasons why balancing failed in
the Warring States Period, contrasting this with the apparent success of that

mechanism in early modern Europe (1495–1815 CE). She proposes a "dynamic of competing logics", consisting of a re-envisaged "logic of balancing" and an opposed "logic of domination". As Hui explains it: "To understand the simultaneous interplay of domination and balancing, we should see politics as strategic interaction between domination-seekers and targets of domination who employ competing strategies and who are simultaneously assisted and obstructed by competing causal mechanisms" (Hui 2005: 11). The logic of balancing includes all means by which concentrations of power might be countered, together with the limits to such power posed by the rising costs and diminishing returns of incorporating ever more distant territories (Gilpin 1981). The logic of domination includes "Machiavellian" manoeuvres and ruthless stratagems, such as the mass slaughter of captives to forestall any revival of defeated polities, but the most telling are "self-strengthening reforms" (Hui 2005: 26–34). These are agent-led transformations of internal structure that increase capabilities in profound ways, giving reformed polities an offensive advantage. In the case of Qin this involved creating a standing army through universal conscription, the centralisation of its tax system, and replacing an aristocratic administration with a meritocratic one – all recognised as critical contributions to its eventual success.

Whereas domination won out in China, which of the two logics will succeed cannot be predicted in advance, since it depends on all manner of contingencies, Hui's scheme offering "similarity in processes and differences in outcomes" (Hui 2005: 177). Although she does not frame the issue in this way, it is clear that these capability-enhancing innovations are more than a prescription for gaining advantage within the system. They transgress the norms of existing practice and represent moves to undermine and destroy that order by a reconfiguration of schemas and resources.

Like most political theorists, Hui does not delve into the deeper psychological motives for seeking domination, leaving us to turn to Hobbes's (1985 [1651]) "drive to dominate", Morgenthau's (1948) *animus dominandi*, or to the social power philosophies of Marx and Weber. We come a little closer to a Darwinian rationale in more recent arguments that the urge to dominate can simply be seen as self-preservation taken to its logical extreme (Mearsheimer 2001). A runaway security dilemma, for example, can force actors to conclude that only the elimination of all potential competitors will guarantee their survival.

Yet the sole emphasis on survival is distorting because, as Watson suggests, while it is a necessary condition of political life it is not, in reality, a sufficient one. We do not seek survival without the inherent goal of wellbeing in the form of personal and group contentment, which is central to the social contract that binds communities of all kinds. The desire to achieve it and fear of losing it are major engines of political action. If one or more polities adopt an expansive solution to insecurity – which cannot be separated from material factors such as demographic and environmental stress – or seeks to enhance its wellbeing at the expense of others, then violent competition is likely to occur and escalate. Where survival and wellbeing are put in serious jeopardy political leaders can, and do, forsake the ethical consensus that makes coexistence possible.

Hui faithfully follows a realist paradigm in which balance of power calculations alone determine the fates of polities. But the Spring and Autumn Period was more than a balance of competitive forces, it was a society of states in which political order was also shaped by moral ideals and institutionalised means of constraining violence. To distinguish the separate roles of these factors would be unproductive because they were mutually sustaining within a single political reality. The change in strategic imperatives in China cannot be considered apart from the accompanying ideological shifts, which makes this transformation a social and cultural as much as it is a material one. It was a set of revolutionary ambitions, a reconfiguration of schemas and resources, and a determined ethical defiance that disrupted the existing order and led into a decisive, if gradual, phase transition. A Lockean culture of rivalry within limits was forsaken for a Hobbesian culture in which violence had practical, but no moral, bounds.

It would therefore be a mistake to believe that we need to choose between realist and idealist factors to explain the relative stability and persistence of a multi-polity ecosystem. Politics can be both principled and pragmatic, the two interwoven in ways that can be difficult or impossible to tease apart, not least because both are subordinate to the greater interest of protecting and promoting subjective and objective wellbeing. Left to its own devices, the isolation and uncertainties of an anarchic political landscape, its division into multiple sovereign polities, does indeed breed a logic of suspicion, aggression, and the ultimate Hobbesian choice of "kill or be killed". This is the appropriate response to an unameliorated state of nature. Here order can only be maintained through self-reliance and a balance of power mechanism.

Yet, a balance of power strategy by itself is politically demanding, wasteful of executive time and resources, and insufficiently stable to guarantee wellbeing in the long term. Thus, whether through enlightened thinking or grim experience, the brutal prospect of a Hobbesian world – which promises few winners but many losers – inspires countervailing social logics that encourage restraint, dialogue, and mutuality. In a stable multi-polity system, these factors stymie the ambitions of would-be consolidators through not one but several mechanisms, building a self-reinforcing cultural, intellectual, and economic dynamic that produces tangible benefits to coexistence. The greater point is that realism and idealism are not opposed principles in politics, since their push and pull constitute attempts to manipulate a brute set of material exigencies into more congenial forms of social life.

HEGEMONIC THEORY AND THE CLASSIC MAYA

The foregoing two sections have put us in a much better position to assess the workings of the Classic Maya political system. The theoretical difficulty of a hegemonic model comes not in understanding how some polities accrue more power than others, but in explaining what prevents them continuing to expand and consolidate that power to create a macro-state or territorial empire. We can posit certain structural impediments: for example, the absence of bureaucratic institutions to administer subjugated territories, or to an especially indelible concept of legitimate rule based on an adherence to local deities. However, like several other rationales, neither of these escapes the potential circularity that they could as easily be the consequences as the causes of political division. Distinguishing cause from effect in a non-linear world can be challenging, and a persuasive argument will be one in which distinct actions and interests consciously or unconsciously serve to block the development of larger formations.

It is no small matter that Classic Maya kings publicly conceded their subordination to other kings, and it is worth noting that all three of the monarchies in our global case studies instituted such relationships in ceremonial and ritualistic form. Informal hierarchies exist without any such trappings and we can only conclude that we are looking at palpable structures rather than ad hoc arrangements. Sponsored installations were acts of formal subjection that can be compared to contracts in the sense used by Lake. They formalise a hierarchical relationship by converting the instability and illegitimacy of coercion into the stability and legitimacy of a rightful compact or covenant. In these terms the subject is not forced but *obliged* to fulfil the expectations of an overlord; a distinction that establishes the rule of that patron as authoritative. We do not have data on the terms of these contracts, and usually cannot know when and to what degree they were coerced or voluntaristic.

A flow of tribute from client to patron, matched by an asymmetrical reciprocation that saw benefits accrue to subject elites, can be assumed in most cases but not quantified. In all the comparative cases we have examined it was tribute, and to a lesser degree booty, that was the primary means by which resources were redistributed from weak to strong polities. The spoils for Maya hegemons were modest by the standards of the Athenian treasury or the trove of goods that the Aztec Triple Alliance extracted at its height. In relative terms, however, the supply of both necessities and preciosities from near and far would have fuelled both political and ritual economies among Maya power-brokers, instilling a reliance that cost them dear when fate dimmed these stars and their gravitational fields waned.

Is there any evidence for "competing logics" determining the fate of Maya power politics? When it comes to balancing, we can certainly identify logistical constraints to the scale of hegemonic expansion, but alliances against a rising power are harder to detect. They are either a truly weak feature or, due to the limits of patrimonial rhetoric, part of our dark matter problem. If client kings fought under the command of a patron monarch such contributions may not have been considered sufficiently heroic to merit their own commemoration. This would definitely be so if client kings sent forces in support of their patron absent of their own leadership. Either way, visibility in the record would only come on those occasions where notable allied fighters fell captive – for which we have a small number of examples.

Where balancing *can* be detected is in episodes of secession and defection. Whether individual polities were conscious of engaging in grand strategy or not, these events are important because they offer a means to thwart the accumulation of overbearing power and thus preserve an anarchic system. Under hegemony, subjects must cooperate in their own domination by acquiescing to their contract. However, since the relative position of subordinant and superordinant can never be static, it is always likely that original terms no longer match a current reality, meaning that its costs and rewards are no longer commensurate with the real or perceived power differential between the two polities as they now stand.

The essence of an anarchical system is a desire and capacity for self-determination, and secession remains an option because of the weak domination exercised by hegemons, which habitually retain client regimes and with them their ability to raise an armed force. In the pursuit of wellbeing and liberty, or just to maximise their rents, clients may calculate that the potential benefits of reneging on a contract outweigh the risks. A sudden opportunity, the defeat of their overlord in a faraway battle or his or her natural death – remembering the personal nature of their bonds – may be enough, although internal events, the demise of their own compliant ruler, or the boost of a local military success might also tip the scales.[9]

This "balance by secession" represents a direct means to counter the concentration of power. A seceding polity may have performed internal balancing to improve its capacity to resist retaliation, or may be acting with others in external balancing – processes that are not directly visible to us. Switching allegiance from one overlord to another would be a variation on the theme, one that not only weakens one hegemon but strengthens its rival. The new overlord may offer better terms or may be exerting its own coercive power by "turning" a rival's client. Caracol was a defector of this general sort, Moral-Reforma another, but there were doubtless more. We saw in Case Study 13 how the small polities along the Usumacinta River and Lacandon regions operated in a volatile environment where loyalties switched as a result of military adventurism.

To review: subjects could be motivated to renege on their contracts if (a) the power of the hegemon approached a point where future resistance might prove impossible and its ambition wholly unchecked, (b) when better terms can be gained from an alternative hegemon, or (c) when their own rising fortunes and power seems sufficient to restore full autonomy, and even to dominate others. In these ways hegemonies can be checked by anti-hegemonial strategies, whether conducted on an individual or group basis. The limits imposed by a balance of power mechanism are joined by the diminishing effectiveness of a low-cost, low-return system at ever greater distance from the core. The persistence of the multi-polity system would be broken only if the logic of domination could gain the upper hand.

We do see certain infrastructural developments at Calakmul and Tikal that could well reflect moves to exploit or solidify their positions. For example, we have seen how the oversized court complexes at these centres may have been involved in socialising subjects as part of a strategy directed at inculcating loyalty and collective elite identity, a schema that would simultaneously provide a group of implicit or explicit hostages. The housing of hostages recurs in several of our comparative studies, where its logic flows from the need to close the distance between patron and client – reducing scores or even hundreds of kilometres to the gap between one palace compound and the next. Additionally, that both Tikal and Calakmul built large permanent marketplaces may well represent efforts to exercise regional control over exchange systems. Though commercial networks were, again, modest in relative terms compared to those of Tenochtitlan and Athens, Mesoamerican precedents suggests a close, symbiotic relationship between tribute, trade, and political power.

What we lack in almost all of our examples of hegemonic societies, including that of the Classic Maya, is evidence for the kind of self-strengthening reforms that enabled Qin to turn itself into a territorial conqueror. To succeed in that, a polity must undertake internal transformations of structure, as well as moving to fully deny to others the ideal of sovereignty and self-determination it claims for itself. Polities capable of reshaping an entrenched concept from inside the system can do so only by developing a new ideological basis, one that explicitly departs from the moral order that sustains a society of states.

The Classic Maya had the kind of coherence we associate with such a society, in which member polities subscribed to a common value system and recognised the legitimacy of each other's claims to sovereign status. It was anarchical in principle but hierarchical in practice and, importantly, this worked to preserve and expand the mosaic of multiple polities rather than to undermine and merge them. The Classic Maya case, therefore, resembles the dynamic equilibrium of the Chinese Spring and Autumn Period, but not the more intensely competitive era of the Warring States – which preserved the unity of an intellectual culture but abandoned the political culture that insisted on at least notional sovereignty for all players. In this phase transition from a

Lockean to a Hobbesian environment, self-preservation could now only be guaranteed through universal domination.

A moral order enlists the unimpeachable authority of the divine in pursuit of highly rational and pragmatic aims, a form of political management in which violence is constrained and the pursuit of wellbeing maximised within commonly accepted bounds. The enduring division of the Classic Maya political landscape, and the lack of effort that even the most powerful polities put into permanent territorial expansion, is testament to the success of that model rather than to a failure of centralisation.

Part of my argument here is that the kind of overkingship exercised by Calakmul and Tikal was a practical realpolitik that never developed a distinctive ideological charter. At heart, the status of *ajaw* adhered to an ideal of lordly solidarity rooted in the founding tenets of Classic Maya political culture. The honorific *kaloomte'* title came to be used in much the same way as the various overking statuses we see in other hegemonic systems, demonstrating that a measure of hierarchy was both practical and ethical. However, the lack of higher ranks – most of all a titular claim to universal rule – shows that the degree of wide mastery periodically attained by Classic Maya hegemons was "never an institution, but merely a prize to be won".

FIFTEEN

SUMMARY AND CONCLUSIONS:
A SOCIETY OF KINGS

The Classic Maya represent a newly important topic for political anthropology and the study of pre-Modern societies. The decipherment of their script offers a trove of primary sources that allow us, uniquely in the ancient Americas, to compare and contrast a rich material record with a significant historical one. Whether our goal is to comprehend social power in its broadest sense, or to understand the nature of specific institutions such as monarchy, complex societies isolated from the cross-fertilisations of the Old World have clear comparative value. As such, what we can learn about the Maya casts useful light on universal themes and will be of wider relevance to the field.

The challenge taken up in this volume has been to explicate the political system of the Classic Maya by means of those written texts, which were utilised diachronically in terms of process and synchronically in terms of structure. The analysis has been one that draws on both anthropological and historical approaches, with contributions from strands within political and complexity theory. In this concluding chapter, I bring together the different facets of the argument and set out my core propositions.

What the combined data make clear is that neither the strong regional state nor the weak peer polity, nor indeed an ideology governed by calendrical cycles, are sustainable interpretations of Classic Maya archaeopolitics. Instead, the evidence consistently supports a hegemonic system, one in which an enduring multitude of polities were arranged within waxing and waning hierarchical orders. Although they were in active competition with one another, there was little or no territorial consolidation or the permanent eradication of rivals – indeed the number of identifiable polities only increased as time wore on.

However, what has been missing from this understanding has been an appreciation of why the system took the form that it did and how it functioned through time. It has been described but not truly analysed, still less explained. The proposals I offer here are therefore not recapitulations of those I have previously advanced, but rather an effort to reconceive and extend those ideas to posit a set of underlying mechanisms. By investigating a larger and better-understood pool of data, examined in reference to a broader range of comparative material and cross-disciplinary political theory, the hegemonic model is here given a conceptual ground on which to stand.

Recognising at the outset that we are dealing with patrimonial rhetoric means that we appreciate that the content and style of the texts are intimately connected to the political effects they sought to achieve. Yet, if we are prepared to look at them not only individually but in the aggregate, they prove to be far from epiphenomenal to the project of understanding the political system of the Classic Period. The particularities of identities, events, and relationships found in the inscriptions are, I have maintained throughout, inherently reflective of the structures that produced them – each a potential outcome of the rules, norms, and conventions that shape, though never determine, the course of political life. But that process cannot be a one-way street since roles, behaviours, and interactions were not simply expressive but, in recursive fashion, constitutive of those structures. The repetition of particular acts, the adoption of specific identities, and the forging of certain engagements were instrumental to their own maintenance and reproduction. Text and image preserve invaluable traces of these processes, yet were not themselves outside them. Not only the content of public monuments but their physical presence and endurance in the world meant that they too played a role and, through a classic conflation of signified and signifier, contributed to the perpetuation of the system.

The issues at the heart of this book are how and why a large number of ostensibly independent polities could coexist, indeed flourish, for centuries without descending into crippling levels of conflict, ultimately to be consumed by expansive empires or macro-states. The reasons Classic Maya polities did not increase in size or structural complexity, and how the system maintained and reproduced itself, can ultimately be discerned in a balance of material and social logics.

The first point to emphasise is that the Classic Maya are by no means an exotic or aberrant case but one with parallels across the world and through time. Global comparisons, here drawn from periods in the histories of Fiji, Ireland, India, and Greece (though others could have been chosen in their place) differ in a great many respects, but the degree to which they correspond offers telling clues to the workings of political tessellation amidst cultural congruity. However, those similarities are apparent only when we cast aside the classificatory mindset and its fixation on form – especially what is, and is not, a state – to focus instead on the ideas and relationships that generate a political ecology.

In each case, we have a self-replicating system in which asymmetrical power relations were manifested not in the appropriation of territory but in the extension of political patronage. Motives might vary as to their priority, but economic gain and enhanced security were consistently at the forefront. Struggles that created, preserved, or resisted patron–client bonds produce turbulence at the unit level, but amount to no more than surface perturbations at the level of the system. The political ecology itself was never in question and it mattered not who filled the dominant and subordinate roles at any one time. While this kind of dynamic equilibrium could be resilient and long-lived, it does not endure indefinitely. In all four of our primary examples the system was brought to an end by the arrival of more powerful foreign actors, who either forced local integration or were themselves system-wide conquerors. But we have also seen how equilibrium could be undone from within. Our fifth comparative case, covering the transition between two eras in Chinese history, shows how internal reforms and the abrogation of long-honoured norms paved the way for one polity to devour all its rivals.

A divided political landscape has, due to the restricted information-gathering and isolated self-reliance of its units, a predisposition toward a Hobbesian culture of mutual suspicion, fear, and violence. Here self-help strategies and the balance of power mechanism are all that separates its members from the ultimate dystopia of "all against all". But polities that co-evolve and maintain intimate social contact possess strategies that mitigate that threat. These expand on the codes of conduct that facilitate intra-communal life, projecting a version of them outward to condition relations between communities. The resulting Lockean culture is still a highly competitive one – it does not reach a Kantian ideal of near-harmonious, law-bound coexistence – but it does place some checks on how that competition is conducted and what its outcomes can be.

One feature that unites the Classic Maya with our global case studies is their acknowledgment of multiple sovereignties as a legitimate social fact. It is this recognition and respect for rights beyond their own that makes each of them more than a system of interacting polities but a more cohesive "society of states". Members of such societies share a resource that others lack, namely an ideological commonwealth that is the wellspring of their shared values and identity. At the same time, competition leads to the development of expansive hegemonies that contradict the concept of local sovereignty. Indeed, we might define hegemony as a mode of dominion that preserves the principle of multiple sovereignties only by converting an absolute definition into a relative one. What seems whole is actually "divisible", and functions by obfuscating the ideal and the real in an "organised hypocrisy". Hegemonies dilute the concept of sovereignty, but in doing so distinguish themselves from territorial empires which, no matter how much administrative authority they leave in local hands, must destroy any semblance of their sovereign status.

With these points in mind I now move to a focussed treatment of the Classic Maya case by means of two interpretive formulations or models based on the evidence currently to hand. The first addresses the issues from a structural and synchronic perspective, the second from a historical and diachronic one. Irreducibly bound, the presence of one necessarily implies the other.

SYNCHRONY

The core unit in Classic Maya political organisation was the individual king-ship, around which cohered a personalised polity that was deemed sovereign and structurally autonomous. The legitimacy of kings stemmed in the first instance from claimed descent from a named dynastic progenitor. But while bloodline might qualify particular candidates, it was their possession and care of specific patron deities that sacralised their role and placed them at the heart as well as at the head of the community. Importantly, the royal lineage was only one among a group of elite families that formed an endogamous caste at the core of the polity, both king and noble sharing the single status of *ajaw*, "lord". The distinction between them was one of degree rather than kind, with the paramount ruler best seen as the highest ranking within a scale of lordship. The privileged position of this collective cohort ultimately rested on their control of violence, but it was their sacerdotal responsibilities on behalf of the community at large that justified and naturalised their distinction from the commoners, those who tilled the land in their service.

The pattern of behaviours producing this distribution of units across the landscape did not arise from some material or environmental exigency – there are clearly other ways in which Maya society might have been constituted in organisational and spatial terms. It was the dispositions of its originators that were the key initial conditions of the system. Whether fictive or real, the idea of kinship between the elite produced an affinity that defined their separation from the population at large.

Successful and self-perpetuating, that founding ethos was manifested in the propagation and spread of Classic Maya polities across a landscape newly available due to the collapse of the previous political order. The division into multiple polities was no barrier to interaction and the flow of ideas, which were achieved by effective, if now largely invisible, means of intellectual exchange.

Some sites were cosmopolitan hubs, others backwaters, but all were linked to an information network that disseminated and promoted their collective identity.

That cultural bundle preserved the coherence and homogeneity of the new society and set out ordering principles. No polity, no kingship, sought to define itself in a novel or idiosyncratic way, but instead replicated the current template down to the smallest detail of regal paraphernalia or phrasing of commemorative text. Each ruler was seen as the localised manifestation of a single archetypal kingship, at the same moment many and one. Through prescribed rituals each king sustained their gods, in return receiving benefaction for themselves and their communities. But they also contributed to the greater task of world order – no matter how many neighbours were performing the exact same rites, on precisely the same days, only a day or two's walk away.

These are all powerful reasons to consider Classic Maya polities collectively. In the same way that events and structures are innately bound to one another, so must the form and functioning of individual polities be seen as the contingent manifestations of potentials offered by the system. And, just as the structure and behaviour of each polity was fashioned by the larger collective, so it reciprocally shaped that collective through time. In its formative stages a political network expands via the agency of its originators. But as it matures its course is no longer centrally directed and instead works holistically from the on-going interactions of all its constituent parts. By that emergent point, the rules, norms, and conventions that shape political practice have no single source or author, they are a possession of the system as a whole.

Classic Maya political ecology meets the criteria for a "society of states", although the personalised nature of its authority makes a "society of kings" the more apt description. It shows three defining attributes of the form: a mutual recognition of sovereignty as an engrained ideal, a common set of patterned interactions, and a collective desire to maintain the system that the persistence of both imply. Yet, no matter how much rational self-interest incentivises cooperation, or what ethnic, linguistic, cultural, or religious commonalities might facilitate it, a more specific essence is required to bind and police such a society. What makes norms ethical, rather than simply pragmatic is the ideological commonwealth I have here called the "moral order". This Durkheimesque social fact embedded coexistence within the deep structure of Classic Maya political culture, rooted in the aforementioned belief that kingship was a localised iteration of a cosmically determined template and part of the fabric of time. Crucially, moral order provides the kind of regulatory authority and centre to political life that a truly anarchical distribution of power would lack. This guiding authority resided in no particular place, but was internalised by its members and in this way distributed across the network.

The bellicose self-representations carved into the monuments speak to the enduring importance of the warrior ideal to royal ideology in general and personal authority in particular. But this patrimonial rhetoric tells us precious little about the actual incidence or character of warfare. The monuments describe conflicts that differed in scale and intensity, but their formulaic presentations in both text and image barely, if at all, distinguish transformative, once-in-a-generation pan-regional contests from the pettiest of border raids. The significance of any given encounter can only be understood within its individual historical matrix. If these were fully known, we might well judge a dozen or so clashes more consequential than all others combined. Make no mistake, competition in a Lockean society of states can be as frequent, disruptive, and deadly as it is in a Hobbesian system of states. But the survival of defeated Classic Maya polities, even the restoration of some captured kings, demonstrates that there were boundaries within which political violence was considered legitimate. Once established, the presence of powerful hegemonies worked to reduce overall levels of conflict by creating zones of common association. This is probably reflected, in part, in the low investment in Classic-era urban fortifications.

The supervision of accession ceremonies and the declarations of lordly ownership we see on the monuments are not mere expressions of relative status, they reference the contracts that converted illegitimate parasitical relationships into legitimate patrimonial ones. Though coercion always plays some role, volunteerism should not be underestimated, as subject polities give up a portion of their liberty and economic rents in exchange for security gains and a share in the benefits of a larger and wealthier elite network. Tribute was the fuel that powered the political machine. Perhaps at times expressed as corvée labour, it was the primary means by which the weak were economically exploited by the strong; a low-cost low-return exaction which offered strong situational advantages over the high-cost high-return strategy of direct territorial control.

The upwardly channelled wealth found its way into the palace economies of the dominant dynasties, where it supported their elevated lifestyles, financed the gifts that maintained client networks, and funded construction projects – not only those of temples and palaces but roads, reservoirs, and perhaps some of the larger agricultural infrastructure. More ephemerally, those same revenues likely funded lavish ceremonies and rituals that promoted hegemonic status at collective gatherings hosted at the capital, as well as supported the military specialists required to intimidate or confront rivals and rebels alike. Finally, it furnished the riches, the jades, pelts, and plumes, that materialised kingly status in life, but were also regularly removed from circulation in the stocking of royal tombs. Although out-of-sight, that interred finery was not entirely out-of-mind and could be seen as a constituent part of the cumulative power and prestige of the ancestral dynasty.

There were several interdependent factors that prevented hegemons from escalating their control to the point at which larger and more integrated formations became possible. First, hegemonic power is self-limiting because it relies on the cooperative acquiescence of its subjects, which were not helpless pawns but accessories in their own domination. Each tolerates its inferior rank, keeps to its contract, only so long as the cost–benefit calculation falls in favour of maintaining that status quo. Each preserves the ambition for greater self-determination inherent to sovereign status, which maximises decision-making liberties and material benefits for its governing elite, and they retain the armed forces that makes resistance feasible.

Moreover, as a patron's zone of authority expands its capacity to enforce its will on an increasing number of clients at ever greater distance correspondingly weakens. The particular time-distance logistics of a world dominated by foot travel would appear to make the low-cost low-return strategy an especially attractive route to political expansion. Hence the expediency and value of contracts which, by adding the moral dimension of obligation, seek to cement attachments without the need for continuous active coercion. Here what most distinguishes hegemony from empire is the absence of the institutional apparatus necessary to stabilise domination.

Next, no long-term, competitive multi-polity system seems to have lacked a balance of power mechanism that regulates relative strength in ways that favour the enduring preservation of that system. Observed switches of allegiance and military alliances are the shadowy remnants of the moves necessary to thwart the consolidation of irresistible power in the Classic era.

Finally, to truly break an entrenched multi-polity society a suitably ambitious contender must gain not only the practical means but the alternative ideology that makes such defiance possible. As long as hegemons subscribe to the same ideals as their clients they cannot overcome the high practical difficulties of converting weak bonds of patronage into strong bonds of domination, the kind necessary to forge true empires or macro-states. Only the abandonment of those ideals, an ethical reinvention together with a corresponding programme of self-strengthening reforms, makes that kind of transformation practical. Though Calakmul and Tikal may have harboured ambitions for universal dominion, there is no evidence that they attempted the moves that would have been necessary to achieve it. The lack of a universal title in the lexicon of the Classic Period – even of an aspirational variety – confirms that such a status would be a transgression of moral order, which could tolerate a ranking of kings, but would be antithetical to the rule of just one.

DIACHRONY

No social system exists in a temporal void, it is always a "historical object". In the terms I have been employing, political structures are sculpted by the interactions of their components through time, such that the relationship between schemas and resources are constantly renewed or re-applied in new contexts. Change takes place as actors respond reflexively to each other's actions and pursue their perceived best advantage within any given set of circumstances.

That a number of the most important Classic-era dynasties ascribed their origins to a single source is an important pointer to their self-perception as a linked movement. Since events at this place are set in the second century CE, squarely within the Protoclassic transition between the Preclassic and Classic, we have good reason to believe that it was a historical location rather than a mythic construct. The Classic Period saw the development of a particular concept of legitimate authority, one clearly springing from Late Preclassic antecedents yet separate and distinct from them. Lordly status was centred on the rank of *ajaw* in both epochs, but the Classic reconfigured its meaning, apparently by fixing power in the hands of one lineage. The position of a paramount ruler was surely no innovation, but in its "dynastic DNA" the Classic system does distinguish itself and offers material corollaries pointing to a meaningful shift in ideology and practice. The early dynastic foundations took place at existing Preclassic sites in the central southern lowlands. These new regimes simply assumed the identities of the places they ruled, as if none had done so before, such that their kings were specified as the "lord of such-and-such place".

The Maya had long been in contact with the great metropolis of Teotihuacan in Central Mexico, but relations took a decisive turn in 378. The authochronous development of Classic Maya kingdoms was interrupted by an intrusive event that unseated and usurped the incumbent Mutul dynasty of Tikal, introducing a patriline directly linked to that of the foreigners. Similar substitutions and subjugations appear to have been enacted across the region, forming a discernible New Order. Its ultimate motivation was presumably economic, offering Teotihuacan greater access to and control over the varied resources of the lowlands, most likely via the tribute that might be extracted from new subjects. However, fourth century Teotihuacan did not tutor the Maya on social and political organisation – the template was already in place – and far from stunting the expansion of the dynastic ideal it seems only to have accelerated it.

As royal groups divided or shifted base they spread outward from the central region, many of their original toponymic titles now evolving into dynastic names. Thus, a good number of the kingdoms established after 378, including Piedras Negras, Palenque, Copan, and Quirigua, were not in situ developments but the result of royal migrations. In a not dissimilar manner, the patron gods that formed such a vital part of royal identity and legitimacy were, in all probability, initially localised and place-specific. Yet by the time we gain clear sight of them at least some had become attached to dynastic lines and moved across the landscape with them.

In the first years of the New Order there was a flurry of imported styles from Central Mexico, but traditional Maya forms reasserted themselves within a generation. It is by no means certain, however, that this reflects an early end to foreign overlordship. That no Tikal ruler carries the uppermost *kaloomte'* title during the fifth century could indicate that it was reserved for a still higher authority. A separate sign of continuing oversight comes in the initiation of the Copan and Quirigua polities in 426, whose legitimising rites seemingly took place at Teotihuacan. Although the sanctioning role of this "Place of Reeds" was to become a potent symbol in later times, here it seems grounded in a practical political reality. The demise of Teotihuacan as a force in the sixth century aligns, likely in causal fashion, with important changes in the Maya lowlands. The recording of military exploits in text as well as image is one such innovation, and this seems to have a direct connection to a newly competitive climate focussed on establishing or resisting regional Classic Maya hierarchies. These developments are especially associated with a budding rival for Tikal in the shape of the Kaanul dynasty of Dzibanche.

By the mid-sixth century Dzibanche overkingship had expanded over a wide area and included former allies or subjects of Tikal. Attacked and overwhelmed in 562, Tikal was subordinated or otherwise subdued and did not return to contention for almost a century. The strength and ambition of the early Snake dynasty can be further gauged by its long-range military expeditions against Palenque in 599 and 611. However, its position must have been seriously jeopardised by the civil conflict that broke out shortly after 630, leading to a defeat for its ruling king in 636 and his demise in 640. This resulted in a lasting transfer of the main royal seat from Dzibanche to Calakmul. Its resolve and capabilities undiminished, the relocated regime succeeded in seizing Tikal in 657 and, in the wake of that victory, acquired a string of new or renewed clients in the 660s – including some that brought it back to the western lowlands of modern-day Tabasco. A period of sustained authority for Calakmul endured until at least 695, when a resurgent Tikal finally bested their great adversary in battle. Calakmul survived that setback and initially held on to its most important possessions, but a second reverse at Tikal's hands around 734 coincides with a sharper decline. The Kaanul dynasty at Calakmul seems to have largely unravelled within the next generation.

Ever linked in binary fashion, Tikal filled some of the power vacuum this produced by seizing the kings of two of Calakmul's leading clients, Naranjo and El Peru, and by mid-century had established the last Classic-era hegemony of any note. Even so, the epigraphic signature of this renewed sphere of influence is negligible. Its scale is more a matter of inference from the gaps in monument commissions at those defeated sites and the wealth implied by immense construction projects at Tikal, whose site core was transformed at this time.

Although the powerful polities of the central lowlands demand most of our attention, it would be a mistake to focus on that region exclusively since important hegemonies also operated elsewhere. The west saw Palenque pitted against Piedras Negras on the one hand and Tonina on the other, often with control of the Tabascan plain or sites along the Usumacinta River at stake. In the north, similar rivalries presumably developed between Coba, Edzna, and Oxkintok, succeeded by Ek Balam, Uxmal, and ultimately Chichen Itza, although our sources on this are very meagre. In all places competition between major powers took place at the regional and pan-regional scale, but always overlaid a great many local rivalries and sub-regional hierarchies.

The rise in prominence of secondary lords during the eighth century, though far from uniform, suggests that some recalibration of status within the Classic cohort might have been underway. If the levelling of position we see at Copan, Yaxchilan, Oxkintok, and across the Río Bec region was part of a wider phenomenon, then the equality innate to the *ajaw* rank seems to have been re-asserting itself at the expense of kings. This would segue neatly into the political realities of the Postclassic era. Hereditary rulership persisted in a number of Postclassic societies, but in others the highest position rotated among elite families. The *ajaw* class survived, but only a much weaker concept of monarchy which was, critically, stripped of the sacralised character it had previously enjoyed.

The great powerbrokers were a key element of Classic political culture at its apogee, and the decline of the most successful, the Kaanul dynasty of Dzibanche-Calakmul, marked an early sign of its dissolution. In network terms, a hub-dominated structure transitioned to a more diffused one, increasing its susceptibility to failures, whether sudden traumas or slow cascades. From about 730 onwards the total number of recorded interactions begins to drop, even though the number of sites erecting monuments rises steeply for up to four decades more. This brief burst marks not strength but weakness, as subject kings once fettered to more powerful ones asserted new liberties. Hyper-localism and its greater reliance on self-help strategies would have both stoked the security dilemma and undermined the collaborative strategies possible under hegemony.

Neither of the ways in which multi-polity systems were extinguished in our full five comparative cases – that is, by the arrival of an external force that successfully unites the entire cultural zone, or by one or more polities enacting the internal reforms that allow them to triumph over all others – apply to the Classic Maya case. Although a good number of causes for the ninth century collapse have been proposed, none by themselves fully explains why their effects proved so devastating, or why no recovery took place. The widespread depopulation of an area once sustaining millions, completed within a few generations, lacks the close historical analogies that might otherwise help us to comprehend it.

Even if much of the collapse story remains opaque, we can chart the key stages in its development. The majority of Classic Maya polities stopped erecting monuments at or not too long before 810, pointing to some significant but unrecorded crisis. Certain polities survived and maintained conservative practices, yet a number of these acknowledge the presence and oversight of lords who used familiar high titles, but carried names and expressed religious ideas that distanced them from conventional Classic Maya kingship. These lords created their own loci of power, basing themselves at hitherto unremarkable capitals such as Ceibal, Ucanal, and Nakum, which were redeveloped and grew in population. The precise manner in which they achieved this position, and how their identities map onto ethnicities or geographic origins, has still to be fully ascertained. However, where such associations can be made they lie with people and cultures far to the west.

Despite their differences, these new powerbrokers were full participants in Classic Maya political culture and can be seen to preserve, assimilate, or even revitalise its traditions. But as the ninth century went on this strategy weakened and non-Maya identities emerged more assertively, shedding light on this group's continuing ties to western societies. All these changes took place in the midst of widespread demographic decline and the progressive extinction of all remaining polities – the cascade that followed a trauma. Evidence for episodic dry periods has emerged from several different sources and current projections suggest that they were sufficiently severe to cause societal distress. How the timing of these events engaged with political, social, cultural, and economic processes to produce direct, compounded, or tangential effects is something only more and better data can establish.

The Classic Maya would not be the first society undone by their own success. Their integrated social, cultural, and economic network generated food surpluses and a population boom, nurtured by political ideals that ensured high levels of division. Such florescence can be seen as taking place, both literally and figuratively, at the "edge of chaos": with this burgeoning populace increasingly vulnerable to any capricious change in climate and an increasingly devolved political landscape that could not rally or unite against any unforeseen threats.

FINAL THOUGHTS

I have presented a view of Classic Maya politics in its full flower that gives primary significance to a set of socially constructed ideals that preserved a divided political landscape by allowing material ambitions and security goals to be pursued without wider consolidation. The kind of dynamic equilibrium that results is not specific to the Maya case but a recurring global pattern, one in which commonly agreed notions of sovereignty guide behaviour and determine what is ethical as well as what is practical in political terms.

In the heyday of nomothetic thinking in the social sciences, the resolution of how and why questions was essentially a matter of collecting sufficient data to trace the linear path from cause to effect. But this kind of thinking cannot adequately explain complex social systems which, being sentient, intersubjective, and reflexive, follow a course that is non-linear and probabilistic. Causality in such systems is dependent on a constellation of variables, each of which has significance only in the presence of others. The divided political landscape and its society of kings, together with the moral order that guided and sustained them, co-evolved. In that sense, no part can be meaningfully prioritised or placed ahead in sequence precisely because each entailed the other in a mutually dependent process.

Thus, even if I have appropriately described a set of entwined material and social logics that shaped the form and trajectory of Classic Maya political life, this always needs to be understood as the result of contingent human action. Although participants have goals in mind, the consequences of their acts are never entirely foreseeable and, while we might retroduce their progress, they were not inevitable. This, in essence, is what a historical perspective and complexity bring to the study of social structures: the acknowledgement of how self-organisation and chaos, as generated by the near-limitless possibilities of agents acting upon each other and the physical world, together bring "similarity in processes and differences in outcomes".

It will surprise no reader to learn that I reject any suggestion that Maya scholarship is succumbing to a "tyranny of the epigraphic record". We are instead, I believe, advancing a new partnership between the textual and material that puts us ever more firmly into the purview of historical archaeologies worldwide; with all the beguiling opportunities and gnawing frustrations that represents. Exploiting these two ways of knowing means recognising their relative strengths and weaknesses depending on the issue at hand – each will disappoint if directed toward questions it is ill-equipped to answer – even as we continue to strive for genuine synergies. While the inscriptions offer a vital resource, it goes without saying that they can only ever tell us a portion of what we would like to know and, even then, only lead us to deeper levels of analysis and interpretation. Still, if we are interested in the way politics is driven not just by material forces but by ideas, things that are not simply ephemeral but might never find direct physical form, then we must take on the challenge of the texts and listen to the stones that now speak.

APPENDIX

AN INVENTORY OF EMBLEM GLYPHS

akankeh
Acanceh

?
Altar de
Sacrificios 1

?
Altar de
Sacrificios 2

?
Altun Ha

ak'e
Bonampak/
Lacanha

xukalnaah?
Bonampak/
Lacanha

kaanul
Calakmul 1/
Dzibanche

suutz'?
Calakmul 2/
Oxpemul 1/Naachtun?

?
Cancuen

k'antumaak
Caracol 1

uxwitz
Caracol 2

?
Ceibal

chak k'uh
Chancala

chan
Chinkultic

?
Coba

joy kaan
Comalcalco

?
Copan

ich? kaan tijo'
Dzibilchaltun

?
Edzna

talol
Ek Balam

?
El Chorro

lakamtuun
El Palma

sak ook wak peet
El Palmar

? wak
El Peru

ch'ajulte'
El Reinado 1

?
El Reinado 2

chak wayib
Holmul

?
Huacatal

ibil?
Itsimte

?
Itzan

juluup?
Ixkun

ho kab
Ixtutz

chan
Jaina

sak tz'i'
Lacanja-Tzeltal

namaan
La Florida

pepe'tuun
La Mar

ch'ate'il
La Rejolla

?
Lamanai

buuk'
Los Alacranes

?
Machaquila

?
Moral-Reforma

ik'a'
Motul de
San José

?
Nakum

sa'al
Naranjo 1

sak chuwen
Naranjo 2

wakam
Nim Li Punit

wuk ?
Oxkintok

?
Oxpemul 2

baakal
Palenque 1

matwiil
Palenque 2

toktahn
Palenque 3

yokib
Piedras Negras 1

k'inil Piedras Negras 2	*wayal* Piedras Negras 3	*pakbuul?* Pomona 1	*pipa'* Pomona 2	*uun* Pusilha
? Quirigua 1	*?* Quirigua 2	*?* Río Azul	*jul(uup)?* Sacul	*wak'ib?* Santa Elena
? Tamarindito- Arroyo de Piedra	*mutul* Tikal/Dos Pilas- Aguateca	*popo'* Tonina 1	*?* Tonina 2	*puhtz'am* Tonina 3
? Uaxactun	*k'anwitznal* Ucanal	*naah kuuma'* Uxul	*baaxwitz* Xultun	*katuutzwitz* Xunantunich?
pa'chan Yaxchilan 1	*kaaj?* Yaxchilan 2	*muwaan* Yaxchilan 3	*yaxa'* Yaxha	*hixwitz* Zapote Bobal- Pajaral-La Joyanca

Currently
unassigned

ak'ab
Ak'ab

anaak'e?
Anaak'e

anayite'
Anaite II?

bital
Bital

komkom
Buenavista del Cayo?

buktuun
Buktuun

chatahn
Chatahn

?
Cloud Bird

?
"Cuychen"

ton
"Hauberg"

?
Itsimte Area

bahlam
Jaguar

jobon
Jobon

jut'
Jut'

koban
Koban

maasal
Maasal

mahk
Mahk

mamis
Mamis

pomoy?
Pomoy

baaxtuun
Quartz Stone

ehmach?
Raccoon

puh
Reed

?
Rubber Ball

siik'
Siik'

?
Site S

?
Site T

?
Small Snake

ek' bahlam
Star Jaguar

tuubal
Tuubal

uxhaabte'
Uxhaabte'

waakchin
Waakchin

?
Xkuy

yopmootz
Yopmootz

NOTES

2 MODELLING THE MAYA

1 Sources referring to a practice of *multepal*, literally "joint rule", have led many to believe in a system of shared, heterarchical governance at Late Postclassic Mayapan. However, under close scrutiny the term more plausibly refers to a hierarchical ranking between powerful families, an interpretation more in keeping with other documentary sources (Ringle and Bey 2001: 273–275).

2 The most accessible introduction to the workings of the Maya calendar is David Stuart's (2011a) *The Order of Days*, while a more exhaustive, if in places dated, description can be found in J. Eric S. Thompson's (1950) *Maya Hieroglyphic Writing: Introduction*. The elements referenced in this book include the Long Count, an accumulative system whose five lowest units are the Bak'tun (144,000 days), K'atun (7,200 days), Tun (360 days), Winal (20 days), and K'in (days). The completion of major stations of the Long Count, dubbed "period endings", were regularly commemorated by the dedication of inscribed monuments. An illustrative example of a K'atun ending would be 9.15.0.0.0, which took place in 731 CE. The Classic Period saw the completion of only two Bak'tun cycles: 9.0.0.0.0 in 435 and 10.0.0.0.0 in 830. The Long Count meshes with two other cycles, a 260-day calendar called the *tzolk'in* and a 365-day calendar called the *haab*. In combination, these two systems form the Calendar Round, a cycle that repeats every 18,980 days or 52 years. This means that every Long Count position has a corresponding Calendar Round which, in the case of 9.15.0.0.0, is 4 Ajaw 13 Yax. The particular meshing of the *tzolk'in* and Long Count ensures that all period endings fall on the *tzolk'in* day of Ajaw "Lord".

3 This book converts Maya Long Count dates into the proleptic Gregorian Calendar using a version of the GMT correlation, 584286, which differs from other versions by one to three days (Martin and Skidmore 2012). It is derived from the account of a solar eclipse that took place in 790 on Poco Uinic Stela 3, which may be the only single-day celestial event referenced in Classic Maya inscriptions. This correlation awaits confirmation or refutation from the discovery of a second such account, since only that will guarantee that the date of that eclipse was recorded correctly.

4 Berlin identified eight emblem glyphs, those of Tikal, Palenque, Copan, Naranjo, Piedras Negras, Yaxchilan, Ceibal (Seibal), and Quirigua, while noting the presence of seven more – including that of the "Snake" – which he could not assign to particular sites. The three-part construction does not include optional phonetic complements or lexical suffixes.

5 One might suppose that the discovery of the expansive battle scene at Bonampak in 1946 would have sparked an immediate challenge to the pacific model (see Figure 44). However, as we will see in Chapter 9, it contributed to the debate in a meaningful way only twenty years later, after the discovery of earthworks at Tikal.

6 The best introduction to Maya decipherment remains Coe (1992) (and its updated editions), while a concise but more specialised description can be found in Zender (2018a). Maya texts in this volume will be represented largely according to the style guide established by George Stuart (1988).

7 This was not true of all work from system theorists, since, somewhat against the grain of the times, Flannery (1972: 399) had argued that ideological factors must be taken into account in social reconstructions.

8   At the time, understanding of this connecting term was rudimentary and glossed as "in the land of". It is now thought to be a transitive verb reading *ukabjiiy*, "he/she supervised it", or instead a relational noun, "his/her doing" (see Chapter 10).

9   Calakmul's heavily eroded inscriptions (see Morley 1933; Ruppert and Denison 1943; Marcus 1987) initially provided no clear examples of the emblem glyph to confirm the attribution and, as will be explained in Case Study 6, the Snake kingdom was long associated with the neutral nickname "Site Q". This introduced further confusion, since the home of most unprovenanced monuments ascribed to Site Q was not Calakmul but La Corona, as explained in Schuster (1997).

10 My original proposal was set out in these terms: "Although such data only seems clear for Site Q, I expect that *Kan* was only the most interactive and successful of a range of 'super-polities'. The outlines of this arrangement are hard to discern since the 'system' was not fixed and admitted many fine distinctions and scales of importance. [...] I see macropolitical organisation not as a concrete system, but simply as a status quo that evolved amongst a limited number of rival polities. The basic political unit was indeed defined by the use of the Emblem Glyph, yet these small kingdoms were also arranged within a semi-fluid map of overlapping spheres of influence, centred on a few (changeable) pre-eminent states" (Martin 1993: 15).
    These sentiments elaborated on those in a letter sent to T. Patrick Culbert (26 May 1992), which was my first use of the term "superpower blocs" for the Classic Maya. It should be noted that the discovery of a *yajaw* statement at Dos Pilas led Stephen Houston and colleagues to detect "the machinations and complexities of superpower politics" in an unpublished paper (Houston et al. 1992: 10).

11 See also Hassig (1988: 18–22). The relevance of the work by Luttwak and Hassig was first brought to our attention by Hanns Prem (pers. comm. 1993).

12 Some colleagues have misconstrued my views on this point. Much of the confusion appears to stem from the title of Martin and Grube (1995) as "Maya Super States", which was devised by the editors of *Archaeology Magazine* in place of the submitted title "Maya Superpowers". The superpowers in question included not only the unusually powerful polities of Tikal and Calakmul, but also lesser rivals such as Palenque, Copan, Tonina, and Piedras Negras (Martin and Grube 1995: 44). I have at no point argued that Tikal and Calakmul shared control of the entire southern lowlands or subsumed all other polities (c.f. Chase and Chase 1998: 13; Chase et al. 2009: 176, 180; Munson and Macri 2009: 425).

13 This limit is derived from a very precise estimation of the weight of maize a warrior and his accompanying retainers could carry in order to sustain themselves over the duration of a campaign, given a marching pace of 2.4 km per hour over an eight-hour day (Hassig 1992: 21, 53; Chase and Chase 1998: 17–18, 23–25). Yet, even if this assessment were to be correct, it does not consider living off the land – a very common form of expropriation in which armies that cannot otherwise be supplied sustain themselves – or for the potential of allied or subject polities to provision a force en route to a distant target.

14 The full list of "primary capitals" in this reconstruction are Calakmul, Caracol, Chichen Itza, Comalcalco, Coba, Copan, Dos Pilas, Dzibilchaltun, Edzna, La Corona, Tikal, Palenque, Piedras Negras, and Uxmal, while "border centres" consist of Izamal, Naranjo, Pomona, Quirigua, Tonina, Santa Rosa Xtampak, and Yaxchilan (Chase and Chase 1998: figure 1).

15 This argument is developed from an MA thesis focusing on an iconographic rather than epigraphic analysis (Savage 2007).

16 Rice's original explanation for the lack of commemoration for a 256-year cycle was that such records appear on monuments still to be discovered, were once to be found in now-eroded and illegible passages, or lie concealed in texts that have yet to be deciphered (Rice 2004: 9, 243). Her suggested translation on the Palace Tablet at Palenque of "since he ended the *may*" (Rice 2004: 245) involves a misidentification of the relevant verb and a different sense of the word *may* (Stuart 2005a: 154, n. 45). I will not address Rice's proposals directly in this book, since comprehensive critiques can already be found in the comments appended to Rice (2013) – especially those of Aldana, Chinchilla, Ciudad and Lacadena, and Grube.

3 ON ARCHAEOPOLITICS

1   Many of the ideas in the chapter were among those explored in a wider theoretical discussion in Martin (2016a).

2   Confusingly, it should be noted that "processualism" has come to describe somewhat different things in archaeology and anthropology. Here, I will keep to the archaeological usage at all times.

3   Service (1971: 157) accepted Fried's (1967) implicit critique of his original categories: "They may be useful for a classification of modern ethnography but not useful if they are to be used in extrapolating from extant stages to extinct ages".

4   See Hodder (1982, 1986), Tilley (1982), and Miller and Tilley (1984).

5   "Nonhuman resources are objects, animate or inanimate, naturally occurring or manufactured, that can be used to enhance or maintain power; human resources are physical strength, dexterity, knowledge, and emotional commitments that can be used to enhance or maintain power, including knowledge of the means of gaining, retaining, controlling, and propagating either human or nonhuman resources" (Sewell 1992: 9).

6   For the appropriateness of linking complexity to practice and agency models see Layton (2003), Bintliff (2007: 46–47), and Beekman (2005). One should note that, here and elsewhere, "complexity" has a very different sense from the "(social) complexity" we find in much anthropological and archaeological literature, as in *Archaeologies of Complexity* (Chapman 2003).

7   In this way, complexity offers a retort to the collapse of faith in objectivity that lies at the heart of poststructuralism and postmodernism, accounting for why phenomena can be understood at large scales but not at smaller ones (Bentley and Maschner 2003: 3–5). Those movements mistook the certainty that there are limits to what we can know for evidence that nothing can be known with certainty.

4 WORLDS IN WORDS

1   Searle (1995: 59–78) ascribes sociocultural meaning, in the form of his "institutional facts", to the existence of "status-functions".

In order to ascribe meaning to a given object X we must first give it the status-function Y. While X can be any kind of thing, those which we generate or enmesh in our sociocultural world are always constituted as a combined X-Y. Since the value Y can exist only by collective agreement within a particular human culture, and we have no way of doing so outside a semiotic system of which by far the most important is language, it follows that X can become an institutional fact only to the extent that it is partly constituted by and in that system.

2   For a historian's rebuttal of archaeological processualism see Finley (1975: 87–93). Other scholars have argued that the processualist critique of culture-history misconceived the methods and goals of historical research (Trigger 1978: 37–41; Snodgrass 1991: 63), and that by focussing only on archaeologically recoverable data they neglected the role of ephemeral events in trains of causation (Kohl 1984: 130–132).

3   The contrast goes beyond mapping and survey, since the excavation of Athens and Sparta would also produce starkly different results. Archaeologists at Classical Athens can, and do, uncover the diverse material goods, many of them imported, that enriched the city. Also recoverable is evidence for the warehouses and docks from which those goods came and went, as well as the boat-pens that speak to its maritime power, whether commercial or military. The nearby hills of the surrounding Attic peninsula show evidence for the silver-mining that contributed so much to the city's coffers and was the source for the huge quantity of minted coins Athens produced and distributed across the Greek world. Compare that to the excavation of landlocked Classical Sparta, where imports were few, coinage banned, and construction very modest indeed. One might encounter the appropriately dated all-male mess halls that constituted a core feature of the Spartan military system – but how could we deduce their function and meaning absent of textual descriptions?

4   The Copan archaeological project developed long-term working relations with epigraphers David Stuart and Linda Schele, iconographers Karl Taube and Barbara Fash, and a range of related specialists to forge a new approach to collaborative research in the Maya area.

5   I reserve some caution when it comes to high K'atun-count ages. Most seem to have a historical basis, but a count of 7 K'atuns (118+ years) on one unprovenanced stela now in the Art Institute of Chicago – perhaps from the Lakamtuun polity – leaves open the possibility that some of these titles may have developed an embellished and honorific function.

6   This can be seen as wider critique of the supposed credulity of ancient people. Were the fantastical claims of Ramesses II in single-handedly rescuing the Egyptian army at Qadesh meant to be taken literally, or was it a rhetorical overstatement understood by a contemporary audience at a symbolic rather than a factual level?

7   Some may even have responded to overblown claims, see Case Study 5.

8   I would not want to give the impression that Classic Maya historiography presents no problems at all. One of the issues involves the chronological "errors" seen in a number of inscriptions. Some might be explained as scribal mistakes, but if so they are blunders that survived review and the more considered process of carving in stone.
     In a few cases texts disagree; as in the account of the Lady of Tikal's birth at the peripheral site of Tres Cabezas, placed one day later than the position recorded on Tikal Stela 23 (Martin and Fialko n.d.). However, seeming anomalies are sometimes no more than a product of our limited knowledge. For example, the death-date for king Itzam K'an Ahk III of Piedras Negras on a looted panel originating in an unidentified dependent centre falls a day earlier than the one inscribed on Piedras Negras Stela 7 and 8. Yet the verbal events differ (*chamiiy*, "died" as opposed to *k'a'ayiiy usaak sak ik'il*, "his spirit-breath flew(?)") and this might well suggest that the moment of death and the departure of the inner life force are not necessarily same-day events.
     Unambiguous discrepancies can be seen on the remarkable Komkom Vase – excavated at Baking Pot, but perhaps originally from Buenavista del Cayo – which carries a 202-glyph painted text (Helmke, Hoggarth, and Awe 2018). Dated to 812 or later, its narrative covers some of the same ground as that on Naranjo Stela 12 from 800, describing stages in a military campaign against Yaxha in 799. The unstated implication is that Komkom was an ally or client supporting the more important Naranjo kingdom. While the events on the vase are much the same as those on the monument, their order and dates differ in most cases (Helmke et al. 2018: 82–88, passim).
     Such divergences could point to localised scriptoria that kept their own records, made calculations, and composed texts. We should not assume that our patchwork of small kingdoms, each proud of its own traditions and institutions, were so well-connected that they shared a fully harmonised record.

9   See Houston (2004: 235) for a call from David Webster to introduce such a term.

10   In line with the arguments made earlier in this chapter, texts are themselves a potential source of power: "Indeed, texts – whether novels, or statute books, or folktales, or contracts – are resources from the point of view of this theory. They, too, are instantiations of schemas in time-space that can be used by actors to generate power" (Sewell 1992: 13).

11   This is comparatively mild stuff. The Annaliste Jacques Le Goff referred to event history as a "cadaver" (quoted in Clark 2004: 89).

12   Many will have been capable and decisive leaders long prepared for the role, but some, especially children, were no more than figureheads for the ambitions of agents that had a surer hand on power, if not the title that should accompany it.

5 IDENTITY

1   E.g. Slotkin (1950); Nadel (1957); Goodenough (1965).

2   See Roys (1957: 6); Edmonson (1965: 7); Scholes and Roys (1968: 55, 384, 390–391 396); Coto (1983 [c.1650]: 440); Laughlin (1988: I:151); Jones (1998: 92–93, 308); also Lacadena and Ciudad (1998: 39–40).

3   Barthel (1968b: 120) identified this sign (T168 in Thompson 1962) as meaning "head man", while Thompson (1972: 151) conjectured that it referred to a "lord" without proposing a specific decipherment.

4   Stuart (1995: 92–193, figure 6.3a) makes a persuasive case that the abstract form originated in a representation of jade jewels.

5   In unpublished work, Stuart has suggested that the sign identified as T533 in the Thompson (1962) catalogue might be logographic **SAAK**

"seed" due to its iconographic association with corn kernels and the consistent phonetic complementation of **ki**.

6   The -*taak* pluralising suffix was first identified in a syllabic spelling of **ch'o-ki-ta-ki** *ch'ok-taak*, "youths/princes" at Oxkintok (Lacadena 1992: 183–184), while substitutional patterns demonstrated that there was also a logographic form, seen in spellings of **AJAW-TAAK** *ajaw-taak*, "lords" at several sites (Stuart 2004b: 1, 2005c: 55–56).

7   The extensive literature on emblem glyphs since Berlin's original paper includes, but is not limited to: Barthel (1968a, 1968b); Marcus (1976); Mathews (1985, 1991); Houston (1986, 1992, 1993); Stuart and Houston (1994); Voss and Eberl (1999); Martin and Grube (2000); Grube (2005); Martin (2005a, 2014a); Graña-Behrens (2006, 2018); Bíró (2007a, 2012a); Tokovinine (2008, 2011, 2013); Wanyerka (2009); Gronemeyer (2012); Helmke and Awe (2012); Helmke and Kupprat (2016); Safronov and Beliaev (2017); Beliaev and Vepretskii (2018); Helmke, Guenter, and Wanyerka (2018).

8   Although an emblem glyph usually fills a single glyph-block, its elements can be divided over two or more blocks, and these instances were key to establishing its correct reading order.

9   Notable dynasties at Altar de Sacrificios, Lacanja-Tzeltal (Sak Tz'i'), Santa Elena, and Xultun are never seen to employ the *k'uhul* prefix on their emblem titles, while the Hixwitz emblem connected to Zapote Bobal, La Joyanca, and Pajaral does so only in a few late contexts.

10   The Appendix features 109 titles that function as emblems, of which fifty-five regularly carry the **K'UH** *k'uh(ul)*, "holy" prefix. A total of seventy-six can be identified with one or more archaeological sites, while the remaining thirty-three are as yet unattributed. The list is not entirely comprehensive, and omits cases that might arguably be names rather than titles, as well as examples too damaged to properly identify. Note that the additional two-part sign often seen at the right-side or base of emblems (for example, Acanceh and Comalcalco, respectively) is the phonetic sign **wa** that serves as a terminal complement to **AJAW** (also seen in Figure 3).

11   It is this method of sign formation that causes disruptions in the normal left–right and top–bottom reading order. Superimposition is one of a number of core script conventions discovered by David Stuart (1995: 38).

12   The toponyms for Tikal and Tamarindito are often prefixed by an additional sign *yax* – likely meaning "first" or "new" in this context – possibly an indication that there were earlier or later places with those same names.

13   Tikal makes reference to Dos Pilas on a small bone from Tikal Burial 116, which records the death of the Dos Pilas king "Itzamnaaj" K'awiil in 726 (Houston 1993: 100). Here he is simply called "Dos Pilas Person" (using its still undeciphered "Shell-Wing Dragon Water" toponym) and denied the Mutul title under dispute.

14   See also Arnauld, Breuil-Martínez, and Ponciano (2004: 49–51); Breuil-Martínez et al. (2004, 2005: 304–307); Gámez, Fitzsimmons, and Forné (2007); and Stuart (2008a).

15   See also Palka (1996); Sachse (1996); Beliaev and Safronov (2004); Bíró (2007b, 2012a); and Tokovinine (2008, 2013).

16   This was apparently the consequence of a conflict that took place shortly before 795 (Demarest, Barrientos, and Fahsen 2006: 832). Yet we also know that these two polities had deep historical connections and an additional legitimatising blood tie should not be discounted (Lacadena 2011: 216–217).

17   Based on a spelling on Yaxchilan Lintel 37 (at B6) of **yo-yo-ki-bi**, Christophe Helmke (pers. comm. 2017) suggests that the original reading of the Piedras Negras emblem glyph was *yoykib,* subsequently elided into *yokib*. Given the propensity of Maya scribes to abbreviate in such contexts we might hold open the possibility that all such collocations were in fact read *yoykib*.

18   It is significant that the transition appears to have taken place between kings that were father and son, Yajawte' K'inich I and K'an I, as seen on their monuments Caracol Stelae 13 (514) and 15 (544?). It was therefore not the consequence of some intrusive dynasty. Interestingly, the first evidence for the emblem glyph of Naranjo also appears around this same time.

19   Given its wide distribution in the region surrounding El Mirador there has long been a suspicion that *chatahn* was a political entity that reaches back into Preclassic times (Boot 1999a, 2005: 505–516; Grube 2004a: 122). Chatahn

was the source area for the majority of codex-style ceramics (of which we will hear more later), where they were produced under the auspices of its late seventh century ruler Yopaat Bahlam. The same name features on a red-on-cream ware vessel excavated at Tintal and this Preclassic site with a significant Late Classic population could be the place in question (Hansen et al. 2006).

20   The referent here is that of the Snake kingdom, in combination spelling **IX-ka-KAAN-AJAW** *ix kaan(ul) ajaw*, "Lady Snake[-Place] Lord".

21   For the **JALAM** reading see Grube (2016).

22   Sometimes called the Woman of Tikal, the elements of her personal name were described in Martin (2003b: n.26) but first collectively read as Ix Uunk'in in Zender (2004: 335).

23   The name of this co-ruler combines that of the Stingray Paddler deity with *bahlam* "jaguar" (Martin 2003b: 20, 2014b). The *kaloomte'* used in his current nickname is simply his prefixed title, an ordering sometimes used in the Early Classic Period.

24   Despite these fantastical dates, the reference to Aj Numsaaj Chan K'inich as the "35th in sequence" of the Square-nosed Serpent and similarly to K'ahk' Tiliw Chan Chahk as the "38th in sequence" would imply a "historical" founding of the dynasty at about 200 BCE.

25   The *kaloomte'* title has suffered a number of faulty readings and mistranslations. These include *batab* (Berlin 1958: 114), *bate* (Kelley 1976: 231), *batel* (Closs 1984), *makuch* (Riese 1988: table 6), and *chakte'* (Fahsen and Schele 1991: 4, n.5). The latter could have some validity as a re-analysis of the hieroglyph that first appears in the Late Classic and survived in some Colonial Period literature (possibly implied by a **-ki** suffix on one version seen on a plate found at Dos Pilas). Very late instances of *kaloomte'* can carry a **ka** phonetic prefix, as if to emphasise a traditional reading.

26   The earliest historical example we have of *kaloomte'* belongs to Foliated Jaguar, who is mentioned on Tikal Stela 31 (see p.120, also Martin 2003b: 6–7). The date does not survive but it certainly fell before 317, and he is explicitly associated with the Ur-Classic site Maguey Metate or Chicha' (Stuart 2014a). The earliest near-contemporary appearances of *kaloomte'* are those ascribed to Sihyaj K'ahk' on a group of monuments at Tikal and Uaxactun after 378.

27   This case appears on Quirigua Stela U, although it surely refers to the king of Copan. Its date has been placed to 480 (Schele 1990b: 2).

28   Examples of verbs represented by a hand-in-action pictograph include **CHOK**, "to scatter", **K'AM/CH'AM**, "to take/receive", **JATZ'**, "to strike", and **TZAK**, "to grasp/conjure".

29   It was the presence of the axe that linked this sign to *baat*, "axe" and thence to *batab*, a title for military-governors in Postclassic Yucatan (Tozzer 1941: 62–64; Berlin 1958: 114). Even though this long-lived reading is now defunct, an association with warrior status has continued to influence some scholars (e.g. Reese-Taylor et al. 2009: 58). Today we might focus our attention on a religious allusion that came to signify the power exercised by great lords.

30   During the Classic Period we see a development in the word for "west" from *ochk'in* to *chik'in*, with glyphic **chi-K'IN-ni** (shown in Figure 6) appearing in addition to, rather than entirely replacing, the spelling **OCH-K'IN-ni**.

31   Given the very incomplete monumental record we have, this listing can only be considered a provisional sketch. At Pusilha a "founder"-type figure is retrospectively ascribed *ochk'in kaloomte'* status for the year 573. Moral-Reforma Stela 5 names two unidentifiable *kaloomte'*, which are surely outsiders, perhaps even foreigners, around 633.

32   On some occasions Shield Jaguar III of Yaxchilan calls himself the *naah* or "first" *kaloomte'*. It is tempting to see this as the introduction of this title after the dramatic revival of the kingdom he engineered. The picture is muddied, however, by his attribution of the *kaloomte'* epithet to his own father, Bird Jaguar III.

33   The *elk'in kaloomte'* title is ascribed to the Dzibanche king K'ahk' Ti' Ch'ich' on a bone found at Calakmul (Martin and Beliaev 2017: 4).

34   We know that Proto-Mayan **kab* underwent a sound-shift to *chab* in Ch'olan-Tzeltalan branch of Mayan language at some point, although exactly when is unclear (Law et al. 2014). However, the spelling of **cha-ba** for "earth" on Halakal Lintel 1 indicates that the shift was occurring during the Classic era. *Chab* may well be the correct value, but in this book I continue to use *kab* for the "earth" sign for the sake of consistency with earlier literature.

35 An early spelling of **BAAH-ka-ba** appears on two vessels from El Zotz, but there it is part of a personal name, Baahkab K'inich, not a title.

36 The only exceptions appear in references produced by their rivals. However, a queen on Calakmul Stela 9 is referred to as *ix baahkab*.

37 By the Postclassic Period the name *bakab* referred to Atlantean bearers of the four world corners (Roys 1933), but during the Classic these figures went under different names (Martin 2015a).

38 The initial reading of this title was *cahal*, following Lounsbury's suggestions on variants of the **ka** syllabogram (Lounsbury 1989). This was amended to *sahal* after the "dotted comb" **sa** sign was distinguished from true **ka** forms in unpublished work by Stuart and the recognition of velar-glottal fricative distinctions in the script, set out by Grube (2004b), led to the current rendering of *sajal*.

39 This small but important list of *sajal*-ruled satellites includes: Miraflores under the control of Palenque; El Cayo, and the sites represented by the New Orleans and Dumbarton Oaks panels under Piedras Negras; and El Chicozapote and La Pasadita as well as the unidentified Laxtunich and Site R under Yaxchilan.

40 Not to be confused with the Lacanha associated with Bonampak.

41 For earlier translations see the detailed summary in Zender (2004: table 2).

42 The text leaves us in no doubt that the *ajk'uhuun* is pictured on this stone, but we must note that the bottom half of the monument is missing and it may have contained additional information.

43 The same possessed term *uti'huun* frequently appears in a more esoteric context as Glyph F, a familiar part of calendrical notation. There it relates to one of nine cycling entities (called Lords of the Night) and specifies their titular relationship to the day at hand (Jackson 2005: 133).

44 Tikal Stela 8 remains an enigmatic monument in more than one respect. See Zender (2004: 334–337) for a detailed description of the chronological problems presented by its text and the reasoning behind his placement on 9.4.2.4.0, 7 Ajaw *G8 8 K'ank'in in 516 (see also Martin 2003b: 42, n.31). The *uti'huun* term appears after a damaged section of text and we should be alert to the possibility that

this obscures some greater complexity to the dynastic relationships there.

45 Since the vessel was owned by a queen from Xultun, who is probably to be identified as the lady who shares the dais, the three visiting *lakam* might hail from that polity.

46 Only the fourth and fifth figures on this vase scene have stated *lakam* titles, but I take it that one for the sixth is omitted for lack of space.

47 The quickest route from El Palmar to Copan would likely be to walk to the Bravo River and take a dugout canoe downstream to the Caribbean. Then one would track the coastline southwards, ultimately reaching the mouth of the Motagua River for a passage upstream toward Quirigua and from there overland to Copan.

48 As further treated in Chapter 6, the first two rulers of the dynasty are ascribed the title *k'uhul toktahn ajaw* in reference to an early capital named *toktahn*. Given that the second king is given a conventional *baakal* emblem in a near-contemporary reference – a carved bowl now in the Dumbarton Oaks collection – it is very likely that the *toktahn* emblem was retrospectively applied to signal the change of royal seat and was not actually used at the time.

49 A lone *joykaan* emblem glyph was identified on an incised clay brick at Comalcalco, and this played a key role in the assignation of this title (Peter Mathews, pers. comm. 1992). The cursive **ka** prefix there suggests a reading of **KAAN** over **CHAN** for the "sky" sign (Christophe Helmke, pers. comm. 2016).

50 The knot-eye device is not related to the tied band read *joy*, but rather to a tied trophy skull that appears in its full form only on a stela now in the Royal Brussels Museum (Martin 2004a: 4, n.10).

51 The chronology of the text lacks an anchor in the Long Count and the placement I use here is that proposed by Schele and Grube (1995: 21) and Ringle and Smith-Stark (1996: 24–25), which is one Calendar Round (52 years) later than those in Zender (2004: 158, 292–294, 306–309, table 8), Stuart (2005a: 124, n.41), and Jackson (2005: 183–187, 306–308). The main evidence for the earlier placement – of which I was once an advocate – is that the lack of a K'inich prefix to the first instance of Janaab Pakal's name seems to identify the earlier, non-ruling lord mentioned on the

sides of the sarcophagus within Palenque's Temple of Inscriptions. However, three factors override this in significance. The first are the three references to the *sajal* Yuhk Mak'abajte' on the sarcophagus of K'inich Janaab Pakal, which strongly imply that this lord was alive between 683 and 689 (Zender 2004: 308–309). In the early scheme it would be 73–79 years since this lord's rise to *yajawk'ahk'* status on the censer-stand, but a more plausible 21–27 years in the later scheme. Next, the royal name at position F1b on the censer-stand seems clearly to be that of K'inich Kaan Bahlam II rather than K'inich Janaab Pakal. The head does have a bird-like appearance appropriate for **JAN (AB)**, but it has the spiral-eye typical of **KAAN** "snake" while lacking any **PAKAL** "shield" sign. Finally, at the end of the text the protagonist Baahis Uchih is described as the *sajal* of the long-deceased K'inich Janaab Pakal, a clear sign that he is the overseer at the beginning of the text, where his **K'INICH** name has been deleted on space grounds alone.

6 CONSTITUTION

1   This is a sub-set of cases where both birth and accession dates are known and, as the sample increases with fresh discoveries, this and other figures will need re-evaluation. The current average from a sample of thirty-five cases differs only slightly from Grube (2006: 150), who obtained a figure of 28.43 years.

2   Among the polities of Postclassic northern lowlands Landa tells us: "If when the lord died, his sons were not fit to govern, and if he had brothers, the oldest or the most forward of his brothers ruled and they taught the heir their customs and their feasts, looking to the time when he should be a man himself. And though the heir was fit to rule, these brothers still held command to the end of their lives, and if there were no brothers, the priests and important people elected a man capable of ruling" (Tozzer 1941: 100).

3   See also Fitzsimmons (2009, table 2) and Grube (2006: 160), which work with slightly smaller samples.

4   The complete logogram for **K'AL** depicts a jade celt lying on a hand, although the principle of superimposition often leads to the object concerned (in this case the *huun* headband) lying over and obscuring the celt. The evidence for *k'al* as "to hold, keep" comes from an entry in one of the word lists of Ch'orti', the closest surviving living language to that represented in the script (Zender 2018b). This works well in most contexts, but in certain scenes the salient feature is that the subject is held above the head. One unique substitution on a vase excavated at Altar de Sacrificios (K3120; www.mayavase.com) shows a small figure holding the celt aloft. The pose is similar to that of two bearers who hold two lords aloft on a composite "sky crocodile" beast, captioned **K'AL-[*la]-ja *ti-CHAN-x-x** *k'alaj ti chan...* "raised? into (the) sky ..." (Mayer 1995: pl.121). Following this argument, the accession act could therefore read "he raises (the) paper (headband) to his head".

5   The decipherment of *pehk* stems from a recognition of the **pe** syllablogram in Landa's "alphabet" within the form **pe-ka-ja**, first made by Werner Nahm.

6   Thanks to Matthew Looper I was able to check my collection of dated accession events against that of the Maya Hieroglyphic Database Project.

7   A similar list appears on Tikal MT.28, an inscribed bone found in Burial 116, which describes the deaths of six or seven high-ranking or royal men and women between 720 and 727 (Jones 1987: table 1, figure 11; Houston 1993: 100, figure 4-3) (see Chapter 5, Note 13).

8   It was David Stuart (pers. comm.) who first recognised the name of Chak Tok Ich'aak II on this monument.

9   It is Alexandre Tokovinine (2013: 9–10) who argues that *nal*, usually translated simply as "place", should more specifically be associated with cultivated crops and the land they grow on – an allusion as much symbolic as it was descriptive.

10   The **CH'EEN** decipherment remains provisional since we lack phonetic data beyond a terminal -*n* supplied by a near-ubiquitous **na** suffix. The best evidence for this sign-set as "cave" comes from the cave of Jolja', where a painted text makes the early variant of the sign the subject of a *hul*, "to arrive" verb (Vogt and Stuart 2005: 160, figure 7.9). Stuart

(2005a: 90) believes that a number of examples of *ch'een*, especially when introduced by *tahn*, "before, the midst", refer to genuine water features such as springs instead of metaphorical allusions. Similarly, Helmke (2009: 85) has argued that isolated instances of *ch'een* refer exclusively to caves.

11 I have argued elsewhere (Martin 2004b: 107–109) that the frequent direction of warfare against the isolated possessed *ch'een* of an opposing king – including *pul*, "burning" events – argues against the literal reading "cave" in those contexts (see Chapter 9).

12 For more detailed discussions of these toponymic expressions see Stuart and Houston (1994: 12–13) and Tokovinine (2013: 19–43), also Houston (2000: 173); Hull (2003: 425–438); Martin (2004b: 106–109); Velásquez (2004a: 85); Vogt and Stuart (2005: 160–162); Bíró (2007a: 96, 2011a: 52–66); Tokovinine (2008: 126–154); and Helmke (2009: 83–86).

13 When possessed, as in *ukab uch'een*, "his earth, his cave" or *tukab tuch'een*, "in his earth, in his cave", it is clear that each term remains distinct within the couplet. Both appear in the Postclassic codices of Yucatan, and the survival of the core concept into the Colonial era is suggested in the Yukatek Maya documents called the Chilam Balams (Roys 1933; Edmonson 1982), where the important regional capital of Mani is referred to as *cabal chen mani*, "earthy cave Mani" (Alfonso Lacadena, pers. comm. 2002). Another potential analogy comes from the highlands, where the K'iche' document of the Popol Vuh uses the couplet *siwan tinamit*, "canyon-citadel" to describe any built-up area of whitewashed structures (Tokovinine 2008: 151).

14 Moon Zero Bird (originally misidentified as a personal name) is mentioned on Tikal Stela 31 (before 317 CE) and on the unprovenanced Leiden Plaque (in 320), while other references appear at Calakmul and Copan. Maguey Metate, spelled **chi-?CHA'-a**, is mentioned at Pusilha (in 81 and 159), Copan (in 159), and appears within titular formulae at Yaxchilan, Tikal, La Florida, and Palenque (though there in reference to a *kaanul* lord). It also appears in iconic form on two codex-style pots, K1384 and K1882, together with names that might well be that of Foliated Ajaw, who additionally appears on K2572 (Grube 2004a: 128). The earliest date associated with this character

comes in 141, recounted at Pol Box, although the featured event is now illegible (Esparza and Pérez 2009: 14). A vessel in the Schaffhausen Museum in Switzerland calls a client of Calakmul's Yuknoom Ch'een II *aj chicha'(?)*, "Maguey Metate Person". Maguey Metate also appears on Dzibanche Fragments 2 and 3, the latter refers to a "capture" event, perhaps the only later historical event it can be linked to (Martin and Velásquez 2016). This could chime with poorly preserved spellings at El Resbalon, close to Dzibanche, that might offer evidence for a *chicha'(?) kaloomte'* in a past timeframe (Guenter 2005a). A substantial Preclassic city, Ichkabal, lies a mere 11 km from Dzibanche and offers itself as one of the contenders for ancient Maguey Metate (Martin and Velásquez 2016: 30, n.26), of which the most prominent is the largest of all Maya cities, El Mirador (Guenter 2005a).

15 Three of these mentions associate Maguey Metate with the term *yajawte'*, "Lord of the Tree", which is a personal title of some sort. Sometimes it seems to work as a statement of lineage, in which "tree" could refer to a descent line using the same metaphor we use in "family tree". However, a variety of other interpretations are equally viable.

16 Nikolai Grube independently reached several of the same conclusions about *huli* (see MacLeod 1990: n.13).

17 Susan Schroeder (1991: 123) tell us: "The importance of arriving was such that the verbal noun *axiliztli*, 'arrival' comes to have almost the sense of 'foundation', and Chimalpahin stresses it as a major factor in substantiating the legitimacy of an *altepetl*".

18 A much later text on a bone from Tikal Burial 116, MT.34, tells us that Sihyaj K'ahk' *ehm*, "comes down" on 8.17.0.15.7 in 377, a date 135 days before his "arrival" at Tikal. A second bone text from the same tomb, MT.35, describes the coming down of Yax Nuun Ahiin from Wiinte'naah on 8.17.2.3.16 in 378, 261 days before his accession. These are most likely the dates on which these characters departed from Teotihuacan and, in the first case especially, denote the time it took for them to reach the Maya lowlands. That said, isotopic analysis suggests that the occupant of Tikal Burial 10, thought to be Yax Nuun Ahiin, was raised in the Peten (Wright 2005). If correct, we should consider if the origins,

ancestry, and early life of Yax Nuun Ahiin were more complex than once believed. I have previously suggested that his mother was a high-ranking woman from Tikal, but in truth the relevant text is eroded and beyond sure reading (Martin 2002: 67, n.14, figure 13).

19 His caption on this vessel reads *sihyaj k'ahk' ch'ahoom wiinte'naah*, "Fire-Born, Censer (or Young Lord) of Wiinte'naah".

20 The Hombre de Tikal sculpture carries a damaged text that seemingly refers to a new "arrival" at Tikal in 406 (Fahsen 1988:figure 4 at C4). This concerns a *kaloomte'* called Sihyaj "Dart", someone who is probably distinct from Sihyaj K'ahk' (Stephen Houston pers. comm. 2019). This is followed by an unread sign prefixed by "2" that is followed by the sequence *kaloomte' mutul* (at E7-F7). Could this whole section describe the arrival of a "second" *kaloomte'* at Tikal, indicating that Sihyaj "Dart" was a successor to Sihyaj K'ahk' in the New Order? There is evidence for at least one other character involved in the entrada project (Dmitri Beliaev pers. comm. 2019), which proves to be a more collective endeavour than previously thought.

21 The breadth of interest in Sihyaj K'ahk' beyond Tikal and Uaxactun might also be measured by the overlord status he is ascribed at Bejucal and Naachtun (see Chapter 10), and less well understood mentions of his name at Palenque (Martin, in Stuart 2005a: 181, n.60), Río Azul (Martin and Grube 2000: 30), and perhaps Río Amarillo, close to Copan, where Altar 1 includes the nominal sequence **SIH-x AJ-WIIN-TE' OCH[K'IN]-ni KALOOM (TE')** *sih(yaj) *k'ahk' aj wiinte'naah ochk'in kaloomte'*. It has previously been suggested that Sihyaj K'ahk' is named at Copan on the early Xukpi Stone (Schele, Grube, and Fahsen 1994).

22 The location of the original, and still unread, Bat toponym used as an emblem referent by Copan is unknown. Stuart (2004a: 216–219) notes a reference to this place on Copan Stela I, attached to a now-missing event that took place in 159 CE, 208 days after a mention of Maguey Metate on the period ending 8.6.0.0.0. There is a Bat referent used in the texts of Calakmul (in 435 and 761), Uxul (in 632), and Naachtun (date lost), though no examples are sufficiently well-preserved to know if it includes the distinctive parts of the Copan compound (Martin 2005a: 9–10).

23 Intriguingly, a person of the same Wak Chan K'awiil name appears on a ceramic vessel where he is identified as a *k'uhul sa'al ajaw*, a ruler of Naranjo (Stanley Guenter, pers. comm. 2004, see Martin 2005b: 7–8). We would normally take this to be a simple namesake, but this centre had close ties to the Tikal dynasty and Wak Chan K'awiil was the great-grandson of a Naranjo king. As a result, we might wonder if Wak Chan K'awiil held high office at Naranjo, perhaps as an exported male heir, before returning to claim the throne of his homeland in 537, a few years before the accession of Aj Numsaaj Chan K'inich at Naranjo in 546. The Tepeu 1 style of the vessel is usually placed no earlier than 550, and we may have one of its earliest examples here.

24 It is possible that the damaged central steps of Dos Pilas Hieroglyphic Stairway 2 describe this "arrival" event (Fahsen 2002; Guenter 2003).

25 The reading **LOK'**, "to emerge, leave" is an unpublished decipherment first made by Alfonso Lacadena.

26 See Zender (2004: 159, n.54) for the grammatical status of such name-lists, which do not employ conjunctions. For the grammatical construction of **yi-ta HUL-*li** see MacLeod (2004: 301), who suggests a translation of "fellow-arrivers".

27 Maya toponyms often conclude with a **la** suffix indicating *-Vl*, although the vowel (*V*) is unknown (Martin and Velásquez 2016: 23, n.3). The full Kaanul reading is therefore insecure and the same can be said of Mutul as well.

28 An isolated block from the Itzan Hieroglyphic Stairway provides a very similar passage of **PAT-ta-li 3-TE'-TUUN** *pahtaal uxte'tuun*, "Three Stones is formed". Conceivably, this is a reference to the same historical episode and is further evidence for its significance for the whole region. That it is directly preceded by the emblem glyph of El Reinado might also suggest their relevance or interest in the matter.

29 The value **KAJ** is suggested by prefixed **ka** signs at Coba and suffixed **ja** signs at Piedras Negras, which are best explained as phonetic complements, the latter confirmed by a spelling of **KAJ-ja-yi** at La Corona. The **yi** component links it to a group of verbs concerned with motion and change that employ **yi** to form -VV*yi* suffixes. Comparable examples include the aforementioned **LOK'-yi** *lok'ooyi*, "emerges, goes out" and **?T'AB-yi** *t'abaayi(?)*, "ascends, goes up" (for the **?T'AB** proposal

see Stuart 1998: 409–417). The verb *kaj* can be found in a variety of Mayan languages and appears in the Paxbolon-Maldonado Papers of Acalan, where it refers to Chontal rulers residing in the town of Tixchel (see Smailus 1975).

30 Stuart (2004c: 5) writes: "Emblem glyphs and localized toponyms do overlap at some sites, but the presence of two different glyphs at Piedras Negras reflects a more normal pattern wherein the two locational terms have different scopes of reference. The **yo-ki-bi** emblem seems an archaic and more generalised name, associated even with mythological dates on the fascinating inscription from Piedras Negras Altar 1. By contrast, the opening passage from Throne 1, discussed above, suggests that Paw Stone might be a true local toponym for the site 'founded' in the Early Classic".

31 A matching construction appears on Piedras Negras Panel 4 in reference to nearby La Mar: *kajaayi tahn ch'een pe(pe)'tuun*, "settles in the midst of La Mar". That event took place around 631 and its agent was the Piedras Negras king K'inich Yo'nal Ahk I (Tokovinine 2013: 81, figure 46d). This phrase could amount to its historical founding but, even if not, references Piedras Negras's dominance over this lesser lordship.

32 As noted in Chapter 5, this could well be a retrospective formula designed to distinguish the kings who ruled at *toktahn* from their descendants. The only Early Classic text we have for Palenque, a small travertine bowl, identifies the second king with a *baakal* referent (K4332 in Kerr 1992: 471; Martin and Grube 2000: 57). Note that K-prefixed numbers throughout this volume refer to roll-out vessel photographs produced by Justin Kerr and posted on the Kerr Archive: www .mayavase.com).

33 The military event recorded here took place on the Long Count date 9.8.17.15.0, just four days before the Dzibanche attack on Palenque on 9.8.17.15.4 (see Chapter 9).

34 It should be noted that the Cancuen emblem glyph is much older, making its first appearance (along with that of Machaquila) further down the Pasión River at Tres Islas (Map 3). However, Tres Islas is barely a site at all, consisting of only a few low platforms (Tomasic and Fahsen 2004), and it has been argued

that the seat of the Early Classic dynasty probably lay at the much more substantial site of El Raudal, 5 km to the east (Tomasic, Quintanilla, and Barrios 2005: 8–10). Interestingly, two of the three stelae found at Tres Islas, dated to 455 and 475 (Mathews 1985: table 3), depict lords dressed as Teotihuacan-style warriors and have texts that back-reference period endings in 396 and 416 CE, soon after the entrada at Tikal. One even refers to a "fourth successor" of the *wiinte'naah ajaw*, a title very similar to the one carried by "Spearthrower Owl" on the Tikal Marcador (Lacadena 2011: 210–211) (see p.242–243).

35 Further evidence comes from a designation ritual performed for Kaan Bahlam in 641, which refers to the *ux tikil ch'oktaak*, "three princes" (Houston 2009: 159, figure 7b).

36 The identifying caption for the first figure in the pictured group on Panel 3 is erased, but the main text makes clear that the visitor is Yopaat Bahlam II of Yaxchilan. I first recognised the relevance of the Yopaat Bahlam name on this monument in 1995 (Martin and Grube 2000: 127).

37 One candidate for the emblem glyph was found on Calakmul Stela 51, from 731 CE, which now stands in the Museo Nacional de Antropología in Mexico City (Marcus 1987: figure 65a). It proved to be a fused compound that shows the abbreviated name of Yuknoom Took' K'awiil emerging from the gaping mouth of a serpent, a variant form of the Kaanul title (Martin 1996d: 4).

38 Blocks of the Dzibanche Captive Stairway carry at least five full Calendar Round dates, as well as three lone *tzolk'in* positions, the latter a feature that implies conflicts separated only by a few days. Only one Calendar Round, 5 Chikchan 3 Yaxk'in, is truly legible, but without a link to the Long Count it floats in time. Stylistically, the portraits of prisoners most closely resemble the one on Uaxactun Stela 19 from 357 CE (see Graham 1986: 177–178). There we see not only the distinctively early back-mounted belt mask (whose headdress spells the victim's name) but the same early treatment of wild wavy hair. On this basis, a fourth century date for the stairway seems likely, and if so this would place 5 Chikchan 3 Yaxk'in to either 8.14.17.5.5 in 334 or 8.17.10.0.5 in 386. If we examine Tikal Stela 39 from 8.17.0.0.0 in 376 (Laporte and Fialko

1990: figure 3.10; Martin and Grube 2008: 28) we see a rather more sophisticated rendering of a prisoner and this arguably makes the earlier position preferable. If correct, we would have not only the earliest recorded warfare, but one of the earliest legible monumental inscriptions from the Classic era.

39 The other three excavated examples appear on: a small carved bone found in a major burial (Velásquez 2008b), a loose block of modelled stucco (Nalda and Balanzario 2014: figure 18), and a sherd from an incised vessel (Velásquez and Balanzario 2016).

40 The conclusion that Dzibanche had been the Early Classic seat of the same Snake kingdom as Calakmul, initially the subject of inference and conjecture (Martin and Grube 2000: 103; Grube 2004a: 117–118; Nalda 2004: 29; Velásquez 2004a: 101–102), progressively took a firm hold (Velásquez 2004b, 2008a, 2008b; Martin 2005a).

41 William Folan of the Universidad Autónoma de Campeche conducted the first archaeological project at Calakmul, with fieldwork in the site core running from 1982 to 1994. The initial write-up of Stela 114 (Pincemin et al. 1998) identifies a bat head sign (at D4), but this is not the emblem glyph in question (at E5). The D4 sign is quite damaged, but could be the avian version of **MAM**, "grandfather/grandson/ancestor". A bat sign serves as a toponym on at least one Calakmul stela, Stela 51 from 731, and this place could refer to the origin of the Bat dynasty (this is seen in an archival photograph of a now-lost portion of the text, recognised and shared with me by Carlos Pallán, pers. comm. 2008).

42 The influence of the intrusive Snake regime can be detected at Uxul. There the Bat emblem appears on one of the last monuments to be erected in the site's original ceremonial core dating to 632. Thereafter Uxul's architectural focus switches to a new complex some 500 m to the east, where two stelae from 662 make references to the oversight of Calakmul's Yuknoom Ch'een II (Grube 2008: 217–220, 224–226). Portraits of Kaanul kings on a series on ballplaying panels from the site's palace emphasise how closely Uxul was affiliated with its giant neighbour (Grube and Delvendahl 2011; Grube et al. 2012). Indeed, a Calakmul stela from 731 was in part carved by an artisan native to Uxul, which may have

been anciently known as Naah Kuuma' (Martin, Houston, and Zender 2015).

43 Waxaklajuun Ubaah Kaan took his name from that of the Teotihuacan war serpent deity, as described in Chapter 7. David Stuart (pers. comm. 2017) noted the name of this king on K6809, a cylinder vessel appropriately decorated with Teotihuacan-inspired imagery.

44 Certain ever-present idiosyncrasies demonstrate that all the vessel texts were copied from a common source (see Carter 2014b: 350–351). Yet, while the names of days and months are consistent, the treatment of their coefficients is cavalier to say the least. We can see this best when comparing K1371 to K6751, both the work of Painter A (Martin 1997a: 849). They share the first ten dated inauguration statements, but of these only two agree as to both their day and month coefficients, and out of twenty coefficients in total only half correspond (even though both vases have some restored portions, very few of the discrepancies can be attributed to those reconstructions). Even more problematically, some of the later dates on K6751 do not coincide with those we know from carved monuments and either we lack some relevant information or there were errors even in the common source text. Yet it should be borne in mind that these texts were not created as historical documents, rather as prestige-imbuing decoration. True codex-style ware was an import to Calakmul from the then-client kingdom of Chatahn to the south, where it was produced in the late 600s and early 700s.

45 The elevation of Ruler 16, K'ahk' Ti' Ch'ich', is assigned to the Calendar Round position 7 Lamat 6 Uo on the dynastic vase K6751. On Lintel 3 of Dzibanche Building 6 we encounter a backward day-count from the period ending 9.6.0.0.0 that takes us to an accession that took place on a matching 7 Lamat 6 Uo, a notation that would have appeared on a preceding lintel, now destroyed. Here it can be firmly equated to 9.5.16.0.8, which fell on 18 April 550 (Martin 2017b). The probability that any two Calendar Rounds match by sheer happenstance is 18,980 to one.

46 A rock carving at Calakmul that can be stylistically placed to the eighth century shows a pair of highly eroded emblems, and it is engaging to wonder if this once showed the

snake and bat titles in tandem, capturing a period of coexistence between them (Martin 2008a).

47 Calakmul Stela 33 tells us that Scroll Serpent celebrated the 9.8.0.0.0 period ending of 593 at a place whose hieroglyph is now much eroded (Martin 2005a: 7, figure 3). Under renewed examination parts of it seem consistent with the snake-head **KAAN** appropriate to Dzibanche, but without a positive identification we must entertain the possibility that it refers to some other place, further complicating the Early Classic history of this dynasty.

7 TRANSCENDENCE

1 For example, after his death in 685 or 686, Yuknoom Ch'een II of Calakmul was simply referred to as K'awiil (Martin 2005a: 8; Helmke and Awe 2016b: 17). Similarly, Sihyaj K'ahk', the nemesis of the pre-378 Tikal dynasty, is called West K'awiil in several texts (Stuart 2000: 478).

2 The recording of a few "off-dated" ceremonies (e.g. Houston 1993: figure 4.9, table 4.1; Zender 2004: 336) leads one to suspect that these rites were far more common than usually supposed, the textual references we normally have being only those falling on the major junctures of the Long Count.

3 The emblem glyph of Edzna was first identified by David Stuart in Grube (2004a: 182), for more examples and Edzna epigraphy more generally see Pallán (2012: 99, figure 7). For a full discussion of the probable Altun Ha emblem see Helmke, Guenter, and Wanyerka (2018).

4 Although horribly eroded, another such grouping of emblem glyphs may appear on the back of Altar de Sacrificios Stela 8, dating to 628, where only that of Copan is recognisable today (see Graham 1972, figure 22).

5 Baron (2013: 172, 204) additionally compares the **u-BAAH-u-CH'AHB[AK'AB]-li** *ubaah uch'ahb yak'abil* expression that describes the relationship between the Triad Progenitor and the Triad gods as an act of "creation" with a matching case at La Corona between the historical ruler K'inich ?-Yook and a deity called Ikiiy. This demonstrates that the term is not restricted to parentage statements and is analogous to the use of **u-BAAH-u-ı-TAHN-na** *ubaah ujuuntahn,* which is used to mean "child

of mother", but also defines metaphysical ties between lords and gods.

6 For an alternative perspective on this issue see Baron (2013: 171–173, 2016: 59–61).

7 As we saw in Chapter 6, *altepetl* was also an entity that was in certain respects comparable to the Maya *kabch'een.*

8 Although distinct beings, here they are often fused together in a visual conflation that I have dubbed "theosynthesis" (Martin 2007a, 2015a).

9 The *wayib* were sufficiently important that they could be built even in the most testing of times. Constructed just before the collapse, Yaxchilan Structure 3 from 808 is the last dated building at the site and one of its smallest (see Chapter 11). Its indifferently carved lintel shows that it was a new *wayib* for several of the kingdom's patron deities.

10 For the specific topic of Classic Maya war gods see Freidel, Schele, and Parker (1993), Martin (1996a), LeFort (1998), and Eberl and Prager (2005).

11 Translated in Houston, Chinchilla, and Stuart (2001: 285–290).

12 David Stuart (2019) recognised the name of the Ucanal victim, Xub(?) Chahk on Yaxha Stela 31 and noted that this was the same person who appears as a prisoner on Caracol Altar 23, commissioned in 800. This unique repetition is hard to explain, but it could reflect a king who was seized by one rival and restored to his throne, but later captured again in a separate conflict with the other.

13 Although it first found publication elsewhere, the relationship between Naranjo Stela 35 and the Yaxha war described on Naranjo Stela 12 is one I recognised in 1992 and first presented in a symposium held in Provo, Utah (Martin 1997b).

14 The relevant passage in the text runs: **CH'AK-ka-u-BAAH ti-yo-OTOOT** "JGU" **u-K'UH-li MA'-CHAHB'[AK'AB]-li K'INICH-LAKAM-TUUN-ni ✶YAX-✶-a-✶AJAW-wa** *ch'ak ubaah ti yotoot* "JGU" *uk'uhuul ma'ch'ahb (ma')ak'abil k'inich lakamtuun yaxa' ajaw,* "Is beheaded in the house of the JGU, the god of (he) without genesis (he) without darkness, K'inich Lakamtuun, lord of Yaxha". Stephen Houston (pers. comm. 2012) made this observation based on an unpublished sketch by Marc Zender, whose matching independent analysis appears in Baron (2013: 207, n.22). The *ma' ch'ahb ma' ak'ab,* "without genesis,

without darkness" couplet is discussed again in Chapter 9. For a detailed treatment of this war see Helmke, Hoggarth, and Awe (2018).

15 The deity names at Dos Pilas-Tikal and Tamarindito are very similar, both consisting of a square-nosed serpent or centipede being, a macaw, and a star. At Dos Pilas and Tikal, but not at Tamarindito, these are joined by a skeletal head that elsewhere represents a firefly (see Stone and Zender 2011: 188–189). Tikal kings impersonate this character on Tikal Stela 16, 19(?), 20, 22(?), and on Temple 4 Lintel 3.

16 This raises a question about the backrack worn by Yihk'in Chan K'awiil on Tikal Temple 4 Lintel 2, which shows a similar reptilian head (Figure 36). It is certainly tempting to see this as the same kind of "captured" supernatural that Case Study 7 examines. However, in this case it is more probably the head of the crocodile-based Cosmic Monster, the full-bodied sky-band, whose damaged tail arches above (Martin 2015a: 192–194) (compare also to K703).

17 In truth, there is greater complexity here because the anthropomorphised serpent is not associated with the conceptual home of the Snake dynasty in this case but rather the Moon Zero Bird location discussed in Chapter 6. This doubtless stems from the common origin Classic Maya dynasties, including that of Kaanul, claimed to this place of importance in the Protoclassic Period (Tokovinine 2013: 119).

18 The unknown verb is a positional root, possibly *hach*, here potentially in the derived transitive form **HACH-ta-ja** *hachtaj*, "raised upon" (Stuart 2005a: 97, n.37).

19 Its platform base is decorated with motifs very much like those that serve as toponymic registers on El Peru monuments, although whether this palanquin was also captured, or specially built for the ceremonial triumph, is less clear (Martin 2000c: 116–121).

20 Nakum, which later became a major site and polity capital, forces itself upon us by virtue of its position on a near-direct line between the two antagonists, and all the more so for lying on the easiest route through the valley cut by the Holmul River. Since no conflict is associated with this arrival we might infer that Tuubal was unresisting of the Tikal advance or perhaps already a client.

21 This sign was first associated with palanquins in Martin (1996a: 227–230), but it was Dmitri

Beliaev (pers. comm. 2000) who suggested **PEET** and then **PIIT/PI'T** as its value.

22 This is presumably a variant of the main local patron deity called *baluun piit*, "JGU" ("The many littered(?) Jaguar God of the Underworld"), which oversees ritual events on Naranjo Stelae 6, 12, 19, and 30 (Martin 2005c).

8 MATRIMONY

1 Daniel Stewart's MA thesis of 2009 collects a sizeable number of genealogical ties, however his list includes misidentifications that produce an overstated total.

2 Confirmation of this value comes where the same crossed-band logograph appears in the month names **CHAK-AT** *chakat* and **IHK'-AT** *ihk'at*, as well as the god name **YOP-a-AT-ta** *yopaat* in a single spelling at Copan.

3 It has been suggested that the core term is *at/aat*, "penis" and signifies the procreative potential of the union (Stephen Houston, pers. comm. 2010), although a contrasting view sees the root as *at*, "companion" (Marc Zender, pers. comm. 2010).

4 A damaged but plausible **ya-AL** *yal*, "the child of" appears between their names on Naranjo Stela 1 (Looper 1992).

5 The identification of La Florida as Namaan comes from both Stanley Guenter and Alexander Safronov (in Zender 2002: 167). Variant spellings of the Namaan referent suggest that it might already have been reduced to Maan, and later still Man, in the Classic Period. Marc Zender (in Houston 2009: 169) first suggested the reading of *chooj/kooj*, "puma" for the sign in which a cat holds the sign for *winik*, "person" in its jaws.

6 The full phrase is **ye-ta-K'ABA'-a IX a-ku-la pa-ta-ha IX sa[ja]-la ya-na-? ya-AJAW-CHAN MUWAAN** *yeet k'aba' ix ahkul patah ? yajaw chan muwaan*, "(the) namesake of Ix Ahkul Patah, Ix Sajal, (the) mother of Yajaw Chan Muwaan". This mother is separately attested on Bonampak Stela 1 (Mathews 1980: 64).

7 A poorly understood series of events in 626 marked by the term *t'abaayi*, "to go up" concern Ix Tz'akab Ajaw, the only known wife of K'inich Janaab Pakal of Palenque. Though reminiscent of "arrival" – we know that she was a foreigner from a site called *uxte'k'uh*, "Three Gods" – *t'abaayi* is always

used in the sense of going elsewhere and we cannot, as yet, link it to marriage (see Bíró 2011b: 3).

8   Tuszyńska (2009) makes a case that these women are concubines rather than wives, but their royal status renders that interpretation unpersuasive to me.

9   The title *ix uxte'tuun kaloomte'* involves the female version of the Calakmul toponym *uxte'tuun*, "Three Stones".

10 This is not something that can be assumed in the other scenes, where attention to accompanying inscriptions is required, since these can be mother–son rather than husband–wife pairs.

11 In some cases, sequential rulers share the same father but different mothers, raising the prospect of polygyny, although no case has the temporal resolution required to exclude serial monogamy.

12 A further text, this one unprovenanced, bears a different name but also refers to a "fourth wife" with **IX-YAX?-K'UH u-4-AT-li?** *ix yax k'uh uchan atanil*, "Lady First? God, the fourth wife of . . ." (Mayer 1995: pl.137) (this could yet be Lady Bone carrying an additional title).

13 See Houston (2014b) for an expansive discussion of concubines (also Note 8, above).

14 My interpretation of Classic Maya polygyny was initially set out in Martin (2010a) and composed in this form in Martin (2014a: 142–144).

15 Diego de Landa describes marriage practices among the Postclassic Maya of Yucatan, but gives conflicting accounts: at one point saying that men took only a single wife, at another that some had more (Landa 1941: 100–101). The distinction may concern commoners as opposed to the highborn.

16 Altar de Sacrificios Stela 8 was erected by the local king Baluun K'uh Ook in 628 (see Graham 1972: figure 18b) and might conceivably name his father as the Tikal king Animal Skull (Houston et al. 1992), or at least a close namesake. He is introduced at C1-D1a by the form **U-BAAH-CH'AHB** *ubaah ch'ahb*, a "child of (father)" expression of the same form as that on Stela 4 at the same site (see Graham 1972: figure 12). Additionally, D4a seems clearly to be a damaged **ya-AL** *y-al*, "child of (mother)" and is followed by a female name. As noted by Stephen Houston (1986:

2–3), the emblem glyph of Altar de Sacrificios changes at about this point. Another example of a local ruler with an outside king as his father evidently comes at Zacpeten (Stuart 2009: 322).

17 Bell (1992: 121) suggests the neologisms of hypergyny, hypogyny, and isogyny better reflect that it is the status of the women that is at issue in these relationships, but I will keep to the traditional transgendered terms.

18 Of the 166 marriages currently known through genealogical statements, only ten per cent or so (n = 17) are clearly exogamous, although the percentage rises when we take into account other kinds of data.

19 The identification of this woman's Palenque origin relies on her emblem glyph title **K'UH-MAT-AJAW-wa** *k'uhul matwiil ajaw*, which refers to a supernatural location prominent in the mythology of that site. Given its unconventional use here we might still regard the link to Palenque with some caution.

20 That the Snake kingdom could choose to send three princesses to La Corona – admittedly over a 200-year span – may seem surprising. While strategic importance might well explain the generous treatment of a small and unsophisticated dependency, there could also be some hint here of the sizeable production of royal offspring through polygyny.

21 This building was dedicated in the same year that Piedras Negras captured a Yaxchilan *sajal*. This demonstrates Yaxchilan's independence from its great rival, which, as Mary Miller has suggested, is the main suspect for Yaxchilan's long and ignominious silence (Miller 1991; Martin and Grube 2000: 123).

22 One of these monuments, Yaxchilan Lintel 53, was the work of her grandson Shield Jaguar IV.

23 Her "east" *kaloomte'* title is almost unique among Snake dynasts – who are either unspecified or ascribed the common "west" designation – and one wonders if this could link her to the old royal seat at easterly Dzibanche rather than the now-dominant capital of Calakmul (Martin 2014a: 350, n.17; Carter 2015: 11).

24 Stela 1 at Dos Caobas, an outlier of Yaxchilan, calls this royal spouse a *ho winikhaab ix ajaw*, "5 K'atun Lady", which means that she could have been born no later than 672 and would have been minimally 37 years old when she

bore Bird Jaguar. If true, this makes it highly probable the marriage was enjoined during the heyday of Calakmul influence rather than after its defeat by Tikal in 695. However, the frequency with which the 5-K'atun Ajaw status appears in the Late Classic makes one suspect that it had, by that time, become something of a titular formula no longer firmly rooted in age-specifics.

25 Tikal-Yaxchilan relations may have been at least cordial. Shield Jaguar III seems to be named on a Tikal vessel (noted by Tatiana Proskouriakoff in the Tikal Archive) – perhaps as a tributary lord (Stuart 1998: 411).

26 For the **we** reading in **che-le-we** *chelew* see Zender, Beliaev, and Davletshin (2016: 36–43).

27 To choose an ethnographic example of polygyny, one leading man of the Brazilian Yanomamo people had 43 children, while his father had 14 children, 143 grandchildren, 335 great-grandchildren and 401 great-great-grandchildren at the time of the research (cited in Gat 2006: 71 – see p.690, n.32 for the original reference).

9 CONFLICT

1 For this point see also Webster (1993: 423, 1998: 350–351).

2 The outer wall of the site depicted in the mural is painted red, while the inner one encircling its sacred precinct is decorated with trapezoid designs. At Ek Balam the inner wall is finely made, stuccoed, and red-painted, while the outer one is undecorated and more crudely constructed (George Bey, pers. comm. 2018). The meaning and depicted locations in the Chichen Itza murals remain a topic of debate. It does not seem beyond the bounds of possibility that the Las Monjas mural impressionistically depicts an assault on Ek Balam, which was certainly eclipsed and replaced by Chichen Itza as a regional power.

3 Some of these fortifications may, of course, have been earlier works that were renewed and re-occupied in later periods.

4 Knorozov's published works do very little to explain his methodology and the route that led him to the *chuhkaj* reading (rendered in his day as *chucah*). It is to be assumed that this was via

the codical images, but this is not something he spells out.

5 *Ubaak* can also serve as the stative expression "(he/she is) the captive".

6 This is the Long Count position 9.17.12.13.14, falling on the Calendar Round 5 Ix 8 Sak.

7 These images are to be found on Tonina Monument 99, Calakmul Stela 9, and the conch shell K4499 illustrated here. The second capture is probably linked to Santa Elena (see p.265) and, coincidentally, the same can be said of the third. The shell has a short surviving text on its other side that presumably identifies the male prisoner depicted close by. He is said to be a *sajal* belonging to Paay Lakam Chahk, a king of Santa Elena who lost a *sajal* to Yaxchilan in 752.

8 The placing of the female figure on the conch shell of Figure 48, close to its opening, may be a sexual allusion intended as a further indignity.

9 Schele and Freidel (1990: 444–446, n.47) identified 42 examples of this "Tlaloc-Venus complex", 39 of them aligned to some kind of planetary phenomenon (although up to 17 days of deviation was allowed). Of these, only seven are said to be wars (their numbers 1, 11, 12, 34, 36, 39, 41) and only two actually were (34, 36).

10 The star war verb has not suffered for a lack of suggested translations, however, each focussed on a particular semantic or iconographic clue. Briefly, these are: *jub*, "to take down" (Stephen Houston, pers. comm. 1992; Stuart 1995: 311–313), *em/ek'em/ek'may*, "to descend" (David Stuart, pers. comm. 1996; Aldana 2005: 313), *hay*, "to destroy" (Erik Boot, pers. comm. 2002), *tz'ay/tz'oy*, "to surrender" (Alfonso Lacadena, pers. comm. 2001), *ch'ay/ch'aykab*, "to be destroyed" (Marc Zender, pers. comm. 2004) and *uk'*, "to weep, lament" (Chinchilla 2006).

11 There is a clear pattern to these phrases, in which the "full" verb of star and falling rain atop the sign for earth is applied to people, whereas the version that includes the suffix **-yi** is applied to places and possessed flint and shield combinations. The distinction is likely to be a grammatical one, but as yet remains unexplained.

12 It is even possible that "flints" and "shields" were in some way analogous to military orders elsewhere in Mesoamerica, specifically the "eagles" and "jaguars" of the Mexica.

13 In Nahautl, the Mexica language, we find a number of paired metaphors that refer to military matters, including *mitlchimalli*, "arrow-shield" with the meaning "war". But we also find *chimalli tlacochtli*, "shield-dart" for "He has a shield, he has a dart" denoting a single warrior (see Francis Karttunen, in Freidel, Schele, and Parker 1993: 472).

14 The protagonist of the attack on Lakamha' in 611 was initially identified as a lord of Pipa', a place closely associated with Pomona (Looper and Schele 1991). Later, however, it was possible to identify the Snake dynasty's Scroll Serpent as the true agent of 611, as well as recognising Lakamha' as the target of the attack in 599 (Martin 1997a: 862, 2000c: 109).

15 Another long-range conflict is revealed by Tonina Monument 153, a panel that shows a captive identified as *aj chiiknahb* or "Calakmul Person". It credits the success to Ruler 4 and therefore occurred at some point between 708 and 723, during the reign of Calakmul king Yuknoom Took' K'awiil (Martin and Grube 2008: 184). It is very likely that this action took place at neither centre, but rather in some intervening area that brought their interests into conflict and may have involved allied engagements rather than a direct clash between the two. Tonina-Calakmul relations seem rather different in the still problematic text on Monument 171, which might place Yuknoom Took' K'awiil in a ballgame with a former Tonina king in 727 (Stuart 2013) (see p.338).

16 Yet even this is retrospectively recorded, being set in stone a half-century or so after the event itself.

17 Houses will burn even when their rooves are wet, so this distribution marks only a preference toward dry weather. It should be noted that over sixty per cent (n = 11) of the *pul* examples come from the single polity of Naranjo, with many of them (n = 6) appearing on a single monument. It is implausible that "burning" was some peculiar regional specialty, and its preponderance here suggests a rhetorical emphasis on physical destruction. It is interesting that the otherwise popular star war is absent at Naranjo.

18 It could be argued that since the Mutul emblem is shared between Tikal and Dos Pilas we cannot know which of these two polities is indicated here. However, given the Dos Pilas affiliations of the attackers it is much more probable that Tikal is intended. Incidentally, we know that a second Yaxha king was married to a Mutul woman, also presumably from Tikal (Teufel 2000: 150–151, figure 107).

19 Similar "exile" episodes involving *t'ab*, "to ascend" (see Stuart 1998: 417) later appear on Naranjo Stela 12, seemingly as the defeated king of Yaxha, K'inich Lakamtuun, retreats to different locations in 799.

20 A similar form, *och(i) ch'een*, appears in supernatural scenes showing armed deities wading waist-high in water, presumably referring in this instance to *ch'een*, "(watery) cave". This may indicate a certain metaphorical level to our *och uch'een* war statements, but it is important to note that none of the mythic examples feature the grammatical possession seen in war events (see K1224, K1248, K1333, K1338, K1343, K1346, K1365, K1366, K1395, K1489, K1562, K1648, K2011, K2096, K2710, K3428, K4117, K5002, K6979, K8201 at www.mayavase.com).

21 It is very likely that an early reference to **OCH-(u)-CH'EEN** appears on the Tikal Marcador (at C6) (Stuart 2014b). This might be the only direct evidence for the use of force in the *entrada*.

22 This "Yopmootz" name is no more than a provisional reading. This referent appears in several different spellings, most centred on a rare and undeciphered "inverted basket" logogram (Boot 1999b). The reading is problematic because their sign sequences are not consistent, apparently disordered for aesthetic reasons. We have versions featuring the logogram of **yo-?-tzi** on K4669 and **yo-?** on a plate not in the Kerr archive, but also **?-mo-yo** on K8728 and a version without the logogram of **mo-yo-tzi** on K7786. The issue is complicated further because the **yo** sign can also be **YOP**, and its regular position ahead of the mystery logogram might suggest that it is an independent word rather than a phonetic complement. Since logograms usually represent CVC units then the "inverted basket" sign is potentially **MOOTZ**. Whatever this site was called and wherever it was situated, it was evidently a player of some note, perhaps somewhere on the scale of El Pilar, the largest site in the area to remain unidentified.

23 See Tokovinine (2008: 301–302) for the association between the *chak tok wayib* title and Holmul.

24 The different analyses to which the data are to be applied use different slices of the sample. For example, a case where we cannot decide between two Long Count positions for a given war event means that it cannot be used in Figure 50. However, if both options fall in November in the GMT correlation then it could appear in Figures 52 and 53.

25 Hassig's "conquests" consist mostly of star war events, although single *chuk* and *jub* events are also mixed in. Of the twenty-five in his tabulation, thirteen are verified star wars for a fifty-two per cent accuracy and this rises to sixty per cent when that from the second group is included. The second group of "captures" are, as one would expect, mostly *chuk* events, but are joined by a single star war, *pul*, and *jub* event. Of his original forty-three conflicts, thirty-four would count today, for an accuracy of seventy-nine per cent.

26 This does not take account of the Dzibanche Captive Stairway (see Case Study 6), to which we will return presently.

27 Analyses courtesy of Emad Khazraee and Joanne Baron (pers. comms. 2019) lead one to conclude that more rigorous and specialised statistical methods are required to settle this issue.

28 The year-bearers examined are the "Ik' set" of the Classic era (Stuart 2004b) rather than the "K'an set" that prevailed in Landa's time.

29 Some events in this analysis should be excluded as sequential parts of single campaigns, as when a *chuk* capture directly follows a *jub* event, and the total number in the sample would fall slightly as a result.

30 The rainfall profile is that given for the Department of Petén, Guatemala, by Hotaling (1995: figures 4 and 5), which he compiled from data in Urrutia (1964) and the World Weather Disc (1988).

31 Maize is the best candidate for this putative wintertime cultivation because other staples, such as root crops, grow throughout the year and require no special tending or management (see Bronson 1966: 271). Maize takes at least three months to mature and intervals between the P4, T1, P1, T2, and P2 would imply overlapping planting and harvesting cycles, or even time-consuming activities such as watering or mulching.

32 It should be noted that almost seventy per cent of the *chuk* events in July and August took place after 720. This type of *canícula* warfare

therefore seems to have become more popular over time, and we might consider the possibility that this was due to a drying climate (see Chapter 11).

33 It would be ironic indeed if data on life-taking conflict would offer a clue to the complexity of life-giving cultivation in the densely inhabited southern lowlands. It goes without saying that any seasonal analysis is dependent on the accuracy of a given correlation. Yet, since the relative dating is fixed – the profiles cannot themselves be changed, only be shifted back or forward en masse to different parts of the year – any close variant of the GMT correlation offers a persuasive fit to the climatological and agricultural constraints.

34 For Classical Greek cases of crop theft see Hanson (1998: 32–40).

35 Figures dressed as armed Teotihuacanos in the late-fourth to sixth centuries include those on Uaxactun Stela 5 (396), Tikal Stela 31 (445), Tres Islas Stelae 1 and 3 (455 and 475), Piedras Negras Panel 12 (514), and Lacanha Stela 7 (593).

36 For example: "[W]e might also consider the economic dimension of the prize, that a prisoner of note represented a much wider set of obligations and resources – be it a ransom that could be extorted or lands and labor, brides and concubines, that might be made tributary to the captor" (Miller and Martin 2004: 166).

37 See Stuart (1995: 352–374, 1998: 410–414), Houston et al. (2006: 242–247) and, especially, McAnany (2010: 269–304) for extensive discussions of tribute and royal finances (see p.339–343).

38 Nuun Bahlam is ascribed the same *uxlajuun tzuk*, "Division 13" designation as Nuun Ujol Chahk. This still-opaque territorial designation encompasses several polities, one of a set of such numbered titles in the eastern half of the southern lowlands that is an important topic for future research (see Tokovinine 2013: 98–110).

10 HIERARCHY

1 The first efforts at interpreting this glyphic term offered "under the auspices of" (Schele 1982: 73; Stuart 1985d: 178), but by the time its role in accession statements was noted in

A Forest of Kings: The Untold Story of the Ancient Maya by Linda Schele and David Freidel (1990: 155, 175), a prepositional form of "in the land of", initially suggested by Peter Mathews, was favoured. However, there was good reason to prefer a more active verbal gloss "by the doing of" (Martin 1993: 3, 8; Martin and Grube 1994a: 7).

2   The **chi** value in **yi-chi-NAL** usually takes the form of a human hand, but there is also a rare acrophonic usage of **CHIH** as **chi** (which can be seen in Figure 61a, b). The **CHIH** sign consists of the maguey plant personified in the form of the rain deity Chahk and refers to the fermented maguey drink called *pulque* today.

3   A spelling on Uxul Stela 12 (B7) (Grube 2008: figure 8.59) is abraded, but could consist of **yi-? ICHON-no-NAL** and supply the otherwise unexpressed medial vowel in *yichonal*.

4   For this reason, Figure 75 – a diagram of political connections – puts examples of the *ila'* relationship under the "Diplomacy" rather than "Hierarchy" category.

5   There are a few examples of possessed forms of the third **AJAW** logogram, a vulture wearing a royal headband. One appears on Naranjo Stela 1 and another on Motul de San José Stela 1.

6   Dmitri Beliaev (2017) offers the 392 date of Río Azul Stela 1 as a correction to previous placements in 393, as well as confirming the presence of the Sihyaj K'ahk' name.

7   The tripod vessel K7528 emerged together with an almost identical counterpart, K7529, that describes its contents as a variety of chocolate called *sa'al kakaw*. *Sa'al* means "maize-gruel" in certain texts, but in this context it more likely refers to the Naranjo referent. Another vessel, K1446, may link the known Naranjo ruler Naatz Chan Ahk to the New Order via the abbreviated statement of subordination *yajaw kaloomte'*, "lord of the *kaloomte'*". Donald Hales (pers. comm. 2018) pointed out the relationship of the name on K7528 to that on an unprovenanced earflare, where it was followed by Río Azul's de facto emblem.

8   Although the relevant inscription is eroded and unclear, there is some suggestion in the strange text on Tikal Stela 1 that Jatz'oom Kuy had at least one Maya wife, implying that Yax Nuun Ahiin had mixed ancestry (Martin 2002: 67) (see Chapter 6, Note 18).

9   Both Jatz'oom Kuy (??) and Sihyaj K'ahk' are Mayan forms, but the proposition is that they

are translations from the language of Teotihuacan. The reading of the former is by David Stuart and, independently, Albert Davletshin. Stuart has suggested that the masked Teotihuacano on Tikal Stela 32 may be a portrait of Jatz'oom Kuy (??).

10 A less complete version of this accession event appears on a block of the Copan Hieroglyphic Stairway (Martin and Grube 2000: 217).

11 Lacanha Stela 7 (O'Neil 2012: figure E.6c) shows a ruler in 593 wearing an identical helmet, and one wonders if this is the very same regalia obtained from Teotihuacan via Piedras Negras some four decades earlier.

12 It is those places where Central Mexican symbolism is most common, Tikal, Copan, Piedras Negras, and to a lesser degree Palenque, that we find some stated historical connection to Teotihuacan or its agents.

13 See some of the chapters in the edited volume Braswell (2003b) for a more sceptical view of Teotihuacan militarism.

14 This damaged compound appears on Tamarindito Stela 2 at C6 (for a drawing see Gronemeyer 2013: pl.5). Consisting of **YAX-EHB-IX?[?]**, this unusual superimposed form resembles the Tikal founder's name, which the Lady of Tikal carries on at least one other occasion. Another potential instance – but no more than a hypothetical one due to its damaged state – appears on Caracol Stela 15 at F4. Here a potential female supervises the accession of the Caracol king K'an I in 531.

15 This ruler has gone under several previous nicknames (Ruler I, Double-Comb, Aj Wosal) and the current **AJ-NUM-sa-ji CHAN-K'INICH** reading by Alexandre Tokovinine relies on a **NUM** reading for the small snake logogram (in Martin et al. 2017).

16 For the identification of K'ahk' Ti' Ch'ich' and his other name Aj Saakil, see Martin and Beliaev (2017). There is no surviving *yajaw* statement linked to Scroll Serpent, but he is named at Caracol as the supervisor of some now-destroyed event (Martin 1997a: 862). The list on Stela 47 passes over a Kaanul king known to us as Yax Yopaat on Dzibanche Monument 16 in 573, while on the dynastic vase K6751 this position is occupied by one Yuknoom Ti' Chan – who are possibly, but not necessarily, the same person (Martin 2017b). We know that there is only a small time-window for this character because Sky

Witness was evidently alive in 572 and Scroll Serpent crowned in 579. Conceivably, the intervening king was too short-lived to be considered worth mentioning, or even that the personal relationship with the Naranjo king had not been established. Even so, this presents us with another of the remaining questions about the Dzibanche attribution. The hope is that additional finds will clarify the dynastic sequence at Dzibanche and ensure that some still more complex scenario is not at work.

17   Even though the victor of 562 cannot be the Caracol king, there are signs that Caracol was involved in the aftermath of this conflict, given various stylistic analogies between the two sites (Coggins 1975). Moreover, the twenty-second king of Tikal, dubbed Animal Skull, was entombed in Burial 195 along with a stucco-covered wooden vessel, now much decayed, that names a Caracol lord, probably as its original owner (Martin 2008c).

18   The connecting term between their names is badly damaged, but it has a **ya** suffix that would be consistent with ***u-*KAB-ya**.

19   This appears in a syntactically unconventional section at the close of Caracol Stela 3 (Beetz and Satterthwaite 1981: figure 4), where the Caracol emblem glyph has been displaced from K'an II's name phrase so that it can conclude the inscription.

20   The relevant *yajaw* statement appears on Dos Pilas HS.4, where it is retrospectively appended to an event in 648 (Houston et al. 1992; Houston 1993: 108).

21   Other cases where this term marks childhood accessions are those of K'ahk' Tiliw Chan Chahk of Naranjo, who was also five years old, and K'inich Janaab Pakal of Palenque, who was twelve.

22   Here on Bonampak Panel 5, the verb involved, **K'AL**, is prefixed by a damaged number, which might be two, three, or four. Given the precedent of Moral-Reforma Stela 4, this figure would appear to indicate the number of (re)installation rites this lord had undergone. If so, it would tell us that the allegiance of Bonampak/Lacanha was switching between Yaxchilan and some other leading power in the first half of the seventh century. Another reference to Bird Jaguar III that could date to within his reign comes on an unprovenanced block, almost certainly part

of a hieroglyphic stairway. It is anomalous because there he carries the only known example of a third emblem glyph for Yaxchilan, whose referent is *muwaan* "hawk", and the carving has stylistic features that are typical of the eighth century.

23   El Peru Stela 20 records the birth of Yuknoom Ch'een II in 600 (Martin 1998), while the accessions of Yuknoom Yich'aak K'ahk' in 686 and Yuknoom Took' K'awiil in 698 appear on El Peru Stela 34 and 43, respectively (Miller 1974; Navarro-Farr and Guenter 2013).

24   This would feature the otherwise unseen possessed form **ya-AJAW-li** for *yajawil*. In another part of this El Reinado text we find a reference to Calakmul in the sequence **AJ-ta-*li 3-TE'-TUUN** *aj tali uxte'tuun*, perhaps meaning "Person who comes from Three Stones". Incongruously, this is the sole subject of the period ending of 9.13.0.0.0 in 692.

25   I am grateful to Arthur Demarest (pers. comm. 2018) for pointing me to this publication.

26   The opening Long Count date on Nim Li Punit Stela 2 is rather weathered, but the key to reconstructing it is the compound of **7-HAAB** (suffixed by **-tu**) seen at F3. This is a "rounded" distance number that counts forward to the period ending 9.15.0.0.0 in 731, the dedicatory date of the monument. It indicates that the accession event took place in 724 and, based on the remains of the month as ***10 Mol**, the best reconstruction for it would be 9.14.12.14.2 6 Ik' 10 Mol. This not inconsistent with the opening date. If the distance number had been written out in full it would have been 7.3.18.

27   Another possibility is that the "Black Copan Lord" refers to a different kingdom in this instance.

28   Wamaaw K'awiil's title on Quirigua Stela I is given as **chi[ku]-NAHB K'UH[a?]-AJAW-wa** for *chiiknahb k'uhul ajaw*. This is notable as one of the earliest appearances of the true *k'uhul ajaw*, "holy lord" epithet, as well as for the seemingly unique conflation between **K'UH** and the phonetic prefix **a**.

29   It is significant that Wamaaw K'awiil is identified as a *k'uhul kaanul ajaw* dynast in what appears to be a near-contemporary context originating at Zapote Bobal (Tunesi 2007). The reference at Quirigua describes events in

736, but was carved a half century or more later, and the shift to the less prestigious *chiiknahb k'uhul ajaw* title presumably better reflects the political reality of that time.

30 The earlier installation of this same noble by the king, an *anaab* who becomes an *ajk'uhuun* – unusually using the *t'abaayi*, "ascends" verb – is recorded on another block (Matteo 2010).

31 The opening date for Altar 13 is very likely 9.19.6.14.4, 9 K'an 7 Sip, which would be the earliest mark we have for this Caracol king. It is followed by the transitive verb **u-CH'AM-wa** *uch'amaw*, "he grasps/receives". This is used in accession events with *k'awiil*, but the mostly effaced object here may be something else. While neither of the terms connecting the two lords is well-preserved, their outlines closely resemble **yi-*chi-*NAL-*la** for *yichonal*.

32 Guenter (1999: 105–106) suggests that their forces were allied in an attack on Tikal that brought down the great city in 817. Certain features of the text on Altar 12 make this an appealing idea, especially with the potential mention of a Nuun Ujol Chahk name, but the critical passages are damaged and remain very hard to understand.

33 El Palma is a small site and it is quite possible that the Lakamtuun kingdom had other, earlier capitals. The large and little-explored site of Benemérito de las Américas must be one candidate (an idea independently reached by Whittaker Schroeder, pers. comm. 2019).

34 In addition, there is a further example of the Santa Elena emblem glyph at Palenque on a now lost stucco fragment illustrated by Jean-Frédéric Waldeck (Pasztory 2011).

35 Here the name of Nuun Hix Lakam Chahk appears in a phrase beginning *ipahsaj*, "then he/she/it opens", which takes place in the company of Shield Jaguar II of Yaxchilan. Although the former carries no identifying title, the Lakam Chahk portion of his name recurs in the names of Santa Elena lords mentioned at Piedras Negras in 706 and Yaxchilan in 752. That combination, seen nowhere else, conforms to the well-known practice in which dynasties make recurring use of particular theonyms. Moreover, a personal inspection of Santa Elena Monument 1 suggests the local ruler who acts under the authority of Palenque's Ajen Yohl Mat between 605 and 611 had

a very similar name: **x-HIX/BAHLAM x-CHAHK**. Whether this is the accession of a new ruler or not, this text indicates that Palenque quickly reasserted itself in the region after the defeat of 599.

36 The Calendar Round is 13 Ak'bal 16 Yax, which equates to 9.11.7.0.3 based on the dedication date of Stela 9 as 9.11.10.0.0 (662).

37 Contact between Piedras Negras and Calakmul is recorded again in 685, when an unprovenanced panel now in the Los Angeles County Art Museum describes the *nahwaj* presentation of a *ko'haw* war helmet and *nuk* pelt (?) to Itzam K'an Ahk III, the same Piedras Negras king who had seized Santa Elena in 662 (Martin and Grube 2000: 144). This event was performed by an *aj baak*, a "prisoner-taker" or war captain, who is said to belong to Yuknoom Ch'een (Grube 1996: 8, figure 8a). This sets up a clear parallel with Itzam K'an Ahk's Panel 2 from 667, which describes his *(u)ch'amaw* receiving/taking of five *ko'haw* helmets in 658 – only four years prior to the war – and Yat Ahk's earlier acquisition of similar items under the oversight of Tajom Uk'ab Tuun, the lord associated with Teotihuacan, in 510 (see p.243). This provokes a question: was the ceremony of 658 itself under the oversight of, or involved gifts from, a foreign power, namely Calakmul?

38 When first photographed by Maudslay most of these gaps were already filled with stone blocks, and at least one adjoining slab that intrudes into the space has not been fully trimmed. It seems likely that an initial plan for captive sculptures was abandoned quite early on.

39 It is not impossible that the entire programme of House C was conceived together. However, the integrated nature of the eastern sculptural programme argues that the dedication date of 661 finalised that part of the building.

40 This, and a similar sculpture, were excavated by Juan Yadeun and published in various print and online outlets in 2011 (see Stuart 2011b, 2011c).

41 Tonina Monument 157 (Graham et al. 2006: 91), also known as the "Lexington Panel", may well provide the anchor for this series with a count of 12.10.15* from a capture event on 9.12.19.16.5 (692) leading to the eighth-of-a-K'atun period ending on 9.13.12.9.0 (704) (Mathews 2001b: table 2).

42   At Tonina the spelling of this toponym always features three elements: a rabbit head, the head of frog or toad that normally represents **e**, and the sign for stone consisting of **TUUN** together with its regular phonetic complement of **ni**. The rabbit head can be read **T'UL**, "rabbit", but much more commonly represents the syllable **pe** (see Dmitri Beliaev and Albert Davletshin, in Houston 2014a). That this is the case here is confirmed by the amphibian head, which works to mark a glottal stop following the *e* vowel, suggesting a reading of *pe'tuun*. However, an example on Piedras Negras Throne 1 shows the rabbit head with a clear "doubler" diacritic, which indicates that the value is to be sounded twice as **pe-pe**. Such markers are regularly omitted in Maya writing, here leaving a single **pe** sign to do the work of two (we see this most clearly on ceramic vessels where *kakaw*, "cacao" is almost always spelled **ka-wa** as a reduction from **²ka-wa**, the standard abbreviation of **ka-ka-wa**). The entire reading of the "Rabbit Stone" toponym is therefore most probably *pepe'tuun*.

43   The possessed title of Buk' Saak was first noted by Yuriy Polyukhovich in a video published online, and description of it appended as a comment to Stuart (2011a).

44   Parts of a fifth shield, Tonina Monument 72, have been found but its text is incomplete. One suspects that a mention of K'awiil Mo' will eventually be found as one of a set of six.

45   An alternative reconstruction could yield *k'ahlaj tuun*, "the stone is held/presented", possibly spread over glyphs E10 and D11 of Stela 2. However, although the day is the appropriate Ajaw position, the Long Count of 9.14.0.10.0 is not a regular period ending (though see p.92 and Zender 2004: 336–337). Given the context of the subsequent accession statement, *k'ahlaj huun* at E10 is preferred here.

11 CODA

1   The era leading up to the collapse is one Mayanists traditionally describe as the Terminal Classic Period. Unfortunately, this label has been assigned different start- and end-dates in different regions by different authors and become increasingly ill-defined as a result. To avoid the difficulties it presents, this volume keeps to common era chronology, where "ninth century" covers most or all of what other scholars refer to when discussing the Terminal Classic.

2   A good number of scholars question the appropriateness of the word "collapse" for the transformations of the ninth century, believing that this privileges the achievements of the Classic and demeans the continuities and innovations of Postclassic society. I have no privileging agenda, but do believe that the termination of a political culture, the abandonment of hundreds of settlements, and the disappearance of millions of people, all in a short timeframe, is one adequately covered by that term.

3   Although some have argued that the populations of certain sites endured beyond the collapse of central authority, the great majority of studies suggest that desertion was closely aligned with the fall of ruling regimes. An illustrative debate is the one regarding the longevity of Copan's occupation and the controversy over the accuracy of obsidian hydration dating (compare Webster and Freter 1990 and Webster 2005 with Andrews and Fash 2005: 420–423).

4   This database includes legible and reconstructible dates, together with a small number of placements made on the basis of clear contextual information. No placements are based exclusively on style. The sole use of style is to assign some dated but unprovenanced monuments to either the northern or southern zone. All records are from free-standing monuments or architectural contexts, except for a few portable objects associated with identifiable sites. If a single building features several dates then only the latest of them is included, while inscribed stela and altar pairs are treated as one record.

5   Scholars working in the Petexbatun region would begin this sequence with Dos Pilas, abandoned in or around 761, since in their view this marks the beginning of an escalation in warfare, ultimately leading to the wider collapse (e.g. Demarest et al. 1997). However, this temporally isolated event more resembles one of the periodic depopulations and resurgences that had always been a feature of Classic Maya political history (see p.229). The crude defences at Dos Pilas enclose a small settlement built within its central plaza and, together with

nearby fortified communities, almost certainly dates to the deeper crisis of some five decades later (Guenter 2014: 173–175).

6   Even later dates are reported for parts of the northern lowlands, reaching well into the tenth century, although almost all of these require some degree of reconstruction (Graña-Behrens 2002: 249–254, table 88). However, few if any scholars would include such aesthetically impoverished commissions as part of the Classic tradition. A secure carved date of 998 is recorded at Chichen Itza, but this is associated with Central Mexican iconography and part of a decidedly intrusive phenomenon. The last stela dedications were part of a revivalist movement at Mayapan in the twelfth and thirteenth centuries.

7   The last known monument at La Milpa, Stela 7 was erected in 780 (Grube 1994a). Although the date of the great building cessation is uncertain, a layer of soil covering one structure contained a sherd of Pabellon pottery (to be discussed momentarily), indicating that the halt occurred in the early rather than the late ninth century (Hammond and Tourtellot 2004: 60).

8   As the post-810 world was described in an earlier paper: "While some centers did persevere for a while, and some former outliers took up kingly traditions, these were very much the shell-shocked survivors of an earlier cataclysm, stalwarts desperately clinging on to a social order whose time was past" (Martin 2003b: 35).

9   The political importance of Coba is inferred from its enormous size and the 98 km long linear causeway it constructed to Yaxuna. The only firm interactions we have for it are the *aj koba'*, "Coba Person" mentioned as a captive on Edzna Stela 18 from 692 (Grube 2003b: 360). In addition, there is a previously unrecognised seizure of someone ascribed the Oxkintok royal title on Coba Stela 6 (at H1–2) from 623. If this were to be the Oxkintok king himself it would count as the most important political interaction we have for the northern lowlands (Martin 2019b).

10 The history of Chichen Itza in the late-ninth and tenth centuries it a critical topic for understanding the northern transition to the Postclassic, but remains frustratingly unclear. The 998 date from the High Priest's Grave is associated with overt signs of Central Mexican presence and is distinct from the Puuc-Chenes regime of the late 800s. A recent Bayesian analysis of radiocarbon dates has helped to re-establish a separation between "Old Chichen" (Chenes-Puuc) and "New Chichen" ("Toltec") periods (Volta and Braswell 2014). There is therefore much to say for a return to traditional, but long disfavoured, readings of the evidence that point to a transformative incursion from the west in the tenth century (see Martin and Grube 2000: 229).

11 Compare Źrałka et al. (2018: figure 15) with Graham (1996: 45).

12 Nicholas Carter (2014a: 197) believes that two pre-Wat'ul K'atel lords, Chan Peet Ajaw and Waxak Peet, together bear one Ceibal emblem glyph on Stela 11 (D2–E1), while I prefer to see Chan Peet Ajaw Waxak Peet as the two-part name of a single lord.

13 I borrow the term "code-switching" from Carter (2014a: 179, 326). A closer look at the physical orientation of the "non-Maya" portraits suggest still deeper levels to the symbolism of this programme. David Stuart (2016) posits that these differing personas are meaningfully aligned toward the particular Maya polities mentioned on the cardinally arranged stelae and reflect how Wat'ul K'atel wants to be seen by them.

14 Unlike Adams, Sabloff, and Willey, Thompson (1970: 42–43) did not see this intrusion as a factor in the collapse, continuing to ascribe that to a peasant's revolt.

15 A similar shift in name-style occurs in the far southeast, where the last lord of Copan in 822, Ukit Took', not only has a name distinct from any of his predecessors but one more typical of those seen in the north (e.g. Guenter 2014: 224). This is only one of a range of late imports to Copan and Quirigua that appear to have a northern origin (e.g. Awe and Helmke 2017). Ukit Took' appears on Copan Altar L, an ideal physical symbol of the collapse since it was left unfinished, with only one of its four sides completed and another started (Barbara Fash, in Fash and Stuart 1991: 175, figure 7.6).

16 Both Guenter (1999: 108) and Carter (2014a: 202) see the name of Olom on Uaxactun Stela 7 (at B11b), dated to 810. However, this is instead the remains of a **K'UH** sign and part of the construction *yichonal uk'uhuul*, "before

his gods" (my thanks go to Dmitri Beliaev who supplied the photograph that confirmed this reading). This leaves the earliest dated record of Olom as the one on Stela 13 at 830.

17   The reading **ye-ta-ja** on Uaxactun Stela 12 (at A4) can be compared with the same spelling on Jimbal Stela 1 (at Y1) (compare Graham 1986: 161 to Jones and Satterthwaite 1982: figure 78) – to be discussed presently. The same relationship appears as **ye-ta** on Ucanal Stela 4 (at D1a) and on Ceibal Stela 9 (at D3) in this same era. The root *et* is widely distributed in Mayan languages and is used to mean "companion" or simply "with" – and here it takes a verbal form we can gloss as "he is accompanied (by)". In earlier times the root *it* served the same or a very similar purpose. The name of the *ochk'in/chik'in kaloomte'* on Uaxactun Stela 12 is not well preserved. As Guenter (1999: 161–163) notes, in beginning with the syllabogram **k'a** it resembles that of a successor to Wat'ul K'atel on Ceibal Stela 20 from this same 889 date. There may well be some relationship here to a name in the rim text of the mould-made vessel K1979.

18   Morley (1937–1938: I:443) dated Ixlu Altar 1 to 10.2.10.0.0 in 879. However, this relied on reading the damaged day coefficient as 2 and the month sign as Ch'en, neither of which can be the case. The coefficient is either "3" or "4", while the month can only realistically be K'ank'in/Uniiw. The only solution that fits these features, plus its half-K'atun statement, is 10.1.10.0.0 4 Ajaw 13 K'ank'in, falling in 859.

19   It has been argued that square cartouches have a long history in the Maya region, with one numbered version seen on Stela 5 at El Zapote, a Tikal satellite, in 435 (Proskouriakoff 1993: 186). Yet here too the association is with the west, being combined with a "ray-and-trapezoid" year sign (Justeson et al. 1985: 69). The name within is the same as that used by a high-ranking woman and a former queen of Tikal (Martin 2002: 57–68). Interestingly, we do see rare Gulf Coast-style day-names before the ninth century. One appears on Moral-Reforma Stela 5 and there may be another on K868.

20   Although some have interpreted the opening numbered square day-sign ("7 Water?") as a date, the lack of a corresponding verb suggests

that the whole text is a name caption to the standing figure – a lord engaged in a mythic re-enactment – probably produced sometime after the last Maya dated monument at Ceibal in 889 (see also Carter 2014a: 176).

21   In several, but not all cases, the square name days and their coefficients are sequential. The significance of this is unknown, although in the Classic Maya system such pairings can refer to events that span two *tzolk'in* positions but fall within a single *haab* day (see Martin and Skidmore 2012: 5). The first Maya sign, a rabbit head, is both syllabic **pe** and logographic **T'UL** "rabbit". While we cannot, with certainty, choose between them, contextual reasons make me prefer the syllabic option.

22   Given the density of Ahk'utu' finds at Nakum, Jarosław Źrałka (2008: 118) has suggested that these pots could have been manufactured at the site. If true, this would further implicate Nakum as a major political centre at this time, and perhaps even the base of Olom, who seems sure to be an outsider at Uaxactun.

23   I diverge with Wyllie (2002: 301–302) on this point, who believes that the Pabellon motifs are examples of an unknown logographic script.

24   I am grateful to Dmitri Beliaev for sharing an image of this vessel.

25   The exceptions are the previously noted *kaloomte'* at Machaquila in 815 and another at Oxpemul in 830 (see Graham 1967: Fig.49; Grube 2008: figures 8.31, 8.33, and 8.40).

26   The nominal phrase of the Mutul lord begins with the title *aj winik baak*, "He of 20 Captives". Although it could be coincidental, the same title recurs at Mountain Cow (close to Caracol) on Altar 1 in 835. Note that the first *kaloomte'* mentioned on the Ixlu altar (at E2) is not attached to a person, but is an independent god name/title.

27   Herein lies the incentive to separate the two opening syllables in the spelling **pa-pa-ma-li-li** into a single short vowel morphemic unit, thus preferring Papmalil over Papamalil.

28   Due to the presence of likely fragments of Stela 24's accompanying Altar 7 in a cache together with Eznab ceramics, the last-but-one ceramic phase at Tikal, Jones and Satterthwaite (1982: 52) concluded that the destruction of these monuments took place in the ninth century.

12 CLASSIC MAYA NETWORKS

1 I refer here to long-distance inter-site roads rather than the shorter intra-site versions, which often take the form of wide processional causeways – as we see at Tikal, Coba, and Caracol, among others (e.g. Folan, Kintz, and Fletcher 1983; Chase and Chase 2001: Shaw 2001, 2008). The unique Coba-Yaxuna roadway has the form and linear routing of those solidly built structures (Folan, Kintz, and Fletcher 1983). Thanks to remote sensing, there has been a rising interest in overland communication routes and the likely courses of ancient Maya roads, together with a concern for their strategic and trade connections (see Freidel et al. 2007; Canuto et al. 2011; also Canuto et al. 2018) (Case Study 9).

2 Stuart (2006c) offers epigraphic evidence from panels found on the Coba-Yaxuna causeway that it was referred to as a *sak bih*, "white road" (c.f. Bolles and Folan 2001: 304 for the argument that this term only gained prominence in the nineteenth century).

3 Lidar scanning has thus far tracked 106 km of paved causeways (Canuto et al. 2018). Most of these emanate from major Preclassic centres, but clearly many would continue to have been used in later times. More detailed surveys will be required to trace the routes of the filigree of lesser roadways that constituted the great bulk of the network.

4 A special case is presented by La Corona, a secondary centre which detailed its interactions with its political masters at Calakmul at length and recorded significant events in Calakmul's history. Under the current archaeological project at La Corona (Canuto and Barrientos 2013) the number of these contacts has risen to at least 25. An anomaly with clear potential to distort the analysis, I have mitigated the problem somewhat by including only the twelve examples known at the inception of that project in 2008. Even so, due to space limitations it is not possible to show all the diplomatic ties to Calakmul and, as with Uxul, each of those lines represents two connections. The same is true for two of the diplomatic lines leading to El Peru.

5 A further caveat is required in cases such as that of Yaxchilan, whose lofty third place in both home and foreign measures is less an artefact of its political importance than of the high textual output of that site and the Usumacinta River region more generally. The opposite problem is posed by major powers at the periphery of the Maya realm. Palenque, Tonina, and Copan lack the number of immediate neighbours that more centrally located polities have, and their counts suffer as a consequence. The case of Caracol is a complete contrast to that of Dzibanche-Calakmul, since it gains its ranking almost exclusively from connections recorded on its own inscriptions at fully ninety-two per cent. Caracol goes unmentioned in the texts of any other site: an emblem glyph on a pot found at Tikal and the supervision of one of its rulers by a lord of Ixkun recorded in the cave texts of Naj Tunich are currently the only exceptions. The idea of a "fame" register is borrowed from Ober (2015: 34). Since it is possible to have a misleading fame value, for example simply because the site in question is a frequent victim of attack, the types of contact always need to be taken into account.

6 The term "edge of chaos" was devised by computer scientist and complexity theorist Charles Langton (see Waldrop 1992: 198–240). It suffers, like the concept of chaos itself, from some loose and sometimes misplaced usage. Nevertheless, I employ it here because it usefully captures the evidently tenuous state of Classic Maya society.

7 Geoffrey Braswell (2005) analysed the original version of my diagram (Martin and Grube 2000: 21) – which then featured thirty-five centres and 194 links – and was the first to note its "small world" properties. Work in the vein of social network analysis, as opposed to network theory, has been conducted by Munson and Macri (2009) and Scholnick, Munson, and Macri (2013). These two works are detailed studies that offer statistical support for understandings that had already been gleaned from the texts themselves.

13 DEFINING CLASSIC MAYA POLITICAL CULTURE

1 I am indebted to Frauke Sachse (pers. comm. 2017) for pointing out this comparison.

2 The white paper headband *huun* was the mark of the *ajaw* status (see p.70) and we see it adorning the foreheads of *sajal, ajk'uhuun,* and *ti'sakhuun* nobles, identifying all as *ajawtaak.*

3   However, this picture needs to be balanced with the recognition of time-depth to some of these features, especially the hotspot of noble visibility in the western region around Yaxchilan, where such royal–noble representations begin as early as the fifth century and number among the earliest monuments known from the region (Zender 2004: 391–392; Bíró 2012b: 92–93).

4   As Hassig (2016: 144) notes, the over-production of elites through polygyny could have had an instrumental role in the ever-greater burden put on the producers that remained, putting new stresses on the system.

5   I am indebted to Charles Golden (pers. comm. 2014) for an update on the ceramic chronology for the region, which ongoing work aims to refine.

6   I have previously summarised the issue in this way: "It may be our notion of the Maya 'polity' that is at fault. We need a definition that sits comfortably with dramatic – if rare – shifts in location, and the transfer of identity and affiliation that affects not only places but whole populations. In essence, these emblem names seem to label royal houses whose connections to specific territories are less intrinsic than habitual" (Martin 2005a: 12).

7   Several of the cases examined by Joffe (1998) do not fulfil his disembedded model and are better explained as strategic relocations.

8   "With the conquest and annexation of neighbouring kingdoms, the original ancestral land and its capital often lost its central position in the framework of the extended imperial kingdom. It was necessary to overcome this marginality by the founding of a new, more centrally situated capital" (Kulke 1995a: 253–254).

9   Classic Maya texts are more reticent on these matters than we would like, with the temple ritual performed by Ix Wak Jalam Chan three days after her arrival at Naranjo a mere hint of the rites necessary to secure an appropriate position within a new dynastic group (and which were only recorded retrospectively to enhance her claims to de facto rulership). This is a special case in more than one respect, since hers became a caretaker regime that asserted its legitimacy by means of her royal Dos Pilas, and therefore Tikal ancestry, but only so as to nurture the continuation of a native line bearing the traditional sa'al emblem of Naranjo.

10   Tokovinine (2011) is the published version of a paper delivered in 2005.

11   This division can also be discerned in the contrast between sites with lengthy counts-of-kings and those without (Houston et al. 2003: 237).

12   There has been a long-running debate about the relationship and direction of cultural influence between the lowlands to the piedmont zone of the Pacific coast, where we see a number of early developments at sites such as Izapa, Takalik Abaj, and El Baúl. The last two of these have Long Count dates falling in the first and second centuries.

13   One instance I have in mind here appears on Moral-Reforma Stela 4, where the third investiture of the local king under the auspices of his counterpart at Palenque is said to have occurred at baakal (Martin 2003c: 47). Normally seen only as a dynastic name, this must either indicate that the event, uniquely, took place at the original home of this royal line, or else baakal is used derivatively to refer to the Palenque polity as a general locale. Another appears on Dos Pilas Panel 19, where a "guardian" of the young prince undergoing a bloodletting ritual is call aj kaanul, "Snake Person". While this person could conceivably hail from Dzibanche, the likelihood that Dos Pilas's overlords at Calakmul are referenced is much greater.

14   "Therefore, the 'T856-la lord' emblem glyph [of Tamarindito] does not indicate one's political control of the region and there is no such thing as a T856-la [Tamarindito] polity, at least not in the Late Classic historical record documented in the available inscriptions" (Tokovinine 2013: 67).

15   Chang (1983: 374) stresses the importance of historical data in determining how clan and political affiliations were arranged in ancient China: "What one cannot do under any circumstances is to look at the location of the towns and then figure out in any quantitative or other way, a geometrical latticework to which the towns should conform".

16   It is associated with dynasts from Uxul (Grube et al. 2012: 22), as well as those from the still unidentified sites of Maasal and Chatahn (Tintal?).

17   The potential for even closer connections to Calakmul emerges on a hieroglyphic stairway found jumbled with others and reset in a series

of new steps in the later history of La Corona (Barrientos, Canuto, and Ponce 2013). This monument – well known from other blocks looted from this same context – is unusual because its protagonist was a noble of the *ajk'uhuun* rank directly subject to the Calakmul king Yuknoom Took' K'awiil. This is what we would expect to find at Calakmul, or if not a secondary site close to it, not a "royal" centre some 88 km distant. The name used for Yuknoom Took' K'awiil is, additionally, the one favoured at Calakmul. This monument may not have been intended for La Corona but instead produced there for shipment to Calakmul – political troubles intervening before the project could be completed.

18 See Stuart (2005b: 379–383) for the two construction phases of the Copan Hieroglyphic Stairway in 710 and 755.

19 After the defeat of 738 the Copan king appears in exactly this construction, with K'ahk' Tiliw Chan Yopaat of Quirigua describing himself as his "guardian/master" of Waxaklajuun Ubaah K'awiil on Quirigua Stela A (at C10–D10) and Stela E (at B19–A20a).

20 Each of these kingdoms is associated with a particular kind of *baak* – presumably "bone" rather than its homonym "captive" in this context.

21 The king in question ruled Motul de San José, yet the vessel belonged to a royal woman from Xultun – indicative of some otherwise unattested relationship between these two polities.

22 This inscription includes two passages in which *k'uk' bahlam*, "quetzal (and) jaguar" refer to literal or metaphorical tribute items. First we have: *yak'aw cha k'al ti ikaatz k'uk' bahlam*, "he gives forty bundles of quetzal (feathers) and jaguar (pelts)". Then a few months later: *k'uk' bahlam ho k'al ti yak'aw ti ikaatz*, "quetzal (feathers) and jaguar (pelts) (numbering) one hundred is given in bundles". These readings and the identification of *k'al*, "twenty" in its combinations of *cha k'al*, "forty", and *ho k'al*, "100" were ones I contributed to the seminar discussion that formed the basis for the published article.

23 Other notable candidates include an enclosed complex in the heart of Yaxha (Christopher Jones, pers. comm. 2007) and low-lying linear features at Sayil (Jeremy Sabloff, pers. comm. 2007).

24 Before the *aj atz'aam* sits a woman holding a green-coloured sphere marked with wavy lines. This is either salt within some form of wrapping or a vegetable, perhaps a squash. If the latter it is presumably offered as an item for barter. In later times we know that cacao beans served as a means of exchange, and bagged presentations of them delivered as tribute during the Classic era could well suggest that this practice had greater antiquity.

25 It should be noted that William Folan's project has informally referred to this compound as the *Mercado*, "market", based entirely on its atypical and suggestive form.

26 The initial papers setting out this hegemonic thesis were Martin (1993), and Martin and Grube (1994a, 1994b, 1995, 2000). Martin and Grube (1994b) is a paper I wrote and presented at the Primer Seminario de las Mesas Redondas de Palenque of that year that, for unaccounted for reasons, found publication as Grube and Martin (1998). Scholars might think it proper to include another paper (Grube, in Hansen 2000a: 547–565), but this is a highly problematic source that should be cited in this regard only after first checking for matching sections that have priority in Martin and Grube (1997).

27 Some colleagues have questioned whether these relations were truly political and might not reflect supervision of a different kind. They suggest that rulers are actually claiming the symbolic support of sites of greater antiquity or prestige, in much the same way that ritual specialists are sanctioned by their peers in highland Guatemala today (e.g. Dennis Tedlock, pers. comm. 2009). But this is where a fuller context is critical to comprehension. The abundant data pointing to a strong correspondence between hierarchy and acts of war makes clear that Classic Maya hegemonies were established, maintained, and undone by force and the threat of force. There were certainly ritual and symbolic dimensions to these relationships –we saw some of this in Chapter 7 – as there was with all Classic Maya political life, but this does not negate their pragmatic significance.

28 Robert Carmack (1981: 177–179), the dean of K'iche' studies, took this to be a mischaracterisation, preferring other sources that describe a radically different, decentralised system consistent with the weak state. Yet the description

in Las Casas is so close to the kind of hegemonic political authority now attested in the Classic lowland regions centuries earlier that we might now prefer to take his testimony at face value.

29   A test-pit dug into the southern portion of the adjacent West Plaza encountered only two stuccoed floors before hitting bedrock, another indicator of the limited antiquity of this part of the site (Ramón Carrasco, pers. comm. 1995).

30   Nikolai Grube (pers. comm. 1999) was the first to recognise the paired *bix* (read as *xan* at the time) and *hul* events.

31   I have earlier noted the presence of subject youths at Piedras Negras from Yaxchilan, Lacanha, and Bonampak in 510 (p.243) and, like the El Cayo heir who goes to Paw Stone in 763 (p.259), these might not be temporary visitors but resident "guests" at Piedras Negras.

32   This is still more apparent in the lidar map of Dzibanche, parts of which have been posted online at the time of writing.

33   There is reason to wonder if some portion of the dynasty was already present at Calakmul by 631. The phrase on Naranjo (actually Caracol) Hieroglyphic Stairway Step VI that describes Yuknoom Head as a lord *ta uxte'tuun*, "at Calakmul" also describes him as *aj chiiknahb*, "Coati(?)-Place Person", implying that he originated from, or was then-resident at, Calakmul (see Case Study 6), although it is also possible that this back-projects a situation relevant at the time of writing in 642. Additionally, Carter (2015) describes a Late Classic painted vessel found at Uaxactun that features a *k'uhul kaanul elk'in kaloomte'* in a scene set in a deeply retrospective and probably legendary 256 BCE. One of the lords who faces the Snake king is called *yax ajaw aj chiiknahb*, "First Lord, Coati(?)-Place Person". One purpose of this scene could be to establish a deep time connection between Dzibanche and Calakmul, reaching back as much as a millennium.

34   It is unclear exactly when Dos Pilas parted ways with Calakmul, but their ties were still being celebrated in text during the reign of Ucha'an K'in Bahlam (Ruler 3) at least as late as 727. That king married into the royal line at Cancuen, conquered Ceibal in 735, and must have continued the longstanding domination

of nearby Arroyo de Piedra and Tamarindito. Importantly, he began to use the *kaloomte'* title on home monuments in 731, a reflection of his new position at the head of a regional hegemony.

14 HEGEMONY IN PRACTICE AND THEORY

1   As with the Maya, there has been a lengthy debate about the nature of the ancient Indian polity and an interpretive progression through "traditional", "feudal", and "segmentary" paradigms (for reviews see Kulke 1995b and Heitzman 1997: 11–20).

2   There is a long history of comparing the Classic Maya to the Classical Greeks, examples of which can be found in Cowgill (1979) and Lowe (1985) (following Wesson 1978).

3   The largest *polis* is usually said to be Sparta at as much as 8,300 km², but this ignores the fifty or so subject *poleis* contained in this area, and other scholars prefer to describe this domain as a regional empire (Hall 2000; Hansen 2000a: 613–614).

4   Thucydides decried the steady corruption of morality during this protracted conflict, which involved massacres and enslavements that violated longstanding norms of conduct.

5   Bull's division of anarchical, multi-polity landscapes into just two ideal types is clearly schematic, yet despite later efforts to introduce transitional steps (Buzan 2004), its usefulness lies in its pared-down clarity.

6   The modern label "autonomous region" captures this same idea of nested authority in a somewhat oxymoronic compound.

7   Compare Waltz (1979: 126): "In anarchy, security is the highest end. Only if survival is assured can states safely seek other goals such as tranquility, profit, and power", with Watson (1992: 252): "Indeed, it is possible to regard all societies of states, with their laws and institutions and codes of conduct, as attempts to ensure order".

8   See also Watson (1992: 261, 314) after Wight (1977).

9   See Webb (1975: 163–164) on the "conditional" nature of such ties, cited in Houston (1993: 146).

REFERENCES

Abercrombie, Nicholas, Stephen Hill, and Bryan S. Turner 1980 *The Dominant Ideology Thesis*. Allen and Unwin, London.

Abrams, Philip 1988 Notes on the Difficulty of Studying the State. *Journal of Historical Sociology* 1(1):58–89.

Adams, Richard E. W. 1971 *The Ceramics of Altar de Sacrificios*. Papers of the Peabody Museum of Archaeology and Ethnology, Harvard University, Vol. 63, No.1. Cambridge.

——1973 Maya Collapse: Transformation and Termination in the Ceramic Sequence at Altar de Sacrificios. In *The Classic Maya Collapse*, edited by T. Patrick Culbert, pp. 133–163. School of American Research. University of New Mexico Press, Albuquerque.

——1977 *Prehistoric Mesoamerica*. University of Oklahoma Press, Norman.

——1981 Settlement Patterns of the Central Yucatan and Southern Campeche Regions. In *Lowland Maya Settlement Patterns*, edited by Wendy Ashmore, pp. 211–257. School of American Research. University of New Mexico Press, Albuquerque.

——1986 Río Azul: Lost City of the Maya. *National Geographic* 169(4):420–451.

Adams, Richard E. W., and Jane Jackson Adams 2003 Volumetric and Stylistic Reassessment of Classic Maya Sites in the Peten, Río Bec, Chenes, and Puuc Hills. *Ancient Mesoamerica* 14:139–150.

Adams, Richard E. W., and Richard C. Jones 1981 Spatial Patterns and Regional Growth among Maya Cities. *American Antiquity* 46 (2):301–322.

Agnew, John 2005 Sovereignty Regimes: Territoriality and State Authority in Contemporary World Politics. *Annals of the Association of American Geographers* 95(2):437–461.

Ajpacaja Tum, Pedro Florentino, M. I. Chox Tum, F. L. Tepaz Raxuleu, and D. A. Guarchaj Ajtzalam 1996 *Diccionario del Idioma K'iche'*: Proyecto Lingüístico Francisco Marroquín, Antigua Guatemala

Aldana, Gerardo 2005 Agency and the "Star War" Glyph: A Historical Reassessment of Classic Maya Astrology and Warfare. *Ancient Mesoamerica* 16(2):305–320.

Ali, Daud 2004 *Courtly Culture and Political Life on Early Medieval India*. Cambridge University Press, Cambridge.

Amin, Samir 1976 *Unequal Development: An Essay on the Social Formations of Peripheral Capitalism*. Harvester Press, Hassocks.

Anaya, Armando, Stanley P. Guenter, and Marc U. Zender 2003 Sak Tz'i', a Classic Maya Center: A Locational Model based on GIS and Epigraphy. *Latin American Antiquity* 14 (2):179–181.

Anaya, Armando, Peter Mathews, and Stanley Guenter 2003 Hallazgo de una caja de madera con inscripciones en Tabasco. *Arqueología Mexicana* 9(61):4–5.

Andrén, Anders 1998 *Between Artifacts and Texts: Historical Archaeology from a Global Perspective*. Plenum Press, New York.

Andrews, George F. 1989 *Comalcalco, Tabasco, Mexico: Maya Art and Architecture*. Second Edition. Labyrinthos, Culver City.

Andrews, E., V. Wyllys, and Barbara W. Fash 1992 Continuity and Change in a Royal Residential Complex. *Ancient Mesoamerica* 3 (1):63–88.

Andrews, E., V. Wyllys, and William L. Fash 2005 Issues in Copán Archaeology. In *Copan:*

The History of an Ancient Maya Kingdom, edited by E. Wyllys Andrews, and William L. Fash, pp. 395–425. School of American Research Press, Santa Fe.

Archivo General de Centro America 1937 Reducción de los Lacandones: Fee de la llegada al peñol y autos de los que en la jornada susedio. *Boletin del Archivo General del Gobierno*, Año II.2:133–184.

Aristotle *Metaphysics*.

Armijo, Ricardo, Miriam Judith Gallegos, and Marc Zender 2000 Urnas Funerarias, Textos Históricos y Ofrendas en Comalcalco. In *Los Investigadores de la Cultura Maya 8, Tomo II*, pp. 312–323. Universidad Autónoma de Campeche, Campeche.

Armillas, Pedro 1951 Mesoamerican Fortifications. *Antiquity* 25:77–86.

Arnauld, M. Charlotte, Véronique Breuil-Martínez, and Erick Ponciano 2004 *La Joyanca (La Libertad, Guatemala): Antigua ciudad maya del noroeste del Petén*. Asociación Tikal, Guatemala City.

Arnauld, Marie-Charlotte, and Alain Breton (eds.) 2013 *Millenary Maya Societies: Past Crises and Resilience*. Electronic document, published online at Mesoweb: www.mesoweb.com/publications/MMS/MMS.pdf

Arnold, C. J. 1986 Archaeology and History: The Shades of Confrontation and Cooperation. In *Archaeology at the Interface: Studies Archaeology's Relationships with History, Geography, Biology and Physical Science*, edited by J. L. Bintliff, and C. F. Gaffney, pp. 32–39. BAR International Series 300. Archaeopress, Oxford.

Aron, Raymond 1961[1938] *Introduction to the Philosophy of History: An Essay on the Limits of Historical Objectivity*. Beacon Press, Boston.

Aulie, Wilbur H., and Evelyn W. de Aulie 1978 Diccionario Ch'ol-Español Español-Ch'ol. Serie de Vocabularios y Diccionarios Indígenas Mariano Silva y Aveces, Núm. 21. Instituto Lingüístico de Verano, Mexico City.

Avendaño y Loyola, Fray Andrés de 1987[1696] *Relation of Two Trips to Peten*, translated by Charles P. Bowditch and Guillermo Rivera. Labyrinthos, Culver City.

Aveni, Anthony, and Lorren Hotaling 1994 Monumental Inscriptions and the Observational Basis of Maya Planetary Astronomy. *Archaeoastronomy* 19:21–54.

Awe, Jamie, and Christophe Helmke 2017 "The Times they are a Changing: Yucatec Influences in Terminal Classic Belize". Paper presented at the Seventh Annual Maya ta the Lago Conference, Davidson School and American Academic Research, Davidson, North Carolina, 27–30 April.

Ayala Falcón, Maricela 1995 The History of Tonina according to its Inscriptions. PhD dissertation, University of Texas at Austin.

Baines, John, and Norman Yoffee 1998 Order, Legitimacy, and Wealth in Ancient Egypt and Mesopotamia. In *Archaic States*, edited by Gary M. Feinman, and Joyce Marcus, pp. 199–260. School of American Research Press, Santa Fe.

Ball, Joseph W., and Jennifer T. Taschek 1991 Late Classic Lowland Maya Political Organization and Central-Place Analysis. *Ancient Mesoamerica* 2(2):149–165.

Barabási, Albert-László 2002 *Linked: The New Science of Networks*. Perseus, Cambridge.

Bardawil, Lawrence W. 1976 Principal Bird Deity in Maya Art: An Iconographic Study of Form and Meaning. In *The Art, Iconography, and Dynastic History of Palenque, Proceedings of the Segunda Mesa Redonda de Palenque, December 14–21, 1974*, edited by Merle Greene Robertson, pp. 195–210. Robert Louis Stevenson School, Pre-Columbian Art Research, Pebble Beach.

Barlow, Robert H. 1987 *Tlatelolco, rival de Tenochtitlan*. Obras de Robert Barlow, Volume 1, edited by Jesús Monjarás-Ruiz, Elena Limón, and Paillés Hernández. Instituto Nacional de Antropología e Historia, Mexico City.

Baron, Joanne Parsley 2013 Patrons of La Corona: Deities and Power in a Classic Maya Community. PhD dissertation, University of Pennsylvania.

———2016 *Patron Gods and Patron Lords: The Semiotics of Classic Maya Community Cults*. University of Colorado Press, Boulder.

———2018a Ancient Monetization: The Case of Classic Maya Textiles. *Journal of Anthropological Archaeology* 49:100–113.

———2018b Making Money in Mesoamerica: Currency Production and Procurement in the Classic Maya Financial System. *Economic Anthropology* 5:210–223.

Barrera Vásquez, Alfredo (editor) 1980 *Diccionario Maya Cordemex*. Ediciones Cordemex, Mérida, Yucatan.

Barrett, John C. 2001 Agency, the Duality of Structure, and the Problem of the Archaeological Record. In *Archaeological Theory Today*, edited by Ian Hodder, pp. 140–162. Polity Press, Cambridge.

Barrientos, Tomás 2014 The Royal Palace of Cancuén: The Structure of Lowland Maya Architecture and Politics at the End of the Late Classic Period. PhD dissertation, Department of Anthropology, Vanderbilt University.

———2015 El Palacio Real de Cancuen: un análisis socio-espacial de la estructura política de las Tierras Bajas Mayas en el siglo VIII. In *XXVIII Simposio de Investigaciones Arqueológicas en Guatemala, 2014*, edited by B. Arroyo, L. Méndez Salinas y, and L. Paiz, pp. 223–238. Museo Nacional de Arqueología y Etnología, Guatemala.

Barrientos, Tomás, Marcello Canuto, Joanne Baron, Yann Desailly-Chanson, and Bruce Love 2011 El Reino de Sak Nikte': Nuevos datos sobre la historia, cronología, asentamiento y medio ambiente en La Corona. In *XXIV Simposio de Investigaciones Arqueológicas en Guatemala, 2010*, edited by Bárbara Arroyo, Lorena Paiz Aragón, Adriana Linares Palma, and Ana Lucía Arroyave, pp. 165–177. Ministerio de Cultura y Deportes, Instituto de Antropología e Historia, and the Asociación Tikal, Guatemala City.

Barrientos, Tomás, Marcello A. Canuto, and Jocelyne Ponce (eds.) 2013 Proyecto Arqueológico La Corona: informe final, temporada 2012. Report submitted to the Dirección General del Patrimonio Cultural y Natural de Guatemala.

Barrientos, Tomás, Rudy Larios, Arthur Demarest, and Luis Fernando Luin 2002 El palacio real de Cancuen: Análisis preliminar de sus características y planes de investigación. In *XV Simposio de Investigaciones Arqueológicas en Guatemala, 2001*, edited by Juan Pedro Laporte, Héctor Escobedo, and Bárbara Arroyo, pp. 283–389. Museo Nacional de Arqueología y Etnología, Ministerio de Cultura y Deportes, Guatemala.

Barthel, Thomas S. 1952 Der Morgensternkult in den Darstellungen der Dresdener Mayahandschrift. *Ethnos* 17:73–112.

———1968a El complejo "emblema". *Estudios de Cultura Maya* 7:159–193.

———1968b Historisches in den klassischen Mayainschriften. *Zeitschrift für Ethnologie*, 93 (1–2):119–156.

Bassie-Sweet, Karen 1991 *From the Mouth of the Dark Cave: Commemorative Sculpture of the Late Classic Maya*. University of Oklahoma Press, Norman.

Baudez, Claude-François 2002 *Une histoire de la religion des Mayas: Du panthéisme au panthéon*. Editions Albin Michel, Paris.

Baudez, Claude, and Peter Mathews 1979 Capture and Sacrifice at Palenque. In *Tercera Mesa Redonda de Palenque*, edited by Merle Greene Robertson, and Donnan Call Jeffers, Vol. IV, pp. 31–40. Pre-Columbian Art Research Institute, San Francisco.

Bazy, Damien, and Takeshi Inomata 2017 Multiple Waves of Political Disintegration in the Classic Maya Collapse. *Journal of Field Archaeology* 42(2):82–96.

Beards, A. 1994 Reversing Historical Skepticism: Bernard Lonergan on the Writing of History. *History and Theory* 33:198–219.

Becker, Marshall J. 1971 The Identification of a Second Plaza Plan at Tikal, Guatemala, and its Implications for Ancient Maya Social Complexity. PhD dissertation, University of Pennsylvania.

———1979 Priests, Peasants, and Ceremonial Centers: The Intellectual History of a Model. In *Maya Archaeology and Ethnohistory*, edited by Norman Hammond, and Gordon R. Willey, pp. 3–20. University of Texas Press, Austin.

———1984 *Theories of Ancient Maya Social Structure*. Occasional Papers in Anthropology

No.53, Museum of Anthropology, University of Northern Colorado, Greeley.

——1999 *Excavations in Residential Areas of Tikal: Groups with Shrines*. Tikal Report 21. University Museum of Archaeology and Anthropology, University of Pennsylvania, Philadelphia.

——2015 Ancient Maya Markets: Architectural Grammar and Market Identifications. In *The Ancient Maya Marketplace: The Archaeology of Transient Space*, edited by Eleanor M. King, pp. 90–110. University of Arizona Press, Tucson.

Becquelin, Pierre, and Claude Baudez 1979 *Tonina, une cité Maya du Chiapas*. Etudes Mésoaméricaines Tome I. Mission archéologique et ethnologique française au Mexique. Editions recherche sur les civilisations, Paris.

Beekman, Christopher S. 2005 Agency, Collectivities, and Emergence: Social Theory and Agent Based Simulations. In *Nonlinear Models for Archaeology and Anthropology: Continuing the Revolution*, edited by Christopher S. Beekman, and William W. Baden, pp. 51–78. Routledge, London.

Beekman, Christopher S., and William W. Baden (eds.) 2005 *Nonlinear Models for Archaeology and Anthropology: Continuing the Revolution*. Routledge, London.

Beetz, Carl P., and Linton Satterthwaite 1981 *The Monuments and Inscriptions of Caracol, Belize*. University Museum Monograph 45. The University Museum, University of Pennsylvania, Philadelphia.

Beliaev, Dmitri D. 2017 Río Azul Dynasty and Polity: New Epigraphic Evidence. Paper presented at the 3rd Annual "Textdatenbank und Wörterbuch des Klassischen Maya" Workshop, Bonn University, December 7–9, 2017.

Beliaev, Dmitri D., and Albert Davletshin 2014 Fundación de las ciudades mayas en el periodo clásico: una aproximación epigráfica. Paper presented at Primera Mesa Redonda del Mayab "Arquitectura y sociedad entre los mayas", Mérida, Mexico, 17–21 October.

Beliaev, Dmitri D., and Alexandr Safronov 2004 Ak'e i Shukal'nakh: Istoriia i Politicheskaia Geografiia Gosudarstv Maiia Verkhnei Usuma-sinty. In *Drevnii Vostok i Antichnyi Mir: Trudy Kafedry Istorii Drevnego Mira*. Vol. 6, pp. 119–142. Istoricheskii Fakul'tet MGU, Moscow.

——2009 Saktz'i', 'Ak'e', and Xukalnaah: Reinterpreting the Political Geography of the Upper Usumacinta Region. Paper presented at the 14th European Maya Conference (13–14 November 2009). www.academia.edu/7982378/SaktziAkeandXukalnaahReinterpretingthePoliticalGeographyoftheUpperUsumasintaRegionwithAlexanderSafronov.

Beliaev, Dmitri, David Stuart, and Camilio Alejandro Luin 2017 Late Classic Vase with a Mention of Sihyaj K'ahk' from the Museo VICAL, Casa Santa Domingo, Antigua Guatemala. *Mexicon* 39(1):2–4.

Beliaev, Dmitri, and Sergei Vepretskii 2018 Los monumentos de Itsimte (Petén, Guatemala): Neuvos datos e interpretaciones. *Arqueología Iberoamericana* 38:3–13.

Bell, Catherine 1997 *Ritual Theory, Ritual Practice*. Oxford University Press, Oxford.

Bell, Ellen E., Robert J. Sharer, Loa P. Traxler, David W. Sedat, Christine W. Carrelli, and Lynn A. Grant 2004 Tombs and Burials in the Early Classic Acropolis at Copan. In *Understanding Early Classic Copan*, edited by Ellen E. Bell, Marcello A. Canuto, and Robert J. Sharer, pp. 131–158. University of Pennsylvania Museum of Archaeology and Anthropology, Philadelphia.

Bell, Karen Elizabeth 1992 The Kingmakers: Women in Ancient Mexico. PhD dissertation, University of Michigan at Ann Arbor.

Bentley, R. Alexander, and Herbert D. G. Maschner (eds.) 2003 *Complex Systems and Archaeology*. University of Utah Press, Salt Lake City.

Berdan, Frances F. 1975 Trade, Tribute and Market in the Aztec Empire. PhD dissertation, Department of Anthropology, University of Texas, Austin.

Berdan, Frances F., Richard E. Blanton, Elizabeth Hill Boone, Mary G. Hodge, Michael E. Smith, and Emily Umberger 1996 *Aztec Imperial Strategies*. Dumbarton Oaks Research Library and Collection, Washington D.C.

Berjonneau, Gérald, and Jean-Louis Sonnery 1985 *Rediscovered Masterpieces of Mesoamerica*. Editions Arts, Boulogne.

Berlin, Heinrich 1951 El Templo de la Inscripciones – VI de Tikal. *Anthropología e Historia de Guatemala* 3(1):33-54.

——1958 El Glifo "Emblema" en las Inscripciones Mayas. *Journal de la Société des Américanistes* 47:111–119.

——1959 *Glifos Nominales en el Sarcófago de Palenque.* Humanidades series, 2(10), pp. 1–8. Universidad de San Carlos de Guatemala, Guatemala.

——1963 The Palenque Triad. *Journal de la Société des Américanistes de Paris* 52:91–99.

——1965 The Inscription of the Temple of the Cross at Palenque. *American Antiquity* 30 (3):330–342.

——1968a The Tablet of the 96 Glyphs at Palenque, Chiapas, Mexico. In *Archaeological Studies in Middle America*, pp. 135–150. Publication 26. Tulane University, Middle American Research Institute, New Orleans.

——1968b Estudios epigraficos II. *Anales de Antropologia e Historia de Guatemala* 20(1):13–24.

Berlo, Janet Catherine 1983 Conceptual Categories for the Study of Texts and Images in Mesoamerica. In *Text and Image in Pre-Columbian Art: Essays on the Interrelationship of the Verbal and Visual Arts*, edited by Janet C. Berlo, pp. 1–39. BAR International Series No.180. Archaeopress, Oxford.

Bernal Romero, Guillermo 2002a U Pakal K'inich Janahb' Pakal, el nuevo gobernador de Palenque. *Lakamha'* 1(4):4–9.

——2002b Análisis epigráfico del Tablero de K'an Tok, Palenque, Chiapas. In *La Organización Social entre los Mayas, Memoria de la Tercera Mesa Redonda de Palenque, Volume I*, coordinated by Vera Tiesler Blos, Rafael Cobos and Merle Greene Robertson, pp. 401–423. Instituto Nacional de Antropología e Historia and Universidad Autónoma de Yucatán, Mexico City and Merida.

——2009 *El Tablero de K'an Tok: Una inscripción glífica Maya del Grupo XVI de Palenque, Chiapas.* Serie testamonios y materiales arqueológicos para el estudio de la cultura Maya 2. Universidad Nacional Autónoma de México, Mexico City.

Betzig, Laura 1993 Sex, Succession, and Stratification in the First Six Civilizations. In *Social Stratification and Socioeconomic Inequality*, edited by Lee Ellis, pp. 37–74. Praeger, New York.

Binford, Lewis R. 1962 Archaeology as Anthropology. In *Contemporary Archaeology*, edited by Mark Leone, pp. 93–101. Southern Illinois University, Carbondale.

——1965 Archaeological Systematics and the Study of Culture Process. *American Antiquity* 31(2):203–210.

——1968a Some Comments on Historical Versus Processual Archaeology. *Southwestern Journal of Anthropology* 28(2):267–275.

——1968b Archaeological Perspectives: In *New Perspectives in Archaeology*, edited by S. R. Binford, and L. R. Binford, pp. 5–32. Aldine, Chicago.

——1977 Historical Archaeology: Is it Historical or Archaeological? In *Historical Archaeology and the Importance of Material Things*, edited by L. Ferguson, pp. 13–22. Society for Historical Archaeology, Tucson.

——1983 *Working at Archaeology.* Academic Press, New York.

Bintliff, John 1991a The Contribution of an *Annaliste*/Structural History Approach to Archaeology. In *The Annales School and Archaeology*, edited by John Bintliff, pp. 1–33. Leicester University Press, Leicester.

——1997 Catastrophe, Chaos and Complexity: The Death, Decay and Rebirth of Towns from Antiquity to Today. *Journal of European Archaeology* 5(2):67–90.

——2003 Searching for Structure in the Past – or Was It "One Damn Thing After Another"? In *Complex Systems and Archaeology*, edited by R. Alexander Bentley, and Herbert D. G. Maschner, pp. 79–83. University of Utah Press, Salt Lake City.

——2007 Emergent Complexity in Settlement Systems and Urban Transformations. In *Historische Geographie der Alten Welt: Grundlagen, Erträge, Perspektiven. Festgabe für Eckart Olshausen*, edited by Ulrich Fellmeth, Peter Guyot, and Holger Sonnabend, pp. 43–82. Georg Olms Verlag, Hildesheim.

Bintliff, John (ed.) 1991b *The Annales School and Archaeology.* Leicester University Press, Leicester.

Bíró, Péter 2005 Sak Tz'i' in the Classic Period Hieroglyphic Inscriptions. *Mesoweb.* www .mesoweb.com/articles/biro/SakTzi.pdf

——2007a Classic Maya Polity, Identity, Migration and Political Vocabulary: Reconceptualisation of Classic Period Maya Political Organisation. *Journal of Historical and European Studies* 1:93–104.

——2007b Las piedras labradas 2, 4 y 5 de Bonampak y los reyes de Xukalnah en el Siglo VII. *Estudios de Cultura Maya* 29:79–96.

——2011a Politics in the Western Mayan Region (I): *Ajawil/Ajawlel* and Ch'e'n. *Estudios de Cultura Maya* 38:41–73.

——2011b On **NUP-** 'To Marry' and the Text of Bonampak Stela 2. Wayeb Notes 38. www .wayeb.org/notes/wayebnotes0038.pdf

——2012a Politics in the Western Mayan Region (II): Emblem Glyphs. *Estudios de Cultura Maya* 39:31–66.

——2012b Politics in the Western Mayan Region (III): The Royal and the Non-royal Elite. *Estudios de Cultura Maya* 40:79–96.

Blanton, Robert E., Gary M. Feinman, Stephen A. Kowalewski, and Peter N. Peregrine 1996 A Dual-Processual Theory for the Evolution of Mesoamerican Civilization. *Current Anthropology* 37(1):1–14.

Bloch, Marc 1954 *The Historian's Craft.* Manchester University Press, Manchester.

Bolles, David, and William J. Folan 2001 An Analysis of Roads Listed in Colonial Dictionaries and Their Relevance to Pre-Hispanic Linear Features in the Yucatan Peninsula. *Ancient Mesoamerica* 12(2):299–314.

Bolles, John S. 1977 *La Monjas: A Major Pre-Mexican Architectural Complex at Chichen Itza.* University of Oklahoma Press, Norman.

Boone, Elizabeth Hill 1991 Migration Histories as Ritual Performance. In *To Change Places: Aztec Ceremonial Landscapes,* edited by David Carrasco, pp. 121–151. University Press of Colorado, Niwot.

Boot, Erik 1999a North of the Lake Petén Itzá: A Regional Perspective on the cha-TAN-na/cha-ta Collocation. Unpublished manuscript.

——1999b A New Naranjo Area Toponym: Yo:tz. *Mexicon* 21(2):39–42.

——2005 *Continuity and Change in Text and Image at Chichén Itzá, Yucatán, Mexico.* CNWS Publications, Leiden.

——2006 A Chochola-Maxcanu Ceramic Vessel in a 1930's Collection in Mérida, Yucatán, Mexico: History and Analysis of Image and Text. *Wayeb Notes.* www.wayeb.org/notes/wayebnotes0024.pdf

Boucher, Sylviane, and Lucía Quiñones 2007 Entre Mercados, Ferias y Festines:Los Murales de la Sub I-4 de Chiik Nahb, Calakmul. *Mayab* 19:27–50.

Bourdieu, Pierre 1977 *Outline of a Theory of Practice,* translated by Richard Nice. Cambridge University Press, Cambridge

——1990 *The Logic of Practice,* translated by Richard Nice. Stanford University Press, Stanford.

Bowditch, Charles P. 1901 Notes on the report to Teobert Maler. In *Researches in the Central Portion of the Usumatsintla Valley: Reports of Explorations for the Museum 1897–1900 Memoirs, 2(1).* Harvard University, Peabody Museum of American Archaeology and Ethnology, Cambridge, MA.

——1910 *Numeration, Calendar Systems, and Astronomical Knowledge of the Mayas.* Harvard University Press, Cambridge, MA.

Brackertz, Ursula 1976 *Zum Problem der Schutzgottheiten griechischer Städte.* Diss. F. U. Berlin.

Brasseur de Bourbourg, Charles-Étienne 1868 *Quatre Lettres sur le Méxique: une exposition absolue du système hieroglyphique mexicain à la fin de l'âge de pierre.* Maisonneuve et Cie, Paris.

Braswell, Geoffrey E. 2003a K'iche'an Origins, Symbolic Emulation, and Ethnogenesis in the Maya Highlands. In *The Postclassic Mesoamerican World,* edited by Michael Smith, and Frances F. Berdan, pp. 297–303. University of Utah Press, Salt Lake City.

——2005 La sociedad de la red de los Mayas Antiguos. In *Los Investigadores de la Cultura Maya 13, Tomo I,* pp. 70–76. Universidad Autónoma de Campeche, Campeche.

Braswell, Geoffrey E. (ed.) 2003b *The Maya and Teotihuacan: Reinterpreting Early Classic Interaction.* Texas University Press, Austin.

Braswell, Geoffrey E., Joel D. Gunn, María del Rosario Domínguez, William J. Folan,

Laraine A. Fletcher, Abel Morales, and Michael D. Glascock 2004a Defining the Terminal Classic at Calakmul, Campeche. In *The Terminal Classic in the Maya Lowlands: Collapse, Transition, and Transformation*, edited by Arthur A. Demarest, Prudence M. Rice, and Donald S. Rice, pp. 162–194. University of Colorado Press, Boulder.

Braswell, Geoffrey E., Christian M. Prager, Cassandra R. Bill, Sonja A. Schwake, and Jennifer B. Braswell 2004b The Rise of Secondary States in the Southeastern Periphery of the Maya World: A Report on Recent Archaeological and Epigraphic Research at Pusilha, Belize. *Ancient Mesoamerica* 15:219–233.

Braudel, Fernand 1972–73 *The Mediterranean and the Mediterranean World in the Age of Philip II*, translated by Sian Reynolds. Two volumes. Collins, London.

——1980 *On History*. Weidenfeld and Nicolson, London.

Bray, Warwick M. 1972 The City-State in Central Mexico at the Time of the Spanish Conquest. *Journal of Latin American Studies* 4 (2):161–185.

Bretschneider, Peter 1995 *Polygyny: A Cross-cultural Study*. Uppsala University, Uppsala and Stockholm.

Breuil-Martínez, Véronique, James L. Fitzsimmons, Laura L. Gámez, Edy Barrios, and Edwin Román 2005 Resultados preliminares de la primera temporada en Zapote Bobal, municipio de La Libertad, Petén. In *XVIII Simposio de Investigaciones Arqueológicas en Guatemala, 2004*, edited by Juan Pedro Laporte, Barbara Arroyo, and Héctor E. Mejía, pp. 296–308. Museo Nacional de Arqueología y Etnología, Guatemala.

Breuil-Martínez, Véronique, Laura Gámez, James Fitzsimmons, Jean Paul Mètailié, Edy Barrios, and Edwin Román 2004 Primeros noticias de Zapote Bobal, una ciudad maya clásica del noroccidente de Petén, Guatemala. *Mayab* 17:61–83.

Bricker, Victoria R. 1986 A Grammar of Mayan Hieroglyphs. *Middle American Research Institute*, Tulane University, Publication 56. New Orleans.

——2002 Evidencia de doble descendencia en las inscripciones de Yaxchilán y Piedras Negras. In *La organización social entre los mayas, Memoria de la Tercera Mesa Redonda de Palenque, Volume I*, coordinated by Vera Tiesler Blos, Rafael Cobos, and Merle Greene Robertson, pp. 125–145. Instituto Nacional de Antropología e Historia and Universidad Autónoma de Yucatán, Mexico City and Merida.

Brinton, Daniel G. 1895 *A Primer of Mayan Hieroglyphics*. Publications of the University of Pennsylvania, Series in Philology, Literature, and Linguistics, Vol.3 No.1. Ginn and Company, Boston.

——1969 *Maya Chronicles*. AMS Press, New York.

Brisch, Nicole (ed.) 2008 *Religion and Power: Divine Kingship in the Ancient World and Beyond*. Oriental Institute Seminars Number 4. The Oriental Institute of the University of Chicago, Chicago.

Bronson, Bennet 1966 Roots and The Subsistence of the Ancient Maya. *Southwestern Journal of Anthropology* 22(3):251–279.

Brown, M. Kathryn, and Travis W. Stanton (ed.) 2003 *Ancient Mesoamerican Warfare*. Altamira Press, Walnut Creek.

Brughmans, Tom 2013 Thinking through Networks: A Review of Formal Network Methods in Archaeology. *Journal of Archaeological Method and Theory* 20(4):623–662.

Buikstra, Jane E., George R. Milner, and Jesper Boldsen 2006 Janaab' Pakal: The Age-at-Death Controversy Revisited. In *Janaab' Pakal of Palenque: Reconstructing the Life and Death of a Maya Ruler*, edited by Vera Tiesler, and Andrea Cucina, pp. 48–59. The University of Arizona Press, Tucson.

Bull, Hedley 1977 *The Anarchical Society: A Study of Order in Politics*. Columbia University Press, New York.

Bull, Hedley, and Adam Watson 1984 Conclusion. In *The Expansion of International Society*, edited by Hedley Bull, and Adam Watson, pp. 425–435. Oxford University Press, Oxford.

Bullard, William R. Jr. 1960 Maya Settlement Pattern in Northeastern Peten, Guatemala. *American Antiquity* 25:355–372.

———1964 Settlement Pattern and Social Structure in the Southern Maya Lowlands during the Classic Period. *Actas y Memorias, XXXV Congreso Internacional de Americanistes* 1, pp. 279–287. Mexico City.

Buzan, Barry 2004 *From International to World Society: English School Theory and the Social Structure of Globalization*. Cambridge University Press, Cambridge.

Buzan, Barry, and Richard Little 2000 *International Systems in World History: Remaking the Study of International Relations*. Oxford University Press, Oxford.

Byrne, Francis J. 1973 *Irish Kings and High-Kings*. B.T. Batsford, London.

Calnek, Edward E. 1982 Patterns of Empire Formation in the Valley of Mexico, Late Post-Classic Period, 1200–1521. In *The Inca and Aztec States 1400–1800: Anthropology and History*, edited by George A. Collier, Renata Rosaldo, and John D. Wirth, pp. 43–62. Academic Press, New York.

Calvin, Inga 1997 Where the *Wayob* Live: A Further Examination of Classic Maya Supernaturals. In *The Maya Vase Book, Volume 5: A Corpus of Roll-out Photographs, by Justin Kerr*, pp. 868–883. Kerr Associates, New York.

Campaña, Luz Evelia 1998 Prospección y sondeo en la área suroeste de la Gran Acropólis. In *Informe de los trabajos arqueológicos, Temporada 1997–1998*, edited by Ramón Carrasco, pp. 59–71. Proyecto Arqueológico Calakmul, Instituto Nacional de Antropología e Historia.

Canuto, Marcello A., and Tomás Barrientos 2013 The Importance of La Corona. *La Corona Notes* 1(1). *Mesoweb*. www.mesoweb.com/LaCorona/LaCoronaNotes01.pdf.

Canuto, Marcello A., Tomás Barrientos, Mary Jane Acuña, Carlos Chiriboga, and Caroline Parris 2011 Siguiendo las huellas del reino Kan: Estudios regionals y definición de rutas de comunicación en el noroccidente de Petén. In *XXIV Simposio de Investigaciones Arqueologicas en Guatemala, 2010*, edited by Bárbara Arroyo, Lorena Paiz Aragón, Adriana Linares Palma, and Ana Lucía Arroyave, pp. 325–340. Ministerio de Cultura y Deportes, Instituto de Antropología e Historia, and Asociación Tikal, Guatemala City.

Canuto, Marcello A., Francisco Estrada-Belli, Thomas G. Garrison, Stephen D. Houston, Mary Jane Acuña, Milan Kováč, Damien Marken, Philippe Nondédéo, Luke Auld-Thomas, Cyril Castanet, David Chatelain, Carlos R. Chiriboga, Tomáš Drápela, Tibor Lieskovský, Alexandre Tokovinine, Antolín Velasquez, Juan C. Fernández-Díaz, and Ramesh Shrestha 2018 Ancient Lowland Maya Complexity as Revealed by Airborne Laser Scanning of Northern Guatemala. *Science* 361:eaau0137.

Canuto, Marcello A., Stanley Guenter, Evangelia Tsesmeli, and Damien Marken 2006 El Reconocimiento de La Corona, 2005. In *Proyecto Arqueológico El Perú-Waka': Informe No. 3, Temporada 2005*, edited by Héctor Escobedo, and David A. Freidel, pp. 455–468. Report submitted to the Instituto de Antropología e Historia, Guatemala, Guatemala City.

Carlson, John B. 1993 Venus-Regulated Warfare and Ritual Sacrifice in Mesoamerica. In *Astronomies and Cultures*, edited by Clive Ruggles, and Nicholas Saunders, pp. 202–252. University of Colorado Press, Niwot.

Carmack, Robert M. 1973 *Quichean Civilization: The Ethnohistoric, Ethnographic, and Archaeological Sources*. University of California Press, Berkeley.

———1981 *The Quiché Mayas of Utatlán: The Evolution of a Highland Guatemala Kingdom*. University of Oklahoma Press, Norman.

Carmean, Kelli, Nicholas Dunning, and Jeff Karl Kowalski 2004 High Times in the Hill Country: A Perspective from the Terminal Classic Puuc Region. In *The Terminal Classic in the Maya Lowlands: Collapse, Transition, and Transformation*, edited by Arthur A. Demarest, Prudence M. Rice, and Donald S. Rice, pp. 424–449. University of Colorado Press, Boulder.

Carneiro, Robert L. 1970 A Theory of the Origin of the State. *Science* 169(3947):733–738.

Carr, E. H. 1961 *What is History?* MacMillan, London.

Carr, R. F., and J. E. Hazard 1961 *Map of the Ruins of Tikal, El Petén, Guatemala. Tikal Report No. 11.* University Museum Monograph 21. The University Museum, University of Pennsylvania, Philadelphia.

Carrasco, Pedro 1984 Royal Marriages in Ancient Mexico. In *Explorations in Ethnohistory: Indians of Central Mexico in the Sixteenth Century,* edited by Herbert J. Harvey, and Hanns J. Prem, pp. 41–81. University of New Mexico Press, Albuquerque.

Carrasco, Ramón 1998 The Metropolis of Calakmul, Campeche. In *Maya Civilization,* edited by Peter Schmidt, Mercedes de la Garza, and Enrique Nalda, pp. 372–385. Thames and Hudson, London and New York.

———2005 The Sacred Mountain: Preclassic Architecture in Calakmul. In *Lords of Creation: The Origins of Sacred Maya Kingship,* edited by Virginia M. Fields, and Dorie Reents-Budet, pp. 62–66, Scala Publishers, London.

Carrasco, Ramón, and Sylviane Boucher 1987 Las Escaleras Jeroglíficas del Resbalón, Quintana Roo. In *Primer Simposio Mundial sobre Epigrafía Maya,* pp. 1–21. Asociación Tikal, Guatemala.

Carrasco, Ramón, and Marinés Colón 2005 El Reino de Kaan y la Antigua Ciudad Maya de Calakmul. *Arqueología Mexicana* 13(75):40–47.

Carrasco, Ramón, and María Cordiero 2012 The Murals of Chiik Nahb Structure Sub 1-4, Calakmul, Mexico. In *Maya Archaeology 2,* edited by Charles Golden, Stephen D. Houston, and Joel Skidmore, pp. 8–59. Precolumbia Mesoweb Press, San Francisco.

Carrasco, Ramón, Verónica Vázquez, and Simon Martin 2009 Daily Life of the Ancient Maya Recorded on Murals at Calakmul, Mexico. *Proceedings of the National Academy of Sciences* 106(46):19245–19249.

Carrasco, Ramón, and Marc Wolf 1996 Nadzca'an: Una Antigua ciudad en el suroeste de Campeche, México. *Mexicon* 18(4):70–74.

Carter, Nicholas P. 2014a Kingship and Collapse: Inequality and Identity in the Terminal Classic Southern Maya Lowlands. PhD dissertation, Brown University.

———2014b Sources and Scales of Classic Maya History. In *Thinking, Recording, and Writing History in the Ancient World,* edited by Kurt F. Raaflaub, pp. 340–371. Wiley Blackwell, Chichester.

———2015 Once and Future Kings: Classic Maya Geopolitics and Mythic History on the Vase of the Initial Series from Uaxactun. *The PARI Journal* 15(4):1–15.

Carver, Martin 2002 Marriages of True Minds: Archaeology with Texts. In *Archaeology: The Widening Debate,* edited by Barry Cunliffe, W. Davies, and Colin Renfrew, pp. 465–496. Oxford University Press and the British Academy, Oxford.

Castellani, Brian, and Frederic Hafferty 2009 *Sociology and Complexity Science: A New Field of Inquiry.* Springer-Verlag Berlin, Heidelberg.

Chamberlain, Robert S. 1948 *The Conquest and Colonization of Yucatán, 1517–1550.* Carnegie Institution of Washington, Publication 582. Washington D.C.

Chang, Kwang-Chih 1974 Urbanism and the King in Ancient China. *World Archaeology* 6 (1):1–14.

———1983 Settlement Patterns in Chinese Archaeology: A Case Study from the Bronze Age. In *Prehistoric Settlement Patterns: Essays in Honor of Gordon Willey,* edited by Evon Z. Vogt, and Richard M. Leventhal, pp. 361–374. University of New Mexico and the Peabody Museum, Cambridge.

Chapman, Robert 2003 *Archaeologies of Complexity.* Routledge, London.

Charles-Edwards, Thomas Mowbray 2000 *Early Christian Ireland.* Cambridge University Press, Cambridge.

Charnay, Désiré 1862 *Cités et Ruines Américaines: Mitla, Palenque, Izamal, Chichen-Itza, Uxmal.* With an introduction by Eugène-Emmanuel Viollet-le-Duc. Morel et Cie., Paris.

Chase, Arlen F. 1985 Troubled Times: The Archaeology and Iconography of the Terminal Classic Southern Lowland Maya. In *The Fifth Palenque Round Table, 1983, Vol. VII,* edited by Merle Greene Robertson, and Virginia M. Fields, pp. 103–114. Pre-Columbian Art Research Institute, San Francisco.

———1992 Elites and the Changing Organization of Classic Maya Society. In *Mesoamerican Elites: An Archaeological Assessment*, edited by Diane Z. Chase, and Arlen F. Chase, pp. 30–49. University of Oklahoma Press, Norman.

Chase, Arlen F., and Diane Z. Chase 1987 Investigations at the Classic Maya City of Caracol, Belize: 1985–1987. *Pre-Columbian Art Research Institute Monograph 3*. Pre-Columbian Art Research Institute, San Francisco.

———1989 The Investigation of Classic Period Maya Warfare at Caracol. *Mayab* 5:5–18.

———1996 The Organization and Composition of Classic Lowland Maya Society: The View from Caracol, Belize. In *Eighth Palenque Round Table, 1993, Vol.X.* edited by Martha J. Macri, and Jan McHargue, pp. 213–222. Pre-Columbian Art Research Institute, San Francisco.

———1998 Late Classic Maya Political Structure, Polity Size, and Warfare Arenas. In *Anatomía de una Civilizacion. Aproximaciones Interdisciplinarias a la Cultura Maya*, edited by Andres Cuidad Ruiz, Yolanda Fernández Marquínez, José Miguel García Campillo, M.a Josefa Iglesias Ponce de León, Alfonso Lacadena García-Gallo, and Luis T. Sanz Castro, pp. 11–29. Sociedad Española de Estudios Mayas, Madrid.

———2001 Ancient Maya Causeways and Site Organization at Caracol, Belize. *Ancient Mesoamerica* 12(2):273–281.

———2004 Terminal Classic Status-linked Ceramics and the Maya "Collapse": De Facto Refuse at Caracol, Belize. In *The Terminal Classic in the Maya Lowlands: Collapse, Transition, and Transformation*, edited by Arthur A. Demarest, Prudence M. Rice, and Donald S. Rice, pp. 343–366. University of Colorado Press, Boulder.

———2015 A New Terminal Classic Altar from Caracol, Belize. *Mexicon* 37(2):47–49.

Chase, Arlen F., Diane Z. Chase, and Michael E. Smith 2009 States and Empires in Ancient Mesoamerica. *Ancient Mesoamerica* 20(2):175–182.

Chase, Arlen F., Diane Z. Chase, John F. Weishampel, Jason B. Drake, Ramesh L. Shrestha, K. Clint Slatton, Jaime J. Awe, and William E. Carter 2011 Airborne LiDAR, Archaeology, and the Ancient Maya Landscape at Caracol, Belize. *Journal of Archaeological Science* 38(2):387–398.

Chase, Arlen F., Nikolai Grube, and Diane Z. Chase 1991 *Three Terminal Classic Monuments from Caracol, Belize*. Research Reports on Ancient Maya Writing 36. Center for Maya Research, Washington, D.C.

Chase, Diane Z., and Arlen F. Chase 1982 Yucatec Influence in Terminal Classic Northern Belize. *American Antiquity* 47(3):596–614.

Chase, Diane Z., Arlen F. Chase, and William A. Haviland 1990 The Classic Maya City: Reconsidering 'The Mesoamerican Urban Tradition'. *American Anthropologist* 92(2):499–506.

Chattopadhyaya, B. D. 1985 Political Processes and Structure of Polity in Early Medieval India: Problems of Perspective. *Social Scientist* 13(6):3–34.

Child, Mark 1999 "Classic Maya Warfare and its Sociopolitical Implications". Paper presented at the Tercera Mesa Redonda de Palenque, Segundo epoca, June 1999.

Chimalpahin, Domingo Francisco de San Antón Muñón 1965 *Relaciones originales de Chalco Amequemecan escritas por Domingo Francisco de San Antón Muñón Chimalpahin Cuauhtlehuanitzin*, translated by Sylvia Rendón. Fonda de Cultura Económica, México.

Chinchilla, Oswaldo 2006 *A Reading for the "Earth-Star" verb in Ancient Maya Writing*. Research Reports on Ancient Maya Writing 56. Center for Maya Research, Washington, D.C.

Christaller, W. 1933 *Die zentralen Orte in Süddeutschland*. G. Fischer, Jena.

Christenson, Allen J. 2003 *Popol Vuh: The Sacred Book of the Maya*. O Books, Winchester.

Clark, Elizabeth A. 2004 *History, Theory, Text: Historians and the Linguistic Turn*. Harvard University Press, Cambridge.

Clark, Grahame 1986 *Symbols of Excellence, Precious Materials as Expressions of Status*. Cambridge University Press, Cambridge.

Clarke, David 1968 *Analytical Archaeology*. Methuen, London.

Clendinnen, Inga 1987 *Ambivalent Conquests: Maya and Spaniard in Yucatan 1517–1570*. Cambridge University Press, Cambridge.

Clignet, Remi 1970 *Many Wives, Many Powers: Authority and Power in Polygynous Families.* Northwestern University Press, Evanston.

Closs, Michael P. 1979 Venus in the Maya World: Glyphs, Gods and Associated Phenomena. In *Tercera Mesa Redonda de Palenque, Vol.IV*, edited by Merle Greene Robertson, and Donnan Call Jeffers, pp. 147–172. Pre-Columbian Art Research Center, Palenque.

——1981 Venus Dates Revisited. *Archaeoastronomy* 4(4):38.

——1984 The Maya Glyph Batel, Warrior. *Mexicon* 6(4):50–52.

——1985 The Dynastic History of Naranjo: The Middle Period. In *The Fifth Palenque Round Table, 1983, Vol. VII*, edited by Merle Greene Robertson, and Virginia M. Fields, pp. 65–78. Pre-Columbian Art Research Institute, San Francisco.

——1988 *The Hieroglyphic Text of Stela 9, Lamanai, Belize.* Research Reports on Ancient Maya Writing 21. Center for Maya Research, Washington D.C.

Cobb, Charles R. 1991 Social Reproduction and the *Longue Durée* in the Prehistory of Midcontinental United States. In *Processual and Postprocessual Archaeologies: Multiple Ways Of Knowing about the Past*, edited by Robert W. Preucel, pp. 168–182. Southern Illinois University, Carbondale.

Coe, Michael D. 1956 The Funerary Temple among the Classic Maya. *Southwestern Journal of Anthropology* 12:387–394.

——1965 A Model of Ancient Community Structure in the Maya Lowlands. *Southwestern Journal of Anthropology* 21(2):97–114.

——1966 An Early Stone Pectoral from Southeastern México. *Studies in Pre-Columbian Art and Archaeology, No. 1.* Dumbarton Oaks Library and Collection. Washington, D.C.

——1974 A Carved Wooden Box from the Classic Maya Civilization. In *Primera Mesa Redonda de Palenque, Part II*, edited by Merle Greene Robertson, pp. 51–58. Robert Louis Stevenson School, Pebble Beach.

——1989 The Hero Twins: Myth and Image. In *The Maya Vase Book: A Corpus of Rollout Photographs of Maya Vases, Volume 1*, edited by Justin Kerr, pp. 161–184. Kerr Associates, New York.

——1992 *Breaking the Maya Code.* Thames and Hudson, London and New York.

Coe, Michael D., and Elizabeth P. Benson 1966 Three Maya Relief Panels at Dumbarton Oaks. *Studies in Pre-Columbian Art and Archaeology No.2.* Dumbarton Oaks, Washington, D.C.

Coe, Michael D., and Justin Kerr 1997 *The Art of the Maya Scribe.* Thames and Hudson, London.

Coggins, Clemency C. 1975 Painting and Drawing Styles at Tikal: A Historical and Iconographic Reconstruction. PhD Dissertation, Harvard University.

Cohen, Abner 1974 *Two-Dimensional Man: An Essay of the Anthropology of Power and Symbolism in Complex Society.* Routledge, London.

——1981 *The Politics of Elite Culture: Explorations in the Dramaturgy of Power in a Modern African Society.* University of California Press, Berkeley.

Cole, Susan G. 1995 *Civic Cult and Civic Identity.* In *Sources for the Ancient Greek City-State, Papers from the Copenhagen Polis Centre 2*, edited by Mogens Herman Hansen, and Kurt Raaflaub, pp. 292–325. Franz Steiner, Stuttgart.

Cortés, Hernán 1971 *Letters from Mexico*, translated by A. R. Pagden. Grossman, New York.

——1986 *Letters from Mexico*, translated by A. R. Pagden. Yale University Press, New Haven.

Coto, Fray Thomas de 1983[c.1650] *Thesavrvs Verborvm: Vocabvlario de la Lengua Cakchiquel V[El] Guatemalteca, Nueuamente hecho y Recopilado con Summo Estudio, Trauajo y Erudicion*, edited by René Acuña. Universidad Nacional Autónoma de México, Mexico City.

Cowgill, George 1979 Teotihuacan, Internal Militaristic Competition, and the Fall of the Classic Maya. In *Maya Archaeology and Ethnohistory*, edited by Norman Hammond, and Gordon R. Willey, pp. 51–62. University of Texas Press, Austin.

Crumley, Carole L. 1976 Toward a Locational Definition of State Systems of Settlement. *American Anthropologist* 78:59–73.

——1979 Three Locational Models: An Epistemological Assessment for Anthropology and Archaeology. In *Advances in Archaeological Method and Theory*, Volume 2, edited by M. B. Schiffer, pp. 141–173. Academic Press, New York.

——1987 A Dialectical Critique of Hierarchy. In *Power Relations and State Formation*, edited by Thomas C. Patterson, and Christine W. Gailey, pp. 155–169. American Anthropological Association, Washington, D.C.

——1995 Heterarchy and the Analysis of Complex Societies. In *Heterarchy and the Analysis of Complex Societies*, edited by Robert M. Ehrenreich, Carole L. Crumley, and Janet E. Levy, pp. 2–5. American Anthropological Association, Arlington.

——2001 Communication, Holism, and the Evolution of Sociopolitical Complexity. In *From Leaders to Rulers*, edited by Jonathan Haas, pp. 19–33. Kluwer Academic/Plenum Publishers, New York.

Ciudad, Andrés, Alfonso Lacadena, Jesús Adánez, and Ma Josefa Iglesias 2013 Crisis y supervivencia en Machaquilá, Petén, Guatemala. In *Millenary Maya Societies: Past Crises and Resilience*, edited by M.-Charlotte Arnauld, and Alain Breton, pp. 73–91. Electronic document, published online at Mesoweb: www.mesoweb.com/publications/MMS/6Ciudadetal.pdf.

Culbert, T. Patrick (ed.) 1973 *The Classic Maya Collapse. School of American Research*. University of New Mexico Press, Albuquerque.

Culbert, T. Patrick 1991a *Classic Maya Political History: Hieroglyphic and Archaeological Evidence. School of American Research Advanced Seminar Series*. Cambridge University Press, Cambridge.

——1991b Polities in the Northeast Peten. In *Classic Maya Political History: Hieroglyphic and Archaeological Evidence*, edited by T. Patrick Culbert, pp. 128–146. School of American Research Advanced Seminar Series. Cambridge University Press, Cambridge.

——1991c Maya Political History and Elite Interaction: A Summary View. In *Classic Maya Political History: Hieroglyphic and Archaeological Evidence*, edited by T. Patrick Culbert,

pp. 311–346. School of American Research Advanced Seminar Series. Cambridge University Press, Cambridge.

Dahlin, Bruce H. 2000 The Barricade and Abandonment of Chunchucmil: Implications for Northern Maya Warfare. *Latin American Antiquity* 11(3):283–298.

——2002 Climate Change and the End of the Classic Period in Yucatan: Resolving a Paradox. *Ancient Mesoamerica* 13(2):327–340.

——2009 Ahead of its Time?: The Remarkable Early Classic Maya Economy of Chunchucmil. *Journal of Social Archaeology* 9(3):341–367.

Dahlin, Bruce H., Christopher T. Jensen, Richard E. Terry, David R. Wright, and Timothy Beach 2007 In Search of an Ancient Maya Market. Latin American Antiquity 18 (4):363–384.

Dávalos, Eusebio, and Arturo Romano 1973 Estudios preliminar de los restos osteológicos encontrados en la Tumba del Templo de las Inscripciones, Palenque. In *El Templo de las Inscripciones, Palenque*, edited by Alberto Ruz, pp. 253–254. Instituto Nacional de Antropología e Historia, Mexico City.

Delvendahl, Kai 2010 Las sedes del poder: Evidencia arqueológica e iconográfica de los conjuntos palaciegos mayas del clásico tardío. Ediciones de la Universidad Autónoma de Yucatán, Merida.

Demarest, Arthur A. 1978 Interregional Conflict and "Situational Ethics" in Classic Maya Warfare. In *Codex Wauchope: A Tribute Roll*, edited by Marco Giardino, Barbara Edmonson, and Winifred Creamer, pp. 101–111. Tulane University, New Orleans.

——1984 Conclusiones y especulaciones acera el El Mirador. *Mesoamérica* 7:138–150.

——1992 Ideology in Ancient Maya Cultural Evolution: The Dynamics of Galactic Polities. In *Ideology and Pre-Columbian Civilizations*, edited by Arthur A. Demarest, and Geoffrey W. Conrad, pp. 135–157. School of American Research Press, Santa Fe.

——1993 The Violent Saga of a Maya Kingdom. *National Geographic* 183(2):94–111.

——2004 After the Maelstrom: Collapse of the Classic Maya kingdoms and the Terminal

Classic in Western Petén. In *The Terminal Classic in the Maya Lowlands: Collapse, Transition, and Transformation*, edited by Arthur A. Demarest, Prudence M. Rice, and Donald S. Rice, pp. 102–124. University of Colorado Press, Boulder.

——2013a The Collapse of the Classic Maya Kingdoms of the Southwestern Petén: Implications for the End of Classic Maya Civilization. In *Millenary Maya Societies: Past Crises and Resilience*, edited by M.-Charlotte Arnauld, and Alain Breton, pp. 22–48. Electronic document, published online at Mesoweb: www.mesoweb.com/publications/MMS/2 Demarest.pdf.

——2013b Ideological Pathways to Economic Exchange: Religion, Economy, and Legitimation at the Classic Maya Royal Capital of Cancuén. *Latin American Antiquity* 24 (4):371–402.

Demarest, Arthur A., Chloé Andrieu, Paola Torres, Mélanie Forné, Tomás Barrientos, and Marc Wolf 2014 Economy, Exchange, and Power: New Evidence from the Late Classic Maya Port City of Cancuen. *Ancient Mesoamerica* 25(1):187–219.

Demarest, Arthur A., Tomás Barrientos, and Federico Fahsen 2006 El apogeo y el Colapso del reinado de Cancuen: Resultados e interpretaciones del Proyecto Cancuen, 2004-2005. In *XIX Simposio de Investigaciones Arqueológicas en Guatemala, 2005*, edited by Juan Pedro Laporte, Bárbara Arroyo, and Héctor Mejía, pp. 757–768. Museo Nacional de Arqueología y Etnología, Guatemala City.

Demarest, Arthur A., Matt O'Mansky, Claudia Wolley, Dirk Van Turenhout, Takeshi Inomata, Joel Palka, and Héctor Escobedo 1997 Classic Maya Defensive Systems and Warfare in the Petexbatun Region. *Ancient Mesoamerica* 8(2):229–253.

Demarest, Arthur A., Prudence M. Rice, and Donald S. Rice (eds.) 2004a *The Terminal Classic in the Maya Lowlands: Collapse, Transition, and Transformation*. University of Colorado Press, Boulder.

Demarest, Arthur A., Prudence M. Rice, and Donald S. Rice 2004b Assessing Collapse, Terminations, and Transformations. In *The Terminal Classic in the Maya Lowlands: Collapse, Transition, and Transformation*. edited by Arthur A. Demarest, Prudence M. Rice, and Donald S. Rice, pp. 545–572. University of Colorado Press, Boulder.

Díaz de Castillo, Bernal 1967 *The Conquest of New Spain*. Kraus Reprint, Nendeln, Liechtenstein.

Dobres, Marcia-Ann, and John E. Robb (eds.) 2000 *Agency in Archaeology*. Routledge, London.

Dornan, Jennifer L. 2002 Agency and Archaeology: Past, Present, and Future Directions. *Journal of Archaeological Method and Theory* 9(4): 303–329.

Douglas, Peter M. J., Mark Pagani, Marcello A. Canuto, Mark Brenner, David A. Hodell, Timothy I. Eglinton, and Jason H. Curtis 2015 Drought, Agricultural Adaptation, and Sociopolitical Collapse in the Maya Lowlands. *Proceedings of the National Academy of Sciences* 112(18):5607–5612.

Drucker, Philip, and John W. Fox 1982 Swidden Didn't Make All That Midden: The Search for Ancient Mayan Agronomies. *Journal of Anthropological Research* 38(2):179–193.

Dumond, D. E. 1961 Swidden Agriculture and the Rise of Maya Civilization. *Southwestern Journal of Anthropology* 17(4):301–316.

Dunning, Nicholas P., and Timothy Beach 1994 Soil Erosion, Slope Management, and Ancient Terracing in the Maya Lowlands. *Latin American Antiquity* 5(1):51–69.

Dunning, Nicholas P., Timothy Beach, and David Rue 1997 The Paleoecology and Ancient Settlement of the Petexbatun Region, Guatemala. *Ancient Mesoamerica* (8):255–266.

Durán, Fray Diego 1967 *Historia de las indias de Nueva España y Islas de Tierre Firme*. Porrúa, Mexico City.

Durkheim, Emile 1915 *The Elementary Forms of the Religious Life, a Study in Religious Sociology*. Translated by Joseph Ward Swain. Macmillan, New York.

——1961 *Moral Education: A Study in the Theory and Application of the Sociology of Education*. Translated by Everett K. Wilson and Herman Schnurer. Free Press of Glencoe, New York.

Dymond D. P. 1974 *Archaeology and History: A Plea for Reconciliation*. Thames and Hudson, London.

Earle, Timothy K. 2011 Chiefs, Chieftaincies, Chiefdoms, and Chiefly Confederacies: Power in the Evolution of Political Systems. *Social Evolution & History* 10(1):27–54.

Eberl, Marcus, and Daniel Graña-Behrens 2004 Proper Names and Throne Names: On the Naming Practice of Classic Maya Rulers. In *Continuity and Change: Maya Religious Practices in Temporal Perspective*, edited by Daniel Graña-Behrens, Nikolai Grube, Christian M. Prager, Frauke Sachse, Stefanie Teufel, and Elisabeth Wagner, pp. 101–120. Proceedings of the 5th European Maya Conference, University of Bonn, December 2000. Saurwein Verlag, Markt Swarben.

Eberl, Marcus, and Christian Prager 2005 B'olon Yokte' K'uh: Maya Conceptions of War, Conflict, and the Underworld. In *Wars and Conflicts in Prehispanic Mesoamerica and the Andes*, edited by Peter Eeckhout, and Geneviève LeFort, pp. 28–36. BAR International Series 1385. Archaeopress, Oxford.

Ebert, Claire E., Keith M. Prufer, Martha Macri, Bruce Winterhalder, and Douglas J. Kennett 2014 Terminal Long Count Dates and the Disintegration of Classic Period Maya Polities. *Ancient Mesoamerica* 24:337–356.

Edmonson, Munro S. 1965 *Quiche-English Dictionary*. Publication 30. Middle American Research Institute, Tulane University, New Orleans.

——1979 Some Postclassic Questions about the Classic Maya. In *Tercera Mesa Redonda de Palenque*, Volume IV, edited by Merle Greene Robertson, and Donnan Call Jeffers, pp. 9–18. Pre-Columbian Art Research Institute, San Francisco.

——1982 *Ancient Future of the Itzá: The Book of Chilam Balam of Tizimin*. University of Texas Press, Austin.

Ehrenburg, Victor 1960 *The Greek State*. Basil Blackwell and Mott, Oxford.

Ember, Carol R., and Melvin Ember 1992 Resource Unpredictability, Mistrust, and War: A Cross-Cultural Study. *The Journal of Conflict Resolution* 36(2):242–262.

Esparza, Octavio Q., and Vania E. Pérez 2009 Archaeological and Epigraphic Studies in Pol Box, Quintana Roo. *The PARI Journal* 9(3):1–16.

Estrada Belli, Francisco 2011 *The First Maya Civilization: Ritual and Power Before the Classic Period*. Routledge, London.

Estrada Belli, Francisco, and Alexandre Tokovinine 2016 A King's Apotheosis: Iconography, Politics, and Text from a Classic Maya Temple at Holmul. *Latin American Antiquity* 27(2):149–168.

Estrada Belli, Francisco, Alexandre Tokovinine, Jennifer M. Foley, Heather Hurst, Gene A. Ware, David Stuart, and Nikolai Grube 2009 A Maya Palace at Holmul, Guatemala and the Teotihuacan "Entrada": Evidence from Murals 7 and 9. *Latin American Antiquity* 20(1):228–259.

Evans, Nicholas P., Thomas K. Bauska, Fernando Gázquez-Sánchez, Mark Brenner, Jason H. Curtis, and David A. Hodell 2018 Quantification of Drought during the Collapse of the Classic Maya Civilization. *Science* 361:498–501.

Evans, R. Tripp 2004 *Romancing the Maya: Mexican Antiquity in the American Imagination, 1820–1915*. University of Texas Press, Austin.

Fahsen, Federico 1988 *A New Early Text from Tikal*. Research Reports on Ancient Maya Writing 17. Center for Maya Research, Washington D.C.

——2002 "Rescuing the Origins of Dos Pilas Dynasty: A Salvage of Hieroglyphic Stairway 2, Structure L5-49". Report to the Foundation for the Advancement of Mesoamerican Studies. www.famsi.org/reports/01098/index

Fahsen, Federico, Arthur A. Demarest, and Luis Fernando Luin 2003 Sesenta años de historia en la escalinata jeroglífica de Cancuen. In *XVI Simposio de Investigaciones Arqueologicas en Guatemala, 2002*, edited by Juan Pedro Laporte, Bárbara Arroyo, Héctor L. Escobedo, and Héctor E. Mejía, pp. 703–713. Museo Nacional de Arqueología y Etnología, Ministerio de Cultura y Deportes, Guatemala.

Fahsen, Federico, and Sarah E. Jackson 2001 El panel de Cancuén: nuevos datos e interpretaciones sobre la dinastía de Cancuén en el periodo Clásico. In *Proyecto Arqueológico Cancuén: Informe Temporada 2001*, edited by Arthur Demarest, and Tomás Barrientos, pp. 21–32. Ministerio de Culturo y Deportes de Guatemala, Guatemala City.

Fahsen, Federico, Jorge Mario Ortiz, Jeannette Castellanos, and Luis Fernando Luin 2003 La Escalinata 2 de Dos Pilas, Petén: Los nuevos escalones. In *XVI Simposio de Investigaciones Arqueológicas en Guatemala, 2002*, edited by Juan Pedro Laporte, Barbara Arroyo, Héctor Escobedo, and Héctor Mejía, pp. 679–692. Museo Nacional de Arqueología y Etnología, Guatemala City.

Fahsen, Federico, and Linda Schele 1991 Curl-Snout Under Scrutiny, Again. *Texas Notes on Pre-Columbian Art, Writing, and Culture 13*. Department of Art, University of Texas at Austin: Austin.

Farrell, Marie Patrice 1997 The Garden City Hypothesis in the Maya Lowlands. PhD dissertation, University of Cincinnati.

Farriss, Nancy M. 1984 *Maya Society Under Colonial Rule: The Collective Enterprise of Survival*. Princeton University Press, Princeton.

Fash, William L. 1989 The Sculpture Façade of Structure 9N-82: Content, Form, and Meaning. In *The House of the Bacabs, Copan, Honduras. Studies in Pre-Columbian Art and Archaeology, No.29*, edited by David Webster, pp. 41–72. Dumbarton Oaks Research Library and Collection, Washington D.C.

——1991a *Scribes, Warriors and Kings: The City of Copán and the Ancient Maya*. Thames and Hudson, London.

——1991b Lineage Patrons and Ancestor Worship among the Classic Maya Nobility: The Case of Copan Structure 9N-82. In *Sixth Palenque Round Table, 1986*, edited by Merle Greene Robertson, and Virginia M. Fields, pp. 68–80. University of Oklahoma Press, Norman and London.

Fash, William, and David Stuart 1991 Dynastic History and Cultural Evolution at Copan. In *Classic Maya Political History: Hieroglyphic and Archaeological Evidence*, edited by T. Patrick Culbert, pp. 147–179. School of American Research Advanced Seminar Series. Cambridge University Press, Cambridge.

Fash, William L., Alexandre Tokovinine, and Barbara W. Fash 2009 The House of New Fire at Teotihuacan and its Legacy in Mesoamerica. In *The Art of Urbanism: How Mesoamerican Kingdoms Represented Themselves in Architecture and Imagery*, edited by William L. Fash, and Leonardo López Luján, pp. 201–229. Dumbarton Oaks, Washington D.C.

Fedick, Scott L. (ed.) 1996 *The Managed Mosaic: Ancient Maya Agriculture and Resource Use*. University of Utah Press, Salt Lake City.

Feeley-Harnik, Gillian 1985 Issues in Divine Kingship. *Annual Review of Anthropology* 14:273–313.

Feinman, Gary, and Jill Neitzel 1984 Too Many Types: An Overview of Sedentary Prestate Societies in the Americas. *Advances in Archaeological Method and Theory* 7:39–102.

Feldman, Lawrence H. 1983 The Structure of Cholan Mayan Surnames in Sixteenth and Seventeenth Century Manuscripts: Features to look for in the Eighth Century Personal Name Hieroglyphs. *Mexicon* 5(3):46–53.

Ferguson, Yale H. 1991 Chiefdoms to City-States: The Greek Experience. In *Chiefdoms: Power, Economy, and Ideology*, edited by Timothy K. Earle, pp. 169–192. School of American Research Advanced Seminar Series. Cambridge University Press, Cambridge.

——2002 The State Concept and a World of Polities Under Perpetual Siege. In *The State, Identity and Violence: Political Disintegration in the Post–Cold War Era*, edited by R. Brian Ferguson, pp. 89–95. Routledge, London.

Ferguson, Yale H., and Richard W. Mansbach 1996 *Polities: Authority, Identities, and Change*. University of South Carolina Press, Columbia.

Finkelstein, Jacob J. 1979 Early Mesopotamia, 2500–1000 BC. In *Propaganda and Communication in World History 1*, edited by Harold D. Lasswell, Daniel Lerner, and Hans Speier, pp. 50–110. University of Hawaii, Honolulu.

Finley, Moses I. 1975 *The Use and Abuse of History*. Chatto and Windus, London.

Fitzsimmons, James L. 2009 *Death and the Classic Maya Kings*. University of Texas Press, Austin.

Flannery, Kent V. 1967 Culture History Versus Culture Process: A Debate in American Archaeology. *Scientific American* 217:119–122.

——1972 The Cultural Evolution of Civilizations. *Annual Review of Ecology and Systematics* 3: 399–426.

Foias, Antonia E. 2013 *Ancient Maya Political Dynamics*. University Press of Florida, Gainesville.

Foias, Antonia E., and Ronald L. Bishop 2005 Fine Paste Wares and the Terminal Classic in the Petexbatun and Pasión Regions, Peten, Guatemala. In *Geographies of Power: Understanding the Nature of Terminal Classic Pottery in the Maya Lowlands*, edited by Sandra L. López, and Antonia Foias, pp. 23–40. BAR International Series 1447. Archaeopress, Oxford

Folan, William J. 1985 Calakmul, Campeche: su centro urbano, estado y región en relación al concepto del resto de la Gran Mesoamerica. *Informacion* 9:161–185.

Folan, William J., E. R. Kintz, and L. A. Fletcher 1983 *Coba, A Classic Maya Metropolis*. Academic Press, London, New York.

Folan, William J., Joyce Marcus, Sophia Pincemin, María del Rosario Carrasco, Laraine Fletcher, and Abel Morales López. 1995 New Data from an Ancient Maya Capital in Campeche, Mexico. *Latin American Antiquity* 6:310–334.

Ford, Anabel 2016 Unexpected Discovery with LiDAR: Uncovering the Citadel at El Pilar in the Context of the Maya Forest GIS. *Research Reports on Belizean Archaeology* 13:87–98.

Forsyth, Donald W. 2005 A Survey of Terminal Classic Ceramic Complexes and their Socioeconomic Implications. In *Geographies of Power: Understanding the Nature of Terminal Classic Pottery in the Maya Lowlands*, edited by Sandra L. López, and Antonia Foias, pp. 7–22. BAR International Series 1447, Archaeopress, Oxford.

Fortes, Meyer 1967 Of Installation Ceremonies. *Proceedings of the Royal Anthropological Institute of Great Britain and Ireland* (1967):5–20.

Fortes, Meyer, and Edward Evan Evans-Pritchard (eds.) 1940 *African Political Systems*. Oxford University Press, London.

Foucault, Michel 1977 *Discipline and Punish: The Birth of the Prison*, translated by Alan Sheridan. Vintage Books, New York.

——1980 *Power/Knowledge: Selected Interviews and Other Writings, 1972–1977*. Harvester Press, Brighton.

Fox, James A., and John S. Justeson 1984 Polyvalence in Mayan Hieroglyphic Writing. In *Phoneticism in Mayan Hieroglyphic Writing*, edited by John S. Justeson, and Lyle Campbell, pp. 17–76. Institute for Mesoamerican Studies, State University of New York at Albany, Albany.

Fox, John W. 1987 *Maya Post-Classic State Formation: Segmentary Lineage Migration in Advancing Frontiers*. Cambridge University Press, Cambridge.

——1994 Political Cosmology among the Quiché Maya. In *Factional Competition and Political Development in the New World*, edited by Elizabeth M. Brumfiel. and John W. Fox, pp. 158–170. Cambridge University Press, Cambridge.

Fox, Richard G. 1977 *Urban Anthropology: Cities in their Cultural Settings*. Prentice-Hall, Englewood Cliffs.

Fox, Robin 1967 *Kinship and Marriage: An Anthropological Perspective*. Penguin Books, London.

Frazer, James G. 1890 *The Golden Bough: A Study in Magic and Religion*. 2 Volumes. MacMillan, London.

Freidel, David A. 1986 Maya Warfare: An Example of Peer Polity Interaction. In *Peer Polity Interaction and Socio-political Change*, edited by Colin Renfrew, and John F. Cherry, pp. 93–108. New Directions in Archaeology, Cambridge University Press, Cambridge.

——1992 The Trees of Life. Ahau as Idea and Artifact in Classic Lowland Maya Civilization. In *Ideology and Pre-Columbian Civilizations*, edited by Arthur A. Demarest, and Geoffrey W. Conrad, pp. 115–133. School of American Research Press, Santa Fe.

——2008 Maya Divine Kingship. In *Religion and Power: Divine Kingship in the Ancient World and Beyond*. Oriental Institute Seminars Number 4, edited by Nicole Brisch, pp. 191–206. The Oriental Institute of the University of Chicago, Chicago.

———2018 Maya and the Idea of Empire. In *Pathways to Complexity, A View from the Maya Lowlands*, edited by M. Kathryn Brown, and George J. Bey III, pp. 363–386. University Press of Florida, Gainesville.

Freidel, David A., Héctor L. Escobedo, and Stanley P. Guenter 2007 A Crossroads of Conquerors: Waka' and Gordon Willey's "Rehearsal for the Collapse" Hypothesis. In *Gordon R. Willey and American Archaeology: Contemporary Perspectives*, edited by Jeremy A. Sabloff, and William L. Fash, pp. 187–208. University of Oklahoma Press, Norman.

Freidel, David, Héctor Escobedo, David Lee, Stanley Guenter, and Juan Carlos Meléndez 2007 El Perú y la ruta terrestre de la Dinastía *Kan* hacia el Altiplano. In *XX Simposio de Investigaciones Arqueológicas en Guatemala, 2006*, edited by Juan Pedro Laporte, Barbara Arroyo, and Héctor E. Mejía, pp. 59–76. Museo Nacional de Arqueología y Etnología, Guatemala.

Freidel, David A., and Linda Schele 1988 Kingship and the Late Preclassic Maya Lowlands: The Instruments and Places of Ritual Power. *American Anthropologist* 90(3):547–567.

Freidel, David, Linda Schele, and Joy Parker 1993 *Maya Cosmos: Three Thousand Years on the Shaman's Path*. William Morrow, New York.

Fried, Morton H. 1967 *The Evolution of Political Society: An Essay in Political Anthropology*. Random House, New York.

Fuentes y Guzmán, Francisco Antonio de 1932–1933 *Recordación Florida: discurso historial y demostración natural, material, militar y política del Reyno de Guatemala*, 3 Volumes. Biblioteca "Goathemala" de la Sociedad de Geografía e Historia, Guatemala City.

Gallie, W. B. 1964 *Philosophy and the Historical Understanding*. Chatto & Windus, London.

Gámez, Laura, James Fitzsimmons, and Mélanie Forné 2007 Epigrafía y Arqueología de *Hixwitz*: Investigaciones en Zapote Bobal, La Libertad, Petén. In *XX Simposio de Investigaciones Arqueológicas en Guatemala, 2006*, edited by Juan Pedro Laporte, Barbara Arroyo, and Héctor E. Mejía, pp. 345–367. Museo Nacional de Arqueología y Etnología, Guatemala.

Gann, Thomas 1927 *Maya Cities*. Duckworth, London.

Gann, Thomas W. F., and J. Eric S. Thompson 1931 *The History of the Maya: From the Earliest Times to the Present Day*. Charles Scribner's Sons, New York.

García Barrios, Ana 2011 Análisis iconográfico preliminar de fragmentos de las vasijas estilo códice procedentes de Calakmul. *Estudios de Cultura Maya* 37:65–97.

García, José Miguel 1991 Edificios y dignatarios: la historia escrita de Oxkintok. In *Oxkintok: Una ciudad maya de Yucatán*, edited by Miguel Rivera, pp. 55–78. Misión Arqueologíca de España eb México, Madrid.

García Moll, Roberto 2004 Shield Jaguar and Structure 23 at Yaxchilan. In *Courtly Art of the Ancient Maya by Mary Miller and Simon Martin*, pp. 268–270. Thames and Hudson, London and New York.

———2005 *Pomoná: un sitio del Clássico Maya en las colinas tabasqueñas*. Instituto Nacional de Antropología e Historia, Mexico City.

Garraty, Christopher P., and Barbara L. Stark (eds.) 2010 *Archaeological Approaches to Market Exchange in Ancient Societies*. University Press of Colorado, Boulder.

Garrison, Thomas, Stephen D. Houston, and Omar A. Alcover 2017 Hilltops and Boundaries: The Lidar Survey of El Zotz and Tikal. Paper presented at the 82nd Meeting of the Society for American Archaeology, Vancouver, British Columbia, 30 March.

———2018 Recentering the Rural: Lidar and Articulated Landscapes among the Maya. *Journal of Anthropological Archaeology* 53:133–146.

Gat, Azar 2006 *War in Human Civilization*. Oxford University Press, Oxford.

Geary, Patrick J. 1994 The Uses of Archaeological Sources for Religious and Cultural History. In *Living with the Dead in the Middles Ages*, edited by Patrick J. Geary, pp. 30–45. Cornell University Press, Ithaca.

Geertz, Clifford 1968 *Islam Observed: Religious Development in Morocco and Indonesia*. University of Chicago Press, Chicago.

———1973 *The Interpretation of Cultures: Selected Essays*. Basic Books, New York.

——1977 Centers, Kings, and Charisma: Reflections on the Symbolics of Power. In *Culture and Its Creators*, edited by J. Ben-David, and T. N. Clark, pp. 150–171. University of Chicago Press, Chicago.

——1980 *Negara: The Theatre State in Nineteenth-Century Bali.* Princeton University Press, Princeton.

Gell, Alfred 1998 *Art and Agency: An Anthropological Theory.* Clarendon, Oxford.

Genet, Jean 1934 *Revue des études Maya-Quiches.* Les Éditions Genet, Paris.

Gibson, Charles 1964 *The Aztec Under Spanish Rule: A History of the Indians of the Valley of Mexico, 1519–1810.* Stanford University Press, Stanford.

Giddens, Anthony 1979 *Central Problems in Social Theory.* University of California Press, Berkeley.

——1984 *The Constitution of Society: Outline of the Theory of Structuration.* University of California Press, Berkeley.

Gill, Richardson 1994 The Great Maya Droughts. PhD dissertation, University of Texas at Austin.

——2000 *The Great Maya Droughts: Water, Life, and Death.* The University of New Mexico Press, Albuquerque.

Gillespie, Susan D. 2000a Maya "Nested Houses": The Ritual Construction of Space. In *Beyond Kinship: Social and Material Reproduction in House Societies*, edited by Rosemary A. Joyce and Susan D. Gillespie, pp. 135–160. University of Pennsylvania Press, Philadelphia.

——2000b Rethinking Ancient Maya Social Organization: Replacing "Lineage" with "House". *American Anthropologist* 102(3):467–484.

Gilpin, Robert 1981 *War and Change in World Politics.* Cambridge University Press, Cambridge.

Giovannini, Adalberto 1994 Greek Cities and Greek Commonwealth. In *Images and Ideologies: Self-Definition in the Hellenistic World*, edited by Anthony Bulloch, Erich S. Gruen, A. A. Long, and Andrew Stewart, pp. 265–286. University of California Press, Berkeley.

Golden, Charles W., and Andrew K. Scherer 2013 Territory, Trust, Growth, and Collapse in Classic Period Maya Kingdoms. *Current Anthropology* 54(4):397–435.

Golden, Charles W., Andrew K. Scherer, Stephen D. Houston, Whittaker Schroder, Shanti Morell-Hart, Socorro del Pilar Jiménez, George Van Kollias, Moises Yerath Ramiro, Jeffrey Dobereiner, and Omar Alcover 2020 Centering the Classic Maya King of Sak Tz'i'. *Journal of Field Archaeology* 45(2):67-85.

Golden, Charles W., Andrew K. Scherer, A. René Muñoz, and Rosaura Vasquez 2008 Piedras Negras and Yaxchilan: Divergent Political Trajectories in Adjacent Maya Polities. *Latin American Antiquity* 19(3):249–274.

González, Arnoldo, and Guillermo Bernal 2000 Grupo XVI de Palenque: Conjuncto arquitectónico de la nobleza provincial. In *Arqueología Mexicana*, 8(45):20–27.

——2012 The Discovery of the Temple XXI Monument at Palenque: The Kingdom of Baakal During the Reign of K'inich Ahkal Mo' Nahb. In *Maya Archaeology 2*, edited by Charles Golden, Stephen D. Houston, and Joel Skidmore, pp. 82–103. Precolumbia Mesoweb Press, San Francisco.

Goodenough, Ward H. 1965 Rethinking 'Status' and 'Role': Toward a General Model of the Cultural Organization of Social Relationships. In *The Relevance of Models in Social Anthropology, A.S.A Monographs 1*, edited by Michael Banton, pp. 1–24. Tavistock Publications, London.

Goodman, Joseph 1905 Maya Dates. *American Anthropologist* 7:642–647.

Goody, Jack 1967 Introduction. In *Succession to High Office. Cambridge Papers in Social Anthropology 4*, edited by Jack Goody, pp. 1–56. Cambridge University Press, Cambridge.

——1968 *The Logic of Writing and the Organisation of Society.* Cambridge University Press, Cambridge.

——1973 Strategies of Heirship. *Comparative Studies in Society and History* 15:3–20.

Graeber, David, and Marshall Sahlins 2017 *On Kings.* Hau Books, Chicago.

Graham, Elizabeth 2002 Perspectives of Economy and Theory. In *Ancient Maya Political Economies*, edited by Marilyn A. Masson, and David A. Freidel, pp. 398–418. Altamira Press, Walnut Creek.

———2006 An Ethnicity to Know. In *Maya Ethnicity: The Construction of Ethnic Identity from Preclassic to Modern Times*, edited by Frauke Sachse, pp. 109–124. Verlag Anton Saurwein, Markt Schwaben.

———2011 *Maya Christians and their Churches in Sixteenth-Century Belize*. University Press of Florida, Gainesville.

Graham, Elizabeth, Scott E. Simmons, and Christine D. White 2013 The Spanish Conquest and the Maya Collapse: How 'Religious' Is 'Change'? *World Archaeology* 45(1):161–185.

Graham, Ian 1986 Corpus of Maya Hieroglyphic Inscriptions, Vol. 5, Part 3: Uaxactun. *Peabody Museum of Archaeology and Ethnology*, Harvard University, Cambridge, MA.

———1988 Homeless Hieroglyphs. *Antiquity* 62 (234):122–126.

———1996 Corpus of Maya Hieroglyphic Inscriptions, Vol. 7 Part 1: Seibal. *Peabody Museum of Archaeology and Ethnology*, Harvard University, Cambridge, MA.

Graham, Ian, Lucia R. Henderson, Peter Mathews, and David Stuart 2006 Corpus of Maya Hieroglyphic Inscriptions, Vol. 9, Part 2: Tonina. *Peabody Museum of Archaeology and Ethnology*, Harvard University, Cambridge, MA.

Graham, Ian, and Eric Von Euw 1992 Corpus of Maya Hieroglyphic Inscriptions, Vol. 4, Part 3: Uxmal, Xcalumkin. *Peabody Museum of Archaeology and Ethnology*, Harvard University, Cambridge, MA.

Graham, John A. 1972 *The Hieroglyphic Inscriptions and Monumental Art of Altar de Sacrificios*, 64(2). Papers of the Peabody Museum of Archaeology and Ethnology, Harvard University Press. Cambridge, MA.

———1973 Aspects of Non-Maya Presences in the Inscriptions and Sculptural Art of Seibal. In *The Classic Maya Collapse*, edited by T. Patrick Culbert, pp. 207–219. University of New Mexico Press, Albuquerque.

Graña-Behrens, Daniel 2002 Die Maya-Inschriften aus Nordwestyukatan, Mexiko. PhD dissertation, University of Bonn.

———2006 Emblem Glyphs and Political Organization in Northwestern Yucatan in the Classic Period (A.D. 300–1000). *Ancient Mesoamerica* 17:105–123.

———2018 New Evidence for Political Hierarchy and Power in the Northern Maya Lowlands (AD 600–1000). *Ancient Mesoamerica* 29 (1):171–195.

Granovetter, Mark S. 1973 The Strength of Weak Ties. *American Journal of Sociology* 78 (6):1360–1380.

Griffeth, Robert, and Carol G. Thomas 1981 Five City-State Cultures Compared. In *The City-State in Five Cultures*, edited by Robert Griffeth, and Carol G. Thomas, pp. 181–207. ABC-Clio, Santa Barbara.

Gronemeyer, Sven 2006 *The Maya Site of Tortuguero, Tabasco, Mexico: Its History and Inscriptions*. Acta Mesoamericana 17. Verlag Anton Sauwein, Markt Schwaben.

———2012 Statements of Identity – Emblem Glyphs in the Nexus of Political Relations. In *Maya Political Relations and Strategies: Proceedings of the 14th European Maya Conference*, edited by Jarosław Źrałka, Wiesław Koszkul, and Beata Golinska. Contributions to New World Archaeology. 4:13–40. Jagiellonian University, Cracow.

———2013 *Monuments and Inscriptions of Tamarindito, Peten, Guatemala*. Acta Mesoamericana 25. Verlag Anton Saurwein, Markt Schwaben.

Gronemeyer, Sven, and Barbara MacLeod 2010 What Could Happen in 2012: A Re-analysis of the 13-Bak'tun Prophecy on Tortuguero Monument 6. *Wayeb Notes* 34. www.wayeb.com/notes/wayebnotes0034.pdf

Grube, Nikolai 1990 A Reference to Waterlily Jaguar on Caracol Stela 16. Copán Note 8. Copan Mosaics Project and Instituto Hondureño de Antropología e Historia, Austin.

———1992 Classic Maya Dance: Evidence from Hieroglyphs and Iconography. *Ancient Mesoamerica* 3:201–218.

———1994a A Preliminary Report on the Monuments and Inscriptions of La Milpa, Orange Walk, Belize. *Baessler-Archiv* 42(2):217–238.

———1994b Hieroglyphic Sources for the History of Northwest Yucatan. In *Hidden among Hills: Maya Archaeology of the Northwest Yucatan Peninsula*. First Maler Symposium, Bonn 1990, Acta Mesoamericana 7, edited by Hanns J.

Prem, pp. 316–358. Verlag Anton Sauwein, Markt Schwaben.

——1994c Epigraphic Research at Caracol, Belize. In Studies in the Archaeology of Caracol, Belize. In *Pre-Columbian Art Research Institute Monograph* 7, edited by Diane Z. Chase, and Arlen F. Chase, pp. 83–122. Pre-Columbian Art Research Institute, San Francisco.

——1996 Palenque in the Maya World. In *Eighth Palenque Round Table, 1993 Vol.X*, edited by Martha Macri, and Merle Greene Robertson, pp. 1–13. Pre-Columbian Art Research Institute, San Francisco.

——2002 Onomástica de los gobernanates mayas. In *La Organización Social entre los Mayas, Memoria de la Tercera Mesa Redonda de Palenque, Volume II*, coordinated by Vera Tiesler Blos, Rafael Cobos, and Merle Greene Robertson, pp. 323–353. Instituto Nacional de Antropología e Historia and Universidad Autónoma de Yucatán, Mexico City and Merida.

——2003a Appendix 2: Epigraphic Analysis of Altar 3 of Altar de los Reyes. In Archaeological Reconnaissance in Southeastern Campeche, México: 2002 Field Season Report by Ivan Šprajc, pp. 34–40. Report submitted to the Foundation for the Advancement of Mesoamerican Studies (FAMSI), www.famsi.org/reports/01014/01014Sprajc01.pdf

——2003b Hieroglyphic Inscriptions from Northwest Yucatan: An Update of Recent Research. In *Escondido en la Selva: Arqueología en el Norte de Yucatán*, edited by Hanns J. Prem, pp. 339–370. Instituto Nacional de Antropología e Historia and University of Bonn, Mexico City and Bonn.

——2004a El Origen de la Dinastía Kaan. In *Los Cautivos de Dzibanché*, edited by Enrique Nalda, pp. 114–131. Instituto Nacional de Antropología e Historia, Mexico City.

——2004b The Orthographic Distinction between Velar and Glottal Spirants in Maya Hieroglyphic Writing. In *The Linguistics of Maya Writing*, edited by Søren Wichmann, pp. 61–82. University of Utah Press, Salt Lake City.

——2005 Toponyms, Emblem Glyphs, and the Political Geography of the Southern Campeche. *Anthropological Notebooks* 11:87–100.

——2006 Ancient Maya Royal Biographies in Comparative Perspective. In *Janaab' Pakal of Palenque: Reconstructing the Life and Death of a Maya Ruler*, edited by Vera Tiesler, and Andrea Cucina, pp. 146–166. The University of Arizona Press, Tucson.

——2008 Monumentos esculpidos: epigrafía e iconografía. In *Reconocimiento arqueológico en el sureste del estado de Campeche, Mexico: 1996–2005*, edited by Ivan Šprajc, pp. 177–231. BAR International Series 1742. Archaeopress, Oxford.

——2016 The Logogram JALAM. Textdatenbank und Wörterbuch des Klassischen Maya, Research Note 3. http://mayawoerterbuch.de/wpcontent/uploads/2016/03/twkmnote003.pdf

Grube, Nikolai, and Kai Delvendahl 2011 Los jugadores de pelota de Uxul, Campeche: Nuevo hallazgos. *Arqueología Mexicana* 14 (112):64–69.

Grube, Nikolai, Kai Delvendahl, Nicolaus Seefeld, and Beniamino Volta 2012 Under the Rule of Snake Kings: Uxul in the 7th and 8th Centuries. *Estudios de Cultura Maya* 40:11–49.

Grube, Nikolai, Alfonso Lacadena, and Simon Martin 2003 Chichen Itza and Ek Balam: Terminal Classic Inscriptions from Yucatan. Notebook for the XXVIIth Maya Hieroglyphic Forum at Texas. Maya Workshop Foundation, University of Texas at Austin.

Grube, Nikolai, and Simon Martin 1998 Política clásica maya dentro de una tradición mesoamericana: Un modelo epigráfico de organización política 'hegemonica'. In *Modelos de entidades políticas mayas. Primer Seminario de Mesas Redondas de Palenque*, edited by Silvia Trejo, pp. 131–146. Instituto Nacional de Antropología e Historia, Mexico City.

Grube, Nikolai, Simon Martin, and Marc Zender 2002a Palenque and its Neighbors. The Proceedings of the XXVIth Maya Hieroglyphic Workshop, 13–14 March 2002. Transcribed and edited by Phil Wanyerka.

——2002b Palenque and its Neighbors. Notebook for the XXVIth Maya Hieroglyphic Forum at Texas. Maya Workshop Foundation, University of Texas at Austin.

Grube, Nikolai, and Werner Nahm 1994 A Census of Xibalba: A Complete Inventory of *Way* Characters on Maya Ceramics. In *The Maya Vase Book: A Corpus of Rollout Photographs of Maya Vases*, edited by Barbara Kerr, and Justin Kerr, Volume 5, pp. 686–715. Kerr Associates, New York.

Grube, Nikolai, and Linda Schele 1990 Royal Gifts to Subordinate Lords. Copán Note 87. Copan Mosaics Project and Instituto Hondureño de Antropología e Historia, Austin.

——1993 Un verbo *nakwa* para "batallar" o "conquistar". Texas Notes on Pre-Columbian Art, Writing, and Culture 55. Department of Art, University of Texas at Austin.

——1994 Tikal Altar 5. Texas Notes on Pre-Columbian Art, Writing, and Culture 66. Department of Art, University of Texas at Austin.

Grube, Nikolai, Linda Schele, and Federico Fahsen 1991 Odds and Ends from the Inscriptions of Quiriguá. *Mexicon* XIII(6): 106–112.

Gruzinski, Serge 1989 *Man-Gods in the Mexican Highlands: Indian Power and Colonial Society*. Stanford University Press, Stanford.

Guenter, Stanley Paul 1999 The Classic Maya Collapse. Unpublished manuscript.

——2002 A Reading of the Cancuén Looted Panel. Mesoweb: mesoweb.com/features/cancuen/Panel.pdf

——2003 The Inscriptions of Dos Pilas associated with B'ajlaj Chan K'awiil. mesoweb.com/features/Guenter/Dos Pilas

——2005a "Altar Chi: Una capital real del Preclásico". Paper presented at the XIX Simposio de Investigaciones Arqueológicas en Guatemala, Guatemala City, 15 July.

——2005b La Corona Find Sheds Light on Site Q Mystery. *The PARI Journal* 6(2):16–18.

——2014 The Classic Maya Collapse: Chronology and Causation. PhD dissertation, Southern Methodist University.

Guiteras Holmes, Calixta 1961 *Perils of the Soul: The World View of a Tzotzil Indian*. Free Press, New York.

Gunn, Joel D., William J. Folan, and Hubert R. Robichaux 1995 A Landscape Analysis of the Candelaria Watershed in Mexico: Insights into Paleoclimates Affecting Upland Horticulture in the Southern Yucatan Peninsula Semi-Karst. *Geoarchaeology* 10(1):3–42.

Haas, Jonathan 1982 *The Evolution of the Prehistoric State*. Columbia University Press, New York.

Haggett, Peter 1965 *Locational Analysis in Human Geography*. St. Martin's Press, New York.

Haldon, John F. 1993 *State Theory and the Tributary Mode of Production*. Verso, London.

Hall, J. M. 2000 Sparta, Lakedaimon and the Nature of Perioikic Dependency. *CPC Papers* 5:73–89.

Halperin, Christina, José Luis Garrido, Miriam Salas, and Jean Baptiste LeMoine 2019 "Convergence Zone Politics and Cultural Affiliations at the Archaeological Site of Ucanal, Guatemala". Paper presented at the 82nd Meeting of the Society for American Archaeology, Albuquerque, 12 April.

Hammond, Norman 1972 Locational Models and the Site of Lubaantun: A Classic Maya Centre. In *Models in Archaeology*, edited by David L. Clarke, pp. 757–800. Methuen, London.

——1974 The Distribution of Late Classic Maya Major Ceremonial Centers in the Central Area. In *Mesoamerican Archaeology: New Approaches*, edited by Norman Hammond, pp. 313–334. University of Texas Press, Austin.

——1991 Inside the Black Box – Defining Maya Polity. In *Classic Maya Political History*, edited by T. Patrick Culbert, pp. 253–284. Cambridge University Press, Cambridge.

Hammond, Norman, and Theya Molleson 1994 Huguenot Weavers and Maya Kings: Anthropological Assessment Versus Documentary Record of Age at Death. *Mexicon* 16(4):75–77.

Hammond, Norman, and Gair Tourtellot 2004 Out with a Whimper: La Milpa in the Terminal Classic. In *The Terminal Classic in the Maya Lowlands: Collapse, Transition, and Transformation*, edited by Arthur A. Demarest, Prudence M. Rice, and Donald S. Rice, pp. 288–301. University of Colorado Press, Boulder.

Hanks, William F. 1990 *Referential Practice: Language and Lived Space among the Maya*. University of Chicago Press, Chicago.

Hansen, Mogens Herman 1995 The Autonomous City-State. Ancient Fact or Modern Fiction? In *Sources for the Ancient Greek City-State, Papers from the Copenhagen Polis Centre 2*, edited by Mogens Herman Hansen, and Kurt Raaflaub, pp. 21–43. Franz Steiner, Stuttgart.

——1998 Polis *and City-State: An Ancient Concept and Its Modern Equivalent*. Acts of the Copenhagen Polias Centre Volume 5. Historisk-filosofiske Meddelelser 76. Munksgaard, Copenhagen.

——2000a Conclusion: The Impact of City-State Cultures on World History. In *A Comparative Study Of Thirty City-State Cultures: An Investigation Conducted by the Copenhagen Polis Centre*, edited by Mogens Herman Hansen, pp. 597–623. Historisk-Filosofiske Skrifter 21. Kongelige Danske Videnskabernes Selskab, Copenhagen.

——2006 *Polis: An Introduction to the Ancient Greek City-State*. Oxford University Press, Oxford.
2007 *The Return of the Polis: The Use and Meaning of the Word Polis in Archaic and Classical Sources*. Steiner, Stuttgart.

Hansen, Mogens Herman (ed.) 2000b *A Comparative Study of Thirty City-State Cultures: An Investigation Conducted by the Copenhagen Polis Centre*. Historisk-Filosofiske Skrifter 21. Kongelige Danske Videnskabernes Selskab, Copenhagen.

——2002 *A Comparative Study of Six City-State Cultures: An Investigation Conducted by the Copenhagen Polis Centre*. Historisk-Filosofiske Skrifter 27. Kongelige Danske Videnskabernes Selskab, Copenhagen.

Hansen, Richard D., Beatriz Balcárcel, Edgar Suyuc, Héctor E. Mejía, Enrique Hernández, Gendry Valle, Stanley P. Guenter, and Shannon Novak 2006 Investigaciones arqueológicas en el sitio Tintal, Petén. In *XIX Simposio de Investigaciones Arqueológicas en Guatemala, 2005*, edited by Juan Pedro Laporte, Barbara Arroyo, and Héctor Mejía, pp. 739–751. Museo Nacional de Arqueología y Etnología, Guatemala City.

Hansen, Thomas Blom, and Finn Stepputat 2006 Sovereignty Revisited. *Annual Review of Anthropology* 35:295–315.

Hanson, Victor Davis 1998 *Warfare and Agriculture in Classical Greece*. University of California Press, Berkeley.

Harrison-Buck, Eleanor 2016 Killing the "Kings of Stone": The Defacement of Classic Maya Monuments. In *Ritual, Violence, and the Fall of Classic Maya Kings*, edited by Gyles Iannone, Brett A. Houk, and Sonja A. Schwake, pp. 61–88. University Press of Florida, Gainesville.

Harrison-Buck, Eleanor, and Patricia A. McAnany 2013 Terminal Classic Circular Architecture in the Sibun Valley, Belize. *Ancient Mesoamerica* 24(2):295–306.

Hassig, Ross 1985 *Trade, Tribute, and Transportation: The Sixteenth Century Political Economy of the Valley of Mexico*. University of Oklahoma Press, Norman.

——1988 *Aztec Warfare: Imperial Expansion and Political Control*. University of Oklahoma Press, Norman.

——1992 *War and Society in Ancient Mesoamerica*. University of California Press, Berkeley.

——2016 *Polygamy and the Rise and Demise of the Aztec Empire*. University of New Mexico Press, Albuquerque.

Haviland, William A. 1967 Stature at Tikal, Guatemala: Implications for Ancient Maya Demography and Social Organization. *American Antiquity* 32(3):316–325.

——1977 Dynastic Genealogies from Tikal, Guatemala: Implications for Descent and Political Organization. *American Antiquity* 42:61–67.

——1981 Dower Houses and Minor Centers at Tikal, Guatemala: An Investigation into the Identification of Valid Units in Settlement Hierarchies. In *Lowland Maya Settlement Patterns*, edited by Wendy Ashmore, pp. 89–117. School of American Research. University of New Mexico Press, Albuquerque.

Heitzman, James 1997 *Gifts of Power: Lordship in an Early Indian State*. Oxford University Press, New Delhi.

Hellmuth, Nicholas M. 1977 Cholti-Lacandon (Chiapas) and Petén-Ytzá Agriculture, Settlement Pattern and Population. In *Social Process in Maya Prehistory*, edited by Norman Hammond, pp. 421–448. Academic Press, London.

Helmke, Christophe 2009 Ancient Maya Cave Usage as Attested in the Glyphic Corpus of the Maya Lowlands and the Caves of the Roaring Creek Valley, Belize. PhD thesis, University College London.

Helmke, Christophe, Christopher R. Andres, Shawn G. Morton, and Gabriel D. Wrobel 2015 For the Love of the Game: The Ballplayer Panels of Tipan Chen Uitz in Light of Late Classic Athletic Hegemony. *PARI Journal* 16(2):1–30.

Helmke, Christophe, and Jaime Awe 2012 Ancient Maya Political Organisation of Central Belize: Confluence of Archaeological and Epigraphic Data. *Contributions in New World Archaeology* 4:59–90.

——2016a Death Becomes Her: An Analysis of Panel 3, Xunantunich, Belize. *PARI Journal* 16(4):1–14.

——2016b Sharper Than a Serpent's Tooth: A Tale of the Snake-Head Dynasty as Recounted on Xunantunich Panel 4. *PARI Journal* 17(2):1–22.

Helmke, Christophe, Stanley P. Guenter, and Phillip Wanyerka 2018 Kings of the East: Altun Ha and the Water Scroll Emblem Glyph. *Ancient Mesoamerica* 29:113–135.

Helmke, Christophe, Julie A. Hoggarth, and Jamie J. Awe 2018 *A Reading of the Komkom Vase Discovered at Baking Pot, Belize.* Precolumbia-Mesoweb Press, San Francisco.

Helmke, Christophe, and Felix A. Kupprat 2016 Where Snakes Abound: Supernatural Places of Origin and Founding Myths in the Titles of Classic Maya Kings. In *Places of Power and Memory in Mesoamerica's Past and Present: How Toponyms, Landscapes and Boundaries Shape History and Remembrance*, edited by Daniel Graña-Behrens, pp. 33–83. Indiana series. Gebrüder Mann Verlag, Berlin.

Helmke, Christophe, and Dorie Reents-Budet 2008 A Terminal Classic Molded-Carved Ceramic Type of the Eastern Maya Lowlands. *Research Reports in Belizean Archaeology, Volume 5*, edited by John Morris, Sherilyne Jones, Jaime Awe, and Christophe Helmke, pp. 37–49. Institute of Archaeology, NICH, Belize.

Hempel, Carl Gustav 1942 The Function of General Laws in History. *The Journal of Philosophy* 39(1):35–48.

Hernández, Elsa C. 1984 *Investigaciones Arqueológicas en el Valle del Rio Tulijá, Tabsaco-Chipas.* Proyecto Tierras Bajas Noroccidentales, Vol. III. Universidad Nacional Autónoma de México, Mexico City.

Hinsley, Francis H. 1966 *Sovereignty.* Basic Books, New York.

Hirth, Kenneth G. 2003 The Altepetl and Urban Structure in Prehispanic Mesoamerica. In *El Urbanismo en Mesoamérica/Urbanism in Mesoamerica, Volume 1*, edited by William T. Sanders, Alba Guadalupe Mastache, and Robert H. Cobean, pp. 58–85. Instituto Nacional de Antropología e Historia and The Pennsylvania State University. Mexico City and University Park.

Hirth, Kenneth G., and Joanne Pillsbury (eds.) 2013 *Merchants, Markets, and Exchange in the Pre-Columbian World.* Dumbarton Oaks Research Library and Collection, Washington D.C.

Hobbes, Thomas 1985[1651] *Leviathan*, edited by C. B. Macpherson. Penguin, Harmondsworth.

Hocart, Arthur M. 1927 *Kingship.* Clarendon Press, Oxford.

——1933 *The Progress of Man: A Short Survey of His Evolution, His Customs and His Works.* Methuen, London.

Hodder, Ian 1982 Theoretical Archaeology: A Reactionary View. In *Symbolic and Structural Archaeology*, edited by Ian Hodder, pp. 1–16. Cambridge University Press, Cambridge.

——1985 Postprocessual Archaeology. In *Advances in Archaeological Method and Theory*, edited by M. B. Schiffer, pp. 1–26. Academic Press, New York.

——1986 *Reading the Past: Current Approaches to Interpretation in Archaeology.* Cambridge University Press, Cambridge.

——1987 The Contribution of the Long-Term. In *Archaeology as Long-Term History*, edited by Ian Hodder, pp. 1–8. Cambridge University Press, Cambridge.

Hodell, David A., Jason H. Curtis, and Mark Brenner 1995 Possible Role of Climate in the Collapse of Classic Maya Civilization. *Nature* 375:391–394.

Hoggarth, Julie A., Matthew Restall, James W. Wood, and Douglas J. Kennett 2017 Drought and Its Demographic Effects in the Maya Lowlands. *Current Anthropology* 58(1):82–113.

Hopkins, Nicholas A. 1991 Classic and Modern Relationship Terms and the "Child of Mother" Glyph (TI:606.23). In *Sixth Palenque Round Table, 1986*, edited by Merle Greene Robertson, and Virginia M. Fields, pp. 255–265. University of Oklahoma Press, Norman.

Hofling, Charles Andrew 2011 *Mopan Maya-Spanish-English Dictionary*. University of Utah Press, Salt Lake City.

Hoppan, Jean-Michel 1996 Nuevos datos sobre las inscripciones de Comalcalco. In *Eighth Palenque Round Table, 1993 Vol.X*, edited by Martha Macri, and Merle Greene Robertson, pp. 153–158. Pre-Columbian Art Research Institute, San Francisco.

Hotaling, Lorren 1995 A Reply to Werner Nahm: Maya Warfare and the Venus Year. *Mexicon* 17(2):32–37.

Houston, Stephen D. 1983a A Reading for the "Flint-Shield" Glyph. In *Contributions to Maya Hieroglyphic Decipherment I*, edited by Stephen D. Houston, pp. 13–25. HRAFlex Books, New Haven.

——1983b Warfare between Naranjo and Ucanal. In *Contributions to Maya Hieroglyphic Decipherment I*, edited by Stephen D. Houston, pp. 31–39. HRAFlex Books, New Haven.

——1986 *Problematic Emblem Glyphs: Examples from Altar de Sacrificios, El Chorro, Río Azul, and Xultun*. Research Reports on Ancient Maya Writing 3. Center for Maya Research, Washington, D.C.

——1987 Appendix II: Notes on Caracol Epigraphy and its Significance. In *Investigations at the Classic Maya City of Caracol, Belize: 1985–1987*, edited by Arlen Chase, and Diane Chase, pp. 85–100. Pre-Columbian Art Research Institute Monograph 3. San Francisco.

——1991 Appendix: Caracol Altar 21. In *Sixth Palenque Round Table, 1986*, edited by Merle Greene Robertson, and Virginia M. Fields,

pp. 38–42. University of Oklahoma Press, Norman.

——1992 Classic Maya Politics. In *New Theories on the Ancient Maya*, edited by Elin C. Danien, and Robert J. Sharer, pp. 65–69. The University Museum, University of Pennsylvania, Philadelphia.

——1993 *Hieroglyphs and History at Dos Pilas: Dynastic Politics of the Classic Maya*. University of Texas Press, Austin.

——1994 Literacy among the Pre-Columbian Maya: A Comparative Perspective. In *Writing Without Words: Alternative Literacies in Mesoamerica and the Andes*, edited by Elizabeth Hill Boone, and Walter D. Mignolo, pp. 27–49. Duke University Press, Durham.

——1996 Symbolic Sweatbaths of the Maya: Architectural Meaning in the Cross Group at Palenque, Mexico. *Latin American Antiquity* 7 (2):132–151.

——1997a The Shifting Now: Aspect, Deixis, and Narrative in Classic Maya Texts. *American Anthropologist* 99(2):291–305.

——1997b A King Worth a Hill of Beans. *Archaeology* 50(3):40.

——1998 Classic Maya Depictions of the Built Environment. In *Function and Meaning in Classic Maya Architecture*, edited by Stephen D. Houston, pp. 333–372. Dumbarton Oaks Research Library and Collection, Washington D.C.

——2000 Into the Minds of Ancients: Advances in Maya Glyph Studies. In *Journal of World Prehistory* 14(2):121–202.

——2004 The Archaeology of Communication Technologies. *Annual Review of Anthropology* 33:223–250.

——2006 Impersonation, Dance, and the Problem of Spectacle among the Classic Maya. In *Archaeology of Performance: Theaters of Power, Community, and Politics*, edited by Takeshi Inomata, and Lawrence S. Coben, pp. 135–155. Altamira Press, Walnut Creek.

——2008a In the Shadow of a Giant. Mesoweb. www.mesoweb.com/zotz/articles/Shadow-of-a-Giant.pdf

——2008b The Epigraphy of El Zotz. *Mesoweb*. www.mesoweb.com/zotz/articles/ZotzEpigraphy .pdf

——2009 A Splendid Predicament: Young Men in Classic Maya Society. *Cambridge Archaeological Journal* 19(2):149–178.

——2012 The Good Prince: Transition, Texting and Moral Narrative in the Murals of Bonampak, Chiapas, Mexico. *Cambridge Archaeological Journal* 22(2):153–175.

——2014a *Pehk* and "Parliaments". *Maya Decipherment*. https://decipherment .wordpress.com/2014/10/07/pehk-and-parliaments

——2014b Concubines and Carnal Commerce. *Maya Decipherment*. https://decipherment .wordpress.com/2014/06/08/courtesans-and-carnal-commerce/

——2016 Crafting Credit: Authorship among Classic Maya Painters and Sculptors. In *Making Value, Making Meaning: Techné in the Pre-Columbian World*, edited by Cathy L. Costin, pp. 391–431. Dumbarton Oaks Research Library and Collection, Washington, D.C.

——2017 Tributary Texts. *Maya Decipherment*. https://decipherment.wordpress.com/2017/ 01/07/tributary-texts/

Houston, Stephen D., Oswaldo Chinchilla, and David Stuart (eds.) 2001 *The Decipherment of Ancient Maya Writing*. University of Oklahoma Press, Norman.

Houston, Stephen D., and Hector Escobedo 1997 Descifrando la politica Maya: Perspectivas arqueologicas y epigraficas sobre el concepto de los estados segmentarios. In *X Simposio de Investigaciones Arqueologicas en Guatemala, 1996*, edited by Juan Pedro Laporte and Hector L. Escobedo, pp. 463–481. Ministerio de Cultura y Deportes, Guatemala.

Houston, Stephen D., Héctor Escobedo, Mark Child, Charles Golden, and René Muñoz 2003 The Moral Community: Maya Settlement Transformation at Piedras Negras, Guatemala. In *The Social Construction of Ancient Cities*, edited by Monica L. Smith, pp. 212–253. Smithsonian Institution Press, Washington, D.C.

Houston, Stephen D., Hector Escobedo, Perry Hardin, Richard Terry, David Webster, Mark Child, Charles Golden, Kitty Emery, and David Stuart 1999 Between Mountains and Sea: Investigations at Piedras Negras, Guatemala, 1998. *Mexicon* 21(1):10–17.

Houston, Stephen D., Charles Golden, A. René Muñoz, and Andrew K. Scherer 2006 *A Yaxchilan-style Lintel Possibly from Retalteco, Petén, Guatemala*. Research Reports on Ancient Maya Writing 61. www.utmesoamerica.org/ pdfmeso/RRAMW61.pdf

Houston, Stephen D., and Takeshi Inomata 2009 *The Classic Maya*. Cambridge University Press, Cambridge.

Houston, Stephen D., and Simon Martin 2016 Through Seeing Stones: Maya Epigraphy as a Mature Discipline. *Antiquity* 90:443–455.

Houston, Stephen D., and Peter Mathews 1985 *The Dynastic Sequence of Dos Pilas, Guatemala*. Pre-Columbian Art Research Institute Monograph 1. Pre-Columbian Art Research Institute, San Francisco.

Houston, Stephen D., and Patricia A. McAnany 2003 Bodies and Blood: Critiquing Social Construction in Maya Archaeology. *Journal of Anthropological Anthropology* 22:26–41.

Houston, Stephen D., John Robertson, and David Stuart 2001 *Quality and Quantity in Glyphic Nouns and Adjectives (Calidad y cantidad en sustantivos y adjetivos glíficos)*. Research Reports on Ancient Maya Writing 47. Center for Maya Research, Washington, D.C.

Houston, Stephen D., and David Stuart 1989 *The Way Glyph: Evidence for "Co-essences" among the Classic Maya*. Research Reports on Ancient Maya Writing 30. Center for Maya Research, Washington D.C.

——1996 Of Gods, Glyphs and Kings: Divinity and Rulership among the Classic Maya. *Antiquity* 70:289–312.

——1998 The Ancient Maya Self: Personhood and Portraiture in the Classic Period. *Res: Anthropology and Aesthetics* 33:73–101.

——2001 Peopling the Classic Maya Court. In *Royal Courts of the Ancient Maya, Volume 1*, edited by Takeshi Inomata, and Stephen D. Houston, pp. 54–83. Westview Press, Boulder.

——2008 "They . . . Accomplished the Matter Betwixt Them": Rediscovered Stucco Fragments from Palenque, Mexico. Unpublished manuscript available at Rediscovered Stucco Glyphs from Palenque. *Maya Decipherment*. https://decipherment.wordpress.com/2008/11/08/rediscovered-stucco-glyphs-from-palenque/

Houston, Stephen D., David Stuart, and John Robertson 1998 Disharmony in Maya Hieroglyphic Writing: Linguistic Change and Continuity in Classic Society. In *Anatomia de una Civilizacion. Aproximaciones Interdisciplinarias a la Cultura Maya*, edited by A. Cuidad Ruiz, Y. Fernández Marquínez, J. M. García Campillo, M. J. Iglesias Ponce de León, A. Lacadena García-Gallo, and L. T. Sanz Castro, pp. 275–296. Sociedad Española de Estudios Mayas, Madrid.

Houston, Stephen D., David Stuart, and Karl A. Taube 1992 Text and Image on the "Jauncy Vase". In *The Maya Vase Book, Volume 3: A Corpus of Roll-Out Photographs*, edited by Justin Kerr, pp. 499–512. Kerr Associates, New York.

——2006 *The Memory of Bones: Body, Being, and Experience among the Classic Maya*. University of Texas Press, Austin.

Houston, Stephen D., Stacey Symonds, David Stuart, and Arthur Demarest 1992 A Civil War of the Late Classic Period: Evidence from Hieroglyphic Stairway 4. Unpublished manuscript.

Houston, Stephen, and Karl Taube 2000 An Archaeology of the Senses: Perception and Cultural Expression in Ancient Mesoamerica. *Cambridge Archaeological Journal* 10(2):261–294.

Hsu, Cho-yun 1990 The Spring and Autumn Period. In *The Cambridge History of Ancient China: From the Origins of Civilization to 221 B.C.*, edited by Michael Loewe, and Edward L. Shaughnessy, pp. 545–586. Cambridge University Press, Cambridge.

Hughes, Jennifer 2016 Cradling the Sacred: Image, Ritual, and Affect in Mexican and Mesoamerican Material Religion. *History of Religions* 56(1):55–107.

Hui, Victoria Tin-bor 2004 Problematizing Sovereignty: Relative Sovereignty in the Historical Transformation of Interstate and State-Society Relations. In *International Interaction in the Post-Cold War World: Moral Responsibility and Power Politics*, edited by Michael C. Davis, Wolfgang Dietrich, Bettina Scholdan, and Dieter Sepp, pp. 83–103. M. E. Sharpe, New York.

——2005 *War and State Formation in Ancient China and Modern Europe*. Cambridge University Press, Cambridge.

Hull. Kerry 2003 Verbal Art and Performance in Ch'orti' and Maya Hieroglyphic Writing. PhD dissertation, University of Texas at Austin.

Hvidtfeldt, Arild 1958 *Teotl and Ixiptlantli: Some Central Conceptions in Ancient Mexican Religion*. Andreassen and Co., Copenhagen.

Iannone, Gyles 2016 Cross-Cultural Perspectives on the Scapegoat King: The Anatomy of a Model. In *Ritual, Violence, and the Fall of Classic Maya Kings*, edited by Gyles Iannone, Brett A. Houk, and Sonja A. Schwake, pp. 23–60. University Press of Florida, Gainesville.

Iannone, Gyles, Brett A. Houk, and Sonja A. Schwake (eds.) 2016 *Ritual, Violence, and the Fall of Classic Maya Kings*. University Press of Florida, Gainesville.

Ikenberry, G. John, and Charles A. Kupchan 1990 Socialization and Hegemonic Power. *International Organization* 44(3):283–315.

Imada, Takatoshi 2008 *Self-Organization and Society*. Springer, Tokyo.

Inden, Ronald 1981 Hierarchies of Kings in Early Medieval India. *Contributions to Indian Sociology* 15:99–125.

——1990 *Imagining India*. Blackwell, Oxford.

Inomata, Takeshi 1997 The Last Day of a Fortified Classic Maya Center: Archaeological Investigations at Aguateca, Guatemala. *Ancient Mesoamerica* 1997:337–351.

——2001 King's People: Classic Maya Courtiers in a Comparative Perspective. In *Royal Courts of the Ancient Maya, Volume 1*, edited by Takeshi Inomata, and Stephen D. Houston, pp. 27–53. Westview Press, Boulder.

——2004 The Spatial Mobility of Non-elite Populations in Classic Maya Society and its Political Implications. In *Ancient Maya Commoners*, edited by Jon C. Lohse, and Fred Valdez Jr., pp. 175–196. University of Texas Press, Austin.

——2008 *Warfare and the Fall of a Fortified Center: Archaeological Investigations at Aguateca.* Vanderbilt Institute of Mesoamerican Archaeology, Volume 3. Vanderbilt University Press, Nashville.

——2014 War, Violence, and Society in the Maya Lowlands. In *Embattled Bodies, Embattled Places: War in Pre-Columbian Mesoamerica and the Andes,* edited by Andrew K. Scherer, and John W. Verano, pp. 25–56. Dumbarton Oaks Research Library and Collection, Washington, D.C.

Inomata, Takeshi, and Stephen D. Houston 2001 *Royal Courts of the Ancient Maya, Volume 1.* Westview Press, Boulder.

——2002 *Royal Courts of the Ancient Maya, Volume 2.* Westview Press, Boulder.

Inomata, Takeshi, Erick Ponciano, Oswaldo Chinchilla, Otto Román, Véronique Breuil-Martínez, and Oscar Santos 2004 An Unfinished Temple at the Classic Maya Centre of Aguateca, Guatemala. *Antiquity* 78:798–811.

Inomata, Takeshi, and Laura R. Stiver 1998 Floor Assemblages from Burned Structures at Aguateca, Guatemala: A Study of Classic Maya Households. *Journal of Field Archaeology* 25(4):431–452.

Inomata, Takeshi, and Daniela Triadan 2000 Craft Production by Classic Maya Elites in Domestic Settings: Data from Rapidly Abandoned Structure at Aguateca, Guatemala. *Mayab* 13:57–66.

——2009 Culture and Practice of War in Maya Society. In *Warfare in Cultural Context: Practice, Agency and the Archaeology of Violence,* edited by Axel E. Nielsen, and William H. Walker, pp. 56–83. The University of Arizona Press, Tucson.

Inomata, Takeshi, Daniela Triadan, Kazuo Aoyama, Victor Castillo, and Hitoshi Yonenobu 2013 Early Ceremonial Constructions at Ceibal, Guatemala, and the Origins of Lowland Maya Civilization. *Science* 340(6131):467–471.

Inomata, Takeshi, Daniela Triadan, Jessica MacLellan, Melissa Burham, Kazuo Aoyama, Juan Manuel Palomo, Hitoshi Yonenobu, Flory Pinzón, and Hiroo Nasu 2017 High-precision radiocarbon dating of political collapse and dynastic origins at the Maya site of Ceibal, Guatemala. *Proceedings of the National Academy of Sciences* 114(6):1293–1298.

Inomata, Takeshi, Daniela Triadan, Erick Ponciano, Estela Pinto, Richard E. Terry, and Marcus Eberl 2002 Domestic and Political Lives of Classic Maya Elites: The Excavation of Rapidly Abandoned Structures at Aguateca, Guatemala. *Latin American Antiquity* 13:305–330.

Isendahl, Christian 2012 Agro-Urban Landscapes: The Example of Maya Lowland Cities. *Antiquity* 86:1112–1125.

Ishihara, Reiko, Karl A. Taube, and Jamie J. Awe 2006 The Water Lily Serpent Masks at Caracol, Belize. In *Research Reports in Belizean Archaeology, Volume 3,* edited by John Morris, Sherilyne Jones, Jaime Awe, and Christophe Helmke, pp. 213–223. Institute of Archaeology, Belmopan.

Ixtlilxochitl, Fernando de Alva 1952 *Obras Históricas,* edited by Alfredo Chavero, 2 vols. Universidad Nacional Autónoma de México, Mexico City.

Jackson, Sarah E. 2005 Deciphering Classic Maya Political Hierarchy: Epigraphic, Archaeological, and Ethnographic Perspectives on the Courtly Elite. PhD dissertation, Harvard University.

——2013 *Politics of the Maya Royal Court: Hierarchy and Change in the Late Classic Period.* University of Oklahoma Press, Norman.

Jackson, Sarah, and David Stuart 2001 The *Aj K'uhun* Title: Deciphering a Classic Maya Term of Rank. *Ancient Mesoamerica* 12:217–228.

Jansen, Maarten, and Gabina Aurora Pérez 2011 *The Mixtec Pictorial Manuscripts: Time, Agency and Memory in Ancient Mexico.* The Early Americas: History and Culture, Volume 1. Brill, Leiden.

Jaski, Bart 2000 *Early Irish Kingship and Succession.* Four Courts Press, Dublin.

Jenkins, Keith 1991 *Rethinking History.* Routledge, London.

Jervis, Robert 1978 Cooperation Under the Security Dilemma. *World Politics* 30(2):167–214.

Joffe, Alexander H. 1998 Disembedded Capitals in Western Asian Perspective. *Comparative Studies in Society and History* 40:549–580.

Johnson, Gregory A. 1972 A Test of the Utility of Central Place Theory in Archaeology. In *Man, Settlement, and Urbanism*, edited by Peter J. Ucko, Ruth Tringham, and G. W. Dimbleby, pp. 769–785. Duckworth, London.

Johnston, Kevin 1985 Maya Dynastic Territorial Expansion: Glyphic Evidence from Classic Centers of the Pasión River, Guatemala. In *Fifth Palenque Round Table, 1983*, edited by Virginia M. Fields, pp. 49–56. Pre-Columbian Art Research Institute, San Francisco.

———2006 Preclassic Maya Occupation of the Itzan Escarpment, Lower Río de la Pasión, Petén, Guatemala. *Ancient Mesoamerica* 17 (2):177–201.

Jones, Christopher 1977 Inauguration Dates of Three Late Classic rulers of Tikal, Guatemala. *American Antiquity* 42:28–60.

———1987 The Life and Times of Ah Cacau, Ruler of Tikal. In *Primer Simposio Mundial sobre Epigraphía Maya*, pp. 107–120. Asociación Tikal, Guatemala.

———1991 Cycles of Growth at Tikal. In: *Classic Maya Political History: Hieroglyphic and Archaeological Evidence*, edited by T. Patrick Culbert, pp. 102–127. School of American Research Advanced Seminar Series. Cambridge University Press, Cambridge.

———1996 Excavations in the East Plaza of Tikal. *Tikal Report 16*. University of Pennsylvania Museum, Philadelphia.

———1999 El comercio y las rutas de intercambio de los mayas. In *Epoca precolombina*. edited by Marian Popenoe de Hatch, pp. 479–486. Historia General de Guatemala 1. Asociación de Amigos del País, Fundacion para la Cultura y el Desarrollo, Guatemala.

———2015 The Marketplace at Tikal. In *The Ancient Maya Marketplace: The Archaeology of Transient Space*, edited by Eleanor M. King, pp. 67–89. University of Arizona Press, Tucson.

Jones, Christopher, and Linton Satterthwaite 1982 The Monuments and Inscriptions of Tikal: The Carved Monuments. *Tikal Report No. 33, Part A*. University Museum Monograph 44. The University Museum, University of Pennsylvania, Philadelphia.

Jones, Christopher, and Robert J. Sharer Forthcoming Archaeological Investigations in the Site Core, Quirigua, Izabal, Guatemala (1975–1979). *Quirigua Reports V* (Museum Monographs). Museum of Archaeology and Anthropology, University of Pennsylvania, Philadelphia.

Jones, Grant D. 1998 *The Conquest of the Last Maya Kingdom*. Stanford University Press, Stanford.

Josserand, J. Kathryn 2002 Women in Classic Maya Hieroglyphic Texts. In *Ancient Maya Women*, edited by Traci Ardren, pp. 114–151. Altamira Press, Walnut Creek.

———2007 The Missing Heir at Yaxchilan: Literary Analysis of a Maya Historical Puzzle. *Latin American Antiquity* 18(3):295–312.

Joyce, Rosemary 2000 High Culture, Mesoamerican Civilization, and the Classic Maya Tradition. In *Order, Legitimacy, and Wealth in Ancient States*, edited by Janet Richards, and Mary Van Buren, pp. 64–76. Cambridge University Press, Cambridge.

Joyce, Thomas A. 1914 *Mexican Archaeology*. Philip Lee Warner, London.

Just, Bryan B. 2006 Visual Discourse of Ninth-Century Stelae at Machaquila and Seibal. PhD dissertation, Tulane University, New Orleans.

Justeson, John S. 1989 Ancient Maya Ethnoastronomy: An Overview of Hieroglyphic Sources. In *World Archaeoastronomy*, edited by Anthony F. Aveni, pp. 76–129. Cambridge University Press, Cambridge.

Justeson, John S., William M. Norman, Lyle Campbell, and Terence Kaufman 1985 *Foreign Impact on Lowland Mayan Language and Script*. Middle American Research Institute, Tulane University, Publication 53, New Orleans.

Kaplan, Martha, 1995 *Neither Cargo nor Cult: Ritual Politics and the Colonial Imagination in Fiji*. Duke University Press, Durham.

Kaplan, Morton A. 1957 *System and Process in International Politics*. Wiley, New York.

Karl, Raimund 2006 Celtoscepticism: A Convenient Excuse for Ignoring Non-Archaeological Evidence? In *Archaeology and Ancient History: Breaking Down the Boundaries*, edited by Eberhard W. Sauer, pp. 185–199. Routledge, London.

Kauffman, Stuart 1993 *The Origins of Order: Self-Organization and Selection in Evolution*. Oxford University Press, Oxford.

Kaufman, Stuart J., Richard Little, and William C. Wohlforth (eds.) 2007 *The Balance of Power in World History*. Palgrave MacMillan, New York.

Kaufman, Terrance S. 2003 A Preliminary Mayan Etymological Dictionary. www.famsi.org/reports/01051/pmed.pdf

Kaufman, Terrence S., and William M. Norman 1984 An Outline of Proto-Cholan Phonology, Morphology and Vocabulary. In *Phoneticism in Mayan Hieroglyphic Writing*, edited by John S. Justeson, and Lyle Campbell, pp. 77-166. Institute for Mesoamerican Studies, Publication No. 9. State University of New York at Albany, Albany.

Kehoe, Alice Beck 1998 *The Land of Prehistory: A Critical History of American Archaeology*. Routledge, New York and London.

———2000 *Shamans and Religion: An Anthropological Exploration in Critical Thinking*. Waveland Press, Long Grove.

Keller, Angela H. 2009 A Road by Any Other Name: Trails, Paths, and Roads in Maya Language and Thought. In *Landscapes of Movement: Trails, Paths, and Roads in Anthropological Perspective*, edited by James E. Snead, Clark L. Erickson, and J. Andrew Darling, pp. 133–157. University of Pennsylvania Museum of Archaeology and Anthropology, Philadelphia.

Kelley, David H. 1962a Glyphic Evidence for a Dynastic Sequence at Quirigua, Guatemala. *American Antiquity* 27: 323–335.

———1962b Fonestismo en la Escritura Maya. *Estudios de Cultura Maya* 2:277–317.

———1965 The Birth of the Gods at Palenque. *Estudios de Cultura Maya* 5:93–134.

———1968 Kakupacal and the Itzas. *Estudios de Cultura Maya* 7:255–268.

———1976 *Deciphering the Maya Script*. University of Texas Press, Austin.

———1977 Maya Astronomical Tables and Inscriptions. In *Native American Astronomy*, edited by A. F. Aveni, pp. 57–74. University of Texas Press, Austin.

Kelley, David H., and K. Ann Kerr 1973 Maya Astronomy and Astronomical Glyphs. In *Mesoamerican Writing Systems*, edited by Elizabeth P. Benson, pp. 179–215. Dumbarton Oaks Research Library and Collections, Washington, D.C.

Kennett, Douglas J., Sebastian F. M. Breitenbach, Valorie V. Aquino, Yemane Asmerom, Jaime Awe, James U. L. Baldini, Patrick Bartlein, Brendan J. Culleton, Claire Ebert, Christopher Jazwa, Martha J. Macri, Norbert Marwan, Victor Polyak, Keith M. Prufer, Harriet E. Ridley, Harald Sodemann, Bruce Winterhalder, and Gerald H. Haug 2012 Development and Disintegration of Maya Political Systems in Response to Climate Change. *Science* 388:788–991.

Kerr, Justin 1992 *The Maya Vase Book: A Corpus of Rollout Photographs of Maya Vases, Volume 3*. Kerr Associates, New York.

Kerr, Barbara, and Justin Kerr 1997 *The Maya Vase Book: A Corpus of Rollout Photographs of Maya Vases, Volume 5*. Kerr Associates, New York.

———2000 *The Maya Vase Book: A Corpus of Rollout Photographs of Maya Vases, Volume 6*. Kerr Associates, New York.

King, Eleanor M. (ed.) 2015 *The Ancient Maya Marketplace: The Archaeology of Transient Space*. The University of Arizona Press, Tucson.

Kingsborough, Edward King, Viscount 1831–1848 *Antiquities of Mexico: Comprising Facsimiles of Ancient Mexican Paintings and Hieroglyphics*. 9 vols. Robert Havell, London.

Kingsley, Melanie J., Charles W. Golden, Andrew K. Scherer, and Luz Midilia Marroquin de Franco 2012 Parallelism in Occupation: Tracking the Pre- and Post-Dynastic Evolution of Piedras Negras, Guatemala, through its Secondary Site, El Porvenir. *Mexicon* 34(5):109–117.

Kistler, S. Ashley 2003 The Search for Five-Flower Mountain: Reevaluating the Cancuen Panel. Mesoweb. www.mesoweb.com/features/kistler/Cancuen.pdf.

Klein, Cecilia F., Eulogio Guzmán, Elisa C. Mandell, and Maya Stanfield-Mazzi 2002 The Role of Shamanism in Mesoamerican

Art: A Reassessment. *Current Anthropology* 43 (3):383–419.

Knapp, A. Bernard (ed.) 1992 *Archaeology, Annales, and Ethnohistory.* Cambridge University Press, Cambridge.

Knappett, Carl (ed.) 2013 *Network Analysis in Archaeology: New Approaches to Regional Interaction.* Oxford University Press, Oxford.

Knorozov, Yuri V. 1952 Древняя письменность Центральной Америки (Drevnyaya pis'mennost' Tsentral'noy Ameriki). *Советская этнография (Sovietskaya Etnografiya)* 3 (2): 100–118.

——1956 New Data on the Maya Written Language. *Journal de la Société des Américanistes* 45:209–217.

——1958 New Data on the Maya Written Language. Proceedings of the Thirty-Second International Congress of Americanists, pp. 284–291. Salt Lake City.

Kohl, Philip L. 1984 Force, History, and the Evolutionist Paradigm. In *Marxist Perspectives in Archaeology*, edited by Matthew Spriggs, pp. 127–134. Cambridge University Press, Cambridge.

Kowalski, Jeff Karl 1989 Who Am I among the Itza?: Links between Northern Yucatan and the Western Maya Lowlands and Highlands. In *Mesoamerica after the Decline of Teotihuacan AD 700–900*, edited by Richard A. Diehl, and Janet C. Berlo, pp. 173–185. Dumbarton Oaks Research Library and Collection, Washington D.C.

——2007 What's "Toltec" at Uxmal and Chichén Itzá? Merging Maya and Mesoamerican Worldviews and World Systems in Terminal Classic to Early Postclassic Yucatan. In *Twin Tollans: Chichén Itzá, Tula, and the Epiclassic to Early Postclassic Mesoamerican World*, edited by Jeff Karl Kowalski, and Cynthia Kristan-Graham, pp. 251–313. Dumbarton Oaks Research Library and Collection, Washington D.C.

Krasner, Stephen D. 1999 *Sovereignty: Organized Hypocrisy.* Princeton University Press, Princeton.

——2001 Rethinking the Sovereign State Model. *Review of International Studies* 27 (1):17–42.

Kuhlken, Robert 1999 Warfare and Intensive Agriculture in Fiji. In *The Prehistory of Food: Appetites for Change*, edited by Chris Gosden, and Jon Hather, pp. 270–287. Routledge, London.

Kulke, Hermann 1993 *Kings and Cults: State Formation and Legitimation in India and Southeast Asia.* Manohar, New Delhi.

——1995a The Early and the Imperial Kingdom: A Processual Model of Integrative State Formation in Early Medieval India. In *The State in India 1000–1700*, edited by Hermann Kulke, pp. 233–262. Oxford University Press, New Delhi.

——1995b Introduction: The Study of the State in Pre-modern India. In *The State in India 1000–1700*, edited by Hermann Kulke, pp. 1–47. Oxford University Press, New Delhi.

Lacadena, Alfonso 1992 El anillo jeroglífico del juego de pelota de Oxkintok, in *Oxkintok 4, Misión Arqueológica de España en México, Proyecto Oxkintok Año 1990*, edited by M. Rivera Dorado, pp. 177–184. Ministerio de Cultura, Madrid.

——1996 A New Proposal for the Transcription of the A-k'u-na/A-k'u-HUN-na Title. *Mayab* 10:46–49.

——2004 Passive Voice in Classic Mayan Texts: CV-*h*-C-*aj* and –*n*-*aj* Constructions. In *The Linguistics of Maya Writing*, edited by Søren Wichmann, pp. 165–194. University of Utah Press, Salt Lake City.

——2005 Los Jeroglíficos de Ek' Balam. *Arqueología Mexicana* 13(76):64–69.

——2008 El título *lakam*: evidencia epigráfica sobre la organización tributaria y militar interna de los reinos mayas del Clásico. *Mayab* 20:23–43.

——2011 Historia y ritual dinásticos en Machaquilá (Petén, Guatemala). *Revista Española de Antropología Americana* 41(1):205–240.

Lacadena, Alfonso, and Andrés Ciudad 1998 Reflexiones sobre la Estructura Política Maya Clássica. In *Anatomía de una Civilizacion. Aproximaciones Interdisciplinarias a la Cultura Maya*, edited by Andres Ciudad, Yolanda Fernández Marquínez, José Miguel García

Campillo, M. A. Josefa Iglesias Ponce de León, Alfonso Lacadena García-Gallo, and Luis T. Sanz Castro, pp. 31–64. Sociedad Española de Estudios Mayas, Madrid.

——2009 Migraciones y llegada: mito, historia y propaganda en los relatos mayas prehispánicos en las tierras bajas. In *Diásporas, migraciones y exilios en el mundo maya*, edited by Mario Humberto Ruz, Joan García Targa, and Andrés Ciudad, pp. 57–78. Sociedad Española de Estudios Mayas and Universidad Nacional Simon Martin Autónoma de México, Mérida.

Lacadena, Alfonso, and Søren Wichmann 2004 On the Representation of the Glottal Stop in Maya Writing. In *The Linguistics of Maya Writing*, edited by Søren Wichmann, pp. 103–162. University of Utah Press, Salt Lake City.

Lake, David 2007 Escape from the State of Nature: Authority and Hierarchy in World Politics. *International Security* 32(1):47–79.

——2009 *Hierarchy in International Relations*. Cornell University Press, Ithaca.

Landa, Fray Diego de 1941[1566] *Landa's Relación de las Cosas de Yucatán*. A translation edited with notes by Alfred M. Tozzer. Papers of the Peabody Museum of American Archaeology and Ethnology 18. Harvard University, Cambridge, MA.

Laporte, Juan Pedro 2004 Terminal Classic Settlement and Polity in the Mopan Valley, Petén, Guatemala. In *The Terminal Classic in the Maya Lowlands: Collapse, Transition, and Transformation*, edited by Arthur A. Demarest, Prudence M. Rice, and Donald S. Rice, pp. 195–230. University of Colorado Press, Boulder.

Laporte, Juan Pedro, and Vilma Fialko C. 1990 New Perspectives on Old Problems: Dynastic References for the Early Classic at Tikal. In *Vision and Revision in Maya Studies*, edited by Flora S. Clancy, and Peter D. Harrison, pp. 33–66. University of New Mexico Press, Albuquerque.

Laporte, Juan Pedro, and Héctor E. Mejía 2002 Ucanal: Una Cuidad del Río Mopan en Petén, Guatemala. *Utz'ib, Serie Reportes 1–2*. Asociación Tikal, Guatemala.

Las Casas, Bartolomé de 1909 *Apologética historia de las Indias*. 2 Vols. Nueva Biblioteca de Autores Españoles, Vol. 13. Bailly, Bailliere e hijos, Madrid.

Last, Jonathan 1995 The Nature of History. In *Interpreting Archaeology: Finding Meaning in the Past*, edited by Ian Hodder, Michael Shanks, Alexandra Alexandri, Victor Buchli, John Carman, Jonathan Last, and Gavin Lucas, pp. 141–157. Routledge, New York.

Latour, Bruno 2005 *Reassembling the Social: An Introduction to Actor-Network-Theory*. Oxford University Press, Oxford.

Laughlin, Robert M. 1975 *The Great Tzotzil Dictionary of San Lorenzo Zinacantan*. Smithsonian Contributions to Anthropology No.19, Smithsonian Institution Press, Washington D.C.

——1988 *The Great Tzotzil Dictionary of Santo Domingo Zinacantán. Volume I: Tzotzil-English*. Smithsonian Contributions to Anthropology No. 31. Smithsonian Institution Press, Washington, D.C.

Law, Daniel A. 2006 A Grammatical Description of the Early Classic Maya Inscriptions. MA Thesis, Brigham Young University.

Law, Danny, John Robertson, Stephen D. Houston, Marc Zender, and David Stuart 2014 Areal Shifts in Classic Maya Phonology. *Ancient Mesoamerica* 25(2): 357–366.

Layton, Robert 2003 Agency, Structuration, and Complexity. In *Complex Systems and Archaeology*, edited by R. Alexander Bentley, and Herbert D. G. Maschner, pp. 103–109. University of Utah Press, Salt Lake City.

LeCount, Lisa J. and Jason Yaeger (eds.) 2010 *Classic Maya Provincial Politics*. University of Arizona Press, Tucson.

Le Goff, Jacques 1988[1978] Préface à nouvelle édition. In *La Nouvelle Histoire*, second edition, edited by Jacques Le Goff, pp. 8–16. Éditions Complexe, Brussels.

Le Plongeon, Augustus 1886 *Sacred Mysteries among the Mayas and the Quichés 11,500 Years Ago: Their Relations to the Sacred Mysteries of Egypt, Greece, Chaldea, and India; or, Free Masonry in Times Anterior to the Temple of Solomon*. Robert Macoy, New York.

——1896 *Queen Móo and the Egyptian Sphinx*. Augustus Le Plongeon, New York.

Lebow, Richard N., and Robert Kelly 2001 Thucydides and Hegemony: Athens and the United States. *Review of International Studies* 27:593–609.

Lee, David F., and Jennifer C. Piehl 2014 Ritual and Remembrance at the Northwest Palace Complex, El Perú-Waka'. In *Archaeology at El Perú-Waka': Ancient Maya Performance of Ritual, Memory, and Power*, edited by Olivia C. Navarro-Farr, and Michelle Rich, pp. 85–101. The University of Arizona Press, Tucson.

LeFort, Geneviève 1998 Gods at War: Of War Protectors, Effigy Idols and Battle Banners among the Classic Maya. *Mayab* 11:12–22.

LeFort, Geneviève, and Robert F. Wald 1995 Large Numbers on Naranjo Stela 32. *Mexicon* 17(6):112–114.

Lehmann, Walter 1907 Ergebnisse und Aufgaben der mexikanistischen Forschung. *Archiv für Anthropologie, New Series* 6(2–3):113–168.

Lentner, Howard H. 2005 Hegemony and Autonomy. *Political Studies* 53:735–752.

Lévi-Strauss, Claude 1963 *Structural Anthropology*, translated by Claire Jacobson and Brooke Grundfest Schoepf. Basic Books, New York.

——1969 *Elementary Structures of Kinship*. Beacon Press, Boston.

——1973 *Tristes Tropiques*, translated by John Weightman and Doreen Weightman. Penguin Books, Harmonsworth.

Lewin, Roger 1992 *Complexity: Life at the Edge of Chaos*. Macmillan, New York.

Lewis, Mark E. 2000 The City-State in Spring-and-Autumn China. In *A Comparative Study of Thirty City-State Cultures: An Investigation Conducted by the Copenhagen Polis Centre*, edited by Mogens Herman Hansen, pp. 359–373. Historisk-Filosofiske Skrifter 21. Kongelige Danske Videnskabernes Selskab, Copenhagen.

Lincoln, Bruce 1994 *Authority: Construction and Corrosion*. University of Chicago Press, Chicago.

Lind, Michael D. 2000 Mixtec City-States and Mixtec City-State Culture. In *A Comparative Study of Thirty City-State Cultures: An Investigation Conducted by the Copenhagen Polis Centre*, edited by Mogens Herman Hansen, pp. 567–580. Historisk-Filosofiske Skrifter 21.

Kongelige Danske Videnskabernes Selskab, Copenhagen.

Liverani, Mario 1999 History and Archaeology in the Ancient Near East: 150 years of a Difficult Relationship. In *Fluchtpunkt Uruk. Archäologische Einheit aus methodischer Vielfalt. Schriften für Hans Jörg Nissen*, edited by Hartmut Kühne, Reinhard Bernbeck, Karin Bartl, and Hans Jörg Nissen, pp. 1–11. M. Leidorf, Rahden/Westf.

——2001 *International Relations in the Ancient Near East, 1600–1100 BC*. Palgrave, Basingstoke.

Lockhart, James 1992 *The Nahuas after the Conquest: A Social and Cultural History of the Indians of Central Mexico, Sixteenth Through Eighteenth Centuries*. Stanford University Press, Stanford.

Looper, Matthew G. 1991 A Reinterpretation of the Wooden Box from Tortuguero. Texas Notes on Pre-Columbian Art, Writing, and Culture 11. Department of Art, University of Texas at Austin, Austin, TX.

——1992 The Parentage of 'Smoking Squirrel' of Naranjo. Texas Notes on Pre-Columbian Art, Writing, and Culture 32. Department of Art, University of Texas at Austin, Austin, TX.

——1999 New Perspectives on the Late Classic Political History of Quiriguá, Guatemala. *Ancient Mesoamerica* 10(2):263–280.

——2003 *Lightning Warrior: Maya Art and Kingship at Quiriguá*. University of Texas Press, Austin.

Looper, Matthew G., Dorie Reents-Budet, and Ronald L. Bishop 2009 Dance on Classic Maya Ceramics. In *To Be Like Gods: Dance in Ancient Maya Civilization*, edited by Matthew G. Looper, pp. 113–150. University of Texas Press, Austin.

Looper, Matthew G., and Linda Schele 1991 A War at Palenque During the Reign of Ah-K'an. Texas Notes on Pre-Columbian Art, Writing, and Culture 25. Department of Art, University of Texas at Austin, Austin, TX.

Lothrop, Samuel K. 1924 *Tulum: An Archaeological Study of the East Cast of Yucatan*. Carnegie Institution of Washington Publication 335. Washington, D.C.

——1927 The Word "Maya" and the Fourth Voyage of Columbus. *Indian Notes* 4:350–363.

Lounsbury, Floyd 1973 On the Derivation and Reading of the "ben-ich" prefix. In *Mesoamerican Writing Systems*, edited by Elizabeth P. Benson, pp. 99–143. Dumbarton Oaks Library and Collection, Washington, D.C.

——1976 A Rationale for the Initial Date of the Temple of the Cross at Palenque. In *The Art, Iconography & Dynastic History of Palenque, Part III: The Proceedings of the Segunda Mesa Redonda de Palenque*, edited by Merle Greene Robertson, pp. 211–222. Robert Louis Stevenson School, Pebble Beach.

——1980 Some Problems in the Interpretation of the Mythological Portion of the Hieroglyphic Text of the Temple of the Cross at Palenque. In *Third Palenque Round Table, 1978*, edited by Merle Greene Robertson, pp. 99–115. University of Texas Press, Austin.

——1982 Astronomical Knowledge and its uses at Bonampak, Mexico. In *Archaeoastronomy in the New World*, edited by Anthony F. Aveni, pp. 143–169. Cambridge University Press, Cambridge.

——1984 Glyphic Substitution: Homophonic and Synonymic. In *Phoneticism in Mayan Hieroglyphic Writing*, Institute for Mesoamerican Studies Publication 9, edited by John S. Justeson, and Lyle Campbell, pp. 167–184. State University of New York at Albany, Albany.

——1985 The Identity of Mythological Figures in the Cross Group Inscriptions of Palenque. In *Fourth Palenque Round Table, 1980, Vol. VI*, edited by Elizabeth P. Benson, and Merle Greene Robertson, pp. 45–58. Pre-Columbian Art Research Institute, San Francisco.

——1989 The Names of a King: Hieroglyphic Variants as a Key to Decipherment. In *Word and Image in Maya Culture: Explorations in Language, Writing and Representation*, edited by William F. Hanks, and Don S. Rice, pp. 73–91. University of Utah Press, Salt Lake City.

Low, Polly 2007 *Interstate Relations in Classical Greece*. Cambridge University Press, Cambridge.

Lowe, John W. G. 1985 *The Dynamics of Apocalypse: A Systems Simulation of the Classic Maya Collapse*. University of New Mexico Press, Albuquerque.

Lowie, Robert H. 1927 *The Origin of the State*. Harcourt, Brace and Company, New York.

Lucero, Lisa J. 1999 Water Control and Maya Politics in the Southern Maya Lowlands. *Archeological Papers of the American Anthropological Association* 9(1):35–49.

——2003 The Politics of Ritual: The Emergence of Classic Maya Rulers. *Current Anthropology* 44(4):523–558.

Lucero, Lisa J., and Barbara W. Fash (eds.) 2006 *Precolumbian Water Management: Ideology, Ritual, and Power*. The University of Arizona Press, Tucson.

Luttwak, Edward N. 1976 *The Grand Strategy of the Roman Empire: From the First Century B.C. to the Third*. John Hopkins University Press, Baltimore.

Mack, William 2015 *Proxeny and Polis: Institutional Networks in the Ancient Greek World*. Oxford University Press, Oxford.

MacLeod, Barbara 1990 The God N/Step set in the Primary Standard Sequence. In *The Maya Vase Book, Volume 2: A corpus of roll-out photographs*, edited by Justin Kerr, pp. 331–347. Kerr Associates, New York.

——2004 A World in a Grain of Sand. In *The Linguistics of Maya Writing*, edited by Søren Wichmann, pp. 291–325. University of Utah Press, Salt Lake City.

Macri, Martha J. 1997 Noun Morphology and Possessive Constructions in Old Palenque Ch'ol. In *The Language of Maya Hieroglyphs*, edited by Martha Macri, and Annabel Ford, pp. 89–96. Pre-Columbian Art Research Institute, San Francisco.

Magaña, Victor, Jorge A. Amador, and Soccoro Medina 1999 The Midsummer Drought over Mexico and Central America. *Journal of Climate* 12(6):1577–1588.

Maler, Teobert 1901–1903 *Researches in the Central Portion of the Usumatsintla Valley: Report of Explorations for the Museum, 1898–1900*. Memoirs of the Peabody Museum of Archaeology and Ethnology 2(1–2). Harvard University, Cambridge, MA.

——1908a *Explorations of the Upper Usumatsintla and Adjacent Region: Altar de Sacrificios, Seibal,*

Itsimté-Sácluk, Cankuen: Report of Explorations for the Museum. Memoirs of the Peabody Museum of Archaeology and Ethnology 4(1). Harvard University, Cambridge, MA.

——1908b *Explorations in the Department of Peten, Guatemala and Adjacent Region Topoxté, Yaxhá, Benque Viejo, Naranjo: Reports of Explorations for the Museum.* Memoirs of the Peabody Museum of Archaeology and Ethnology 4(2). Harvard University, Cambridge, MA.

——1910 *Explorations in the Department of Peten, Guatemala and Adjacent Region: Motul de San José, Peten-Itza: Reports of Explorations for the Museum.* Memoirs of the Peabody Museum of Archaeology and Ethnology 4(3). Harvard University, Cambridge, MA.

——1911 *Explorations in the Department of Peten, Guatemala: Tikal.* Memoirs of the Peabody Museum of Archaeology and Ethnology 5 (1). Harvard University, Cambridge, MA.

Malkin, Irad 2011 *A Small Greek World: Networks in the Ancient Mediterranean.* Oxford University Press, Oxford.

Marcus, Joyce 1973 Territorial Organization of the Lowland Classic Maya. *Science* 180: 911–916.

——1976 *Emblem and State in the Classic Maya Lowlands: An Epigraphic Approach to Territorial Organization.* Dumbarton Oaks, Washington, D.C.

——1987 *The Inscriptions of Calakmul: Royal Marriage at a Maya City in Campeche, Mexico.* Museum of Anthropology, University of Michigan Technical Report 21. Ann Arbor.

——1992a *Mesoamerican Writing Systems: Propaganda, Myth, and History in Four Ancient Civilizations.* Princeton University Press, Princeton.

——1992b Royal Families, Royal Texts: Examples from the Zapotec and Maya. In *Mesoamerican Elites: An Archaeological Assessment,* edited by Diane Z. Chase, and Arlen F. Chase, pp. 221–237. University of Oklahoma Press, Norman.

——1993 Ancient Maya Political Organization. In *Lowland Maya Civilization in the Eighth Century A.D.,* edited by Jeremy A. Sabloff, and John S. Henderson, pp. 111–171. Dumbarton Oaks Research Library and Collection, Washington, D.C.

——1998 The Peaks and Valleys of Ancient States. In *Archaic States,* edited by Gary M. Feinman, and Joyce Marcus, pp. 59–94. School of American Research Press, Santa Fe.

Martin, Simon 1993 "Site Q": The Case for a Classic Maya Super-Polity. www.mesoweb.com/articles/martin/SiteQ.pdf

——1996a Tikal's "Star War" against Naranjo. In *Eighth Palenque Round Table, 1993 Vol.X,* edited by Martha Macri, and Merle Greene Robertson, pp. 223–236. Pre-Columbian Art Research Institute, San Francisco.

——1996b Calakmul y el enigma del glifo Cabeza de Serpiente. *Arqueología Mexicana,* 3 (18):42–45.

——1996c "Lords and Overlords: Decoding Political Hierarchy at Piedras Negras, Guatemala". Paper presented at the conference: Maya Kings and Warfare in the Usumacinta Basin, British Museum, London. 22–26 June 1996.

——1996d Calakmul en el Registro Epigráfico. In *Proyecto Arqueológico de la Biosfera de Calakmul: Temporada 1993–1994,* edited by Ramón Carrasco. Centro Regional de Yucatán, Instituto Nacional de Antropología e Historia, Merida.

——1997a The Painted King List: A Commentary on Codex-style Dynastic Vases. In *The Maya Vase Book, Volume 5: A Corpus of Roll-out Photographs,* edited by Barbara Kerr, and Justin Kerr, pp. 846–867. Kerr Associates, New York.

——1997b "Supernatural Patrons and Mythic Paradigms." Paper given at the conference Maya Religion, 7 April 1997. Brigham Young University, Provo.

——1998 Investigación Epigráfica de Campo: 1995–1998. In: *Proyecto Arqueológico de la Biosfera de Calakmul: Temporada 1995–1998,* edited by Ramón Carrasco, Centro Regional de Yucatán, unpublished report to INAH.

——1999 The Queen of Middle Classic Tikal. In *Pre-Columbian Art Research Newsletter.* Pre-Columbian Art Research Institute, San Francisco.

——2000a Los Señores de Calakmul. *Arqueología Mexicana* 7(42):40–45.

——2000b At the Periphery: The Movement, Modification and Re-use of Early Monuments in the Environs of Tikal. In *The Sacred and the Profane: Architecture and Identity in the Southern Maya Lowlands*, edited by Pierre R. Colas, Kai Delvendahl, Marcus Kuhnert, and Annette Pieler, pp. 51–62. Acta Mesoamericana 10, Markt Schwaben.

——2000c Nuevos Datos Epigráficos sobre la Guerra Maya del Clásico. In *La Guerra entre los Antiguos Mayas*, Memoria de la Primera Mesa Redonda de Palenque 1995, edited by Silvia Trejo, pp. 105–124. Instituto Nacional de Antropología e Historia, Mexico City.

——2001a The Power in the West – The Maya and Teotihuacan. In *Maya: Divine Kings of the Rainforest*, edited by Nikolai Grube, pp. 98–111. Könemann, Cologne.

——2001b "The War in the West: New Perspectives on Tonina and Palenque". Paper presented at Four Corners of the Maya World, 19th Maya Weekend, 23–25 March 2001. University of Pennsylvania Museum of Archaeology and Anthropology, Philadelphia.

——2001c Under a Deadly Star – Warfare among the Classic Maya. In *Maya: Divine Kings of the Rainforest*, edited by Nikolai Grube, pp. 174–185. Könemann, Cologne.

——2001d Court and Realm: Architectural Signatures in the Classic Maya Southern Lowlands. In *Royal Courts of the Ancient Maya, Volume 1*, edited by Takeshi Inomata, and Stephen D. Houston, pp. 168–194. Westview Press, Boulder.

——2002 The Baby Jaguar: An Exploration of its Identity and Origins in Maya Art and Writing. In *La Organización Social entre los Mayas, Memoria de la Tercera Mesa Redonda de Palenque, Volume I*, coordinated by Vera Tiesler Blos, Rafael Cobos, and Merle Greene Robertson, pp. 49–78. Instituto Nacional de Antropología e Historia and Universidad Autónoma de Yucatán, Mexico City.

——2003a Historiography and the Classic Maya Monumental Tradition. A paper presented at the Fifth World Archaeological Congress, 21–24 June, Washington D.C.

——2003b In Line of the Founder: A View of Dynastic Politics at Tikal. In *Tikal: Dynasties, Foreigners, and Affairs of State*, edited by Jeremy A. Sabloff, pp. 3–45. School of American Research Advanced Seminar Series, James Curry, Oxford.

——2003c Moral-Reforma y la Contienda por el Oriente de Tabasco. *Arqueología Mexicana* 9 (61):44–47.

——2004a A Broken Sky: The Ancient Name of Yaxchilan as Pa' Chan. *The PARI Journal* 5 (1):1–7.

——2004b Preguntas epigráficas acerca de los escalones de Dzibanché. In *Los Cautivos de Dzibanché*, edited by Enrique Nalda, pp. 104–115. Instituto Nacional de Antropología e Historia, Mexico City.

——2004c "Pakal at War: Recovering the Political History of 7th-Century Palenque through its Art and Writing." Paper presented at the symposium New Discoveries in the Art of the Ancient Maya, 17 April, National Gallery of Art, Washington D.C.

——2005a Of Snakes and Bats: Shifting Identities at Calakmul. *Precolumbian Art Research Institute (PARI) Journal* 6(2):5–15.

——2005b Caracol Altar 21 Revisited: More Data on Double Bird and Tikal's Wars of the Mid-Sixth Century. *Precolumbian Art Research Institute (PARI) Journal* 6(1):1–9.

——2005c "Treasures from the Underworld: Cacao and the Realm of the Black Gods". Paper presented at Maya Chocolate and Precious Delights, 23rd University of Pennsylvania Museum Maya Weekend, 9–11 April 2005, Philadelphia.

——2006a On Pre-Columbian Narrative: Representation Across the Word-Image Divide. In *A Pre-Columbian World*, edited by Jeffrey Quilter, and Mary Miller, pp. 55–105. Dumbarton Oaks Research Library and Collection, Washington D.C.

——2006b Cacao in Ancient Maya Religion: First Fruit from the Maize Tree and other Tales from the Underworld. In *Chocolate in Mesoamerica: A Cultural History of Cacao*, edited by Cameron McNeil, pp. 154–183. University Press of Florida, Gainesville.

——2007a "Theosynthesis in Ancient Maya Religion". Paper presented at the 12th European Maya Conference The Maya and their Sacred Narratives: Text and Context of Maya Mythologies. 3–8 December, Geneva.

Martin, Simon 2007b A Provisional Report on the Murals of Structure 1 of the Chiik Nahb Acropolis. In *Proyecto Arqueológico de Calakmul: Temporada 2006*, edited by Ramón Carrasco, Centro Regional de Yucatán, report submitted to INAH.

——2008a "Reading Calakmul: Epigraphy of the Proyecto Arqueológico de Calakmul 1994–2008". Paper presented at the VI Mesa Redonda de Palenque, 16–21 November, Palenque, Mexico.

——2008b Wives and Daughters on the Dallas Altar. www.mesoweb.com/articles/martin/Wives&Daughters.html

——2008c A Caracol Emblem Glyph at Tikal. *Maya Decipherment*. https://decipherment.wordpress.com/2008/06/07/a-caracol-emblem-glyph-at-tikal/

——2009a "On the Trail of the Serpent State: The Unusual History of the Kan Polity". Paper presented at the 33rd Maya Meetings at Texas History and Politics of the Snake Kingdom, 23 February–1 March. University of Texas at Austin.

——2009b "A Time for War: A Return to Statistical Approaches in Studying Classic Maya Conflict". Paper presented at the 14th European Maya Conference Maya Political Relations and Strategies, 9–14 November, Jagiellonian University and the Polish Academy of Arts and Sciences, Cracow, Poland.

——2010a "Here Comes the Bride: Marriage Politics in the Classic Maya Lowlands Revisited". Paper presented at the 15th European Maya Conference Maya Society and Socio-Territorial Organization, 29 November–4 December 2010, Museo de América de Madrid, Spain.

——2010b Biografía de K'inich Janaab' Pakal. In *Misterios de un rostro maya: la máscara funeraria de K'inich Janaab' Pakal de Palenque*, edited by Laura Filloy Nadal, pp. 71–89. Instituto Nacional de Antropología y Historia, Mexico City.

——2012a Escritura. In *Calakmul: Patrimonio de la Humanidad*, pp. 155–175. Grupo Azabache, Mexico City.

——2012b Carved Bowl. In *Maya Art at Dumbarton Oaks*, edited by Joanne Pillsbury, Miriam Doutriaux, Reiko Ishihara-Brito, and Alexandre Tokovinine, pp. 108–119. Pre-Columbian Art at Dumbarton Oaks No. 4, Dumbarton Oaks Research Library and Collection, Washington, D.C.

——2012c Hieroglyphs from the Painted Pyramid: The Epigraphy of Chiik Nahb Structure Sub 1–4, Calakmul, Mexico. In *Maya Archaeology 2*, edited by Charles Golden, Stephen D. Houston, and Joel Skidmore, pp. 60–81. Precolumbia Mesoweb Press, San Francisco.

——2014a The Classic Maya Polity: An Epigraphic Approach to a Pre-Hispanic Political System. PhD thesis, University College London.

——2014b Early Classic Co-Rulers on Tikal Temple VI. *Maya Decipherment*. https://decipherment.wordpress.com/2014/11/22/early-classic-co-rulers-on-tikal-temple-vi/

——2015a The Old Man of the Maya Universe: A Unitary Dimension to Ancient Maya Religion. In *Maya Archaeology 3*, edited by Charles Golden, Stephen D. Houston, and Joel Skidmore, pp. 186–227. Precolumbia Mesoweb Press, San Francisco.

——2015b The Dedication of Tikal Temple VI: A Revised Chronology. *PARI Journal* 15 (3):1–10.

——2016a Reflections on the Archaeopolitical: Pursuing the Universal within a Unity of Opposites. In *Political Strategies in Pre-Columbian Mesoamerica*, edited by Sarah Kurnick, and Joanne P. Baron, pp. 241–277. University of Colorado Press, Boulder.

——2016b Ideology and the Early Maya Polity. In *The Origins of Maya States*, edited by Loa P. Traxler, and Robert J. Sharer, pp. 507–544. University of Pennsylvania Museum, Philadelphia.

——2017a The Caracol Hieroglyphic Stairway. *Maya Decipherment*. https://decipherment.wordpress.com/2008/06/07/the-caracol-hieroglyphic-stairway/

———2017b Secrets of the Painted King List: Recovering the Early History of the Snake Dynasty. *Maya Decipherment.* https:// decipherment.wordpress.com/2017/05/05/ secrets-of-the-painted-king-list-recovering-the-early-history-of-the-snake-dynasty/

———2019a Time, Narrative, and Historical Consciousness among the Classic Maya (Telling Time: Historical Thinking and the Ancient Maya). In *Historical Consciousness and the Use of the Past in the Ancient World*, edited by John Baines, Henriete van der Blom, Yi Samuel Chen, and Tim Rood, pp. 133–152. Equinox, Sheffield.

———2019b A Northern War: Coba vs. Oxkintok. *Maya Decipherment.* https:// mayadecipherment.com/2019/12/31/a-northern-war-coba-vs-oxkintok/

Martin, Simon, and Dmitri Beliaev 2017 K'ahk' Ti' Ch'ich': A New Snake King from the Early Classic Period. *The PARI Journal* 17(3):1–7.

Martin, Simon, and Vilma Fialko n.d. Notes on the Inscription of Tres Cabezas Stela 1. Unpublished manuscript.

Martin, Simon, Vilma Fialko, Alexandre Tokovinine, and Fredy Ramirez 2016 Contexto y texto de la Estela 47 de Naranjo-Sa'aal, Peten, Guatemala. In *XXIX Simposio de investigaciones Arqueológicas en Guatemala 2015, tomo II*, pp. 615–628. Ministerio de Cultura y Deportes, Instituto de Antropología e Historia, Asociación Tikal, Guatemala.

Martin, Simon, and Nikolai Grube 1994a Evidence for Macro-Political Organization among Classic Maya Lowland States. www.mesoweb.com/articles/Martin/Macro-Politics.pdf

———1994b "Classic Maya Politics within a Mesoamerican Tradition: An Epigraphic Model of 'Hegemonic' Political Organization". Paper presented at the Primer Seminario de las Mesas Redondas de Palenque, Palenque, México, 29 September–1 October.

———1995 Maya Superstates. *Archaeology* 48 (6):41–46.

———1997 Evidence for Macro-Political Organization among Classic Maya Lowland States. Revised draft. www.mesoweb.com/articles/Martin/Macro-Politics2.pdf

———2000 *Chronicle of the Maya Kings and Queens: Deciphering the Dynasties of the Ancient Maya.* Thames and Hudson, London.

———2008 *Chronicle of the Maya Kings and Queens: Deciphering the Dynasties of the Ancient Maya.* Second edition. Thames and Hudson, London.

Martin, Simon, Stephen Houston, and Marc Zender 2015 Sculptors and Subjects: Notes on the Incised Text of Calakmul Stela 51. *Maya Decipherment.* https://decipherment .wordpress.com/2015/01/07/sculptors-and-subjects-notes-on-the-incised-text-of-calak mul-stela-51/

Martin, Simon, and Dorie Reents-Budet 2010 A Hieroglyphic Block from the Region of Hiix Witz, Guatemala. *The PARI Journal* 11(1):1–6.

Martin, Simon, and Joel Skidmore 2012 Exploring the 584286 Correlation between the Maya and European Calendars. *The PARI Journal* 13(2):3–16.

Martin, Simon, Alexandre Tokovinine, Elodie Treffel, and Vilma Fialko 2017 La Estela 46 de Naranjo Sa'al, Petén, Guatemala: Hallazgo y texto jeroglífico. In *XXX Simposio de Investigaciones Arqueológicas en Guatemala, Tomo II*, edited by Bárbara Arroyo, Luis Méndez Salinas, and Gloria Ajú Álvarez, pp. 669–684. Ministerio de Cultura y Deportes, Instituto de Antropología e Historia y Asociación Tikal, Guatemala City.

Martin, Simon, and Erik Velásquez 2016 Polities and Places: Tracing the Toponyms of the Snake Dynasty. *The PARI Journal* 17(2):23–33.

Martínez Hernández, Juan (ed.) 1929 *Diccionario de Motul, Maya-Español atribuido a Fray Antonio de Ciudad Real y arte de lengua Maya por Fray Juan Coronel.* Talleres de la Compañía Tipografica Yucateca, Merida.

Masson, Marilyn A., and David A. Freidel (eds.) 2002 *Ancient Maya Political Economies.* Altamira Press, Walnut Creek.

Masson, Marilyn A., and David A. Freidel 2012 An Argument for Classic Era Maya Market Exchange. *Journal of Anthropological Archaeology* 31(4):455–484.

Matheny, Ray T. 1987 Early States in the Maya Lowlands during the Late Preclassic Period:

Edzna and El Mirador. In *City States of the Maya*, edited by Elizabeth P. Benson, pp. 1–44. Rocky Mountain Institute for Pre-Columbian Studies, Denver.

Mathews, Peter 1975 "The Lintels of Structure 12, Yaxchilan, Chiapas". Paper presented at the Annual Conference of the Northeastern Anthropological Association, Wesleyan University, October.

——1977 Naranjo: The Altar of Stela 38. Unpublished manuscript.

——1979 Notes on the Inscriptions of "Site Q". Manuscript on file, Department of Archaeology, University of Calgary, Alberta.

——1980 Notes on the Dynastic Sequence of Bonampak, Part 1. In *Third Palenque Round Table, 1978, Part 2*, edited by Merle Greene Robertson, pp. 60–73. Pre-Columbian Art Research Institute, San Francisco.

——1982 Dynastic Sequence of Tonina, Chiapas, Mexico. In *Toniná: Une Cité Maya du Chiapas*. Etudes Mésoaméricaines Tome II, edited by Pierre Becquelin, and Claude Baudez, pp. 894–902. Editions recherche sur les civilisations, Paris.

——1985 Early Classic Monuments and Inscriptions. In *A Consideration of the Early Classic Period in the Maya Lowlands*, edited by Gordon R. Willey, and Peter Mathews, pp. 5–55. Institute for Mesoamerican Studies, Publication No. 10. State University of New York, Albany.

——1988 The Sculpture of Yaxchilan. PhD dissertation, Yale University.

——1991 Classic Maya Emblem Glyphs. In *Classic Maya Political History: Hieroglyphic and Archaeological Evidence*, edited by T. Patrick Culbert, pp. 19–29. School of American Research Advanced Seminar Series. Cambridge University Press, Cambridge.

——2000 Guerra en las tierras bajas occidentales mayas. In *La Guerra entre los Antiguos Mayas*, Memoria de la Primera Mesa Redonda de Palenque 1995, edited by Silvia Trejo. pp. 125–153. Instituto Nacional de Antropología e Historia, Mexico D.F.

——2001a[1979]Notes on the Inscriptions on the Back of Dos Pilas Stela 8. In *The Decipherment of Ancient Maya Writing*, edited by Stephen Houston, Oswaldo Chinchilla, and David Stuart, pp. 394–415. University of Oklahoma Press, Norman.

——2001b The Dates of Tonina and a Dark Horse in its History. *The PARI Journal* 11(2):1–6.

Mathews, Peter, and John S. Justeson 1984 Patterns of Sign Substitution in Maya Hieroglyphic Writing: The "Affix Cluster". In *Phoneticism in Mayan Hieroglyphic Writing*, edited by John S. Justeson, and Lyle Campbell, pp. 185–231. Institute for Mesoamerican Studies, State University of New York at Albany, Publication 9. Albany.

Mathews, Peter, and Linda Schele 1974 Lords of Palenque: The Glyphic Evidence. In *Primera Mesa Redonda de Palenque, Part I*, edited by Merle Greene Robertson, pp. 63–75. Robert Louis Stevenson School, Pebble Beach.

Mathews, Peter, and Gordon R, Willey 1991 Prehistoric Polities of the Pasion Region. In: *Classic Maya Political History: Hieroglyphic and Archaeological Evidence*, edited by T. Patrick Culbert, pp. 30–71. School of American Research Advanced Seminar Series. Cambridge University Press, Cambridge.

Matteo, Sebastián F. C. 2010 Un nuevo monumento atribuido a La Corona, Petén, Guatemala. *Mexicon* 32(5):102–104.

Maudslay, Alfred P. 1889–1902 *Biologia Centrali-Americana: Archaeology*, 5 Vols. R. H. Porter, Dulau & Co., London.

Maxwell, Judith M., and Robert M. Hill II 2006 *The Kaqchikel Chronicles: The Definitive Edition*. University of Texas Press, Austin.

May Hau, J., R. Cohuah Muñoz, R. Gonzalez Heredia, and William J. Folan 1990 *El Mapa de las Ruinas de Calakmul, Campeche, Mexico*. Universidad Autonoma de Campeche, CIHS.

Mayer, Karl Herbert 1978 *Maya Monuments: Sculptures of Unknown Provenance in Europe*. Acoma Books, Ramona.

——1980 *Maya Monuments: Sculptures of Unknown Provenance in the United States*. Acoma Books, Ramona.

——1991 *Maya Monuments: Sculptures of Unknown Provenance, Supplement 3.* Verlag von Flemming, Berlin.

——1995 *Maya Monuments: Sculptures of Unknown Provenance, Supplement 4.* Verlag von Flemming, Berlin.

McAnany, Patricia A. 1993 The Economics of Social Power and Wealth among Eighth-Century Maya Households. In *Lowland Maya Civilization in the Eighth Century A.D.*, edited by Jeremy A. Sabloff, and John S. Henderson, pp. 65–89. Dumbarton Oaks Research Library and Collection, Washington, D.C.

——1995 *Living with the Ancestors: Kinship and Kingship in Ancient Maya Society.* University of Texas Press, Austin.

——2010 *Ancestral Maya Economies in Archaeological Perspective.* Cambridge University Press, Cambridge.

McAnany, Patricia A., and Shannon Plank 2001 Perspectives on Actors, Gender Roles, and Architecture at Classic Maya Courts and Households. In *Royal Courts of the Ancient Maya, Volume 1: Theory, Comparison and Synthesis*, edited by Takeshi Inomata, and Stephen D. Houston, pp. 84–129. Westview Press, Boulder.

Mearsheimer, John 2001 *The Tragedy of Great Power Politics.* W. M. Norton, New York.

Medina, Paulo H. 2012 Maya Warfare: Implications of Architecture that Infers Violence in the Preclassic Maya Lowlands. MA thesis, California State University Los Angeles.

Medina-Elizalde, Martín, Stephen J. Burns, David W. Lea, Yemane Asmerom, Lucien von Gunten, Victor Polyak, Mathias Vuille, and Karmalkar Ambarish 2011 High Resolution Stalagmite Climate Record from the Yucatán Peninsula spanning the Maya Terminal Classic Period. *Earth and Planetary Science Letters* 298:255–262.

Medina-Elizalde, Martín, and Eelco Rohling 2012 Collapse of Classic Maya Civilization Related to Modest Reduction in Precipitation. *Science* 335:956–959.

Michelet, Dominique, Phillippe Nondédéo, and Charlotte Arnauld 2005 Río Bec, una excepción? *Arqueología Mexicana* 13:58–63.

Michelon, Oscar (ed.) 1976 *Diccionario de San Francisco.* Bibliotheca Linguistica Americana, Vol. 2. Akademische Druck- u. Verlagsanstalt, Graz.

Miller, Daniel, and Christopher Tilley 1984 Ideology, Power and Prehistory: An Introduction. In *Ideology, Power and Prehistory*, edited by Daniel Miller, and Christopher Tilley, pp. 1–15. Cambridge University Press, Cambridge.

Miller, Jeffrey 1974 Notes on a Stela Pair Probably from Calakmul, Campeche, Mexico. In *Primera Mesa Redonda de Palenque, Part I*, edited by Merle Greene Robertson, pp. 149–162. Robert Louis Stevenson School, Pebble Beach.

Miller, Mary Ellen 1986 *The Murals of Bonampak.* Princeton University Press, Princeton.

——1991 "Some Observations on the Relationship between Yaxchilan and Piedras Negras". Paper presented at XVth Maya Meetings at Texas, University of Texas at Austin, 9–10 March.

——1993 On the Eve of Collapse: Maya Art of the Eighth Century. In *Lowland Maya Civilization in the Eighth Century A.D.*, edited by Jeremy A. Sabloff, and John S. Henderson, pp. 355–411. Dumbarton Oaks Research Library and Collection, Trustees for Harvard University, Washington, D.C.

——1995 Maya Masterpieces Revealed at Bonampak. *National Geographic* 187(2):50–69.

Miller, Mary Ellen, and Claudia Brittenham 2013 *Spectacle of the Late Maya Court: Reflections on the Murals of Bonampak.* University of Texas Press, Austin.

Miller, Mary Ellen, and Stephen D. Houston 1987 The Classic Maya Ballgame and its Architectural Setting: A Study of Relations between Text and Image. *Res: Anthropology and Aesthetics* 14:46–65.

Miller, Mary, and Simon Martin 2004 *Courtly Art of the Ancient Maya.* Thames and Hudson, London.

Milner, Murray 1994 *Status and Sacredness: A General Theory of Status Relations and an Analysis of Indian Culture.* Oxford University Press, New York.

Mitchell, Melanie 2009 *Complexity: A Guided Tour.* Oxford University Press, Oxford.

Moertono, Soemarsaid 1968 *State and Statecraft in Old Java: A Study of the Late Mataram Period, 16th to 19th Century.* Cornell University Press, Ithaca.

Moholy-Nagy, Hattula 2008 *The Artifacts of Tikal: Ornamental and Ceremonial Artifacts and Unworked Material.* Tikal Report No.27, Part A. University of Pennsylvania Museum of Archaeology and Anthropology, Philadelphia.

Molloy, John P., and William L. Rathje 1974 Sexploitation among the Late Classic Maya. In *Mesoamerican Archaeology: New Approaches*, edited by Norman Hammond, pp. 431–444. Duckworth, London.

Montgomery, John 1994 Sculptors of the Realm: Hieroglyphic Inscriptions and Monumental Art of Piedras Negras Ruler 7. PhD dissertation, University of Texas at Austin.

——1995 Sculptors of the Realm: Hieroglyphic Inscriptions and Monumental Art of Piedras Negras Ruler 7. MA thesis, University of New Mexico.

de Montmollin, Olivier 1989 *The Archaeology of Political Structure: Settlement Analysis in a Classic Maya Polity.* Cambridge University Press, Cambridge.

——1995 *Settlement and Politics in Three Classic Maya Polities.* Monographs in World Archaeology No.24. Prehistory Press, Madison.

Morales, Paulino L. 1993 Estructuras de planta circular: Nuevas referencias para las Tierras Bajas Mayas Centrales. In *VI Simposio de Investigaciones Arqueológicas en Guatemala, 1992*, edited by Juan Pedro Laporte, Héctor Escobedo, and S. Villagrán de Brady, pp. 262–279. Museo Nacional de Arqueología y Etnología, Guatemala.

Moreland, John F. 1992 Restoring the Dialectic: Settlement Patterns and Documents in Medieval Central Italy. In *Archaeology, Annales, and Ethnohistory*, edited by Bernard A. Knapp, pp. 112–129. Cambridge University Press, Cambridge.

——2001 *Archaeology and Text.* Duckworth, London.

——2006 Archaeology and Texts: Subservience or Enlightenment. *Annual Review of Anthropology* 35:135–151.

Morgan, Lewis Henry 1877 *Ancient Society; or Researches in the Lines of Human Progress from Savagery, through Barbarism to Civilization.* H. Holt and Company, New York.

Morgenthau, Hans J. 1948 *Politics among Nations: The Struggle for Power and Peace.* Alfred A. Knopf, New York.

Morley, Sylvanus 1911 The Historical Value of the Books of Chilan Balam. *American Journal of Archaeology* 15(2):195–214.

——1915 *An Introduction to the Study of the Maya Hieroglyphs.* Bureau of American Ethnology Bulletin 57. Smithsonian Institution, Washington D.C.

——1920 *The Inscriptions at Copan.* Publication No. 219, Carnegie Institution of Washington, Washington D.C.

——1933 The Calakmul Expedition. *Scientific Monthly* 37:193–206.

——1937–1938 *Inscriptions of Peten.* Carnegie Institution of Washington Publication 437, 5 Vols. Washington, D.C.

——1946 *The Ancient Maya.* Stanford University Press, Stanford.

Mouzelis, Nicos P. 1995 *Sociological Theory: What Went Wrong? Diagnosis and Remedies.* Routledge, London.

Munson, Jessica L., and Martha J. Macri 2009 Sociopolitical Network Interactions: A Case Study of the Classic Maya. *Journal of Anthropological Archaeology* 28:424–438.

Musisi, Nakanyike B, 1991 "Elite Polygyny" and Buganda State Formation. *Signs* 16 (4):757–786.

Nadel, Siegfried F. 1957 *The Theory of Social Structure.* Free Press, Glencoe.

Nahm, Werner 1994 Maya Warfare and the Venus Year. *Mexicon* 16(1):6–10.

——1997 Hieroglyphic Stairway 1 at Yaxchilan. *Mexicon* 19(4):65–69.

Nalda, Enrique 2004 Dzibanché: El context de los cautivos. In *Los Cautivos de Dzibanché*, edited by Enrique Nalda, pp. 13–55. Instituto Nacional de Antropología e Historia, Mexico City.

Nalda, Enrique, and Sandra Balanzario 2014 El estilo Río Bec visito desde Dzibanché y Kohunlich. *Journal de la Société des Américanistes* 100(2):179–209.

Navarro-Farr, Olivia, and Stanley Guenter 2013 "Royal Interment and Enduring Social

Memory: The Archaeology of Burial 61 at El Perú-Waka's Principal Public Shrine". Paper presented at the 10th Annual Tulane Maya Symposium Kaanal: The Snake Kingdom of the Classic Maya. Tulane University, New Orleans, 22–24 February.

Netting, Robert M. 1977 Maya Subsistence: Mythologies, Analogies, Possibilities. In *The Origins of Maya Civilization*, edited by Richard E. W. Adams, pp. 299–333. School of American Research. University of New Mexico Press, Albuquerque.

Nicholson, Henry B. 1971 Religion in pre-Hispanic Central Mexico. In *Handbook of Middle American Indians 10: Archaeology of Northern Mesoamerica*, edited by Gordon F. Ekholm, and Ignacio Bernal, pp. 395–446. University of Texas Press, Austin.

Nielsen, Axel E., and William H. Walker 2009 The Archaeology of War in Practice. In *Warfare in Cultural Context: Practice, Agency and the Archaeology of Violence*, edited by Axel E. Nielsen, and William H. Walker, pp. 1–14. The University of Arizona Press, Tucson.

Noble Bardsley, Sandra 1994 Rewriting History at Yaxchilan: Inaugural Art of Bird Jaguar IV. In *Seventh Palenque Round Table 1989*, edited by Merle Green Robertson, and Virginia Fields, pp. 87–94. Pre-Columbian Art Research Institute, San Francisco.

Nondédéo, Phillippe, Charlotte Arnauld, and Dominique Michelet 2013 Río Bec Settlement Patterns and Sociopolitical Organization. *Ancient Mesoamerica* 24(2):373–396.

Nondédéo, Phillippe, Alfonso Lacadena, Juan Ignacio, and Julien Hiquet 2016 « Teotihuacanos y Mayas en la 'entrada' de 11 Eb' (378 d. C.): nuevos datos de Naachtun, Peten, Guatemala ». Paper presented at the 21st European Maya Conference: Hierarchy and Power in the Maya World, 17–22 October, Russian State University for the Humanities, Moscow.

North, Douglas C., John J. Wallis, and Barry R. Weingast 2009 *Violence and Social Order: A Conceptual Framework for Interpreting Recorded Human History*. Cambridge University Press, Cambridge.

Novick, Peter 1988 *That Noble Dream: The "Objectivity Question" and the American Historical Profession*. Cambridge University Press, Cambridge.

Oakeshott, Michael 1983 *On History and Other Essays*. Blackwell, Oxford.

Ober, Josiah 2015 *The Rise and Fall of Classical Greece*. Princeton University Press, Princeton.

Ó Corráin, Donncha 1972 *Ireland Before the Normans*. Gill and Macmillan, Dublin.

Offner, Jerome 1983 *Law and Politics in Aztec Texcoco*. Cambridge University Press, Cambridge.

Ohnuki-Tierny, Emiko 1990 Introduction: The Historicization of Anthropology. In *Culture Through Time: Anthropological Approaches*, edited by Emiko Ohnuki-Tierny, pp. 1–25. Stanford University Press, Stanford.

Okoshi, Tsubasa, 1994 Ecab: Una revision de la geografía política de una provincia Maya Yucateca del periodo postclásico tardio. In *Memorias del Primer Congreso Internacional de Mayistas*, pp. 280–287. Universidad Nacional Autónoma de México, Mexico City.

———2009 *Códice de Calkini*. Universidad Nacional Autónoma de México, Mexico City.

Okoshi, Tsubasa, and Sergio Quezada 2008 Vivir con Fronteras. Espacios Mayas Penninsulares del Siglo XVI. In *El Territorio Maya, Memoria de la Quinta Mesa Redonda de Palenque*, edited/coordinated by Rodrigo Liendo Stuardo, pp. 137–149. Instituto Nacional de Antropología e Historia, Mexico City.

Okoshi, Tsubasa, Lorraine A. Williams-Beck, and Ana Luisa Izquierdo (eds.) 2006 *Nuevas perspectivas sobre la geografía política de los Mayas*. Universidad Nacional Autónoma de México, Universidad Autónoma de Campeche, and the Foundation for the Advancement of Maya Studies Inc., Mexico City.

O'Neil, Megan E. 2012 *Engaging Ancient Maya Sculpture at Piedras Negras, Guatemala*. University of Oklahoma Press, Norman.

Ong, Walter J. 1982 *Orality and Literacy*. Routledge, London.

Orejel, Jorge L. 1990 The "Axe-Comb" Glyph (T333) as ch'ak. Research Reports on Ancient

Maya Writing 32. Center for Maya Research, Washington D.C.

Ortner, Sherry B. 1984 Theory in Anthropology since the Sixties. *Comparative Studies in Society and History* 26:126–166.

——2006 *Anthropology and Social Theory: Culture, Power and the Acting Subject.* Duke University Press, Durham.

Ostwald, Martin 1982 *Autonomia: Its Genesis and Early History.* The American Philological Association, American Classical Studies 11. Scholars Press, Chicago.

Otzoy, Simón 1999 *Memorial de Sololá: Edición Facsimilar del Manuscrito Original.* Comisión Interuniversitaria Guatemalteca de Commemoración del Quinto Centenario del Descubrimiento de América, Guatemala City.

Ouweneel, Arij 1990 Altepeme and Pueblos de Indios: Some Comparative Theoretical Perspectives on the Analysis of the Colonial Indian Communities. In *The Indian Community of Colonial Mexico: Fifteen Essays on Land Tenure, Corporate Organizations, Ideology, and Village Politics,* edited by Arij Ouweneel, and Simon Miller, pp. 1–37. Latin America Series 58. CEDLA, Amsterdam.

——1995 "Tlahtocayotl" to "Gobernadoryotl": A Critical Examination of Indigenous Rule in 18th-Century Central Mexico. *American Ethnologist* 22(4):756–785.

Page, John L. 1938 Appendix II: The Climate of Petén, Guatemala. In *The Inscriptions of Peten. Carnegie Institution of Washington Publication 437, Volume IV,* pp. 349–353. Carnegie Institution, Washington, D.C.

Palka, Joel W. 1995 Classic Maya Social Inequality and the Collapse and Dos Pilas, Peten, Guatemala. PhD dissertation, Vanderbilt University.

——1996 Sociopolitical Implications of a New Emblem Glyph and Place Name in Classic Maya Inscriptions. *Latin American Antiquity* 7 (3):211–227.

——1999 Classic Maya Parentage and Social Structure with Insights on Ancient Gender Ideology. In *From the Ground Up: Beyond Gender Theory in Archaeology,* edited by Nancy L. Wicker, and Bettina Arnold, pp. 41–48.

BAR International Series 812. Archaeopress, Oxford.

Pallán, Carlos 2012 A Glimpse from Edzna's Hieroglyphics: Middle, Late and Terminal Processes of Cultural Interaction between the Southern, Northern and Western Lowlands. In *Maya Political Relations and Strategies: Proceedings of the 14th European Maya Conference,* edited by Jarosław Źrałka, Wiesław Koszkul, and Beata Golinska. Contributions to New World Archaeology 4:89–110. Jagiellonian University, Cracow.

Parsons, Talcott 1951 *The Social System.* Free Press, Glencoe.

Pascual, Arturo, and Erik Velásquez 2012 Relaciones y estrategias polítcas entre El Tajín y diversas entidades Mayas durante el signo IX D.C. In *Maya Political Relations and Strategies: Proceedings of the 14th European Maya Conference,* edited by Jarosław Źrałka, Wiesław Koszkul, and Beata Golinska. Contributions to New World Archaeology 4:205–227. Jagiellonian University, Cracow.

Pasztory, Esther 2011 *Jean-Frédéric Waldeck: Artist of Exotic Mexico.* University of New Mexico Press, Albuquerque.

Patterson, Thomas C. 1989 History and the Post-Processual Archaeologies. *Man* 24:555–566.

Pauketat, Timothy R. 2000 The Tragedy of the Commoners. In *Agency in Archaeology,* edited by Marcia-Anne Dobres, and John Robb, pp. 113–129. Routledge, London.

——2001 Practice and History in Archaeology: An Emerging Paradigm. *Anthropological Theory* 1:73–98.

——2007 *Chiefdoms and Other Archaeological Delusions.* Altamira, New York.

Pendergast, David A. 1989 The Products of their Times: Iconography in Social Context. In *Cultures in Conflict: Current Archaeological Perspectives,* edited by Diane C. Tkaczuk, and Brian C. Vivian, pp. 69–72. The Archaeological Association of the University of Calgary, Calgary.

——1990 *Excavations at Altun Ha: 1964–1970, Vol.3.* Royal Ontario Museum, Toronto.

Perlman, Shalom 1991 Hegemony and *Arkhe* in Greece: Fourth-Century Views. In *Hegemonic*

Rivalry: From Thucydides to the Nuclear Age, edited by Richard Ned Lebow, and Barry Strauss, pp. 269–288. Westview Press, Boulder.

Pincemin, Sophia, Joyce Marcus, Lynda Florey Folan, William J. Folan, María del Rosario Domínquez Carrasco, and Abel Morales López 1998 Extending the Calakmul Dynasty Back in Time: A New Stela From a Maya Capital in Campeche, Mexico. *Latin American Antiquity* 9(4):310–327.

Pines, Yuri 2012 *The Everlasting Empire: The Political Culture of Ancient China and its Imperial Legacy*. Princeton University Press, Princeton.

Pollock, Harry E. D. 1936 *Round Structures of Aboriginal Middle America*. Carnegie Institution of Washington Publication 471, Washington D.C.

Pongratz-Leisten, Beate 2011 A New Agenda for the Study of the Rise of Monotheism. In *Reconsidering the Concept of Revolutionary Monotheism*, edited by Beate Pongratz-Leisten, pp. 1–40. Eisenbrauns, Winona Lake.

Porter, Anne 2010 Akkad and Agency, Archaeology and Annals: Considering Power and Intent in Third Millennium BCE Mesopotamia. In *Agency and Identity in the Ancient Near East: New Paths Forward*, edited by Sharon R. Steadman, and Jennifer C. Ross, pp. 166–180. Equinox, London.

Potter, Daniel R., and Eleanor M. King 1995 A Heterarchical Approach to Lowland Maya Socioeconomies. In *Heterarchy and the Analysis of Complex Societies*, edited by Robert M. Ehrenreich, Carole L. Crumley, and Janet E. Levy, pp. 17–32. Archaeological Papers of the American Anthropological Association 6, Arlington.

Prager, Christian M. 2013 Übernatürliche Akteure in der Klassischen Maya-Religion: Eine Untersuchung zu intrakultureller Variation und Stabilität am Beispiel des *k'uh* "Götter"-Konzepts in den religiösen Vorstellungen und Überzeugungen Klassischer Maya-Eliten (250 – 900 n.Chr.). PhD dissertation, University of Bonn.

Prager, Christian M., and Elisabeth Wagner 2008 "Historical Implications of the Early Classic Hieroglyphic Text on the Step of Structure 10L-11-Sub-12 at Copan (CPN 3033)". Paper presented at the VI Mesa Redonda de Palenque: Arqueología, Imagen y Texto. 16–21 November, Palenque, Mexico.

Price, T. Douglas, James H. Burton, Robert J. Sharer, Jane E. Buikstra, Lori E. Wright, Loa P. Traxler, and Katherine A. Miller 2010 Kings and Commoners at Copan: Isotopic Evidence for Origins and Movement in the Classic Maya Period. *Journal of Anthropological Archaeology* 29(1):15–32.

Prigogine, Ilya, and Isabelle Stengers 1984 *Order Out of Chaos: Man's New Dialogue with Nature*. Bantam Books, New York.

Proskouriakoff, Tatiana 1950 *A Study of Classic Maya Sculpture*. Carnegie Institution of Washington Publication 593. Washington, D.C.

——1960 Historical Implications of a Pattern of Dates at Piedras Negras, Guatemala. *American Antiquity* 25:454–475.

——1963 Historical Data in the Inscriptions of Yaxchilan, Part I. *Estudios de Cultura Maya* 3: 149–167.

——1964 Historical Data in the Inscriptions of Yaxchilan, Part II. *Estudios de Cultura Maya* 4: 177–201.

——1978 Olmec Gods and Maya God-Glyphs. In *Codex Wauchope*, edited by Marco Giardino, Barbara Edmonson, and Winifred Creamer, pp. 113–117. Tulane University, New Orleans.

——1993 *Maya History*, edited by Rosemary A. Joyce. University of Texas Press, Austin.

Puleston, Dennis E., and Donald W. Callender, Jr. 1967 Defensive Earthworks at Tikal. *Expedition* 9(3):40–48.

Quezada, Sergio 1993 *Pueblos y caciques yucatecos 1550–1580*. El Colegio de México, Mexico City.

——2014 *Maya Lords and Lordship: The Formation of Colonial Society in Yucatán, 1350–1600*, translated by Terry Rugeley. University of Oklahoma Press, Norman.

Raaflaub, Kurt A. 2004 Archaic Greek Aristocrats as Carriers of Cultural Interaction. In *Commerce and Monetary Systems in the Ancient World: Means of Transmission and Cultural Interaction*, edited by Robert Rollinger, and Christoph Ulf, pp. 197–217. Franz Steiner Verlag, Stuttgart.

Radcliffe-Brown, A. R. 1940 Preface. In *African Political Systems*, edited by M. Fortes, and E. E. Evans-Pritchard, pp. xi–xxiii. Oxford University Press, Oxford.

——1941 The Study of Kinship Systems. *The Journal of the Royal Anthropological Institute of Great Britain and Ireland* 71(1/2):1–18.

Rands, Robert L. 1952 Some Evidences of Warfare in Classic Maya Art. PhD dissertation, Columbia University.

——1973 The Classic Maya Collapse: Usumacinta Zone and the Northwestern Periphery. In *The Classic Maya Collapse*, edited by T. Patrick Culbert, pp. 165–206. University of New Mexico Press, Albuquerque.

——1977 The Rise of Classic Maya Civilization in the Northwestern Zone: Isolation and Integration. In *The Origins of Maya Civilization*, edited by Richard E. W. Adams, pp. 159–180. University of New Mexico Press, Albuquerque.

——2007 Palenque and Selected Survey Sites: The Preclassic. In *Palenque: Recent Investigations at the Classic Maya Center*, edited by Damian B. Marken, pp. 25–56. Altamira Press, Lanham.

Rands, Robert L., Ronald L. Bishop, and Jeremy A. Sabloff 1982 Maya Fine Paste Ceramics: An Archaeological Perspective. In *Analyses of Fine Paste Ceramics*, edited by Jeremy A. Sabloff, pp. 315–338. Memoirs of the Peabody Museum of Archaeology and Ethnology, Vol. 15, No. 2. Harvard University, Cambridge.

Redmond, Elsa M. (ed.) 1998 *Chiefdoms and Chieftaincy in the Americas*, edited by Elsa M. Redmond. University Press of Florida, Gainesville.

Reed, Nelson A. 2001 *The Caste War of Yucatán*. Stanford University Press, Stanford.

Reents-Budet, Dorie J. 1991 The "Holmul Dancer" Theme in Maya Art. In *Sixth Palenque Round Table, 1986*, edited by Merle Greene Robertson, and Virginia M. Fields, pp. 217–222. University of Oklahoma Press, Norman.

——1994 *Painting the Maya Universe: Royal Ceramics of the Classic Period*. Duke University Press, Durham.

Reents-Budet, Dorie J., Ellen E. Bell, Loa P. Traxler, and Ronald L. Bishop 2004 Early Classic Ceramic Offerings at Copan: A Comparison of the Hunal, Margarita, and Sub-Jaguar Tombs. In *Understanding Early Classic Copan*, edited by Ellen E. Bell, Marcello Canuto, and Robert J. Sharer, pp. 159–190. University of Pennsylvania Museum Press, Philadelphia.

Reese-Taylor, Kathryn, Peter Mathews, Julia Guernsey, and Marlene Fritzler 2009 Warrior Queens among the Classic Maya. In *Blood and Beauty: Organized Violence in the Art and Archaeology of Mesoamerica and Central America*, edited by Heather Orr, and Rex Koontz, pp. 39–72. Cotsen Institute of Archaeology, University of California-Los Angeles.

Reisch, George 1991 Chaos, History, and Narrative. *History and Theory* 30(1):1–20.

Relación de la Genealogía 1941 Relación de la genealogía y linaje de los Señores que han señoreado esta tierra de la Nueva España, después que se acuerdan haber gente en estas partes.... In *Nuevo colección de documentos originales para historia de México*, Volume 3, edited by Joaquín García Icazbalceta, pp. 240–256. Editorial Chávez Hayhoe, Mexico City.

Relaciones de Yucatán 1898–1900 Coleccion de documentos inéditos relativos al descubrimiento conquista y organización de las antiguas posesiones españolas de ultamar, 2nd Series. Real Academia de Historia (España), Madrid.

Renfrew, Colin 1982 Polity and Power: Interaction, Intensification, and Exploitation. In *An Island Polity: The Archaeology of Exploitation in Melos*, edited by Colin Renfrew, and Malcolm Wagstaff, pp. 264–290. Cambridge University Press, Cambridge.

——1986 Introduction: Peer Polity Interaction and Socio-Political Change. In *Peer Polity Interaction and Socio-Political Change*, edited by Colin Renfrew and John F. Cherry, pp. 1–18. Cambridge University Press, Cambridge.

Renfrew, Colin, and John F. Cherry (eds.) 1986 *Peer Polity Interaction and Socio-Political Change*. Cambridge University Press, Cambridge.

Restall, Matthew 1997 *The Maya World: Yucatec Culture and Society, 1550–1850*. Stanford University Press, Palo Alto.

Rice, Don S., Prudence M. Rice, and Timothy Pugh 1998 Settlement Continuity and Change in the Central Petén Lakes Region: The Case of Zacpetén. In *Anatomía de una civilización: aproximaciones interdisciplinarias a la cultura maya*, edited by Andres Cuidad Ruiz, Yolanda Fernández Marquínez, José Miguel García Campillo, M.a Josefa Iglesias Ponce de León, Alfonso Lacadena García-Gallo, and Luis T. Sanz Castro, pp. 207–252. Sociedad Española de Estudios Mayas, Madrid.

Rice, Prudence 2004 *Maya Political Science: Time, Astronomy, and the Cosmos*. University of Texas Press, Austin.

——2013 Texts and the Cities: Modeling Maya Political Organization. *Current Anthropology* 54(6):684–715.

Ricoeur, Paul 1983–1984 *Time and Narrative, Volumes 1–3*, translated by Kathleen McLaughlin and David Pellauer. University of Chicago Press, Chicago.

Riese, Berthold 1980 Die Inschriften von Tortuguero, Tabasco. Materialien der Maya-Inschiften Dokumentation 5. Hamburg.

——1984a Kriegsberichte der Klassischen Maya. *Baessler-Archiv*, n.F. 30:255–321.

——1984b Hel Hieroglyphs. In *Phoneticism in Mayan Hieroglyphic Writing*, edited by John S. Justeson, and Lyle Campbell, pp. 263–286. Institute for Mesoamerican Studies, Publication 9. State University of New York, Albany.

——1988 Epigraphy of the Southeast Zone in Relation to Other Parts of Mesoamerica. In *The Southeast Classic Maya Zone*, edited by Elizabeth H. Boone, and Gordon R. Willey, pp. 67–94. Dumbarton Oaks, Washington, D.C.

——1992 The Copan Dynasty. In *Handbook of Middle American Indians, Supplement 5*, edited by Victoria R. Bricker, pp. 128–153. University of Texas Press, Austin.

Ringle, William M. 1985 Notes on Two Tablets of Unknown Provenance. In *The Palenque Round Table Series, Vol. VIII*, edited by Merle Greene Robertson, and Virginia M. Fields, pp. 151–158. Pre-Columbian Art Research Institute, San Francisco.

——1988 *Of Mice and Monkeys: The Value and Meaning of T1016, the God C Hieroglyph*. Research Reports on Ancient Maya Writing 18. Center for Maya Research, Washington D.C.

——1996 Birds of a Feather: The Fallen Stucco Inscription of Temple XVIII, Palenque, Chiapas. In *Eighth Palenque Round Table, 1993, Vol.X*, edited by Martha J. Macri, and Jan McHargue, pp. 45–61. Pre-Columbian Art Research Institute, San Francisco.

Ringle, William M., and George J. Bey III 1988 *Preliminary Report of the Ek Balam Project*. Report submitted to the Centro Regional Sureste Instituto Nacional de Antropología e Historia, Mexico.

Ringle, William M., and George J. Bey III 2001 Post-Classic and Terminal Classic Courts of the Northern Maya Lowlands. In *Royal Courts of the Ancient Maya, Volume 2*, edited by Takeshi Inomata, and Stephen D. Houston, pp. 266–307. Westview Press, Boulder.

Ringle, William M., George J. Bey III, Tara Bond Freeman, Craig A. Hanson, Charles W. Houck, and J. Gregory Smith 2004 The Decline of the East: The Classic to Postclassic Transition at Ek Balam, Yucatán. In *The Terminal Classic in the Maya Lowlands: Collapse, Transition, and Transformation*, edited by Arthur A. Demarest, Prudence M. Rice, and Donald S. Rice, pp. 485–516. University of Colorado Press, Boulder.

Ringle, William M., Tomás Gallareta, and George J. Bey III 1998 The Return of Quetzalcoatl: Evidence for the Spread of a World Religion during the Epiclassic Period. *Ancient Mesoamerica* 9(2):183–232.

Ringle, William M., and Thomas C. Smith-Stark 1996 *A Concordance to the Inscriptions of Palenque, Chiapas, Mexico*. Middle American Research Institute, Tulane University, Publication 62. New Orleans.

Robb, John E. (ed.) 1999 *Material Symbols: Culture and Economy in Prehistory*. Center for Archaeological Investigations, Occasional Paper No.26. Southern Illinois University, Carbondale.

Ross, Jennifer, and Sharon R. Steadman 2010 Agency and Identity in the Ancient Near East:

New Paths Forward. In *Agency and Identity in the Ancient Near East: New Paths Forward*, edited by Sharon R. Steadman, and Jennifer C. Ross, pp. 1–10. Equinox, London.

Rossi, Franco D., William A. Saturno, and Heather Hurst 2015 Maya Codex Book Production and the Politics of Expertise: Archaeology of a Classic Period Household at Xultun, Guatemala. *American Anthropologist* 117(1):116–132.

Routledge, David 1985 *Matanitū: The Struggle for Power in Early Fiji*. University of the South Pacific, Suva.

Roys, Ralph L. 1933 *The Book of Chilam Balam of Chumayel*. Carnegie Institution of Washington, Publication 438, Washington D.C.

——1943 *The Indian Background of Colonial Yucatan*. Carnegie Institution of Washington, Publication 548, Washington, D.C.

——1957 *The Political Geography of the Yucatan Maya*. Carnegie Institution of Washington, Publication 548. Washington D.C.

——1962 Literary Sources for the History of Mayapan. In *Mayapan, Yucatan, Mexico*, edited by Harry E. D. Pollock, Ralph L. Roys, Tatiana Proskouriakoff, and A. Ledyard Smith, pp. 24–86. Publication 619. Carnegie Institution of Washington, Washington, D.C.

Ruhl, Thomas, Nicholas P. Dunning, and Christopher Carr 2018 Lidar Reveals Possible Network of Ancient Maya Marketplaces in Southwestern Campeche, Mexico. *Mexicon* 40(3):83–91.

Runciman, W. G. 1982 Origins of States: The Case of Archaic Greece. *Comparative Studies in Society and History* 24(3):351–377.

Ruppert, Karl, and John H. Denison Jr. 1943 Archaeological Reconnaissance in Campeche, Quintana Roo, and Petén. *Carnegie Institution of Washington, Publication 543*. Washington D.C.

Ruppert, Karl, J. Eric S. Thompson, and Tatiana Proskouriakoff 1955 *Bonampak, Chiapas, Mexico*. Carnegie Institution of Washington, Publication 602, Washington D.C.

Russell, Bradley W. 2013 Fortress Mayapan: Defensive Features and Secondary Functions of a Postclassic Maya Fortification. *Ancient Mesoamerica* 24(2):275–294.

Rutherford, Ian 2007 Network Theory and Theoric Networks. *Mediterranean Historical Review* 22(1):23–37.

Ruz, Alberto 1954 La Pirámide-Tumba de Palenque. *Cuadernos Americanos* 13(2):141–159.

——1973 El Templo Inscripciones, Palenque. Instituto Nacional de Antropología e Historia. Colección Científica 7. Mexico City.

——1976 Nuevas Interpretacion de la Inscripcion Jeroglifica en la Sarcófago del Templo de las Inscripciones. In *The Art, Iconography and Dynastic History of Palenque Part III, Segunda Mesa Redonda de Palenque, Mexico, 1974*, edited by Merle Greene Robertson, pp. 87–93. Pre-Columbian Art Institute, Pebble Beach.

——1977 Gerontocracy at Palenque? In *Social Process in Maya Prehistory*, edited by Norman Hammond, pp. 287–295. Academic Press, London.

Sabloff, Jeremy A. 1975 Excavations at Seibal: Ceramics. In *Excavations at Seibal, Department of Peten, Guatemala*. Memoirs of the Peabody Museum of Archaeology and Ethnology, Volume 13, Number 2. Harvard University, Cambridge, MA.

——1986 Interaction among Classic Maya Polities. In *Peer Polity Interaction and Socio-Political Change*, edited by Colin Renfrew, and John F. Cherry, pp. 109–116. Cambridge University Press, Cambridge.

Sabloff, Jeremy A., and Gordon R. Willey 1967 The Collapse of Maya Civilization in the Southern Lowlands: A Consideration of History and Process. *Southwestern Journal of Anthropology* 23(4):311–336.

Sachse, Frauke 1996 "A New Identification of the Bonampak Emblem Glyph". Paper presented at the First European Maya Conference Maya Kings and Warfare at the Usumacinta Basin. British Museum, London, 22–26 June.

——2008 Over Distant Waters: Places of Origin and Creation in Colonial K'iche'an Sources. In *Pre-Columbian Landscapes of Creation and Origin*, edited by John E. Staller, pp. 123–160. Springer, New York.

Sachse, Frauke, and Allen J. Christenson 2005 Tulan and the Other Side of the Sea:

Unraveling a Metaphorical Concept from Colonial Guatemalan Highland Sources. Mesoweb. www.mesoweb.com/articles/tulan/Tulan.pdf.

Safronov, Alexandr 2006 Gosudarstva Maya Zapadnogo Regiona V Klassicheskiy Period. PhD Dissertation, Moscow State University.

Safronov, Alexandr, and Dmitri Beliaev 2017 La epigrafía de Uaxactun depués un siglo, 1916–2016. In *XXX Simposio de Investigaciones Arqueológicas en Guatemala, Tomo II*, edited by Bárbara Arroyo, Luis Méndez Salinas, and Gloria Ajú Álvarez, pp. 515–528. Ministerio de Cultura y Deportes, Instituto de Antropología e Historia y Asociación Tikal, Guatemala City.

Sahagún, Fray Bernardino de 1979 *Códice Florentino. Historia general de las cosas de la Nueva España*, 3 Volumes. Facsimile, Mexico City.

Sahlins, Marshall D. 1981 *Historical Metaphors and Mythical Realities: Early History of the Sandwich Islands Kingdom*. University of Michigan Press, Ann Arbor.

——1985 *Islands of History*. Chicago University Press, Chicago.

——1991 The Return of the Event, Again: With Reflections of the Beginnings of the Great Fijian War of 1843 to 1855 between the Kingdoms Bau and Rewa. In *Clio in Oceania: Towards an Historical Anthropology*, edited by Aletta Biersack, pp. 37–100. Smithsonian Institution Press, Washington, D.C.

——2004 *Apologies to Thucydides: Understanding History as Culture and Vice Versa*. Chicago University Press, Chicago.

Sahlins, Marshall D., and Elman R. Service (eds.) 1960 *Evolution and Culture*. University of Michigan Press, Ann Arbor.

Sanders, William T. 1962 Cultural Ecology of the Maya Lowlands, 1. *Estudios de Cultural Maya* 2:79–121.

——1963 Cultural Ecology of the Maya Lowlands. *Estudios de Cultural Maya* 3:203–241.

Sanders, William T., and Barbara J. Price 1968 *Mesoamerica: The Evolution of a Civilization*. Random House, New York.

Sanders, William T., and David Webster 1988 The Mesoamerican Urban Tradition. *American Anthropologist* 90:521–546.

Sanderson, Stephen K. 1995 *Social Transformations: A General Theory of Historical Development*. Blackwell, Oxford.

Santley, Robert S. 1989 Writing Systems, Political Order, and the Internal Structure of Early States in Precolumbian Mesoamerica. In *Cultures in Conflict: Current Archaeological Perspectives*, edited by Diane C. Tkaczuk, and Brian C. Vivian, pp. 90–99. The Archaeological Association of the University of Calgary, Calgary.

——1990 Demographic Archaeology in the Maya Lowlands. In *Pre-Columbian Population History in the Maya Lowlands*, edited by T. Patrick Culbert, and Don S. Rice, pp. 325–343. University of New Mexico Press, Albuquerque.

Saturno, William A., Franco D. Rossi, David Stuart, and Heather Hurst 2017 A Maya Curia Regis: Evidence for a Hierarchical Specialist Order at Xultun, Guatemala. *Ancient Mesoamerica* 28(2):423–440.

Saturno, William A., David Stuart, and Boris Beltrán 2006 Early Writing at San Bartolo, Guatemala. *Science* 311:1281–1283.

Saturno, William A., Karl A. Taube, and David Stuart 2005 *The Murals of San Bartolo, El Petén, Guatemala, Part 1: The North Wall*. Ancient America 7. Center for Ancient American Studies, Barnardsville.

Sauer, Eberhard W. 2006 The Disunited Subject: Human History's Split into 'History' and 'Archaeology'. In *Archaeology and Ancient History: Breaking Down the Boundaries*, edited by Eberhard W. Sauer, pp. 17–45. Routledge, London.

Savage, Christopher T. 2007 Alternative Epigraphic Interpretations of the Maya Snake Emblem Glyph. MA Thesis, University of Central Florida.

Sayes, Shelley Ann 1984 Changing Paths of the Land: Early Political Hierarchies in Cakaudrove, Fiji. *The Journal of Pacific History* 19(1):3–20.

Scarborough, Vernon L., Fred Valdez Jr., and Nicholas Dunning (eds.) 2003 *Heterarchy, Political Economy, and the Ancient Maya: The Three Rivers Region of the East-central Yucatán Peninsula*. The University of Arizona Press, Tucson.

Schele, Linda 1982 *Maya Glyphs: The Verbs*. University of Texas Press, Austin.

——1984a Some Suggested Readings for the Event and Office of Heir-Designate at Palenque. In *Phoneticism in Mayan Hieroglyphic Writing*, edited by John S. Justeson, and Lyle Campbell, pp. 287–305. Institute for Mesoamerican Studies, State University of New York at Albany, Publication 9, Albany.

——1984b Human Sacrifice among the Classic Maya. In *Ritual Human Sacrifice in Mesoamerica*, edited by Elizabeth Boone, pp. 6–48. Dumbarton Oaks Research Library and Collection, Washington, D.C.

——1985 The Hauberg Stela: Bloodletting and the Mythos of Maya Rulership. In *The Fifth Palenque Round Table, 1983, Vol. VII*, edited by Merle Greene Robertson, and Virginia M. Fields, pp. 135–149. Pre-Columbian Art Research Institute, San Francisco.

——1990a *Ba* as "First" in Classic Period Titles. Texas Notes on Precolumbian Art, Writing, and Culture No.5, University of Texas at Austin.

——1990b Early Quirigua and the Kings of Copan. Copán Note 75. Copan Mosaics Project and Instituto Hondureño de Antropologia e Historia, Austin.

——1991a The Demotion of Chak-Zutz': Lineage Compounds and Subsidiary Lords. In *Sixth Palenque Round Table, 1986*, edited by Merle Greene Robertson, and Virginia M. Fields, pp. 6–11. University of Oklahoma Press, Norman.

——1991b The Owl, Shield, and Flint Blade. *Natural History* 100(11):6–11.

——1991c Some Observations on the War Expressions at Tikal. Texas Notes on PreColumbian Art, Writing, and Culture No.16, University of Texas at Austin.

——1991d An Epigraphic History of the Western Region. In *Classic Maya Political History*, edited by T. Patrick Culbert, pp. 72–101. Cambridge University Press, Cambridge.

——1992a A New Look at the Dynastic History of Palenque. In *Handbook of Middle American Indians, Supplement 5*, edited by Victoria R. Bricker, pp. 82–109. University of Texas Press, Austin.

——1992b The Founders of Lineages at Copan and other Maya Sites. *Ancient Mesoamerica* 3 (1):135–144.

——1992c Workbook for the XVIth Maya Hieroglyphic Workshop at Texas, 14–15 March. University of Texas at Austin.

——1994 Some Thoughts on the Inscriptions of House C. In *Seventh Palenque Round Table, 1989, Volume IX*, edited by Merle Greene Robertson, and Virginia M. Fields, pp. 1–10. Pre-Columbian Art Research Institute, San Francisco.

Schele, Linda, and David Freidel 1990 *A Forest of Kings: The Untold Story of the Ancient Maya*. William Morrow, New York.

Schele, Linda, and Nikolai Grube 1994 Notes on the Chronology of Piedras Negras Stela 12. Texas Notes on Precolumbian Art, Writing, and Culture 70. Center for the History and Art of Ancient American Culture, University of Texas at Austin.

——1995 Notebook for the Maya Hieroglyphic Workshop at Texas, March 9–18, 1995. Department of Art and Art History, University of Texas at Austin.

Schele, Linda, Nikolai Grube, and Federico Fahsen 1994 The Xukpi Stone: A Newly Discovered Early Classic Inscription from the Copán Acropolis, Part II: A Commentary on the Text. Copán Note 114. Copán Acropolis Project and Instituto Hondureño de Antropología e Historia, Austin.

Schele, Linda, and Peter Mathews 1991 Royal Visits and Other Intersite Relationships. In *Classic Maya Political History*, edited by T. Patrick Culbert, pp. 226–252. Cambridge University Press, Cambridge.

——1998 *The Code of Kings: The Language of Seven Sacred Maya Temples and Tombs*. Scribner, New York.

Schele, Linda, Peter Mathews, and Floyd Lounsbury 1977 Parentage Expressions from Classic Maya Inscriptions. Unpublished manuscript.

Schele, Linda, and Paul Matthews 1994 The Last Lords of Seibal. Texas Notes on Precolumbian Art, Writing, and Culture 68. Center for the History and Art of Ancient American Culture, University of Texas at Austin.

Schele, Linda, and Mary Ellen Miller 1986 *The Blood of Kings: Dynasty and Ritual in Maya Art*. Sotheby's and Kimbell Art Museum, Fort Worth.

Schellhas, Paul 1904 Representation of Deities of the Maya Manuscripts. *Papers of the Peabody Museum of Archaeology and Ethnology* 4(1). Harvard University Press, Cambridge, MA.

——1936 Fifty Years of Maya Research. *Maya Research* 3(2):129–139.

——1945 Die Entzifferung der Mayahieroglyphen ein unlösbares Problem? *Ethnos* 10:44–53.

Scherer, Andrew K., and Charles Golden 2009 Tecolote, Guatemala: Archaeological Evidence for a Fortified Late Classic Maya Political Border. *Journal of Field Archaeology* 34 (3):285–305.

——2014 War in the West: History, Landscape, and Classic Maya Conflict. In *Embattled Bodies, Embattled Places: War in Pre-Columbian Mesoamerica and the Andes*, edited by Andrew K. Scherer, and John W. Verano, pp. 57–92. Dumbarton Oaks Research Library and Collection, Washington, D.C

Scholes, France V., and Ralph L. Roys 1968 *The Maya Chontal Indians of Acalan-Tixchel: A Contribution to the History and Ethnography of the Yucatan Peninsula*. Second Edition. University of Oklahoma Press, Norman.

Scholnick, Jonathan B., Jessica L. Munson, and Martha J. Macri 2013 Positioning Power in a Multi-Relational Framework: A Social Network Analysis of Classic Maya Political Rhetoric. In *Network Analysis in Archaeology: New Approaches to Regional Interaction*, edited by Carl Knappett, pp. 95–124. Oxford University Press, Oxford.

Schroeder, Susan P. 1991 *Chimalpahin and the Kingdoms of Chalco*. The University of Arizona Press, Tucson.

Schuster, Andrea 1997 The Search for Site Q. *Archaeology* 50(5):42–45.

Scott, James C. 1990 *Domination and the Arts of Resistance: Hidden Transcripts*. Yale University Press, New Haven.

Searle, John R. 1995 *The Construction of Social Reality*. Free Press, New York.

Service, Elman R. 1962 *Primitive Social Organization*. Random House, New York.

——1971 *Cultural Evolutionism: Theory and Practice*. Holt, Rinehart, and Winston, New York.

——1975 *Origins of the State and Civilization*. Norton, New York.

Sewell, William H. Jr. 1992 A Theory of Structure: Duality, Agency, and Transformation. *American Journal of Sociology* 98(1):1–29.

——2005 *Logics of History: Social Theory and Social Transformation*. University of Chicago Press, Chicago.

Shanks, Michael, and Ian Hodder 1995 Processual, Postprocessual and Interpretive Archaeologies. In *Interpreting Archaeology*, edited by Ian Hodder, Michael Shanks, Alexandra Alexandri, Victor Buchli, John Carmen, Jonathan Last, and Gavin Lucas, pp. 3–29. Routledge, London.

Shanks, Michael, and Christopher Tilley 1987 *Re-constructing Archaeology*, Cambridge University Press, Cambridge.

Sharer, Robert J. 1978 Archaeology and History of Quirigua, Guatemala. *Journal of Field Archaeology* 5:51–70.

——1993 The Social Organization of the Late Classic Maya: Problems of Definition and Approaches. In *Lowland Maya Civilization in the Eighth Century A.D.*, edited by Jeremy A. Sabloff, and John S. Henderson, pp. 91–109. Dumbarton Oaks Research Library and Collection, Washington, D.C.

——2003 Founding Events and External Interaction at Copan, Honduras. In *The Maya and Teotihuacan: Reinterpreting Early Classic Interaction*, edited by Geoffrey E. Braswell, pp. 143–165. Texas University Press, Austin.

——2004 External Interaction at Early Classic Copan. In *Understanding Early Classic Copan*, edited by Ellen E. Bell, Marcello Canuto, and Robert J. Sharer, pp. 299–317. University of Pennsylvania Museum Press, Philadelphia.

Sharer, Robert J., Loa P. Traxler, David W. Sedat, Ellen E. Bell, Marcello A. Canuto, and Christopher Powell. 1999 Early Classic Architecture beneath the Copan Acropolis. *Ancient Mesoamerica* 10:3–23.

Shaw, Justine M. 2001 Maya Sacbeob: Form and Function. *Ancient Mesoamerica* 12 (2):261–272.

——2008 *White Roads of the Yucatan*. The University of Arizona Press, Tucson.

Sheets, Payson, and Thomas L. Sever 1991 Prehistoric Footpaths in Costa Rica: Transportation and Communication in a Tropical Rainforest. In *Ancient Road Networks and Settlement Hierarchies in the New World*, edited by Charles D. Trombold, pp. 53–65. Cambridge University Press, Cambridge.

Shennan, Stephen 1993 After Social Evolution: A New Archaeological Agenda? In *Archaeological Theory: Who Sets the Agenda?*, edited by Norman Yoffee and Andrew Sherratt, pp. 53–59. Cambridge University Press, Cambridge.

Shermer, Michael 1993 The Chaos of History: On a Chaotic Model That Represents the Role of Contingency and Necessity in Historical Sequences. *Nonlinear Science Today* 2(4):1–13.

——1995 Exorcising Laplace's Demon: Chaos and Antichaos, History and Metahistory. *History and Theory* 34(1):59–83.

Sheseña, Alejandro 2015 *Joyaj Ti 'Ajawlel: La ascensión al poder entre los Mayas clásicos*. Afinita Editorial and Universidad de Ciencias y Artes de Chiapas, Mexico City.

Shook, Edwin 1952 *The Great Wall of Mayapan*. Current Reports 2. Carnegie Institution of Washington, Cambridge.

Slotkin, James Sydney 1950 *Social Anthropology*. The Macmillan Company, New York.

Smailus, Ortwin 1975 *El Maya-Chontal de Acalan: Análisis lingüístico de un documento de los anos 1610–1612*. Centro de Estudios Mayas, Cuaderno 9. Universidad Nacional Autónoma de México, Mexico City.

Smith, A. Ledyard 1950 *Uaxactun, Guatemala: Excavations of 1931–1937*. Publication 588, Carnegie Institution of Washington, Washington D.C.

——1982 Major Architecture and Caches. In *Excavations at Seibal, Department of Peten, Guatemala*. Memoirs of the Peabody Museum of Archaeology and Ethnology, Volume 15, Number 1. Harvard University Press, Cambridge, MA.

Smith, Adam T. 2001 The Limitations of Doxa: Agency and Subjectivity from an Archaeological Point of View. *Journal of Social Archaeology* 1(2):155–171.

——2003 *The Political Landscape: Constellations of Authority in Early Complex Polities*. University of California Press, Berkeley.

——2011 Archaeologies of Sovereignty. *Annual Review of Anthropology* 40:415–432.

Smith, Michael 1984 The Aztlan Migrations of the Nahuatl Chronicles: Myth or History? *Ethnohistory* 31(3):153–186.

——1986 The Role of Social Stratification in the Aztec Empire: A View from the Provinces. *American Anthropologist* 88:70–91.

——2000 Aztec City-States. In *A Comparative Study of Thirty City-State Cultures: An Investigation Conducted by the Copenhagen Polis Centre*, edited by Mogens Herman Hansen, pp. 581–595. Historisk-Filosofiske Skrifter 21. Kongelige Danske Videnskabernes Selskab, Copenhagen.

——2014 The Aztec Paid Taxes, Not Tribute. *Mexicon* 36(1):19–22.

Snodgrass, Anthony 1991 Structural History and Classical Archaeology. In *The Annales School and Archaeology*, edited by John Bintliff, pp. 57–72. Leicester University Press, Leicester.

Sosa, John, and Dorie Reents 1980 Glyphic Evidence for Classic Maya Militarism. *Belizean Studies* 8(3): 2–11.

Sourvinou-Inwood, Christiane 1990 What is *Polis* Religion? In *The Greek City: From Homer to Alexander*, edited by Oswyn Murray, and Simon Price, pp. 295–322. Clarendon Press, Oxford.

Southall, Aidan W. 1956 *Alur Society: A Study in Processes and Types of Domination*. Heffer, Cambridge.

——1965 A Critique of the Typologies of States and Political Systems. In *Political Systems and the Distribution of Power*, pp. 113–140. A.S.A Monographs 2. Praeger, New York.

——1988 The Segmentary State in Africa and Asia. *Comparative Studies in Society and History* 30(1):52–82.

Spinden, Herbert J. 1913 *A Study of Maya Art: Its Subject Matter and Historical Development*. Memoirs of the Peabody Museum of Archaeology and Ethnology 6. Harvard University Press, Cambridge, MA.

——1916 Portraiture in Central American Art. In *Holmes Anniversary Volume; Anthropological Essays Presented to William Henry Holmes in Honor of the Seventieth Birthday, December 1st 1916, by his Friends and Colaborers*, pp. 434–450. J. W. Bryan, Washington, D.C.

Spores, Ronald 1974 Marital Alliances in the Political Integration of Mixtec Kingdoms. *American Anthropologist* 76(2):297–311.

——1984 *The Mixtecs in Ancient and Colonial Times*. University of Oklahoma Press, Norman.

Šprajc, Ivan 2015 *Exploraciones arqueológicas en Chactún, Campeche, México*. Inštitut za antropološke in prostorske študije. Založba ZRC, Ljbuljana.

Stein, Burton 1977 The Segmentary State in South Indian History. In *Realm and Region in Traditional India*, edited by Richard G. Fox, pp. 3–51. Vikas Publishing House, New Delhi.

Stephens, John Lloyd 1841 *Incidents of Travel in Central America, Chiapas, and Yucatan*. 2 vols. J. Murray, London.

Steward, Julian 1955 *Theory of Culture Change: The Methodology of Multilinear Evolution*. University of Illinois Press, Urbana.

Stewart, Daniel M. 2009 Parentage Statements and Paired Stelae: Signs of Dynastic Succession for the Classic Maya. MA Thesis, Brigham Young University.

Stone, Andrea 1983 The Zoomorphs of Quirigua, Guatemala. PhD dissertation, University of Texas at Austin.

——1989 Disconnection, Foreign Insignia and Political Expansion: Teotihuacan and the Warrior Stelae of Piedras Negras. In *Mesoamerica after the Decline of Teotihuacan AD 700–900*, edited by Richard A. Diehl, and Janet C. Berlo, pp. 153–172. Dumbarton Oaks Research Library and Collection, Washington D.C.

Stone, Andrea, and Marc Zender 2011 *Reading Maya Art*. Thames and Hudson, London.

Stout, Sam D., and Margaret Streeter 2006 A Histomorphometric Analysis of the Cortical Bone of Janaab' Pakal's Rib. In *Janaab' Pakal of Palenque: Reconstructing the Life and Death of a Maya Ruler*, edited by Vera Tiesler, and Andrea Cucina, pp. 60–67. The University of Arizona Press, Tucson.

Strogatz, Steve H. 2003 *Sync: How Order Emerges from Chaos in the Universe, Nature, and Daily Life*. Penguin, Harmondsworth.

Stuart, David 1985a The "Count-of-Captives" Epithet in Classic Maya Writing. In *Fifth Palenque Round Table, 1983, Volume VII*, edited by Virginia M. Fields, pp. 97–101. Pre-Columbian Art Research Institute, San Francisco.

——1985b Epigraphic Evidence of Political Organization in the Usumacinta Drainage. *Maya Decipherment:* https://decipherment.wordpress.com/2013/11/19/early-thoughts-on-the-sajal-title/

——1985c *A New Child-Father Relationship Glyph*. Research Reports on Ancient Maya Writing 2. Center for Maya Research, Washington D.C.

——1985d The Inscriptions on Four Shell Plaques from Piedras Negras, Guatemala. In *Fourth Palenque Round Table, 1980, Volume IV*, edited by Elizabeth P. Benson, pp. 175–183. Pre-Columbian Art Research Institute, San Francisco.

——1985e *The Yaxha Emblem Glyph as Yax-ha*. Research Reports on Ancient Maya Writing 1. Center for Maya Research, Washington D.C.

——1987 *Ten Phonetic Syllables*. Research Reports on Ancient Maya Writing 14. Center for Maya Research, Washington D.C.

——1988 Blood Symbolism in Maya Iconography. In *Maya Iconography*, edited by Elizabeth Benson, and Gillett Griffin, pp. 175–221. Princeton University Press, Princeton.

——1989 Hieroglyphs on Maya Vessels. In *The Maya Vase Book: A Corpus of Rollout Photographs of Maya Vases, Volume 1*, edited by Justin Kerr, pp. 149–160. Kerr Associates, New York.

——1992 Hieroglyphs and Archaeology at Copán. *Ancient Mesoamerica* 3:169–184.

——1993 Historical Inscriptions and the Maya Collapse. In *Lowland Maya Civilization in the Eighth Century A.D.*, edited by Jeremy A. Sabloff, and John S. Henderson, pp. 321–354. Dumbarton Oaks Research Library and Collection, Washington D.C.

——1995 A Study of Maya Inscriptions. PhD Dissertation, Vanderbilt University.

——1996 Kings of Stone: A Consideration of Stelae in Maya Ritual and Representation. *Res: Anthropology and Aesthetics* 29/30: 149–171.

——1997 Kinship Terms in Mayan Inscriptions. In *The Language of Maya Hieroglyphs*, edited by Martha J. Macri, and Anabel Ford, pp. 1–11. Pre-Columbian Art Research Institute, San Francisco.

——1998 "Fire Enters His House": Architecture and Ritual in Classic Maya Texts. In *Function and Meaning in Classic Maya Architecture*, edited by Stephen D. Houston, pp. 373–425. Dumbarton Oaks Research Library and Collection, Washington, D.C.

——2000 The Arrival of Strangers: Teotihuacan and Tollan in Classic Maya History. In *Mesoamerica's Classic Heritage*, edited by David Carrasco, Lindsay Jones, and Scott Sessions, pp. 465–513. University Press of Colorado, Boulder.

——2002 Comment on Klein et al., "The Role of Shamanism in Mesoamerican Art: A Reassessment". *Current Anthropology* 43 (3):410–411.

——2003 "La identificacion de Hixwitz". Paper presented at the XV Simposio de Investigaciones Arqueologicas en Guatemala, Museo Nacional de Arqueología y Etnología de Guatemala.

——2004a The Beginnings of the Copan Dynasty: A Review of the Hieroglyphic and Historical Evidence. In *Understanding Early Classic Copan*, edited by Ellen E. Bell, Marcello Canuto, and Robert J. Sharer, pp. 215–247. University of Pennsylvania Museum of Archaeology and Anthropology, Philadelphia.

——2004b New Year Records in Classic Maya Inscriptions. *The PARI Journal* 5(2):1–6.

——2004c The Paw Stone: The Place Name of Piedras Negras, Guatemala. *The PARI Journal* 4(3):1–6.

——2005a A Foreign Past: The Writing and Representation of History on a Royal Ancestral Shrine at Copan. In *Copan: The History of an Ancient Maya Kingdom*, edited by E. Wyllys Andrews, and William L. Fash, pp. 373–394. School of American Research Press, Santa Fe.

——2005b *The Inscriptions from Temple XIX at Palenque: A Commentary*. Pre-Columbian Art Research Institute, San Francisco.

——2005c A Brief Introduction to Maya Writing. In Sourcebook for the 29th Maya Hieroglyph Forum, 11–16 March, pp. 3–109. Department of Art and Art History, The University of Texas at Austin.

——2005d Glyphs on Pots: Decoding Classic Maya Ceramics. In Sourcebook for the 29th Maya Hieroglyph Forum, 11–16 March, pp. 110–165. Department of Art and Art History, The University of Texas at Austin.

——2005e Ideology and Classic Maya Kingship. In *A Catalyst for Ideas: Anthropological Archaeology and the Legacy of Douglas W. Schwartz*, edited by Vernon L. Scarborough, pp. 257–285. School of American Research Press, Santa Fe.

——2006a The Palenque Mythology. In Sourcebook for the 30th Maya Meetings, 14–19 March, pp. 85–194. The Mesoamerican Center, Department of Art History, University of Texas at Austin.

——2006b Vulture Hill: The Place Name of Bonampak. *Maya Decipherment*. https://decipherment.wordpress.com/2008/03/16/bonampaks-place-name/

——2006c The Inscribed Markers of the Coba-Yaxuna Causeway and the Glyph for Sakbih. Mesoweb. www.mesoweb.com/stuart/notes/Sacbe.pdf

——2007a Inscriptions of the River Cities: Yaxchilan, Piedras Negras and Pomona. In Sourcebook for the XXXI Maya Meetings, 9–14 March. Mesoamerican Center; Department of Art and Art History, University of Texas at Austin.

——2007b The Origin of Copan's Founder. *Maya Decipherment*. https://decipherment.wordpress.com/2007/06/25/the-origin-of-copans-founder/

——2007c[2000] The Maya Hieroglyphs for Mam, "Grandfather, Grandson, Ancestor". https://decipherment.wordpress.com/2007/09/29/the-mam-glyph/

——2007d "White Owl Jaguar": A Tikal Royal Ancestor. *Maya Decipherment*. https://

decipherment.wordpress.com/2007/11/04/white-owl-jaguar-a-tikal-royal-ancestor/

——2008a A Stela from Pajaral, Guatemala. *Maya Decipherment.* https://decipherment.wordpress.com/2008/05/31/a-stela-from-pajaral-guatemala/

——2008b A Childhood Ritual on the Hauberg Stela. *Maya Decipherment.* https://decipherment.wordpress.com/2008/03/27/a-childhood-ritual-on-the-hauberg-stela/

——2009 The Symbolism of Zacpeten Altar 1. In *The Kowoj: Identity, Migration, and Geopolitics in Late Classic Petén, Guatemala*, edited by Prudence M. Rice, and Don S. Rice, pp. 317–326. University Press of Colorado, Boulder.

——2010a Shining Stones: Observations on the Ritual Meaning of Early Maya Stelae. In *The Place of Stone Monuments: Context, Use, and Meaning in Mesoamerica's Preclassic Transition*, edited by Julia Guernsey, John E. Clark, and Barbara Arroyo, pp. 283–298. Dumbarton Oaks Research Library and Collection, Washington D.C.

——2010b Some Working Notes on the Text of Tikal Stela 31. Mesoweb. www.mesoweb.com/stuart/notes/Tikal.pdf.

——2011a *The Order of Days: The Maya World and the Truth about 2012.* Harmony Books, New York.

——2011b New Captive Sculptures from Tonina. *Maya Decipherment.* https://decipherment.wordpress.com/2011/07/07/new-captive-sculptures-from-tonina/

——2011c An Update on the Tonina Captives. *Maya Decipherment.* https://decipherment.wordpress.com/2011/08/13/an-update-on-the-tonina-captives/

——2012a The Name of Paper: The Mythology of Crowning and Royal Nomenclature on Palenque's Palace Tablet. In *Maya Archaeology 2*, edited by Charles Golden, Stephen D. Houston, and Joel Skidmore, pp. 116–142. Precolumbia Mesoweb Press, San Francisco.

——2012b Notes on a New Text from La Corona. *Maya Decipherment.* https://decipherment.wordpress.com/2012/06/30/notes-on-a-new-text-from-la-corona/

——2012c The Hieroglyphic Stairway at El Reinado, Guatemala. Mesoweb. www.mesoweb.com/stuart/Reinado.pdf

——2013 Notes on a Curious Ballgame. *Maya Decipherment.* https://decipherment.wordpress.com/2013/06/11/report-toninas-curious-ballgame/

——2014a A Possible Sign for Metate. *Maya Decipherment.* https://decipherment.wordpress.com/2014/02/04/a-possible-sign-for-metate/

——2014b Naachtun's Stela 24 and the Entrada of 378. *Maya Decipherment.* https://decipherment.wordpress.com/2014/05/12/naachtuns-stela-24-and-the-entrada-of-378/

——2015 Preliminary Notes on Two Recently Discovered Inscriptions from La Corona, Guatemala. https://decipherment.wordpress.com/2015/07/17/preliminary-notes-on-two-recently-discovered-inscriptions-from-la-corona-guatemala/

——2016 "Ceibal in Historical Context: Geo-Politics, Cosmology and the Design of Structure A-3". Paper presented at the 2016 Maya Meetings, Archaeology and History of the Pasión River, 12–16 January. The University of Texas at Austin, Austin.

——2019 A Captive's Story: Xub Chahk of Ucanal. *Maya Decipherment.* https://mayadecipherment.com/2019/06/23/a-captives-story-xub-chahk-of-ucanal/

Stuart, David, Marcello A. Canuto, and Tomás Barrientos 2015 The Nomenclature of La Corona Sculpture 1(2). Mesoweb. www.mesoweb.com/LaCorona/LaCoronaNotes02.pdf.

Stuart, David, Nikolai Grube, and Linda Schele 1989 A Substitution Set for the "Macuch/Batab" Title. Copán Note 58. Copán Mosaics Project and the Instituto Hondureño de Antropología e Historia. Copán, Honduras.

Stuart, David, and Stephen D. Houston 1994 *Classic Maya Place Names.* Studies in Pre-Columbian Art and Archaeology No.33. Dumbarton Oaks Research Library and Collection, Washington, D.C.

Stuart, David, Stephen D. Houston, and John Robertson 1999 Recovering the Past: Classic Mayan Language and Classic Maya Gods. Notebook to the XXIIIrd Linda Schele Forum on Maya Hieroglyphic Writing, 13–14 March. University of Texas at Austin.

Stuart, David, and George E. Stuart 2008 *Palenque: Eternal City of the Maya*. Thames and Hudson, London.

Stuart, George E. 1988 *A Guide to the Style and Content of Research Reports on Ancient Maya Writing*. Special supplement to Research Reports on Ancient Maya Writing 15. Center for Maya Research. Washington D.C.

Sugiyama, Saburo 2004 Governance and Polity at Classic Teotihuacan. In *Mesoamerican Archaeology*, edited by Julia A. Hendon, and Rosemary A. Joyce, pp. 97–123. Blackwell Publishing, Malden.

Szymański, Jan 2010 Round Structures in Pre-Columbian Maya Architecture. *Contributions in New World Archaeology NS* 2:35–71.

Tainter, Joseph A. 1996 Valuing Complexity. In *Debating Complexity: Proceedings of the 26th Annual Chacmool Conference*, edited by Daniel A. Meyer, Peter C. Dawson, and Donald T. Hanna, pp. 10–15. The Archaeological Association of the University of Calgary, Calgary.

Tambiah, Stanley J. 1976 *World Conqueror and World Renouncer: A Study of Buddhism and Polity in Thailand against a Historical Background*. Cambridge Studies in Social Anthropology 15. Cambridge University Press, Cambridge.

——1977 The Galactic Polity: The Structure of Traditional Kingdoms in Southeast Asia. In *Anthropology and the Climate of Opinion*, edited by Stanley A. Freed, pp. 69–97. Annals of the New York Academy of Science 293, New York.

Taube, Karl A. 1985 The Classic Maya Maize God: A Reappraisal. In *Fifth Palenque Round Table, Vol. VII*, edited by Merle Greene Robertson, pp. 171–181. Pre-Columbian Art Research Institute, San Francisco.

——1988 A Prehispanic Katun Wheel. *Journal of Anthropological Research* 44(2):183–203.

——1992a *The Major Gods of Ancient Yucatan*. Studies in Precolumbian Art and Archaeology No.32. Dumbarton Oaks Research Library and Collection, Washington D.C.

——1992b The Temple of Quetzalcoatl and the Cult of Sacred War at Teotihuacan. *Res: Anthropology and Aesthetics* 21:53–87.

——2000 The Turquoise Hearth: Fire, Self-Sacrifice, and the Central Mexican Cult of War. In *Mesoamerica's Classic Heritage*, edited by David Carrasco, Lindsay Jones, and Scott Sessions, pp. 271–340. University Press of Colorado, Boulder.

——2001 The Breath of Life: The Symbolism of Wind in Mesoamerica and the American Southwest. In *The Road to Aztlan: Art from a Mythic Homeland*, edited by Virginia M. Fields, pp. 102–123. Los Angeles County Museum of Art, Los Angeles.

——2003 Maws of Heaven and Hell: The Symbolism of the Centipede and Serpent in Classic Maya Religion. In *Antropología de la Eternidad: La Muerte en la Cultura Maya*, edited by Andrés Ciudad, Mario Humberto Ruza Sosa, and M.a Josefa Iglesias Ponce de León, pp. 405–442. Sociedad Española de Estudios Mayas, Madrid.

——2004a Flower Mountain: Concepts of Life, Beauty, and Paradise among the Classic Maya. *Res: Anthropology and Aesthetics* 45:69–98.

——2004b Structure 10L-16 and its Early Classic Antecedents: Fire and the Evocation and Resurrection of K'inich Yax K'uk' Mo'. In *Understanding Early Classic Copan*, edited by Ellen E. Bell, Marcello A. Canuto, and Robert J. Sharer, pp. 265–295. University of Pennsylvania Museum of Archaeology and Anthropology, Philadelphia.

Taube, Karl A., William A. Saturno, David Stuart, and Heather Hurst 2010 *The Murals of San Bartolo, El Petén, Guatemala. Part 2: The West Wall*. Ancient America 10. Center for Ancient American Studies, Barnardsville.

Tate, Carolyn 1992 *Yaxchilan: The Design of a Ceremonial City*. University of Texas Press, Austin.

Teeple, John 1930 *Maya Astronomy*. Carnegie Institution of Washington Publication 403, Washington, D.C.

Terry, Richard E., Daniel A. Blair, and Eric G. Coronel 2015 Soil Chemistry in the Search for Ancient Maya Marketplaces. In *The Ancient Maya Marketplace: The Archaeology of Transient Space*, edited by Eleanor M. King, pp. 138–167. The University of Arizona Press, Tucson.

Teufel, Stefanie 2000 Interpretación de artefactos del Entierro 49. In *El sitio Maya de Topoxté:*

investigaciones en una isla del Lago Yaxhá, Petén, Guatemala, edited by Wolfgang W. Wurster, pp. 149–158. Materialien zur allgemeinen und vergleichenden Archäologie, Band 57. P. von Zabern, Mainz am Rhein.

Thapar, Romila 2002 *Early India: From the Origins to AD 1300.* Allen Lane, London.

Thayer, Bradley A. 2000 Bringing in Darwin: Evolutionary Theory, Realism, and International Politics. *International Security* 25(2):124–153.

——2004 *Darwin and International Relations: On the Evolutionary Origins of War and Ethnic Conflict.* University Press of Kentucky, Lexington.

Thomas, Carol G. 1981 The Greek Polis. In *The City-State in Five Cultures*, edited by Robert Griffeth, and Carol G. Thomas, pp. 31–69. ABC-Clio, Santa Barbara.

Thomas, Cyrus 1882 *A Study of the Manuscript Troano. Contributions to North American Ethnology*, Volume 5, pp. 1–237. U.S. Department of the Interior, Washington D.C.

Thomas, Nicholas 1986 Planets around the Sun: Dynamics and Contradictions of the Fijian *Matanitu*. Oceania Monograph 31, University of Sydney, Sydney.

Thompson, Edward H. 1886 Archaeological Research in Yucatan. *Proceedings of the American Antiquarian Society* 4:248–254.

Thompson, John Eric S. 1927 *Civilization of the Mayas.* Leaflet No.25. First edition. Field Museum of Natural History, Chicago.

——1930 Ethnology of the Mayas of Southern and Central British Honduras. *Field Museum of Natural History Anthropological Series* 17(1).

——1932 *Civilization of the Mayas.* Leaflet No.25. Second edition. Field Museum of Natural History, Chicago.

——1950 *Maya Hieroglyphic Writing: Introduction.* Carnegie Institute of Washington, Publication 589. Washington D.C.

——1953 Review of Y. V. Knorosov – The Ancient Writing of the Peoples of Central America. *Yan* 2:174–178.

——1954 *The Rise and Fall of Maya Civilization.* University of Oklahoma Press, Norman.

——1959 Systems of Hieroglyphic Writing in Middle America and Methods of Deciphering Them. *American Antiquity* 4(1):349–364.

——1960 *Maya Hieroglyphic Writing: An Introduction.* Second edition. University of Oklahoma Press, Norman.

——1962 *A Catalog of Maya Hieroglyphs.* University of Oklahoma Press, Norman.

——1965 Maya Hieroglyphic Writing. In *Archaeology of Southern Mesoamerica*, edited by Gordon R. Willey, pp. 632–658. Handbook of Middle American Indians 3. University of Texas Press, Austin.

——1970 *Maya History and Religion.* University of Oklahoma Press, Norman.

——1972 *A Commentary on the Dresden Codex.* American Philosophical Society, Philadelphia.

Thucydides *Historia.*

Tilley, Christopher 1982 Social Formation, Social Structures and Social Change. In *Symbolic and Structural Archaeology*, edited by Ian Hodder, pp. 26–38. Cambridge University Press, Cambridge.

Tokovinine, Alexandre 2005a The Dynastic Struggle and the Biography of a *Sajal*: "I Was with That King". In *Wars and Conflicts in Prehispanic Mesoamerica and the Andes*, edited by Peter Eeckhout, and Geneviève LeFort, pp. 37–49. BAR International Series 180. Archaeopress, Oxford.

Tokovinine, Alexandre 2005b Reporte Epigráfico de la Temporada de 2005. Investigaciones en la región de Holmul, 2005, edited by Francisco Estrada-Belli, pp. 347–387.

——2007 Of Snakes, Kings, and Cannibals: A Fresh Look at the Naranjo Hieroglyphic Stairway. *The PARI Journal* 7(4):15–22.

——2008 The Power of Place: Political Landscape and Identity in Classic Maya Inscriptions. PhD dissertation, Harvard University.

——2011 People of a Place: Re-interpreting Classic Maya Emblem Glyphs. In *Ecology, Power, and Religion in Maya Landscapes*, edited by Christian Isendahl, and Bodil Liljefors-Persson, pp. 81–96. Verlag Anton Saurwein, Möckmuhl.

——2013 *Place and Identity in Classic Maya Narratives. Studies in Pre-Columbian Art and Archaeology, No.37.* Dumbarton Oaks Research Library and Collection, Washington, D.C.

Tokovinine, Alexandre, and Dmitri Beliaev 2013 People of the Road: Traders and

Travelers in Ancient Maya Words and Images. In *Merchants, Markets, and Exchange in the Pre-Columbian World*, edited by Kenneth G. Hirth, and Joanne Pillsbury, pp. 169–200. Dumbarton Oaks Research Library and Collection, Washington, D.C.

Tokovinine, Alexandre, and Vilma Fialko 2007 Stela 45 of Naranjo and the Early Classic Lords of Sa'aal. *PARI Journal* VII(4):1–14.

Tokovinine, Alexandre, and Marc Zender 2012 Lords of Windy Water: The Royal Court of Motul de San José in Classic Maya Inscriptions. In *Motul de San José: Politics, History, and Economics in a Maya Polity*, edited by Antonia E. Foias, and Kitty F. Emery, pp. 30–66. University Press of Florida, Gainesville.

Tomasic, John, and Federico Fahsen 2004 Exploraciones y excavaciones preliminares en Tres Islas, Petén. In *XVII Simposio de Investigaciones Arqueológicas en Guatemala, 2003*, edited by Juan Pedro Laporte, Barbara Arroyo, Hector Escobedo, and Hector Mejía, pp. 794–809. Museo Nacional de Arqueología y Etnología, Guatemala.

Tomasic, John, Claudia M. Quintanilla, and Edy Barrios 2005 Excavaciones en el sitio arqueológico Tres Islas, Río Pasión, Petén. In *XVIII Simposio de Investigaciones Arqueológicas en Guatemala, 2004*, edited by Juan Pedro Laporte, Barbara Arroyo, and Hector Mejía, pp. 389–399. Museo Nacional de Arqueología y Etnología, Guatemala.

Tourtellot, Gair, and Jason J. González 2004 The Last Hurrah: Continuity and Transformation at Seibal. In *The Terminal Classic in the Maya Lowlands: Collapse, Transition, and Transformation*, edited by Arthur A. Demarest, Prudence M. Rice, and Donald S. Rice, pp. 60–82. University of Colorado Press, Boulder.

Townsend, Richard F. 1979 *State and Cosmos in the Art of Tenochtitlan*. Studies in Pre-Columbian Art and Archaeology, No.20. Dumbarton Oaks Research Library and Collection, Washington D.C.

Tozzer, Alfred M. 1941 *Landa's Relación de las Cosas de Yucatán*. A translation edited with notes by Alfred M. Tozzer. Papers of the Peabody Museum of American Archaeology and Ethnology 18. Harvard University, Cambridge.

Traxler, Loa P. 2004 Redesigning Copan: Early Architecture of the Polity Center. In *Understanding Early Classic Copan*, edited by Ellen E. Bell, Marcello Canuto, and Robert J. Sharer, pp. 53–64. University of Pennsylvania Museum Press, Philadelphia.

Trigger, Bruce G. 1978 *Time and Traditions: Essays on Archaeological Interpretation*. Columbia University Press, New York.

——1989 *A History of Archaeological Thought*. First Edition. Cambridge University Press, Cambridge.

Trik, Helen, and Michael E. Kampen 1983 The Graffiti of Tikal. *Tikal Report No. 31*. University Museum Monograph 57. The University Museum, University of Pennsylvania, Philadelphia.

Tsukamoto, Kenichiro, and Octavio Esparza 2015 Ajpach' Waal: The Hieroglyphic Stairway of the Guzmán Group of El Palmar, Campeche, Mexico. In *Maya Archaeology 3*, edited by Charles Golden, Stephen D. Houston, and Joel Skidmore, pp. 30–55. Precolumbia Mesoweb Press, San Francisco.

Tsukamoto, Kenichiro, Javier López Camacho, Luz Evelia Campaña Valenzuela, Hirokazu Kotegawa, and Octavio Q. Esparza Olguín. 2015 Political Interactions among Social Actors: Spatial Organization at the Classic Maya Polity of El Palmar, Campeche, Mexico. *Latin American Antiquity* 26 (2):200–220.

Tunesi, Raphael 2007 A New Monument Naming Wamaaw K'awiil of Calakmul. *The PARI Journal* 8(2):13–19.

Turner, Ellen S., Norman I. Turner, and Richard E. W. Adams 1981 Volumetric Assessment, Rank Ordering, and Maya Civic Centers. In *Lowland Maya Settlement Patterns*, edited by Wendy Ashmore, pp. 37–70. University of New Mexico Press, Albuquerque.

Turner, B. L. II 1974 Prehistoric Intensive Agriculture in the Mayan Lowlands: New Evidence from the Río Bec Region. PhD dissertation, University of Wisconsin, Madison.

Turner, Victor 1974 *Dramas, Fields, and Metaphors: Symbolic Action in Human Society*. Cornell University Press, Ithaca.

Tuszyńska, Boguchwala 2009 Some Notes on Wives and Concubines. Wayeb Note 31. www.wayeb.org/notes/wayebnotes0031.pdf

Urcid, Javier 1993 Bones and Epigraphy: The Accurate Versus the Fictitious. Texas Notes on Pre-Columbian Art, Writing, and Culture 42. Department of Art, University of Texas at Austin.

Urrutia, Claudio (ed.) 1964 *Atlas Climatológico de Guatemala*. Observatorio Nacional, Instituto Agropecuario Nacional, Guatemala City.

Valdés, Juan Antonio, and Federico Fahsen 2004 Disaster in Sight: The Terminal Classic at Tikal and Uaxactun. In *The Terminal Classic in the Maya Lowlands: Collapse, Transition, and Transformation*, edited by Arthur A. Demarest, Prudence M. Rice, and Donald S. Rice, pp. 140–161. University of Colorado Press, Boulder.

Valdés, Juan Antonio, Federico Fahsen, and Gaspar Muñoz Cosme 1997 *Estela 40 de Tikal: Hallazgo y Lectura*. Instituto de Antropología e Historia de Guatemala and Agencia Española de Cooperación Internacional, Guatemala City.

Valencia, Rogelio 2015 El rayo, la abundancia y la realeza. Análisis de la naturaleza del dios K'awiil en la cultura y la religión mayas. PhD thesis, Universidad Complutense, Madrid.

Van de Mieroop, Marc 1999 *Cuneiform Texts and the Writing of History*. Routledge, London.

Vargas de la Peña, Leticia, and Víctor Castillo 2006 Ek' Balam, un antiguo reino localizadoen el oriente de Yucatán. In *Nuevas ciudades, nuevas patrias: fundación y relocalización de ciudades en Mesoamérica y el Mediterráneo antiguo*, edited by M.a Josefa Iglesias Ponce de León, Rogelio Valencia, and Andres Ciudad, pp. 191–207. Sociedad Española de Estudios Mayas, Madrid.

Vargas, Leticia, and Victor R. Castillo 2014 Las construcciones monumentales de Ek' Balam. In *The Archaeology of Yucatán*, edited by Travis W. Stanton, pp. 377-393. Archaeopress

Pre-Columbian Archaeology 1, Archaeopress, Oxford.

Vasquez, John A. 2003 The New Debate on Balancing: A Reply to My Critics. In *Realism and the Balancing of Power: A New Debate*, edited by John. A. Vasquez, and Colin Elman, pp. 87–113. Prentice Hall, Englewood Cliffs.

Velásquez, Erik 2004a Los Escalones Jeroglíficos de Dzibanché. In *Los Cautivos de Dzibanché*, edited by Enrique Nalda, pp. 78–103. Instituto Nacional de Antropología e Historia, Mexico City.

———2004b "Los posibles alcances territoriales de la influencia política de Dzibanché durante el Clásico temprano: nuevas alternativas para interpretar las menciones epigráficas tempranas sobre Kaan". Paper presented at the V Mesa Redonda de Palenque, Palenque, Mexico.

———2005 The Captives of Dzibanche. *PARI Journal* 6(2):1–4.

———2008a Los posibles alcanes territoriales de la influencia política de Dzibanché durante el Clásico temprano: Nuevas alternativas para interpretar las menciones históricas sobre la entidad política de Kan. In *El Territorio Maya, Memoria de la Quinta Mesa Redonda de Palenque*, edited/coordinated by Rodrigo Liendo Stuardo, pp. 323–352. Instituto Nacional de Antropología e Historia, Mexico City.

———2008b "En Busca de Testigo Cielo (ca. 561–572 d.C.): El Punzón de Hueso del Edificio de los Cormoranes de Dzibanché." Paper presented at the VI Mesa Redonda de Palenque, 16–21 November, Palenque, Mexico.

———2011 Gobernantes simultáneos en el señorío de Ik': evidencia epigráfica de un atípico sistema de organización política en la región del lago Petén Itzá. In *XXIV Simposio de Investigaciones Arqueológicas en Guatemala 2010*, edited by Bárbara Arroyo López, Lorena Paiz Aragón, Adriana Linares Palma, and Ana Lucía Arroyave Prera de Rosito, pp. 973–987. Museo Nacional de Arqueología y Etnología, Ministerio de Cultura y Deportes, Instituto de Antropología e Historia, Asociación Tikal, Guatemala City.

Velásquez, Erik, and Sandra Balanzario 2016 "Rulers of the Kanu'l Dynasty from the

Perspective of Dzibanche, Quintana Roo, Mexico". Paper presented at the 81st Meeting of the Society for American Archaeology, Orlando, FL, 6–10 April.

Vepretskii, Sergei, and Philipp Galeev 2016 "Hiix Witz and Kaanul: New Evidence for the Development of the Late Classic Maya Secondary Polity at Zapote Bobal". Paper presented at the 21st European Maya Conference Hierarchy and Power in the Maya World, 17–22 October, Russian State University for the Humanities, Moscow.

Villagutierre Soto Mayor, Juan de 1933 *Historia de la conquista de la provincia de el Itzá, reducción, y progressos de la de el Lacandón*. Biblioteca "Goathemala" de la Sociedad de Geografía e Historia, Vol.9. Tipografía Nacional, Guatemala City.

Villagutierre Soto Mayor, Juan de 1985 *Historia de conquista de Itzá*, edited by J. M. García Añoveros. Col. Crónicas Americas, 13. *Historia* 16, Madrid.

Villaseñor, Rafael E. 2012 Estrella y las guerras del Clásico Maya. *Kin Kaban* 1 (1):27–43. www.ceicum.org/Datos/2012-1/PDF/2012127-43.pdf

Villela, Khristaan 1993 The Classic Maya Secondary Tier: Power and Prestige at Three Polities. MA thesis, University of Texas at Austin.

Vlassopoulos, Kostas 2007 *Unthinking the Greek Polis: Ancient Greek History Beyond Eurocentrism*. Cambridge University Press, Cambridge.

Vogt, Evon Z. 1969 *Zinacantan: A Maya Community in the Highlands of Chiapas*. Belknap Press and Harvard University Press, Cambridge

Vogt, Evon Z., and David Stuart 2005 Ritual Caves among the Ancient and Modern Maya. In *In the Maw of the Earth Monster: Mesoamerican Ritual Cave Use*, edited by James E. Brady, and Keith M. Prufer, pp. 155–185. University of Texas Press, Austin.

Volta, Beniamino, and Geoffrey E. Braswell 2014 Alternative Narratives and Missing Data: Refining the Chronology of Chichen Itza. In *The Maya and their Central American Neighbors: Settlement Patterns, Architecture, Hieroglyphic Texts, and Ceramics*, edited by Geoffrey E. Braswell, pp. 356–402. Routledge, Abingdon.

Voorhies, Barbara (ed.) 1989 *Ancient Tribute and Trade: Economies of the Soconusco Region of Mesoamerica*. University of Utah Press, Salt Lake City.

Voss, Alexander, and Markus Eberl 1999 Ek Balam: A New Emblem Glyph from the Northeastern Yucatán. *Mexicon* 21(5):124–131.

Wagner, Elizabeth 1995 Thoughts on the chak te-/kaloom te- title. Unpublished manuscript.

Wald, Robert 1997 Politics of Art and History at Palenque: Interplay of Text and Iconography on the Tablet of the Slaves. Texas Notes on Pre-Columbian Art, Writing, and Culture 80. Department of Art, University of Texas at Austin.

Waldrop, Mitchell M. 1992 *Complexity: The Emerging Science at the Edge of Order and Chaos*. Simon and Schuster, New York.

Walker, Richard L. 1953 *The Multi-state System of China*. The Shoe String Press, Hamden.

Waltz, Kenneth N. 1979 *Theory of International Politics*. Addison-Wesley, Reading.

Wanyerka, Phillip J. 1996 A Fresh Look at a Maya Masterpiece. *Cleveland Studies in the History of Art* 1:72–97.

———2009 Classic Maya Political Organization: Epigraphic Evidence of Hierarchical Organization in the Southern Maya Mountains Region of Belize. PhD Dissertation, Southern Illinois University at Carbondale.

Watanabe, John M. 2004 Some Models in a Muddle: Lineage and House in Classic Maya Social Organization. *Ancient Mesoamerica* 15:159–166.

Watson, Adam 1992 *The Evolution of International Society: A Comparative Historical Analysis*. Routledge, Abingdon.

———2007 *Hegemony and History*. Routledge, Abingdon.

Watts, Duncan J. 1999 *Small Worlds: The Dynamics of Networks between Order and Chaos*. Princeton University Press, Princeton.

———2003 *Six Degrees: The Science of a Connected Age*. W. W. Norton, New York.

Watts, Duncan J., and Steve H. Strogatz 1998 Collective Dynamics of 'Small-World' Networks. *Nature* 393:440–442.

Webb, Malcolm C. 1975 The Flag Follows Trade: An Essay on the Necessary Interaction of Military and Commercial Factors in State Formation. In *Ancient Civilization and Trade*, edited by Jeremy A. Sabloff, and Carl C. Lamberg-Karlovsky, pp. 155–209. School of American Research Seminar Series, University of New Mexico Press, Albuquerque.

Weber, Max 1951 *The City*. Glencoe Press, Glencoe.

——1978 *Economy and Society: An Outline of Interpretive Sociology*, edited by Guenther Roth, and Claus Wittich. University of California Press, Berkeley.

Webster, David 1975 Warfare and the Origins of the State: A Reconsideration. *American Antiquity* 40(4):464–470.

——1976a Lowland Maya Fortifications. *Proceedings of the American Philosophical Society* 120:361–371.

——1976b *Defensive Earthworks at Becan, Campeche, Mexico*. Middle American Research Institute, Publication 41. Tulane University, New Orleans.

——1977 Warfare and the Evolution of Maya Civilization. In *The Origins of Maya Civilization*, edited by Richard E. W. Adams, pp. 353–372. University of New Mexico Press, Albuquerque.

——1978 Three Walled Sites of the Northern Lowlands. In *Journal of Field Archaeology* 5:375–390.

——1993 The Study of Maya Warfare: What It Tells Us about the Maya and What It Tells Us about Maya Archaeology. In *Lowland Maya Civilization in the Eighth Century A.D.*, edited by Jeremy A. Sabloff, and John S. Henderson, pp. 415–444. Dumbarton Oaks Research Library and Collection, Washington, D.C.

——1998 Warfare and Status Rivalry: Lowland Maya and Polynesian Comparisons. In *Archaic States*, edited by Gary M. Feinman, and Joyce Marcus, pp. 311–351. School of American Research Press, Santa Fe.

——1999 Ancient Maya Warfare. In *War and Society in the Ancient and Modern Worlds: Asia, The Mediterranean, Europe, and Mesoamerica*, edited by Kurt Raaflaub, and Nathan Rosenstein, pp. 333–360. Center for Hellenic Studies, Washington D.C. and Harvard University Press, Cambridge.

——2000 The Not So Peaceful Maya: A Review of Maya War. *Journal of World Prehistory* 14(1):65–119.

——2002 *The Fall of the Ancient Maya: Solving the Mystery of the Maya Collapse*. Thames and Hudson, London.

——2005 Resource Management at Copán. In *Copan: The History of an Ancient Maya Kingdom*, edited by E. Wyllys Andrews, and William L. Fash, pp. 33–72. School of American Research Press, Santa Fe.

——2006 The Mystique of the Ancient Maya. In *Archaeological Fantasies*, edited by Garrett G. Fagan, pp. 129–153. Routledge, Oxford.

Webster, David (ed.) 1989 *The House of the Bacabs, Copan, Honduras*. Studies in Pre-Columbian Art and Archaeology, No.29. Dumbarton Oaks Research Library and Collection, Washington D.C.

Webster, David, and AnnCorinne Freter 1990 Settlement History and the Classic Collapse at Copan: A Redefined Chronological Perspective. *Latin American Antiquity* 1(1):66–85.

Webster, David, Timothy Murtha, Kirk D. Straight, Jay Silverstein, Horacio Martinez, Richard E. Terry, and Richard Burnett 2007 The Great Tikal Earthwork Revisited. *Journal of Field Archaeology* 32:41–64.

Webster, David, Jay Silverstein, Timothy Murtha, Horacio Martinez, and Kirk D. Straight 2004 *The Tikal Earthworks Revisited*. Occasional Paper in Anthropology No.28, Department of Anthropology, The Pennsylvania State University, University Park.

Wendt, Alexander 1992 Anarchy is What States Make of It: The Social Construction of Power Politics. *International Organization* 46 (2):399–403.

——1999 *Social Theory of International Politics*. Cambridge University Press, Cambridge.

Werness, Maline Diane 2003 Pabellon Molded-Carved Ceramics: A Consideration in Light of the Terminal Classic Collapse of Classic Maya Civilization. MA thesis, University of Texas at Austin.

——2010 Chocholá Ceramics of Northwestern Yucatán. PhD dissertation, University of Texas at Austin.

Wesson, Robert G. 1978 *State Systems: International Pluralism, Politics, and Culture.* Free Press, New York.

Westermarck, Edward 1921 *A History of Human Marriage.* Fifth Edition. Macmillan and Company, London.

White, Douglas R. 1988 Rethinking Polygyny: Co-wives, Codes, and Cultural Systems. *Current Anthropology* 29(4):531–558.

White, Douglas R., and Michael L. Burton 1988 Causes of Polygyny: Ecology, Economy, Kinship, and Warfare. *American Anthropologist* 90 (4):871–887.

White, Leslie A. 1949 *The Science of Culture: A Study of Man and Civilization.* Farrar, Straus, New York.

Whitecotton, Joseph W. 1977 *The Zapotecs: Princes, Priests, and Peasants.* University of Oklahoma Press, Norman.

Wichmann, Søren, and Albert Davletshin 2006 Writing with an Accent: Phonology as a Marker of Ethnic Identity. In *Maya Ethnicity: The Construction of Ethnic Identity from Preclassic to Modern Times,* edited by Frauke Sachse, pp. 99–107. Acta Mesoamericana, Vol. 19. Anton Saurwein, Markt Schwaben.

Wickersham, John M. 1994 *Hegemony and Greek Historians.* Rowman and Littlefield, Lanham.

Wienold, Götz 1994 Writing, Inscription, and Text. In *Origins of Semiosis: Sign Evolution in Nature and Culture,* edited by Winfried Nöth, pp. 455–478. Mouton de Gruyter, Berlin.

Wight, Martin 1977 *Systems of States.* Leicester University Press, Leicester.

———1991 The Three Traditions of International Theory. In *International Theory: The Three Traditions,* edited by G. Wight, and B. Porter, pp. 7–24. University of Leicester Press, Leicester.

Willey, Gordon R. 1974 The Classic Maya Hiatus; A Rehearsal for the Collapse? In *Mesoamerican Archaeology: New Approaches,* edited by N. Hammond, pp. 417–430. University of Texas Press, Austin.

———1990 General Summary and Conclusions. In *Excavations at Seibal, Department of Peten, Guatemala.* Memoirs of the Peabody Museum of Archaeology and Ethnology, Volume 17, Number 4. Harvard University Press, Cambridge, MA.

Willey, Gordon R., and Philip Phillips 1958 *Method and Theory in American Archaeology.* University of Chicago Press, Chicago.

Williams, Thomas 1859 *Fiji and the Fijians,* edited by George Stringer Rowe. D. Appleton and Company, New York.

Wisdom, Charles 1950 Materials on the Chorti Language. *Microfilm Collection of Manuscripts on Middle American Cultural Anthropology, No. 28.* Transcribed and transliterated by Brian Stross. University of Chicago Library, Chicago.

Wobst, Martin H. 1978 The Archaeo-Ethnology of Hunter-Gatherers or the Tyranny of the Ethnographic Record in Archaeology. *American Antiquity* 43(2):303–309.

Wohlforth, William C., Richard Little, Stuart J. Kaufman, David Kang, Charles A. Jones, Victoria Tin-Bor Hui, Arthur Eckstein, Daniel Deudney, and William L. Brenner 2007 Testing Balance-of-Power Theory in World History. *European Journal of International Relations* 13(2):155–185.

Wolf, Eric R. 1982 *Europe and the People Without History.* University of California Press, Berkeley.

World Weather Disc 1988 World Airfield Summaries, Seattle.

Wright, Lori E. 2005 In Search of Yax Nuun Ayiin I: Revisiting the Tikal Project's Burial 10. *Ancient Mesoamerica* 16:89–100.

Wyllie, Cherra 2002 Signs, Symbols, and Hieroglyphs of Ancient Veracruz: Classic to Postclassic Transition. PhD dissertation, Yale University.

Yaeger, Jason, and David A. Hodell 2008 The Collapse of Maya Civilization: Assessing the Interaction of Culture, Climate, and Environment. In *El Niño: Catastrophism, and Culture Change in Ancient America,* edited by Daniel H. Sandweiss, and Jeffrey Quilter, pp. 187–242. Dumbarton Oaks Research Library and Collection, Washington, D.C.

Yoffee, Norman 2005 *Myths of the Archaic State: The Evolution of the Earliest Cities, States, and Civilizations.* Cambridge University Press, Cambridge.

Zender, Marc 2001 "The Conquest of Comalcalco: Warfare and Political Expansion in the

Northwestern Periphery of the Maya Area". Paper presented at the 19th Maya Weekend, University of Pennsylvania, Philadelphia, 23–25 March.

——2002 The Toponyms of El Cayo, Piedras Negras, and La Mar. In *Heart of Creation: The Mesoamerican World and the Legacy of Linda Schele*, edited by Andrea Stone, pp. 166–184. University of Alabama Press, Tuscaloosa.

——2004 A Study of Classic Maya Priesthood. PhD thesis, University of Calgary.

——2005a The Raccoon Glyph in Classic Maya Writing. *The PARI Journal* 5(4):6–11.

——2005b Teasing the Turtle from its Shell: **AHK** and **MAHK** in Maya Writing. *The PARI Journal* 6(3):1–14.

——2007 "Mexican Associations of the Early Classic Dynasty of Turtle Tooth I of Piedras Negras". Paper presented at the Hieroglyphic Forum, 31st Annual Maya Meetings at Texas, University of Texas at Austin, 10–15 March.

——2018a Theory and Method in Maya Decipherment. *The PARI Journal* 18(2):1–48.

——2018b "*K'ahlaj sakhuun tu'baah* (the crown was held above him): Rethinking Classic Maya Coronation Ceremonies". Paper presented at the 8th Annual Maya at the Lago Conference, Davidson, NC, 27 April.

Zender, Marc, and Karen Bassie 2002 The Wooden Offering Container of Aj K'ax B'ahlam of Tortuguero. *Kislak Foundation*. www .jaykislakfoundation.org/tortuguero.html.

Zender, Marc, Dmitri Beliaev, and Albert Davletshin 2016 The Syllabic Sign **we** and Apologia for Delayed Decipherment. *The PARI Journal* 17(2):35–56.

Zender, Marc, Ricardo Armijo, and Miriam Judith Gallegos 2001 Vida y Obra de Aj Pakal Tahn, un sacerdote del siglo VIII en Comalcalco, Tabasco. In *Los Investigadores de la Cultura Maya 9, Tomo II*, pp. 387–398. Universidad Autónoma de Campeche, Campeche.

Zettler, Richard 2003 Reconstructing the World of Ancient Mesopotamia: Divided Beginnings and Holistic History. *Journal of the Economic and Social History of the Orient* 46 (1):3–45.

Zhang, Yongjin 2001 System, Empire and State in Chinese International Relations. *Review of International Studies* 27(5):43–63.

Źrałka, Jarosław 2008 *Terminal Classic Occupation in the Maya Sites Located in the Area of Triangulo Park, Peten, Guatemala*. Jagiellonian University Press, Cracow.

Źrałka, Jarosław, and Bernard Hermes 2012 Great Development in Troubled Times: The Terminal Classic at the Maya Site of Nakum, Petén, Guatemala. *Ancient Mesoamerica* 23:161–187.

Źrałka, Jarosław, Christophe Helmke, Simon Martin, Wiesław Koszkul, and Juan Luis Velásquez 2018 The Monolithic Monuments of Nakum, Guatemala. *PARI Journal* 19:1–28.

INDEX

Abrams, Philip, 39
Acalan, 16–17
accession events, 24, 32–33, 60, 109–115, 140, *See*
    also kingship
  age at, 106
  ajaw as a verb, 110, 252, 275
  as *ajk'uhuun*, 89
  as Banded Bird, 95
  as *kaloomte'*, 79, 83, 140, 348
  as *sajal*, 87, 98, 259
  as *yajawk'ahk'*, 93, 100
  at a hegemon's home seat, 253
  chum "to sit", 79, 87, 89, 99, 106, 109, 111, 113
  depictions, 113, *114–115*, 132
  identified by Proskouriakoff, 103
  in the Preclassic, 113
  joy "to surround, process", 110–111
  k'al "to raise, present", 110–111, 243, 249, 252,
    252, 273, 406n4, 418n22
  k'am/ch'am "to grasp, receive", 110–111, 124
  of ancestral kings, 77
  supervised or overseen, 95, 100, 113–115, *113–115*,
    163, 188, 237, 239, 241, 243, 245–246,
    248–250, *252*, 254, 256–259, 263, 266,
    268, 273, 352, 388
  taking a regnal name, 111, 193, 252
  timing, 112, *112*
  witnessed by gods or ancestors, 163–164
Adams, Richard E. W., 27, 289, 421n14
agency and practice theories, 41, 51, 62, 64, 394,
    401n6, *See* also recursion
agriculture, 5, 225, 227, *See* also warfare
  beans, 223, 225
  cacao, 228, 347
  cotton, 228
  fruits, 225
  maize, 112, 149, 164, 216, 223, 225–227, 416n31
  manioc, 225
  modified landscapes, 3, 226, 230, 256
  nuts, 225
  squash, 223, 225
  sweet potatoes, 225
"agro-urban" landscape, 225
Aguateca, 332
  as co-capital, 73, 207

destruction of, 200, 258, 282–283
exile at, 235
fortifications at, 203
halted construction, 282
influx of people, 330
kaloomte' at, 81
monuments
  Altar M, 282
  Stela 12, 282
mutul emblem glyph, 73, 161–162
patron gods of, 162
silent after 810 CE or earlier, 281
Ahk'utu' ceramics, 293, 422n22, *See* also
    mould-made ceramics
Ahkal Mo' Nahb I, 96, 130, 132
aj atz'aam "salt person", 342, *343*, 425n24
Aj Chak Maax, 205, *206*
Aj K'ax Bahlam, 95
Aj Numsaaj Chan K'inich (Aj Wosal),
    171
  accession date, 408n23
  as 35th successor, 404n24
  as child ruler, 245
  as client of
    Dzibanche, 245–246
  impersonates Juun Ajaw, 246, 417n15
  tie to Holmul, 248
Aj Saakil, *See* K'ahk' Ti' Ch'ich'
Aj Sak Maax, 259
Aj Sak Teles, 97
aj tz'ihb. See literati, the
ajaw. See royal titles
ajaw as a verb. *See* accession events
Ajaw Bot, 95
ajaw day-name, 34, 147, 399n2
ajaw day-sign, *148*
Ajen Yohl Mat
  as patron of
    Santa Elena, 249, 263, 268, 419n35
  death date, 210
  war against
    Dzibanche, 210
ajk'in. See literati, the
ajk'uhuun. See noble titles
Aldana, Gerardo, 217, 220

CPSIA information can be obtained
at www.ICGtesting.com
Printed in the USA
LVHW060217040722
722702LV00009B/197

9 781108 705233